THE SOUTH

A Documentary History

---

by

INA WOESTEMEYER VAN NOPPEN

Professor of History
Appalachian State Teachers College

D. VAN NOSTRAND COMPANY, INC.

PRINCETON, NEW JERSEY

TORONTO   LONDON

NEW YORK

D. VAN NOSTRAND COMPANY, INC.
120 Alexander St., Princeton, New Jersey (*Principal office*)
257 Fourth Avenue, New York 10, New York

D. VAN NOSTRAND COMPANY, LTD.
358, Kensington High Street, London, W.14, England

D. VAN NOSTRAND COMPANY (Canada), LTD.
25 Hollinger Road, Toronto 16, Canada

PRINTED IN THE UNITED STATES OF AMERICA

Preface

Over a period of twenty years I have been collecting the documents contained within the pages of this book. The individual selections, being brief, make interesting reading for pleasure as well as for study. Most of them are as fascinating historical material as is found in popular current magazines.

The selections have been used repeatedly in my classes in American history and in history of the South. For several years I have mimeographed the majority of them and have used them as part of the required reading material in my classes, The Old South, and The New South. Graduate students have taken them into their classrooms and allowed junior high school and senior high school students to read them. With proper guidance from the teacher, such primary source materials enrich the history course, making it more alive and more meaningful. American history classes in the junior high schools of one of the South's largest cities have a unit on the Civil War. In this documentary history about 150 pages are devoted to sectionalism and the Civil War. The chapter on sectionalism makes graphic the differences between the North and the South as people then saw them. The portion on the Civil War gives the reader a mental image of civilian life as well as of military campaigns, of the totality of that war, in its effects on the entire population of the South.

Most of the documents are not available to the average teacher, student, or lay reader in any other form. A few of the selections are from books which are available in their entirety in reprints. In such cases the student, after reading the excerpt, hunts up the complete work and reads it from beginning to end; the selections here serve to motivate further reading.

The textbook that I have used along with the documents is Francis Butler Simkins, A HISTORY OF THE SOUTH. These works complement each other adequately to make desirable the adoption of the two books as texts for courses in Southern history.

My history of the South is told by people who lived the life and shared the problems described within its pages. These people have been allowed to tell their own stories and make their own comments, some more interestingly than others. Great names in Southern history stand out prominently in the collection; others are better known to scholars than to average read-ers. Some of the selections may lack literary quality, but they all add to the reader's understanding of the traditions, customs, capacities, and limitations of society in the Southern part of the United States from the sixteenth cen-tury to the present.

For encouragement and assistance in preparing this documentary history I acknowledge my debt to the following good friends: Professor Francis Butler Simkins, who encouraged me over a period of years and who wrote the introduction; Dr. D. J. Whitener, Dean and Head of the Department of Social Studies, Appalachian State Teachers College; and Mr. Leonard Eury, Librarian, who borrowed books from other libraries for my use; and to the Staff of the Library of the University of North Carolina for their generosity in allowing me complete use of their facilities, with special thanks to the Staff of the Southern Historical Collection; and most especially to my husband, John James Van Noppen, who studied the literature of Southern history along with me and passed judgment on documents many times the number chosen; also to my twin daughters, Mary and Anne; my son, Jack; and my sister, Mary Gaffney, for their loving help in every stage of the pro-duction of this book.

I. W. V. N.

Contents

Introduction

By Francis Butler Simkins

Those of us who write about the American South should assume that the region between the Potomac and the Rio Grande possesses characteristics that distinguish it from the rest of the United States. Observers who were not born in the region testify to these differences in books of travel. Native Southerners have the differences impressed upon them when they venture forth to other sections of the United States. We see no excuse for writing about a South that is assumed to be a mere geographical division of a unified country. The implication from the writings of Sinclair Lewis that all America is one colorless Main Street is least applicable to the South.

Writers about the Southern province of the United States should not allow the urges of Americans for national unity to cause them to assume that the Southern variations from the national norm are evil merely because they are variations. If historians, they should regard as lacking in generosity those who scold the South because of its differences; their duty as objective scholars does not demand that they follow the example of numerous patriotic Southerners by resorting to a continuous apology for the Southern differential. To do so convicts them of a narrow nationalism.

There is, says Donald Davidson, the reality of Southern regionalism acknowledged in the vocabulary of the Southern people if not in the solemn documentation of Southern scholars and politicians. We should have no trouble in agreeing with a distinguished Northern scholar who, after residing for many years in a Southern university town, lived in a Western city, and then returned to spend his old age in the Southern university town. Out of such an experience Norman Foerster was able to write that the people of the state in which he finally settled "impress one at once with their different voices, different accent, their sense of manners, the courtesy which appears in all classes, their organic folkiness (as if of one family), their awareness of the past as a force both hampering and helping."

The most obvious explanation of these regional variations is the South's unique and unchanging climate. There the winter is neither long nor very cold; in summer for fifty afternoons the temperature climbs to ninety degrees in the shade; throughout the year there is greater humidity, more sunshine, and less wind than in other regions of the United States. At certain seasons there are torrential rains, and along the Gulf of Mexico the growing season lasts nine months.

The imprint of this distinct climate has a powerful effect on the destiny of the region. The long, hot seasons—"the cruel sunshine" of which the German immigrant Ludwig Lewisohn speaks—favored the creation of the kingdoms of tobacco, rice, sugar, and cotton, slowed the tempo of living, and encouraged the employment of a labor imported from a hotter land. The poorer soils, eroded and leached by the torrential rains, gave both the blacks and whites of the South excuse for their poverty and leisurely life.

The primary problem of the European migrants to America was adjustment to a new and virgin country. Those who settled in the northern part of the United States largely solved this problem by stopping in a climate like that they left behind in Europe. The settlers of the South, on the other hand, faced a climate so hot for half the year that they were almost frightened out of their wits by the heat of the noonday sun. Strange semitropical diseases—malaria, hookworm, and yellow fever—punished Southerners for three centuries. Apparently rich soils were deceptive because of their shallowness. Soil exhaustion early became a curse on the land. This deterioration was hastened by the fact that the nature of the Southern climate worked against agricultural diversity. The South could produce triumphantly only a few crops, having, at least in the not remote past, surrendered its bid for national markets in grains and dairy products to regions where the sun is not so searing.

The radical differences between the climate of the South and that of Northern Europe has been hampering. This was the main reason that not since the last decades of the eighteenth century has the South attracted much immigration. This has meant the domination of the soil by persons of English descent. They are a people who, despite their many virtues, do not handle the land with the same intensive care as do persons of other European stock.

Moreover, the comparatively mild winters of the South have led the inhabitants of the section to give an overabundance of time to outdoor recreations—hunting, fishing, horsemanship, and other less purposeful activities. Mechanical creations have been neglected. This has prevented the development of master mechanics and the consequent making of machinery and the establishment of enriching industries. Down to the present the South is almost completely lacking in mechanical inventiveness, and what industry it has developed is largely imported from the North.

Yet successful adjustments to the climate of the South have enabled the North European race to live and multiply there for the past three hundred years. "Not elsewhere the world over," wrote an English geographer in 1907, "have Englishmen dwelt continuously in large numbers under semitropical conditions for as much as three generations." Since 1907 the descendants of the English colonists have demonstrated an inventiveness which may before long make the traditional handicaps of a semitropical climate seem superstitions of the past. Yellow fever, malaria, and hookworm have been banished through the adoption of sanitary precautions. The bright sun is no longer considered a cruel destroyer but a beneficent goddess whose direct rays possess both esthetic and curative properties. Air conditioning negates at least in part the debilitating effects of the Southern summers. The early and long growing seasons have led to the creation of the kingdoms of vegetables, fruits, cattle, and pine which are as economically significant as the older kingdoms of rice, tobacco, sugar, and cotton.

The greatest achievement of the South is the triumph of people of northern origin over a semitropical climate. The adjustments necessary for this triumph have given the region below the Potomac distinctive characteristics.

Even more distinctive is what one of the section's most distinguished scholars calls "the central theme" of Southern history. This is the doctrine of White Supremacy under which effective use of a large mass of Negro laborers has been made without the African heritage entering in the blood stream of the white race. For 338 years two biologically aggressive races both fully capable of increasing and multiplying have lived close to each other without merging into a mulatto race.

There has been, it is true, extensive race mixture as evidenced by the presence of a numerous mulatto population. But the mixing has almost always been between the white man and the colored or black woman. For the white woman to cohabit with a Negro has from the time of the first coming of the black man been regarded as the worst of crimes. Everywhere in the South the possession of a recognized degree of Negro blood relegates a person to a lower caste from which there is no escape this side of the Pearly Gates. The absolute rigidity of the Southern caste line makes possible the continued existence of a pure white race.

In the opinion of most Southern whites, a rigid enforcement of the prevailing caste lines is necessary to prevent the mongrelization that has overtaken those countries of Latin America in which Negro colonization has been extensive. The South regards as the worst period of its history, not when Northern armies slew its youth, devastated its fields and cities, and freed its slaves, but when outsiders, with the support of victorious armies, tried to iron out the regional caste lines. "All the misfortunes of war itself," says a Southern scholar writing about his section in the *Encyclopaedia Britannica,* "are insignificant when compared with the suffering of the people during the era of Reconstruction." The sinister word *radical* possesses little significance to the orthodox Southerner except in connection with the demand that race relations be altered. The maintenance of White Supremacy over the Negroes is the essence of Southernism; abolish it and much of the regional consciousness would cease to exist.

Factors additional to the peculiarities of geography and race attitudes enter into the explanation of the Southern differential. Outstanding among them is the prevalence of the country-gentleman ideal. This is a pattern of society adopted from the English, justified by the physiocratic philosophy of the French, and taking root naturally in a predominantly agricultural region. Seemingly working against this conception is the emergence of constantly growing cities and towns. But this development has been effective only in a statistical and material sense. Southern urban communities are inhabited by country folk come-to-town. They build their houses and gardens country style. Their major interest is to be able to be successful in business in order to establish country estates where they can spend their mellowing years amid horses, chickens, and hogs. They are primarily interested in country sports—hunting, fishing, and horsemanship. Their interest in museums, theaters, libraries, musicals, and other urban diversions is at a minimum. Their charm is expressed in such rural diversions as dinners, dances, and the races.

Historians of Europe are in the habit of saying that everything stops with the Pyrenees. That is to say, Spain has not in the past few centuries been stirred by the progressive movements that have convulsed Italy and the nations of Northern Europe. The cause is the deep piety of the Spanish people. American historians are in the habit of saying that all progressive movements stop with the Potomac. The reason again is the deep piety of the Southern people.

The religiosity of the South is perhaps more widespread than that of any other area of Christendom. Seventy-odd per cent of the Southern people of both races profess some form of orthodox Christianity. This comparatively high percentage has increased in the past half century and signs point to its continued growth in the next half century. The irreligious or the non-religious exist only among the lower classes too ignorant to understand the teachings of Christ. One seldom or never meets a native Southerner of the middle or upper classes who does not affirm the Christian beliefs. Ethical culture, that is, belief in virtue without revelation, has not been appreciated in the South since the death of Thomas Jefferson. It is almost beyond the conception of the average Southerner to envisage a person being good without being godly.

The unrelenting hold of "the old-time religion" upon Southerners helps to keep the section in old-time grooves. It largely explains why the section, in the face of revolutions in transportation, industry and education, retains its cultural identity in the twentieth century. The Word of God as revealed in the Book continues to provide the Southern masses with an unchanging and certain truth before which the demonstrations of scientists and social reformers are negligible. The modern Southerner accepts scientific technology, but he refuses to be separated from the view "that man holds a position in the universe under divine guidance"; he refuses to convert science into a religion or a philosophy of life.

Such elementary orthodoxy explains not only the difficulty of arousing Southern churches to the need of social reform but also the indifferences of Southerners to nonreligious changes except those of a political or purely practical nature. Public forums, even in the larger cities, are rare, and street-corner orators discoursing on other than religious themes are unknown. Those interested in liberal or radical reforms despairingly admit that the pervading influence of religion has re-created an Old South unwilling to grow into a New South.

Additional factors explain the successful determination of the South to keep its identity. One is a powerful nativism largely untouched by the stream of foreign immigration that has influenced other sections of the United States. The Southerner, despite his provincial prejudices and the memory of having a hundred years ago fought the other sections of the United States, is a vociferous patriot. He is as ready as the inhabitant of any other section of the country to confront in battle the foe of the United States, be he Spaniard, German, Japanese, or Russian. At the time of World War II, for example, Canadians began calling their air corps the Royal Texas Air Force, and an Alabama congressman asserted that the federal government "had to start selective service to keep our Southern boys from filling up the army."

Hot biscuits bind the Southern province together with an authority almost as intimate as White Supremacy. They are a mixture of flour, lard, soda, and buttermilk, lightly kneaded, rolled, cut out, and baked until brown and served while still hot. Hot biscuits are but the most outstanding examples of the peculiarities of the Southern diet. There are several varieties of corn bread, the ever-popular fried chicken, and the endless varieties of pork—the spare ribs, the backbone, fresh ham, boiled, baked, or fried country-cured ham. There are also string beans, black-eyed peas, mustard, collards, and the potlikker left in the vegetable container which is reputed to have magic nutritive value, especially for pickaninnies.

Outsiders complain that Southern dishes are overcooked, overgreasy, and overjuicy. But their absence in strange places is among the potent reasons why Southerners wish to return home.

The tragic experiences of 1861-65 effected the greatest changes that have overtaken the South. It destroyed the bid for national independence, freed the slaves, and impoverished much of the ruling class. The Confederate States were defeated largely because the Southern people did not give them adequate support.

But the great defeat increased the love of section and the hatred or suspicion of the North. In any but a literal sense, it may be said that the Confederacy was not born until after it was dead. The Lost Cause became a symbol around which the South rallied with a unanimity never known before. There were no regrets that the war had been fought, a glorification rather than a condemnation of the chieftains who had led the section in defeat, a tragic joy in the fact that a son or brother had made the supreme sacrifice for what was considered the worthiest of causes. The Union was restored, and the South learned not to regret this fact; but the land of the defunct Confederacy ever since this restoration possesses an ingrown pride in its bid to destroy the national unity.

The South as a regional entity survives today because of its geography, its pride of race, its ruralism, its nativism, its peculiar diet, and the memory of its part in a great civil struggle. Yet powerful forces have been at work for no less than 137 years trying to iron out or blast out the section's peculiarities. First, in 1820, came the Missouri controversy in which the enemies of Southern aspirations attempted to confine the Southern institution of slavery east of the Mississippi River. Then for more than thirty years came the bombardment of the Abolitionists against the peculiarities of the social and moral order that existed south of the Mason and Dixon Line. Next came the march of righteous legions who ripped the Southern Confederacy wide open in order to restore the Union and eradicate slavery. After this terrible invasion came Reconstruction in which, by Acts of Congress, attempts were made to exorcise those distinctions of race on which the South insisted.

Failing in this, the opponents of the Southern way tried methods other than war and law. For several decades after Reconstruction they unleashed a propaganda campaign against the uglier aspects of the South's practice of race distinctions. Held up to ridicule and condemnation were the Ku Klux Klan, the share-crop and convict lease systems, the chain gang, and the one-party organizations. With the cooperation of Southern progressives, new industries and new devices changed the landscape of many previously somnolent Southern communities and led young persons to sprout ideas different from those of their grandparents.

But when this brought no genuine change of the Southern heart, Federal decrees and laws were again resorted to. In the 1940's and 1950's the Presidents of the United States proposed certain economic and social reforms designed to lift the section below the Potomac out of its traditional grooves. In 1954 the Supreme Court of the United States hit hard at the color line by declaring unconstitutional the separation of the two races in schools. This was an attempt to effect intimate contacts between the opposite races in an institution in which marriages are spawned. Seemingly a body blow from the highest authority in the land was aimed at the whole system of race distinctions and White Supremacy.

The South has reacted favorably at times to suggestions from the majority section of the nation that it change its contrary ways. It accepted with good grace the let-us-have-peace sentiments expressed at Appomattox. It has heeded that suggestion that it give the Negroes certain rights—better schools, better wages, better protections against diseases, and better housing. It has embraced with greatest alacrity the American notion that universal education is the sovereign remedy for many social ills. It welcomes Northern industry as the way to get out of the slough of agricultural poverty. There is a changing South that has taken on many of the social and physical features of the ever-changing North.

But, as the Southern novelist Stark Young sapiently observes, the changing South is still the South. Despite the changes which the disruptions of 1865 and subsequent years made inevitable, the distinctive culture of the section has not been destroyed. In politics, to cite the most obvious example, the South responded to the suggestion that the Negro be given the equalities listed in the Declaration of Independence by reducing the race to political impotence. The opening, since 1937, of the Democratic primaries to Negroes by the Federal courts effected a change more technical than real. While there has been a considerable increase in colored voters, these new voters merely won the privilege of ratifying procedures already determined by the white bosses of the local Democratic organizations. An unchanging caste system generally prevented Negroes from becoming candidates for office or from advocating policies contrary to the will of the dominant whites. The sum total of the Negroes' political gains is an occasional membership on a school board or city council. Almost never does a single Negro appear among the several thousand members of the legislatures of the Southern states.

That "close cohabitation and association of black and white" which a Northern traveler observed in the 1850's has vanished from the land by the 1950's. Immediately after the Civil War the races separated in church, and for the cultural give and take of the plantation was substituted a dual school system which sealed off the children of one race from those of the other. Miscegenation, the means through which a numerous mulatto race was created, and through which caste lines were softened, gradually disappeared. Despite Supreme Court decisions, immutable custom makes for increased residential segregation, especially in the newer sections of the cities. There are new towns in Virginia in which no Negroes live. In many places the blacks live so far away from white settlements that the whites find it impractical to hire Negro servants. It is now almost possible for a middle-class white to live many years in a Southern city without direct contacts with blacks. The Supreme Court decision ordering the mixture of races in the public schools has, three years after its promulgation, proved completely unenforceable in all communities of the Deep South.

The region gets practically all its reading materials and educational plans out of the North. This information is often hostile to the regional concepts. But among Southerners there is the education that does not educate. This is caused by the survival of traditions and by the temperament of a people inclined to be leisurely and unintellectual. Northern bias in textbooks is offset by effective instruction in local concepts that survive the indoctrination of the schools. The home, not the school, dominates the cultural outlook of Southerners. It is remarkable how seldom problems raised in classrooms are discussed in the market place or around the dinner table, how unused is the public to listening to the collective opinions of teachers or students, and how beneficial lessons in a subject as pervading as cooking have difficulty in influencing the home diet.

The Southern habit of reading almost exclusively books of Northern origin is as old as *Uncle Tom's Cabin*. A book, even about the South and by a Southerner, wins little attention from Southerners unless published in New York City. In order to win the approval of this literary capital of America, the Southern author often feels obligated to use critical realism or romantic irony involving the repudiation of the Southern tradition.

There is danger, however, of overemphasizing literary materials in measuring the outlook of a people as nonliterary as those of the South. Most Southerners do not take to heart the realistic writings about their section, nourishing themselves on the self-flattery of historical romances. Many among the minority who read the new realism do not connect it with life; for them it is a vicarious escape into a sentimental world which they do not actually wish to enter. They do their sinning within the covers of books. They are like the virtuous ladies who satisfy hidden desires to be evil by reading about lust in slick magazines.

Those among the investigators about the South's past who have delved in widely scattered documents can now rest from their tedious labors. This is because Ina Woestemeyer Van Noppen has brought together, with pertinent comments, a goodly portion of the documents on which a fair appraisal of the region's history can be based. The reader, on the basis of Mrs. Van Noppen's sizable compilation, can determine for himself what he believes the proper conclusions should be. Or, again on the basis of this collection of documents, he may have the dangerous but pleasurable experience of drawing his own conclusions from the evidence. Or he can philosophically let the documents speak for themselves.

Mrs. Van Noppen begins her extensive documentation of the South's history with accounts of Spanish explorations as told by the Spanish themselves and ends with an account in a Washington magazine in 1956 of the material prosperity that has overtaken the region in the middle of this century. Interlarding these, are articles that give as complete a story of the culture and labor of the Southern people as can be found in print.

There are accounts of the Indians, the romantic delusions and actual findings of the English explorers, and the sufferings of the Jamestown settlers. Then are displayed documents on the epic expansion of English America beyond Jamestown; the development of the great Southern paradox: slavery along with the English passion for self-government; the struggle between the Tidewater oligarchs and the people of the Back Country; life in the Virginia plantation house as revealed by the diarist Fithian; the problems of labor in tobacco and rice fields; the trade in overseas luxuries; the coming of non-English immigrants; the amazing religious tolerance or indifference of eighteenth-century Southerners; the invasion of the sectarians from the North; the expostulations of the Revolutionary Fathers; and the clash of arms between the colonists and the mother country.

Next Mrs. Van Noppen arrays her exhibits to demonstrate how the South developed into a distinct province through the use of Negro slave labor for the growing of cotton. Then are described the movement of people beyond the mountains, the founding of towns, and the inauguration of steamboat and railroad. Southern society both in its plebeian and patrician aspects gets much attention. Among the things described are the position of the lady in the provincial society and the diversions of the slaves. The place of the school in the Old South is revealed by chatty observers rather than by the uncritical reports of the educational officials. And as a prelude to the Civil War come full extracts from the utterances of the participants in the sectional controversy. Much attention is given to the Pro-Slavery Argument.

The section on the Civil War begins with Jefferson Davis' justification of Secession before the United States Senate and with a summary by a British periodical of the economic grievances of the seceding states. Then follow accounts of the relative strength of the two contenders in the internecine struggle, of the great battles of the war, of conditions on the home front and in the prison camps, and of the effects of the blockade. The terrible march of William T. Sherman is revealed by the bewildered reports of Confederate officers. This is followed by descriptions of the surrender at Appomattox and of the privations experienced by the inhabitants of a conquered and gutted land. Documents illustrate the several plans for the restoration of the Union, the reaction of the region below the Potomac to Radical Reconstruction, the beginning of formal schooling for the blacks, the war of words between Yankee missionaries and the defenders of the Southern way of life, and the settlement of the social alignment of the freedmen, and of the complexities of land tenure.

The next section of this compilation begins with brilliant characterizations of those who assumed power after Reconstruction, with the explanation of how the Negro was frightened out of politics, and with an account of the rise of industry through Northern capital and skill. Life among the workers in the new industries is contrasted with rural stagnation. The rise of the Southern businessman to take the place of the ante-bellum planter is noted.

The causes of the Farmers' Revolt are given by the participants in that curious episode in the region's history. Analyses are made of the oppressions imposed upon the farmers by the nonagricultural portion of the population. Next come documents illustrating the attempts to regulate the trusts, to disfranchise the Negro legally, and to impose Prohibition. The sections on the post-Reconstruction period close with a description of the renewal of White Democracy and the rise of the much-maligned Dixie Demagogues.

Descriptions of life among the Negroes begin with an article by a judicious portrayer of American life, James Viscount Bryce. A group of writers delineate the injustices imposed upon Negroes by Southern courts and mobs. Defenses and condemnations of racial segregation accompany an account of the development of an autonomous Negro society.

The evangel of the New South, second only in importance to industry, is education. The documents devoted to this endeavor begin with an account of the training given ladies of the upper classes of Virginia who did not go to a university or college. Then follow fervent criticisms of the inadequacies of Southern schools, especially of colleges for women, and praises of those who are credited with remedying these inadequacies. The problems of Negro education are attacked from all angles. The opinions of Thomas Nelson Page are set against those of William E. Burghardt Du Bois.

Southern characteristics are best explained in the sections of this book devoted to religion, imaginative literature, and social diversions. The religious topic is opened with Edwin McNeill Poteat, Jr's., description of the prevailing power of orthodoxy. This article is followed by English travelers' descriptions of the part religion plays in the life of the Southerner and then proof of the good that comes from the much-abused Negro churches.

The section on imaginative writers starts with illustrations from Thomas Nelson Page and William Faulkner of the South's utter lack of the Marxian concept of class struggle. The Negro in "Marse Chan" is set against the poor white in *Absolom, Absolom!* This is followed by the section on recreational life: baseball, football, theatricals, and woman's clubs.

The last division of *The South: A Documentary History* tells of efforts to redeem the region from being "The Nation's Economic Problem No. 1." The document defining it as such precedes glowing accounts of progress in diversification of crops and industry that bids fair to lead the South into a prosperity equal to that of the rest of the country.

Ina Woestemeyer Van Noppen presents in twenty-two chapters the various phases of Southern life through more than 350 years. She has done this successfully, not in her own words, but through the testimony of persons on the spot—natives, Northerners, and foreigners. Thereby do we get a series of pictures varied enough to bring the accusation of being disjointed. But out of this variety develops a concept nearer reality than any attempt that has been made, through vigorous interpretation to create a unity. Brought to the reader's attention is a South composed of many Souths, geographic, cultural and political; yet, the South, despite its many discordant aspects, is a distinct province bound together by racial attitudes, religion, rural psychology, and other traits listed at the beginning of this Introduction.

FRANCIS B. SIMKINS

1

European Beginnings in the New World

THE SPANISH EXPLORERS

The age of exploration and discovery is one of the most thrilling and exciting periods in the history of mankind. The voyages of Columbus and Magellan, the conquests of Cortez and Pizarro, are more amazing than fiction. The new world thus opened up for exploration and colonization inspired in man the lure of the new, the unknown, the dream that he too might achieve greatly, acquire glory for his country and wealth and prestige for himself. The world could become his "oyster which he with his sword would ope." The call of the wild new world was now a clear call to brave hearts and red-blooded men. It was a ringing challenge that led men to leave homes and hearths, the old, the staid, the secure. It offered the unparalleled thrill of discovery and a hitherto unrealizable hope for gold and glory.

The Spanish explorers or members of their expeditions left accounts of their routes, descriptions of land and people, and impressions—our earliest available information concerning the history of the South. The influence of the Spanish on the subsequent English settlements may be illustrated by the following examples: Spanish success with tropical agricultural products led English settlers to attempt to produce the same staples; possible Spanish attacks conditioned the location of the English colonies. Thus Jamestown was planted far enough up the James River to escape attacks by sea; Georgia was created as a buffer state between Spanish Florida and the Carolinas. Furthermore the Spanish first imported Negro slaves for a labor supply in the New World.

Among the preserved accounts of Spanish expeditions is one describing a journey from Tampa Bay to Mexico which lasted eight years, 1528 to 1536. Alvar Nunez da Vaca, the author, was a member of the party of Panfilo de Narvaez, who had been directed to colonize from Mexico to Florida. Motivated by a desire for gold and a curiosity concerning the interior of the continent, the band of men experienced starvation, shipwreck and death, only three members surviving to tell the story of the expedition. His narrative inspired other Spaniards to undertake similar ventures, and translations of the account appeared in England to arouse interest among adventurers there. The following account is from *The Journey of Alvar Nunez da Vaca and his companions from Florida to the Pacific, 1528-1536,* translated from his own account by Fanny Bandelier, New York, A. S. Barnes and Company, 1905, pp. 1-41.

On the 27th day of the month of June, 1527, the Governor Panfilo de Narvaez departed from the port of San Lucar de Barrameda, with authority and orders from your Majesty to conquer and govern the provinces that extend from the river of the Palms to the Cape of Florida, these provinces being on the main land. The fleet he took along consisted of five vessels, in which went about 600 men. . . . We arrived at the Island of Santo Domingo, where we remained nearly forty-five days, supplying ourselves with necessary things, especially horses. Here more than 140 men of our army forsook us, who wished to remain, on account of the proposals and promises made them by the people of the country. [After wintering in Cuba a party of 400 men and eighty horses, on four vessels and one brigantine, departed and] . . . we crossed to the coast of Florida, sighting land on Tuesday, the 12th day of the month of April. We coasted the way of Florida, and on Holy Thursday cast anchor at the mouth of a bay, at the head of which we saw certain houses and habitations of Indians.

On that same day the clerk, Alonso Enriquez, left and went to an island in the bay and called the Indians, who came and were with him a good while, and by way of exchange they gave him fish and some venison. The day following (which was Good Friday) the Governor disembarked, with as many men as his little boats would hold, and as we arrived at the huts or houses of the Indians we had seen, we found them abandoned and deserted, the people having left that same night in their canoes. One of those houses was so large that it could hold more than 300 people. The others were smaller, and we found a golden rattle among the nets. The next day the Governor hoisted flags in behalf of Your Majesty and took possession of the country in Your Royal name, exhibited his credentials, and was acknowledged as Governor according to Your Majesty's commands. . . . He then ordered the remainder of the men to disembark, also forty-two horses left (the others having perished on account of the great storms and the long time they had been on sea), and these few that remained were so thin and weak that they could be of little use for that time. The next day the Indians of the village came, and, although they spoke to us, as we had no interpreters we did not understand them; but they made many gestures and threats, and it seemed as if they beckoned to us to leave the country. Afterward, without offering any molestation, they went away.

After another day the Governor resolved to penetrate inland to explore the country and see what it contained. We went with him—the commissary, the inspector and myself, with forty men, among them six horsemen, who seemed likely to be of but little use. We took the direction of the north, and at the hour of vespers reached a very large bay, which appeared to sweep far inland. After remaining there that night and the next day, we returned to the place where the vessels and the men were. . . . [Later] we followed the shore of the bay, and after a march of four leagues, captured four Indians, to whom we showed maize in order to find out if they knew it, for until then we had seen no trace of it. They told us that they would take us to a place where there was maize and they led us to their village, at the end of the bay nearby, and there they showed us some that was not yet fit to be gathered. . . . We inquired of the Indians (by signs) . . . and they gave us to understand that, very far from there, was a province called Apalachen in which there was much gold. They also signified to us that in that province we would find everything we held in esteem. They said that in Apalachen there was plenty.

So, taking them as guides, we started, and after walking ten or twelve leagues, came to another village of fifteen houses, where there was a large cultivated patch of corn nearly ready for harvest, and also some that was already ripe. After staying there two days, we returned to the place where we had left the purser . . . and pilots [and told them] what we saw and the news the Indians had given us.

The next day . . . the Governor . . . told us that he had in mind to penetrate inland, while the vessels should follow the coast as far as the harbor; since the pilots said and believed that, if they went in the direction of the Palms they would reach it soon. On this he asked us to give our opinions. *

I replied that it seemed to me in no manner advisable to forsake the ships until they were in a safe port, held and occupied by us. . . . The commissary was of the contrary opinion saying, that we should not embark, but follow the coast in search of a harbor . . . while the vessels with the other men would follow to the same port. . . .

The Governor clung to his own idea . . . [and] forth-with ordered the people who were to go with him to get ready, providing themselves with what was necessary for the journey. . . .

On Saturday, the 1st of May, the day on which all this had happened, he ordered that they should give to each one of those who had to go with him, two pounds of ship-biscuit and one-half pound of bacon, and thus we set out upon our journey inland. [Thus the wanderings of this party started, and pursuing a northerly course, they reached the head of

Apalachee Bay in the Gulf of Mexico, after experiencing many trials such as hunger, illness, and Indian treachery. Finding none of the treasures they sought, Narvaez attempted escape for his party by sea.]

. . . the Governor . . . called them to his presence all together, and each one in particular, asking their opinion about this dismal country, so as to be able to get out of it and seek relief, for in that land there was none.

One-third of our people were dangerously ill, getting worse hourly, and we felt sure of meeting the same fate, with death as our only prospect, which in such a country was much worse yet. And considering these and many other inconveniences and that we had tried many expedients, we finally resorted to a very difficult one, which was to build some craft in which to leave the land. It seemed impossible, as none of us knew how to construct ships. We had no tools, no iron, no smithery, no oakum, no pitch, no tackling; finally, nothing of what was indispensable. Neither was there anybody to instruct us in shipbuilding, and, above all, there was nothing to eat, while the work was going on, for those who would have to perform the task. Considering all this, we agreed to think it over. Our parley ceased for that day, and everyone went off, leaving it to God, Our Lord, to put him on the right road according to His pleasure.

The next day God provided that one of the men should come, saying that he would make wooden flues, and bellows of deerskin, and as we were in such a state that anything appearing like relief seemed acceptable, and we told him to go to work, and agreed to make of our stirrups, spurs, cross-bows and other iron implements the nails, saws and hatchets and other tools we so greatly needed for our purpose.

In order to obtain food while the work proposed was in progress we determined upon four successive raids into Aute [an Indian village], with all the horses and men that were fit for service, and that on every third day a horse should be killed and the meat distributed among those who worked at the barges and among the sick. The raids were executed with such people and horses as were able, and they brought as many as four hundred fanegas of maize, although not without armed opposition from the Indians. We gathered plenty of palmettos, using their fibre and husk, twisting and preparing it in place of oakum for the barges. The work on these was done by the only carpenter we had, and progressed so rapidly that, beginning on the fourth day of August, on the twentieth day of the month of September five barges of twenty-two elbow lengths each were ready, caulked with palmetto oakum and tarred with pitch, which a Greek called Don Teodoro made from certain pines. Of the husk of palmettos, and of the tails and manes of the horses we made ropes and tackles, of our shirts sails, and of the junipers that grew there we made the oars, which we thought were necessary, and such was the stress in which our sins had placed us that only with very great trouble could we find stones for ballast and anchors for the barges, for we had not seen a stone in the whole country. We flayed the legs of the horses and tanned the skin to make leather pouches for carrying water.

During that time some of the party went to the coves and inlets for sea-food, and the Indians surprised them twice, killing ten of our men in plain view of the camp, without our being able to prevent it. We found them shot through and through with arrows, for, although several wore good armor, it was not sufficient to protect them, since, as I said before, they shot their arrows with such force and precision. According to the sworn statements of our pilots, we had travelled from the bay, to which we gave the name of the Cross, to this place, two hundred and eighty leagues, more or less.

In all these parts we saw no mountains nor heard of any, and before embarking we had lost over forty men through sickness and hunger, besides those killed by Indians. On the twenty-second day of the month of September we had eaten up all the horses but one. We embarked in the following order: In the barge of the Governor there were forty-nine men, and as many in the one entrusted to the purser and the commissary. The third barge he placed in charge of Captain Alonse del Castillo and of Andrés Dorantes, with forty-eight men; in another he placed two captains . . . with forty-seven men. The last one he gave to the inspector and to me, with forty-nine men, and, after clothing and supplies were put on board, the sides of the barges only rose half a foot above the water. Besides, we were so crowded as to be unable to stir. So great is the power of need that it brought us to venture out into such a troublesome sea in this manner, and without any one among us having the least knowledge of the art of navigation.

THE AMERICAN INDIANS

One cause of the uncertainty of European colonization in America was the presence of the red men, who were to be found along the entire coastal plain, a few hundred in some places, thousands in confederated neighborhoods elsewhere, living partly by hunting and fishing and in some measure by agriculture. At times they were hospitable to the invading white men, helping the strangers to plant native crops and giving the best of their food supply when needed, yet at other times destroying the settlements and people to protect the land of which they considered themselves owners and masters.

Indian life in the interior of the continent is described in the following narrative by the Gentleman of Elvas. Hernando de Soto received from the Spanish government a grant to settle the entire region north of the Gulf of Mexico. With six hundred soldiers he left the Florida coast, perhaps at Tampa Bay, in May,

1539. They marched north to the Savannah River, west to the Blue Ridge Mountains, southwest almost to the Gulf of Mexico near Mobile, then north to cross the Mississippi River near Memphis. Crossing through the Ozarks, the party reached eastern Oklahoma, then returned to the Mississippi River, where de Soto died of fever and was buried in the waters of the great river. The Gentleman of Elvas who wrote this account was a member of the expedition. While his account may be indefinite in details, having been written after his return from the expedition, it is the best narrative of this journey available. The text, from *Narratives of the Career of Hernando de Soto*, translated by Buckingham Smith, and edited by Edward G. Bourne, was published by Williams Barker Company, New York, 1904; reprinted, 1922, Allerton Book Co., and the following extract is from Volume I, pp. 3-91, *passim.*

Hernando de Soto had . . . nothing more than blade and buckler. . . . [He] went with Hernando Pizarro to conquer Peru. According to the report of many persons who were there, he distinguished himself over all the captains and principal personages present. . . . Hence, . . . bringing together in time, from portions falling to his lot, one hundred and eighty thousand cruzados, . . . which he brought with him to Spain, . . . [of which] the Emperor borrowed a part. . . . In Seville [he showed] himself . . . at court, spent largely, and went about attended by . . . his dependents, and by many others who there came about him. . . . The Emperor made him Governor of the Island of Cuba and Adelantado of Florida, with title of Marquis to a certain part of the territory he should conquer.

After Don Hernando had obtained the concession, a fidalgo arrived at Court from the Indies, Cabeca de Vaca by name, who had been in Florida with Narvaez; and he stated how he with four others had escaped, taking the way to New Spain; that the Governor had been lost in the sea, and the rest were all dead. . . .

[Hernando de Soto prepared an expedition to explore Florida. Among those who offered their services were some from Portugal and others from Castile.] He commanded a muster to be made, to which the Portuguese turned out in polished armour, and the Castilians very showily, in silk over silk, pinked and slashed. As such luxury did not appear to him becoming on such occasion, he ordered a review to be called for the next day, when every man should appear with his arms. . . . Those that Soto liked and accepted of were passed, counted, and enlisted; six hundred men in all followed him to Florida. . . .

[De Soto left Spain in 1539, and in March, 1540, we find him in the vicinity of Apalache where Narvaez became discouraged and abandoned his explorations. On the twenty-first of March the party reached a town called Toalli.] The houses of this town were . . . roofed with cane, after the fashion of tile. They are kept very clean: some have their sides so made of clay as to look like tapia. Throughout the cold country every Indian has a winter house, plastered inside and out, with a very small door, which is closed at dark, and a fire being made within, it remains heated like an oven, so that clothing is not needed during the night-time. He has likewise a house for summer, and near it a kitchen, where fire is made and bread baked. Maize is kept in a barbacoa, which is a house with wooden sides, like a room, raised aloft on four posts, and has a floor of cane. The difference between the houses of the masters, or principal men, and those of the common people is, besides being larger than the others, they have deep balconies on the front side, with cane seats, like benches; and about are many barbacoas, in which they bring together the tribute their people give them of maize, skins of deer, and blankets of the country. These are like shawls, some of them made from the inner bark of trees, and others of grass resembling nettle, which, by treading out, becomes like flax. The women use them for covering, wearing one about the body from the waist downward, and another over the shoulder, with the right arm left free, after the manner of the Gypsies: the men wear but one, which they carry over the shoulder in the same way, the loins being covered with a bragueiro of deer-skin, after the fashion of the woollen breech-cloth that was once the custom of Spain. The skins are well dressed, the colour being given to them that is wished, and in such perfection, that, when of vermilion, they look like very fine red broadcloth; and when black, the sort in use for shoes, they are of the purest. The same hues are given to blankets. . . .

[At the town of Achese, the Governor sent to call the Cacique from the farther side of the river, and spoke to him. The Cacique expressed good will.] The Governor responded, . . . and thanked him, and . . . told him that he was the child of the Sun, coming from its abode, and that he was going about the country, seeking for the greatest princ. there, and the richest province. The Cacique stated that farther on was a great lord, whose territory was called Ocute. He gave him a guide, who understood the language, to conduct him thither. . . . A high cross, made of wood, was set up in the middle of the town-yard; and as time did not allow more to be done, the Indians were instructed that it was put there to commemorate the suffering of Christ, who was God and man; that he had created the skies and the earth, and had suffered for the salvation of all, and therefore, that they should revere that sign; and they showed by their manner that they would do so.

The Governor set out on the first of April, and advanced through the country . . . and on the tenth arrived at Ocute. The Cacique sent him a present, by two thousand Indians, of many rabbits and partridges, maize, bread, many dogs, and two turkeys. On account of the scarcity of meat, the dogs were as much esteemed by the Christians as though they had been fat sheep. There was such want of salt, also, that oftentimes, in many places, a sick man had nothing for his nourishment, and was wasting away to bone, of some ail that elsewhere might have found a remedy, when sinking under pure debility he would say: "Now, if I had but a slice of meat, or only a few lumps of salt, I should not thus die."

The Indians never lacked meat. With arrows they get abundance of deer, turkeys, conies, and other wild animals, being very skilful in killing game, which the Christians were not; and even if they had been, there was not the opportunity for it, they being on the march the greater part of their time; nor did they, besides, ever dare to straggle off. Such was the craving for meat, that when the six hundred men who followed Soto arrived at a town, and found there twenty or thirty dogs, he who could get sight of one and kill him, thought he had done no little. . . .

[In October the expedition reached a town called Casiste, near the Black Warrior River, in the present state of Alabama. The Governor sent the master of the camp, Luis de Moscoco, with fifteen cavalry, to inform the Cacique of his approach.]

The Cacique was at home, in a piazza. Before his dwelling, on a high place, was spread a mat for him, upon which two cushions were placed one above another, to which he went and sat down, his men placing themselves around, some way removed, so that an open circle was formed about him, the Indians of highest rank being nearest to his person. One of them shaded him from the sun with a circular umbrella, spread wide, the size of a target, with a small stem, and having deer-skin extended over cross-sticks, quartered with red and white, which at a distance made it look of taffeta.

✓   ✓   ✓

The following description of the Indians of Virginia is taken from Robert Beverley, *The History and Present State of Virginia,* written in 1705, F. Fayram and J. Clarke, London, 1705, 1722 Edition, pp. 139-140, 9-10.

The *Indians* are of the middling and largest stature of the *English:* They are straight and well proportion'd, having the cleanest and most exact Limbs in the world: They are so perfect in their outward frame, that I never hear of one single *Indian,* that was either dwarfish, crooked, bandy-legg'd, or otherwise mis-shapen, . . .

Their Colour, when they are grown up, is a Chesnut brown and tawny; but much clearer in their Infancy. Their Skin comes afterwards to harden and grow blacker, by greasing and Sunning themselves. They have generally coal black Hair, and very black Eyes, which are most commonly grac'd with that sort of Squint which many of the *Jews* are observ'd to have. Their Women are generally Beautiful, posssessing an uncommon delicacy of Shape and Features, and wanting no Charm, but that of a fair Complexion.

The Men wear their Hair cut after several fanciful Fashions, sometimes greas'd, and sometimes painted. The Great Men, or better sort, preserve a long Lock behind for distinction. They pull their Beards up by the roots with a Muscle-shell; both Men and Women do the same by the other parts of their Body for Cleanliness sake. The Women wear the hair of the Head very long, either hanging at their backs, or brought before in a single Lock, bound up with a Fillet of Peak, or Beads. . . . It is commonly greased, and shining black, but never painted. . . .

The Ladies of Distinction wear deep Necklaces, Pendants, and Bracelets, made of small Cylinders of the Conque shell, which they call *Peak:* They likewise keep their Skin clean, and shining with Oyl, while the Men are commonly bedaub'd all over with Paint. . . .

The manner of the *Indians* treating their young Children is very strange, for instead of keeping them warm, at their first entry into the World, and wrapping them up, with I don't know how many Cloaths, according to our fond custom; the first thing they do, is to dip the Child over Head and Ears in cold Water, and then to bind it naked to a convenient Board, having a hole fitly plac'd for evacuation; but they always put Cotton, Wool, Furr, or other soft thing, for the Body to rest easy on, between the Child and the Board. In this posture they keep it several months, till the Bones begin to harden, the Joynts to knit, and the Limbs to grow strong; and when they let it loose from the Board, suffering it to crawl about, except when they are feeding, or playing with it.

While the Child is thus at the Board, they either lay it flat on its back, or set it leaning on one end, or else hang it up by a string fasten'd to the upper end of the Board for that purpose. The Child and Board being all this while carry'd about together. As our Women undress their Children to clean them and shift their Linnen, so do they theirs to wash and grease them.

The method the Women have of carrying their Children after they are suffer'd to crawl about, is very particular; they carry them at their backs in Summer, taking one Leg of the Child under their Arm, and the Counter-Arm of the Child in their Hand over their Shoulder; the other Leg hanging down, and the Child all the while holding fast with its other Hand; but in Winter they carry them in the hollow of their Match-coat at their back, leaving nothing but the Child's Head out. . . .

The method of the *Indian* Settlements is altogether by Cohabitation, in Townships, from fifty to five hundred Families in a Town, and each of these Towns is commonly called a Kingdom. Sometimes one King has the command of several of these Towns, when they happen to be united in his Hands, by Descent or Conquest; but in such cases there is always a Vice-regent appointed in the dependent Town, who is at once Governor, Judge, Chancellour, and has the same Power and Authority which the King himself has in the Town where he resides. This Viceroy is oblig'd to pay his Principal some small Tribute, as an acknowledgement of his submission, as likewise to follow him to his Wars, whenever he is requir'd.

The manner the *Indians* have of building their Houses is very slight and cheap; when they would erect a *Wigwang,* which is the *Indian* name for a House, they stick Saplins into the ground by one end, and bend the other at the top, fastening them together by strings made of fibrous Roots, the rind of Trees, or of the green Wood of the white Oak, which will rive into Thongs. The smallest sort of these Cabbins are conical like a Bee-hive; but the larger are built in an oblong form, and both are cover'd with the Bark of Trees, which will rive off into great flakes. Their Windows are little holes left open for the passage of the Light, which in bad weather they stop with Shutters of the same Bark, opening the Leeward Windows for Air and Light. Their Chimney, as among the true Born *Irish,* is a little hole in the top of the House, to let out the Smoak, having no sort of Funnel, or anything within, to confine the Smoak from ranging through the whole Roof of the Cabbins, if the vent will not let it out fast enough. The Fire is always made in the middle of the Cabbin. Their Door is a Pendant Mat, when they are near home; but when they go abroad, they barricado it with great Logs of Wood set against the Mat, which are sufficient to keep out Wild Beasts. There's never more than one Room in a House, except in some Houses of State, or Religion, where the Partition is made only by Mats, and loose Poles. . . .

Their Cookery has nothing commendable in it, but that it is perform'd with little trouble. They have no other Sauce but a good Stomach, which they seldom want. They boil, broil, or toast all the Meat they eat, and it is very common with them to boil Fish as well as Flesh with their *Homony;* This is *Indian* Corn soaked, broken in a Mortar, husked, and then boil'd in Water over a gentle Fire, for ten to twelve hours, to the consistence of Furmity. . . .

They have two ways of Broyling, *viz.* one by laying the Meat itself upon the Coals, the other by laying it upon Sticks rais'd upon Forks at some distance above the live Coals, which heats more gently, and drys up the Gravy; this they, and we also from them, call Barbacueing. . . .

Their Food is Fish and Flesh of all sorts. . . . They eat all sorts of Peas, Beans, and other Pulse, both parched and boiled. They make their Bread of *Indian* Corn, Wild Oats, or the Seed of the Sunflower. But when they eat their Bread, they eat it alone, and not with their Meat. . . . They delight much to feed on Roasting-ears; that is, the *Indian* Corn, gathered green and milky, before it is grown to its full bigness, and roasted before the Fire. . . .

THE BEGINNING OF ENGLISH PLANTATIONS

For almost a century before the settlement of Jamestown, the imagination of English writers had been caught by the discoveries being made in the new Western World. Sir Thomas More, in 1516, published his *Utopia,* in which he described a supposed traveler who accompanied Amerigo Vespucci to South America and remained behind to reach home by traveling westward by land and sea. Among the places visited by the traveler was the island of Utopia, or *Nowhere,* an aristocratic republic where everybody worked but where the members of the laboring population were slaves, the Utopians devoting their energies to learning and science. More's idea of establishing an ideal society in the new world caught the fancy of Sir Humphrey Gilbert and other visionaries of sixteenth century England. The text of the following excerpt from More's *Utopia* is from the *Roxburge Library of Classics,* edited by Nathan Haskell Cole, Forrest Morgan, and Caroline Ticknor, The Roxburge Press, New York, 1904, Vol. VIII, pp. 2749-2759, *passim.*

They have built over all the country farmhouses for husbandmen, which are well contrived, and furnished with all things necessary for country labor. Inhabitants are sent by turns from the cities to dwell in them; no country family has fewer than forty men and women in it, besides two slaves. There is a master and a mistress set over every family; and over thirty families there is a magistrate.

Every year twenty of this family come back to the town, after they have stayed two years in the country; and in their room there are other twenty sent from the town, that they may learn country work from those that have been already one year in the country, as they must teach those that come to them the next from the town. By this means such as dwell in those country farms are never ignorant of agriculture. . . .

The chief and almost the only business of the . . . magistrates is to take care that no man may live idle, but that every one may follow his trade diligently: yet they do not wear themselves out with perpetual toil, from morning to night, as if they were beasts of burden, which as it is indeed a heavy slavery, so it is everywhere the common course of life amongst all mechanics except the Utopians; but they, dividing the day and night into twenty-four hours, appoint six of these for work; three of which are before dinner, and three after. Then they sup, and at eight o'clock, counting from noon, go to bed and sleep eight hours. The rest of their time besides that taken up in work, eating, and sleeping, is left to every man's discretion; yet they are not to abuse that interval to luxury and idleness, but must employ it in some proper exercise according to their various inclinations, which is for the most part reading.

ᛋ   ᛋ   ᛋ

Queen Elizabeth granted to Sir Humphrey Gilbert a patent for discovery and colonization in America. He made a voyage in 1578-79 and made plans to establish a colony. In 1583 he sailed for Newfoundland with five ships and two hundred and sixty men. Explorations were made; but his ship was sunk on the return voyage and Gilbert lost his life. His half-brother, Sir Walter Raleigh, applied for and received a renewal of the patent. The following accounts illustrate Raleigh's efforts to plant a colony in present North Carolina. The text is from *Explorations,*

Descriptions, and Attempted Settlements of Carolina, 1584-1590, collected by Richard Hakluyt, 1600; reprint edited by David Leroy Corbitt, State Department of Archives and History, Raleigh, 1948.

THE FIRST VOYAGE MADE TO THE COASTS OF AMERICA WITH TWO BARKS, WHEREIN WERE CAPTAINS M. PHILIP AMADAS AND M. ARTHUR BARLOW WHO DISCOVERED PART OF THE COUNTRY NOW CALLED VIRGINIA, ANNO 1584. WRITTEN BY ONE OF THE SAID CAPTAINS, AND SENT TO SIR WALTER RALEIGH, KNIGHT, AT WHOSE CHARGE AND DIRECTION THE SAID VOYAGE WAS SET FORTH.

The 27th day of April, in the year of our redemption, 1584, we departed from the west of England, with two barks well furnished with men and victuals. . . .

The tenth of May we arrived at the Canaries, and the tenth of June in this present year, we were fallen with the Islands of the West Indies. . . . At which islands we found the air very unwholesome, and our men grew for the most part ill disposed: so that having refreshed ourselves with sweet water, and fresh victuals, we departed the twelfth day of our arrival there. . . .

The second of July we found shoal water, where we smelled so sweet and strong a smell as if we had been in the midst of some delicate garden abounding with all kinds of odoriferous flowers, by which we were assured that the land could not be far distant; . . . the fourth of the same month we arrived upon the coast, which we supposed to be a continent and firm land, and we sailed along the same a hundred and twenty English miles before we could find any entrance or river issuing into the sea. The first that appeared unto us we entered, though not without some difficulty, and cast anchor about three harquebus-shot within the haven's mouth, on the left hand of the same; and, after thanks given to God for our safe arrival thither, we manned our boats and went to view the land adjoining and to take possession of the same in the right of the Queen's most excellent majesty as the rightful Queen princess of the same, and after delivered the same over to your use, according to her majesty's grant and letters patent, under her highness' great seal. Which being performed according to the ceremonies used in such enterprises, we viewed the land about us, being where we first landed very sandy and low toward the water side, but so full of grapes as the very beating and surge of the sea overflowed them, of which we found such plenty . . . that I think in all the world the like abundance is not to be found; and myself having seen those parts of Europe that most abound, find such difference as were incredible to be written. . . .

This island had many goodly woods full of deer, conies, hares and fowl, even in the midst of summer, in incredible abundance; . . . the highest and reddest cedars of the world, far bettering the cedars of the Azores . . . ; pines, cypress, sassaphras, . . . the tree that bears the rind of black cinnamon . . . and many other of excellent smell and quality.

We remained by the side of this island two whole days before we saw any people of the country. The third day we espied one small boat rowing towards us, having in it three persons; this boat came to the island side . . . and, . . . two of the people remaining, the third came along the shore side towards us, and we being then all within board, he walked up and down and upon the point of land next unto us. . . . [We] rowed to the land . . . never making any show of fear or doubt. And after he had spoken of many things not understood by us, we brought him, with his own good liking, aboard the ships, and gave him a shirt, a hat and some other things, and made him taste of our wine and meat, which he liked very well; and after having viewed both barks he departed. . . .

The next day there came to us divers boats, and in one of them the king's brother, accompanied by forty or fifty men, very handsome and goodly people, and in their behavior as mannerly and civil as any of Europe. . . . When we came to shore with our weapons he never moved from his place, . . . nor never mistrusted any harm to be offered from us, but sitting still, he beckoned us to come and sit by him, which we performed, and, being set, he made all signs of joy and welcome, striking on his head and breast, and afterwards on ours, to show we were all one, smiling and making show the best he could of all love and familiarity. After he had made a long speech to us, we presented him with divers things, which he received very joyfully and thankfully. . . .

After we had presented . . . [the king's brother] with such things as we thought he liked, we likewise gave somewhat to the others that sat with him on the mat; but presently he arose and took all from them and put it into his own basket, . . . as the rest were but his servants and followers. A day or two after this we fell to trading with them, exchanging some things we had for chamoys, buff and deer skins. When we showed him all our packet of merchandise, of all things that he saw, a bright tin dish most pleased him, which he presently took up and clapt it before his breast, and after making a hole in the brim thereof and hung it about his neck, making signs that it would defend him against his enemies' arrows; for these people maintain a deadly and terrible war with the people and the king adjoining. We exchanged our tin dish for twenty skins, worth fifty crowns. They offered us a good exchange for our hatchets and axes and for knives, and would have given anything for swords, but we would not depart with any. . . .

When we first had sight of this country some thought the first land we saw to be the continent, but after we entered into the haven we saw before us another mighty sea; for there lieth along the coast a tract of islands two hundred miles in length, adjoining the ocean sea, and between the islands two or three entrances. When you are entered between them (these islands being very narrow for the most part, as in most places six miles broad, in some places less, in few more), then there appeared another great sea, containing in breadth in some places forty and in some fifty, in some twenty miles over, before you come unto the continent, and in this enclosed sea there are above a hundred islands of divers bigness, whereof one is sixteen miles long. . . .

We brought home also two of the savages, being lusty men, whose names were *Wanchese* and *Manteo*.

↑   ↑   ↑

The island on which Amadas and Barlow explored was Roanoke Island. In 1585 Raleigh sent a colonizing expedition to the island, but Indian troubles and fear of the Spanish led the settlers to abandon the colony when Drake stopped there after a raid on the Spanish West Indies. A third expedition to Roanoke Island under the command of John White arrived in 1587. The colonists remained, and White sailed to England for supplies. His return to the colony was delayed three years because of the Spanish Armada, and upon his arrival at the island in 1590 he found no trace of the colonists. The following account of that disappointing experience is from David Leroy Corbitt, reprint of *Explorations, Descriptions, and Attempted Settlements of South Carolina, 1584-1590,* by Richard Hakluyt, 1600, State Department of Archives and History, Raleigh, 1948, pp. 122-123.

. . . We came to the place where I left our colony in the year *1586*. In all this way we saw in the sand the print of savages' feet of two or three sorts trodden in the night; and as we entered up the sandy bank, upon a tree, in the very brow thereof were curiously carved these fair Roman letters, C R O: which letters we presently knew to signify the place, where I should find the planters seated, according to a secret token agreed upon between them and me at my last departure from them; which was, that in any ways they should not fail to write or carve on the trees or posts of the doors the name of the place where they should be seated; for at my coming away they were prepared to remove from Roanoke fifty miles into the main. Therefore at my departure from them in An. 1587, I willed them, that if they should happen to be distressed in any of those places, that then they should carve over the sign or name a cross + in this form; but we found no such letters of distress. And having well considered of this, we passed toward the place where they were left in sundry houses, but we found the houses taken down, and the place very strongly enclosed with a high palisado of great trees, with curtains and flankers, very fort-like; and one of the chief trees or posts at the right side of the entrance had the bark torn off, and five foot from the ground in fair capital letters, was graven C R O A T A N, without any cross or sign of distress; this done, we entered into the palisado, where we found many bars of iron, two pigs of lead, four iron-fowlers, iron locker shot, and such like heavy things thrown here and there, almost overgrown with grass and weeds. From thence we went along the water side toward the point of the creek, to see if we could find any sign of their boat or pinnace, but we could perceive no sign of them, nor any of the last falcons or small ordnance which was left with them at my departure from them. At our return from the creek, some of our sailors meeting us, told us that they had found where divers chests had been hidden, and long since digged up again and broken up, and much of the goods in them spoiled and scattered about, but nothing left of such things as the savages knew any use of, undefaced. . . . Presently Captain Cook and I went to the place, which was in the end of an old trench, made two years past by Captain Amadas, where we found five chests that had been carefully hidden of the planters, and of the same chests three were my own, and about the place many of my things, spoiled and broken. . . . this could be no other but the deed of the savages. . . .

THE FIRST PERMANENT SETTLEMENT

A comedy entitled *Eastward Hoe* written by George Chapman, Ben Jonson, and John Marston, in 1605, illustrates the interest in Virginia at that time. Alexander Brown quoted the following lines from the play to illustrate how the authors joked about this subject of popular interest. Brown's work, *The Genesis of the United States,* Houghton Mifflin Co., Boston, 1890, two volumes, covers the period 1605-1616, and deals chiefly with the movement in England which was responsible for the establishment of Virginia. The materials are letters, broadsides, charters, and other documents. The extract is from Vol. I, pp. 29-32, *passim.*

Act II, Scene 1

Quicksilver. . . . Well, dad, let him [Sir William Petronell Flash] have money; all he could anyway get is bestowed on a ship, nowe bound for Virginia; the frame of which voyage is so closely convaide that his new lady nor any of his friends know it. Notwithstanding, as soone as his ladies hand is gotten to the sale of her inheritance, and you have furnisht him with money, he will instantly hoyst saile and away.

Security. Now, a franck gale of wind go with him, Maister Franck! we have too fewe such knight adventurers. Who would not sell away competent certenties to purchase (with any danger) excellent uncertenties? Your true knight venturer ever does it. Let his wife seale today, he shall have his money today. . . .

Act III

Enter a Messenger.

Messenger. Sir Petronel, here are three or fowre gentlemen desire to speak with you.

Petronel. What are they?

Quicksilver. They are your followers in this voyage, knight Captaine Seagul and his associates; I met them this morning, and told them you would be here.

Petronel. Let them enter, I pray you; I know they long to be gone, for their stay is dangerous.

Enter Seagul, Scapethrift, and Spendall.

Seagul. God save my honorable Collonell!

Petronel. Welcome, good Captaine Seagul, and worthy gentlemen; if you will meete my friend Franck here, and mee, at the Blewe Anchor Taverne by Billingsgate this evening, wee will there drinke to our happy voyage, be merry, and take boate to our ship with all expedition. . . .

Act III, Scene 2

Enter Seagull, Spendall, and Scapethrift in the Blewe Anchor Taverne, with a Drawer.

Seagull. Come, drawer, pierce your neatest hogsheads, and lets have cheare—not fit for your Billingsgate taverne, but for our Virginian Colonel; he will be here instantly.

Drawer. You shal have al things fit, sir; please you have any more wine?

Spendal. More wine, slave! whether we drinke it or no, spill it, and draw more.

Scapethrift. Fill all the pottes in your house with all sorts of licour, and let 'hem waite on us here like souldiers in their pewter coates; and though we doe not emploi them now, yet we will maintaine 'hem till we doe.

Drawer. Said like an honorable captaine; you shal have all you can commaund, sir.   *Exit Drawer*

Seagull. Come, boyes, Virginia longs till we share the rest of her maiden-head.

Spendall. Why, is she inhabited alreadie with any English?

Seagull. A whole countrie of English is there, man, bread of those that were left there in '79; they have married with the Indians, and make 'hem bring forth as beautiful faces as any we have in England; and therefore the Indians are so in love with 'hem, that all the treasure they have they lay at their feete.

Scapethrift. But is there such treasure there, Captaine, as I have heard?

Seagull. I tell, thee, golde is more plentifull there then copper is with us; and for as much redde copper as I can bring Ile have thrise the weight in gold. Why, man, all their dripping-pans and their chamber-potts are pure gould; and all the chaines with which they chaine up their streets are massie gold; all the prisoners they take are fetered in gold; and for rubies and diamonds they goe forth on holydayes and gather 'hem by the seashore to hang on their childrens coates, and sticke in their children's caps, as commonly as our children weare saffron-gilt brooches and groates with hoales in 'hem.

Scapethrift. And is it a pleasant countrie withall?

Seagull. As ever the sunne shind on: temperate and ful of all sorts of excellent viands; wilde bore is as common there as our tamest bacon is here; venison as mutton. And then you shall live freely there, without sargeants, or courtiers, or lawyers, or intelligencers. . . . Therfor your meanes to advancement, there it is simple, and not preposterously mixt. You may bee an alderman there, and never be scavinger; you may be any other officer, and never be a slave. You may come to preferment enough, and never be a pandar; to riches and fortune enough, and have never the more villainie nor the lesse witte. Besides, there wee shall have no more law then conscience, and not too much of eyther; serve God enough, eate and drink inough, and "enough is as good as a feast."

Spendall. Gods, me! and how farre is it thether?

Seagull. Some six weekes saile, no more, with any indifferent good winde. And if I get to any part of the coaste of Affrica, ile saile thether with any wind; or When I come to Cape Finister, ther's a foreright winde continuall wafts us till we come to Virginia. See, our collonell's come.

Enter Sir Petronell Flash with his followers. . . . .

Sir Petronell. . . . Wee'll have our provided supper brought a bord Sir Francis Drake's ship, that hath compast the world, where, with full cups and banquets, wee will doe sacrifice for a prosperous voyage. [Drake's ship, the Golden Hind, was preserved in the Deptford dockyard as a memorial of the first English voyage around the world, the cabin being turned into a banqueting house.]

ᶠ   ᶠ   ᶠ

Many plans were proposed for colonizing Virginia. Some attempted to persuade Parliament to plant a colony. The following paper from the British Museum, believed to have been written in 1605, offered to Parliament fourteen arguments in favor of such a public settlement, among which are the following, quoted from Alexander Brown, Editor, *The Genesis of the United States,* Boston, Houghton Mifflin Company, Boston, 1890, Vol. I, pp. 37-39.

The Realme of Englande is an Islande impossible to be otherwise fortified then by strong shippes and able mariners and is secluded from all corners with those of the maine continent, therefore fit abundance of vessels be prepared to exporte and importe merchandise. . . . .

The life of shipping resteth in number of able Mariners and worthy Chieftaines, which cannot be maintained without assurance of rewarde of honorable meanes to be imployed and sufficient seconde of their adventurs.

It is honorable for a state rather to backe an exploite by a publique consent then by a private monopoly. . . . .

That Realme is most compleet and wealthie which hath sufficient to serve itselfe or can finde the meanes to exporte of the naturall comodities then [if] it hath occasion necessarily to importe, consequently it muste insue that by a publique consent, a Collony transported into a good and plentiful climate able to furnish our wantes, our monies and wares that nowe run into the handes of our adversaries or cowld frendes shall passe unto our frendes and naturall kinsmen and from them likewise we shall receive such things as shalbe most available to our necessities, which intercourse of trade maye rather be called a home bread trafique then a forraigne exchange.

ᛩ   ᛩ   ᛩ

The plan adopted by the English government was for the King to grant land to two groups of interested adventurers, known as the London and Plymouth Companies, who would undertake to settle the colonies. Both companies were incorporated by the same charter, issued in April, 1606. A brief description of this first charter is contained in a document by Arthur Wodenoth, "A Short Collection of the Most Remarkable Passages from the originall to the Dissolution of the Virginia Company," London, 1651, quoted by Brown, *op. cit.*, Vol. I, p. 51.

The Continent of *Virginia* discovered in the time of Q.Elizabeth (who gave it that name) was in the beginning of K.*James* his reign much advanced in reputation, and the advantages promised thereby seemed then worthy the best consideration how to make it a Plantation for the *English*. Whereupon many worthy Patriots, Lords, Knights, Gentlemen, merchants and others held consultation, which produced a large subscription of Adventurers, . . . [who procured a patent] establishing and impowering a Councell of State, as well as a generall Company, Whereby the whole affairs of the Plantation whould in *perpetuity bee governed.*

ᛩ   ᛩ   ᛩ

On the twentieth of December, 1606, three ships embarked to begin the settlement financed by the London Company. The directions for the colony were written by His Majesties Council for Virginia. The following extract is from Neill's *Virginia Company of London*, pp. 4-8, quoted by Brown, *op. cit.*, Vol. I, pp. 76-77.

First, Whereas the good ship called the Sarah Constant and the ship called the Goodspeed, with a pinnace called the Discovery are now ready victualed, riged, and furnished for the said voyage; . . . [we] do ordain and appoint that Capt. Christopher Newport shall have the sole charge to appoint such captains, soldiers, and marriners, as shall either command or be shiped to pass in the said ships or pinnace. . . .

And whereas we have caused to be delivered unto the said Captain Newport, Captain Barthol. Gosnold and Captain John Ratcliffe, several instruments close sealed with the Counsels seal aforesaid containing the names of such persons as we have appointed to be of his Majesties Counsel in the said country of Virginia, we do ordain and direct that the said Captain Christopher Newport, Captain Bartholomew Gosnold, and Captain John Ratcliffe, or the survivor or survivors of them, shall within four and twenty hourse next after the said ship shall arrive upon the said coast of Virginia and not before open and unseal the said Instruments and declare and publish unto all the company the names therein set down, and that the persons by us therein named are . . . his Majesties Counsel of his first Colony in Virginia. . . .

The following instructions for the Council in Virginia are quoted from Hening's *Statutes at Large* in Brown, *op. cit.*, Vol. I, pp. 67-75, *passim*. . . . .

. . . we do specially ordaine . . . [that the] president and councells, and the ministers of the said several colonies . . . with all diligence, care, and respect, doe provide, that the true word, and service of God and Christian faith be preached, planted, and used, not only within every of the said several colonies, and plantations, but alsoe as much as they may amongst the salvage people which doe or shall adjoine unto them. . . .

. . . we doe hereby establish and ordaine, that the said several colonies and plantations, and every person and persons of the same, severally and respectively, shall within every of their several precincts, for the space of five years, next after their first landing upon the said coast of Virginia and America, trade together all in one stocke or devideably, but in two or three stocks at the most, and bring not only all the fruits of their labours there, but alsoe all such other goods and commodities which shall be brought out of England, or any other place, into the same collonies, into severall magazines or store houses, for that purpose to be made, and erected there . . . and that every person of every the said several colonies and plantations shall be furnished with all necessaries out of those several magazines or storehouses which shall belong to the said colony and plantation. . . .

George Percy, who was president of the colony from September, 1609, to May, 1610, wrote a detailed account of the first voyage to Jamestown and of the first events of that settlement. The following extract illustrates the insecurity of those first settlers. It is quoted from Brown, *op. cit.*, Vol. I, pp. 152-168, *passim*.

On Saturday the twentieth of December in the yeere 1606. the fleet fell from London, and the fift of January we anchored in the Downes; but the winds continued contrarie so long, that we were forced to stay there some time, where wee suffered great stormes, but by the skilfulnesse of the Captaine wee suffered no great losse or danger. . . . The six and twentieth day of Aprill about foure a clocke in the morning, wee descried the Land of Virginia: the same day wee entered into the Bay of Chesupioc directly, without any let or hindrance; there wee landed and discovered a little way, but we could find nothing worth speaking of, but faire meddows and goodly tall Trees, with such Fresh-waters running through the woods, as I was almost ravished at the first sight of.

At night, when we were going aboard, there came the Savages creeping upon all foure, from the Hills like Beares, with their Bowes in their mouthes, charged us very desperately in the faces, hurt Captaine Gabrill Archer in both his hands, and a sayler in two places of the body very dangerous. After they had spent their Arrowes, and felt the sharpnesse of our shot, they retired into the Woods with a great noise, and so left us. . . . . .

The nine and twentieth day we set up a Crosse at Chesupioc Bay, and named that place Cape Henry. . . . [After exploring for several days, and having various encounters with the Indians] the twelfth day [of May] we went backe to our ships, and discovered a point of Land called Archer's Hope, which was sufficient with a little labour to defend ourselves against any Enemy. The soile was good and fruitfull, with excellent good Timber. There are also great store of Vines in Bignesse of a man's thigh, running up to the tops of the Trees in great abundance. . . .

The thirteenth day we came to our seating place in Paspihas countrey, some eight miles from the point of Land. . . . The fourteenth we landed all our men which were set to worke about the fortifications and others to watch and ward as it was convenient. The first night of our landing, about midnight, there came some Savages sayling close to our quarter; presently there was an alarum given; upon that the savages ran away, and we were not troubled any more by them that night. . . . .

The fifteenth day of June, we had built and finished our Fort which was triangle wise, having three Bulwarkes at every corner like a halfe Moone, and four or five pieces of Artillerie mounted in them, we had made ourselves sufficiently strong for these Savages, we had also sowne most of our Corne on two Mountaines, it sprang a mans height from the ground, this countrey is a fruitfull soile, bearing many goodlie and fruitfull Trees, as Mulberries, Cherries, Walnuts, Cedars, Cypresse, Sassafras, and Vines in great abundance. . . .

Captaine Newporte being gone for England, leaving us (one hundred and foure persons) verie bare and scantie of victualls, furthermore in warres and in danger of the Savages, we hoped after a supply which Captaine Newport promised within twentie weeks. . . .

The sixt of August there died John Asbie of the bloudie Flixe [dysentery]. The ninth day died George Flowre of the swelling. The tenth day died

William Bruster gentleman, of a wound given by the Savages, and was buried the eleventh day.

The fourteenth day Jerome Alicock, Ancient, died of a wound, the same day Francis Midwinter, Edward Moris Corporall died suddenly. The fifteenth day, there died Edward Brown and Stephen Galthrope. The sixteenth day, there died Thomas Gower, Gentleman. The seventeeth day, there died Thomas Mounslie. The eighteenth, . . . Robert Pennington, and John Martine Gentleman. . . . The two and twentieth of August, there died Captaine Bartholomew Gosnold, one of our Councell, he was honourably buried, having all the Ordnance in the Fort shot off with many vollies of small shot. . . . There were never Englishmen left in a forreigne Countrey in such misery as we were in this new discovered Virginia. Wee watched every three nights, lying on the bare cold ground, what weather soever came, and warded all the next day, which brought our men to bee the most feeble wretches, our food was but a small can of Barlie sod in water to five men a day, our drinke cold water taken out of the River, which was at a flood verie Salt, at a low tide full of slime and filth, which was the destruction of many of our men. Thus we lived for the space of five moneths in this miserable distresse, not having five able men to man our Bulwarkes upon any occasion.

⚜ ⚜ ⚜

Captain John Smith was an explorer and soldier of fortune who served against the Turks, after which he returned to England and participated in organizing the London Company. He was one of the first colonists in Virginia and a member of the governing council, active in exploration and in obtaining food from the Indians for the starving settlers. In 1608 he became President of the colony, serving for about a year. He wrote several accounts of the early history of Virginia, including his *General History of Virginia,* the Fourth Book of which he compiled from the narratives of other men many years after he returned to England. The following extract from that book is quoted from Captain John Smith, "Works," edited by Edward Arber, *The English Scholar's Library,* The Editor, Birmingham, England, 1884, pp. 497-499, 573-578.

THE STARVING TIME

The day before Captaine *Smith* returned for *England* with the ships [3 Oct., 1609], Captaine *Davis* arriued in a small Pinace, with some sixteen proper men more: . . . the Saluages no sooner vnderstood *Smith* was gone, but they all reuolted, and did spoile and murther all they incountered. . . . Now we all found the losse of Captaine *Smith,* yea his greatest maligners could now curse his losse: as for corne prouision and contributions from the Saluages, we had nothing but mortall wounds, with clubs and arrowes; as for our Hogs, Hens, Sheepe, Horse, or what liued, our commanders, officers, and Saluages daily consumed them, some small proportions sometimes we tasted, till all was deuoured; then swords, armes, pieces, or any-

thing, wee traded with the saluages, whose cruell fingers were so oft im-
brewed in our blouds, that what by their crueltie, our gouernours indiscretion, and the losse of our ships, of fiue hundred within six moneths after
Captaine *Smiths* departure, there remained not past sixtie men, women and
children, most miserable and poore creatures; and those were preserued
for the most part by roots, herbes, acornes, walnuts, berries, now and then
a little fish: they that had startch in these extremities, made no small vse of
it; yea, euen the very skinnes of our horses. Nay, so great was our famine,
that a Saluage we slew and buried, the poorer sort took him up againe and
eat him; . . . and one amongst the rest did kill his wife, powdered [salted]
her, and had eaten part of her before it was knowne; for which hee was
executed, as hee well deserued. . . . This was that time, which still to this
day [1624] we called the staruing time; . . . the occasion was our owne,
for want of prouidence industrie and gouernment, and not the barrennesse
and defect of the Countrie, as is generally supposed. . . . This in ten
daies more, would have supplanted us all with death.

But God that would not that this Countrie should be vnplanted, sent
Sir *Thomas Gates,* and Sir *George Sommers* with one hundred and fiftie
people . . . to preserue us. . . .

THE MASSACRE UPON THE TWO AND TWENTIETH OF MARCH, 1622

Sir *Francis Wyat* at his arriual was aduertised he found the Countrey
setled in such a firme peace, as most men there thought sure and vnuiolable,
not onely in regard of their promises, but of a necessitie. The poore weake
Saluages being euery way bettered by vs, and safely sheltred and defended,
whereby wee might freely follow our businesse: and such was the conceit of
this conceited peace, as that there was seldome or neuer a sword, and sel-
domer a peece [used], except for a Deere or Fowle; by which assurances
the most plantations were placed straglingly and scatteringly, as a choice
veine of rich ground inuited them, and further from neighbours the better.
Their houses [were] generally open to the Saluages, who were alwaies
friendly fed at their tables, and lodged in their bed-chambers; which made
the way plaine to effect their intents, and the conuersion of the Saluages as
they supposed.

Having occasion to send to *Opechankanough* about the middle of March,
hee vsed the Messenger well, and told him he held the peace so firme, the
sky should fall or he dissolued it; yet such was the treachery of those people,
when they had contriued our destruction, euen but two daies before the
massacre, they guided our men with much kindness thorow the woods,
and one *Browne* that liued among them to learne the language, they sent
home to his Master. Yea, they borrowed our boats to transport themselues
ouer the Riuer, to consult on the deuillish murder that insued, and of our
vtter extirpation, which God of his mercy (by the meanes of one of them-

selues conuerted to Christianitie) preuented; and as well on the Friday morning that fatall day, being the two and twentieth of March, as also in the euening before, as at other times they came vnarmed into our houses, with Deere, Turkies, Fish, Fruits, and other prouisions to sell vs: yea in some places sat downe at breakfast with our people, whom immediately with their own tools they slew most barbarously, not sparing either age or sex, man woman or childe; so sudden in their execution, that few or none discerned the weapon or blow that brought them to their destruction. In which manner also they slew many of our people at seuerell works in the fields, well knowing in what places and quarters each of our men were, in regard of their familiaritie with vs, for the effecting that great masterpeece of work their conuersion: and by this meanes that fatall morning vnder the bloudy and barbarous hands at that perfidious and inhumane people, three hundred and forty seuen men, women and children; mostly by their owne weapons; and not being content with their liues, they fell againe vpon the dead bodies, making as well as they could a fresh murder, defacing, dragging, and mangling their dead carkases into many peeces, and carrying some parts away in derision, with base and brutish triumph. . . .

[The natives had] warning giuen them one from another in all their habitations, though farre asunder, to meet at the day and houre appointed for our destruction at al our seuerall Plantations; some directed to one place, some to another. . . . Some entring their houses vnder colour of trading, so took their advantage; others drawing vs abroad vnder faire pretences; and the rest suddenly falling vpon those that were at their labours.

✓   ✓   ✓

The Spanish government kept in close touch with the efforts of England to colonize Virginia, through a system of espionage. Spies within the colony and in the Council for Virginia in England reported to the Spanish ambassador, who in turn wrote the information to the King of Spain. On March 16, 1606, this ambassador, Don Pedro de Zuniga, sent to the King a warning of the plans for a settlement. Late in the nineteenth century the text of this letter and of subsequent correspondence was obtained in Spain by the American ambassador, J. L. M. Curry and published in Alexander Brown, Editor, *The Genesis of the United States,* Houghton Mifflin Company, Boston, 1890. The following extracts are from Vol. I, pp. 45-46, and Vol. II, pp. 737-8, 743.

Letter from Don Pedro de Zuniga . . . . They also propose to do another thing, which is to send 500 or 600 men, private individuals of this kingdom to people Virginia in the Indies, close to Florida. They sent to that country some small number of men in the years gone by, and having afterwards sent again, they found a part of them alive.

They brought 14 or 15 months ago about ten natives, that they might learn English, and they have kept some of them here in London and others in the country, teaching and training them to say how good that country is for people to go there and inhabit it. The chief leader in this business is the Justiciario Chief Justice, Sir John Popham, who is a very great Puritan and exceedingly desirous, whatever sedition may be spoken of, to say that he does it in order to drive out from here thieves and traitors to be drowned in the sea. I have not yet spoken to the king about this; I shall do so when I see in what way they will try to satisfy me in the council. [Popham may have told Zuniga that the purpose of the undertaking was to drive thieves out of England, merely to quiet the latter's objections to the enterprise.]

On October 17, 1614, Don Diego Sarmiento y Acuna, a later ambassador, wrote:

The ship in which they offered me that Don Diego de Molino should be brought in, has returned without him. Two Englishmen, who were in the same vessel and whom I had charged, without the one knowing of the other, to bring me a very detailed account of the state in which matters were over there—to see if it agreed with what I have been told by others—and likewise informing me of all that had occurred there, why Don Diego de Molino did not come, or whether he had died. . . . They have returned and brought me letters from Don Diego, which one had sewed between the soles of his shoes, while the other had them in a coil of rope, as I herewith send it to Y.M.; because they knew that they would be searched and carefully examined, and if they found that they carried letters from Don Diego, they would hang them, without saying a word, and besides would learn what Don Diego had written.

✔ ✔ ✔

Don Diego de Molino (or Molina), to whom the second letter referred, was a spy sent out on a Spanish caravel to spy out conditions in the English colony. He was one of three men, one of whom died, the second being hanged when it was discovered that he was an Englishman. Don Diego de Molina was kept a prisoner for five years, despite the efforts of the Spanish government to secure his release; he was returned to his own country in 1616. While in Virginia he wrote the following description to the Spanish government. The text is from a letter from Don Diego de Molino to Don Diego Sarmiento y Acuna, June 14, 1614, quoted in Alexander Brown, *The Genesis of the United States,* Houghton Mifflin Company, Boston, 1890, Vol. II, p. 743.

There are here three settlements: this in which I have been three years, altho' now they have ordered us to a prison in a stockade a mile distant, with orders not to speak to me, because the Marshall, says, I persuade and have persuaded Edward 'Colaque' [Coles] that he should flee with five other persons to Florida, as he put him to work. . . . The other settlement is 20 leagues up the river, which they made 3 years ago. They have made still another three leagues higher up this Spring, where almost all the people are, who altogether, and in all parts amount to two hundred fifty persons, men, women and children. Three stockades which they have at the mouth of the river have been dismantled, and thus there are in them only six or seven men. I take it for granted that the King, our Master, would do a work worthy of his greatness, if he were to take these people away from here, and I am convinced that the Lord brought me hither by such extraordinary and unheard of events in order to become the Moses of these unfortunate people—not, as they say, as a spy. . . .

2

Expansion of the English Colonies

MARYLAND

George Calvert, first Lord Baltimore, persuaded King Charles I to grant him land north of the Potomac River. As the charter was granted after his death, his son, Cecilius Calvert, received the proprietary rights to the land between Virginia and forty degrees north latitude, and sent an expedition of more than two hundred immigrants to establish a colony in 1634. A group of Virginians had already established homesteads and fur trading arrangements with the Indians of the Chesapeake Bay region, and the rival interests struggled for possession of Maryland until 1638 when the king rejected the petition of the Virginians. Some characteristics of the new colony are described in a tract written in 1666 by George Alsop, a former indentured servant, from which the following extracts are taken. The text is from his *A Character of the Province of Maryland*, 1666, reprinted as Fund Publication, No. 15, Maryland Historical Society, Baltimore, 1880, pp. 44-49.

MARY-LAND, not from the remoteness of her situation, but from the regularity of her well-ordered Government, may (without sin, I think) be called *Singular:* And though she is not supported with such large Revenues as some of her Neighbours are, yet such is her wisdom in a reserved silence, and not in pomp, to shew her well-conditioned Estate, in relieving at a distance the proud poverty of those that wont be seen they want, as well as those which by undeniable necessities are drove upon the Rocks of pinching wants. . . . .

Here every man lives quietly, and follows his labour and implyment desiredly; and by the protection of the Laws, they are supported from those molestious troubles that ever attend upon the Commons of other States and Kingdoms, as well as from the Aquafortial operation of great and eating Taxes. Here's nothing to be levyed out of the Granaries of Corn; but contrarywise, by a Law every Domestick Governor of a family is enjoyned to make or cause to be made so much Corn by a just limitation, as shall be sufficient for him and his Family. . . .

Once every year within this Province is an Assembly called, and out of every respective County (by the consent of the people) there is chosen a number of men, and to them is deliver'd up the Grievances of the Country; and they maturely debate the matters, and according to their Consciences make Laws for the general good of the people. . . . .

Common Ale-houses (whose dwellings are the only Receptacles of debauchery and baseness, and those Schools that train up Youth, as well as Age, to ruine), in this Province there are none; neither hath Youth his swing or range in such a profuse and unbridled liberty as in other Countries; for from an ancient Custom at the primitive seating of the place, the Son works as well as the Servant, (an excellent cure for untam'd Youth) so that before they eat their bread, they are commonly taught how to earn it; which makes them by that time Age speaks them capable of receiving that which their Parents indulgency is ready to give them, and which partly is by their own laborious industry purchased, they manage it with such a serious, grave, and watching care, as if they had been Masters of Families, trained up in that domestick and governing power from their Cradles.

NORTH CAROLINA

About 1653 Virginians began to move into the region of Albemarle Sound and the Chowan River, a migration which was encouraged by the Virginia Assembly. Among the men of prominence who encouraged the expansion were Edward Bland, a merchant of Virginia, who made an expedition into the region north of the Chowan River in 1650, and Francis Yeardley, son of Sir George Yeardley, former governor of Virginia, who financed several expeditions from Virginia into Carolina. The following narrative is quoted from Edward Bland, *The Discovery of New Brittaine*, 1650, reprinted by Joseph Sabin, New York, 1873.

Who ever thou art that desirest the Advancement of Gods glory by conversion of the Indians, the Augmentation of the English Common-wealth, in extending its liberties; I would advise thee to consider the present benefit and future profits that will arise in the wel setling Virginia's Confines, especially that happy Country of New Brittaine, in the Latitude of 35. and 37. degrees, of more temperate Clymate than that the English now inhabit, abounding with great Rivers of long extent, and encompassing a great part . . . of Virginia's continent; a place so easie to be settled in, in regard that Horse and Cattle in foure or five dayes may be conveyed for the benefit of the Undertakers, and all inconveniences avoyded which commonly attend New Plantations, being supplied with necessaries from the Neighborhood of Virginia.

That the Assembly of Virginia (as may be seene by their Order since my returne hereto procured) have conceived a hundred to be a sufficient

force and competence for the establishment of that country in which Tobacco will grow larger and more in quantity. Sugar canes are supposed
naturally to be there, or at least if implanted will undoubtedly flourish:
For we brought with us thence extraordinary Canes of twenty-five foot long
and six inches round; there is also great store of fish, and the Inhabitants
relate that there is plenty of Salt made to the sunne without art; Tobacco
Pipes have beene seene among these Indians tipt with Silver, and they
weare Copper Plates about their necks: They have two Crops of Indian
Corne yearly, whereas Virginia hath but one. What I write, is what I have
proved; I cordially wish some more then private Spirits would take it into
their consideration, so may it prove most advantagious to particular and
publick ends; for which so prayeth,

Your faithfull servant,
Edward Bland

✓   ✓   ✓

Francis Yeardley's "Narrative of Excursions into Carolina, 1654," is reprinted
from *State Papers of John Thurloe,* Thomas Birch, London, 1742, Vol. II,
pp. 273-274.

. . . we find [in Carolina] a most fertile, gallant, rich soil, flourishing in
all the abundance of nature, especially in the rich mulberry and vine, a
serene air, and temperate clime, and experimentally rich in precious minerals; and lastly, I may say, parallel with any place for rich land, and
stately timbers of all sorts; a place indeed unacquainted with our Virginia's nipping frosts, no winter, or very little cold to be found there.
[Yeardley arranged to purchase land from the Roanoke Indians on the
following terms:] I dispatched a boat with six hands, one being a carpenter,
to build [the Indian chief] an English house, my promise . . . being to
comply in that matter. I sent 200L. sterling, in trust, to purchase and pay
for what land they should like, the which in little time they effected, and
purchased, and paid for three great rivers, and also such others as they
should like of southerly; and in solemn manner took possession of the
country, in the name, and on the behalf, of the commonwealth of England;
and actual possession was solemnly given them by the great commander,
and all the great men of the rest of the provinces, in delivering them a
turf of the earth with an arrow shot into it; and so the Indians totally left
the lands and rivers to us, retiring to a new habitation, where our people
built the great commander a fair house, the which I am to furnish with
English utensils and chattels. . . . .

I am lastly, Sir, a suitor to you, for some silkworm eggs, and materials for
the making of silk, and what other good fruits, or roots, or plants, may be
proper for such a country. Above all, my desire is to the olive, some trees

of which could we procure, would rejoice me; for wine we cannot want with industry. . . .

ᛉ   ᛉ   ᛉ

From Nansemond, the most southern settlement of Virginia, planters moved into the wilderness to the southwest, until a considerable number of families made clearings in Albemarle. Of this settlement George Chalmers, in his *Political Annals of the Province of Carolina,* wrote the following account. The text is from B. R. Carroll, Editor, *Historical Collections of South Carolina,* Harper and Brothers, New York, 1836, Vol. II, pp. 283-4.

At the epoch of the Carolinian patent of 1663, a small plantation had been . . . , for some years, established within its boundaries, on the northeastern shores of the river Chowan, which was now honoured with the name of Albemarle. . . . But as it was so distant from the seat of Virginian government, the inhabitants yielded little obedience to its power, and had lived for some time without any perceivable rule. And nothing could be more wise than the appointment of Sir William Berkeley, the governor of Virginia, as general superintendent of the affairs of the county of Albemarle. In September, 1663, he was empowered, by the proprietaries, to nominate a governor and council of six, who were authorized to rule that little community according to the powers granted by the royal charter; to confirm former possessions, and to grant lands to everyone, allowing them three years to pay the quitrents; to make laws, with the consent of the delegates of the freemen, for the general good, transmitting them for the approbation of the proprietaries. . . . Berkeley . . . appointed Drummond, a man of sufficient prudence and abilities, the first governor, with other officers. . . . Such is the early history of North Carolina.

ᛉ   ᛉ   ᛉ

In 1666 the Carolina proprietors published "A Brief Description of the Province of Carolina," hoping to attract settlers. This document contained a description of a settlement started in 1664 on the Cape Fear River, and a statement of the privileges to be enjoyed by the colonists. It ended with a cordial invitation to would-be planters and indentured servants. The text of the following extract is from B. R. Carroll, Editor, *Historical Collections of South Carolina,* Harper and Brothers, New York, 1836, Vol. II, pp. 11-17, *passim.*

In the midst of this fertile Province, in the Latitude of 34 degrees, there is a colony of *English* seated, who landed there the 29 of May, *Anno* 1664. and are in all about 800 persons, who have overcome all the difficulties that attend the first attempts, and have cleared the way for those that come after, who will find good houses to be in whilst their own are in building; good forts to secure them from their enemies; and many things brought from other parts there, increasing to their no small advantage. The entrance into the River, now called *Cape-Feare* River, the situation of the

Cape, and trending of the Land, is plainly laid down to the eye in the Map annexed. The River is barred at the entrance, but there is a channel close abord the Cape that will convey in safety a ship of 300 Tons, and as soon as a ship is over the Bar, the River is 5 or 6 fathom deep for a 100 miles from the Sea; this Bar is a great security to the Colony against a forreign Invasion, the channel being hard to find by those that have not experience of it, and yet safe enough to those that know it. . . . Up the River about 20 or 30 mile, . . . they have made a Town, called Charlestown. . . .

Is there therefore any younger Brother who is born of Gentile blood, and whose Spirit is elevated above the common sort, and yet the hard usage of our Country hath not allowed suitable fortune; he will not surely be afraid to leave his Native Soil to advance his Fortunes equal to his Blood and Spirit, and so he will avoid those unlawful ways too many of our young Gentlemen take to maintain themselves according to their high education, having but small Estates; here, with a few Servants and a small Stock a great Estate may be raised, although his Birth have not entitled him to any of the Land of his Ancestors, yet his Industry may supply him so, as to make him the head of as famous a family. . . .

If any Maid or single Woman have a desire to go over, they will think themselves in the Golden Age, when Men paid a Dowry for their Wives; for if they be but Civil, and under 50 years of Age, some honest Man or other, will purchase them for their Wives.

SOUTH CAROLINA

By 1660 Barbados, in the West Indies, was a flourishing English colony, already believed by the planters to be overpopulated. A group of these planters engaged William Hilton to explore the Carolina coast, and after receiving an encouraging report from him two Barbadian planters and Sir William Berkeley, governor of Virginia, they persuaded King Charles II to grant to themselves and five other associates the area between 31° and 36° north latitude and extending westward to the "south seas." The proprietors encouraged immigrants from Virginia and Barbados to attempt settlements. The first such settlement, described in the preceding selection, was soon abandoned. A second village called Charlestown, located on the Ashley River, was relocated in 1680 at the junction of the Ashley and Cooper rivers, the present site of Charleston. Several pamphlets were published in England advertising the advantages of that part of Carolina. The following, attributed to Thomas Ashe, described the agricultural products of that colony in 1682. The text is from B. R. Carroll, Editor, *Historical Collections of South Carolina*, Harper & Brothers, New York, 1836, Vol. II, pp. 67-69, 81-83.

Gardens as yet they have not much improved or minded, their Designs having otherwise more profitably engaged them in settling and cultivating their Plantations with good Provisions and numerous Stocks of Cattle; which

two things by Planters are esteemed the basis and Props of all New Plantations and Settlements; before which be well accomplished and performed,
nothing to any purpose can be effected; . . . but now their Gardens begin
to be supplied with such Herbs and Flowers which to the Smell or Eye are
pleasing and agreeable, viz. The Rose, Tulip, Carnation, and Lilly &c.
Their Provision which grows in the Field is chiefly Indian Corn, which
produces a vast Increase, yearly, yielding Two plentiful Harvests, of which
they make wholesome Bread, and good Bisket, which gives a strong, sound,
and nourishing Diet. . . . At Carolina they have lately invented a way of
makeing with it good sound Beer; but it's strong and heady. . . .

   Tobacco grows very well . . . but finding a great deal of trouble in the
Planting and Cure of it, and the great quantities which Virginia, and other
of His Majesties Plantations make, rendring it a Drug over all Europe;
they do not much regard or encourage its Planting. . . . Tarr made of the
resinous Juice of the Pine (which boyl'd to a thicker Consistence is Pitch)
they make great quantities yearly, transporting several Tuns to Barbadoes,
Jamaica, and the Caribbe Islands. Indigo they have made, and that good:
the reason why they have desisted I can not learn. . . . .

The Principal place where the English are now settled lies scituated on a
point of Land about two Leagues from the Sea, between Ashly and Cooper
Rivers, . . . the place called Charles Town, . . . very commodiously scituated from many other Navigable Rivers that lie near it on which Planters
are seated; by the advantage of Creeks, which have a Communication from
one great River to another, at the Tide or Ebb the Planters may bring
their Commodities to the Town as to the Common Market and Magazine
both for Trade and Shipping. . . . At our being there was judged in the
Country a 1000 or 1200 Souls; but the great Numbers of Families from
England, Ireland, Berbadoes, Jamaica, and the Caribees, which daily Transport themselves thither, have more than doubled that Number. . . . to
encourage People to Transport themselves thither, the Lord Proprietors
give unto all Masters and Mistresses of Families, to their Children, Men-
Servants and Maid-Servants if above sixteen years of Age, fifty to all such
under . . . Acres of Land to be held for ever, annually paying a Penny an
Acre to the Lord Proprietors to commence in 2 Years after it's survey'd.

GEORGIA

   The last English colony to be established in North America was Georgia.
Widespread unemployment and economic distress in England had resulted in the
imprisonment of many persons for debt. James Oglethorpe, a member of Parliament, a philanthropist and a promoter, proposed the establishment of a new
Crown colony to which debtors might be exported as settlers. His plan was
broadened to include persecuted Protestants from continental Europe. In 1732

a charter was granted to a board of trustees who were to serve for twenty-one years, enjoying both legislative and executive powers. Persons of high estate, as well as impoverished ones, were allowed to settle in the new colony. Several motives prompted the English government to support this project. It might serve as an outlet for excess population, a market for English manufactures, and as a buffer colony between the Spanish settlements and the English. Georgia promised to be a utopia. The following description of Savannah, the first settlement in Georgia, was written in 1735, when the colony was two years old. The text is from *A New Voyage to Georgia,* an extremely rare pamphlet reprinted in *Collections of the Georgia Historical Society,* Savannah, Vol. II, 1842, p. 40.

Savannah is a very pleasant town, being situated on a beautiful bluff, at least sixty feet high, on the said river; it is a fine navigable river, so that ships of any burden may come up to the town, and a great many miles above; the town is very regularly laid out, and they now have at least forty houses in it; they are at present obliged to have all their things up by a crane from the water, but I understand Mr. Oglethorpe has laid some scheme for another contrivance; the houses are all of them of the same size, that is twenty-two by sixteen. . . . The honorable trustees have a beautiful garden there, consisting of ten acres, where are a great many white mulberry trees, vines, and orange trees raised, on purpose for the poor people. . . . I do not in the least question, but by the great assistance they have had from England, which has been laid out to the best advantage, and the good economy of the honorable trustees, it will, in a few years time, become a flourishing country. The chief manufacture they go upon is silk and wine, and it will not be long before they will bring both to perfection. I think it is the pleasantest climate in the world; for it is neither too warm in the summer, nor too cold in the winter. They certainly have the finest water in the world, and the land is extra-ordinary good; this may certainly be called the land of Canaan.

✔ ✔ ✔

Within the first ten years of settlement a group of the settlers sent petitions to the English government protesting against the arbitrary rule of the trustees. These were answered by various reports prepared at the direction of the trustees. The two following selections are written from the point of view of the trustees. The text of the first is from *An Account Showing the Progress of the Colony of Georgia in America, From Its First Establishment,* published per order of the Honourable the Trustees, London, 1741; reprinted as No. 5, September, 1897, *Colonial Tracts,* George P. Humphrey, Rochester, New York, pp. 3-22, *passim.* The second is from "A State of the Province of Georgia," a paper drawn up at the suggestion of the Trustees, by William Stephens, Esq., Secretary of the Colony; reprinted in *Collections of the Georgia Historical Society,* Savannah, Vol. II, 1842, pp. 71-78, *passim.*

In pursuance of his majesty's charter, and in order to fulfill the good intents and purposes therein expressed, it was thought necessary for the trustees to send over such poor people and foreign Protestants as were willing to live in Georgia, not only to cultivate the lands, but at the same time to strengthen his majesty's colonies. For which purpose they considered each inhabitant both as a planter and a soldier; and they were therefore to be provided with arms for their defence, as well as tools for their cultivation and to be taught the exercise of both, and towns were to be laid out for their settlements, and lands allotted to each of them for their maintenance as near to those towns as conveniently could be, that they might never have occasion to be too far distant from their towns, which were to be regarded as garrisons. . . .

As the military strength of the province was particularly to be taken care of, . . . each lot of land was to be considered as a military fief, and to contain so much in quantity as would support such planter and his family; and fifty acres were judged sufficient. . . .

The persons sent over were poor indigent people . . . ; they were maintained at the expense of the government during their voyage, and their passage was paid for them and they were provided with tools, arms, seeds, and other necessaries, and supported from the public store, many of them at least for four years . . . from their first landing. . . . It was thought necessary to require the inhabitants to cultivate their lands within a limited time, in order to raise raw silk, which was intended to be one of the products there, a certain proportion of white mulberry trees were to be planted on every ten acres of land when cleared, with a power for the trustees to reenter on the parts that should remain uncultivated. . . .

And as other persons applied to the trustees for grants of land in order to go over and settle there at their own expense, particular grants were made . . . under the following conditions: viz., That they should within twelve months from the date of their grants, go to and arrive in Georgia with one man-servant for every fifty acres granted them, and should with such servants abide, settle, inhabit, and continue there for three years. That they should within ten years clear and cultivate one-fifth part of the land granted them, and within the next ten years clear and cultivate three-fifths more of the said lands, and plant one thousand white mulberry trees upon every one hundred acres thereof when cleared. And that they should not at any time hire, keep, lodge, board, or employ any negroes within Georgia on any account whatsoever without special leave; . . . and every such man servant when requested there-unto by any writing under the hand and seal of the master, [would be granted] twenty acres of land under the same tenure. . . .

The number of people sent on the charity from the beginning to the ninth of June, 1733 . . . amounted to one hundred and fifty-two; of whom one hundred and forty-one were Britons, and eleven were foreign protestants. The men numbered sixty-one. . . . On the island of Tybee, at the entrance of the river, a beacon was erected ninety feet high, which has been of great service, not only to ships entering the river Savannah, but to those likewise which sail by the coast, there being none like it all along the coast of America. . . .

About fifteen miles from Savannah is a village called Abercorn; about twenty miles further up the river is the town of Ebenezer, where the Saltsz-burgers are settled with two ministers, one of whom computed that the number of his congregation in June, 1738, consisted of one hundred and forty-six.

✓   ✓   ✓

Narrative of William Stephens.

[Augusta] was laid out by the trustees' orders in the year 1735, which has thriven prodigiously; there are several warehouses thoroughly well furnished with goods for the Indian trade, and five large boats belonging to the different inhabitants of the town, which can carry about nine or ten thousand weight of deerskins each, making four or five voyages at least in a year to Charleston, for exporting to England; and the value of each cargo is computed to be from twelve to fifteen hundred pounds sterling. Hither all the English traders, with their servants, resort in the spring; and it is computed above two thousand horses come thither at that season; and the traders, packhorsemen, servants, townsmen, and others, depending upon that business, are moderately computed to ·be six hundred white men, who live by their trade, carrying upon packhorses all kinds of proper English goods; for which the Indians pay in deer-skins, beaver, and other furs; each Indian hunter is reckoned to get three hundred weight of deer-skins in a year. This is a very advantageous trade to England, since it is mostly paid for in woollen and iron. . . .

At Augusta there is a handsome fort, where there is a small garrison of about twelve or fifteen men, besides officers; and one reason that drew the traders to settle the town of Augusta, was the safety they received from this fort, which stands upon high ground on the side of the river Savannah, which is there one hundred and forty yards wide, and very deep; another reason was the richness and fertility of the land. The great value of this town of Augusta occasioned the General to have a path marked out, through the woods, from thence to Old Ebenezer. . . .

[At Darien] Scotts Highlanders are settled; the buildings are mostly huts, but tight and warm; and they have a little fort. They have been industrious in planting, and have got into driving of cattle, for the supply of the regiment, &c.; but this last year most of them going voluntarily into the war, little was done at home, where their families remained.

Below the town of Darien, is the town of Frederica, where there is a strong fort, and brick store-houses, many good buildings in the town, some of which are brick. . . .

It ought not here to be passed over, how ready the country is to receive a number of German families, accustomed to husbandry, such as usually come once a year down the Rhine to Holland, and embark thence for America or the East Indies. . . . The terms are, they pay half their passage themselves on embarking, and six weeks after their arrival, to pay the other half, which they generally do, with private contracts to the people; but in case they do not, then they may be bound by the ship's master for four or five years, if they are above twenty-one years of age; but if under, they may be bound until the age of twenty-one, if men, and eighteen if girls. . . .

THE WESTWARD MOVEMENT

Not long after Virginians trekked southward to lay out plantations south of the Dismal Swamp, in Albemarle, their westward advance began. The fur trade of the coastal region in Virginia had been exhausted. John Lederer, a German and an agent of the Governor of Virginia, one of the first explorers to have recorded a trip to the crest of the Appalachians, gave the following advice to anyone who wished to follow his trail to trade with the Indians. The text is from *The Discoveries of John Lederer, in Three Several Marches from Virginia to the West of Carolina, 1669-1670:* Collected and Translated out of the Latine from his Discourse and Writings by Sir William Talbot (London, 1672), reprinted, Rochester, 1902, p. 29.

If you barely designe a home-trade with neighbour-Indians, for skins of deer, beaver, otter, wild-cat, fox, racoon, etc., your truck is a sort of course trading cloth, of which a yard and a half makes a matchcoat or mantle fit for their wear: as also axes, hoes, knives, sizars, and all sorts of edg'd tools. Guns, powder, and shot, etc. are commodities they will greedily barter for: but to supply the Indians with arms and ammunition, is prohibited in all English governments.

In dealing with the Indians, you must be positive and at a word: for if they perswade you to fall any thing in your price, they will spend time in higgling for further abatements, and seldom conclude any bargain. Sometimes you may with brandy or strong liquor dispose them to an humour of giving you ten times the value of your commodity; and at other times they are so hide-bound, that they will not offer half the market-price, especially if they be aware that you have a designe to circumvent them with drink, or that . . . you have a desire to their goods, which you must seem to slight and disparage.

To the remoter Indians, you must carry other kinde of truck, as small looking-glasses, pictures, beads, and bracelets of glass, knives, sizars, and all manner of gaudy toys and knacks for children, which are light and portable. For they are apt to admire such trinkets, and will purchase them at any rate, either with their currant coyn of small shells, which they call roanoack or peack, or perhaps with pearl, vermilion, pieces of christal.

❧   ❧   ❧

From 1670 on, scattered settlements were made west of the Fall Line. Hugh Jones, a Jamestown clergyman, wrote a history of Virginia in which he described these settlements. The text is from Hugh Jones, *The Present State of Virginia,* London, 1724, reprinted for Joseph Sabin, New York, 1865, pp. 14, 59.

[Colonel Alexander Spotswood, Governor of Virginia,] built a Fort called *Christianna,* which tho' not so far back, yet proved of great Service and Use; where at his sole Expense (I think) I have seen Seventy-seven *Indian Children* at a Time at School, under the careful Management of the worthy *Mr. Charles Griffin,* who lived there some years for that purpose. . . . .

Beyond *Col. Spotswood's* Furnace above the Falls of the *Rappahannock* River, within view of the vast *Mountains,* he has founded a Town called *Germanna,* for some *Germans* sent thither by *Queen Anne,* who are now removed up farther. Here he has Servants and Workmen of most handycraft Trades; and he is building a Church, Court House and Dwelling-House for himself: and with his Servants and Negroes he has cleared Plantations about it, proposing great Encouragement for people to come and settle in that uninhabited Part of the World, lately divided into a County.

Beyond this are seated the Colony of *Germans* or *Palatines,* with Allowance of good Quantities of rich Land, at easy or no Rates, who thrive very well, and live happily, and entertain generously.

Governor *Spotswood,* when he undertook the great Discovery of the *Passage* over the *Mountains* [in 1716,] attended with sufficient Guard and Pioneers and Gentlemen, with a sufficient Stock of Provision, with abundant Fatigue *passed* these *Mountains,* and cut *his Majesty's name* in a *Rock* upon the *Highest* of them, naming it MOUNT GEORGE; and in complaisance the Gentlemen from the Governor's Name, called the Mountain next in Height, *Mount Alexander.*

For this Expedition they were obliged to provide a great quantity of Horse-Shoes; (Things seldom used in the lower Parts of the Country, where there are few Stones:) Upon which Account the Governor upon their Return presented each of his Companions with a Golden Horse-Shoe, (some of which I have seen studded with valuable Stones resembling the Heads of Nails) with this inscription on one Side: *Sic juvat transcendere montes* (Thus it aids one to climb over mountains): and on the other is written the tramontane Order. This he instituted to encourage Gentlemen to venture backwards, and make Discoveries, and new Settlements: Any Gentleman being entitled to wear this Golden Shoe that can prove his having drank *His Majesty's Health* upon Mount George.

❧   ❧   ❧

Speculation was an important feature of expansion in America. Many young men became proprietors, making a business of buying lands and selling them at a higher figure to actual settlers. These speculators encouraged families to move out to unoccupied parts of the colonies. Often these vast tracts were given to promoters with the understanding that they would locate settlers on them.

Typical of grants instrumental in the settlement of the Shenandoah Valley of Virginia was that of 118,491 acres of land to Sir John Randolph in 1736, which was later conveyed to William Beverley. The following letter was written by Beverley requesting that a friend in the House of Burgesses secure such a grant for him. The text is from the Virginia *Calendar of State Papers,* arranged and edited by William P. Palmer, *et al.,* printed under the authority and direction of H. W. Flournoy, Secretary of the Commonwealth, Richmond, 1875, Vol. I, pp. 217-218.

April 30th, 1732

Dear Sir,

I am persuaded that I can get a number of people from Pensilvania to settle on Shenondore, if I can obtain an order of Council for some Land there, and I beg ye favour of you to get me an order at the first Council held after you receive this, for fifteen thousand acres of Land, lying on both sides of ye main River of Shenondore to include an old field, called and known by ye name of Massanutting Town, and running back & above & below the same on ye said river to include the Quantity; . . . for ye northern men are fond of buying land there, because they can buy it, for six or seven pounds pr. hundred acres, cheaper than they can take up land in pensilvania and they don't care to go as far as Wmsburg. . . .

I am

Dear Sir, your most obedient
humble servant W. Beverley

✠   ✠   ✠

Beverley said that people from Pennsylvania would settle on the land, and after he had received the grant he sent agents into Lancaster, Chester, and other counties of eastern Pennsylvania, to post circulars and advertise the attractions of the unsettled valley. The geographical situation made penetration from Pennsylvania to this back country of Virginia especially convenient. In 1738 the tide of German and Scotch-Irish immigration to the valley began, and by 1745 it was at its height. Settlers came on horseback and brought their possessions on pack horses. At first these settlers traded at Lancaster, Pennsylvania, and at New Castle, Delaware; but gradually their trade shifted to Williamsburg and later to Richmond. Among their products were butter, cheese, ginseng, hemp, skins, and furs.

William Byrd, a Virginia land speculator, planned to secure his settlers directly from Europe. The following request for a land grant was read at a Council held in Williamsburg in June, 1735. It is from the Virginia *Calendar of State Papers,* edited by William P. Palmer, *et al.,* 1875, Vol. I, p. 223.

On the *Petition* of Wm. Byrd Esqr sett forth that he speedily Expects a Number of Switzers, and other foreign Protestants to come over to this county & praying that 100,000 Acres of Land may be granted him for their Accommodation & Settlement, to be taken up in one or more Tracts, . . . free & Discharged from the Purchase of rights & upon the terms on which other Remote Frontier Lands have been granted— It is ordered the Petitioner have leave to take up 100,000 acres of land . . . on Condition of settling one family at least upon every 1000 acres, within the space of two years from & after the last Day of October next ensuing the date hereof.

✓   ✓   ✓

In the years 1759 and 1760 the Reverend Andrew Burnaby toured the Shenandoah Valley and was much pleased with the settlements there. The text of his description is from his *Travels Through the Middle Settlements in North America in the Years 1759 and 1760*, T. Payne, London, Third Edition, 1798, pp. 43-44.

The River Shenando rises a great way to the southward from under this Great North-Ridge. It runs through Augusta county, and falls into the Potowmac somewhere in Frederic. At the place where I ferried over, it is only about a hundred yards wide; and indeed it is no where, I believe, very broad. It is exceedingly romantic and beautiful, forming great variety of falls, and is so transparent, that you may see the smallest pebble at the depth of eight or ten feet. . . . The low grounds upon the banks of this river are very rich and fertile; they are chiefly settled by Germans, who gain a comfortable livelihood by raising stock for the troops, and sending butter down into the lower parts of the country. I could not but reflect with pleasure on the situation of these people; and think if there is such a thing as happiness in this life, that they enjoy it. Far from the bustle of the world, they live in the most delightful climate, and the richest soil imaginable: they are everywhere surrounded with beautiful prospects and sylvan scenes; lofty mountains, transparent streams, falls of water, rich vallies, and majestic woods; the whole interspersed with an infinite variety of flowering shrubs, constitute the landscape surrounding them: they are subject to few diseases; are generally robust; and live in perfect liberty; they are ignorant of want, and acquainted with but few vices. Their inexperience of the elegancies of life, precludes any regret that they possess not the means of enjoying them: but they possess what many princes would give half their dominion for, health, content, and tranquillity of mind.

✓   ✓   ✓

In 1737 the British Crown granted to Murray Cymble and James Huey, two merchants of London, warrants for 1,200,000 acres of land in North Carolina, upon condition that they settle 6000 Protestants on the land and pay as quitrents four shillings per acre. These two merchants were acting merely as trustees for one Henry McCulloch, another London merchant, and his associates. One of the associates, Arthur Dobbs, received 200,000 acres. Later Dobbs was made Governor of North Carolina, and in one of his reports to the Board of Trade and Plantations he described conditions on his western lands. The text of his report is from

William L. Saunders, Editor, *Colonial Records of North Carolina, 1662-1776,* P. M. Hale, etc., Raleigh, 1886-90, Vol. V, pp. 353ff.

I sett out on the 17th of June to view my Lands, and at the same time the Western frontier and fix a place to station our Frontier Company. . . . I took my roote by the Heads of New River in Onslow County, called the rich Lands. . . .

There are at present 75 families on my Lands. I viewed betwixt 30 and 40 of them, and except two there was not less than 5 or 6 to 10 children in each family, each going barefooted in their shifts in warm weather, no woman wearing more than a shift and one thin petticoat; They are a colony from Ireland removed from Pennsylvania, of what we call Scotch Irish Presbyterians who with others in the neighboring Tracts had settled together in order to have a teacher of their own opinion and choice; Besides these there are 22 families of German or Swiss, who are all an industrious people, they raise horses cows and hogs with a few sheep, they raise Indian Corn, wheat, barley, rye and oats and make good butter and tolerable cheese, and they have gone into indigo with good success, which they sell at Charles Town, having a waggon road to it, tho' 200 miles distant, because our roads are not yet shortened, and properly laid out, and from the many merchants there, they afford them English goods cheaper, than at present in this Province, the trade being in fewer hands they take a much higher price. This year they have suffered much by the dry season, having not had as much rain from the middle of March to July, as to enter the earth 2 inches, and since only chance thunder showers, so that great part of their indigo is so short as not to yield a Crop, and their corn hurt, the air is fine, water good, running springs from each Hill and the Country so healthy that few or none have died since their settlement 7 or 8 years ago, they sow flax for their own use and cotton, and what Hemp they have sown is tall and good, All these high hills which they call barren, and won't take are excellent for vines, with which they are overspread but burnt down yearly, that few are left to bear grapes, the whole soil rich red loaming soil intermixed with marchasites and spar. . . .

⸱   ⸱   ⸱

America was highly advertised in Europe, and many groups came from Germany and Switzerland to settle on the cheap lands of the interior. The following memorial of a group of Swiss people who wished to settle in North Carolina will illustrate the difficulties faced by such parties of immigrants. The text is from William L. Saunders, Editor, *Colonial Records of North Carolina, 1662-1776,* P. M. Hale, etc., Raleigh, 1886-90, Vol. IV, p. 18.

MAY IT PLEASE YOUR EXCELLENCY,

We have been informed by a little Boock printed in Berne that the King of England wants Maun that are brought up to country Buissiness and know how to improve Land and make Butter and Cheese, in the Royal Province of Carolina wich as wee heard is a land flowing with milck and Honey, wee think ourselves happy to bekome the Subjects of so great and generous a King and usefull to the most charitable Nations under Heaven.

Wee have sold our small Substance in our native country and meight have paid our expences But as wee were instead of fourteen days, fourteen Weeks upon the Rhine where the Armees have made all things scarce wee have laid out all our money and must now beg your Excellency to recommend us and our wives and children to the Kings bounty that he may send us to that blesses Country in the Two Boathes commanded by Captain Thomson, who has been so good to the Saltzburgers while our Captain has been so hard to us and wee shall for ever pray that God may bless the King and his good people

To his Excellency My Lord Harrington one of his Majesty's Principall Secretaries of State London.

✓ ✓ ✓

Alexander Hewit, a Presbyterian clergyman and a resident of Charleston, published a history of South Carolina in 1779, in which he referred to the migration of Scotch-Irish to the Carolinas. This migration was encouraged by the planters of the coastal plain who feared the dangers of Indians, Spanish, or French attacks, and revolt of their slaves at home. Settlers in the back country could be brought in to help quell such a revolt and could absorb Indian attacks. The text is from B. R. Carroll, Editor, *Historical Collections of South Carolina*, Harper and Brothers, New York, 1836, Vol. I, pp. 484-490.

[After the French and Indian War] The assembly appropriated a large fund for bounties to foreign Protestants, and such industrious poor people of Britain and Ireland as should resort to the province within three years, and settle on the inland parts. Two townships, each containing 48,000 acres, were laid out; one on the Savannah, called Mecklenburgh, and the other on the waters of the Santee . . . called Londonderry; to be divided among emigrants, allowing one hundred acres for every man, and fifty for every woman and child, that should come and settle in the back woods. . . . .

Besides foreign Protestants, several persons from England and Scotland resorted to Carolina after the peace. But of all other countries none has furnished the province with so many inhabitants as Ireland. In the northern counties of that kingdom the spirit of emigration seized the people to such a degree, that it threatened almost a total depopulation. Such multitudes of husbandmen, labourers and manufacturers flocked over the Atlantic, that the landlords began to be alarmed, and concert ways and means for preventing the growing evil. Scarce a ship sailed for any of the plantations that was not crowded with men, women, and children. But the bounty allowed new settlers in Carolina proved a great encouragement, and induced numbers of these people, notwithstanding the severity of the climate, to resort to that province. The merchants finding this bounty equivalent to the expenses of the passage, from avaricious motives persuaded the people to embark for Carolina, and often crammed such numbers of them into their ships that they were in danger of being stifled during the passage, and sometimes were landed in such a starved and sickly condition, that numbers of them died before they left Charleston. Many causes may be assigned for this spirit of emigration that prevailed so much in Ireland: some, no doubt, emigrated from a natural restlessness of temper and a desire of roving abroad, without any fixed object in view. Others were enticed over by flattering promises from friends and relations, who had gone before them. But of all other causes of emigration oppression at home was the most powerful and prevalent. . . .

Nor were these the only sources from which Carolina, at this time, derived strength and an increase of population. For, notwithstanding the vast extent of territory which the provinces of Virginia and Pennsylvania contained, yet such was the nature of the country, that a scarcity of improvable lands began to be felt in these colonies, and poor people could not find spots in them unoccupied equal to their expectations. Most of the richest valleys in these more populous provinces lying to the east of the Alleghany mountains were either under patent or occupied, and, by the royal proclamation at the peace, no settlements were allowed to extend beyond the sources of the rivers which empty themselves into the Atlantic. In Carolina the case was different, for there large tracks of the best lands as yet lay waste, which proved a great temptation to the northern colonists to migrate to the south. Accordingly, about this time, above a thousand families, with their effects, in the space of one year resorted to Carolina, driving their cattle, hogs, and horses over-land before them. Lands were allotted them on the frontiers, and most of them being only entitled to small tracts, such as one, two, or three hundred acres, the back settlements by this means soon became the most populous parts of the province. The frontiers were not only strengthened and secured by new settlers, but the old ones on the maritime parts began also to stretch backward and spread their branches, in consequence of which the demand for lands in the interior parts every year increased. The governor and council met once a month for the purpose of granting lands and signing patents, and it is incredible what numbers of people attended those meetings in order to obtain them; so that, from the time in which America was secured by the peace, Carolina made rapid progress in population, wealth, and trade. . . .

⸾   ⸾   ⸾

Before the Revolutionary War some pioneer families had pushed westward along the river valleys in the eastern part of present Tennessee. Three distinct settlements were made, each with a distinct self-organized government. While they were within the territory of North Carolina they were beyond the protection of her laws. The Watauga settlers, declared trespassers on Cherokee hunting grounds, and unable to secure title from either North Carolina or the Indians, leased their land for a ten-year period, and drew up the Articles of the Watauga Association, believed to be the first written constitution drawn up and adopted by a group of native-born Americans. A group of settlers on the Cumberland River, and a third on the Holston, French Broad, and Big Pigeon Rivers, later also drew up articles of association. While the Watauga constitution has perished, the records of the Cumberland Association are still in existence. From those minutes the following agreement is quoted. The text is from *The American Historical Magazine,* Nashville, Tennessee, April, 1902, pp. 115-116, 123-124; and July, 1902, pp. 254-266.

North Carolina, Cumberland River, Jan. 7th, 1783.

The manifold suffering and distress that settlers here have from time to time undergone, even almost from our first settling; with the desertion of the greater number of the first adventurers, being so discouraging to the remaining few, that all administration of justice seemed to cease from amongst us; which, however weak, whether in constitution, administration, or execution, yet has been construed in our favor, against those whose malice or interest would insinuate us a people fled to a hiding place from justice, and the revival of them again earnestly recommended; and now having a little respite granted, and numbers returning to us, it appears highly necessary that for the common weal of the whole, the securing of the peace, the performance of contract between man and man, together with the suppression of vice, again to revive our former manner of proceedings, pursuant to the plan agreed upon at our first settling here, and to proceed accordingly, until such times as it shall please the Legislature to grant us the salutary benefit of the law duly administered amongst by their authority.

To this end, previous notice having been given to the several stations to elect twelve men of their several stations, whom they thought most proper for the business, and being elected to meet at Nashborough the 7th day of January, 1783, accordingly there met at the time and place aforesaid,

Col. Jas. Robertson	Heydon Wells
Capt. Geo. Freeland	Jas. Maulding
Thos. Molloy	Ebenezer Titus
Isaac Linsey	Sam'l Barton
David Rounsevall	Andrew Ewin

constituting into a committee for the purpose aforesaid, by voluntarily taking the following oath, viz.:

I, A. B., do solemnly swear that, as a member of committee, I will do equal right and justice according to the best of my skill and judgment in the decision of all causes that shall be laid before me, without fear, favor or partiality. So help me God.

The committee so constituted proceeded to elect Andrew Ewin to be their clerk, John Montgomery to be sheriff of the district and Col. James Robertson to be their chairman. . . .

The following items will illustrate the business transacted by the Committee from time to time.

March 4th, 1783
. . . It being thought necessary for our better defense, in these times of danger, that officers be chosen in each respective station to embody the inhabitants for their greater safety: Accordingly there was made choice of at Nashborough Station, William Pruit for captain; Sam'l Martin and Jno. Buchanan, 1st and 2nd lieutenants, and William Overall, ensign. [Officers were chosen for Freeland's Station, Heatonsburg, Mansco's Station, and Maulding's Station.]

April 1st, 1783
On motion made ordered, that a road be opened from Nashborough to Mansco's Station, and thence to Maulding's Station. [Overseers were chosen for different projects, and each was directed to call together as many of the inhabitants of their respective stations as they could, to assist in opening the roads. Two courts were established, an inferior court composed of any three members of the committee of twelve, with final jurisdiction in cases where damage did not exceed one hundred dollars; and a superior court for criminal cases or ones involving amounts in excess of one hundred dollars.]

January 20, 1783
Records of Marks and Brands
February 11th, 1783, James Robertson records his stock mark, thus: A crop off each ear, and under kell in each, and brand this -R. Feby. 11th, John McAdams records his stock mark, thus: A crop off the right ear and whole through it, and a swallow fork in the left. [A total of 19 owners registered their marks and brands.]

In many instances speculators were in advance of actual settlers, and both speculators and settlers defied the Proclamation Line. The leading speculator was Colonel Richard Henderson, Judge in the colonial courts of North Carolina and one of the best authorities on the laws of that province and the British Empire. He is believed to have learned of Kentucky from Daniel Boone, and he employed Boone to explore western lands in behalf of a company which he was organizing. The judge, in the name of the company, in 1775, purchased from 17,000,000 to 20,000,000 acres of land from the Cherokee Indians for a sum of 10,000 pounds sterling in money and goods, chiefly in the bounds of Kentucky and Tennessee. Daniel Boone was sent with thirty ax-men to cut a path for the settlers, the path becoming famous as the "Wilderness Road." In 1775 Henderson met his prospective settlers at the site of the future Boonesboro and outlined a plan for the democratic government of the proposed new state, which was to be named Transylvania. Henderson was soon required to give up the colony because his claim was declared by the highest court of Virginia to be illegal.

The following selection is a warning to the British government from Governor Martin of North Carolina, pointing out the disrespect shown by the colonists to the Proclamation Line. The text is from William L. Saunders, Editor, *Colonial Records of North Carolina, 1662-1776*, P. M. Hale, etc., Raleigh, Vol. IX, p. 1175.

In spite of all the measures taken by the Superintendent of Indian Affairs the White people are continually obtaining from the Indians Cessions and Leases of the Lands they hold and under these pretences the Settlements are extended far beyond the present established Boundaries between this Province and the Indians. I submit to your Lordship's consideration the expediency of his Majesty's making further purchases of the Indian Lands. There prevails an opinion I find which is industriously cultivated by Henderson the famous invader . . . that people may take up lands of the Indians by lease although they cannot purchase of them without militating against the King's Proclamation of the 7th of October 1763, and accordingly I understand his bargain with the Cherokee Indians that at first I understood to be a purchase is now reported to be a Lease for 999 years to a tract of Country four hundred miles square to which I am informed many of the wretched and desperate people of this Province talk of resorting upon the invitation given out by Henderson whose doctrine is clearly in my opinion contrary to the express words as well as to the meaning and design of the Royal Proclamation referred to.

↑   ↑   ↑

A Kentucky fever rose; in the Blue-Grass region where the cane in the cane-brakes was 10 to 12 feet high and there were salt licks in abundance, the land was unoccupied by Indians and it seemed a veritable paradise. Similar conditions existed in the limestone basins of Tennessee. Both areas attracted farmers of Virginia and North Carolina, who felt an impatience at the disappearance of their game, the exhaustion of their soil, and at their inability to get out of debt. Harrodsburg and Boonesboro, Kentucky's first two settlements, were stockaded "stations" with high walls enclosing a group of cabins to protect the families against Indian attacks. The men went out each day to their "clearings" taking their axes and rifles. After new stations had been built further on to break the

Indians' attacks, families could risk moving out of the stations to private farms.

Harry Toulmin, an English clergyman who came to America to select a site for a settlement of his friends, having investigated Mason and Washington Counties in Kentucky, wrote the following words of advice. The text from Harry Toulmin, *The Western Country in 1793,* edited by Marion Tinling and Godfrey Davies, The Huntington Library & Art Gallery, San Marino, California, 1948, p. 80, is used by permission of the Henry E. Huntington Library and Art Gallery.

A man who comes in the fall to settle in the woods with a family of three or four children should be able to purchase fifty or sixty bushels of Indian corn, and as much bacon as will serve them for five or six months, a cow or two, two or three ewes, a sow, a horse, a plow, a hoe, and axe. When a man is going to settle, he leaves his wife and family in some neighboring cabin, puts up a little shed for himself, and cuts down the timber, which will be wanted in building his log cabin. When this is ready he gives notice to his neighbors, who assemble and raise the building for him. He provides meat and bread for them, and sometimes a little whiskey. If he can begin to clear about Christmas, and is industrious, and knows something of the work, he may easily clear ten acres, and put them in Indian corn, which will more than furnish his family and stock with necessary provisions. He must have assistance in rolling his logs, but he repays it by helping those who help him. His wife spins the wool for clothing, and the weaver is paid either in toll from the cloth or in corn. Many begin in the woods without having any stock but a horse. The prevailing size of the estates are [sic] from one hundred to five or six hundred acres. Some are no more than fifty, and some have 150,000. Leased estates are generally from fifty to two hundred acres. Probably three-fourths are tenants, but many of them have land of their own on the frontiers.

3

Colonial Self-Government

BASIC PRINCIPLES

There are three key factors to be observed in British settlement of the New World: it was encouraged by the Crown; it came about because of private initiative and enterprise; it was conditioned by English ideals and principles which had developed over the centuries. The following excerpts from the patent granted by Queen Elizabeth to Sir Walter Raleigh illustrate all three factors. The text is from Richard Hakluyt's *Explorations, Descriptions, and Attempted Settlements of Carolina, 1584-1590,* edited by David Leroy Corbitt, State Department of Archives and History, Raleigh, 1948, pp. 5-9, *passim.*

Elizabeth by the grace of God of England, France and Ireland, Queen, defender of the faith, &c. To all people to whom these presents shall come, greeting; Know ye, that of our special grace, certain science, and mere motion, we have given and granted . . . to our trusty and well beloved servant, Walter Raleigh Esquire, and to his heirs and assigns for ever, free liberty and license . . . to discover, search, find out, and view such heathen and barbarous lands . . . not actually possessed of any Christian prince, nor inhabited by Christian people . . . and the same to have, hold, occupy and enjoy to him, his heirs and assigns forever. . . . And the said Walter Raleigh, his heirs and assigns, and all such as from time to time, by license of us, our heirs and successors, shall go to travel thither to inhabit or to remain, there to build and fortify. . . .

And we do grant . . . to all . . . persons, being of our allegiance, . . . that with the assent of the Said Walter Raleigh, his heirs or assigns, shall . . . hereafter travel to such lands . . . and to every of their heirs, . . . being borne within our said realms of England and Ireland, or in any other place within our allegiance, and which hereafter shall be inhabiting within any the lands . . . with such license, . . . shall and may have all the privileges of free denizens, and persons native of England, and within our allegiance in such ample manner and form, as if they were borne and

46

personally resident within our said realm of England, any law, custom, or usage to the contrary notwithstanding.

REPRESENTATIVE GOVERNMENT IN VIRGINIA

In 1618 the Virginia Company adopted a "great charter of priviledges, orders and Lawes"; Virginia was the first colony with a written constitution. In 1619 Sir George Yeardley, the newly appointed governor, invited the settlements to send delegates to Jamestown to cooperate in making laws. In 1624 the charter was revoked and Virginia became a royal colony. As new colonies were established they followed the same pattern, going through a period of company or proprietary ownership, and eventually becoming royal colonies modeled after the plan developed in Virginia: an English governor appointed by the King, an appointed council, a representative assembly, a hierarchy of courts resembling those of England, and some form of representative local government. This plan of government was described by Robert Beverley in *The History and Present State of Virginia,* 1705. The following text is from the 1722 Edition, F. Fayram and J. Clarke, London, pp. 201-207.

[The] first settlement of this Country was under the direction of a Company of Merchants incorporated. . . . [A] Council was nominated by the Corporation, and the President annually chosen by the People.

. . . In the year 1610 this Constitution was altered, and the Company obtain'd a new Grant of his Majesty: whereby they themselves had the nomination of the Governor, who was oblig'd to act only by advice in Council.

. . . In the year 1620, an Assembly of Burgesses was first call'd, from all the inhabited parts of the Country, who sat in consultation with the Governor and Council, for setling the Publick Affairs of the Plantation; and so the form of Government became perfect.

. . . When the Company was dissolv'd, the King continued the same method of Government, by a Governour, Council, and Burgesses; which three being united, were call'd the General Assembly.

. . . This General Assembly debated all the weighty Affairs of the Colony, and enacted Laws for the better government of the People; and the Governor and Council were to put them in execution.

. . . The Governor and Council were appointed by the King, and the Assembly chosen by the People. . . .

In the General Assembly, the Council make the Upper-House, and claim an entire Negative Voice to all Laws, as the House of Lords in *England*. . . .

The Burgesses of Assembly are elected, and return'd from all parts of the Country, *viz.* from each County two, and from James City one; which make up in all fifty one Burgesses, besides one Burgess to be sent by the Colledge, as the Charter directs. . . . The Freeholders are the only Electors, and where-ever they have a Free-hold, (if they be not Women or under

Age) they have a Vote in the Election. The method of summoning the Free-holders, is by publication of the Writ, together with the day appointed by the Sheriff for Election, at every Church and Chappel in the County, two several Sundays successively. The Election is concluded by plurality of votes. . . .

The Country is divided into twenty five Counties, and the Counties as they are in bigness, into fewer or more Parishes. . . .

They have two sorts of Courts, that differ only in jurisdiction; namely, the General Court, and the County-Courts. . . . The General Court, is a Court held by the Governour and Council, who by Custom, are the Judges of it, in all civil Disputes; but in all criminal Cases, they are made Judges by the Charter. . . . From this court there is no appeal, except the thing in demand exceed the value of three hundred pounds, Sterling; in which case, an Appeal is allowed to the Queen and Council in *England* and there determin'd by a Committee of the Privy Council, call'd the Lords of Appeals. . . .

The way of impanneling the Juries to serve in this Court, is thus: The Sheriff and his Deputies every Morning that the Court sits, goes about the Town, summoning the best of the Gentlemen, who resort thither, from all part of the Country . . . to these Courts as well to see Fashions, as to dispatch their particular Business. . . .

The County-Courts are constituted by Commission from the Governor, with advice of Council. They consist of eight or more Gentlemen of the County, called Justices of the Peace, the Sheriff being only a Ministerial Officer. This Court is held Monthly, and has Jurisdiction of all Causes within the County, not touching Life or Member: But in case of hog-stealing, they may Sentence the Criminal to lose his Ears; which is allow'd by a particular Act for that purpose. . . .

Besides this Monthly Court, there is a day appointed, to be kept annually by the Justices of the said Court, for the care of all Orphans and of their Estates; and for the binding out and well ordering of such fatherless Children, who are either without any Estate, or have very little. . . . The Boys are bound till one and twenty years of Age, and the Girls till eighteen: At which time, they who have taken any care to improve themselves, generally get well Married, and live in Plenty, tho they have not a farthing of paternal Estate. . . .

They have in each Parish a convenient Church, built either of Timber, Brick, or Stone, and decently adorn'd with every thing necessary for the celebration of Divine-Service. . . .

The people are generally of the Church of England, which the Religion establisht by Law in that Country, from which there are very few Dissenters. Yet liberty of Conscience is given to all other Congregations pretending to Christianity, on condition they submit to all Parish Duties. . . .

The Maintenance for a Minister there, is appointed by Law at 16,000 pounds of Tobacco *per Annum*, (be the Parish great or small) as also a Dwelling-House and Glebe, together with certain Perquisites for Marriages and Funeral Sermons. . . . In some Parishes . . . there are stocks of Cattle and Negroes, on the Glebes, which are also allow'd to the Minister, for his Use and Incouragement; he only being accountable for the surrender of the same value, when he leaves the Parish.

For the Well-governing of these, and all other Parochial Affairs, a Vestry is appointed in each Parish. These Vestries consist of twelve Gentlemen of the Parish, and were at first chosen by the vote of the Parishoners; but upon the Death of one, have been continued by the Survivor's electing another in his place. . . . They choose two from among themselves to be Church-Wardens . . . to see the Orders, and Agreements of the Vestry perform'd; to collect all the Parish's Tobacco's and distribute them to the several Claimers; and to make up the Accounts of the Parish, and to present all Profaneness and Immorality. By these the Tobacco of the Minister is collected, and brought home to him in Hogsheads convenient for Shipping.

DEVIATIONS FROM THE VIRGINIA MODEL

From the colonial ventures English promoters expected profits, such as markets for manufacturers, opportunities to creditors for extending credit, cargoes to shipowners, dividends to stockholders in the corporations, and profits from the Indian trade. Laws passed by Parliament with respect to the English plantations and by colonial legislatures all reflect these expectations. In Carolina the proprietors attempted to establish a preconceived plan for promoting their own interests, for keeping their colony's government in conformity with the English monarchy, and for preventing the development of democracy within their province. The plan, credited to John Locke, the "Fundamental Constitutions," was never adopted by the Assembly and was consequently not operative. In 1719 South Carolina became a royal colony, as did North Carolina in 1729. The following portions of the "Fundamental Constitutions" are quoted from William L. Saunders, Editor, *Colonial Records of North Carolina, 1662-1776*, P. M. Hale, etc., Raleigh, 1886-90, Vol. I, pp. 185-205, *passim*.

March 1, 1669

Our sovereign Lord the King, having out of his royal grace and bounty, granted unto us the Province of Carolina, with all the royalties, properties, jurisdictions and privileges of a County Palatine . . . , for the better settlement of the government of the said place, and establishing the interests of the Lords Proprietors with equality, and without confusion; and that the government of this Province may be made most agreeable to the Monarchy under which we live, and of which this Province is a part; and that we may avoid erecting a numerous democracy: We, the Lords and proprietors of the Province aforesaid, have agreed to the following form of government. . . .

1st. The eldest of the Lords Proprietors shall be Palatine; and upon the decease of the Palatine the eldest of the seven surviving proprietors shall always succeed him.

2d. There shall be seven other chief officers . . . , which places shall be enjoyed by none but the Lords Proprietors. . . .

3d. The whole Province shall be divided into Counties; each county shall consist of eight signiories, eight baronies and four precincts; each precinct shall consist of six colonies.

4th. Each signiory, barony, and colony shall consist of twelve thousand acres. . . . .

9th. There shall be just as many Landgraves as there are Counties, and twice as many Casiques, and no more. These shall be the hereditary nobility of the Province. . . . .

16th. In every signiory, barony, and manor, the respective Lord shall have power in his own name to hold court leet there, for trying all causes, both civil and criminal. . . . .

95th. No man shall be permitted to be a freeman of Carolina, or to have any estate or habitation within it, that doth not acknowledge a God, and that God is publicly and solemnly to be worshipped.

✓   ✓   ✓

The one English colony that received financial aid from the mother country was Georgia. Because there was not the motive of individual profit in this settlement, and control had to be placed in the hands of some public-spirited individual or group, the following plan of government was used. The text is from *An Account Showing the Progress of the Colony of Georgia in America, From Its First Establishment,* Published Per Order of the Honourable the Trustees, London, MDCCXLI; reprinted as No. 5, September, 1897, *Colonial Tracts,* published by George P. Humphrey, Rochester, New York, p. 3.

His majesty King George the Second, by his letters patent bearing the date of the ninth of June, one thousand seven hundred and thirty-two, reciting amongst many other things, that many of his poor subjects were, through misfortune and want of employment, reduced to great necessities and would be glad to be settled on any of his majesty's provinces of America, where, by cultivating the lands waste and desolate, they might not only gain a comfortable subsistence, but also strengthen his majesty's realms; and that the provinces in North America had been frequently ravaged by Indian enemies, more especially that of South Carolina, whose southern frontier continued unsettled and lay open to the neighboring savages; and that to relieve the wants of the said poor people, and to protect his majesty's subjects in South Carolina, a regular colony of the said, should be settled and established in the southern frontiers of Carolina; did, for the considerations aforesaid, constitute a corporation by the name of the Trustees for Establishing the Colony of Georgia in America, with capacity to purchase and take lands, to sue and be sued, to have a common seal . . . , with restraining clauses, that no member of the said corporation should have any salary, fee, perquisite, benefit, or profit whatsoever for acting therein. . . .

The said corporation for the term of twenty-one years from the date of the said letters patent [was authorized] to form and prepare laws, statutes, and ordinances for the government of the said colony . . . and . . . after the end of the said twenty-one years, the governor, and all officers, civil and military, within the province should be appointed by his majesty, his heirs and successors.

MERCANTILISM

At the time the colonies were settled, England was practicing mercantilism, that economic control of commerce, industry, and labor which attempted to produce a strong national state; gradually this concept broadened, with a self-sufficient empire as its objective. The Acts of Trade and Navigation passed between 1650 and 1767 subordinated the colonial interests to those of the mother country. Some provisions of those acts created great dissatisfaction in the South, because their enforcement affected the profits from the staple crops. Others favored the Southern colonies. The two following clauses are from Danby Pickering, *The Statutes at Large,* from the Thirty-ninth of Q. Elizabeth, to the Twelfth of K. Charles II, inclusive, J. Bentham, Cambridge, 1763, Vol. VII, pp. 459, 503.

NAVIGATION ACT OF 1660

. . . And it is further enacted—That from and after the first day of April, . . . [1661,] no sugars, tobacco, cotton-wool, indicoes, ginger, fustick, or other dying wood, of the growth, production or manufacture of any *English* plantations in *America, Asia,* or *Africa* shall be shipped, carried, conveyed or transported from any of the said *English* plantations to any land . . . other than to such other English plantations as do belong to his Majesty. . . . .

. . . it is hereby enacted . . . That no person or persons whatsoever shall or do from and after the first day of *January* in the year of our Lord one thousand six hundred and sixty, set, plant, improve to grow, make or cure any tobacco, either in seed, plant or otherwise . . . within the kingdom of *England,* dominion of *Wales,* islands of *Guernsey* or *Jersey,* or town of *Berwick* upon *Tweed,* or in the kingdom of *Ireland,* under the penalty of

the forfeiture of all such tobacco, or the value thereof, or the sum of forty
shillings for every rod or pole of ground so planted. . . .

✓   ✓   ✓

The Commissioners of Plantations sent a query to Governor Berkeley of Virginia in 1670, which he answered the following year. Among the questions which
he answered was one concerning trade. The report is quoted from William Waller
Hening, Editor, *Statutes at Large,* Samuel Pleasants, Jr., Richmond, 1823, Vol. II,
pp. 511-517.

[Question] 19. What obstructions do you find to the improvement of
the trade and navigation of the plantations within your government?

Answer. Mighty and destructive, by that severe act of parliament which
excludes us the having any commerce with any nation in Europe but our
own, so that we cannot add to our plantation any commodity that grows
out of it, as olive trees, cotton or vines. Besides this, we cannot procure
any skilful men for one now hopefull commodity, silk; for it is not lawful
for us to carry a pipe stave, or barrel of corn to any place in Europe out
of the king's dominions. If this were for his majesty's service or the good
of his subjects, we should not repine, whatever our sufferings are for it;
but on my soul, it is the contrary for both. And this is the cause why
no small or great vessells are built here; for we are most obedient to all laws,
whilst the New England men break through, and men trade to any place
that their interest lead them.

[Question] 20. What advantages or improvement do you observe that
may be gained to your trade or navigation?

Answer. None, unless we had liberty to transport our pipe staves, timber
and corn to other places besides the king's dominions.

GOVERNMENTAL PROBLEMS OF THE EXPANDING FRONTIER

As counties were formed in the interior, the county seats became the centers
of economic life of the newly organized areas. Some of these were mere hamlets,
but others attracted the trade of a wide region. The charter granted to Hillsborough, North Carolina, illustrates the economic functions served by such a
town. The text is from William L. Saunders, Editor, *Colonial Records of North
Carolina, 1662-1776,* P. M. Hale, etc., Raleigh, 1886-90, Vol. VIII, pp. 216-217.

. . . We, of our Special Grace, . . . do give and grant to the . . . said
Town of Hillsborough forever full power and authority to have hold and
keep a Market weekly at the . . . Court House in the said town of Hillsborough that is to say on every Saturday throughout the year with all the
priviledges immunities to a weekly public market belonging or pertaining.
And also two Fairs yearly to be held and kept at the said Court House on

the first Tuesdays in May and November to continue for that and the two following days for the sale and vending all manner of black Cattle, Provisions Goods, Wares and Merchandizes whatsoever and that during the continuance of the said Fair and for one day immediately preceding and one day immediately succeeding the same all persons coming to bring at and going from the said Fair together with their black Cattle Goods Wares and Merchandizes whatsoever shall be exempt and priviledged from all arrests and attachments and executions except for Breach of the Peace and for carrying into Execution the Judgments Orders and Decrees hereinafter mentioned. And we give . . . Authority to the Justice of the Peace of the said County of Orange for the time being or any three of them, summarily to hear and determine all such Controversies and Debates as may during the continuance of the said Fair arise among the Buyers and Sellers in the Course of their Dealings and Transactions at the Fair. . . .

✓   ✓   ✓

Farmers of the interior were handicapped by their distance from seaports or water transportation, especially in exporting commodities that were subject to inspection before sale. Settlers in the back country of North Carolina petitioned the Governor and his Council for the establishment of an inspection station at Hillsborough, and the petition was granted. This excerpt from the petition is from William L. Saunders, Editor, *Colonial Records of North Carolina, 1662-1776*, P. M. Hale, etc., Raleigh, 1886-90, Vol. VIII, p. 80a.

TO HIS EXCELLENCY WILLIAM TRYON ESQUIRE CAPTAIN GENERAL AND GOVERNOR IN CHIEF IN AND OVER HIS MAJESTY'S PROVINCE OF NORTH CAROLINA.

To the Honourable Member of his Majesty's Council, To the Speaker and gentlemen of the House of Assembly of the Province of North Carolina, the Petition of the County of Orange humbly sheweth,

That whereas by reason of the Great Distance we your petitioners live from any Publick Inspections, whereto we may carry Tobacco Hemp, and other Commodity's, that we your Petitioners are Greatly Discouraged, from attempting the making Tobacco & the Cultivation of Hemp, Two of the most valuable as we apprehend profitable Branches (the Quality of the soil of this Country being Particularly suited to those articles) of Husbandry from consideration after a long and laborious process of preparing them for sale, that the Possessor is obliged to be at the further Trouble, Labour, and Expence, of Transporting those Weighty and Bulky Articles at least one Hundred miles by Land, before he can be Certain that his Commodity will pass an Inspection, or that he shall receive any satisfaction or Recompence, for the Fruits of his Long Industry, For Remedy whereof we your Petitioners most humbly pray, that for the Mutual Benefit of the Trader, & the Industrious Laborer & Planter that a Publick Inspection

may be established at the Town of Hillsborough, in the County afore-
said Under such Rules & Regulations & Restrictions as to you in your
Great Wisdom and Goodness may seem meet, and your Petitioners as in
Duty bound shall ever pray &c. . . .

WEST VERSUS EAST

On two notable occasions groups of colonists rebelled against colonial governors
and took up arms against the governors' forces. In 1676 Nathaniel Bacon led a
group of planters in opposition to Governor Berkeley of Virginia, who had failed
to maintain a peaceful frontier with the Indians. The movement broke up when
Bacon died suddenly, and the defeated rebels fled westward. Bacon's laws were
the laws passed at an Assembly held during the period called Bacon's Rebellion,
in June, 1676. They were repealed by the king's instructions and proclamation,
and also by act of the succeeding session. They illustrate the grievances of the
people of Virginia at that time. Acts I-III dealt with carrying on war against
Indian enemies. The following selections, Acts VI and XVI, are quoted from
William Waller Hening, Editor, *Statutes at Large*, Samuel Pleasants, Jr., Richmond,
1823, Vol. II, pp. 356, 361.

Act VI. An Act for chooseing of Vestries
WHEREAS the long continuance of vestries in severall parishes in the
country is presented a greivance, for remedy whereof for the future, *Bee
it enacted by the governor, councell and burgesses of this grand assembly,
and by the authority thereof,* that it shall and may be lawfull at any time
after publication hereof, for the freeholders and freemen of every parish
within this country by the majoritie of votes to elect and make choice of
(if they see fitt) certaine freeholders or substantiall householders to the
number of twelve within their respective parishes . . . to be the vestrie
of the parish, where they are soe chosen to order, regulate and mannage
the parochiall affaires thereof, and such election of a vestrie to be made
in Easter weeke, and once in every three yeares. . . .

An Act for the suppressing of ordinaries
WHEREAS it is most aparently found that the many ordinaries in severall
parts of the country are very prejudiciall, and this assembly finde the same
to be a generall greivance presented from most of the counties, Bee it therefore enacted . . . that no ordinaries, ale houses, or other tipling houses
whatsoever, by any the inhabitants of this country, be kept in any part
of the country except it bee in James Citty, and at each side of the Yorke
river, at the two great ferries of that river; *Provided,* . . . that those
at the ferries . . . as aforesaid, be admitted in their said ordinaries to sell
and utter man's meate, horsemeate, beer and syder, but no other strong
drinke whatsoever. . . . Whosoever shall presume to sell any sorte of
drunke or liquor whatsoever by retail . . . and thereof be lawfully con-

victed . . . shall pay to the informer for each time hee shall . . . bee thereof lawfully convicted . . . one thousand pounds of tobacco. . . .

✓   ✓   ✓

Almost a century later in the interior of North Carolina a group known as Regulators took the law into their own hands because the Piedmont region was not fairly represented in the Assembly and because they believed the king's tax collectors were oppressing them. The Assembly passed an act making rioters guilty of treason, and Governor Tryon called together troops to give battle to the Regulators, who, when defeated, were required to take an oath of allegiance to the government, seven being executed for treason. The following text is from William L. Saunders, Editor, *Colonial Records of North Carolina, 1662-1776,* P. M. Hale, etc., Raleigh, 1886-90, Vol. VIII, pp. 81, 235, 681, 717-727, *passim.* The final passage is quoted from John H. Wheeler, *Historical Sketches of North Carolina,* Lippincott, Grambo and Co., Philadelphia, 1851, Vol. II, pp. 16-17.

A PETITION TO GOVERNOR TRYON AND THE COUNCIL AND ASSEMBLY. . . .

The humble Petition of us Inhabitants of Orange and Rowan Countys, true and faithful subjects of his Majesty King George the Third Sheweth,

That we your poor Petitioners, now do and long have laboured under many and heavy Exactions, Oppressions and Enormity, committed on us by Court Officers, in every Station. . . . may it please you to consider of and pass an Act to divide the several Countys within this Province, into proper Districts, appointing a Collector in each, to raise and collect the several Taxes, laid or to be laid, by Law, who shall be accountable, and make all Returns to a County _____ to be nominated _____ with the Assembly. This method will (we humbly conceive) effectually prevent the Sheriffs from robbing and plundering the Country spending their ill got gains in Riot, purchasing Estates, or bearing off the same into other provinces, as they frequently do, to our unspeakable prejudice, who are required to make good the Defficiencys, And may it please you to consider of and pass an Act, to Tax every one in proportion to his Estates; however equitable the Law as it now stands, may appear to the Inhabitants of the Maritime parts of the Province, where estates consist chiefly in Slaves, . . . tho' their Estates are in proportion (in many instances) as of one Thousand to one, for all to pay equal, is with Submission, very grievous and oppressive . . .

The rebellion developed as petitions such as the above were disregarded.

North Carolina
Hillsborough District
At a Superor Court of Justice begun and held for the district afore-mentioned at the Court House in Hillsborough . . .

Present

The Honorable Richard Henderson, Associate Justice

Monday 24th [1770]

. . . Several persons stiling themselves Regulators assembled together in the Court Yard under the conduct of Harmon Husbands, James Hunter, Rednap Howell, William Butler, Samuel Devinney, & many others insulted some of the gentlemen of the Bar, & in a violent manner went into the Court House, and forcibly carried out some of the attorneys, and in a cruel manner beat them. They then insisted that the Judge should proceed to the Tryal of their Leaders, who had been indicted in a former Court, and that the Jury should be taken out of their party.

Therefore the Judge finding it impossible to proceed with honor to himself and Justice to his Country, adjourned the Court till tomorrow morning at 10 o'clock, and took advantage of the night & made his escape, and the Court adjourned to Court in Course.

ꜰ ꜰ ꜰ

Governor Tryon sent letters similar to the following to the Colonels of the Colonial militia.

Newbern 20th Nov 1770

COLONEL JOHN SIMPSON,

From the Reports generally prevailing in the Country that the Body of People who stile themselves the Regulators intend coming to Newbern during the sitting of the ensuing . . . Legislative Body, I think proper hereby to command you to assemble your Regiment on the first notice you can get that the Insurgents are on their march, and to obstruct and oppose them in their progress through the Country to Newbern, and even to repel force with force, but should you find it out of your Power to collect a sufficient number of men in time to effect that purpose, I must require you in case they do come down to follow them in Newbern with all possible expedition with your whole Regiment in order to protect the Legislature and preserve the Peace of the Government. . . .

ꜰ ꜰ ꜰ

On May 16, 1771, a battle was fought between the Regulators and Governor Tryon's troops, which was described by the Governor in the following official report.

My Lord:—I have the happiness to inform your Lordship, that it has pleased God to bless his Majesty's arms in this province with signal victory over the Regulators.

The action began before twelve o'clock, on Thursday the 16th instant, five miles to the westward of Great Alamance River, on the road leading from Hillsborough to Salisbury. . . .

The action was two hours. But after about half an hour the enemy took to tree fighting, and much annoyed the men who stood at the guns, which obliged me to cease the artillery for a short time, and advance the first line to force the rebels from their covering. This succeeded, and we pursued them a mile beyond their camp, and took many of their horses, and the little provision and ammunition they left behind them. . . .

4

Colonial Life and Labor

From the narratives of the early settlements, in Chapter 2, may be noted some of the most important problems that faced the struggling little colonies. Land was cleared, defense against the Indians and the Spanish was established, livestock was introduced, cultivation of tobacco, rice, and naval stores developed; from the Indians new native foods were made available and methods of preparing them were learned; trade with the Indians provided furs for foreign commerce.

In Virginia for a while the company had a monopoly of the trade, and land was not privately owned. At first there was one large plantation, operated on a communistic basis. The term, "plantation," as used in the fifteenth and sixteenth centuries in England meant "colony"; thus it was applied to the settlement of Jamestown, and to others as they developed. Toward the end of the seventeenth century a committee was set up within the Privy Council, to have charge of colonial affairs; this committee was called the "Committee for Trade and Plantations." In the second stage of the economic life of Virginia, semi-public plantations were established, when the stockholders in the company were allowed to take up tracts of land ranging in size from 80,000 to 200,000 acres, upon which they were required to settle a specified number of persons, reckoned in hundreds; hence, these plantations were called "hundreds." As this system of landholding proved unpopular, the land was gradually disposed of to private owners. As tobacco culture developed, many large farms, individually owned, were devoted to this crop, under a system of regimented labor; these farms were called "plantations," and the word came to have an industrial meaning.

LIFE IN THE PIONEER STAGE

Life at first was very primitive, and houses were built of logs placed vertically in palisade fashion and roofed with thatch. People did not usually gather in towns, but built their houses apart from each other. Gradually a spirit of permanence

58

The Cupola House, the oldest house standing today in Edenton, North Carolina, was built in 1758. Its cupola was an observatory for watching the coming and going of boats on Albermarle Sound.

developed, as a few brick houses and many more framed ones were built. Only a few towns developed in the South. The text of the following account is from *Tracts and Other Papers Relating Principally to the Origin, Settlement, and Progress of the Colonies in North America*, edited and printed by Peter Force, Washington, 1844, Vol. III, No. 14. It was written by John Hammond in 1656 in a book entitled *Leah and Rachel, or Two Fruitful Sisters, Virginia and Mary-land*, to induce new settlers to locate in the two colonies.

The Country [Virginia] is not only plentifull but pleasant and profitable, pleasant in regard to the brightnesse of the weather, the many delightfull rivers, on which the inhabitants are settled (every man almost living in sight of a lovely river) the abundance of game, the extraordinary good neighbourhood and loving conversation they have one with the other.

Pleasant in their building, which although for the most part they are but one story besides the loft, and built of wood, yet contrived so delightfull, that your ordinary houses in England are not so handsome, for usually the rooms are large, daubed and whitelimed, glazed and flowered, and if not glazed windows, shutters which are made very pritty and conveni-ent. . . .

The manner of living and trading there is thus, each man almost lives a free-holder, nothing but the value of 12d. a year to be paid as rent, for every 50 Acrees of land; firing costs nothing every man plants his own corne and neede take no care for bread if anything be bought, it is for comodity, exchanged presently, or for a day, payment is usuall made but once a year, and for that Bill taken (for accounts are not pleadable).

In summer when fresh meat will not keep (seeing every man kils of his own, and quantities are inconvenient) they lend from one to another, such portions of flesh ás they can spare, which is repaied again when the bor-rowers kils his.

If any fall sick, and cannot compasse to follow his crope which if not followed, will soon be lost, the adjoyning neighbour, will either voluntarily or upon a request joyn together, and work in it by spels, untill the honour recovers, and that gratis, so that no man by sicknesse loose any part of his years worke. . . .

By their labours is produced corne and Tobacco, and all other growing provisions, and this Tobacco however low-rated, yet a good maintenance may be had out of it, (for they have nothing of necessity but cloathing to purchase), or can this mean price of Tobacco long hold, for these reasons, First that In England it is prohibited, next that they have attained of late those sorts equall with the best Spanish, Thirdly that the sicknesse in Holland is decreasing, which hath been a great obstruction to the sail of tobacco.

ﾉ   ﾉ   ﾉ

The importance of tobacco in the economy of the Southern colonies was great; soil and climate were appropriate for its growth, especially in Virginia and Maryland. A letter written by John Pory, Secretary of Virginia, in 1619, described this significant crop: it soon became the staple of Maryland also, as illustrated by the second account below. The texts are from (a) *Collections of the Massachusetts Historical Society,* Massachusetts Historical Society, Boston, 1792, Vol. IX, Fourth Series, pp. 9-16, (b) George Alsop, *A Character of the Province of Maryland,* 1666, reprinted as Fund Publication No. 15, Maryland Historical Society, Baltimore, 1880, pp. 67-69.

. . . (a) All our riches for the present doe consiste in Tobacco, wherein one man by his owne labour hath in one yeare raised to himselfe to the value of 200L sterling; and another by the means of sixe servants hath cleared at one crop a thousand pound English. These be true, yet indeed rare examples, yet possible to be done by others. Our principall wealth (I should have said) consisteth in servants; But they are chardgeable to be furnished with armes, apparell & bedding, and for their transportation, and casuall both at sea, & for their first yeare commonly at lande also: But if they escape, they prove very hardy, and sound able men. Nowe that your lordship may knowe, that we are not the veriest beggers in the worlde, our cowekeeper here of James citty on Sundays goes accowtered all in freshe flaming silke; and a wife of one that in England had professed the black arte, not of a scholler, but of a collier of Croydon, weares her rough bever hatt with a faire perle hatband, and a silken suite thereto correspondent. But to leave the Populace, and to come higher; the governor here, who at his first coming, besides a great deale of worth in his person, brought onely his sword with him, was at his late being in London, together with his lady, out of his meer gettings here, able to disburse very near three thousand pounde to furnish himself for his voiage. . . .

(b) Tobacco is the only solid Staple Commodity of this Province Maryland: the use of it was first found out by the *Indians* many Ages agoe, and transferr'd into Christendom by that great discoverer of *America* Columbus. It's generally made by all the Inhabitants of this Province, and between the months of *March* and *April* they sow the seed (which is much smaller than the Mustard-seed) in small beds and patches digg'd up and made so by art, and about May the Plants commonly appear green in those beds: in *June* they are transplanted from their beds, and set in little hillocks in distant rowes, dug up for the same purpose; some twice or thrice they are weeded, and succoured from their illegitimate Leaves that would be peeping out from the body of the Stalk. They top the several Plants as they find occasion in their predominating rankness: About the Middle of *September* they cut the Tobacco down, and carry it into houses, (made for that purpose) to bring it to its purity: And after it has attained, by a convenient attendance upon time, to its perfection, it is then tyed up in bundles, and packt into Hogs-heads, and then laid by for the Trade.

Between November and January there arrives in this Province Shipping to the number of twenty sail and upwards, all Merchant-men loaden with Commodities to Trafique and dispose of, trucking with the Planter for Silks, Hollands, Serges, and Broad-clothes, with other necessary Goods, priz'd at such and such rates as shall be judg'd on is fair and legal, for Tobacco at so much the pound, and advantage on both sides considered; the Planter for his work, and the Merchant for adventuring himself and his Commodity into so far a Country: Thus is the Trade on both sides drove on with a fair and honest *Decorum*. . . .

Tobacco is the current Coyn of *Mary-Land,* and will sooner purchase Commodities from the Merchant, then money. I must confess the *New-England* men that trade into this Province, had rather have fat Pork for their Goods, than Tobacco or Furrs, which I conceive is, because their bodies being fast bound up with the cords of restringent Zeal, they are fain to make use of the lineaments of this *Non-Canaanite* creature physically to loosen them. . . .

Medera-Wines, Sugars, Salt, Wickar-Chairs, and Tin Candlesticks, is the most of the Commodities they bring in: They arrive in *Mary-Land* about *September,* being most of them Ketches and Barkes, and such small Vessels, and those dispersing themselves into several small Creeks of this Province, to sell and dispose of their Commodities, where they know the Market is most fit for their small Adventures.

✓ ✓ ✓

Descriptions of life on Southern plantations in the middle of the colonial period pictured a life of plenty, gracious homes and hospitality at the beginning of the eighteenth century in Virginia, North Carolina, and Georgia, respectively.

✓ ✓ ✓

Robert Beverley's description of the hospitality of Virginia planters, followed by his criticism of the apparent lack of industry, and a sketch of the buildings to be found in Virginia in 1705, are from his *The History and the Present State of Virginia,* F. Fayram and J. Clarke, London, 1705, 1722 Edition, pp. 249-251.

The inhabitants are very Courteous to Travellers, who need no other Recommendation, but the being Human Creatures. A Stranger has no more to do, but to inquire upon the Road, where any Gentleman, or good House-keeper Lives, and there he may depend upon being received with Hospitality. This good Nature is so general among their People, that the Gentry when they go abroad, order their Principal Servant to entertain all Visitors, with everything the Plantation affords. And the poor Planters, who have but one Bed, will very often sit up, or lie upon a Form or Couch all night, to make room for the weary Traveller, to repose himself after his Journey. . . .

A Thousand . . . Advantages that Country naturally affords, which its Inhabitants make no manner of use of. They can see their Naval Stores daily benefit other People, who sent thither to build Ships; while they, instead of promoting such Undertakings among themselves, and easing such as are willing to go upon them, allow them no manner of Encouragement, but rather the contrary. They receive no Benefit nor Refreshment from the Sweets, and precious things they have growing amongst them, but make use of the Industry of *England* for all such things.

What Advantages do they see the Neighbouring Plantations make of their Grain and Provisions, while they, who can produce them infinitely better, not only neglect the making a Trade thereof, but even a necessary Provision against an accidental Scarcity, contenting themselves with a supply of Food from hand to mouth, so that if it should please God, to send them an unseasonable Year, there would not be found in the Country, Provision sufficient to support the People for three Months extraordinary.

By reason of the unfortunate Method of the Settlement, and want of Cohabitation, they cannot make a beneficial use of their Flax, Hemp, Cotten, Silk, Silk-grass, and Wool, which might otherwise supply their Necessities, and leave the Produce of Tobacco to enrich them, when a gainful Market can be found for it. . . .

The Private Buildings are of late very much improved; several Gentlemen . . . having built themselves large Brick Houses of many Rooms on a Floor, and several Stories high, as also some Stone-Houses: but they don't covet to make them lofty, having extent enough of Ground to build upon. . . . They always contrive to have large Rooms, that they may be cool in Summer. Of late they have made their Stories much higher than formerly, and their Windows large, and sasht with Cristal Glass; and they adorn their Apartments with rich Furniture.

All their Drudgeries of Cookery, Washing, Daries, &c. are perform'd in Offices detacht from the Dwelling-Houses, which by this means are kept more cool and Sweet.

Their Tobacco-Houses are all built of Wood, as open and airy as is consistent with keeping out the Rain; which sort of Building, is most convenient for the curing of their Tobacco.

Their common covering for Dwelling-Houses is Shingle, which is an Oblong Square of Cypress or Pine-Wood.

ィ   ィ   ィ

This description of life in North Carolina is from John Lawson, *History of North Carolina, Containing the Exact Description and Natural History of That Country Together with the Present State Thereof* . . . , 1714, reprinted, O. H. Perry & Co., Raleigh, 1860, pp. XVII, 136-137.

The gentlemen seated in the country, are very courteous, live very noble in their houses, and give very genteel entertainment to all strangers and others that come to visit them. . . .

We have yearly abundance of Strangers come among us, who chiefly strive to go southerly to settle, because there is a vast tract of rich land betwixt the place we are seated in and Cape Fair, and upon that river, and more southerly which is inhabited by none but a few Indians, who are at this time well affected to the English, and very desirous of their coming to live among them. The more southerly the milder winters, with the advantage of purchasing the lords land at the most easy and moderate rate of any lands in America, nay, allowing all Advantages thereto annexed, I may say the universe does not afford another; besides, men have a great advantage of choosing good and commodious tracts of land at the first seating of a country or river, whereas the latter settlers are forced to purchase smaller dividends of the old standers, and sometimes at very considerable rates; as now in Virginia and Maryland where a thousand acres of good land cannot be bought under twenty shillings an acre, besides two shillings yearly acknowledgement for every hundred acres; which sum, be it more or less, will serve to put the merchant or planter here into a good posture of buildings, slaves, and other necessaries, when the purchase of his land comes to him on such easy terms and as our grain and pulse thrives with us to admiration, no less do our stocks of cattle, horses, sheep and swine multiply. . . .

✔   ✔   ✔

William Bartram's *The Travels of William Bartram,* James and Johnson, Philadelphia, 1791; reprinted for Johnson, London, 1792, deals with the author's explorations in South Carolina, Georgia, and westward to the Mississippi River in 1773 and the following few years. This book, first published in 1791, is said to have influenced Coleridge to want to found an ideal colony for poets and philosophers in America; Wordsworth took the book with him to Germany in 1798. The following extracts are from pp. 4-13, *passim,* 307-308.

I concluded to make an excursion into Georgia. . . . I arrived in Savannah, the capital, where . . . the governor, Sir J. Wright, . . . received me with great politeness, shewed me every mark of esteem and regard, and furnished me with letters to the principal inhabitants of the state, which were of great service to me. Another circumstance very opportunely occurred on my arival: the assembly was then sitting in Savannah, and several members lodging in the same house where I took up my quarters, I became acquainted with several worthy characters, who invited me to call at their seats occasionally, as I passed through the country; particularly the hon. B. Andrews, esq., a distinguished, patriotic, and liberal character. This Gentleman's seat, and well-cultivated plantations, are situated near the south-road, which I often travelled; and I seldom passed his house without calling to see him, for it was the seat of virtue, where hospitality, piety, and philosophy, formed the happy family; where the weary traveller and stranger found a hearty welcome, and from whence it must be his own fault if he departed without being greatly benefited. . . . I viewed with pleasure this gentleman's exemplary improvements in agriculture; particularly in the growth of rice, and in his machines for shelling that valuable grain, which stands in the water almost from the time it is sown, until a few days before it is reaped, when they draw off the water by sluices, which ripens it all at once, and when the heads or panicles are dry ripe, it is reaped and left standing in the field, in small ricks, until all the straw is quite dry, when it is hauled, and stacked in the barn yard. The machines for cleaning the rice are worked by the force of water. They stand on the great reservoir which contains the waters that flood the rice-fields below. . . .

I rode [two days] through swamps, creeks, and pine forests, [when] . . . I came to a small plantation by the side of another swamp: the people were remarkably civil and hospitable. The man's name was M'Intosh, a family of the first colony established in Georgia, under the conduct of general Oglethorpe. Was there ever such a scene of primitive simplicity, as was here exhibited. . . : The venerable grey-headed Caledonian smilingly meets me coming up to his house. "Welcome, stranger; come in and rest; the air is now very sultry; it is a very hot day." I was there treated with some excellent venison, and here found friendly and secure shelter from a tremendous thunder storm. . . .

On another occasion, when Bartram left Charleston and traveled about sixty miles into Georgia, he wrote the following description of his hosts for a night.

In the evening I took up my quarters at a delightful habitation, though not a common tavern. Having ordered my horse a stable and provender, and refreshed my spirits with a draught of cooling liquor, I betook myself to contemplation in the groves and lawns. Directing my steps toward the river, I observed in a high Pine forest on the border of a savannah, a great number of cattle herded together, and on my nearer approach discovered it to be a cow pen; on my coming up I was kindly saluted by my host and his wife, who I found were superintending a number of slaves, women, boys and girls, that were milking the cows. Here were about forty milch cows and as many young calves; for in these southern countries the calves run with the cows a whole year, the people milking them at the same time. The pen, including two or three acres of ground, more or less, according to the stock, adjoining a rivulet or run of water, is enclosed by a fence: in this enclosure the calves are kept while the cows are out at range: a small part of this pen is partitioned off to receive the cows, when they come up at evening: here are several stakes drove into the ground, and there is a gate in the partition fence for a communication between the two pens. When the milkmaid has taken her share of milk, she looses the calf, who strips the cow, which is next morning again turned out to range.

I found these people, contrary to what a traveller might perhaps, reasonably expect, from their occupation and remote situation from the capital or any commercial town, to be civil and courteous: and though educated as it were in the woods, no strangers to sensibility, and those moral virtues which grace and ornament the most approved and admired characters in civil society. . . . On my observing to him [my host] that his stock of horned cattle must be very considerable to afford so many milch cows at one time, he answered, that he had about fifteen hundred head: "my stock is but young, having lately removed from some distance to this place; I found it convenient to part with most of my old stock and begin here anew; Heaven is pleased to bless my endeavours and industry with success even beyond my own expectations.

✓   ✓   ✓

While in Virginia and Maryland planters traded directly from their own wharves with agents of English merchants, in South Carolina trade centered at Charleston. The tidewater area where the rich plantations were located was swampy and unhealthful. Wealthy planters often built town houses in Charleston and spent a part of every year there. Charleston grew as a trading center and a cultural center as well. John Lawson, in his *History of North Carolina,* . . . 1714, reprinted, O. H. Perry and Co., Raleigh, 1860, pp. XIII-XIV, described Charleston as it was in 1714.

The town has very regular and fair streets, in which are good buildings of brick and wood; and since my coming thence, has had great additions of beautiful, large brick buildings, besides a strong fort. . . . They have a considerable trade both to Europe and the West Indies, whereby they became rich, and are supplied with all things necessary for trade, and genteel Living, which several other places fall short of. Their co-habiting in a town, has brought to them ingenious people of most sciences, whereby they have tutors amongst them that educate their youths a-la-mode.

They are absolute masters over the Indians, and carry so strict a hand over such as are within the circle of their trade, that none does the least injury to any of the English, but he is presently sent for and punished with death, or otherwise, according to the nature of the fault. They have an entire friendship with the neighboring Indians of several nations, which are a very warlike people, ever faithful to the English. . . .

✓   ✓   ✓

F. Yonge, in *A Narrative of the Proceedings of the People of South Carolina, in the Year 1719,* reprinted in B. R. Carroll, Editor, *Historical Collections of South Carolina,* Harper and Brothers, New York, 1836, Vol. II, pp. 144-145, described one of the Indian wars on the Carolina frontier, the Yamassee War.

. . . after some Years Intercourse and Dealing between the Inhabitants and several Nations of the *Indians,* with whom they traded, as they do now, for several Thousand Pounds a Year, the said *Indians,* unanimously agreed to destroy the whole Settlement, by murdering and cutting to pieces all the Inhabitants, on a Day they had agreed on; and altho' some private Intimations were given the People of their design, it was totally disbelieved; so that on that certain Day, in the year 1715, they killed all, or most of the Traders that were with them in their Towns; and going among the Plantations, murdered all who could not fly from their Cruelty, and burned their Houses. The occasion of this Conspiracy, which was so universal, that all the *Indians* were concerned in it, except a small Clan or two that lived amongst the Settlements, insomuch, that they amounted to between Eight and Ten Thousand Men, was attributed to some ill Usage they had receiv'd from the Traders, who are not (generally) Men of the best Morals. . . . In this War near 400 of the Inhabitants were destroy'd, with many Houses and Slaves, and great Numbers of Cattle, especially to the southward near Port-Royal, from whence the Inhabitants were entirely drove, and forced into the Settlements near *Charles-Town.*

This Town being fortified, they had time to think what to do; and not mustering above 1200 Men, they sent to *Virginia* and the neighbouring Colonies for Assistance; and for want of Money, of which they have very little in the Country, they formed *Bills of Credit* to pass current in all Payments, . . .

✓   ✓   ✓

Life in Charleston in 1763 was described in *A Short Description of the Province of South Carolina,* printed for John Hinton, London, reprinted in B. R. Carroll, Editor, *Historical Collections of South Carolina,* Harper and Brothers, New York, 1836, Vol. II, pp. 478-479.

The men and women who have a right to the class of gentry (who are more numerous here than in any other colony in North America) dress with elegance and neatness: The personal qualities of the ladies are much to their credit and advantage; they are generally of middling stature, genteel and slender; they have fair complexions, without the help of art, and regular features; their air is easy and natural; their manner free and unaffected; their eyes sparkling, penetrating, and inchantingly sweet: They are fond of dancing, an exercise they perform very gracefully; and many sing well, and play upon the harpsicord and guitar with great skill; nor are they less remarkable for goodness of heart, sweetness of disposition, and that charming modesty and diffidence, which command respect whilst they invite love, and equally distinguish and adorn the sex—in short, all who have the happiness of their acquaintance, will acquit me of partiality, when I say they are excelled by none in the practice of all the social virtues, necessary for the happiness of the other sex, as daughters, wives, or mothers.

The weather is much too hot in summer, for any kind of diversion or exercise, except riding on horseback, or in chaises (which few are without) in the evenings and mornings; and this is much practiced. In the autumn, winter, and spring, there is variety and plenty of game for the gun or dogs; the gentlemen are not backward in the chase. During this season there is once in two weeks a dancing-assembly in Charlestown, where is always a brilliant appearance of lovely, well-dress'd women: We have likewise a genteel playhouse, where a very tolerable set of actors called the American company of comedians, frequently exhibit; and often concerts of vocal and instrumental music, generally performed by gentlemen.

The foregoing selections have illustrated the transition from seventeenth century pioneer conditions, where plantations were largely self-sufficient, to a period of greater cultural maturity, based on the accumulation of wealth. Production of a staple crop on a large scale required credit, and English merchants were willing to extend credit only to large planters. Small farmers had to go to their wealthy neighbors to obtain credit advances. These planters became the respected leaders of the Southern colonies. They were successful economically, could build fine homes, could live more elaborately than their poorer neighbors. As land became more scarce in the old settled regions, sons and daughters of the wealthy planters tended to intermarry and thus limit their group which was becoming an aristocracy. Each succeeding generation came to place greater emphasis on birth, breeding, and education. This process was repeated in every area where the plantation system matured.

A society that was in the process of development was apt to be extravagant and ostentatious in building fine homes and in living. In time more restraint, conservatism, intellectual attainment, and good manners developed.

✔   ✔   ✔

Philip V. Fithian, a tutor in the family of Robert Carter of Westmorland County, Virginia, kept a diary and also wrote a series of letters to Northern friends in which he described the life of the wealthy Virginia planters. The following text is from the *Journal and Letters of Philip Vickers Fithian, 1773-1774: A Plantation Tutor of the Old Dominion,* edited by Hunter Dickinson Farish, Colonial Williamsburg, Inc., Williamsburg, 1943, used by permission of the publisher.

Letters of Philip V. Fithian to the Reverend Enoch Green.

Westmorland. Novr. 2d 1773

Revd. Sir.

. . . I am situated in the *Northern-Neck,* in a most delightful country;

in a civil, polite neighborhood; and in a family remarkable for regularity, and economy, tho' confessedly of the highest quality and greatest worth of any in Virginia. . . .

Respect of your humble Servt
Philip V. Fithian

Revd Sir.   Decemr 1st 1773.

. . . [I] arrived at the Hon. Robert Carters, of Nomini, in Westmorland County, the 28th [of October]. I began to teach his children the first of November. He has two sons, and one Nephew; the oldest Son is turned of seventeen, and is reading Salust and the Greek grammer; the others are about fourteen, and in English grammer, and Arithmetic. He has besides five daughters which I am to teach english, the eldest is turned of fifteen, and is reading the spectator; she is employed two days in every week in learning to play the Forte-Piana, and Harpsicord—the others are smaller, and learning to read and spell. Mr. Carter is one of the Councellors in the general court at Williamsburg, and possest of as great, perhaps the clearest fortune according to the estimation of people here, of any man in Virginia; he seems to be a good scholar, even in classical learning, and is a remarkable one in english grammer; notwithstanding his rank, which in general seems to countenance indulgence to children, both himself and Mrs. Carter have a manner of instructing and dealing with children far superior, I may say it with confidence, to any I have ever seen, in any place, or in any family. They keep them in perfect subjection to themselves, and never pass over an occasion of reproof; and I blush for many of my acquaintances when I say that the children are more kind and complaisant to the servants who constantly attend them than we are to our superiors in age and condition. . . .

I am, Sir, yours,
Philip V. Fithian

Entries from Fithian's Diary.

Monday 13

Mr. Carter is preparing for a voyage in his Schooner, the Hariot, to the Eastern Shore in Maryland, for oysters: there are of the party, Mr. *Carter,* Captain *Walker,* Colonel *Richd. Lee,* & Mr Lancelot Lee. With Sailors to work the vessel—I observe it is a general custom on Sundays here, with Gentlemen to invite one another home to dine, after Church; and to consult about, determine their common business, either before or after Service— It is not the Custom for Gentlemen to go into Church til the Service is beginning, when they enter in a Body, in the same manner as they come out; I have known the Clerk to come out and call them in to prayers.—They stay also after the Service is over, usually as long, sometimes longer, than the parson was preaching— Almost every Lady wears a red Cloak; and when they ride out they tye a white handkerchief over their Head and face, so that when I first came into Virginia, I was distress'd whenever I saw a Lady, for I thought She had the Tooth-Ach.—The People are extremely hospitable, and very polite both of which are most certainly universal Characteristics of the Gentlemen in Virginia—some swear bitterly, but the practice seems to be generally disapproved— I have heard that this Country is notorious for Gaming, however this be, I have not seen a Pack of *Cards,* nor a *Die,* since I left home, nor gaming nor Betting of any kind except at the Richmond-Race. Almost every Gentleman of Condition, keeps a Chariot and Four: many drive with six Horses. . . .

Wednesday 15

. . . In the morning so soon as it is light a Boy knocks at my Door to make a fire; after the Fire is kindled, I rise which now in the winter is commonly by Seven, or a little after . . . ; the Bell rings for eight o'clock (for Mr. Carter has a large good Bell of upwards of 60 Lb. which may be heard some miles, & this is always rung at meal Times; . . . and at half after eight the Bell rings for Breakfast . . . ; the dinner-Bell rings commonly about half after two, often at three, but never before two. . . . I have to myself in the Evening, a neat Chamber, a large Fire, & Candle & my Liberty, either to continue in the school room, in my own Room, or to sit over at the great House with Mr. and Mrs. Carter— We go into Supper commonly about half after eight or at nine & I usually go to Bed between ten and Eleven. . . .

Friday 17.

I dismissed the children this morning til' monday on account of Mr Christian's *Dance* which, as it goes through his Scholars in Rotation, happens to be here to Day. . . . There came to the dance three Chariots, two Chairs, & a number of Horses. Towards Evening . . . [I] walked down, with a number of young Fellows to the River; after our return I was strongly solicited by the young Gentlemen to go in and dance. I declined it, however, and went to my room not without Wishes that it had been a part of my Education to learn what I think is an innocent and an ornamental, and most certainly, in this province is a necessary qualification for a person to appear even decent in Company!

Mrs. *Carter* in the Evening, sent me for Supper a Bowl of hot Green Tea, & several Tarts. I expected that they would have danced till late in the Night, but intirely contrary to my Expectation, the Company were separated to their respective apartments before half after nine *oClock.*

Saturday 18

Rose by Seven, Sent for Mr Carters Barber and was drest for Breakfast— We went in to Breakfast at ten; . . . There were present of Grown persons

Mr and Mrs *Carter,* Mrs Lee, and Miss Jenny Corbin; young Misses about
Eleven; & Seven young Fellows, including myself;—After Breakfast, we all
retired into the Dancing-Room, & after the Scholars had their Lesson
singly round Mr Christian, very politely requested me to step a *Minuet;*
I excused myself however, but signified my peculiar pleasure in the Accuracy of their performance— There were several Minuets danced with
great ease and propriety; after which the whole company Joined in Country-
dances, and it was indeed beautiful to admiration, to see such a number of
young persons, set off by dress to the best Advantage, moving easily, to the
sound of well performed Music, and with perfect regularity. . . . When it
grew too dark to dance, the young Gentlemen walked over to my Room,
and we conversed til half after six: Nothing is now to be heard in Conversation, but the *Balls,* the *Fox-hunts* the fine *entertainments,* and the *good
fellowship,* which are to be exhibited at the approaching Christmas. . . .
     When the candles were lighted we all repaired, for the last time, into
the dancing Room; first each couple danced a Minuet; then all joined as
before in the country Dances, these continued till half after Seven when
Mr. Christian retired; and at the proposal of several, (with Mr. Carters
approbation) we played *Button,* to get Pauns for Redemption; here I
could join with them, and indeed it was carried on with sprightliness and
Decency; in the course of redeeming my Pauns, I had several Kisses of the
Ladies!—Early in the evening came colonel Philip Lee, in a travelling
Chariot from Williamsburg— Half after eight we were rung in to Supper;
the room looked luminous and splendid; four very large candles burning
on the table where we supp'd, three others in different parts of the Room;
a gay, sociable Assembly, & four well instructed waiters!—So soon as we
rose from supper, the company form'd into a semi-circle round the fire,
& Mr. Lee, by the voice of the Company was chosen Pope, and Mr. Carter,
Mr. Christian, Mrs. Carter, Mrs. Lee, and the rest of the Company were
appointed Friars, in the Play call'd "break the Popes neck". . . . we were
all dismiss'd by ten, and retired to our several Rooms.

1   *1*   *1*

Andrew Burnaby, in *Travels Through the Middle Settlements in North America
in the Years 1759 and 1760,* T. Payne, London, Third Edition, 1798, p. 28, described Virginia society.

The women [in Virginia] are, generally speaking handsome, though not
to be compared with our fair country-women in England. They have but
few advantages, and consequently are seldom accomplished; this makes
them reserved, and unequal to any interesting or refined conversation.
They are immoderately fond of dancing, and indeed it is almost the only
amusement they partake of: but even in this they discover want of taste
and elegance, and seldom appear with that gracefulness and ease, which

these movements are calculated to display. Towards the close of an evening when the company are pretty well tired with country dances, it is usual to dance jiggs; a practice originally borrowed, I am informed from the Negroes. These dances are without method or regularity: a gentleman and a lady stand up, and dance about the room, one of them retiring, the other pursuing, then perhaps meeting, in an irregular fantastic manner. After some time, another lady gets up, and then the first lady must sit down, she being, as they term it, cut out: the second lady acts the same part which the first did, till somebody cuts her out. The gentlemen perform in the same manner. The Virginian ladies, excepting these amusements, and now and then going upon a party of pleasure into the woods to partake of a barbecue, chiefly spend their time in sewing and taking care of their families: they seldom read or endeavour to improve their minds; however, they are in general good housewives.

✓   ✓   ✓

While the society of the seacoast region was deepening its culture and the planters were becoming more and more like the country gentlemen of the mother country, those on the western fringe of settlement were repeating the pioneer process. This process was re-enacted many times in the transit of civilization across the continent. Francois Andre Michaux in his *Travels to the West of the Alleghany Mountains*, B. Crosby and Company, London, Second Edition, 1805, p. 283, observed as late as 1802 this type of pioneer life.

Eight tenths of the inhabitants of this part of the country . . . [upper Carolina] reside . . . in log-houses, isolated in the woods, which are left open in the night as well as the day. They live in the same manner with regard to their domestic affairs, and follow the same plan of agriculture. Notwithstanding there are many of them whose moral characters, perhaps, . . . are not . . . unspotted . . . it is probably altered by associating with the Scotch and Irish who come every year in great numbers to settle in the country, and who teach them a part of their vices and defects, the usual attendants on a great population. The greater part of these new adventurers go into the upper country, where they engage to serve, for a year or two, those persons who have paid the captain of the ship for their passage.

TRADE OF THE SOUTHERN COLONIES

The London Company wanted Virginia to complement the economy of England. The leaders experimented with cotton, rice, indigo, silk, hemp, and flax. The colonists learned by bitter experience that they must first produce their own food supply. Then they perfected tobacco culture and cure, and concentrated on that. Tobacco became the staple crop of Virginia and later of Maryland. As new colonies were established, they too were expected to help to round out the economic life of England, but not to compete with the Mother country. The trade of the Southern colonies has been referred to in several of the preceding narratives. B. R. Carroll, Editor, in *Historical Collections of South Carolina,* Harper and Brothers, New York, 1836, Vol. II, pp. 128-129, 234-256, *passim,* 264-271, *passim,* made available summaries of the trade of that province at several dates in the colonial period: (A) Peter Purry, "Description of the Province of South Carolina, 1731," and (B) J. Dodsley, "A description of South Carolina," 1761, are examples.

A. The trade of *Carolina* is now so considerable, that of late Years there has sail'd from thence Annually above 200 Ships, laden with merchandizes of the Growth of the Country, besides 3 Ships of War, which they commonly have for the Security of the Commerce, and last Winter they had constantly 5, the least of which had above 100 Men on Board. It appears by the Custom-house Entries from *March* 1730, to *March* 1731, that there sailed within that time from *Charles-Town* 207 Ships most of them for *England,* which carried among other Goods 41,957 Barrels of Rice about 500 Pound Weight per Barrel, 10754 Barrels of Pitch, 2063 of Tar, and 1159 of Turpentine; of Deer Skins 300 Casks, containing 8 or 900 each; besides a vast Quantity of *Indian* Corn, Pease, Beans, &c. Beef, Pork, and other salted Flesh, Beams, Planks, and Timber for Building, most part of Cedar, Cypress, Sassafras, Oak, Walnut and Pine.

They carry on a great trade with the Indians, from whom they get these great Quantities of Deer Skins, and those of other Wild Beasts, in Exchange for which they give them only Lead, Powder, coarse Cloth, Vermillion, Iron Ware, and some other Goods, by which they have a very considerable Profit.

B.   AN ACCOUNT

Of . . . Commodities of South Carolina . . . exported . . . at the Port of Charles-town. . . . from . . . November 1747 to . . . November 1748 . . . [*Abridged*]

Commodities	Amount of Value, in South-Carolina Currency
	£
Rice	618,750
Indian Corn	19,654
Beef	11,466
Pork	31,140
Pitch	12,422
Indigo	117,353
Skins Deer	252,000
Leather	18,123

[A comparison of the lists of exports for 1731 and 1747 will reveal one important new staple, indigo. Of the production of indigo, the author wrote,] An Acre of good Land may produce about Eighty Pounds Weight of good Indigo; and one Slave may manage Two Acres and upwards, and raise Provisions besides, and have all the Winter Months to saw Lumber and be otherwise employed in; but as much of the Land-hitherto used for Indigo is improper, I am persuaded that not above Thirty Pounds Weight of good Indigo per Acre, can be expected from the Land at present cultivated. Perhaps we are not conversant enough in this Commodity, either in the Culture of the Plant, or in the Method of managing or manufacturing it, to write with certainty. . . .

But I cannot leave this subject without observing how conveniently and profitable, as to the charge of Labour, both Indigo and Rice may be managed by the same Persons, for the Labour attending Indigo being over in the Summer Months, those who were employed in it may afterwards manufacture Rice in the ensuing Part of the Year, when it becomes most laborious; and after doing all this, they will have some Time to spare for sawing Lumber and making Hogsheads, and other Staves, to supply the Sugar Colonies. . . .

I cannot help expressing my surprise and Concern to Find that there are annually imported into this Province, considerable quantities of Fine *Flanders Laces,* the Finest Dutch Linens, and French Cambricks, Chints, Hyson Tea, and other East India Goods, Silks, Gold and Silver Lace, &c.

By these means we are kept in low circumstances; . . . . for the Riches of all the Colonies must at length Centre in the Mother Country, more especially when they are not encouraged to go upon Manufactories, and when they do not rival her in produce. . . .

The Inhabitants of South Carolina have not any Manufactures of their own but are supplied from Great Britain with all their Cloathing, and the other Manufactures by them consumed. . . .

The only commodity of Consequence produced in South Carolina is Rice, and they reckon it as much their staple commodity, as Sugar is to Barbadoes and Jamaica, or Tobacco to Virginia, and Maryland. . . . The production of Rice in South Carolina which is of much prodigious Advantage was owing to the following Accident.

A Brigantine from the Island of Madagascar, happened to put into that Colony: —They had a little Seed Rice left, not exceeding a Peck or Quarter of a Bushel, which the Captain offered and gave a Gentleman by the name of Woodward:— from a Part of this he had a very good Crop, but was very ignorant for some years how to clean it:—it was soon dispersed over the Province, and by frequent experiments and observations, they found out ways of producing and manufacturing it, to so great Perfection, that it is said to exceed any other Rice in value:— The Writer of this hath seen the said Captain in Carolina where he received a handsome Gratuity from the Gentlemen of that Country, in acknowledgement of the Service he had done that Province.

It is likewise reported, that Mr. Du Bois, Treasurer of the East India Company did send to that Country a small Bag of Seed Rice, some short time after; from whence it is reasonable to suppose there might come those two sorts of that Commodity, the one called Red-Rice in Contradistinction to the White Rice, from the redness of the inner husk or rind of this Sort, though they both clear and become alike White. . . .

The Trade between South Carolina and Great Britain, one year with another, employs Twenty two Sail of Ships. Those Ships bring from Great Britain to South Carolina all sorts of Wollen Cloths, Stuffs, and Druggetts; Linens, Hollands, Printed Calicoes and Linens; Silks and Muslins; Nails of all sizes, Hoes, Hatchetts, and all kinds of Iron-wares; Bedticks, Strong Beer, Bottled Cider, Raisins, Fine Earthen wares, Pipes, Paper, Rugs, Blankets, Quilts; Hats from 28 to 12s. price; Stockings from 1 to 8s. price; Gloves; Pewter Dishes and Plates; Brass and Copper wares; Guns, Powder, Bulletts, Flints, Glass Beads, Cordage, Wollen and Cotton cards, Steel Hand mills, Grind-stones; Looking and Drinking Glasses; Lace, Thread coarse and fine; Mohair, and all Kinds of Trimmings for Cloaths, Pins, Needles, &c.

. . . [The] commodities and manufactures . . . [that] are sent from South Carolina to Great Britain . . . are not sufficient to pay for European Goods, and negro Slaves with which the English Merchants are continually supplying the South Carolina people. . . .

Besides the twenty two sail of Ships which trade between South Carolina and Great Britain . . . there enter and clear annually at the Port of Charles-Town, about Sixty sail of Ships, Sloops, and Brigantines, which are employed in carrying on the . . . Trade between South Carolina and other Countries.

The Trade between South Carolina and Jamaica, Barbadoes, the British Leeward Islands, the Island of St. Thomas, (a Danish Sugar Colony), and Curaso (a Dutch Sugar Colony).

The Commodities sent from South Carolina to those Places are beef, Pork, Butter, Candles, Soap, Tallow, Myrtle wax candles, Rice, some Pitch and Tar, cedar and pine boards, Shingles, Hoop Staves and Heads for Barrels.

The Commodities sent in return from those places to South Carolina, are Sugar, Rum, Molasses, Cotton, Chocolate made up, Cocoa Nuts, Negro Slaves, and Money.

The Trade between South Carolina and New England, New York and Pennsilvania.

The Commodities sent from South Carolina to other Northern Colonies, are tanned hides, small Deer Skins, Gloves, Rice, Slaves taken by the Indians in War, some Tar and Pitch.

The Commodities sent in return from those other Northern Colonies, to South Carolina are, Wheat, Flour, Biscuit, Strong Beer, Cyder, Salted Fish, Onions, Apples, Hops.

The Trade between South Carolina and the Madeira, and Western Islands (belonging to Portugal).

The commodities sent from South Carolina to those Islands, are Beef, Pork, Butter, Rice, Casks, Staves, Heading for Barrels, &c.

The Commodities sent in return from those Islands to South Carolina are Wines. N. B. The Salt used in South Carolina is brought from the Bahama Islands. From Guinea, and other parts of the Coast of Africa, Negroe Slaves are imported into South Carolina; But the Ships which bring them there, being sent from England with effects to purchase them, the Carolina Returns for the same are sent thither.

LABOR

Two types of labor, indentured servants and Negro slaves, have been mentioned repeatedly in the preceding selections. The former predominated during the seventeenth century and decreased during the eighteenth, when the pattern of slave labor developed. To those who contemplated taking the extreme step of going to America as servants, the following advice was given. The text is from John Hammond, *Leah and Rachel* . . . , in Peter Force, Editor, *Tracts and Other Papers, Relating Principally to the Origin, Settlement, and Progress of the Colonies in North America,* printed by P. Force, Washington, 1844, p. 11. It was written in 1656.

Let such as are so minded not rashly throw themselves upon the voyage, but observe the nature, and enquire the qualities of the persons with whom they ingage to transport themselves, or if (as not acquainted with such as inhabit there, but go with Merchants and Mariners, who transport them to others), let their covenant be such, that after their arrival they have a fortnights time assigned them to enquire of their Master, and make choyce of such as they intend to expire their time with, nor let that brand of selling of servants, be any discouragement to deter any from going, for if a time must be served, it is all one with whom it be served, provided they be people of honest repute, with whom the Country is well replenished.

And be sure to have your contract in writing and under hand and seal, for if ye go over upon promise made to do this or that, or to be free or your own men, it signifies nothing, for by a law of the Country (waving all promises) any one coming in, and not paying their own passages, must serve if men or women four years, if younger according to their years, but where an Indenture is, that is binding and observing.

The usual allowance for servants is (besides their charge of passage defrayed) at their expiration, a years provision of corne, dubble apparrell, tooles necessary, and land according to the custome of the Country, which is an old delusion, for there is no land accustomary due to the servant, but to the Master, and therefore that servant is unwise that will not dash out that custom in his covenant, and make that due of land absolutely his own, which although at the present, not of so great consequence; yet in few years will be worth much more, as I shall hereafter make manifest. . . .

The labour servants are put to, is not so hard nor of such continuance as Husbandmen, nor Handecraftmen are kept at in *England,* I said little or nothing is done in winter time, none ever work before sun rising nor after sun set, in the summer they rest, sleep or exercise themselves five houres in the heat of the day, Saturdayes afternoon is alwayes their own, the old Holidayes are observed and the Sabboath spent in good exercises.

The Women are not (as is reported) put into the ground to worke, but occupie such domestique imployments and housewifery as in England, that is dressing victuals, righting up the house, milking, imployed about dayries, washing, sowing, &c., and both men and women have times of recreations as much or more than in any part of the world besides. . . .

✓　　　✓　　　✓

Daniel DeFoe's novel, *The Fortunes and Misfortunes of the Famous Moll Flanders,* 1722, was propaganda encouraging moral derelicts to rehabilitate themselves by becoming indentured servants in America. The following excerpts are from the title page and preface, 1840 Edition, Oxford.

The Fortunes and Misfortunes of the Famous Moll Flanders, &c. Who was Born in NEWGATE, and during a Life of continu'd Variety Threescore Years, besides her Childhood, was Twelve Years a *Whore,* five Times a *Wife* (whereof once to her own Brother), Twelve Years a *Thief,* Eight Years a Transported *Felon* in Virginia, at last grew *Rich,* liv'd *Honest,* and died a *Penitent.* Written from her own Memorandums. . . .

Her application to a sober life and industrious management at last in Virginia, with her transported spouse, is a story fruitful of instruction, to all the unfortunate creatures who are obliged to seek their re-establishment abroad, whether by misery of transportation or other disaster; letting them know that diligence and application have their due encouragement, even in the remotest parts of the world, and that no case can be so low, so despicable, or so empty of prospect, but that an unwearied industry will go a great way to deliver us from it, will in time raise the meanest creature to appear again in the world, and give him a new cast for his life.

✓　　　✓　　　✓

The following account of Negro slavery in the English colonies is from Alexander Hewit's *Historical Account of South Carolina and Georgia,* originally published in London in 1779, reprinted in B. R. Carroll, Editor, *Historical Collections of South Carolina,* Harper and Brothers, New York, 1836, Vol. I, pp. 348-358, *passim.*

By this trade being torn from those nearest connexions, . . . and with irons, and cooped up in a ship, oppressed with the most gloomy apprehensions, many of them sicken and die through fear and regret. The provisions made for the voyage by the merchants and masters of ships, who consult their worldly interests more than the dictates of humanity, we may be sure are neither of the best kind, nor distributed among them in the most plentiful manner. After their arrival they are sold and delivered over to the colonists, to whose temper, language and manners they are utter strangers; where their situation for some time, in case of harsh usage, is little better than that of the dumb beasts, having no language but groans in which they can express their pains, nor any friend to pity or relieve them. . . .

After the sale the puchasers become vested with the absolute property of them, according to the laws, usages, and customs of the trade, and whatever hardships are thereby imposed on those foreigners, the planters are so far excusable, having the sanction of the supreme legislature for the purchase they make. The laws of England, from necessity or expediency, have permitted such labourers to be imported among them; and therefore, on their part, the purchase, however injurious, cannot be illegal. Having acquired this kind of property, it then lies with the colonists to frame laws and regulations for the future management of their slaves. . . . All laws framed with respect to them, give their masters such authority over them as is under few limitations. Their power of correction may be said to be only not allowed to extend to death. However severely beat and abused, no negro can bring action against his owner, or appear as an evidence against white men, in any court of law or justice. . . . A common place of correction is instituted, to which they are sent to receive such a number of stripes as their owners shall order, and such blunders have been committed in giving and executing those orders, that the innocent sometimes have suffered along with the guilty. . . . At the decease of their masters they descend, like other estates of inheritance, to the heir at law, and sometimes to thoughtless and giddy youth, habituated from their earliest days to treat them like brutes. At other times, no doubt, they are more fortunate, but their condition of life evidently subjects them to harsh usage even from the best of masters, and we leave the world to judge what they have to expect from the worst.

Indeed, it must be acknowledged, in justice to the planters of Carolina in general, that they treat their slaves with as much, and perhaps more tenderness, than those of any British colony where slavery exists; yet a disinterested stranger must observe, even among the best of masters, several instances of cruelty and negligence in the manner of managing their slaves. Comparatively speaking, they are well clothed and fed in that province, which, while they continue in health, fits and qualifies them for their task. When they happen to fall sick, they are carefully attended by a physician; in which respect their condition is better than that of the poorest class of labourers in Europe. . . .

But there is another circumstance which renders their case still more wretched and deplorable. Good masters and mistresses, whose humanity and a sense of interest will not permit them to treat their negroes in a harsh manner, do not always reside at their plantations. Many planters have several settlements a considerable distance from the place where they usually live, which they visit only three or four times a year. In their absence the charge of the negroes is given to overseers, many of whom are ignorant and cruel, and all totally disinterested in the welfare of their charge. In such a case it can scarcely be expected that justice will be equally dispensed, or punishments inflicted. The negroes, however, lay entirely at the mercy of such men. . . .

RELIGION

The Church of England was officially "established" in the five Anglo-American Southern colonies. Tithes were collected by law, and in early Virginia no one was allowed to vote unless he was a member of the Church of England. An act of the Virginia House of Burgesses provided for a glebe, or tract of one hundred acres of farmland to be set aside, together with a fixed salary, usually paid in tobacco, for ministers. The establishment of the church in the other Southern colonies was somewhat tardy, and except in South Carolina the churches were wanting in vitality and power. The principal difficulty was to secure a sufficient number of ministers.

Captain John Smith, in his *Pathway to Erect a Plantation,* described the first places of divine worship in Virginia. The following extract was reprinted in *Collections of the Massachusetts Historical Society,* Massachusetts Historical Society, Boston, 1792-, Vol. III, Third Series, p. 44.

When I went first to *Virginia,* I well remember, wee did hang an awning (which is an old saile) to three or foure trees to shadow us from the Sunne; our walls were rales of wood; our seats unhewed trees till we cut plankes, our Pulpit a bar of wood nailed to two neighboring trees, in foul weather we shifted into an old rotten tent; and this came by way of adventure for new; this was our Church, till wee built a homely thing like a barne, set upon Cratchets, covered with rafts, sedge, and earth; so was also the walls: the best of our houses of like curiosity, but the most farre much worse workmanship, that could neither well defend wind nor rain, yet we had daily Common Prayer morning and evening, every Sunday two Sermons, and every three moneths the holy Communion, till our Minister died, but our Prayers daily with an Homily on Sundaies; we continued two or three yeares after, till more Preachers came. . . .

⚹   ⚹   ⚹

A letter written by William Gale from Perquimans at the close of the seventeenth century, describing life in Albemarle at that time, emphasized the lack of cultural and religious advantages. The following text is quoted in Samuel A'Court Ashe, *History of North Carolina*, Charles Van Noppen, Publisher, Greensboro, North Carolina, 1908, Vol. I, p. 152.

Our greatest grievance is want of books and pleasing conversation. The Quakers are here very numerous, but as for Independents, Anabaptists, Presbyterians, and other sectaries, they have little or no place here. Most who profess themselves doctors and attorneys are scandals to the profession. The decay of Christian piety is in such large characters that he who runs may read. The second of January last it pleased God to make me happy in a son, who bears the name of his grandfather, but he has the unhappiness to be unchristened, to my great grief, the only minister we have had of the Church of England having left us before my son was born, but it was no loss to religion, for he was ye monster of ye age.

✓   ✓   ✓

In 1701 a great missionary agency, the Society for the Propagation of the Gospel in Foreign Parts, was organized and chartered. Its purpose was to provide for the "better support and Maintenance of an Orthodox Clergy in Forreigne Parts." While its main object was work among the English settlers, conversion of Indians and Negro slaves was also undertaken. From that time on most of the work of the Anglican Church in America was done under the auspices of the so-called "Venerable Society." Occasionally a complaint was registered against a missionary; in some instances the Society dismissed men against whom complaints were brought. The following complaint was sent to the Bishop of London. The text is from William L. Saunders, Editor, *Colonial Records of North Carolina, 1662-1776*, P. M. Hale, etc., Raleigh, 1886-90, Vol. IV, p. 263.

SO. CAROLINA CHARLESTOWN SEPT 6TH [1737]
MY LORD BISHOP OF LONDON

I have lately recd a letter from his excellency the Governor of N. Carolina of which the following is a paragraph concerning the ill behavior of Mr. Boyd the Honble Society's missionary in that Colony.

After having expressed much concern that no farther assistance was to be expected from the honble Society towards the propagating of religion in that Colony than the one Missionary, already there, His excellency subjoins concerning him and says, "But what makes the matter still worse is that this very missionary is one of the vilest and most scandalous persons in the government. . . . I have heard such accounts of his behaviour as are really shocking, particularly that on a Sunday, this spring, at noon day he was seen by many persons lying dead drunk (& fast asleep) on the great road to Virginia, with his horses bridle tied to his leg this I have been assured of by several persons of the best credit As he is under your inspection I hope you will take some notice of such horrid practices. . . ."

I humbly crave your Ldships blessing, & am, My Lord,

A. GARDEN

✓   ✓   ✓

In the following selection James Moir, a missionary, reported to the Secretary of the Venerable Society some of his difficulties. The text is from William L. Saunders, Editor, *Colonial Records of North Carolina, 1662-1776,* P. M. Hale, etc., Raleigh, 1886-90, Vol. IV, p. 605.

WILMINGTON APRIL 22d 1742.

REVEREND SIR, [to the secretary]

When I was in London I signified to you that this part of the Province where I am Missionary is about 150 miles in breadth along the coast and that in some places they have settled upwards of 150 miles back from the sea. The Inhabitants are very much scattered, and most of them live at a great distance from one another which renders it impossible for me to serve them as I could wish the generality of them are extremely ignorant, I baptized 210 children. . . .

In this county which is pretty large we have about 3000 Inhabitants, two thirds whereof are Negroes, I take one half of the whites to be Dissenters of various denominations—notwithstanding I ride twice a year betwixt this and the Neuse and Make all the inquiries I can, it is not possible for me to know the number of Inhabitants and what they profess   we have no churches no Glebes, no Parsonage Houses, nothing so far as I can see, that discovers in the People the least intention of providing the necessary travelling charges. We are wretchedly accommodated and at extravagant rates. We are subject to so many inconveniences that I am ashamed to mention them, and don't at all wonder to hear former Missionaries were much dissatisfied & had so little inclination to stay in this Province. . . .

I am, Revd Sir, &c.,

James Moir

✓   ✓   ✓

The church was handicapped by the absence of bishops in America. The Society had no authority over missionaries except to employ or discharge them. The Bishop of London was too far removed from the colonies to supervise the work in America. Governors of the colonies and church leaders in England urged the creation of a colonial episcopate, but several factors prevented their success. The government in England was following the policy of "salutary neglect" toward the colonies. Another factor was the wish of the planter aristocracy to maintain control of the local churches through the office of vestryman, which caused them to oppose the appointment of an American bishop. The following selections illustrate the conflict between the planters and the church. The texts are from William L. Saunders, Editor, *Colonial Records of North Carolina, 1662-1776,* P. M. Hale, etc., Raleigh, 1886-90, Vol. IV, p. 604, and Vol. V, p. 315.

NO. CAROLINA BATH TOWN April 16:1742

REVEREND SIR [TO THE SECRETARY]

In obedience to the order of the Honorable Society to me I send by this a true and faithful account of my services this year. . . .

I do beg the favour of you to inform their Honours with my endeavours, to promote goodness, christianity and the true Religion among the inhabitants within my mission, but immorality is arrived to that head among so many, that it requires not only some time but great patience to conquer it; because upon my preaching upon any prevalent & predominant Sin, I must be prepared to stand the persecution of those who are guilty of it, especially in my resident Parish, in which adultery, Incest, Blasphemy, and all kinds of profaneness has got such deep root.

I shall be more large in my next, In the mean time I stand the oppression of an inveterate and obstinate Parish, govern'd by twelve Vestry men, whose only endeavour is to hinder & obstruct the service of God, being performed, they themselves never coming to hear the word of God, and dissuading as much as possible others from it and who in a particular manner exercise their malice daily against me, by depriving me of my quietness of mind and the enjoyment of the small Salary of L37:10ˢ per annᵐ allow'd by law, & which I am obliged to have recourse to recover, having had nothing these 4 years for the support of my Family, but what is allow'd to me by the Honᵇˡᵉ Society, for whom my humble Prayers to God, & my humble respect to your Reverence & begging the continuance of your favour, am

Revᵈ Sir, your most &c.,
John Garzia

Letter from Governor Dobbs to the Board of Trade.

. . . the Assembly is determined to give a proper Encouragement to learned and pious Clergymen and to encourage Schools; but am of Opinion it wou'd be of great Service to his Majesty & to Britain and great Satisfaction to the Inhabitants, if a Bishop was appointed or a Clergyman with Episcopal power to confirm the Youth, to visit & keep the Clergy to their Duty, and to concur in putting the Laws in Execution by removing them if convicted by a Jury of any gross Immorality, non Residence or Inattention to their Cure, and to put Persons qualified into orders, without the Expense trouble & Delay of going to be ordained and licensed by the Bishop of London, without giving them any other Judicial power spiritual Courts as in Britain. . . .

✓   ✓   ✓

One of the most detailed accounts of the work of an Anglican missionary is *The Carolina Backcountry on the Eve of the Revolution; The Journal and Other Writings of Charles Woodmason, Anglican Itinerant,* edited by Richard J. Hooker, University of North Carolina Press, Chapel Hill, 1953, reprinted by permission of the publisher. Woodmason was of the English gentry class and entered upon his ministry as a mature person, having lived in London, on the Peedee River as a planter for almost a decade, and as a statesman in Charleston for several years.

He returned to England especially to be ordained as a minister, and entered upon his duties in 1766. The following selection from his diary was written at the end of the second year of his ministry, pp. 60-63, *passim*.

Saturday September 30) Rode down the Country on the West Side the Wateree River into the Fork between that and the Congaree River—This is out of my Bounds—But their having no Minister, and their falling (therefrom) continually from the Church to Anabaptism, inclin'd me to it—The People received me gladly and very kindly. Had on Sunday 4—a Company of about 150—Most of them of the Low Class—the principal Planters living on the Margin of these Rivers.

Baptiz'd 1 Negro Man—2 Negro Children—and 9 White Infants and married 1 Couple—The People thanked me in the most kind Manner for my Services—I had very pleasant Riding but my Horse suffered Greatly. The Mornings and Evenings now begin to be somewhat Cool, but the Mid day heat is almost intolerable—Many of these People walk 10 or 12 Miles with their Children in the burning Sun—Ought such to be without the Word of God, when so earnest, so desirous of hearing it and becoming Good Christians, and good Subjects! How lamentable to think, that the Legislature of this Province will make no Provision—so rich, so luxurious, polite a People! Yet they are deaf to all Solicitations, and look on the poor White People in a Meaner Light than their Black Slaves, and care less for them. Withal there is such a Republican Spirit still left, so much of the Old Leaven of Lord Shaftsbury and other the 1st principal Settlers still remains, that they seem not at all disposed to promote the Interest of the Church of England—Hence it is that above 30,000£ Sterling have lately been expended to bring over 5 or 6000 Ignorant, mean, worthless, beggarly Irish Presbyterians, the Scum of the Earth, and Refuse of Mankind, and this, solely to ballance the Emigrations of People from Virginia, who are all of the Established Church. . . .

It will require much Time and Pains to New Model and form the Carriage and Manners, as well as Morals of these wild Peoples—Among this Congregation not one had a Bible of Common Prayer—or could join a Person or hardly repeat the Creed or Lords Prayer—Yet all of 'em had been educated in the Principles of our Church. So that I am obliged to read the Whole Service, omitting such Parts, as are Repetitious, and retaining those that will make the different Services somewhat Uniform—Hence it is, that I can but seldom use the Litany, because they know not the Responses.

It would be . . . a Great Novelty to a Londoner to see one of these Congregations—The Men with only a thin Shirt and pair of Breeches or Trousers on—barelegged and barefooted—the Women bareheaded, barelegged and barefoot with only a thin Shift and under Petticoat—Yet I cannot break [them] of this—for the heat of the Weather admits not of any [but] thin Cloathing—I can hardly bear the Weight of my Whig and Gown, during Service. The Young Women have a most uncommon Practise, which I cannot break them off. They draw their Shift as tight as possible to the Body, and pin it close, to shew the roundness of their Breasts, and slender Waists (for they are generally finely shaped) and draw their Petticoat close to their Hips to shew the fineness of their Limbs—so that they might as well be in Puri Naturalibus—Indeed Nakedness is not censurable or indecent here, and they expose themselves often quite Naked, without Ceremony—Rubbing themselves and their Hair with Bears Oil and tying it up behind in a Bunch like the Indians—being hardly one degree removed from them—In few Years, I hope to bring about a Reformation, as I have already done in several Parts of the Country. . . .

Thus You have a Journal of two Years—In which have rode near Six thousand Miles, almost on one Horse. Wore my Self to a Skeleton and endured all the Extremities of Hunger, Thirst, Cold, and Heat. Have baptized near 1200 Children—Given 200 or more Discourses—Rais'd almost 30 Congregations—Set on foot the building of sundry Chapels Distributed Books, Medicines, Garden Seed, Turnip, Clover, Timothy Burnet, and other Grass Seeds—with Fish Hooks—Small working Tools and variety of Implements to set the Poor at Work, and promote Industry to the amount of at least One hundred Pounds Sterling: Roads are making—Boats building—Bridges framing, and other useful Works begun thro' my Means, as will not only be of public Utility, but make the Country side wear a New Face, and the People become New Creatures. And I will venture to attest that these small, weak Endeavours of mine to serve the Community, has (or will) be of more Service to the Colony, than ever Mr. Whitfield's Orphan House was, or will be.

✟   ✟   ✟

Religious toleration developed in England during the seventeenth century and was reflected in America. In 1623-24 the Virginia House of Burgesses passed laws requiring all residents to attend the church of England; in 1649 a statute was written by Lord Baltimore and adopted by the Maryland Assembly providing for freedom of conscience in that colony, and the Fundamental Constitutions drawn up for Carolina in 1669 provided for religious toleration which was by that time an accepted ideal of liberal-minded Englishmen. The following law is quoted from William Waller Hening, Editor, *The Statutes at Large,* Samuel Pleasants, Jr., Richmond, 1823, Vol. I, pp. 122-124.

No. of the Acts

1. THAT there shall be in every plantation, where the people use to meete for the worship of God, a house or roome sequestred for that purpose, and not to be for any temporal use whatsoever, and a place empaled in, sequestered only to the buryal of the dead.

2. That whosoever shall absent himselfe from divine service any Sunday without an allowable excuse shall forfeite a pound of tobacco, and he that absenteth himselfe a month shall forfeit 50 lb. of tobacco.

3. That there be an uniformity in our church as neere as may be to the canon's in England; both in substance and circumstance, and that all persons yeild readie obedience unto them under paine of censure.

John V. L. McMahon, *An Historical View of the Government of Maryland*, F. Lucas, Jr., Cushing and Sons, and W. and J. Neal, Baltimore, 1831, Vol. I, p. 277, quotes the Maryland Toleration Act of 1649.

Whereas the enforcing of the conscience, in matters of Religion, hath frequently fallen out to be of dangerous Consequence in these commonwealthes where it hath been practised; and for the more quiet and peaceable government of the province, and the better to preserve mutual Love and unity amongst the Inhabitants. . . . No person *professing to believe in Jesus Christ,* shall be in anywise molested or discountenanced, in respect of his religion, nor in the free exercise thereof, nor in any way compelled to the beleife or exercise of any other Religion.

✓   ✓   ✓

From the "Fundamental Constitutions of Carolina," in B. R. Carroll, Editor, *Historical Collections of South Carolina,* Harper and Brothers, New York, 1836, Vol. II, pp. 386-387, the following provisions are quoted.

100. In the terms of communion of every church or profession, these following shall be three; without which no agreement or assembly of men, under pretence of religion, shall be accounted a church or profession within these rules:

1. "That there is a GOD.

2. "That GOD is publicly to be worshipped.

3. "That it is lawful and the duty of every man, being thereunto called by those that govern, to bear witness to truth; and that every church or profession shall, in their terms of communion, set down the external way whereby they witness a truth as in the presence of GOD, whether it be by laying hands on, or kissing the Bible, as in the church of England, or by holding up the hand, or any other sensible way."

102. No person of any other church or profession shall disturb or molest any religious assembly.

109. No person whatsoever shall disturb, molest, or persecute another for his speculative opinions in religion, or his way of worship.

✓   ✓   ✓

Instructions sent by the English Government to Governor Dobbs of North Carolina and to Governor John Reynolds of Georgia in 1753 provided for religious liberty but supported the established church. The following quotation is from William L. Saunders, Editor, *Colonial Records of North Carolina, 1662-1776*, P. M. Hale, etc., Raleigh, 1886-90, Vol. V, p. 1136.

You are to permit a liberty of conscience to all persons except Papists so as they are contented with a quiet and peaceable enjoyment of the same not giving scandal or offense to the Government.

You shall take especial care that God Almighty be devoutly and duly served throughout your government the Book of Common Prayer as by law established read each Sunday and Holiday and the blessed Sacrament administered according to the rights of the Church of England.

You shall take care that the Churches already built be well and orderly kept and that more be built as the Province by God's blessing shall be improved and that besides a competent maintenance to be assigned to the Minister of each Orthodox Church a convenient House to be built at the common charge for each Minister and a competent proportion of land assigned him for a Glebe and exercise of his industry.

✶ ✶ ✶

Among the dissenters of the Southern colonies, the first of whom were probably Quakers, George Fox journeyed along the coast of Maryland, Virginia, and the Carolinas in 1672 and planted Quaker meetings. He was followed by other Quaker missionaries who were entertained in the homes of the people and held local meetings keeping Quaker ideals alive. Meetings were held in homes of members and no effort was made to establish a professional ministry.

The history of the Baptists in the South began in the seventeenth century; during that period the political, economic, and religious unrest in England caused many people to leave the Anglican Church. Many became independents in religion, and some eventually formed the Baptist Church. Baptists did not believe in infant baptism, were very democratic, and joined themselves together in associations through which they carried on a correspondence and achieved some unity of purpose. Charles Town, South Carolina, was the seat of the oldest Baptist church in either of the Carolinas; it may have been formed in 1683.

Between 1660 and 1690 large numbers of Scottish Covenanters came to America, some of whom settled in Maryland. Through their invitation the first Presbyterian missionary, Frances Makemie, came to America from Ireland. From that time the number of independent, isolated Presbyterian congregations gradually increased. However, the greatest growth in all of the dissenting denominations came with the immigration of people to the back country of the Southern colonies in the eighteenth century. This growth was accompanied by the "Great Awakening," a revival that swept the colonies from New England to Georgia.

George Whitefield was the most influential evangelist of the revival. The following account of his work is from Alexander Hewit, *The History of South Carolina,* reprinted in B. R. Carroll, Editor, *Historical Collections of South Carolina,* Harper and Brothers, New York, 1836, Vol. I, pp. 405-410, *passim.*

In the annals of Georgia the famous George Whitfield may not be unworthy of some notice. . . . Actuated by religious motives, this wanderer several times passed the Atlantic to convert the Americans, whom he addressed in such a manner as if they had been all equal strangers to the privileges and benefits of religion with the orginal inhabitants of the forest. However, his zeal never led him beyond the maritime parts of America, through which he travelled, spreading what he called the true evangelical faith among the most populous towns and villages. . . . Wherever he went in America, as in Britain, he had multitudes of followers. . . .

As George Whitfield appeared in such different lights in the successive stages of life, it is no easy matter to delineate his character without an uncommon mixture, and vast variety of colours. He was in the British empire not unlike one of those strange and erratic meteors which appear now and then in the system of nature. In his youth, as he often confessed and lamented, he was gay, giddy, and profligate; so fondly attached to the stage, that he joined a company of strolling actors and vagabonds, and spent a part of his life in that capacity. At this period, it is probable he learned that grimace, buffoonery, and gesticulation, which he afterward displayed from the pulpit. From an abandoned and licentious course of life, he was converted; and, what is no uncommon thing, from one extreme he ran into the other, and became a most zealous and indefatigable teacher of religion. Having studied some time at Oxford, he received ordination in the church of England; yet he submitted to none of the regulations of that or any other church, but became a preacher in churches, meeting-houses, halls, fields, in all places, and to all denominations, without exception. Though little distinguished for genius or learning, yet he possessed a lively imagination, much humour, and had acquired considerable knowledge of human nature and the manners of the world. His pretensions to humanity and benevolence were great, yet he would swell with venom, like a snake, against opposition and contradiction. His reading was inconsiderable, and mankind being the object of his study, he could, when he pleased, raise the passions, and touch the tone of the human heart to great perfection. By this affecting eloquence and address, he impressed on the minds of many, especially of the more soft and delicate sex, such a strong sense of sin and guilt, as often plunged them into dejection and despair. As his custom was to frequent those larger cities and towns, that are commonly best supplied with the means of instruction, it would appear that the love of fame and popular applause was his leading passion; yet, in candour it must be acknowledged, that he always discovered a warm zeal for the honour of God and the happiness of men. While he was almost worshipped by the vulgar, men of superior rank and erudition found him the polite gentleman, and the facetious and jocular companion. Though he loved good cheer, and frequented the houses of the rich, or more hospitable people of America, yet he was an enemy to all manner of excess and intemperance. . . . Though, in prayer, he commonly addressed the second person of the Trinity in a familiar and fulsome style, and, in his sermons, used many ridiculous forms of speech, and told many of his own wonderful works, yet these seemed only shades to set off to greater advantage the luster of his good qualities. In short, though it is acknowledged that he had many oddities and failings, and was too much the slave of party and vain-glory, yet in justice it cannot be denied, that religion in America owed not a little to the zeal, diligence, and oratory of this extraordinary man.

✓   ✓   ✓

In the following selection, Morgan Edwards, the first historian of the Baptist denomination in America, described the rapid growth of the Baptist Church in North Carolina as a result of the Great Awakening. The text is from a mimeographed copy of an unpublished manuscript, "Materials towards a History of the Baptists in the Province of North Carolina," Vol. IV; the manuscript is in the possession of the Library of the American Baptist Convention in Chester, Pennsylvania.

Next to Virginia, southward, is North Carolina; a poor and unhappy province, where superiors make compaints of the people and the people of their superiors; which complaints, if just, show the body politic to be like that of Israel in the time of Isaiah "From the sole of the feet to the crown of the head without any soundness, but wounds and bruises and putrifying sores." These complaints rose to hostilities at Alamance Creek May.16.1771, where about 6000 appeared in arms and fought each other, 4000 Regulators killing three Tryonians; and 2000 Tryonians killing twelve Regulators, besides lodging in the trees an incredible number of bals which the hunters have since picked out, and therewith have killed more deer and turkies than they killed of their antagonists. In this wretched province have been some baptists since the settlement in 1695; but no society of them till about the year 1742, when one was formed about Quehuky: these came hither from Isle-of-wight county in Virginia, having one William Sojourner to their minister. In 12 years this society had spread her branches through the north and northeast parts, and become 16 churches. They were all General-baptists. But about 1751 they began to embrace the sentiments of the Particular-baptists, and have since come into these sentiments, except Mer Parker and his church, and some others. The cause was, partly the conversation of lay-man, commonly called the Stay-maker: His name was William Wallis; but chiefly, a visit which Mer Gano paid them in 1753. On his arrival he sent to the ministers, requesting an interview, which they declined, and appointed a meeting among themselves to consult what to do? Mer Gano, hearing of it, went to their meeting, and addressed them. . . .

In 1755 a small company from Connecticut came and settled in the forks of Capefear river at a place called Sandy-creek, they were 16 souls in number, having Shubal Stearns to their minister: these were the beginning of what are commonly, tho improperly, called Separat-baptists, who soon spread thro the province, to South-carolina and Georgia, and northward to Virginia. . . . Near the same time (1742) the Tunker-baptists from Pennsylvania arrived in this province, and settled about the branch of the Pedee. . . . .

Besides Separatists, they are sometimes called Newlights, because, in their manner, they resemble those devout people to the northward who, in 1740, acquired the names of Separatists and Newlights: the ministers resemble those in tones of voice and action of body; and the people in crying out under the ministry, falling—down as in fits, and awaking in extacies; and both ministers and people resemble those in regarding impulses, visions, and revelations. But it must be observed yt. these things are not true of all the separate Baptists; there are some exceptions: neither do all regard the nine Christian rites, but only baptism, the Lords supper, and imposition of hands. Of the separate baptists there are 9 churches in Northcarolina. . . .

SANDY-CREEK

. . . in the county of Guilford. The place of worship is 30 feet by 26, built in 1762, on land given by Seamore York. No estate, no salary except presents. . . . Here ruling elders, eldresses, and deaconnesses are allowed. . . . This is their present state. They had their beginning, Nov. 22, 1755, when the following persons arrived to the place. viz. Shubal Stearns and wife, Peter Stearns and wife, Ebenezer Stearns and wife. . . . The Stearns travelled hither from Boston. . . . As soon as they arrived to Sandy creek they built a little meeting house on the spot where the present stands. Very remarkable things may be said of this church. . . . It began with 16 souls; and in a short time increased to 606, spreading its branches to deep-river and Abbots-creek, which branches are gone to other provinces; and most of the members of this church have followed them, in so much that in 17 years it is reduced from 606 to 14 souls, and is in danger of becoming extinct. The cause of this dispersion was the abuse of power which too much prevailed in the province and caused the inhabitants at least to rise up in arms, and fight for their privileges; but being routed (May 16, 1771) they despaired of seeing better times, and therefore quitted the province. It is said that 1500 families departed since the battle of Alamance, and, to my knowledge, great many more are only waiting to dispose of their plantations in order to follow them. . . .

But to return . . . Sandy-Creek is the mother of all the Separate-baptists. From this Zion went forth the word, and great was the company of them who published it; it, in 17 years, has spread branches westward as far as the great river Mississippi; southward as far as Georgia; eastward to the sea and Chesopeck bay; and northward to the waters of the Potowmack. . . .

✓   ✓   ✓

The Presbyterian Church made a great growth because of the multitudes of Scotch-Irish who were moving into the back country at the time of the Great Awakening. Dr. Alexander Hewit, a Presbyterian minister, described the characteristics of the church. The text is from Hewit, *The History of South Carolina,* in B. R. Carroll, Editor, *Historical Collections of South Carolina,* Harper and Brothers, New York, 1836, Vol. I, pp. 316-317.

The first clergymen having received their ordination in the church of Scotland, the fundamental rules of the association were framed according to the forms, doctrines, and disciplines of that establishment, to which they agreed to conform as closely as their local conditions would admit. These ministers adopted this mode of religious worship, not only from a persuasion of its conformity to the primitive apostolic form, but also from a conviction of its being, of all others the most favourable to civil liberty, equality, and independence. Sensible that not only natural endowments, but also a competent measure of learning and acquired knowledge were necessary to qualify men for the sacred function, and enable them to discharge the duties of it with honour and success, they associated on purpose to prevent deluded mechanics, and illiterate novices from creeping into the pulpit, to the disgrace of the character, and the injury of religion. In different parts of the province, persons of this stamp had appeared, who cried down all establishments, both civil and religious, and seduced weak minds from the duties of allegiance, and all that the presbytery could do was to prevent them from teaching under the sanction of their authority. But this association of Presbyterians having little countenance from government, and no name or authority in law, their success depended wholly on the superior knowledge, popular talents and exemplary life of their ministers. From time to time clergymen were afterwards sent out at the request of the people from Scotland and Ireland; and the colonists contributed to maintain them, till at length funds were established in trust by private legacies and donations, to be appropriated for the support of Presbyterian ministers, and the encouragement of that mode of religious worship and government.

✶   ✶   ✶

The first Presbyterian minister regularly settled in the colony of Virginia was John Craig of Dunagor, County Antrim, Ireland. From his manuscript volume of memoirs, William K. Foote quoted in his *Sketches of Virginia, Historical and Biographical,* Philadelphia, J. B. Lippincott Company, 1856, pp. 28-33, *passim.* (Parts not enclosed in quotation marks are paraphrased by Foote.)

"I was born August 17th, 1709, in the parish of Dunagor, County Antrim, Ireland, of pious parents, the child of their old age, tenderly loved, but in prudent government, and by early instructions in the principles of religion as I was capable of receiving them. . . ." About the age of fourteen or fifteen, he made profession of religion. . . . He . . . spent some years in reading Algebra, and the Mathematics generally, Logic, Metaphysics, Pneumatics and Ethics—and also Geography and History, ecclesiastical and profane: and then he repaired to Scotland, and in the college at Edinburgh, attained to the degree of A.M. Anno Domini, 1732. . . .

"America was then much in my mind accompanied with the argument— that service would be most pleasing and acceptable, where most needful and wanting—which raised in me a strong desire to see the part of the world."

He attended the Synod of Philadelphia, in September 1734, and delivered his letters of introduction to the members. . . . "I taught school one year, and read two years more. Being invited by the Presbytery, I entered on trials, and was licensed by the Presbytery of Donegal, 1737. I was sent to a new settlement in Virginia of our own country people, near 300 miles distant. From the dream I had before I left Ireland, I knew it to be the plot in Christ's vineyard, where I was to labor. . . .

"From them I had a call, and durst not refuse it, although I well saw it would be attended with many great difficulties. I accepted the call—the place was a new settlement, without a place of worship, or any church order, a wilderness in the proper sense, and a few Christian settlers in it, with numbers of the heathen travelling among us, but generally civil, though some persons were murdered by them about that time. They march about in small companies from fifteen to twenty, sometimes more or less. They must be supplied at any house they call at with victuals, or they become their own stewards and cooks, and spare nothing they choose to eat and drink. . . ." The Act of Assembly forming Augusta County, passed 1738. The first court was held in 1745. Kentucky, and all Virginia claimed in the west, belonged to it. Mr. Craig goes on—"When we were erected into a county and parish, and had ministers inducted, of which we had two, they both in their turns wrote to me, making high demands. I gave no answer, but still observed our own rules when there were no particular laws against them. . . ."

Of the congregation Mr. Craig says—"It was large by computation, about thirty miles in length, and near twenty in breadth. The people agreed to have two meeting-houses, expecting they would become two congregations, which is now come to pass. That part now called Tinkling Spring was most in numbers, and richer than the other, and forward, and had the public management of the affairs of the whole settlement: their leaders close-handed about providing necessary things for pious and religious uses, and could not agree for several years upon a plan or manner, where or how to build their meeting-house, which gave me very great trouble to hold them together, their disputes ran so high. . . . As to the other part of the congregation, now called Augusta, the people were fewer in numbers, and much lower as to their worldly circumstances, but a good-natured, prudent, governable people, and liberally bestowed a part of what God gave them for religious and pious uses, and now enjoy the benefit. . . . I had no trouble with them about their meeting-house, but to moderate and direct them when they met. They readily fixed on the place, and agreed on the plan for building it, and contributed cheerfully money and labor to accomplish the work, all in the voluntary way, what every man pleased.

As to my private and domestic state of life when fixed in the congregation, I purchased a plantation and began to improve upon it: and June 11th, 1744, married a young gentlewoman of a good family and character, born and brought up in the same neighborhood where I was born, daughter of Mr. George Russel, by whom I had nine children. . . .

What made the times distressing and unhappy to all the frontiers was the French and Indian war, which lay heavy on us, in which I suffered a part as well as others. When General Braddock was defeated and killed, our country was laid open to the enemy, our people were in dreadful confusion and discouraged to the highest degree. Some of the richer sort that could take some money with them to live upon, were for flying to a safer place of the country. My advice was then called for, which I gave, opposing that scheme as a scandal to our nation, falling below our brave ancestors, making ourselves a reproach among Virginians, a dishonor to our friends at home, an evidence of cowardice, want of faith, and a noble Christian dependence on God, as able to save and deliver from the heathen; it would be a lasting blot to our posterity." Mr. Craig urged the building forts in convenient neighborhoods, sufficient to hold twenty or thirty families, secure against small arms, and on alarms to flee to these places of refuge. One of which was to be the church. The proposition was acted upon very generally—"They required me to go before them in the work which I did cheerfully, though it cost me one-third of my estate. The people readily followed, and my congregation in less than two months was well fortified.

✓   ✓   ✓

The Presbyterians established schools as well as churches. At first these were log colleges conducted by Presbyterian preachers. Hampton-Sidney College and Washington and Lee University had their beginnings as academies in colonial Virginia. Graduates of these academies went out to establish new congregations. A letter by the Reverend Samuel Houston described the establishment of one of these schools. The text is from William K. Foote, *Sketches of Virginia, Historical and Biographical,* J. B. Lippincott Company, Philadelphia, 1856, p. 60.

. . . before the struggle for independence took place N. P. [New Providence] kept the Sabbath with great strictness, and family worship was almost universal. . . . shortly before the war, some men whose sons were growing up, felt a desire for having them, or part of them, educated liberally, chiefly with a view to the ministry of the gospel. Accordingly a small grammar school was formed in the neighborhood of Old Providence, composed of Samuel Doak, John Montgomery, Archibald Alexander, James Houston, William Tate, Samuel Greenlee, William Wilson, and others, which greatly increased and drew youths from distant neighborhoods. This grammar school was moved to the place near Fairfield, called Mount Pleasant; it was, in 1776, established at Timber Ridge meeting-house, and named Liberty Hall.

✓   ✓   ✓

A similar school was that established by David Caldwell, pastor of the Presbyterian churches at Buffalo and Alamance, in North Carolina. The following account is from Eli W. Caruthers, *A Sketch of the Life and Character of the Rev. David Caldwell,* Swain and Sherwood, Greensboro, 1844, pp. 28ff.

[On March 3, 1768, David Caldwell was appointed pastor of the above mentioned churches.] At this time there were probably not more than three or four, if so many, regularly settled ministers of the Presbyterian denomination in the State; but in the course of this year several others were settled, so that if David Caldwell was not the very first, he was among the first, who settled here, and made North Carolina their permanent residence. Having lived much longer too, and in many ways exerted a more extensive and lasting influence than any other belonging to that eventful period, it may be said . . . that his history if more identified with that of the country, at least so far as literature, enlightened piety, and good morals are concerned, than the history of any one man who has lived in it; and this seems to be the opinion of those who knew him best, and who are the most competent judges. . . . It was manifest that, situated as his congregations were, he could not depend on them for such a support as would enable him to devote himself exclusively to the work of the ministry; for they promised him only two hundred dollars; and that was to be paid in grain, if the people chose, at a stipulated price, which was wholly inadequate to the support of a family. He therefore purchased a tract of land, containing some two or three hundred acres; and on that he raised the most of his provisions. As soon, too, as he was prepared for it, he commenced a classical school at his own house, which he continued, with two or three short interruptions, until he was disqualified by the infirmities of age. This was an employment in which he not only excelled, as he certainly did, but in which he took great delight; and therefore it would, in all probability, have been a matter of choice with him, if his circumstances had not made it necessary. . . . But it was clearly necessary if he would maintain his family in comfort, and it was obviously necessary for the prosperity of the church in this region, and for the improvement of the community at large; for there were then no institutions of the kind in the State, or none of much value and permanence. . . .

Being a thorough scholar himself in all that he professed to teach, and having a peculiar tact for the management of boys, as well as a facility in communicating instruction, he soon became so celebrated a teacher that he had students from all the States south of the Potomac; and according to the testimony of those who were better judges of the matter than the writer, he was certainly instrumental in bringing more men into the learned professions than any other man of his day, at least in the Southern States. Many of these became eminent, as statesmen, lawyers, judges, physicians, and ministers of the gospel. . . . Five of his scholars became governors of different States; many more members of Congress. . . . Probably no man in the Southern States has a more enviable reputation as a teacher, or was more beloved by his pupils.

EDUCATION

Frequent references have been made in the preceding selections to education in the Southern colonies. There were private tutors in the homes of the planters and wealthier citizens, and boys were sometimes sent to Harvard or to England to complete their education. The one college established in a Southern colony was William and Mary at Williamsburg. The following account of the founding of William and Mary, 1705, from Robert Beverley, *The History and Present State of Virginia*, F. Fayram and J. Clarke, London, 1705, 1722 Edition, pp. 87-89, 230-232.

Anno 1690. *Francis Nicholson,* Esq; being appointed Lieutenant-Governour under Lord *Effingham,* arrived . . . [in Williamsburg.] He studied Popularity, discoursing freely of Country Improvements. He made his Court to the People, by instituting Olympick Games, and giving Prizes to all those, that should excel in the Exercises of Riding, Running, Shooting, Wrestling, and Backsword. When the Design of a College was communicated to him, he foresaw what interest it might create him with the Bishops in *England,* and therefore promised it all imaginable Encouragement. The first Thing desired of him in its Behalf, was the Calling of an Assembly; but this he wou'd by no Means agree to, being under Obligations to Lord *Effingham,* to stave off Assemblies as long as he could, for fear there might be further Representations sent over against his Lordship, who was conscious to himself, how uneasie the Country had been under his Despotick Administration.

When that could not be obtain'd, then they proposed, that a Subscription might pass thro' the Colony, to try the Humour of the People in general, and see what voluntary Contributions they could get towards it. This he granted, and he himself, together with the Council, set a generous Example to the other Gentlemen of the Country; so that the Subscriptions at last amounted to about Two Thousand Five Hundred Pounds, in which Sum is included the generous Benevolences of several Merchants of *London.*

Anno 1691, an Assembly being called, this Design was moved to them, and they espoused it heartily; and soon after made an Address to King *William* and Queen *Mary* in its Behalf, and sent the Reverend Mr. James Blair their Agent to *England,* to sollicite their Majesties Charter for it.

It was proposed, that Three Things should be taught in this College, *viz.* Languages, Divinity, and Natural Philosophy.

They appointed a certain Number of Professors, and their Salaries. And they form'd Rules for the Continuation, and good Government thereof in Perpetuity. . . .

Their Majesties were well pleased with that pious Design of the Plantation, and granted a Charter, according to their Desire; in obtaining which, the Address and Assiduity of Mr. *Blair,* their Agent, was highly to be admired.

Their Majesties were graciously pleased, to give near Two Thousand Pounds Sterling, the Ballance due upon the Account of Quit-Rents, towards the Founding the College; and towards the Endowing of it, they allow'd Twenty Thousand Acres of choice Land, together with the Revenue arising by the Penny *per* Pound, on Tobacco exported from Virginia and Maryland to the other Plantations.

It was a great Satisfaction to the Archbishops and Bishops to see such a Nursery of Religion founded in that new World; especially for that it was begun in an Episcopal Way, and carried on wholly by zealous Conformists to the Ch. of *England.*

[When Beverley wrote his History, in 1705, the College had not made much progress.] When the last Governor was removed, which was before any room was finished in the College, and the Boys were taught by the College-Master, in a little School-House close by it; it had more Scholars than it has now. Which Misfortune has happen'd, by reason of the late confusion, occasion'd by the furious proceedings of the present Governor, so that many chose to send their Sons to *England,* and others to keep theirs at Home, rather than put them to the hazard of being harassed, and living in the Combustion which that Gentleman makes among them.

The Method of Teaching is likewise very much impair'd by the chief Masters minding his Country Affairs; For by this means he is obliged to live several Miles from the College, upon his own Plantation; so that he cannot give that Attendance and Application, which was design'd, by appointing so good a Salary, as 100 £. *per Annum* besides Perquisites.

The College Revenue is behind-hand, and the *Maryland Duty* of 1 d. *per Pound,* has not been paid in of late, so that several of the Established Salaries are in arrear.

✓ ✓ ✓

The query from the Commissions of Plantations which Governor Berkeley answered in 1671 contained one question concerning education. The Governor's reply is quoted from William Waller Hening, Editor, *Statutes at Large,* Samuel Pleasants, Jr., Richmond, 1823, Vol. II, p. 317.

[Question] 23. What course is taken about the instructing the people, within your government in the christian religion; and what provision is there made for the paying of your ministry?

Answer. The same course that is taken in England out of town; every man according to his ability instructing his children. We have forty eight parishes, and our ministers are well paid, and by my consent should be better *if they would pray oftener and preach less.* But of all other commodities, so of this, *the worst are sent us,* and we had few that we could boast of, since the persecution in *Cromwell's* tiranny drove divers worthy men hither. But, I thank God, *there are no free schools* nor hundred years, for *learning* has brought disobedience, and heresy, and sects into the world, and *printing* has divulged them, and libels against the best government. God keep us from both!

✓ ✓ ✓

Hugh Jones, *The Present State of Virginia,* London, 1724, reprinted for Joseph Sabin, New York, 1865, p. 70, touched upon schools very briefly.

In most Parishes are *Schools* (little Houses being built on Purpose) where are taught *English* and *Writing;* but to prevent the sowing the Seeds of Dissention and Faction it is to be wished that the Masters or Mistresses should be such as are approved or licensed by the Minister and Vestry of the Parish, or Justices of the County; the Clerks of the Parishes being generally most proper for this purpose.

✓ ✓ ✓

Schools were taught by the missionaries sent to the colonies by the Venerable Society. A chapter from Humphrey's *History of the Propagation of the Gospel in*

Foreign Parts, reprinted in B. R. Carroll, Editor, *Historical Collections of South Carolina,* Harper and Brothers, New York, 1836, Vol. II, pp. 537-568, *passim,* describes this work.

The missionaries represented frequently to the society the great want of schools in this province [South Carolina] for the instruction of the children in the principles of religion, and teaching convenient learning. Dr. Le Jeau at Gooscreek, did very earnestly press the society to allow a salary for a schoolmaster in his parish, and they appointed Mr. Dennis schoolmaster in the year 1710; he had a good number of scholars for several years till the Indian war broke out, which dispersed the people and all his scholars. The society appointed also the Rev. Mr. Guy to be schoolmaster in Charles-town, and also curate or assistant to the minister of Charles-town, because that cure seemed too laborious for one person. There is now a handsome school-house built by act of assembly, and the schoolmaster allowed a salary of 100 £. proclamation money. Upon Mr. Guy's being removed to the care of a parish, Mr. Morrit was fixed schoolmaster here; but being lately chose minister of a parish, and leaving the school, the society have appointed the Rev. Mr. Lambert, schoolmaster and catechist, or afternoon preacher there; and accounts have been transmitted to the society, that he discharges his duty with diligence, and hath been very useful in training up the youth.

The people of this whole country are thoroughly sensible to the necessity of schools, for the Christian education of their children, and have, in several places, taken measures for founding of schools. An act of assembly was passed in the year 1724, for establishing of a free school in the town of Dorchester, in the parish of St. George. Upon this occasion some of the most considerable gentlemen of this colony, wrote to the society, "The chief source of irreligion and immorality here, is the want of schools; and we may justly be apprehensive, that if our children continue longer to be deprived of opportunities of being instructed, Christianity will of course decay insensibly, and we shall have a generation of our own, as ignorant as the native Indians." This act hath been transmitted to Great Britain for the royal assent. The people of St. Paul's parish have lately raised a sum of money by voluntary subscriptions, for founding a free-school; and Mr. Whitmarsh of this parish, lately deceased, hath left 500 £. for this purpose; they have now good hopes of raising a sufficient fund for building and endowing one. The Rev. Mr. Ludlam, late the society's missionary at Gooscreek, bequeathed all his estate, which hath been computed to be about 2000 £. Carolina money, for building and endowing a school at Gooscreek. . . . The late Richard Beresford, Esq. of St. Thomas's parish, in this colony, has been a great promoter of the founding of schools. He died in March 1722, and by his will bequeathed the annual profits of his estate, which was very considerable, in trust, to be paid to the vestry of that parish. . . . He directed the vestry to apply one-third of the yearly profits of his estate for the support of one or more schoolmasters; who should teach reading, accounts, mathematicks, and other liberal learning; and the remaining two thirds, towards the support and maintenance of the children of the poor of that parish, who should be sent to this school. . . .

It is now to be hoped this necessary work, of the education of the youth, will be carried on with success; which the society have always strove to the utmost of their power to promote; . . . .

5

The Spirit of Liberty and Organized Resistance

I. THE SPIRIT OF LIBERTY

The leadership in the South in the American Revolution was almost entirely from the members of the aristocracy: the documents which illustrate the thoughts of the leaders came chiefly from the pens of Virginians. If we pause to review the political system of colonial Virginia, we remember the following characteristics: property qualifications for voting existed; within the colony the county courts were so powerful that a quasi-federal system existed there: a man might sit in the House of Burgesses to represent a county other than the one in which he lived; a member of the House of Burgesses or of the governor's council was usually a man who had served in a hierarchy of offices, from vestryman in his local parish, to the county court, and then to the House of Burgesses. In addition to these experiences, the aristocrat was usually a landowner and a planter, and therefore conservative in respect to property rights.

Our Southern aristocrat was a product of the Age of Reason, because his education and his library introduced him to the current intellectual thought of the mother country. Newton's law of gravitation had inspired men to seek for reason and order in every part of their world; John Locke's Essay on Human Understanding and his two Treatises on Civil Government led men to believe that they could bring their ideas in harmony with a universal natural order. The truth about all things might be inferred by observation of the behavior of the world. Locke's ideas must have been very influential in shaping the thoughts of these statesmen of Virginia, because some of the documents we are about to examine bear a close relationship to Locke's ideas.

The text of the following is from John Locke, "An Essay Concerning the True, Original, Extent and End of Civil Government," reprinted in *The World's Great*

Thinkers, Man and State: The Political Philosophers, edited by Saxe Commins and Robert N. Linscott, Random House, New York, 1947, pp. 59, 129-132, *passim,* used by permission of the publishers.

To understand political power aright, and derive it from its original, we must consider what state all men are naturally in, and that is a state of perfect freedom to order their actions and dispose of their possessions and persons as they think fit, within the bounds of the law of nature, without asking leave, or depending upon the will of any other man.

A state also of equality, wherein all the power and jurisdiction is reciprocal, no one having more than another; there being nothing more evident than that creatures of the same species and rank, promiscuously born to all the same advantages of nature, and the use of the same faculties, should also be equal one amongst another without subordination or subjection, unless the Lord and Master of them all should by any manifest declaration of His will set one above another, and confer on him by an evident and clear appointment an undoubted right to dominion and sovereignty. . . .

If man in the state of nature be so free, as has been said, if he be absolute lord of his own person and possessions, equal to the greatest, and subject to nobody, why will he part with his freedom, this empire, and subject himself to the dominion and control of any other power? To which it is obvious to answer, that though in the state of nature he hath such a right, yet the enjoyment of it is very uncertain, and constantly exposed to the invasion of others. For all being kings as much as he, every man his equal, and the greater part no strict observers of equity and justices, the enjoyment of the property he has in this state is very unsafe, very unsecure. This makes him willing to quit this condition, which, however free, is full of fears and continual dangers; and it is not without reason that he seeks out and is willing to join in a society with others, who are already united, or have a mind to unite, for the mutual preservation of their lives, liberties, and estates, which I call by the general name, property. . . .

But though men when they enter into society give up the equality, liberty and executive power they had in the state of nature into the hands of society, to be so far disposed of by the legislative as the good of the society shall require; yet it being only with an intention in everyone the better to preserve himself, his liberty and property (for no rational creature can be supposed to change his condition with an intention to be worse), the power of the society, or legislative constituted by them, can never be supposed to extend farther than the common good, but is obliged to secure everyone's property by providing against those three defects above-mentioned that made the state of nature so unsafe and uneasy. And so whoever has the legislative or supreme power of any commonwealth is bound to govern by established standing laws, promulgated and known to the people, and not by extemporary decrees; by indifferent and upright judges, who are to decide controversies by those laws; and to employ the force of the community at home only in the execution of such laws, or abroad, to prevent or redress foreign injuries, and secure the community from inroads and invasion. And all this to be directed to no other end but the peace, safety, and public good of the people.

ʃ   ʃ   ʃ

Patrick Henry, a lawyer and a brilliant orator, the son of a Scotch farmer of the piedmont region, then the frontier in Virginia, was an exception to the usual members of the House of Burgesses in that, always during the revolutionary era, he was on the side of the plain people. After the passage of the Stamp Act, Henry presented the following resolutions which were adopted by the Virginia House of Burgesses in 1765. The resolutions are from the *Journals of the House of Burgesses of Virginia, 1761-1765,* edited by John Pendleton Kennedy, The Colonial Press, E. Wadding Co., Richmond, 1907, p. 360.

Resolved, That the first Adventurers and Settlers of this his Majesty's Colony and Dominion of *Virginia* brought with them, and transmitted to their Posterity, and all other his Majesty's Subjects since inhabiting in this his Majesty's said Colony, all the Liberties, Privileges, Franchises, and Immunities, that have at any time been held, enjoyed, and possessed, by the people of *Great Britain.*

Resolved, That by two royal Charters, granted by King *James* the First, the Colonists aforesaid are declared entitled to all the Liberties, Privileges, and Immunities of Denizens and natural Subjects, to all Intents and Purposes, as if they had been abiding and born within the Realm of *England.*

Resolved, That the Taxation of the People by themselves, or by Persons chosen by themselves to represent them, who can only know what Taxes the People are able to bear, or the easiest Method of raising them, and must themselves be affected by every Tax laid on the People, is the only Security against a burdensome Taxation, and the distinguishing Characteristick of *British* Freedom, without which the ancient Constitutions cannot exist.

Resolved, That his Majesty's liege People of this his most ancient and loyal Colony have without Interruption enjoyed the inestimable Right of being governed by such Laws, respecting their internal Polity and Taxation, as are derived from their own Consent, with the Approbation of their Sovereign, or his Substitute; and that the same hath never been forfeited or yielded up, but hath been constantly recognized by the Kings and People of *Great Britain.*

ʃ   ʃ   ʃ

Nine years later, after Lord Dunmore dissolved the colonial assembly, the legislators gathered at Raleigh Tavern under the leadership of Patrick Henry and issued calls for a Virginia convention and a continental congress. In March 1775, Henry, representing his county at the Virginia Convention of Delegates delivered an address, the exact text of which is not in existence, but which is known, as reconstructed by his biographer, William Wirt, by most Americans. The text of the address is from *The Roxburghe'Library of Classics,* edited by Nathan Haskell Dole, Forest Morgan, and Carolina Ticknor, the Roxburghe Press, New York, 1904, Vol. XV, pp. 4916-4919.

MR. PRESIDENT,—No man thinks more highly than I do of the patriotism, as well as abilities, of the very worthy gentlemen who have just addressed the House. But different men often see the same subject in different lights; and, therefore, I hope that it will not be thought disrespectful to those gentlemen if, entertaining as I do, opinions of a character very opposite to theirs, I shall speak forth my sentiments freely and without reserve. This is no time for ceremony. The question before the House is one of awful moment to this country. For my own part I consider it as nothing less than a question of freedom or slavery; and in proportion to the magnitude of the subject ought to be the freedom of the debate. It is only in this way that we can hope to arrive at the truth, and fulfill the great responsibility which we hold to God and our country. Should I keep back my opinions at such a time, through fear of giving offense, I should consider myself as guilty of treason toward my country, and of an act of disloyalty toward the majesty of heaven, which I revere above all earthly kings.

Mr. President, it is natural to man to indulge in the illusions of hope. We are apt to shut our eyes against a painful truth, and listen to the song of that siren, till she transforms us into beasts. Is this the part of wise men, engaged in a great and arduous struggle for liberty? Are we disposed to be of the number of those who, having eyes, see not, and having ears, hear not, the things which so nearly concern their temporal salvation? For my part, whatever anguish of spirit it may cost, I am willing to know the whole truth; to know the worst and to provide for it.

I have but one lamp by which my feet are guided; and that is the lamp of experience. I know of no way of judging the future but by the past. And judging by the past, I wish to know what there has been in the conduct of the British ministry for the last ten years to justify those hopes with which gentlemen have been pleased to solace themselves and the House? Is it that insidious smile with which our petition has been lately received? Trust it not, sir; it will prove a snare to your feet. Suffer not yourselves to be betrayed with a kiss. Ask yourselves how this gracious reception of our petition comports with these warlike preparations which cover our waters and darken our land. Are fleets and armies necessary to a work of love and reconciliation? Have we shown ourselves so unwilling to be reconciled that force must be called in to win back our love? Let us not deceive ourselves, sir. These are the implements of war and subjugation; the last arguments to which kings resort. I ask gentlemen, sir, what means this martial array, if its purpose be not to force us to submission? Can gentlemen assign any other possible motives for it? Has Great Britain any enemy, in this quarter of the world, to call for this accumulation of navies and armies? No, sir, she has none. They are meant for us; they can be meant for no other. They are sent over to bind and rivet upon us those chains which the British ministry have been so long forging. And what have we to oppose to them? Shall we try argument? Sir, we have been trying that for the last ten years. Have we anything new to offer on the subject? Nothing. . . . Our petitions have been slighted; our remonstrances have produced additional violence and insult; our supplications have been disregarded; and we have been spurned with contempt, from the foot of the throne. In vain, after these things, may we indulge the fond hope of peace and reconciliation. There is no longer any room for hope. If we wish to be free—if we mean to preserve inviolate those inestimable privileges for which we have been so long contending—if we mean not basely to abandon the noble struggle in which we have been so long engaged, and which we have pledged ourselves never to abandon, until the glorious object of our contest shall be obtained, we must fight! An appeal to arms and to the God of Hosts is all that is left us!

They tell us, sir, that we are weak; unable to cope with so formidable an adversary. But when shall we be stronger? Will it be the next week, or the next year? Will it be when we are totally disarmed, and when a British guard shall be stationed in every house? Shall we gather strength by irresolution and inaction? . . .

It is in vain, sir, to extenuate the matter. Gentlemen may cry peace, peace—but there is no peace. The war is actually begun! The next gale that sweeps from the north will bring to our ears the clash of resounding arms! Our brethren are already in the field! Why stand we here idle? What is it that gentlemen wish? What would they have? Is life so dear, or peace so sweet, as to be purchased at the price of chains and slavery? Forbid it, Almighty God! I know not what course others may take; but as for me, give me liberty, or give me death!

✓   ✓   ✓

Among the individuals in America who wrote letters to the people of Great Britain explaining the point of view of the colonies, was James Iredell, a young man of twenty-three, who had come to North Carolina from England at the age of seventeen to act as Comptroller of the Customs at Edenton. In addition to carrying out the duties of his office he studied law, and in 1770 he received a license from Governor Tryon to practice law in the Inferior Courts of the province. He made many friendships with leaders of the colony, and in September, 1774, he wrote his message, "To the Inhabitants of Great Britain." The text is from Griffith J. McRee, *Life and Correspondence of James Iredell,* D. Appleton and Company, New York, 1857, Vol. I, pp. 205-220, *passim.*

FRIENDS AND FELLOW SUBJECTS:—United as we are by the strongest ties of affection and interest, descended from the same revered ancestors, and possessed equally of the blessings of a most happy Constitution, it is greatly to be lamented that differences should arise between us, which too fatally tend to disturb the harmony of a connection highly beneficial and honorable to both. Yet such, I have the concern to say, have heretofore arisen, and are now again occasioned, by an attempt in your Parliament to exercise a supreme authority over us, to which we cannot possibly conceive they are at all entitled upon any view of policy, justice, or the real nature of our Constitution. . . . Colonies planted originally by men emigrating from their own country, where they unhappily feared freedom was near losing its existence, in search of this desired blessing among woods and deserts, which they thought preferable to all kinds of ease and luxury enjoyed by a humiliating tenure; increased by the surprising industry of the first settlers, and by the blessing of Providence, to an amazing degree, and come at length to enjoy a pretty comfortable state of maintenance, secured to them, as they fondly hoped, by sanctions of a most sacred and inviolable nature. In these possessions they long lived easy and happy, flattering themselves that they should be permitted to enjoy freely property procured for them by the severe labor and virtue of their ancestors, and that the valuable blessings of the British Constitution, bestowed on them by their charters, would never be infringed. In this state of confidential security and hope, these Colonies continued at the commencement of the late war, when disputes arose between our sovereign and the French king about the limits of a part of this Continent. It was an object of great importance to both countries: yours had long discovered and felt the great advantages reaped from a connection with us, and was naturally jealous of having any part of so useful a country unjustly encroached upon;—ours was eminently endangered by so near and formidable an enemy being invested with the great power which so large extent of territory as he claimed gave him. Thus situated, the war was on this account of great advantage to both; both engaged in it, therefore, with great cheerfulness and alacrity, and the success was answerable to our most sanguine wishes. America showed an uncommon ardor of exertion; . . . no endeavors were spared on *our* part to co-operate in all *your* plans and regulations. Duty and affection prompted us with unsolicited zeal to prove ourselves worthy of a connection with the greatest (because the freest and most virtuous) state on earth. . . . At this time, I venture to say, America would voluntarily have gone any lengths to serve you, so much did she admire the generous turn of your minds. . . . You, yourselves, witnessed to the honorable exertion of our abilities; you thought we spent more than could be expected from us, or was properly our due proportion, and you ordered each of the Provinces to be refunded the surplus of its real share. Here was period for good offices, and mutual obligations, to begin upon new terms of confidence, and to increase from year to year with added fervor and affection. Here was glorious disposition

to cultivate. . . . But, alas! this delightful prospect was but ideal: ou
happiness was soon to be blasted; Freedom was to be banished from ou
soil, endeared to us because it was laboriously tilled by our fathers; an
we were cruelly and infamously told that we were, for the future, to be i
absolute subjection to the British Parliament.

It is an obvious and sufficient answer to this extraordinary claim—of
sovereign dominion in your Parliament over us—that, if it in truth exist
we are possessed of no *liberty;* we have nothing we can call *our own.* Th
charters granted by our Sovereigns, instead of being considered a
pledges of the honor and sacred faith of kings, were a mere snare an
delusion to induce our forefathers to come abroad, with the utmost diff
culty, expense, and hazard, and for many years almost entirely at thei
own risk, to make out of the wilderness, by their own and their children'
labor, a fine country for you to spoil in. You are the *real proprietors, w*
only the *tenants at will,* of these possessions. For this is exactly the case, i
any part of our property is at your command. *What part* shall be receive
must be according to your judgment, if you can tax us *constitutionally*
. . . What becomes of confidence in government, of reliance on the mos
sacred contracts of the state? But your Parliament, I suppose, can do n
wrong: they are immaculate, and none of their proceedings can ever caus
any real injury as to *us;* though you sometimes complain of them your
selves. Our complaints, you will say, are evidently founded in faction an
injustice, in heated and erroneous ideas of the Constitution, and i
endeavors to form a new system of government, destructive of that beautifu
theory in political discourses—the necessity of an absolute power residin
somewhere in every state. . . .

We have hitherto been forward and zealous in the grant of our money
to a degree your Parliament thought to be extraordinary and profuse; an
we should always, I am sure, be readier to give too much than too little
if you would allow us the merit of offering it ourselves. But we conten
for an exclusive right of the disposal of our own property, because it i
one of the most essential privileges of the British Constitution, and tha
which is the principal guard and protection of all the others. When th
people have the grant of their own money, and a share in making the law
by which they are to be governed; unless they are either blind to thei
own interest, or wicked and despicable enough to betray it, they have
every possible human tie for their own welfare and happiness. If they ha
the *latter,* without the *former,* and this resided in the Crown, their libertie
might be easily taken from them; because the Crown, by raising money *a*
libitum upon the subject, could easily provide the means of effecting an
maintaining encroachments upon the people's rights; and might also rui
them by wanton depredations on their property. But when the people
have in *their* hands the only means of supporting Government, by the abso
lute disposition of their property, they can take care that the administration

of their affairs is faithfully and wisely conducted; or, as an elegant writer of yours expresses it, by withholding supplies, peaceably admonish their Sovereign of his duty. It is needless to add, they have then something *they can call their own.*

These principles you like very well, when applied to yourselves, but you would willingly deprive us of the benefit of them. . . .

A power of taxing, and of harassing us with cruel, oppressive, and inconvenient laws, we will not give you; because it is a *novel* claim, and can never be exercised but to our destruction. . . . But we are ready, at any time, to enter into a fair negotiation, by which means to concert a plan of cementing the general interest of the empire upon a broad basis, at once securing *a proper union of counsel* and *authority,* and the *individual freedom* of *each member of the empire,* so far as is consistent with the *general welfare.*

✓   ✓   ✓

Edmund Burke, British orator and political philosopher, whose speeches are monuments in English literature, in his address on "Conciliation with America," delivered before the House of Commons in 1775, showed a profound understanding of the American point of view. The following excerpts from that address are from *The Roxburghe Library of Classics,* edited by Nathan Haskell Dole, *et al.,* The Roxburghe Press, New York, 1904, Vol. XX, pp. 6921-6923, *passim.*

. . . First, the people of the colonies are descendants of Englishmen. England, sir, is a nation which still, I hope, respects, and formerly adored, her freedom. The colonists emigrated from you when this part of your character was most predominant, and they took this bias and direction the moment they parted from your hands. They are therefore not only devoted to liberty, but to liberty according to English ideas, and on English principles. . . .

There is . . . a circumstance attending these colonies, which, in my opinion, . . . makes the spirit of liberty still more high and haughty [in the Southern colonies] than in those to the northward. It is, that in Virginia and the Carolinas they have a vast multitude of slaves. Where this is the case in any part of the world, those who are free are by far the most proud and jealous of their freedom. Freedom is to them not only an enjoyment, but a kind of rank and privilege. Not seeing there, that freedom, as in countries where it is a common blessing, and as broad and general as the air, may be united with much abject toil, with great misery, with all the exterior of servitude, liberty looks, amongst them, like something that is more noble and liberal. I do not mean, sir, to commend the superior morality of this sentiment, which has at least as much pride as virtue in it; but I cannot alter the nature of man. The fact is so; and these people of the southern colonies are much more strongly, and with a higher and more stubborn spirit, attached to liberty, than those to the northward.

. . . In such a people, the haughtiness of domination combines with he spirit of freedom, fortifies it, and renders it invincible.

✓　　✓　　✓

The Virginia statesman of the Revolutionary generation is exemplified by George Mason. A plantation owner, trustee of the town of Alexandria, justice of his county court, vestryman of Truro Parish, and member of the House of Burgesses, he wrote the Fairfax Resolves, the Virginia Declaration of Rights, and most of the Virginia constitution. The influence of Locke may be seen in the Declaration of Rights, 1776. The text is from William Waller Hening, Editor, *Statutes at Large* Samuel Pleasants, Jr., Richmond, 1823, Vol. I, pp. 47-49.

A Declaration of Rights made by the Representatives of the Good people of Virginia, assembled in full and free Convention; which rights do pertain to them, and their posterity, as the basis and foundation of Government

I. That all men are by nature equally free and independent, and have certain inherent rights, of which, when they enter into a state of society they cannot, by any compact, deprive or divest their posterity; namely, the enjoyment of life and liberty, with the means of acquiring and possessing property, and pursuing and obtaining happiness and safety.

II. That all power is vested in, and consequently derived from, the people; that Magistrates are their trustees and servants, and at all times amenable to them.

III. That government, is or ought to be, instituted for the common benefit, protection, and security, of the people, nation, or community. Of all the various modes and forms of government, that is best, which is capable of producing the greatest degree of happiness and safety, and is most effectually secured against the danger of mal-administration; and that when any government shall be found inadequate or contrary to these purposes, a majority of the community hath an indubitable, unalienable and indefeasible right, to reform, alter, or abolish it, in such manner as shall be judged most conducive to the public weal. . . .

II. ORGANIZED RESISTANCE

At the First Continental Congress in Philadelphia, on October 18, 1774, a Continental Association was organized; modeled upon a Virginia Association framed in August, it was joined by the delegates from twelve provinces. These delegates pledged that their provinces would cease all importation from Great Britain, effective December first, would discontinue the slave trade on that date, and would embargo exports to the British Empire after September first, 1775. This pledge was enforced by local agencies through boycott and publicity. Wilmington and New Hanover County, North Carolina, at a meeting of the freeholders, chose a Committee of Safety to carry into execution the pledge made to the Continental Association, and the following excerpts from their proceedings and minutes illustrate the efforts made by local committees to make the Association a success. The text is from Alfred Moore Waddell, *A History of New Hanover County and the Lower Cape Fear Region,* 1723-1800, Vol. I, pp. 89-90.

. . . Upon a suggestion to the committee that Mr. Arthur Mabson hath imported in his schooner from the West Indies, some slaves which are now at his plantation near this town; it is ordered that the sense of this committee relative thereto be made known to Mr. Mabson, and that Mr. McLain write to him for that purpose, which he hath done as follows, to-wit:

Wilmington, Dec. 17, 1774.

Sir: The committee for the town, chosen to observe the conduct of all persons touching the association of the General Congress, have resolved that all slaves imported into this river, since the first day of December, instant, shall be re-shipped to the place from whence they came as soon as possible, and being informed that you have, contrary to the express letter of the said association, imported slaves from the West Indies, which you now have at your plantation, it is expected that you will give a particular account of the number thereof, and take such steps as may satisfy the committee that you intend, on your part, to adhere strictly to the regulations laid down by your representatives.

I am, Sir, your obd't servant.

(Signed)
ARCHIBALD M'LAINE

Mr. Mabson.

WILMINGTON, NOVEMBER 26, 1774.

The Committee, finding that several gentlemen intended to start horses, which they have had for some time in keeping, for the Wilmington subscription purse on Monday the 28th inst., and the general Congress having particularly condemned horse racing as an expensive diversion, the Committee thought proper to send the following admonitory circular letter to the several gentlemen who had kept horses for the race, to wit:

Wilmington, November 26, 1774.

Sir: The Continental Congress, lately held at Philadelphia, representing the several American colonies, from Nova Scotia to Georgia, associated and agreed among other things, for themselves and their constituents, to "discountenance and discourage every species of extravagance and dissipation, and especially all horse racing, and all kinds of gaming, cock-fighting, exhibitions of shows and plays and other expensive diversions and entertainments," and we being the majority of the committee, chosen by the freeholders of Wilmington to observe the conduct of all persons touching the association of the said Congress, think it our indispensable duty to inform you that in our opinion the avowed intention of running horses for the subscription purse near this town on the 28th inst., if carried into execution, will be subversive to the said association, and a breach of the resolves of the general Congress; and that if the gentlemen who intended to enter horses for said purse (of whom we understand you are one) persist in running the race, we shall be under the disagreeable necessity of bearing public testimony against a proceeding which immediately strikes at the ground of the association and resolves, by disuniting the people.

You must be sensible, Sir, that the Americans have not the most distant prospect of being restored to their former rights or of succeeding in their attempts to defeat a venal and corrupt ministry and Parliament, but by an unanimous adherence to the resolutions and advice of their representatives in the late general Congress; and as a friend to your country we have no doubt but you will readily relinquish an amusement that however laudable in other respects, is certainly attended with considerable expense, and even destruction to many individuals; and may very justly be condemned at a time when frugality should be one of our leading virtues.

We shall only add that nothing will so effectually tend to convince the British Parliament that we are in earnest in our opposition to their measures, as a voluntary relinquishment of our favorite amusements. Those who will take the trouble of making observations on mankind must soon be convinced that the people who abandon their pleasures for the public good are not to be biased by any other consideration. Many will cheerfully give up their property to secure the remainder. He only is the determined patriot who willingly sacrifices his pleasure on the altar of freedom.

We are, &c. which was signed by all of the committee present . . .

↗   ↗   ↗

On June 7, 1776, Richard Henry Lee, from Virginia, presented a resolution for independence to the Continental Congress. A committee of five was appointed to write a declaration of independence, but Thomas Jefferson drafted the document drawing upon Mason's Declaration of Rights. The text is quoted from *The Roxburghe Library of Classics,* edited by Nathan Haskell Dole, *et al.,* The Roxburghe Press, New York, 1904, Vol. XX, pp. 6944-6947.

When in the Course of human events, it becomes necessary for one people to dissolve the political bands which have connected them with another and to assume among the powers of the earth, the separate and equal station to which the Laws of Nature and of Nature's God entitle them a decent respect to the opinions of mankind requires that they should declare the causes which impel them to the separation.

We hold these truths to be self-evident, that all men are created equal that they are endowed by their Creator with certain unalienable Rights that among these are Life, Liberty, and the pursuit of Happiness. That to secure these rights, Governments are instituted among Men, deriving their just powers from the consent of the governed. That whenever any form of

overnment becomes destructive of these ends, it is the Right of the
eople to alter or abolish it, and to institute a new Government, laying its
oundation on such principles and organizing its powers in such form, as
o them shall seem most likely to effect their Safety and Happiness. Pru-
ence, indeed, will dictate that Governments long established, should not
e changed for light and transient causes; . . . The history of the present
ing of Great Britain is a history of repeated injuries and usurpations,
ll having in direct object the establishment of an absolute tyranny over
hese States. . . .

Nor have We been wanting in attentions to our British brethren. We
ave warned them from time to time of attempts by their legislature to
xtend an unwarrantable jurisdiction over us. We have reminded them of
he circumstance of our emigration and settlement here. We have appealed
o their native justice and magnanimity, and we have conjured them by
he ties of our common kindred to disavow these usurpations, which
rould inevitably interrupt our connections and correspondence. They too
ave been deaf to the voice of justice and consanguinity. We must, there-
ore, acquiesce in the necessity, which denounces our Separation, and
old them, as we hold the rest of mankind, Enemies in War, in Peace
riends.

We, therefore, the Representatives of the United States of America, in
General Congress, Assembled, appealing to the Supreme Judge of the
World for rectitude of our intentions, do in the Name, and by Authority
of the good People of these Colonies, solemnly publish and declare, That
hese United Colonies are, and of Right ought to be Free and Independent
tates; that they are Absolved from all Allegiance to the British Crown,
nd that all political connection between them and the State of Great
Britain, is and ought to be totally dissolved; and that as Free and Inde-
endent States, they have full Power to levy War, conclude Peace, contract
Alliances, establish Commerce, and to do all other Acts and Things
vhich Independent States may of right do.

And for the support of this Declaration, with a firm reliance on the
rotection of divine Providence, we mutually pledge to each other our
Lives, our Fortunes and our sacred Honor.

✓   ✓   ✓

While a larger percentage of the population of Georgia was loyal to England
han was true of any other Southern colony, the resistance to the Intolerable Acts
ook about the same form there as in the other colonies. On July 27, 1774, the
atriotic citizens assembled at the Liberty Pole at Tondee's Tavern in Savannah. A
ommittee was appointed and charged with the preparation of resolutions expres-
ive of the rebel sentiments of the community and of the determination of Georgia
t an early date to join her sister colonies in opposition to the enforcement of
he Intolerable Acts. Another committee solicited supplies for the suffering poor
f Boston. Six hundred pounds of powder were taken from the king's magazine
n Savannah on May 11, 1775, and distributed among the parties of the rebellion.

A council of Safety was created as in other colonies, and a Provincial Congress sent an address to Governor Wright. From the governor's letters to Lord Dartmouth, Secretary of State for the Colonies, we may construct a narrative of events in Georgia. The text is from *Collections of the Georgia Historical Society*, Savannah, 1873, Vol. III, pp. 183-187, *passim*.

Gov. Sir Jas. Wright to Sec. Lord Dartmouth.

SAV. IN GEORGIA the 17th of June, 1775.

MY LORD,

It gives me much concern to acquaint Your Lordship that on Thursday the 13th Inst. the Liberty Folks here assembled in the Town of Sav. and put up a Liberty Tree and a Flagg and in the Evening paraded about the Town I am informed to the number of 300, some say 400. . . .

This happened My Lord on the 1st day of the Meeting of the Court of Sessions, when the Chief Justice gave an excellent charge very properly adapted to the present times. However the Liberty Tree and Flagg were kept up from Tuesday Morning till now and is still flying in contempt and defiance of the Court and of all Law and Government and which here as well as elsewhere seems now nearly at an end. And it has been debated whether or not to stop the Courts and shut the Port but this I am assured is laid aside for the present although very probably will be resumed hereafter. But they have entered into an Association as your Lordship will see by the inclosed Paper and whatever is agreed upon by the Continental Congress, will undoubtedly be adopted and carried into execution here, and will meet with little or no opposition, for those who disapprove of these things and wish well to the Government say "Why should they expose their lives and properties to the resentment of the people when no support or protection is given them by Government." And therefore they find it most prudent to waive opposition and remain quiet. . . .

We have accounts from Carolina that they have agreed to raise two Regiments of foot of 750 each and one of horse of 500.

My Lord, I presume again to repeat my humble request to have leave to return to England, and have the honor to be with perfect esteem My Lord, Your Lordship's

most obliged & most obed^t Ser

JAS. WRIGHT

Another letter from Governor Wright to Lord Dartmouth.

SAVANNAH IN GEORGIA the 17th of June 1775

MY LORD,

. . . we are . . . of the opinion that a Fort should be erected on some proper part of the Common, with buildings and barracks suitable for such number of men, as it may be thought necessary to send, if any should, and then the Governor and Officers would be in a state of security, whereas now they are and must be exposed to every kind of insult and violence the people may choose to offer them.

SAVANNAH IN GEORGIA the 8th July 1775

MY LORD,
. . . I wrote your Lordship in my Letter No. 51 that our Inlet was Guarded by Boats with Many Arm'd Men from Carolina, Since which several have gone down there from Savannah: all waiting the Arrival of a Ship Expected from London with Gun Powder, it is said to seize upon the Gun Powder, those from Carolina to take the Gun Powder out belonging to the Inhabitants of their Province and those from hence to take out the Powder belonging to this Province, at least this is what is given out. . . .

And My Lord, I have just been informed that Mr. Barnard Elliott (a Capt. in the Troops Raising by South Carolina) is in the back parts of this Province Inlisting Men without having made the least Application to me, or taking any Notice at all.

SAVANNAH IN GEORGIA 18th of July 1775

MY LORD,
. . . On the 13 instant of night two Gentlemen came here from Charles Town sent as I was informed by the Council of Safety there and they have Prevail'd on the Congress to let them have 5000 weight of the Gun Powder and which they carried away with them, and I am Informed that some of the Liberty People here, Assisted in Putting on board the Vessell they came in a brass field Piece and Carriage belonging to His Majesty, this I did not hear of till Afterwards, but if I had I could not have Prevented it.

I understand the Congress have agreed to send 2000 weight of Gun Powder into the Indian Country as a Present from the People and it is Particularly Agreed that the Indians be Acquainted that it is not from the *King* or from *Government* or from the *Superintendent* or from the *Traders* but from the *People of the Province* and I am much afraid this will raise strange Ideas amongst the Indians and be attended with very bad consequences. They have appointed here what they call a Council of Safety and very nearly followed the example of the Carolinians Except as to Raising an Army, it was proposed to raise 350 men but after great debates that was carried in the Negative and this Province having now Join'd with the others, I am well Informed that the Gentlemen who come from Carolina Assured the Congress here, that if they should on any Account want Assistance they should Immediately have it to the amount of 1000 men.

SAVANNAH IN GEORGIA the 29th of July 1775

My Lord,

Since my last of the 18th instant No. 54 the Council of Safety as they Call themselves, have in a Solemn Manner forbid the Rector of the Parish to preach any more in the Church, and he has been so much threatened that on the 25th instant he left the town and went over into Carolina, the reason given for this is, because he refused to Preach a Sermon and observed a Fast which had been directed by the Continental Congress, to be observed throughout all the Colonies. . . . And My Lord on the 24th instant about 9 o'clock at night I heard a very great Huzzaing in the Streets and on Sending out found they had seized upon one Hopkins a Pilot and were Tarring and Feathering him, and Soon after they brought him in a Cart along by my House and such a Horrid Spectacle I really never Saw, they made the Man stand up in a Cart with a Candle in his Hand and a great many Candles were Carried round the Cart and thus they went through most of the Streets in town for upwards of three Hours.

And on Inquiring what he had done, I was informed that he had behaved disrespectfully towards the Sons of Liberty and Drank some Toasts which gave great offence. . . .

III. THE WAR IN THE SOUTH

Much of the Revolutionary War was fought on Southern soil. The royal governors of Virginia, the Carolinas, and Georgia felt very insecure from the time the first Continental Congress convened. Frequent appeals to Lord Dartmouth, Secretary of State for the Colonies, for troops, were unanswered. Governor Martin of North Carolina forbade the assembling of a Provincial Congress to appoint delegates to a second Continental Congress in Philadelphia; however, no attention was paid to his proclamation. Bands of minutemen were organized in defiance of the governor's orders. In June, 1775, Governor Martin took refuge on a sloop of war after sending his family to New York. In the Cape Fear valley were hundreds of Scotch Highlanders who had been permitted to come to America within the preceding twenty-five years under an oath of allegiance to the Crown. Governor Martin sent emissaries to organize these Highlanders. Early in 1776 Martin was notified that Lord Cornwallis and seven regiments were soon to sail to relieve him, along with additional help from Major-General Clinton. A call was issued by Governor Martin to all of his Majesty's faithful servants to come to the coast to join the oncoming British soldiers. The Committee of Safety of the New Bern district commanded the Minutemen in that district to join forces from other parts of the province in suppressing the insurrection of the Highlanders. The battle fought at Moore's Creek Bridge between Tories and Patriots was a Patriot victory.

When Cornwallis and Clinton reached the Cape Fear and learned of the defeat of the Tories, they delayed about a month and went on to South Carolina, accompanied by Governor Martin. This ended royal government in North Carolina.

The following report of the Battle of Moore's Creek Bridge was sent to the President of the Provincial Congress at New Bern by Colonel James Moore. The text is from Alfred Moore Waddell, *A History of New Hanover County and the Lower Cape Fear Region, 1723-1800*, Vol. I, pp. 169-170.

I then dispatched an express to Colonel Caswell, who was on his march to join us with about eight hundred men, and directed him to return and take possession of Corbett's Ferry over Black River, and by every means to obstruct, harass and distress them in their march. At the same time I directed Colonel Martin and Colonel Thackston to take possession of Cross Creek in order to prevent their return that way. Colonel Lillington and Colonel Ashe I ordered by a forced march to endeavor if possible, to reinforce Colonel Caswell; but if that could not be effected to take possession of Moore's Creek Bridge while I proceeded back with the remainder of our army to cross the Northwest at Elizabethtown so as either to meet them on their way to Corbett's Ferry, or fall in their rear and surrender them there. On the 23rd I crossed the river at Elizabethtown, where I was compelled to wait for a supply of provisions until the 24th at night, having learned that Colonel Caswell was almost entirely without. Just when I was prepared to march I received an express from Colonel Caswell, informing me that the Tories had raised a flat which had been sunk in Black River about five miles above him, and by erecting a bridge had passed in with the whole army. I then determined as a last expedient to proceed immediately in boats down the Northwest River to Dollerson's Landing, but as we could not possibly march that night, for the want of horses for the artillery, I dispatched an express to Moore's Creek Bridge to learn the situation of affairs there, and was informed that Colonel Lillington, who had the day before taken his stand at the bridge was, that afternoon, reinforced by Colonel Caswell, and that they had raised a small breastwork and destroyed a part of the bridge.

The next morning, the 27th at the break of day, an alarm gun was fired, immediately after which, scarce allowing our people a moment to prepare, the Tory army, with Captain McLeod at the head, made their attack on Colonel Caswell and Colonel Lillington, and finding a small intrenchment next the bridge on our side empty, concluded that our people had abandoned their post, and in the most furious manner advanced within thirty paces of our breastwork and artillery, where they met a very proper reception. Captain McLeod and Captain Campbell fell within a few paces of the breastwork, the former of whom received upward of twenty balls in his body; and in a very few minutes their whole army was put to flight, and most shamefully abandoned their General, who was next day taken prisoner. The loss of the enemy in this action, from the best accounts we have been able to learn, is about thirty killed and wounded, but as numbers of them must have fallen into the creek, besides many more that were carried off. I suppose their loss may be estimated at about fifty. We had only two wounded, one of them died this day.

✓   ✓   ✓

Having abandoned the plan to occupy North Carolina in 1776, Clinton, joined by Cornwallis, decided to attack Charleston, South Carolina. On June 28, 1776, British warships under Sir Peter Parker were repulsed at the American palmetto log fort on Sullivan's Island, commanded by General William Moultrie. All of the British ships were damaged and there were over 200 casualties, while at the fort there were ten dead and twenty-one wounded. Clinton's troops were withdrawn, and there was no more active warfare in the South until 1778, when on December 29th the British occupied the town of Savannah and re-established royal government in Georgia. On January 29th Augusta was seized. In September, 1779, General Benjamin Lincoln with 1400 American troops and Admiral d'Estaing with a French fleet of thirty-five ships and 4000 men attempted to retake Savannah, but failed. Clinton decided to make an increased effort to win the South, and in December, 1779, left New York with 8000 troops, to capture Charleston. The attack began on April 11 and lasted until May 12 when General Benjamin Lincoln surrendered the 5400 man garrison and four American ships. Clinton then returned to New York, leaving Cornwallis to hold Georgia and South Carolina, and if possible, to extend the territory he held.

The following report from General Lincoln to General Washington explains the reasons for his surrender of Charleston. The text is from the *State Records of North Carolina, 1777-1790,* edited by Walter Clark, Nash Brothers, Goldsboro, 1898, Vol. XV, pp. 46-47.

Hostilities again commenced in the evening of the Ninth [of May, 1780] with a more incessant and heavy fire than ever, which continued until the 11th, when, having prior thereto received an address from the principal inhabitants of the town and a number of the Country militia, signifying that the terms acceded to by General Clinton, as they related to them, were satisfactory, and desired that I would propose my acceptance of them, and a request from the Lieutenant-Governor and Council that the negotiations might be renewed—the militia of ye Town having thrown down their arms—our provisions, saving a little rice, being exhausted, the troops on the line being worn down with fatigue, having for a number of days been obliged to lay upon the blanket—our harbour closely blocked up —completely invested by land nine thousand men at least, the flower of the British Army in America, besides the large force which at all times they could draw from their marine, and aided by a great number of blacks in all their laborious employments, the garrison at this time, exclusive of the sailors, but little exceeding twenty-five hundred men, part of whom had thrown down their arms—the citizens in general discontented and clamourous—the enemy being within twenty yards of our lines, and preparing to make a general assault by sea and land—many of our cannon dismounted and others silenced from the want of shot—a retreat being judged impracticable, and every hope of timely succour cut off—we were induced to offer and accede to the terms executed on the 12th. . . .

Your most obedient Servant,

B. LINCOLN.

General Horatio Gates was commissioned by Congress in 1780 to assemble a Southern army, with a nucleus of soldiers from the Continental Army detached from Washington's command. In August Gates attempted to take the British supply base and post at Camden, South Carolina, but was defeated and forced to retreat to Hillsboro, North Carolina. He lost between 800 and 900 dead and 1000 prisoners.

The deposed governor of North Carolina, Josiah Martin, witnessed the engagement at Camden and wrote a lengthy report of it to the British Secretary of State. The text of the following excerpt from his message is from the *State Records of North Carolina, 1777-1790,* edited by Walter Clark, Nash Brothers, Goldsboro, 1898, Vol. XV, p. 49.

It is with inexpressible satisfaction that I have the Honor to offer to your Lordship my sincerest congratulations on a victory gained over the Rebel Army by His Majesty's Forces under the command of Earl Cornwallis on the 16th inst., of which I had the Honor and Happiness to be a Spectator, and which I am warranted to say was in all its circumstances as glorious, compleat and critical as has been obtained by the Arms of Britain for Ages. In one word, my Lord, it could receive no additional splendour. Everything was achieved that was to be acquired by the General's magnanimity, bravery and vigour of troops, the Enemy's Army, of much more than three times our strength, being intirely routed after a very sharp action of three-quarters of an hour, with the loss of 1,500 Men Killed, Wounded and Prisoners, together with their whole artillery, consisting of 8 pieces of Brass Ordnance, 130 Waggons, many Colours, and the greatest part of their Arms, Ammunition, Accoutrements and Baggage. . . .

From the time the Rebel Army assembled at Hillsborough, early in June, every devise had been practised upon the adherents of the usurpation in this Province to prepare them for a new Revolt. . . . By the latter end of July, or sooner, they were joining the Rebel Armies. . . .

[Now, Great Britain's cause and interests, as a result of] . . . this action, may be fairly said to be rescued, saved, redeemed.

✓ ✓ ✓

In September Cornwallis began an invasion of North Carolina. Major Patrick Ferguson, said to have been one of the best British officers in America, raised a large body of Tories who, combined with his own corps of regulars, gave him 1125 men. With this force Ferguson screened Cornwallis' left flank, and as Cornwallis moved along the central road by way of Salisbury, Ferguson's detachment marched towards the mountains. A force of American frontiersmen from several counties in and west of the Blue Ridge in North and South Carolina, the present Tennessee, and Virginia, caught Ferguson on King's Mountain on the border between the Carolinas, and inflicted defeat, capturing or killing the entire force. Ferguson was among those killed. Cornwallis then retreated to South Carolina.

Colonel William Campbell, co-commander with Colonel Isaac Shelby, described the battle in the following letter. General George Washington sent his congratulations to the Army. The text of the two following selections is from the *State Records of North Carolina, 1777-1790*, edited by Walter Clark, Nash Brothers, Goldsboro, 1898, Vol. XV, pp. 126-127, 131-132.

A.

WILKES COUNTY, CAMP ON BRIAR CREEK, OCTOBER 20th, 1780.

DEAR SIR:

Ferguson and his party are no more in circumstances to injure the citizens of America. We came up with him in Craven County in South Carolina, posted on a height called King's Mountain, about twelve miles north of the Cherokee Ford on Broad River, about two O'clock in the evening of the 7th inst., we having marched the whole night before Col. Shelby's regiment and mine began the attack, and sustained the whole fire of the enemy for about ten minutes, while the other troops were forming around the height upon which the enemy was posted. The firing became general, and as heavy as you can conceive for the number of men. The advantageous situation of the enemy, being the top of the steep ridge, obliged us to expose ourselves exceedingly, and the dislodging of them was almost equal to driving men from strong breastworks, though in the end we gained the point of the ridge, where my regiment fought, and drove them along the summit of it to the other end, where Col. Cleveland and his countrymen were. They were driven into a huddle, and the greatest confusion; the flag for surrender was immediately hoisted, and as soon as our troops could be notified of it the firing ceased, and the survivors surrendered themselves at discretion.

We fought an hour and five minutes, in which time two hundred and twenty-five were killed of the enemy, and one hundred and thirty wounded; the rest, making about seven hundred regulars and Tories, were taken prisoners. Ferguson was killed near the close of the action. The victory was complete to a wish; and I think it was won by about seven hundred men who fought bravely. . . .

WILLIAM CAMPBELL

B.   WASHINGTON'S GENERAL ORDER
            HEADQUARTERS, TOTOWAY, October 27, 1780.

The General has the pleasure to congratulate the army on an important advantage lately gained in North Carolina over a corps of fourteen hundred men, British troops and new levies, commanded by Col. Ferguson.

The militia of the neighboring Country, under Cols. Williams, Shelby and others, having assembled to the number of about three thousand men, a detachment of sixteen hundred was sent on horseback to fall in with Ferguson's party on its march to Charlotte. They came up with the enemy at a place called King's Mountain, advantageously posted, and gave him a total defeat, in which Col Ferguson and a hundred and fifty of his men were killed, eight hundred made prisoners, and fifteen hundred stand of arms taken. On our part, the loss was inconsiderable. We have only to regret that the brave Col. Williams is mortally wounded.

These advantages will, in all probability, have a very happy influence on operations in that quarter, and are a proof of the spirit and resources of the country.

✢   ✢   ✢

In December, 1780, Nathaniel Greene succeeded Gates in command of the Southern army. He sent Daniel Morgan into western South Carolina and at Cowpens Morgan defeated Tarleton severely. With Cornwallis pursuing him, Morgan joined Greene in North Carolina. A battle at Guilford Court House was a very costly victory for the British. Greene then undertook a campaign to regain South Carolina, and although he lost some battles he succeeded by September in freeing the state of the British except in the vicinity of Charleston.

In the meantime Cornwallis marched into Virginia to stop the flow of supplies and recruits from that state into the South. After raiding Virginia far into the interior he was checked by Lafayette, Von Steuben, and Anthony Wayne. His decision to establish a base on the seacoast by which he might receive aid from Clinton in New York was the cause of his defeat. At Yorktown he was hemmed in by American and French troops under Washington and Rochambeau and the French fleet under DeGrasse. On October 19th the British force of 8000 surrendered to Washington. By the end of 1782 all of the Southern seaports had been evacuated by the British.

The text of the following selection is from James Thacher, *Military Journal of the American Revolutionary War from 1775 to 1783,* Hurlburt, Kellogg and Company, Hartford, 1861, pp. 344-347.

October 18, 1781. It is now ascertained that Lord Cornwallis, to avoid the necessity of a surrender, has determined on the bold attempt to make his escape in the night of the 16th, with a part of his army, into the country. His plan was to leave sick and baggage behind, and to cross with his effective force over to Gloucester Point, there to destroy the French legion and other troops, and to mount his infantry on their horses and such others as might be procured, and thus push their way to New York by land. A more preposterous and desperate attempt can scarcely be imagined. Boats were secretly prepared, arrangements made, and a large proportion of his troops actually embarked and landed on Gloucester Point, when, from a moderate and calm evening, a most violent storm of wind and rain ensued. The boats with the remaining troops were all driven down the river, and it was not till the next day that his troops could be returned to the garrison at York.

At an early hour this forenoon General Washington communicated to Lord Cornwallis the general basis of the terms of capitulation, which he deemed admissible, and allowed two hours for his reply. Commissioners were soon afterward appointed to prepare the particular terms of agreement. The gentlemen appointed by General Washington are Colonel Laurens, one of his aide-de-camps, and Viscount Noailles of the French army. They have this day held an interview with the two British officers on the part of Lord Cornwallis; the terms of capitulation are settled, and being confirmed by the commanders of both armies, the royal troops are to march out tomorrow and surrender their arms.

19th. This is to us a most glorious day; but to the English, one of bitter chagrin and disappointment. Preparations are now making to receive as captives that vindictive, haughty commander and that vanquished army who, by their robberies and murders, have so long been a scourge to our brethren of the Southern states. Being on horseback, I anticipate a full share of satisfaction in viewing the various movements in the interesting scene. The stipulated terms of capitulation are similar to those granted to General Lincoln at Charleston the last year. The captive troops are to march out with shouldered arms, colors cased, and drums beating a British or German march, and to ground their arms at a place assigned for the purpose. The officers are allowed their side arms and private property, and the generals and such officers as desire it are to go on parole to England or New York. The marines and seamen of the King's ships are prisoners of war to the navy of France, and the land forces to the United States. All military and artillery stores are to de delivered up unimpaired. The royal prisoners are to be sent into the interior of Virginia, Maryland, and Penn-

ylvania in regiments, to have their officers near them, Lord Cornwallis
o man and dispatch the *Bonetta* sloop of war with dispatches to Sir Henry
Clinton at New York without being searched, the vessel to be returned and
he hands accounted for.

At about twelve o'clock, the combined army was arranged and drawn
up in two lines extending more than a mile in length. The Americans
were drawn up in a line on the right side of the road, and the French occupied the left. At the head of the former, the great American commander,
mounted on his noble courser, took his station, attended by his aides. At
he head of the latter was posted the excellent Count Rochambeau
and his suite. The French troops, in complete uniform, displayed a martial
and noble appearance; their band of music, of which the timbrel formed
a part, is a delightful novelty, and produced while marching to the ground
a most enchanting effect. The Americans, though not all in uniform nor
their dress so neat, yet exhibited an erect, soldierly air, and every countenance beamed with satisfaction and joy. The concourse of spectators from
he country was prodigious, in point of numbers was probably equal to the
military, but universal silence and order prevailed. It was about two
o'clock when the captive army advanced through the line formed for their
reception. Every eye was prepared to gaze on Lord Cornwallis, the object of
peculiar interest and solicitude, but he disappointed our anxious expecta-
ions; pretending indisposition, he made General O'Hara his substitute as
he leader of his army. This officer was followed by the conquered troops
in a slow and solemn step, with shouldered arms, colors cased, and drums
beating a British march. Having arrived at the head of the line, General
O'Hara, elegantly mounted, advanced to his Excellency, the Commander-
in-chief, taking off his hat, and apologized for the nonappearance of Earl
Cornwallis. With his usual dignity and politeness, his Excellency pointed
to Major General Lincoln for directions, by whom the British army was
conducted into a spacious field, where it was intended they should ground
their arms. The royal troops, while marching through the line formed
by the allied army, exhibited a decent and neat appearance, as respects
arms and clothing, for their commander opened his store, and directed
every soldier to be furnished with a new suit complete, prior to their capitu-
ation. But in their line of march we remarked a disorderly and unsoldierly
conduct, their step was irregular, and their ranks frequently broken. But
it was in the field, when they came to the last act of the drama, that the
pirit and pride of the British soldier was put to the severest test: here
their mortification could not be concealed. Some of the platoon officers
appeared to be exceedingly chagrined when giving the words, "Ground
arms," and I am a witness that they performed this duty in a very unofficer-
like manner and that many of the soldiers manifested a *sullen temper,*
throwing their arms on the pile with violence, as if determined to render

them useless. This irregularity, however, was checked by the authority of General Lincoln. After having grounded their arms and divested themselves of their accounterments, the captive troops were conducted back to Yorktown, and guarded by our troops till they could be removed to the place of their destination.

6

The Cotton Kingdom

It would be impossible to think of the history of the South after the Revolutionary War without thinking at the same time of cotton. Even before Eli Whitney invented the cotton gin the four southernmost states grew a great deal of cotton, and the poor were almost entirely clothed with it. Yet cotton was not a staple, because of the difficulty of separating the seeds from the fiber. Whitney's invention was relatively simple and, hence, inexpensive to manufacture. By its use as much cotton could be cleaned in a day as a hand picker could do in a year. Immediately cotton was planted in quantity.

Francois Andre Michaux, visiting Tennessee in 1802, described agriculture in some detail. The following excerpts are from his *Travels to the West of the Allegheny Mountains,* B. Crosby and Company, London, Second Edition, 1805, pp. 241-243, 278-279.

The culture [of cotton] infinitely more lucrative than that of corn and tobacco, is, as before observed, the most adhered to in West Tennessea. There is scarcely a single emigrant but what begins to plant his estate with it the third year after his settling the country. Those who have no negroes cultivate it with the plough, nearly in the same manner as Indian wheat, taking particular care to weed and throw new earth upon it several times in the course of the season. Others lay out their fields in parallel furrows, made with the hoe, from twelve to fifteen inches high. It is computed that one man, who employs himself with this alone, is sufficient to cultivate eight or nine acres, but not to gather in the harvest. A man and a woman, with two or three children, may, notwithstanding, cultivate four acres with the greatest ease, independent of the Indian wheat necessary for their subsistence; and calculating upon a harvest of three hundred and fifty pounds per acre, which is very moderate according to the extreme fertility of the soil, they will have, in four acres, a produce of fourteen hundred pounds of cotton. Valuing it at the rate of eighteen dollars per hundred weight, the lowest price to which it had fallen at the epoch of the last peace, when I was in the country, gives two hundred and fifty-two dollars; while the same number of acres, planted with Indian wheat, or sown with corn, would yield only at the rate of fifty bushels per acre; and twenty-five bushels of corn, about fifty dollars, reckoning the Indian wheat at thirteen pence, and the corn at two shillings and two pence per bushel; under the supposition that they can sell it at that price, which is not always the case. This light sketch demonstrates with what facility a poor family may acquire speedily, in West Tennessea, a certain degree of independence, particularly after having been settled five or six years, as they procure the means of purchasing one or two negroes, and of annually increasing their number. The species of cotton which they cultivate here is somewhat more esteemed than that described by the name of green-seed cotton in which there is a trifling distinction in point of colour.

The cottons which are manufactured in West Tennessea are exceedingly fine, and superior in quality to those I saw in the course of my travels. The legislature of this state, appreciating the advantage of encouraging this kind of industry, and of diminishing, by that means, the importation of English goods of the same nature, has given, for these two years past, a premium of ten dollars to the female inhabitant who, in every county, presents the best manufactured piece; for in this part, as well as in Kentucky, the higher circles wear, in summer time, as much from patriotism as from economy, dresses made of cottons manufactured in the country. At the same time they are convinced that it is the only means of preserving the little specie that is in the country, and of preventing its going to England. . . .

The low price to which tobacco is fallen in Europe, within these few years, has made them give up the culture of it in this part of the country. That of green-seed cotton had resumed its place, to the great advantage of the inhabitants, many of whom have since made their fortunes by it. The separation of the seed from the felt that envelopes them is a tedious operation, and which requires many hands, is now simplified by a machine for which the inventor has obtained a patent from the federal government. The legislature of South Carolina paid him, three years since, the sum of a hundred thousand dollars, for all the inhabitants belonging to the state to have the privilege of erecting one. This machine, very simple, and the price of which does not exceed sixty dollars, is put in motion by a horse or by a current of water, and separates from the seed three or four hundred pounds of cotton per day; while by the usual method, a man is not able to separate above thirty pounds. This machine, it is true, has the inconvenience of shortening by haggling it; the wool, on that account, is rather inferior in point of quality, but this inconvenience is, they say, well compensated by the saving of time, and more particularly workmanship.

✓ ✓ ✓

During the eighteen-thirties English people showed considerable interest in America. A number of English travelers wrote descriptions of their travels, which were published serially in periodicals as well as in book form.

While many of them were critical of the slave system, their reports give us an understanding of life in the South. These accounts are replete with evidence concerning the large plantations which they visited, slave labor, and the expansion of the cotton-growing South.

Captain Basil Hall, in *Travels in North America in the Years 1827 and 1828,* Carey, Sea and Carey, 1829, Vol. II, pp. 228-234, described a "sea island" plantation.

On looking at the map of America, abreast of Georgia a number of islands will be observed, such as Tybee, Ossabaw, Sapelo, and St. Simon's. These make no great show on paper, but they are very important in commerce, as being the spots on which the finest of cotton is raised. In strictness, what is called, technically, "Sea Island Cotton," is not confined to these insular districts, but grows at various places on the main coast, and also for some distance from the sea, in the swampy regions bordering on most of the great rivers. The term is now used, therefore, to describe a particular sort of cotton, the essential characteristic of which is the length of fibre or staple, in contradistinction to the less valuable kind, with a short staple, which, from growing further from the sea, at a higher level, has acquired the name of Upland cotton, or, in the brevity of commercial language, "Uplands." . . .

On a "Sea Island" plantation which I visited, there were 122 slaves employed in the culture of cotton. Of these, 70 were men and women, between the ages of fourteen and fifty—48 children under the age of fourteen—and 4 superannuated.

39 of them were called full hands.

16 three-quarter hands.

11 half hands.

4 quarter hands.

Making in all, out of the 70 persons, 57½ "Taskable hands." Those actually in the field were 44 taskables, while the remaining 13½ were employed as cart drivers, nurses, cooks for the negroes, carpenters, gardeners, house servants, and stock-minders—what we should call in Scotland herds; in England, I believe, herdsmen.

The ground under tillage consisted of 200 acres of cotton, and 25 of Indian corn, potatoes, and other things of that description. This gave about 5 acres to a full hand in the field. Several ploughs were occasionally used, the ploughmen being included in the 44 field hands. . . .

With respect to the amount of labour performed by the slaves in the culture and preparation of cotton, I may mention, that in all cases of tasking—whether this term be applied to field or to housework—a three-quarter, a half, or a quarter hand, is required to work only that proportion of a task per day. . . . This method of tasking, or defining their work, is that which the slaves prefer to any other. Active hands get through their proportion generally by the middle of the day, others in two-thirds of the day, after which, they are left to employ the balance, as it is rather well called, or what remains of daylight, in their own fields, in fishing, or in dancing;—in short, as they please. The driver puts them to work in the morning, and sees that all is properly executed before they go away.

The young slaves, of course, come in as one-quarter hands, and are gradually raised. Every negro knows his rate, and lawful task, so well, that if he thinks himself imposed upon by the driver, he appeals at once to the master. . . .

The stated allowance of food to every slave, over fourteen years of age, is nine quarts of Indian corn per week, and for children from five to eight quarts. This is said to be more than they can eat, and the surplus is either sold, or is given to the hogs and poultry which they are always allowed to rear on their own account. A quart of salt monthly is also allowed, and salt fish, as well as salf beef occasionally, but only as a favour, and can never be claimed as a right. A heaped-up bushel of sweet potatoes is considered equal to the above allowance, and so are two pecks of rough, that is un-husked, rice or paddy. But this is not thought so substantial a food as the Indian corn.

On the plantation to which these details refer, the negroes are allowed three holydays at Christmas, when they have plenty of beef and whisky. At the end of this period they are often, I am told, completely done up with eating, drinking, and dancing. On that plantation, they are allowed to have as much land as they choose to plant, and the master's family is supplied entirely with poultry and eggs from the free work of the slaves, who are . . . paid. . . .

The slaves are generally dressed in what is called White Welsh plains, for winter clothing. This costs about 80 cents . . . a yard in Charleston. They prefer white cloth, and afterwards die it of a purple colour to suit their own fancy. Each man gets seven yards of this, and the women six yards, —the children in proportion. Each grownup negro gets a new blanket every second year, and every two children in like manner one blanket. The men receive also a cap, and the women a handkerchief, together with a pair of strong shoes, every winter. A suit of homespun cotton, of the stuff called Osnaburgs, is allowed to each person for summer dress.

It is very disagreeable to speak of the punishments inflicted on these negroes, but a slave-holder must be more or less of a despot in spite of himself; for the laws neither do, nor can they, effectually interfere in the details of discipline. The master must enforce obedience to his orders, and maintain general subordination, however kind-hearted he may be, by the only means which the nature of the whole system leaves in his power. . . .

It is a great mistake . . . to suppose that the slaves labour sulkily, and under perpetual exercise of the lash. On the contrary, from constant habit, they do, in point of fact, go about their work with cheerfulness; and as their tasks are limited to what can be readily performed, it is in the power of every slave who chooses, to escape punishment for any length of time. . . . It ought to be recollected, in due fairness to slave-holders—a class of men who are entitled to a large share of our indulgence—that many ships of war, many regiments, and, I fear, I may add, many domestic establishments, to say nothing of schools, are often—as I have witnessed in all quarters of the globe—the scenes of as revolting tyranny as any rice or cotton plantation can well be. The scale may be smaller, but the principle is exactly the same. In fairness to the planters, we ought also to recollect, that the slave-holders, or by far the greater number of them, are not possessed of that character by any voluntary act of their own. Most of these gentlemen have succeeded to their property by inheritance, or have been obliged by duty to themselves and their families to engage in the particular profession, if I may call it so. They cannot, therefore, and they ought not, consistently with their duty, to disentangle themselves from the obligations which have devolved upon them, as the masters of slaves.

✓   ✓   ✓

Two views of life on the "sea island" plantations of Georgia are compared in the following section. The "pro" side of the argument was written by Sir Charles Lyell, the eminent scientist, who visited Hopeton Plantation by mere chance, on one of his exploring expeditions. The account is quoted from his book, *A Second Visit to the United States,* Harper and Brothers, New York, 1850, Vol. I, pp. 261-263. The "con" point of view was written by Frances Anne Kemble as a letter to the Editor of the London *Times,* and later incorporated in the author's *Journal of a Residence on a Georgia Plantation,* Harper and Brothers, New York, 1863, pp. 308-315. As an actress, Fanny Kemble came to America to appear on the American stage and married Senator Pierce Butler who owned a plantation adjacent to Hopeton, on Butler's Island, Georgia. Miss Kemble admitted that she was prejudiced against slavery: "For I am an Englishwoman, in whom the absence of such a prejudice would be disgraceful."

Pro	*Con*
During a fortnight's stay at Hopeton, [the plantation of Mr. Hamilton Couper of Georgia] we had the opportunity of seeing how the planters live in the South, and the condition and prospects of the negroes on a well-managed estate. The relations of the slaves to the owners resembles nothing in the northern states. There is an hereditary regard and often an attachment on both sides, more like	On some of the great Southern estates, the owners are habitual absentees, utterly unknown to their serfs, and enjoying the proceeds of their labor in residences as far remote as possible from the sands and swamps where their rice and cotton grow, and their slaves bow themselves under the eye of the white overseer, and the lash of the black driver. . . . Some travel in Eu-

Pro

that formerly existing between lords and their retainers in the old feudal times of Europe, than to anything now to be found in America. The slaves identify themselves with the master, and their sense of their own importance rises with his success in life. But the responsibility of the owners is felt to be great, and to manage a plantation with profit is no easy task; so much judgment is required, and such a mixture of firmness, forbearance, and kindness.

There are 500 negroes on Hopeton estate, a great many of whom are children, and some old and superannuated. The latter class, who would be supported in a poor-house in England, enjoy here, to the end of their days, the society of their neighbors and kinsfolk, and live at large in separate houses assigned to them. . . .
We visited the hospital at Hopeton, which consisted of three separate wards, all perfectly clean and well-ventilated. One is for men, another for women, and a third for lying-in women. The latter are always allowed a month's rest after their confinement, an advantage rarely enjoyed by hardworking English peasants. . . .
The negro mothers are often so ignorant and indolent, that they can not be trusted to keep awake and administer medicine to their own

Con

rope, and few, whose means permit the contrary, ever pass the entire year on their plantations. Great intervals of many years pass, and no master ever visits some of these properties: what species of attachment do you think the slave entertains for him? In other cases, the visits made will be of a few days in one of the winter months, the estate and its cultivators remaining for the rest of the year under the absolute control of the overseer, who, provided he contrives to get a good crop . . . into the market for his employers, is left to the arbitrary exercise of a will seldom uninfluenced for evil by the combined effects of the grossest ignorance and habitual intemperance.
Your authority next states that the infirm and superannuated slaves no longer capable of ministering to their master's luxuries, on the estate that he visited, were ending their lives among all the comforts of home, with kindred and friends around them, in a condition which he contrasts, at least by implication, very favorably with the work-house, the last refuge provided by the social humanity of England for the pauper laborer when he has reached . . . old age. On the plantation where I lived the Infirmary was a large room, the walls of which were simply mud and laths; the floor, the soil itself, damp with perpetual drippings from holes in the roof; and the open space which served for a window was protected only by a broken shutter, which, in order to exclude the cold, was drawn so near as almost to exclude the light at the

Pro

children; so that the mistress has often to sit up all night with a sick negro child.

If we place ourselves in the condition of the majority of the population, that of servants, we see at once how many advantages we should enjoy over the white race in the same rank of life in Europe. In the first place, all can marry; and if a mistress should lay on any young woman here the injunction so common in English newspaper advertisements for a maid of all work, "no followers allowed," it would be considered an extraordinary act of tyranny.

The laborers begin work at six o'clock in the morning, have an hour's rest at nine for breakfast, and many have finished their as-

Con

same time. Upon this earthen floor, with nothing but its hard, damp surface beneath him, no covering but a tattered shirt and trowsers, and a few sticks under his head for a pillow, lay an old man of upward of seventy, dying. . . . and so, like a worn-out hound, with no creature to comfort or relieve his last agony, with neither Christian solace nor human succor near him, with neither wife, nor child, nor even friendly fellow-being to lift his head from the knotty sticks on which he had rested it, or drive away the insects that buzzed round his lips and nostrils like those of a fallen beast, died this poor old slave, whose life had been exhausted in unrequited labor, the fruits of which had gone to pamper the pride and feed the luxury of those who cared neither for his life nor his death. . . .

The next note of admiration elicited from your "impartial observer" is bestowed upon the fact that the domestic servants were *allowed* . . . to marry. . . . surely it is a gross mockery to apply such a word to a bond which may be holy in God's sight, but which did not prevent the owner of a plantation where my observations were made from selling and buying men and their so-called wives and children into divided bondage, nor the white overseer from compelling the wife of one of the most excellent and exemplary of his master's slaves to live with him.

"Work," continues your authority, "began at six in the morning; at nine an hour's rest was allowed for breakfast, . . ." Certainly this was a pat-

signed task by two o'clock, all of them by three o'clock. In summer they divide their work differently, going to bed in the middle of the day, then rising to finish their task, and afterward spending a great part of the night in chatting, merry-making, preaching, and psalm-singing.

tern plantation, and I can only lament that my experience lay amid such far less favorable circumstances. The negroes among whom I lived went to the fields at daybreak, carrying with them their allowance of food, which toward noon, and not till then, they ate, cooking it over a fire which they kindled as best they could where they were working; their *second* meal in the day was at night, after their labor was over, having worked at the very least six hours without rest or refreshment since their noonday meal.

After the Revolutionary War Middle Georgia received many planters from the Carolinas and Virginia, and land was in great demand. Much of the territory was still occupied by Indians. Georgia at that time included all of the area east of the Mississippi River between Florida and South Carolina. Settlement took place rapidly, especially after the War of 1812. Cotton was the principal product of Middle Georgia. By piecing together the narratives of several travelers we have a glimpse of America in the process of rapid growth.

Adam Hodgson, in 1819, visited Augusta. The following extract is from his *Letters from North America During a Tour in the United States and Canada,* 2 vols., Hurst, London, 1824, Vol. I, p. 104.

[As we approached Augusta] we found ourselves surrounded by immense cotton plantations, and all "the pomp and circumstance" of commerce; carts coming in from the country with cotton, and crowding the streets, or rather avenues, of this rural town; tradesmen and agents bustling about in different directions; wharfs loaded with bales; and steam-boats darkening the air with their black exhalations. . . .

I left Augusta . . . with the intention of proceeding overland to Mobile or New Orleans. . . . After travelling about twenty-eight miles, we stopped for the night at Mrs. Harris's tavern, a small country inn by the way side. Two female Negroes were hand-picking cotton by the kitchen fire, where I took my seat, till I was unexpectedly invited to another room, where a fire had been made for me. The first question my landlady asked me, was the price of cotton at Augusta; a question which was eagerly repeated wherever I stopped.—Indeed, the fluctuations in this article came home to "the business and bosoms" of the poorest family, since every one is concerned more or less in its cultivation. While my hostess poured out my coffee, I asked her if there were any schools in the neighbourhood. She said, Oh, yes; there was an academy to which her daughter went when cotton was thirty cents per pound; that she paid three hundred dollars per annum simply for board, and fifty more for learning the pī -ā-no! but that, as cotton had fallen to fifteen cents she could not afford to buy an instrument, and supposed her daughter must forget her music.

✓   ✓   ✓

James S. Buckingham, in *The Slave States of America*, Fisher, Son, and Company, London, 1842, Vol. I, pp. 174-175, 193, described the distribution of land by the state of Georgia.

[In Georgia] 100,000 square miles of territory were ceded by the legislature to the general government, soon after the incorporation of the several States into the Union, for the purpose of forming the new States of Alabama and Mississippi. . . . The general government undertook . . . to extinguish . . . all the Indian titles to the Cherokee lands within the limits of the newly circumscribed state of Georgia. Several hundred thousand acres being thus left at their disposal, a lottery was formed of the whole, and they were thus distributed:—First, a survey was made of all these lands; then they were marked off into townships and sections, and numbered in consecutive order. Each section of 160 acres was designated by a particular number, and tickets corresponding to these numbers were put into a wheel, as into any ordinary lottery. Every person residing in Georgia, at the time of the drawing, who had been living six months in the State, was entitled to a draw, if a single man or woman; and every married man had a draw for himself, his wife, and each of his children, however many, and however young; and there were sections enough for all. Accordingly, men of large families, and who were fortunate in obtaining lands in a good position, were made rich; there were no blanks, except that some sections were sandy, others marshy, and others woody, and therefore worth less than others; but as nothing was paid for the privilege of a draw, no one could lose by such a lottery. As there were known to be many, however, who if they drew good lands would have no capital to work them, but would be obliged to sell out, it was not difficult to speculate upon their shares; and accordingly, land jobbers from the north went about and bought up men's chances for a small sum, never paying more than 50 dollars, and getting many for 5 dollars, by which large fortunes were made in this way. One gentleman told me that he sold a lot which came to him through this lottery for 500 dollars, within a week after he had drawn it; others had cultivated their lots, and these were now worth 20 dollars an acre, or upwards of 3,000 per lot. These fluctuations of fortune produced, as lotteries everywhere have done, a spirit of speculation and gambling, which it is easy to engender but very difficult to subdue; and the effects of this continue to the present day, in speculations, jobbing, and lotteries, of which Augusta is still full. . . .

When the Indian titles to large tracts [in Georgia] were extinguished by the general government paying to them a compensation or purchase-money for the same, . . . and when [the lottery was conducted] . . . certain localities were reserved by the State government of Georgia, for the formation of towns, and . . . [Macon] was one of them. Accordingly, the town of Macon, so called after a wealthy citizen of Carolina, was laid out by the state-surveyor, and the ground sold in lots to private purchasers for building. It was soon after incorporated with all the municipal privileges of a city. Since that period it has gone on increasing in wealth and population, till the present year, when it numbers upwards of 8,000 inhabitants, of whom about 5,000 are whites, and 3,000 slaves and coloured people; and though only fifteen years old, its exports of cotton amounted last year to 5,000,000 dollars and its imports to 4,000,000 dollars. Macon has a Female College . . . which is sufficiently spacious to accommodate 200 boarders, and to educate 200 day-scholars besides. . . . Though the building is not yet finished, there are already 150 young ladies, from 10 to 18 years of age, receiving their education there; . . . the value of land in this locality has so increased, that a gentleman wishing to erect a country mansion on the hill, surrounded by a garden, had to pay 3,000 dollars . . . per acre, which, five years ago might have been had for 100 dollars, and fifteen years ago might have been had for 1¼ dollar; so rapid is the increase of value in land by augmented population, and increased demand for it. . . .

The small settlement of Carnesville Georgia . . . presented a very perfect specimen of a gradually forming American village, rising into the dignity of a country-town. In its centre was the Court House of the district, and within a few yards of this were the signposts of three hotels. Not far off was seen the symbol of a doctor of medicine, with his name and title at full length, under a rudely delineated pestle-and-mortar, as the emblem of his profession. Right opposite to him, in a small wooden cabin of a single room, was the office of another professional man, the attorney-at-law; and within a few doors of these, were the shops of a blacksmith, a carpenter, and a saddler, with one large grocery store, at which everything sold by grocers, ironmongers, drapers, stationers, and haberdashers, in larger places, were to be found. The whole population did not exceed 250, including black and white; but as the proportion of the former grows less and less as you leave the coast and approach the mountains, there were probably not more than fifty coloured persons among the whole. . . .

✓   ✓   ✓

The ceaseless movement of people westward is sketched in Adam Hodgson,
Letters from North America During a Tour in the United States and Canada,
Hurst, London, 1824, Vol. I, p. 138.

[We] arrived at Line Creek, which, we were told, forms . . . the present
boundary between the Creek Nation and Alabama. We had travelled that
day about forty miles, and had passed as usual many large parties of emigrants, from South Carolina and Georgia, and many gangs of slaves. Indeed,
at the edges of the creeks and on the banks of the rivers, we usually found
a curious collection of sans soucis, carts, Jersey waggons, heavy waggons,
little planters, Indians, Negroes, horses, mules, and oxen; the women and
little children sitting down frequently for one, two or three, and sometimes
five or six hours, to work or play, while the men were engaged in the almost
hopeless task of dragging or swimming their vehicles and baggage to the
opposite side. Often a light carriage, with a sallow planter and his lady,
would bring up the rear of a long cavalcade, and indicate the removal of
a family of some wealth, who, allured by the rich lands of Alabama, or
the sugar plantations on the Mississippi, had bidden adieu to the scenes of
their youth, and undertaken a long and painful pilgrimage through the
wilderness.

✓   ✓   ✓

Some causes of the great migration are given by James S. Buckingham in *The
Slave States of America.* Fisher, Son, and Company, London, 1842, Vol. I, p. 173,
and Vol. II, p. 106, and quoted from the Augusta, Georgia *Constitutionalist* for 1839.

The farmers of Georgia could not have pursued a more fatal course than
they have done for the last thirty years. The growing of cotton on broken
lands, is the most ready way that can be adopted, to utterly destroy them.
Hence we have thousands of acres that were once fertile, and richly repaid
labour, now worthless, to the last degree—nothing but sterile red clay, full
of gullies. And what has the planter received as an equivalent for his ruined
land? Why, in most cases, nothing but an increased number of negroes,
who now consume the almost entire production of his worn out land. And
a few years more, going on at this rate, he must either remove West, be
sold out by the Sheriff, or live in extreme poverty. . . . .

In an upland region in Northwestern Georgia, the Buckingham party
spent the night at a farmhouse inn. The climate of this elevated region
being not sufficiently warm for the cultivation of cotton, the soil is devoted
to the growth of wheat, oats, and maize, or Indian corn. . . . One of the
farmers, who was upwards of sixty-five years of age, told me that he had
made up his mind to emigrate next year, to the valley of the Mississippi:

and when I asked him what could induce him, now so far advanced in life, and with a large family, to move so far from his home, he replied, that there was too much aristocracy here for him! I asked him who or what constituted the aristocracy of which he spoke. He said they were the rich men of these parts, who bought up all the land at extravagant prices, and left none for the poorer citizens to purchase; the prices which he deemed so extravagant being from ten dollars an acre for the freehold property. I asked him if he could not rent land from these proprietors, and live by farming in this way. He said, yes; but added, that the rent demanded was extravagant, also, amounting to ten barrels of corn for a small farm of twenty acres; which in sterling money would be about one dollar per acre for annual rent, without tithes or other imposts, and no expense of manure or draining.

✔ ◦ ✔ ✔

To Captain Basil Hall's *Travels in North America in the Years 1827 and 1828*, Carey, Sea and Carey, 1829, Vol. II, p. 261, we are indebted for the following account of the establishment of Columbus, Georgia.

[When one of the lotteries took place] the State government reserved a portion of the country, five miles square . . . upon which they proposed to found a city. The situation chosen for this purpose was a spot on the left bank of the Chatahoochie, which is the boundary line between the State of Georgia and Alabama. The new city was to commence at the lower end of a long series of falls, or more properly speaking, rapids, over which this great river dashes for some miles in a very picturesque manner. . . .

By a law of the State of Georgia, it was arranged that 60 days should elapse, after this portion of land reserved for the city was completely surveyed, before any of the building lots could be sold. The lots were to consist of half an acre each, and the whole five miles square was to be distinctly marked out in streets, on paper, and being numbered and lettered accordingly, they were to be advertised for sale over the whole Union. These sixty days were considered sufficient to enable adventurers, settlers, landspeculators, merchants, and all others so disposed, to come to the spot preparatory to the auction.

The project took like wildfire; and the advantages of the new city being loudly proclaimed over the land, people flocked from all quarters to see and judge of it for themselves. We arrived, fortunately, just in the nick of time to see the curious phenomenon of an embryo town—a city as yet without any name, or any existence in law or fact, but crowded with inhabitants, ready to commence their municipal duties at the tap of an auctioneer's hammer. . . .

After threading our way for some time amongst the trees, we came in sight, here and there, of huts made partly of planks, partly of bark, and at last reached the principal cluster of houses, very few of which were above two or three weeks old. These buildings were of all sizes, from a six-feet box or cube, to a house with half-a-dozen windows in front. There were three hotels, the sign belonging to one of which, I could observe, was nailed to a tree still growing untouched, in the middle of the street. Another had glazed windows, but the panes of glass were fixed in their places merely for the time, by a little piece of putty at each corner. Everything indicated hurry. The direction and width alone of the future streets were adhered to, but no other description of regularity could be discovered. As none of the city lots were yet sold, of course no one was sure that the spot upon which he had pitched his house would eventually become his own. Every person, it seemed, was at liberty to build where he could find room, it being understood, that forty days after the sale would be allowed him to remove his property from the ground on which it stood, should he not himself become its purchaser. In consequence of this understanding, many of the houses were built on trucks—a sort of low, strong wheels, such as cannon are supported by—for the avowed purpose of being hurled away when the land should be sold. At least sixty frames of houses were pointed out to me, lying in piles on the ground, and got up by carpenters on speculation, ready to answer the call of future purchasers. At some parts of this strange scene, the forest, which hereabouts consists of a mixture of pines and oaks, was growing as densely as ever; and even in the most cleared streets some trees were left standing, I do not know why. As yet there had been no time to remove the stumps of the felled trees, and many that had been felled, were left in their places; so that it was occasionally no easy matter to get along. Anvils were heard ringing away merrily at every corner; while saws, axes, and hammers were seen flashing amongst the woods all round. Stage-coaches, travelling-wagons, carts, gigs, the whole family of wheeled vehicles, innumerable, were there. Grocery stores and bakeries were scattered about in great plenty—and over several doors was written, "Attorney at Law."

One of the commissioners, from the State of Georgia, who had the management of this extraordinary experiment in colonization, assured me, there were upwards of nine hundred inhabitants already collected together, though it was expected that four months must still elapse before the sale could take place, or the city have any legal existence!

✓   ✓   ✓

Columbus was a frontier town. Proximity to Indian territory was a factor that contributed to lawlessness. In *Blackwood's Edinburgh Magazine,* 1843, Vol. 54, p. 782, in an article entitled "Adventures in Texas," was the following paragraph concerning Columbus, Georgia.

In the whole of the south-western states there was no place that could boast of being the resort of so many outlaws as the town of Sodoma. It is situated, or was situated, . . . in Alabama, on Indian ground, and was the harbour of refuge for all the murderers and outcasts from the western and south-western parts of the Union. Here, under Indian government, they found shelter and security; and frightful were the crimes and cruelties perpetrated at this place. Scarcely a day passed without an assassination, not secretly committed, but in broad sunlight. Bands of these wretches, armed with knives and rifles, used to cross the Chatahoochie, and make inroads into Columbus; break into houses, rob, murder, ill-treat women, and then return in triumph to their dens, laden with booty, and laughing at the laws. It was useless to think of pursuing them, or of obtaining justice, for they were on Indian territory; and many of the chiefs were in league with them. At length General Jackson and the government took it up. The Indians were driven over the Mississippi, the outlaws and murderers fled, Sodoma itself disappeared; and, released from its troublesome neighbors, Columbus is now as flourishing a state [*sic*] as any in the west.

✓   ✓   ✓

Most of Alabama was ceded to the United States by the Indians, after Andrew Jackson's campaign of 1814. Although Mississippi, too, was troubled by Indians, vigorous efforts were made by the English during their control of Florida, 1763-1783, to secure settlers. Grants of land were made to men who had fought against the French; these varied from one hundred to twenty-five thousand acres, located in the vicinity of Vicksburg, Natchez, and Claiborne County. Tories settled in this area as well as in Alabama, forming the nucleus of a conservative and aristocratic society. After the War of 1812 planters from the cotton growing states flocked into Mississippi, although only the southern quarter and a strip along the Mississippi River were free of Indians and open to settlement. By 1835 the Indian titles had been extinguished and all of Mississippi had been thrown open to settlement.

A readable account of the settlement of Alabama and Mississippi is to be found in Joseph G. Baldwin, *The Flush Times of Alabama and Mississippi,* American Book Company, New York, 1853, from which the following is quoted, pp. 82-100, *passim.*

This country was just settling up. Marvellous accounts had gone forth of the fertility of its virgin lands; and the productions of the soil were commanding a price remunerative to slave labor as it had never been remunerated before. Emigrants came flocking in from all quarters of the Union, especially from the slaveholding States. The new country seemed to be a reservoir, and every road leading to it a vagrant stream of enterprise and adventure. Money, or what passed for money, was the only cheap thing to be had. Every cross-road and every avocation presented an opening,— through which a fortune was seen by the adventurer in near perspective. Credit was a thing of course. To refuse it—if such a thing was ever done—

were an insult for which a bowie-knife were not a too exemplary a means of redress. The State banks were issuing their bills by the sheet, like a patent steam printing-press *its* issues; and no other showing was asked of the applicant for the loan than an authentication of his great distress for money. Finance, even in its most exclusive quarter, had thus already got, in this wonderful revolution, to work upon the principles of the charity hospital. If an overseer grew tired of supervising a plantation and felt a call to the mercantile life, even if he omitted the compendious method of buying out a merchant wholesale, stock, house and good will, and laying down at once, his bull-whip for the yard-stick—all he had to do was to go to New York, and present himself in Pearl-street with a letter avouching his citizenship, and a clean shirt, and he was regularly given a thorough ticket to speedy bankruptcy.

Under this stimulating process prices rose like smoke. Lots in obscure villages were held at city prices; lands bought at the minimum cost of government, were sold at from thirty to forty dollars per acre, and considered dirt cheap at that. . . . Society was wholly unorganized: there was no restraining public opinion: the law was well-nigh powerless—and religion scarcely was heard of except as furnishing the oaths and *technics* of profanity. . . .

Money, got without work, by those unaccustomed to it, turned the heads of its possessors, and they spent it with a recklessness like that with which they had gained it. The pursuits of industry neglected, riot and coarse debauchery filled up the vacant hours. . . .

The groceries—*vulgice*—doggeries, were in full blast in those days, no village having less than a half-dozen all busy all the time; gaming and horse-racing were polite and well patronized amusements. I knew a Judge to adjourn two courts (or court twice) to attend a horse-race, at which he officiated judicially and ministerially, and with more appropriateness than in the judicial chair. Occasionally the scene was diversified by a murder or two, which though perpetrated from behind a corner, or behind the back of the deceased, whenever the accused *chose* to stand his trial, was always found to have been committed in self-defence, securing the homicide an honorable acquittal *at the hands of his peers.* . . .

The condition of society may be imagined: —vulgarity—ignorance—fussy and arrogant pretension—unmitigated rowdyism—bullying insolence, if they did not rule the hour *seemed* to wield unchecked dominion . . . the modest, unobtrusive, retiring men of worth and character (for there were many, perhaps a majority of such) were almost lost sight of in the hurly-burly of those strange and shifting scenes.

Even in the professions were the same characteristics visible. Men dropped down into their places as from the clouds. Nobody knew who or what they were, except as they claimed, or as a surface view of their characters indicated. Instead of taking to the highway and magnanimously calling upon the wayfarer to stand and deliver, or to the fashionable larceny of credit without prospect or design of paying, some unscrupulous horse-doctor would set up his sign as "Physician and Surgeon," and draw his lancet on you, or fire at random a box of pills into your bowels, with a vague chance of hitting some disease unknown to him, but with a better prospect of killing the patient, whom or whose administrator he charged some ten dollars a trial for his marksmanship.

A superannuated justice or constable in one of the old States was metamorphosed into a lawyer; and though he knew not the distinction between a *fee tail* and a *Female*, would undertake to construe, off-hand, a will involving all the subtleties of *uses* and *trusts*.

But this state of affairs could not last for ever: society cannot always stand on its head with its heels in the air.

The Jupiter Tonans of the White House saw the monster of a free credit prowling like a beast of apocalyptic vision, and marked him for his prey. Gathering all his bolts in his sinewy grasp, and standing back on his heels, and waving his wiry arm, he let them all fly, hard and swift upon all the hydra's heads. Then came a crash, as "if the ribs of nature broke," and a scattering, like the burstings of a thousand magazines, and a smell of brimstone, as if Pandemonium had opened a window next to earth for ventilation,—and all was silent. The beast never stirred in his tracks. To get down from the clouds to level ground, the Specie Circular was issued without warning, and the splendid lie of a false credit burst into fragments. . . . Its effect was like that of a general creditor's bill in the chancery court, and a marshalling of all the assets of the trades-people. Gen. Jackson was no fairy; but he did some very pretty fairy work, in converting the bank bills back into rags and oak-leaves. Men worth a million were insolvent for two millions: promising young cities marched back again into the wilderness. The ambitious town plat was reannexed to the plantation, like a country girl taken home from the city. The frolic was ended, and what headaches, and feverish limbs the next morning! . . . The only question was as to the means of escape, and the nearest and best route to Texas. The sheriff was as busy as a militia adjutant on review day; and the lawyers were mere wreckers, earning salvage. . . . .

Many were the instances of suffering; of pitiable misfortune, involving and crushing whole families; of pride abased; of honorable sensibilities wounded; of the provision for old age destroyed; of hopes of manhood overcast; of independence dissipated, and the poor victim without help, or hope, or sympathy, forced to petty shifts for a bare subsistence. . . ; but there were too many examples of this sort for the expenditure of a useless compassion; just as the surgeon after a battle, grows case-hardened, from an excess of objects of pity.

✓   ✓   ✓

Thomas Dabney moved his family and slaves from Virginia to Mississippi in
1835. Years later his daughter, Susan Dabney Smedes, wrote *Memorial of a Southern Planter,* James Pott and Company, New York, 1888, a partial biography of
her father, in which she described their removal to Mississippi. The following
extract is from pp. 47-50 of her work.

Thomas went through a large part of Alabama, Louisiana, and Mississippi looking at the country before deciding on a body of land in Hinds
Country, Mississippi. He succeeded in purchasing four thousand acres
from half a dozen small farmers.

The ancestors of both Thomas and Sophia Dabney had been slave-
owners. The family servants, inherited for generations, had come to be
regarded with great affection, and this feeling was warmly returned by
the negroes. The bond between master and servant was, in many cases, felt
to be as sacred and close as the ties of blood.

During the course of years many of the Elmington negroes had intermarried with the negroes on neighboring estates.

When the southern move was decided on, Thomas called his servants
together and announced to them his intention to remove, with his family,
to Mississippi. He further went on to say that he did not mean to take one
unwilling servant with him. His plan was to offer to buy all husbands and
wives, who were connected with his negroes, at the owners' prices, or he
should, if his people preferred, sell those whom he owned to any master or
mistress whom they might choose. No money difficulty should stand in the
way. Everything should be made to yield to the important consideration
of keeping families together.

Without an exception, the negroes determined to follow their beloved
master and mistress. They chose rather to give up the kinspeople and
friends of their own race than to leave them. . . .

When it was resolved to leave Virginia, the baby boy was named Vir-
ginius, after the beloved State that had given birth to his ancestors. This
child, the youngest of four brothers, was but six months old when, in
September, 1835, the long journey southward was begun.

Sophia's father and mother and her two sisters, one married to Mr. Lewis
Smith, with her husband and two children, Augustine Dabney, with his
wife and family, and other kinsfolk and friends had become quite infatuated with the desire to go with Thomas to Mississippi, and a number of
these arranged to undertake the move along with him. Mr. Charles Hill
took charge of the carriages that held the white families, while Thomas had
the care of the negroes and wagons. The journey was made with so much
care and forethought that not a case of serious illness occurred on the
route. The white families were quartered at night, if practicable, in the

houses that they found along the way. Tents were provided for the negroes. The master himself, during the entire journey, did not sleep under a roof. The weather was perfect; no heavy rains fell during the two months. He wrapped himself in his great-coat, with sometimes the addition of a blanket, and slept all night in their midst, under one of the travelling wagons. . . .

❧ ❧ ❧

Comments concerning absentee ownership of lands in Alabama and Mississippi were frequently made. The following is from Sir Charles Lyell, *A Second Visit to the United States,* Harper and Brothers, New York, 1850, Vol. II, p. 70.

One of the evils, tending greatly to retard the progress of the southern states, is absenteeism, which is scarcely known in the North. The cheapness of land, caused by such rapid emigration to the South and West, and the frequent sales of the estates of insolvents, tempts planters to buy more land than they can manage themselves, which they must therefore give in charge to overseers. Accordingly, much of the property in Alabama belongs to rich Carolinians, and some wealthy slave-owners of Alabama have estates in Mississippi. With a view of checking the increase of these "pluralities," a tax has recently been imposed on absentees.

❧ ❧ ❧

At the time that this rapid expansion was taking place the steamboat was coming into use on the rivers, facilitating the export of cotton. Captain Basil Hall, in 1827-1828, remarked about this trade. The comment is from his *Travels in North America in the Years 1827 and 1828,* Carey, Sea and Carey, 1829, Vol. II, pp. 275-276.

On our way from Montgomery to Mobile . . . by steamboat we called at about 20 different places to take on bales of cotton. Indeed we soon found we had got completely into the country of that great staple, for nothing else seemed to be thought or talked of. Numberless persons came on board at each landing-place, some to take a passage, some merely to gossip—but whatever might be the ostensible object, cotton was the sole topic. Every flaw of wind from the shore wafted off the smell of that useful plant; at every dock or wharf we encountered it in huge piles or pyramids of bales, and our decks were soon choked up with it. All day, and almost all night long, the captain, pilot, crew, and passengers, were talking of nothing else; and sometimes our ears were so wearied with the sound of cotton! cotton! cotton! that we gladly hailed a fresh inundation of company in hopes of some change—but alas! Wiggin's Landing, or Chocktaw Creek, or the towns of Gaines, or Cahawba, or Canton, produced us nothing but fresh importations of the raw material. "What's cotton at?" was the first eager enquiry. "Ten cents." "Oh, that will never do!" From the cotton in the market, they went to the crops in the fields—the frost which had nipped their shoots —the bad times—the overtrading—and so round to the prices and prospects again and again, till I wished all the cotton in the country at the bottom of the Alabama!

⁂

By 1854 the twenty stops for cotton on the steamboat voyage from Montgomery to Mobile had been multiplied by ten, as reported by Frederick Law Olmsted in his *A Journey in the Seaboard Slave States,* Dix and Edwards, New York, 1856, p. 549.

Montgomery is a very prosperous town, with very pleasant suburbs, and a remarkably enterprising population, among which there is a considerable proportion of Northern and foreign-born business-men and mechanics.

I spent a week here very pleasantly, and then left for Mobile, on the steamboat, Fashion, a clean and well-ordered boat, with polite and obliging officers. We were two days and a half making the passage, the boat stopping at almost every bluff and landing to take on cotton, until she had a freight of nineteen hundred bales, which was built up on the guards, seven or eight tiers in height and until it reached the hurricane deck. The boat was thus brought so deep that her guards were in the water, and the ripple of the river constantly washed over them. There are two hundred landings on the Alabama river, and three hundred on the Bigby (Tombeckbee of the geographers), at which the boats advertise to call, if required, for passengers or freight. This, of course, makes the passage exceedingly tedious.

⁂

Between 1810 and 1820 Louisiana began to attract cotton planters. This vast area, ceded by Spain to France and purchased by the United States in 1803, was now a part of the public domain of the United States. That portion which became the state of Louisiana doubled its population between 1810 and 1820, and during the next decade the planters continued to pour into the country. In southern Louisiana the land which had been used by the Creoles for herding was bought at constantly rising prices because here there was no clearing to be done; the planter could put in his first crop immediately, build his house, and live without great hardship. In this area travelers noticed the prevalence of self-made planters, who were interested in horse-racing, cards, dancing, and speculation. Books and fine arts were not highly regarded, but these planters built elaborate homes, went to summer resorts, traveled in Europe, and entertained lavishly.

Many Creoles retained their plantations and their homes in New Orleans, and it was their lives and customs that our travel accounts emphasized as making that city unique and interesting. The travelers enjoyed the Creoles' love of life, their beautiful women, and their old-world characteristics.

Timothy Flint was a protestant minister from New England who worked in the
Mississippi Valley. He first approached New Orleans by river boat, visiting Natchez
and Baton Rouge. His interest in religious work is evident, as he usually described
the churches in the towns through which he journeyed. He later became Principal
of the Seminary of Rapide, Louisiana. The following account is from his *Recollections of the Last Ten Years,* Boston, 1826, pp. 284, 289, 290, 297.

Natchez is romantically situated, in two divisions. The river business is
transacted at the town "under the hill," as it is called, a repulsive place, the
centre of all that is vile, from the upper and lower country. At the proper
season a thousand boats are lying here at the landing, and the town is
full of boatmen, mulattoes, houses of ill fame, and their wretched tenants,
in short, the refuse of the world. The fiddle screaks jargon from these
faucibus orci. You see the unhappy beings dancing; and here they have
what are called "rows," which often end in murder. The town is situated
on the summit of a bluff, three hundred feet in height, from which you
look upon the cultivated strip of Concordia, on the opposite shore, in the
state of Louisiana, and the boundless and level cypress swamps beyond. On
the eastern side, the country is waving, rich and beautiful; the eminence
is crowned with neat country houses. The town itself is quiet, the streets
broad, some of the public buildings handsome, and the whole has the
appearance of comfort and opulence. It is the principal town in this
region for the shipment of cotton, with bales of which, at the proper
season, the streets are almost barricaded. Some of the planters who reside
here are opulent. I remember to have heard of a Mrs. Turner spoken of, as
possessing a great plantation, and "force," as the phrase is. The income
of the planters is, in some seasons, from ten to forty thousand dollars a
year. The Baptists, Methodists, and Presbyterians, have each a church
here. The Presbyterian church and society is large and respectable. A
stranger is kindly received by the opulent people of this town,—city, I should
say, for they call it so. It has a charming atmosphere of quietness and
repose. . . .

Below Baton Rouge the banks on both sides of the river become uniform
The levée is continuous. The cultivation of cotton, sugar cane, and rice
has become regular. The breadth of the cultivated lands is generally two
miles; a perfectly uniform strip, conforming to the shape of the river, and
every where bounding the deep forests of the Mississippi swamp with a regu
lar line. In the whole distance to New Orleans, plantation touches planta
tion. I have seen in no part of the United States such a rich and highly
cultivated tract of the same extent. It far exceeds that on the banks of
the Delaware. Noble houses, massive sugar-houses, neat summer-houses
and numerous negro villages succeed each other in such a way, that the
whole distance has the appearance of one continued village. The house

are airy and neat, some of them splendid, and in the midst of orange groves and pretty gardens, in which are the delicious cape jessamine, a flowering shrub, multitudes of altheas, bowers of the multiflora rose, and a great variety of vines and flowering shrubs, that flourish in this mild climate. . . .

One hundred miles from the mouth of the Mississippi, and something more than a thousand miles from the mouth of the Ohio, just below a sharp point of the river, is situated on its east bank, the city of New Orleans, the great commercial capital of the Mississippi Valley. The position for a commercial city is unrivalled, I believe, by any one in the world. At a proper distance from the Gulf of Mexico,—on the banks of a stream which may be said almost to water a world,—but a little distance from Lake Ponchartrain, and connected with it by a navigable canal, . . . penetrated in all directions either by *Bayous* formed by nature, or canals which cost little more trouble in making than ditches,—steamboats visiting it from fifty different shores,—possessing the immediate agriculture of its own state, the richest in America, and as rich as any in the world, with the continually increasing agriculture of the upper country, its position far surpasses that of New York itself. It has one dreary drawback—the insalubrity of its situation. Could the immense swamps between it and the bluffs be drained, and the improvements commenced in the city be completed; in short, could its atmosphere ever become a dry one, it would soon leave the great cities of the Union behind.

Great efforts are making towards this result. Unhappily, when the dog-star rises upon its sky, the yellow fever is but too sure to come in its train. Notwithstanding the annual, or at least the biennial visits of this pestilence; although its besom sweeps off multitudes of unacclimated poor, and compels the rich to fly; notwithstanding the terror, that is everywhere associated with the name of the city, it is advancing in population. When I visit the city, after the absence of a season, I discover an obvious change. New Buildings have sprung up, and new improvements are going on. Its regular winter population, between forty and fifty thousand inhabitants, is five times the amount which it had, when it came under the American government. The external form of the city on the river side is graduated in some measure to the curve of the river. The street that passes the levée, and conforms to the course of the river, is called Levée street, and is the one in which the greatest and most active business of the city is transacted. The upper part of the city is principally built and inhabited by Americans, and is called the "fauxbourg St. Mary." The greater number of the houses in this fauxbourg are of brick, and built in the American style. . . . The ancient part of the city, as you pass down Levéé street towards the Cathedral, has in one of the clear, bright January mornings, that are so common at that season, an imposing and brilliant aspect. There is something fantastic and unique in the appearance, I am told, far more resembling European cities, than any other in the United States. The houses are stuccoed externally, and this stucco is white or yellow, and strikes the eye more pleasantly than the dull and sombre red of brick. . . .

The streets are broad, and the plan of the city is perfectly rectangular and uniform. There are in the limits of the city three malls, or parade grounds, of no great extent, and not yet sufficiently shaded, though young trees are growing in them. They serve as parade grounds, and in the winter have a beautiful carpet of clover, of a most brilliant green.

Its most conspicuous public buildings, are the cathedral, the Presbyterian church, the charity hospital, and the New Orleans college. The cathedral, to me who profess to know nothing of architecture, is a most imposing fabric, not so much from its size, as its structure, the massiveness of its walls, and within, its wonderful adaptation in my mind to excite religious feelings. Under its stone pavements are deposited the illustrious dead. In niches and recesses are figures of the saints, in their appropriate dress, and with those pale and unearthly countenances that are so fully in keeping with the ideal image which I have formed of them. . . .

This city exhibits the greatest variety of costume, and foreigners; French, Spanish, Portuguese, Irish in shoals, in short, samples of the common people of all the European nations, Creoles, all the intermixtures of Negro and Indian blood, the moody and ruminating Indians, the inhabitants of the Spanish provinces, and a goodly woof to this warp, of boatmen, "half horse and half alligator"; and more languages are spoken here than in any other town in America. There is a sample, in short, of every thing. In March the town is most filled; the market shows to the greatest advantage; the citizens boast of it, and are impressed with the opinion that it surpasses any other. In effect, this is the point of union between the North and the South. The productions of all climes find their way hither, and for fruits and vegetables, it appears to me to be unrivalled. In a pleasant March forenoon, you see, perhaps, half the city here. The crowd covers half a mile in extent. The negroes, mulattoes, French, Spanish, Germans, are all crying their several articles in their several tongues. They have a wonderful faculty of twanging the sound through their noses, as shrill as the notes of a trumpet. In the midst of this Babel trumpeting, "un picalion, un picalion," is the most distinguishable tune.

ノ   ノ   ノ

The alluvial lands of the Red River in Louisiana were made available to cotton planters when the United States government in 1833 removed a huge raft 128 miles or more in length which had obstructed navigation. In 1839 the Indians were removed from the areas above the raft, and the land was immediately sought by cotton planters. The following experiences are taken from a story which appeared, unsigned, in *Blackwood's Edinburgh Magazine,* Vol. 56, 1844, p. 640.

It was just nine years and two months since I had first come into possession of my "freehold of these United States," as the papers specified it.
Five thousand dollars had procured me the honour of becoming a Louisi-
anian planter; upon the occurrence of which event, I was greeted by my
friends and acquaintances as the luckiest of men. There were two thousand acres, "with due allowance for fences and roads," according to the
usual formula; and the wood alone, if I might believe what was told me,
was well worth twenty thousand dollars. For the preceding six months,
the whole of the western press had been praising the Red River territory
to the very skies; it was an incomparable sugar and cotton ground, full
sixteen feet deep of river slime—Egypt was a sandy desert compared to
it—and as to the climate, the zephyrs that disported themselves there
were only to be paralleled in Eldorado and Arcadia. I like a ninny as I was,
although fully aware of the puffing propensities of our newspaper editors,
especially when their tongues, or rather pens, have been oiled by a few
handfuls of dollars, fell into the trap, and purchased land in the fever-
hole in question, where I was assured that a habitable house and two negro
huts were already built and awaiting me. The improvements alone, the
land speculator was ready to take his oath, were worth every cent of two
thousand dollars. In short, I concluded my blind bargain, and in the
month of June, prepared to visit my estate. . . .

I had four negroes with me, including old Sybille, who was at that
time full sixty-five years of age; Caesar, Tiberius, and Vitellius, were the
three others. We are fond of giving our horses and negroes these high sound-
ing appilations, as a sort of warning, I am inclined to think, to those
amongst us who sit in high places; for even in our young republic there is
no lack of would-be Caesars.

[Because of the annual scourge of yellow fever] the steamers had left
off running below Baton Rouge, so I resolved to leave my gig at New
Orleans, procuring in its stead a sort of dearborn or railed cart, in which I
packed the whole of my traps, consisting of a medley of blankets and
axes, harrows and ploughshares, cotton shirts and cooking utensils. Upon
the top of all this I perched myself; and those who had known me only
three or four months previously as the gay and fashionable Mr. Howard,
one of the leaders of the *ton,* the deviser and proposer of fetes, balls, and
gaieties of all kinds, might well have laughed, could they have seen me
half buried amongst pots and pans, bottles and bundles, spades and mat-
tocks, and suchlike useful but homely instruments. . . . Our town beauties
—ay, the most fashionable and elegant of them—think nothing of install-
ing themselves, with their newly wedded husbands, in the aforesaid dear-
borns, and moving off to the far west, leaving behind them all the comforts and luxuries among which they have been brought up. Whoever
travels in our backwoods, will often come across scenes and interiors such
as the boldest romance writer would never dare to invent. Newly married

couples, whose childhood and youth have been spent in the enjoyment of all the superfluities of civilization, will buy a piece of good land far in the depths of forests and prairies, and found a new existence for themselves and their children. One meets with their dwellings in abundance—log-houses, consisting for the most part of one room and a small kitchen: on the walls of the former the horses' saddles and harness, and the husband's working clothes, manufactured often by the delicate hands of his lady; in one corner a harp or piano; on the table, perhaps, a few numbers of the North American or Southern reviews, and some Washington or New York papers. A strange mixture of wild and civilized life. It is thus that our Johnsons, our Livingstons, and Ranselaers, and hundreds, ay, thousands of families, our Jeffersons and Washingtons commenced; and truly it is to be hoped, that the rising generation will not despise the custom of their forefathers, or reject this healthy means of renovating the blood and vigour of the community.

[At the end of the third day we reached Baton Rouge] and the following morning we started for the Red River in the steamboat Clayborne. By nightfall we reached my domain. . . .

. . . what I exclaimed, I am sure I do not remember; but I know that my hair stood on end, when I beheld for the first time, the so-called improvements on my new property. The habitable and comfortable house was a species of pigsty, built out of the rough branches of trees, without doors, windows, or roof. There was I to dwell, and in a season when the thermometer was ranging between ninety-five and a hundred degrees. The very badness of things, however, stimulated us to exertion; we set to work and in two days had built a couple of very decent huts, the only inconvenience of which was, that when it rained hard we were obliged to take refuge under a neighbouring cotton-tree. Fortunately, out of the two thousand acres, there really were fifty in a state of cultivation, and that helped us. I planted and kept house as well as I could; in the daytime I ploughed and sowed; and in the evening I mended harness and the holes in my inexpressibles. With society I was little troubled, seeing that my nearest neighbour lived five-and-twenty miles off. The first summer passed in this manner; the second was a little better; and the third still—until at last the way of life became endurable.

⁕   ⁕   ⁕

The rapid expansion of the 1830's brought into cultivation the west bank of the Mississippi River, in Arkansas, and pioneer life developed there along the patterns established three decades earlier in Tennessee and Kentucky. George W. Featherstonehaugh, in his *Excursion Through the Slave States,* John Murray, London, 1844, Vol. I, p. 335, described this way of life.

All these settlers are, in fact, drawn from the poorest classes of Tennessee, Kentucky, and Louisiana. Where they are agriculturists they are hard-working, enterprising men, always busy, fencing, ploughing, chopping timber, setting traps for the wolves, hunting the panthers that destroy their swine, and are continually occupied without a moment's relaxation. With them the ceremony of eating is an affair of a few moments; the grand object is to fill the stomach as quick as possible with the usual food; this from long habit they prefer to anything else, and the women having got into a daily routine without any motive for changing it in the slightest degree, and, indeed, without even suspecting that it would be agreeable to anybody to do so, go on preparing the same disgusting coffee, pork, bread and butter, three times a day, as long as they live.

If the settler is merely a hunter and a squatter, you find a poor cabin and no farm, a cow perhaps that comes in from the woods once every two or three days to get a little salt, and that then only give a teacup of milk. But in most cases when you arrive, the owner of the mansion is not at home, and in his place you find six or seven ragged wild-looking imps, and a skinny, burnt up dirty female, who tells you that he "is gone to help a neighbor to hunt up an old painter that's been arter all the pigs; he ain't been hum in a week, and I reckon he's stopt somewhar to help shuck corn (the stripping the maize from the husk when it is ripe): we han't got nothing in the house but a little corn that I pounds as I uses it, and a couple of racoons jist to sarve us till he gits back." The corn they consume is paid for in deer-skins, and the heavier debts of the squatter he literally liquidates with bears' oil. If he has to negotiate the purchase of a horse to the amount of 50 dollars, the items of the appropriation are as follows: On or before Christmas he is "to turn in" 15 gallons of bar (bear) oil, the current value of which is one dollar per gallon; twelve deer-skins at 75 cents each; then he is to go with a "negur" to Big Swamp to help "hunt up" some young horses that were taken there six months ago to pasture, and is to have a dollar a day for that service; and as to the rest he "is to git along with it somehaw or other."

This curious bargain I took down from the mouth of one of these fellows who had been born in the woods, had never even been in a village, and knew nothing of the arts and customs of society.

✦   ✦   ✦

A somewhat idealistic view of a cotton plantation was given in an article by T. B. Thorpe, "Cotton and Its Cultivation," in *Harper's New Monthly Magazine,* New York, 1850-, Vol. 8, March, 1854, pp. 452-456.

The cotton region, extending as it does over more than two thirds of the geographical division of the Union, possesses therefore every variety of scenery, and, consequently, cotton plantations, unlike sugar estates, are made picturesque by the combinations of hill and dale. Some favorite site, which commands a view of the surrounding country, is generally chosen for the "residence," while a gushing stream hard by will form the nucleus of the "quarters." The roads follow the favorable suggestion of the surface of the country, and, of course, wind pleasantly through the cultivated fields and untouched woodland.

The preparations for planting cotton begin in January; at this time the fields are covered with the dry and standing stalks of the "last year's crop." The first care of the planter is to "clean up" for plowing. To do this, the "hands" commence by breaking down the cotton stalks with a heavy club, or pulling them up by the roots. These stalks are then gathered into piles, and at nightfall set on fire. This labor, together with "housing the corn," repairing fences and farming implements, consume the time up to the middle of March or the beginning of April, when the plow for the "next crop" begins its work. First, the "water furrows" are run from five to six feet apart, and made by a heavy plow, drawn either by a team of oxen or mules. This labor, as it will be perceived, makes the surface of the ground in ridges, in the centre of which is next run a light plow, making what is termed "the drill," or depository of the seed: a girl follows the light plow, carrying in her apron the cotton seed, which she profusely scatters in the newly-made drill; behind this sower follows "the harrow," and by these various labors the planting is temporarily completed.

From two to three bushels of cotton seed are necessary to plant an acre of ground; the quantity used, however, is but of little consequence, unless the seed is imported, for the annual amount collected at the gin-house is enormous, and the surplus, after planting, is either left to rot, to be eaten by the cattle, or scattered upon the fields for manure.

If the weather be favorable, the young plant is discovered making its way through in six or ten days, and the "scraping" of the crop, as it is termed, now begins. A light plow is again called into requisition, which is run along the drill, throwing the *earth away from the plant:* Then come the laborers with their hoes, who dexterously cut away the superabundant shoots and the intruding weeds, and leave a single cotton-plant in little hills generally two feet apart.

Of all the labors of the field, the dexterity displayed by the negroes in "scraping cotton" is most calculated to call forth the admiration of the novice spectator. The hoe is a rude instrument, however well made and handled; the young cotton-plant is as delicate as vegetation can be, and springs up in lines of solid masses, composed of hundreds of plants. The field-hand, however, will single one delicate shoot from the surrounding multitude, and with his rude hoe he will trim away the remainder with all the boldness of touch of a master, leaving the incipient stalk unharmed and alone in its glory; and at nightfall you can look along the extending rows, and find the plants correct in line, and of the required distance of separation from each other.

The planter, who can look over his field in early spring, and find his cotton "cleanly scraped" and his "stand" good, is fortunate; still, the vicissitudes attending the cultivation of the crop have only commenced. Many rows, from the operations of the "cut-worm" and from multitudinous causes unknown, have to be replanted, and an unusually late frost may destroy all his labors, and compel him to commence again. But, if no untoward accident occurs, in two weeks after the "scraping," another hoeing takes place, at which time the plow throws the furrow *on to the roots* of the now strengthening plant, and the increasing heat of the sun also justifying the sinking of the roots deeper in the earth. The pleasant month of May is now drawing to a close, and vegetation of all kinds is struggling for precedence in the fields. Grasses and weeds of every variety, with vines and wild flowers, luxuriate in the newly-turned sod, and seem to be determined to choke out of existence the useful and still delicately-grown cotton.

It is a season of unusual industry on the cotton plantations, and woe to the planter who is outstripped in his labors, and finds himself "overtaken by the grass." The plow tears up the surplus vegetation, and the hoe tops it off in its luxuriance. The race is a hard one, but industry conquers; and when the third working over of the crop takes place, the cotton plant, so much cherished and favored, begins to over-top its rivals in the fields— begins to cast a *chilling shade of superiority* over its now intimidated groundlings, and commences to reign supreme.

Through the month of July, the crop is wrought over for the last time; the plant, heretofore of slow growth, now makes rapid advances toward perfection. The plow and hoe are still in requisition. The "water furrows" between the cotton rows are deepened, leaving the cotton growing as it were upon a slight ridge; this accomplished, the crop is prepared for the "rainy season," should it ensue, and so far advanced that it is, under any circumstances, beyond the control of art. Nature must now have its sway.

On some plantations there is no "overseer"; the owner manages his place with the help of a skillful and trustworthy negro, termed the "driver." These drivers are very ambitious, and are, like their masters, exceedingly sensitive if a stranger, or other disinterested person, gives an unfavorable opinion of the general appearance of the crop under their management. If much grass is seen in the cotton field, it is supposed to be an unfavorable testimony of the industry or skill of the driver. Upon a certain occasion, a gentleman riding along a cotton field remarked to the negro manager, "You have a good deal of grass in your crop." The negro felt mortified, and, anxious to break the force of the insinuation, coolly replied, "It is poor ground, master, that won't bring grass." The finest intellect could not, under the circumstances, have said a better thing.

The "cotton bloom," under the matured sun of July, begins to make its appearance. The announcement of the "first blossom" of the neighborhood is a matter of general interest; it is the unfailing approach of the busy season of fall; it is the evidence that soon the labor of man will, under a kind Providence, receive its reward.

It should perhaps here be remarked, that the color of cotton in its perfection is precisely that of the blossom—a beautiful light, but warm cream color. In buying cotton cloth, the "bleached" and "unbleached" are preceptibly different qualities to the most casual observer; but the dark hues and harsh look of the "unbleached domestic" comes from the handling of the artisan and the soot of machinery. If cotton, pure as it looks in the field, could be wrought into fabrics, they would have a brilliancy and beauty never yet accorded to any other material in its natural or artificial state. . . .

. . . The size of the cotton-plant depends upon the accident of climate and soil. The cotton of Tennessee bears very little resemblance to the luxuriant growth of Alabama and Georgia; but even in those favored states the cotton-plant is not every where the same, for in the rich bottom lands it grows to a commanding size, while in the more barren regions it is an humble shrub. In the rich alluvium of Mississippi the cotton will tower beyond the reach of the tallest "picker," and a single plant will contain hundreds of perfect "bolls"; in the neighboring "piney-woods" it lifts its humble head scarcely above the knee, and is proportionably meagre in its produce of fruit.

The growing cotton is particularly liable to accidents, and suffers immensely in "wet seasons" from the "rust" and "rot." The first named affects the leaves, giving them a brown and deadened tinge, and frequently causes them to crumble away. The "rot" attacks the "boll." It commences with a black spot on the rind, which increasing, seems to produce fermentation and decay. Worms find their way to the roots; the caterpillar eats into the "boll" and destroys the staple. It would be almost impossible to enumerate all the evils the cotton-plant is heir to, all of which, however, sink into nothingness compared with the scourge of the "army-worm." . . . We once witnessed the invasion of the army-worm, as it attempted to pass from a desolated cotton-field to one untouched. Between these two fields was a wide ditch, which had been deepened, to prove a barrier to the onward march of the worm. Down the perpendicular sides of the trench the caterpillars rolled in untold millions, until its bottom, for nearly a mile in extent, was a foot or two deep in a living mass of animal life. . . .

The season of cotton picking commences in the latter part of July, and continues without intermission to the Christmas holidays. . . . The field hands are each supplied with a basket and bag. The basket is left at the head of the "cotton-rows"; the bag is suspended from the "picker's" neck by a strap, and is used to hold the cotton as it is taken from the boll. When the bag is filled it is emptied into the basket, and this routine is continued through the day. Each hand picks from two hundred and fifty to three hundred pounds of "seed cotton" each day, though some negroes of extraordinary ability go beyond this amount.

If the weather be very fine, the cotton is carried from the field direct to the packing-house; but generally it is first spread out on scaffolds, where it is left to dry, and picked clean of any "trash" that may be perceived mixed up with the cotton. Among the most characteristic scenes of plantation life is the returning of the hands at nightfall from the field, with their well-filled baskets of cotton upon their heads. Falling unconsciously "into line," the stoutest leading the way, they move along in the dim twilight of a winter day with the quietness of spirits rather than human beings.

The "packing-room" is the loft of the gin-house, and is over the gin-stand. By this arrangement the cotton is conveniently shoved down a causeway into the "gin-hopper." . . . With constant attention, a gin-stand, impelled by four mules, will work out four bales of four hundred and fifty pounds each a day; but this is more than the average amount. Upon large plantations the steam-engine is brought into requisition, which, carrying any number of gins required, will turn out the necessary number of bales per day.

The *baling* of the cotton ends the labor of its production on the plantation. The power which is used to accomplish this end is generally a single but powerful screw. The ginned cotton is thrown from the packing-room down into a reservoir or press, which, being filled, is tramped down by the negroes engaged in the business. When a sufficient quantity has been forced by "foot labor" into the press, the upper door is shut down, and the screw is applied, worked by horse. By this process the staple becomes almost as solid a mass as stone. By previous arrangement, strong Kentucky bagging has been so placed as to cover the upper and lower side of the pressed cotton. Ropes are now passed round the whole and secured by a knot; a long needle and a piece of twine closes up the openings in the bagging; the screw is then run up, the cotton swells with tremendous power inside of its ribs of ropes—the baling is completed, and the cotton is ready for shipment to any part of the world.

ɉ　　　ɉ　　　ɉ

The mass of ordinary farmers had no slaves and farmed under 200 acres of land; almost half of the slave-holders owned less than five slaves. Mark Twain gave us a description of a "one-horse cotton plantation" in *The Adventures of Huckleberry Finn,* C. L. Webster and Company, New York, 1885, 1899 edition, pp. 284-285.

Phelps' was one of these little one-horse cotton plantations, and they all look alike. A rail fence round a two-acre yard; a stile made out of logs sawed off and up-ended in steps, like barrels of a different length, to climb over the fence with, and for the women to stand on when they are going to jump on to a horse; some sickly grass-patches in the big yard, but mostly it was bare and smooth, like an old hat with the nap rubbed off;

big double log-house for the white folks—hewed logs, with the chinks stopped up with mud or mortar, and these mud-stripes had been white-washed some time or another; round-log kitchen, with a big broad, open but roofed passage joining it to the house; log smokehouse back of the kitchen; three little log nigger-cabins in a row t'other side of the smoke-house; one little hut all by itself away down against the back fence, and some outbuildings down a piece the other side; ash-hopper and big kettle to bile soap in by the little hut; bench by the kitchen door, with bucket of water and a gourd; hound asleep there in the sun; more hounds asleep round about; about three shade trees away off in a corner; some currant bushes and gooseberry bushes in one place by the fence; outside of the fence a garden and a watermelon patch; then the cotton fields begin, and after the fields the woods.

✓   ✓   ✓

The majority of Southern planters did not conserve their soil, because labor was expensive and land was cheap. One slave's labor would produce more cotton or tobacco on new land than on worn-out soil; consequently the planters made frequent moves in search of new, fertile plantations. Yet some of the planters studied scientific agriculture and introduced new ideas to rehabilitate their lands. Leaders were George Washington, Thomas Jefferson, John Taylor of Caroline, and, a generation later, Edmund Ruffin of Virginia. An agricultural revolution in the upper South in the 1830's was aided by the establishment of agricultural fairs and farm magazines. Sir Charles Lyell, in *A Second Visit to the United States,* Harper and Brothers, New York, 1850, Vol. I, p. 207, observed signs of the new era in Virginia.

The whites who live west of the Blue Ridge are about equal in number to those who live east of it; but the eastern division, or lower country, owns a greater number of slaves, and in the right of them has more votes. The western men are talking loudly of a convention to place them on a more equal footing, some even desiring a separation into two states. There has also been a suggestion that it might be well to allow a single county to declare itself free, without waiting for the emancipation of others. Among other signs of approaching change, I am told that several new settlers from the north have made a practical demonstration that slave labor is less profitable, even east of the Blue Ridge, than that of free whites. As we sailed down the Potomac from Washington, a landed proprie-tor of Fairfax County pointed out to me some estates in Virginia, on the right bank of the river, in which free had been substituted for slave labor since I was here in 1841. Some farmers came from New Hampshire and Connecticut, and, having bought the land at five dollars an acre, tilled it with their own hands and those of their family, aided in some cases by a few hired whites. To the astonishment of the surrounding planters, be-fore the end of four years, they had raised the value of the soil from five to forty dollars per acre, having introduced for the first time a rotation of corn and green crops, instead of first exhausting the soil, and then letting it lie fallow for years to recover itself. They have also escaped the ruinous expense of feeding large bodies of negroes in those seasons when the harvest is deficient.

✓   ✓   ✓

Some of the plantations in the newer Southwestern states were operated scientifically. Solon Robinson, a Northern agricultural writer, visited an exemplary plantation in Mississippi. The following description is from his "Notes of Travel in the Southwest," No. VII, from *The Cultivator*, Vol. II (Oct. 1845), pp. 303-4, and quoted in Albert Lowther Demaree, *The American Agricultural Press*, Columbia University Press, New York, 1941, p. 284.

I visited . . . the plantation of Captain Wm. Eggleston, of Holmes county, who is one of the good farmers of Mississippi. He is a Virginian from Amelia county. . . .

The 17th of February was an uncomfortably warm day. The peas in Captain E.'s garden several inches high, lettuce in full head, and other things in proportion. Captain Eggleston has about 1,400 acres of land under cultivation, and upon which live 20 whites, and 150 blacks, 70 of which are field hands; about one-third of his land is kept in corn and oats, the proportion of corn being as two to one. He keeps up a continued rotation of crops, and puts all the manure that he can upon the corn, which averages about 25 to 30 bushels to the acre; plants corn and sows oats in February. He is now working 43 mules and horses, and 28 oxen, and makes 560 bales a year, which he has to haul 10 or 12 miles. He also raises all the grain and meat required upon the plantation, feeding his negroes at the rate of 3½ lbs. clear bacon per head per week, with about a peck and a half of corn meal, besides vegetables and fruit, melons, &c. . . . he gets his flour from Virginia, and asserts that no other will keep well through the summer.

I saw in his garden some fine fig trees, which as far north as this produce remarkably well. Peaches are unfailing, but with grapes he has not been successful. . . . And now a word of Captain Eggleston's system of cultivation. His place is all hilly, thin, oak land, very light soil, that melts away in water not *quite* as easy as salt or sugar; and yet he has scarcely a gully upon the whole farm; but he has more than 20 miles of side hill ditches, which are so constructed that they take up all the surface water before it passes far enough over the ground to form gullies. . . .

Leaving Captain Eggleston on the 18th, the first plantation I passed was one that once had been a very fine one, of comparative level and rich soil, now in utter ruins: Cause—debt, law and taxes. Fences, buildings and lands all in ruins; the former rotted and fallen down, and the latter gullied away.

✓   ✓   ✓

The panic of 1837 brought bankruptcy to many southern planters. Texas, which drew off the Mexican yoke and became an independent republic in 1836, was a land of opportunity. Mr. J. A. Orr, in "A Trip from Houston to Jackson, Mississippi, in 1845," *Mississippi Historical Society Publications,* 1898-1914, Jackson, Vol. IX, pp. 175-176, described the exodus from Mississippi to Texas during the depression.

It is a beautiful and fertile country through Holmes, Yazoo, and Madison Counties. . . . Many plantations had been recently opened, prior to 1837 and on some of them elegant residences had been erected. The owners had freely endorsed for each other in the banks, and hundreds of thousands of dollars had been invested in negroes, brought from Virginia and the Carolinas. When the storm broke over the banks the suits were so numerous in the courts that some of the lawyers had their declarations in *assumpsit* printed by the quire, leaving blanks only for the names of the debtor, creditor, and the amounts. In each of these counties an immense number of judgments had been obtained and the aggregate indebtedness had run into millions. A great number of these plantations in 1845 were uncultivated. The fences had fallen down, the homes and outhouses were tenantless and bespoke widespread desolation. We learned the history of the times from lawyers at Lexington, Yazoo City, and Canton. . . . We were told that as a general thing on the evening before abandonment these large plantations would present no unusual appearance. The stock would be in the stables, properly attended to; the cows would be in the cowpen; the hogs would be called and fed; the sheep would be herded; the plantation negroes would be in their proper place, and over all the hush of evening and the stillness of night would fall. On the morning following the smoke would curl from the chimneys, from residence and quarters, the cows would be lowing in the pen, the sheep bleating in the fold, the hogs in their place; not a wagon gone, not a vehicle missing; the meat left in the smokehouse, the poultry raising their usual disturbance—and not a human being, nor horse, nor mule, nor saddle, nor bridle on the whole place. Every negro, every horse, every mule spirited away in the darkness of the night—the negro women and children on horses and mules, the men on foot, all, all, in a double-quick march for Texas, then a foreign government. The first object was to get across the county line, the next to cross the Mississippi River, and the next to cross the line of the Republic of Texas. All this had to be done before the executions could issue and be placed in the hands of the sheriffs of the different counties. Family carriages were left motionless to avoid creating any suspicion, the white families having taken their trips to neighboring towns, where the stage lines would convey them to points of safety—generally steamboat landings on the Mississippi—on their way to Texas.

Between 1840 and 1860 the Texas immigration reached fever stage, as described by Sir Charles Lyell in *A Second Visit to the United States,* Harper and Brothers, New York, 1850, Vol. II, pp. 55-56, and Vol. I, p. 209.

The morning after our arrival at Claiborne, [Alabama,] we found at the inn a family of "movers" on their way to Texas, sitting in the verandah enjoying the warm sunshine after a shower of rain. . . .

The movers, who were going to Texas, had come down 200 miles from the upper country of Alabama, and were waiting for some others of their kindred who were to follow them with their heavy wagons. One of these families is carrying no less than forty negroes, and the cheerfulness with which these slaves are going, they know not where, with their owners, notwithstanding their usual dislike to quit the place they have been brought up in, shows a strong bond of union between the master and "his people." In the last fifteen months 1300 whites, and twice that number of slaves, have quitted Alabama for Texas and Arkansas, and they tell me that Monroe County has lost 1500 inhabitants. "Much capital," said one of my informants, "is leaving this state, and no wonder; for if we remain here, we are reduced to the alternative of high taxes to pay the interest on money so improvidently borrowed from England, or to suffer the disgrace of repudiation, which would be doubly shameful, because the money was received in hard cash, and lent out, often rashly, by the state, to farmers for agricultural improvements. Besides," he added, "all the expenses of Government were in reality defrayed during several years by borrowed money, and the burthen of debt thrown on posterity. The facility with which your English capitalists, in 1821, lent their cash to a state from which the Indians were not yet expelled, without reflecting on the migratory nature of the white population, is astonishing! The planters who got grants of your money, and spent it, have nearly all of them moved off and settled beyond the Mississippi. . . . ."

Texas prolongs the duration of negro slavery in Virginia, aggravating one of its worst consequences, the internal slave trade, and keeping up the price of negroes at home. They are now selling for 500, 750, and 1000 dollars each, according to their qualifications. There are always dealers at Richmond, whose business it is to collect slaves for the southern market; and, until a gang is ready to start for the south, they are kept here well fed, and as cheerful as possible. In a court of the jail, where they are lodged, I see them every day amusing themselves by playing at quoits. How much this traffic is abhorred, even by those who encourage it, is shown by the low social position held by the dealer, even when he has made a large fortune. When they conduct gangs of fifty slaves at a time across the mountains to the Ohio river, they usually manacle some of the men, but on reaching the Ohio river, they no longer have any fear of their attempting an escape, and they then unshackle them.

7

Southern Society

By 1860 the South had over 12,000,000 people, all kinds of people, white, black, Indians; Americans of Anglo-Saxon, German, Scotch, Irish, French, Spanish and Swiss stock, but mostly descendants of Northern Europeans, and mostly several generations removed from their European origin, because after 1800 not many immigrants came into the South. Some of the people were of the gentry; some were ambitious, hard-working farmers, as neat and orderly in their farming methods as their wives were in their housekeeping; others were shiftless and aimless because they could easily gain a living without hard work. Some lived on land so poor that they lived very meagerly; some lived in areas so isolated that they lost contact with the outside world, and for them progress stood still. Travelers in the South commented on these conditions and readers of travel books came to think of the South in terms of extremes, the very rich and the very poor. But in fact the majority of Southern people were neither rich nor poor, but just comfortable.

It is customary in discussing the people of the Old South to divide the population into social classes. While such classification is entirely artificial because there were no actual class lines, the device enables us to describe the ways of life of some of the people.

Randolph Abbott Shotwell, the author of the following sketch, was the son of a minister who accepted a charge in North Carolina at about the beginning of the Civil War. Young Shotwell fought in the Confederate army and then went to Rutherfordton, North Carolina, to settle while recovering from fever and ague. Purchasing the fragments of a printing office, he published the weekly *Western Vindicator*. *The Papers of Randolph Abbott Shotwell*, edited by J. G. de Roulhac Hamilton, Raleigh, the North Carolina Department of Archives and History, 1931, pp. 279-297, *passim*, contained this description, reprinted here by the permission of the publishers.

In many respects the inhabitants of this magnificent [region] are as rugged, and uncultured as its corrugated mountain crags. Yet, the diversity

Sketch by Captain Basil Hall with the Camera Lucinda. This etching represents the town of Columbus, Georgia, before the advertised sale of lots.

Ellerslie Plantation in Louisiana, as it appears today.

of population is as great as between the sterile "ridge-barrens" and the alluvial river bottoms, with loam four feet deep. There are classes of society that seem a distinct race of people. Whole sections will be covered with log-cabin dwellers who own only a few, worthless acres, showing the red-clay seams of long washing of the rains without cultivation or care; thriftless, uneducated beings, who live little better than negroes—in rude log huts, "chinked" with clay, and lighted by the door, and perhaps a square hole with clap-board shutters, but no glass—warmed by a huge fire-place —filling the whole end of the single room, and surmounted by a ragged stone, or wood and plaster, chimney; while the only furniture consists of a bed, two or three slab stools, a pine table, a box cup-board nailed against the wall, a string of red peppers hanging, with a few small bags of "yarbs" and simples from the rafters, a frying pan, and flat bake-oven on the hearth, a wash tub, and a couple of gourds dangling from a pole! . . . The small patches of garden truck, with hunting and fishing and an occasional day's work, for more energetic neighbors serves to supply the family with food; the women spin, weave, and make all their clothes, and the family do not see as much as $20 in money all the year. There are, I say, whole sections peopled in such style and I have drawn no exaggerated picture I am sorry to say! Yet it may be a few miles farther on brings us to a handsome brick mansion with a number of outhouses, barns, cattle yard, etc.: and every indication of cultivated comfort. Stopping here we have our horse carried to the stables by a servant and we are shown into a neatly furnished parlor with its piano, pictures, books, periodicals, etc., etc. Inquiring further, we find that these people are well-informed, and in appearance as well as in style of living, are entirely different from the others.

Nowhere is this disparity of social circumstances so marked, and so well-recognized, as in the Rutherford region. Owing to peculiar location of the counties of Rutherford and Polk, they are almost isolated from railway and mail facilities. A boy driving a blind mule, in a shackling buggy, which stopped by the wayside on nearly every trip, brought a mail from Cherryville—36 miles distant—twice-a-week; and this very uncertain route often interrupted by freshets, accidents, drunkenness of the carrier, or failure of the wheezy old engines on the railroad to arrive at Cherryville, furnished the only regular communication with the exterior world.

But the social and educational differences in Rutherford were due mainly to the unusual diversity in wealth. In the village of Rutherfordton, and along the alluvial "bottoms," or margins of the streams, were many families of wealth, intelligence, and cultivation.

They were generally ex-slave-holders . . . who possessed the means to educate their children at distant schools; and though greatly impoverished by the war, still owned large tracts of land, or other property which enabled them to preserve a semblance of former comfort. To these must be added the professional gentry—lawyers, physicians, clergymen, and some others; the whole comprising an intelligent, genteel class, as distinct from the majority as a separate race. These families of whom there are perhaps 100 in Rutherford, in many cases intermarried until there are few that have not some claim of kinship or connectionship. All of this class were true as steel to the South during the War, and in no single instance that I am aware of have since deserted the faith for which we fought.

In addition to these there were some one or two hundred families of less property, and less education, who lived in considerable comfort having substantial frame, or log-covered, dwellings, and having reputation for respectability and "good-living." The majority of these were Democrats or Conservatives, after the war; but here and there a family would lean to-ward Radicalism through the mis-guidance of the Logan influence. Still lower in the scale of wealth, refinement, and social recognition, were the majority; the "one-horse croppers," the farm-laborers, tenants, and idlers —living in little log cabins out in barren "old fields," or on the wooded side-hills, owning neither land, nor property—ignorant of even the first rudiments of education—scarce able to tell you the name of the capital of the State—and wholly unable to give any account of the outside world. . . . As a branch of this class are the illicit-distillers—who frequent the wildest woodlands, and plant their two or three gallon still worms upon the most secluded portion of the innumerable rivulets that rattle across the country from the foot of the mountain ranges. . . .

✓   ✓   ✓

The Southern aristocracy was not a closed society. Indentured servants, pioneer farmers, and merchants succeeded in entering this group by marriage or by growing up with the group in a newly developing area. If they did not at first possess the high degree of culture which is usually attributed to the Southern gentry, succeeding generations could acquire it through education, association, and travel.

In illustrating the life of this group, excerpts from a number of sources have been pieced together to form a composite picture. Some were written in the eighteenth century and others in the middle of the nineteenth. Such disregard for the continuity of time may be excused on the grounds that the South was a land of tradition and that many of the same ideals and customs were observed during the entire ante-bellum period.

John Pendleton Kennedy, under the pseudonym of "Mark Littleton," published a series of sketches entitled *Swallow Barn,* Carey, Philadelphia, 1832, one of the first fictional presentations of the Southern country gentleman and the plantation tradition. The following excerpt is from Chapter II.

Swallow Barn is an aristocratic old edifice which sits, like a brooding hen, on the southern bank of the James River. . . . The master of this lordly domain is Frank Meriwether. He is now in the meridian of life—

somewhere about forty-five. Good cheer and an easy temper tell well upon him. The first has given him a comfortable, portly figure, and the latter a contemplative turn of mind, which inclines him to be lazy and philosophical.

He has some right to pride himself on his personal appearance, for he has a handsome face, with a dark blue eye and a fine intellectual brow. His head is growing scant of hair on the crown, which induces him to be somewhat particular in the management of his locks in that locality, and these are assuming a decided silvery hue.

It is pleasant to see him when he is going to ride to the Court House on business occasions. He is then apt to make his appearance in a coat of blue broadcloth, astonishingly glossy, and with an unusual amount of plaited ruffle strutting through the folds of a Marseilles waistcoat. A worshipful finish is given to this costume by a large straw hat, lined with green silk. There is a magisterial fulness in his garments which betokens condition in the world, and a heavy bunch of seals, suspended by a chain of gold, jingles as he moves, pronouncing him a man of superfluities.

It is considered rather extraordinary that he has never set up for Congress: but the truth is, he is an unambitious man, and has a great dislike to currying favor—as he calls it. . . . He has of late embarked on the millpond of county affairs, and notwithstanding his amiable character and his doctrinary republicanism, I am told he keeps the peace as if he commanded a garrison, and administers justice like a Cadi.

He has some claim to supremacy in this last department; for during three years he smoked segars in a lawyer's office in Richmond, which enabled him to obtain a bird's-eye view of Blackstone and the Revised Code. Besides this, he was a member of a Law Debating Society, which ate oysters once a week in a cellar; and he wore, in accordance with the usage of the most promising law students of that day, six cravats, one over the other, and yellow-topped boots, by which he was recognized as a blood of the metropolis. Having in this way qualified himself to assert and maintain his rights, he came to his estate, upon his arrival at age, a very model of landed gentlemen. Since that time his avocations have had a certain literary tincture; for having settled himself down as a married man, and got rid of his superfluous foppery, he rambled with wonderful assiduity through a wilderness of romances, poems, and dissertations, which are now collected in his library, and with their battered blue covers, present a lively type of an army of continentals at the close of the war, or a hospital of invalids. These have all, at last, given way to the newspapers—a miscellaneous study very attractive and engrossing to country gentlemen. This line of study has rendered Meriwether a most perilous antagonist in the matter of legislative proceedings.

A landed proprietor, with a good house and a host of servants, is naturally a hospitable man. A guest is one of his daily wants. A friendly face is a necessary of life, without which the heart is apt to starve, or a luxury without which it grows parsimonious. Men who are isolated from society by distance, feel these wants by instinct, and are grateful for the opportunity to relieve them. In Meriwether, the sentiment goes beyond this. It has, besides, something dialectic in it. His house is open to every-body, as freely almost as an inn. But to see him when he has the good fortune to pick up an intelligent, educated gentleman—and particularly one who listens well!—a respectable, assentatious stranger! All the better if he has been in the Legislature, or better still, if in Congress. Such a person caught within the purlieus of Swallow Barn, may set down one week's entertainment as certain—inevitable, and as many more as he likes—the more the merrier. He will know something of the quality of Meriwether's rhetoric before he is gone.

Then again, it is very pleasant to see Frank's kind and considerate bearing towards his servants and dependents. His slaves appreciate this, and hold him in most affectionate reverence, and, therefore, are not only contented, but happy under his dominion.

Meriwether is not much of a traveller. He has never been in New Eng-land, and very seldom beyond the confines of Virginia. He makes now and then a winter excursion to Richmond, which, I rather think, he considers as the centre of civilization; and towards autumn, it is his custom to journey over the mountain to the Springs, which he is obliged to do to avoid the unhealthy season in the tide-water region. But the upper country is not much to his taste, and would not be endured by him if it were not for the crowds that resort there for the same reason which operates upon him; and I may add—though he would not confess it—for the op-portunity this concourse affords him for discussion of opinions.

He thinks lightly of the mercantile interest, and, in fact, undervalues the manners of the large cities generally. He believes that those who live in them are hollow-hearted and insincere, and wanting in that substantial intelligence and virtue, which he affirms to be characteristic of the coun-try. . . .

He is somewhat distinguished as a breeder of blooded horses; and, ever since the celebrated race between Eclipse and Henry, has taken to this occupation with a renewed zeal, as a matter affecting the reputation of the state. It is delightful to hear him expiate upon the value, importance, and patriotic bearing of this employment, and to listen to all his technical lore touching the mystery of horse-craft. He has some fine colts in training, which are committed to the care of a pragmatical old negro, named Carey, who, in his reverence for the occupation, is the perfect shadow of his master.

✓   ✓   ✓

Hospitality was one of the most frequently mentioned traits of all Southerners. James Kirke Paulding, a New Yorker, in *Letters from the South, Written During an Excursion in the Summer of 1816,* J. Eastburn and Company, New York, 1817, Vol. I, Letter III, pp. 22-29, wrote as follows:

Dear Frank,

The first settlers of Virginia generally located larger tracts than those to the north, because they saw more clearly its prospective value, or the early introduction of slaves enabled them to cultivate more extensively. Hence arose the distinction subsisting between the two parts of the Union—the one occupied by farmers, cultivating farms, the other by planters, cultivating plantations.

To this day, the land in the occupancy of individuals lies mostly in large tracts, some of them containing several thousand acres. In one of my late excursions previous to setting out on my *grand tour,* I spent several days at the seat of one of these planters; who, by the way, was a lady, and such a one you will not see every day, Frank. In the place of general description, which is for the most part vague and unsatisfactory, take the following picture; which, however, is a favourable one; as the establishment was one of the most liberal and hospitable of any in Virginia.

The master of the house, at least the gentleman who officiated as such, was a son-in-law of the family, who dressed exceedingly plain, and who, I soon found, was a well-educated, lively, good-humoured, sensible man. . . . A stranger here, is just as much at home as a child in its cradle. Indeed I have heard a story of a gentleman from our part of the world, who stopped here, *en passant,* with his wife, carriage, and servants; forgot in a little time that he was not at home, and staid more than half a year!

. . . Here the ladies attend, as usual, to their own amusements and employments. You are told the carriage or horses are at your service—that you can fish, hunt, or lounge, or read, just as you please; and every one makes his choice.

✓   ✓   ✓

The breeding and racing of fine horses held an important place in the life of the gentry. The priority of that sport in Charleston may be seen from the following account from Irving, *History of the Turf,* pp. 10-11, quoted by Henry Edmund Ravenel in *Ravenel Records,* The Franklin Printing and Publishing Co., Atlanta, 1898, pp. 46-47.

We will commence with the proceedings at the New Market course at Charleston, S. C., season of 1786; and here it may be remarked, that if ever there was a "golden age of racing" in South Carolina, or rather, if ever there was a period destined to be the commencement of a new era in the annals of racing in this State, that period is the one to which we are now referring.

Whether we consider the elevated character of the gentlemen of the turf, the attraction that the races possessed at that time and for many subsequent years, "For all sorts and conditions of men," youth anticipating its delight for weeks beforehand—the sternness of age relaxing by their approach, lovers becoming more ardent, and young damsels setting their caps with greater taste and dexterity, the quality of the company in attendance, the splendid equipages, the liveried outriders that were to be seen daily on the course, the gentlemen attending the races in fashionable London-made clothes, the buckskin breeches and top boots, the universal interest pervading all classes, from the judge on the bench to the little schoolboy with his satchel on his back, the kind greeting of the town and country, the happy meeting of old friends whose residences were at a distance, affording occasions of happy intercourse and festivity, the marked absence of all care, except the care of the horses—the total disregard of the value of time, except by the competitors in the races, who did their best to save and economize it—everything combined to render race week in Charlston emphatically the carnival of the State, when it was unpopular, if not impossible, to be out of spirits, and not to mingle with the gay throng.

The best idea we can give of the moral influence of race week (as exerted formerly) is to state that the courts of justice used daily to adjourn, and all the schools were regularly let out, as the hour for starting the horses drew nigh; with one consent the stores in Broad and King streets were closed— all business being suspended on the joyous occasion—the feelings of the good people partaking of the rapidity of the races themselves; in fact it was no uncommon sight to see the most venerable and distinguished dignitaries of the land, clergymen and judges, side by side on the course, taking a deep interest in the animated and animating scene around them.

With such a stimulus to propriety and the preservation of good morals, no wonder that order, and sobriety, and good fellowship prevailed as abundantly as they did in those days. We must not omit to notice that, in the early days of racing in South Carolina, the gentlemen of the turf, like the ancient nobles, Hiero and others, never ran their horses for the pecuniary value of the prize to be won, but solely for the honor that a horse of their own breeding and training should distinguish himself.

Mr. Daniel Ravenel and many other high-minded turfmen of those days expressed great disapprobation at any departure from the good old customs of their fathers, and did all in their power to prevent a change, when it was proposed. The prize used to be not a purse of gold or silver, but a *piece of plate*.

✓   ✓   ✓

Dancing was a favored entertainment in the Old South, and instruction in dancing was an essential part of the education of a young lady or gentleman. Many of the mansions contained large ballrooms. The following two selections illustrate the impressions of two travelers, each of whom attended a ball. The first is from Basil Hall, *Travels in North America in the Years 1827 and 1828*,

Carey, Sea and Carey, 1829, Vol. II, p. 195; the second is from Frederick Law
Olmsted, *A Journey in the Seaboard Slave States*, Dix and Edwards, New York,
1856, p. 646.

1. The room was large, the ball handsomely got up, and everything ordered in the best style, with one small exception—the ladies and gentlemen
appeared to be entire strangers to one another. The ladies were planted
firmly along the walls, in the coldest possible formality, while the gentlemen, who, except during the dance, stood in close column near the door,
seemed to have no fellow-feeling, nor any wish to associate with the opposite sex.

In the ordinary business of their lives—I mean their busy, money-
making, electioneering lives—the Americans have little or no time for
companionship, that I could ever see or hear of, with the women, still
less for any habitual confidential intercourse. Consequently, when they
come together for the express purpose of amusement, those easy and
familiar habits which are essential to the cheerfulness of a ballroom, or indeed of any room, are rarely to be found.

2. I attended a Creole ball, while at Washington [Louisiana]. The ladies
were, on an average, more beautiful, better formed, and more becomingly
dressed, as well as much better dancers, than they would be found in a
country ball room at the North; but, what was chiefly remarkable, was the
exquisite skill and taste displayed in the dressing of their hair. The ball
was conducted with the greatest propriety; and broke up earlier than public
balls usually do at the North.

ꞋꞋ   ꞋꞋ   ꞋꞋ

The place of women in the life of the Southern home was one of honor and
respect. While the participation of women in public life was unthought of, their
influence over husbands and sons was not to be overlooked. The mother developed ability as an administrator and social worker on her own plantation. The
following selections illustrate the different capacities in which women functioned.
The first was written by Mrs. Julia Gardiner Tyler, wife of ex-President John
Tyler, in reply to the Duchess of Sutherland, who had sent an address to the
women of America calling for nationwide action to end slavery. It was quoted
by Mary R. Beard, in *America Through Women's Eyes*, Macmillan, New York,
1933, pp. 136-138, with permission of the publisher.

The second illustrates the chivalric ideal and the veneration in which women were
held in the South. In the eyes of chivalrous Southerners of the better class all
"ladies" were held to be queens of love and beauty, without stain and without
reproach. Each Southerner in the manner of one of the knights of King Arthur
dedicated himself to the worship of and service to his lady fair. This attitude was
derived to some degree from the novels of Sir Walter Scott. It is quoted from the
Diary of David Schenck, May, 1858, from the Southern Historical Collection, Library
of the University of North Carolina, Chapel Hill, North Carolina.

The third is quoted from James S. Buckingham, *The Slave States of America,* Fisher, Son, and Company, London, 1842, Vol. II, p. 182.

The fourth is an exposition on "Woman's Rights" from George Fitzhugh, *Sociology for the South,* Morris, Richmond, 1854, pp. 213-220, *passim.*

1. Woman, in the United States, with but few exceptions, confines herself within that sphere for which the God who created her seems to have designed her. Her circle is, literally and emphatically, that of her family; and such is she content that it shall be, Within that circle her influence is felt over the relations of life, as mother, mistress—and as she discharges the duty of one or all of these relations, so is she respected or otherwise. . . . She knows nothing of political conventions, or conventions of any other sort than such as are held under suitable pastors of the Church, and are wholly directed to the advancement of the Christian religion. Such is emphatically the case of the women of the Southern States. Do you ascertain the nature of their employments, you must enter the family circle, and, believe me, good sisters of England, you would find in their Christian deportment, and perfect amiability of manners, enough, at once, to inspire you with the most exalted respect and esteem. . . .

It is the province of women in the Southern States to preside over the domestic economy of the estates and plantations of their husbands—it is emphatically their province to visit the sick, and attend to the comfort of all the laborers upon such estates. . . . The women of the Southern States are, for the most part, well educated; indeed they yield not in this respect to any females on earth, and they have peculiar opportunities of acquiring knowledge in regard to the public concerns of the world. Politics is almost universally the theme of conversation among the men, in all their coteries and social gatherings, and the women would be stupid indeed, if they did not gather much information from this abundant source. Hence they are not ignorant of the rapid growth of their beloved country.

2. May, the happy month of flowers and beauty and gladness—the fairest of the year opened with a most glorious fete. It has been long since our gentle ladies have honored this beautiful month with a floral festival and for the enjoyment of the present return— The ladies of Mrs. Alexander's boarding school very appropriately concluded on a rural Pic Nic as the fittest celebration and to that end invited the young men to join them and spent the day in festivity. A train of six buggies and three carriages left town at 8 Ock. and with glad hearts and joyful smiles drove out to a green, shady spot on the river some two miles from town, where a cool spring and murmuring rivulet lent their inviting attractions to the spot. Here we spent the morning in the fullest sense of enjoyment—some fishing, some wreathing flowers, while others rowed in the boat, up and down the placid stream and made

the bank echo with vocal music, nor must we forget the crowning of our
floral queen—

Miss L—a A—

L— is young and very fair
With blue eyes and auburn hair
Her *cheeks* as rosy as the blush of morn
And lips as ruby as e'er eyes look^d on
Her countenance oh! how gentle and kind
The symbol of grace and purity of mind.
Her *voice* so musical, it dies on the ear
Like the note of the swan, as its death draws near.
Her temper as calm and serene
As the crystal lake at even is seen.
It ripples when swept by pleasure's breeze
But knows not the wave which anger may cause.
Nature now so kind to fortune's call
Gave a noble intellect to crown it all.
And man for once, in rapture took
A gaze on what he sought—*A perfect work.*

3. [American women] affect to be, and I think generally are, indifferent to
what may be called party politics; . . . still they are not, as supposed, so
wholly disregarded as not to be flattered and appealed to by political orators, and by the newspapers, whenever the occasion presents itself for doing
so with effect. Accordingly, the ladies are present at the celebrations of
American Independence, as in the instance just reported; they are toasted
at their political dinners, and they dance at the political balls. In the great
struggle between the Nullifiers of South Carolina and the General Government of the United States, they took a very prominent part; and retain
at the present day more of the enthusiastic feelings of that period than the
men.

4. Nothing in the signs of the times exhibits in stronger relief the fact, that
free society is in a state of dissolution and thaw, of demoralization and
transition, than the stir about woman's rights. . . . Northern newspapers
are filled with the sufferings of poor widowed needlewomen, and the murders of wives by their husbands. Woman *there* is in a false position. Be she
white, or be she black, she is treated with kindness and humanity in the
slave-holding South. . . . If American women wish to participate in the
hard labor of men, they are right to curtail the petticoat. Queens wear
the longest trains because they have the least occasion to labor. The broom
girls of Bavaria have to work hard for a living, and find it necessary to

amputate the nether impediments. In France, woman draws the plough and the canal boat. She will be condemned to like labors in America, so soon as her dress, her education and coarse sentiments fit her for such labors. Let her exhibit strength and hardihood, and man, her master, will make her a beast of burden. So long as she is nervous, fickle, capricious, delicate, diffident and dependent, man will worship and adore her. Her weakness is her strength, and her true art is to cultivate and improve that weakness. Woman naturally shrinks from public gaze, and from the struggle and competition of life. Free society has thrown her into the arena of industrial war, robbed her of the softness of her own sex, without conferring on her the strength of ours. In truth, woman has but one right, and that is the right to protection. The right to protection involves the obligation to obey. A husband, a lord and master, whom she should love, honor and obey, nature designed for every woman—for the number of males and females is the same. If she be obedient, she is in little danger of mal-treatment; if she stands upon her rights, is coarse and masculine, man loathes and despises her, and ends by abusing her. Law, however well intended, can do little in her behalf. True womanly art will give her an empire and a sway far greater than she deserves. . . . Women would do well to disguise strength of mind or body, if they possess it, if they would retain their empire. . . .

We would infinitely prefer to nurse a sickly woman, to being led about by a masculine blue stocking.

✓   ✓   ✓

At about the beginning of the nineteenth century many planters in the tidewater region of South Carolina began migrating from their plantations about the middle of May to escape the sickness known as "country fever." Leaving overseers in charge of the Negroes, they stayed away until the first killing frost in October or November. Some had town houses in coastal towns; others sought summer resorts. Adam Hodgson, in *Letters from North America During a Tour in the United States and Canada,* Hurst, London, 1824, Vol. I, pp. 48-51, reported such migration.

The best society here, [Charleston] is much superior to any which I have yet seen in America. It consists of a few old patrician families, who form a select circle, into which the "novi homines," unless distinguished by great personal merit, find it extremely difficult to gain admission. Strangers, well introduced, and of personal respectability, are received with much liberality and attention. Many of the old gentlemen were well educated at English colleges, and retain something of their original attachment to the mother country, notwithstanding their sensibility to recent calumny and misrepresentation. Their manners are extremely agreeable, resembling the more polished of our country gentlemen, and are formed on the model of what in England we call "the old school." They are, however, the last of their generation, and will leave a blank much to be deplored when they pass away. The young ladies of patrician families are delicate, refined, and intelligent, rather distant and reserved to strangers, but frank and affable to those who are familiarly introduced to them by their fathers and brothers. They go very early into company, are frequently married at sixteen or eighteen years of age, and generally under twenty, and have retired from the vortex of gay society, before even the fashionable part of my fair countrywomen would formally have entered it. They often lament that the high standard of manners to which they have been accustomed seems doomed to perish with the generation of their fathers. The fact is, that the absence of the privileges of primogeniture, and the consequent repeated subdivision of property, are generally effecting a change in the structure of society in South Carolina, and will shortly efface its most interesting and characteristic features.

I arrived at Charleston immediately after the races, which are a season of incessant gaiety. They usually take place in February, when all the principal families visit their town-houses in Charleston, for three or four weeks, collecting from their plantations, which are at a distance of from 30 to 150 miles. During this short interval, there is a perpetual round of visits. About the beginning of March, they return to the retirement of their plantations, often accompanied by the strangers with whom they have become acquainted. As a large proportion of the plantations are in the swamps, where a residence in the summer months would probably be fatal from a fever of a bilious nature, from which the natives themselves are not exempt, the families return about the beginning of June to the city, where they remain till the first frost, which is looked for with great anxiety towards October. They then go back to their plantations until February. Some, instead of coming into the city in June, retire to the mountains, or to the springs of Ballston and Saratoga, in the State of New York, where a large concourse of persons assemble from every part of the United States and from Canada, and, by the reciprocation of civilities, and a better acquaintance with each other, gradually lose their sectional and colonial prejudices.—Although these springs are from a thousand to fifteen hundred miles from the Southern States, the inhabitants of Georgia and Carolina speak of them with as much familiarity as our Londoners speak of Bath or Cheltenham. Some of the planters spend the hot months on Sullivan's Island, at the mouth of the Bay, where even strangers may generally remain with impunity. . . .

⁘ ⁘ ⁘

Most of the people in the South would fall into the group called the "Middle Class." They lived on their own farms or plantations, or in the towns and villages. They were educated in the schools available in their communities and sometimes sent their sons and daughters away to acade-

mies and colleges, were deeply religious, and might be called the "backbone of the South." Many of them were of non-English stock, Scotch-Irish, and Germans, who came up the Shenandoah Valley from Pennsylvania and settled in the Piedmont section of Virginia and the Carolinas before the Revolutionary War, and whose children and children's children made their way farther west with successive waves of migration. Not a few of these people settled in the towns which developed as marketing centers sprinkled throughout the farming areas.

Daniel R. Hundley, in *Social Relations in Our Southern States,* H. B. Price, New York, 1860, divided Southern society into several distinct types. He devoted Chapter Two to "The Middle Classes," from which the following is quoted.

As in all other civilized communities, the middle classes of the South constitute the greater proportion of her citizens, and are likewise the most useful members of her society. . . . Jackson was nearly full-blooded Scotch-Irish, . . . Calhoun was the son of a middle-class planter; while the well-beloved and eloquent Harry of the West, as is well known, came of English Baptist parentage, and noble-hearted Patrick Henry sprung directly from the bosom of the people.

But not only have the Middle Classes of the South helped to furnish these great leaders, as well as many others of less note; they have always exercised a healthy and sensible influence upon both national and state politics from the adoption of our Federal Constitution to the present day. Had it not been for them, the law of descent never would have been changed in Virginia, or materially in any of the other Southern States. . . . So, also, was the extension of the elective franchise bitterly opposed by the major part of the gentry. . . .

In a majority of cases the middle-class planter is a kind master, works not infrequently in company with his slaves, and always attends to their wants in sickness or their necessities in old age. . . .

[Of the women of the Middle Class, he wrote:] Modest and virtuous, chaste in speech and manners; they are, besides, very industrious house-keepers, kind-hearted mistresses, and the most devoted of wives and mothers; although, we are free to confess, they are not infrequently quite simple and unsophisticated and easily gulled or deceived, knowing at best but little of the world and its manifold follies, and caring even less for its empty vanities and trumpery.

ϒ ϒ ϒ

The following letter was written by Harry Toulmin to James Leight in 1793, and is quoted from Toulmin, *The Western Country in 1793,* edited by Marion Tinling and Godfrey Davies, The Huntington Library and Art Gallery, San Marino, California, 1948, pp. 57-58.

The town of Winchester, which is in the heart of the Shenandoah Valley . . . is one of the most important towns in Virginia. It contains ,660 inhabitants. But they are a motley set of Germans, Irish, Scots, and Anglo-Americans (or Americans descended from Englishmen). Various mechanical arts are carried on here. There are saddlers, hatters, shoemakers, weavers, braziers, smiths, clock-makers, riflesmiths, cabinetmakers, a painted-hairman, an earthenware-maker, a coachmaker, a wagon-maker, buckskin breeches makers, etc. The stores, or shops, are numerous and considerable. They obtain their goods from Philadelphia, Baltimore, and Alexandria, but principally from Philadelphia, and dispose of them to people of the town, of the neighborhood, and of the back country. Multitudes of horses, sometimes bringing hemp, come down every spring and return loaded with the products of Europe and the West Indies, but principally with salt and iron. . . .

You would be astonished at the multiplicity of cattle which pour through this town from the back country to the north, and of wagons and horses with emigrants from the north and east to Kentucky. Several thousands have gone down the river this year, and I, after waiting some weeks for the rising of the waters, propose following them tomorrow.

✓   ✓   ✓

There were many smaller towns such as the one described in the following passage from Francois Andre Michaux, *Travels to the West of the Allegheny Mountains,* B. Crosby and Company, London, Second Edition, 1805, p. 265.

Morganton, the principal town of the county of Burke [North Carolina] contains about fifty houses built of wood, and almost all inhabited by tradesmen. One warehouse only, supported by a commercial house at Charleston, is established in this little town, where the inhabitants, for twenty miles round, come and purchase mercey and jewellery goods from England, or give in exchange a part of their produce, which consists chiefly of dried hams, butter, tallow, bear and stag skins, and ginseng, which they bring from the mountains.

✓   ✓   ✓

A half century later New York was the entrepôt center which served as obscure a town as Wilkesboro, at the edge of the Blue Ridge Mountains in North Carolina. The following business letter from *Happy Valley History and Genealogy,* by Thomas Felix Hickerson, published by the author, Chapel Hill, 1940, illustrates some of the stock-in-trade of a rural store. The following letter is from pp. 128-129.

New York, Mar. 12, 1848

Dear Brother: . . . .

Your Hardware, Crockery, shoes, and a box of Yankee notions, are on the Jonas Smith, which vessel advertised to sail yesterday, but will not get off before tomorrow evening, but will certainly go on Tuesday if no before.

When I finished paying your bills on yesterday morning, I was a littl frightened at the amount, which is $4322.97. Don't be frightened man Don't jump so! Don't swear!!!

Dry goods, hats, etc., were so cheap, that I could not help buying. A least they seemed cheap to me, and I hope that you will not regret the amt. of the purchases. I am rather more scared about the quantity of hats shoes, and bonnets than anything else. After I had filled your bill for hats I met with a lot of mens and boys wool hats, drab and black at $3.50 and some quite passable silk hats at $9.00 and could not resist the temptation so I bought 2 doz. of the silk and 6 doz. wool. And as for bonnets, you had better give away your old ones if you can't sell, and make room for the new ones.

I wrote to you last week, telling you that the most of your goods were on board the Athalia and that she sailed the first of the week (on Tuesday morning I believe).

Nails were so high that I could not buy for you, as you limited me to 4 cents, but I sent on a few kegs for father, and you must call on him for pay if they are lost.

I neglected to send you a duplicate of the drug bill, but believe that prices range about as usual except that castor oil and some articles are a good deal higher than common. . . .

Yours affectionately,
Thos. I. Lenoir.

To James Gwyn, Esq.
Wilkesboro,
Wilkes County, N. C.

✓   ✓   ✓

The farmer of the South often started as a herdsman, a native of the immense and lonely frontier, locating at the edge of the settlements and at a safe distance from the Indians. He preempted a tract of land, perhaps intending to purchase it as soon as it was surveyed. Here he acquired a character and tradition of his own, living his obscure life in contentment and plenty. He engaged in agriculture to the extent of his family's needs, but livestock grazing was his chief occupation. Later, if he turned to planting or farming, he continued to raise livestock extensively, driving his stock to market on the hoof, as described in the following passage from James S. Buckingham, *The Slave States of America,* Fisher, Son, and Company, London, 1842, Vol. II, p. 203.

About a mile after quitting the village, we came on the banks of a river called "The French Broad" [just outside Asheville, North Carolina.] . . . As we passed its bank, we observed a ferry, at which persons drew themselves across by a cord, in a slender canoe, and the horses and carriages forded the stream a little below. . . .

On our way we met a small caravan, as it might be termed, of fine horses, and beautiful mules, conducted by two drovers, one of whom rode in advance, the other in the rear; and the cattle were driven like sheep, without halter, bridle, or other fastening, between the two. These were all proceeding, to the number of about a hundred, from Kentucky and Ohio to South Carolina and Georgia for sale; and some idea may be formed of the extent of this traffic, when it is mentioned that not less than 10,000 horses and mules, from these middle or western States come down every year for sale to the purchasers in the Atlantic States, and the cities of the coast, as many as 500 at a time frequently passing through Greenville in a single day. The horses were quite as fine as ordinary horses seen at fairs and markets in England; but the mules were by far the most beautiful I had ever seen, surpasing even the finest of those in Spain and Portugal.

✓   ✓   ✓

J. F. H. Claiborne, in "A Trip Through the Piney Woods, 1841-42," *Publications of the Mississippi Historical Society,* Vol. IX, pp. 521-522, quoted from the *Natchez Free Trader and Gazette,* delineated the activities of some of the herdsmen of Mississippi.

Many of the people here are herdsmen, owning large droves of cattle, surplus increase of which are annually driven to Mobile. These cattle are permitted to run in the range or forest, subsisting in the summer on the luxuriant grass with which the teeming earth is clothed, and in winter on green rushes or reeds, a tender species of cane that grows in the brakes or thickets in every swamp, hollow and ravine. The herdsmen have pens or stampedes at different points in the forest, where at suitable times they salt the cows, and once or twice a year they are all collected and marked and branded. This is a stirring period and quite an incident in the peaceful and somewhat monotonous life of the woodsman. Half a dozen of them assemble, mounted on low built, shaggy, but muscular and hardy horses of that region, and armed with raw hide whips of prodigious size, and sometimes with a catching rope or lasso, plaited of horsehair. They scour the woods in gallant style, followed by a dozen or more fierce looking dogs; they dash through swamps and morass, deep ravines, and swim rivers, sometimes driving a herd of a thousand heads to the pen, or singling out and separating with surprising dexterity a solitary steer which has become incorporated with another herd. In this way, cheering each other with loud shouts and making the woods ring with the crack of their long whips and the trampling of the flying cattle, they gallop thirty or forty miles a day and rendezvous at night at the *stamping ground.*

✓   ✓   ✓

Daniel R. Hundley, in *Social Relations in Our Southern States,* H. B. Price, New York, 1860, p. 199, commented on the capabilities and traits of character of the Southern yeomen.

The usual weapon of the Southern Yeoman is the deadly rifle—even i his sports—and this he handles with such skill as few possess, even i America. . . . With his rifle the Yeoman shoots squirrels, ducks, dee bear, buffalo, and whatever else he pleases. The best riflemen are found i Georgia, Mississippi, Tennessee, and Kentucky—the *best,* perhaps, in th last-named and chivalrous Commonwealth. Herein turkey-shooting is prac ticed by all classes, but chiefly by the yeomen. A live turkey is securel fastened to a stake at a distance of one hundred paces, and you pay fiv or ten cents for the privilege of each shot; if you hit the fowl in the head th carcass is yours, but any other *hit* is considered *foul,* and so passes fo nothing. This is the kind of school in which were trained the hunting-shir heroes of King's Mountain, and those unerring riflemen who, at the memora ble battle of New Orleans, made such havoc in the ranks of Pakenham' veterans. So also were trained those brave defenders of Texan independenc —Crockett, Travis, and their compeers. . . .

The Southern Yeoman much resembles in his speech, religious opinions household arrangements, indoor sports, and family traditions, the middl class farmers of the Northern States. He is fully as intelligent as the latter and is on the whole much better versed in the lore of politics and th provisions of our Federal and State Constitutions. This is chiefly owing t the public barbecues, court-house-day gatherings, and other holiday oc casions, which are more numerous in the South than in the North, and ir the former are nearly always devoted in part to political discussions of on kind or another. . . .

So far as hospitality goes, the Yeomen of the South are not a whit be hind the Southern Gentleman, or any other class of gentlemen the world over. . . . Besides being given to hospitality, although in a primitive way, . . . the Yeomen of the South are also quite social and gregarious in their instincts, and delight much in having all kinds of frolics and family gather ings during the long winter evenings. On all such occasions, nearly, some thing serviceable is the ostensible cause of their assembling, though the time is devoted almost wholly to social pleasures: sometimes, 'tis true, there is a wedding, or a birthday-party, or a candy pulling; but much more frequently it is a corn-husking, or the everlasting quilting—this last being the most frequent and most in favor of all the merrymakings which call the young people together. . . . The old women and old men sit demurely beside the blazing kitchen fire, and frighten one another with long-winded ghost stories; thus leaving the young folks all to themselves in the "big room," wherein is also the quilt-frame, which is either suspended at the corners by ropes attached to the ceiling, or else rests on the tops of four chairs. Around this assemble the young men and the young maidens. . . . Meanwhile the children play hide and seek, in-doors and out, whoop ing, laughing, and chattering like so many magpies; and, in the snug

himney-corner, Old Bose, the faithful watch-dog, stretches himself out to
his full length and dozes comfortably in the genial warmth of the fire.

✓ ✓ ✓

Robert Lee Stowe, Sr., was born in 1866, in a little log cabin on the banks of
he Catawba River in Gaston County, North Carolina. His early memories center
around this scene two miles below the present town of Belmont. The following
description of homes of Gaston County before the Civil War is from his *Early
History of Belmont and Gaston County, North Carolina,* privately published,
Belmont, 1951, pp. 10ff.

From about 1800 to 1850 quite a lot of homes were built along the
Catawba River. [The earliest settlers had come about 1750.] These houses
were built by the landowners for their own use and were practically all
alike. Some of the houses had cellars, others did not, but the plan of all
the houses was virtually the same. They consisted of one large room, probably twenty-five by thirty feet, one and a half stories high. The lower story
consisted of one large room used as a bedroom and living room combined.
The half-story was used as a bedroom and storage room, and was reached
by a stairway or ladder. There was generally a kitchen in the yard where
the cooking was done, and the people either ate in the kitchen or had
the food carried into the living room. The barns, stables and other storage
houses were built some distance away. These dwelling houses were built of
hewn logs, generally post oaks, and the cracks between the logs were
daubed with mud. They were covered with split boards and the earlier
ones used wooden pegs instead of nails to hold the boards in place. At
a later date many nails were used which were made in the blacksmith
shops. After lumber and nails were available many of these houses had
shed rooms or porches built on one or both sides, and some of them were
weatherboarded and ceiled. Some had a partition in the large room down-
stairs, making two rooms. They had large fireplaces and could be kept
comfortably warm in winter.

The houses described above were the homes of the more prosperous
people. The tenants and poor people lived in one-room cabins, which was
bedroom, kitchen and living room combined. Sometimes they had a little
kitchen built away from the cottage in which to do their cooking.

To show how the landowners lived—if you will excuse a little personal
history—I will describe the place where I was born and lived until I was
fourteen years of age. . . . The dwelling house was built like the one I
described. . . . There was a large barn some distance from the house with a
big stable which would accommodate several horses. The cow lot was
about forty feet from the barn on one side and another building stood
about seventy-five feet from the barn on the other side. This building contained two stables, a wagon shed and a gear room. Some distance from

this building in the general direction of the dwelling was a corn crib and forty or fifty feet to the south was another crib. About thirty or forty feet from the crib was a . . . house used for storing grain and heavy groceries. A short distance from this house was a smokehouse, which was built of heavy logs and the cracks chinked so that no one could see inside. There was a heavy padlock and hasp and staple for fastening the door, made of heavy lumber, and for a considerable distance around the staple were driven nails made in the blacksmith shop. I suppose this was done to keep anyone from sawing the staple out and opening the door. . .

About thirty feet away from the dwelling was a kitchen where the cooking was done. About one hundred feet to the east was a wheat storage house with a wagon shed. A branch ran in front of the house about eighty yards away, and across the branch was the spring coming out of the hill on the south side of the branch. A short distance below the spring was a spring house. The branch flowing from the spring had been widened out and flat rocks placed on the bottom on which sat the milk pans and other utensils. The spring house, which was ten or twelve feet square, was built over this. A short distance from the path which led to the spring was a small log house which we called the straw house because the broom straw used for making brooms, along with other material, was stored here.

Close to the path to the spring was the ash hopper. I remember the ash hopper very well because it was my job to carry water and pour it on the ashes to drain off and make lye which was used in making soap. The ash hopper was a triangular affair in which the ashes were deposited and when water was poured in the lye drained off into a trough. People made their own soap in those days, and saved all the grease from the kitchen for this purpose. They also saved all the ashes and when a sufficient amount had been accumulated they would put the ashes in the ash hopper and saturate them with water, collect the lye as it drained out through the ashes, and boil it with the grease to make soap. The soap for washing clothes was left in a semi-liquid state, but that used for toilet soap was boiled down until it was hard and then cut into cakes. It was pretty hard on the hands, but very effective in removing the dirt. . . .

The cows furnished milk and butter, the sheep wool to make the clothes, the geese the feathers to make feather beds, and the bees honey for sweetening. When cattle were butchered for beef the hides were preserved and sent to a tannery to make leather for making shoes. There were shoemakers over the country who made these shoes, and a pair was supposed to last a boy all winter. The wool from the sheep was carded and spun by hand into yarn which was woven into cloth by the women.

✔   ✔   ✔

Travelers commented on the "poor whites" of the Old South, referring to them as "poor white trash." If these people cultivated fields at all they did it in a careless fashion. The only occupation of the men was hunting; consequently they had dogs in numbers. The women and children did the work. Some authors believed that competition with plantation economy had pushed them into the pine barrens and sand hills; another theory was that they were descended from the scum of Europe, sent here as indentured servants during colonial days. Today we believe that many of them were afflicted by malaria and hookworm; the latter made its victim lazy and apathetic; persons afflicted by hookworm frequently craved a certain sweet clay which was commonly found in the region inhabited by the so-called "clay-eaters."

Frederick Law Olmsted's description of life in the turpentine forests in North Carolina illustrates this type of people. It is quoted from *A Journey in the Seaboard Slave States,* Dix and Edwards, New York, 1856, p. 348.

Among . . . [the white people inhabiting the turpentine forests] there is a large number, I should think a majority, of entirely uneducated, poverty-stricken vagabonds. I mean by vagabonds, simply, people without habitual, definite occupation or reliable means of livelihood. They are poor, having almost no property but their own bodies; and the use of these, that is, their labor, they are not accustomed to hire out statedly and regularly, so as to obtain capital by wages, but only occasionally by the day or job, when driven to it by necessity. A family of these people will commonly hire, or "squat" and build, a little log cabin, so made that it is only a shelter from rain, the sides not being chinked, and having no more furniture or pretension to comfort than is commonly provided a criminal in the cell of a prison. They will cultivate a little corn, and possibly a few roods of potatoes, cowpeas and coleworts. They will own a few swine, that find their living in the forest; and pretty certainly, also, a rifle and dogs; and the men, ostensibly, occupy most of their time in hunting. A gentleman from Fayetteville told me that he had, several times, appraised, under oath, the whole household property of families of this class at less than $20. If they have need of money to purchase clothing, etc., they obtain it by selling their game or meal. If they have none of this to spare, or an insufficiency, they will work for a neighboring farmer for a few days, and they usually get for their labor fifty cents a day, *finding themselves.* The farmers say, that they do not like to employ them, because they cannot be relied upon to finish what they undertake, or to work according to directions; and because, being white men, they cannot "drive" them.

✓   ✓   ✓

The women of this class were described by Daniel R. Hundley in *Social Relations in Our Southern States,* H. B. Price, New York, 1860, p. 257.

If anything, after the first freshness of their youth is lost, the women are even more intolerable than the men—owing chiefly to their disgusting habit of snuff-dipping, and even sometimes pipe-smoking. The vile practice of snuff-dipping prevails, sometimes, also, among the wives and daughters of the Yeomanry, and even occasionally among otherwise intelligent members of the Southern Middle Classes, particularly in North Carolina. The usual mode is, to procure a straight wooden tooth-brush—one made of the bark of the hickory-nut tree preferred—chew one end of the brush until it becomes soft and pliant, then dab the same while still wet with saliva into the snuff-bottle, and immediately stick it back into the mouth again with the fine particles of snuff adhering; then proceed to mop the gums and teeth adroitly, to suck, and chew, and spit to your heart's content. Ah! it is almost as decent as smoking cigars, and is fully as distingue as chewing tobacco.

✔   ✔   ✔

The mountains became the masters of the people who came to settle within their walled areas. Isolation retarded the evolution of economic life, and subsistence farming did not give way to progress. In writing of the mountains, visitors usually lumped all of the occupants into one group, which they classed perhaps a little above the sand-hillers and other poor whites. There were varying degrees of prosperity in the mountains just as there were in other sections of the South. The Appalachian mountains are ridges interspersed with valleys that vary in width, all of which are very fertile. The first settlers chose those rich valleys, built rude log cabins, and eventually replaced them with more comfortable houses. They were isolated, it is true, and, since they had no communications with the outside world they produced practically everything their families needed; in addition, they grew corn to fatten their livestock. Settlers on the narrower valleys and slopes were not so blessed. Their homes were naturally more meager. Often it was necessary for the son of a valley farmer to farm land a little less desirable than that of his father, because the available land was limited. Living was poorest for those who built their homes on the steep mountainsides.

The mountaineer loved his environment, as the following account by John Muir will show. When a mountain man felt the fever to seek more fertile fields, he sought them in some distant mountains. Thus the Ozarks were peopled by pioneers from the Appalachian region.

The following account is from John Muir, *A Thousand-Mile Walk to the Gulf*, Houghton Mifflin Company, New York, 1916, pp. 34-41, *passim*. In August, 1867, Muir started from Indianapolis on a botanizing walk. Traveling twenty-five miles per day, keeping a journal, he crossed Kentucky, Tennessee, a corner of North Carolina, Georgia, and Florida. On September 16 he was in the Cumberland Mountains, and after spending the night with a mountaineer he was taken by his host for a view of the mountains.

"I will take you," said he [Muir's host], "to the highest ridge in the country, where you can see both ways. You will have a view of all the world on one side of the mountains and all creation on the other. Besides, you, who are travelling for curiosity and wonder, ought to see our gold mines." I agreed to stay and went to see the mines. Gold is found in small quantities throughout the Alleghanies, and many farmers work at mining a few weeks or months every year when their time is not more valuable for other pursuits. In this neighborhood miners are earning from half a dollar to two dollars a day. There are several large quartz mills not far from here. Common labor is worth ten dollars a month.

September 17. Spent the day in botanizing, blacksmithing, and examining a grist mill. Grist mills, in the less settled parts of Tennessee and North Carolina, are remarkably simple affairs. A small stone, that a man might carry under his arm, is fastened to the vertical shaft of a little home-made, boyish-looking, back-action water-wheel, which, with a hopper and a box to receive the meal, is the whole affair. The walls of the mill are of undressed poles cut from seedling trees and there is no floor, as lumber is dear. No dam is built. The water is conveyed along some hillside until sufficient fall is obtained, a thing easily done in the mountains.

On Sundays you may see wild, unshorn, uncombed men coming out of the woods, each with a bag of corn on his back. From a peck to a bushel is a common grist. They go to the mill along verdant foot-paths, winding up and down over hill and valley, and crossing many a rhododendron glen. The flowers and shining leaves brush against their shoulders and knees, occasionally knocking off their coon-skin caps. The first arrived throws his corn into the hopper, turns on the water, and goes to the house. After chatting and smoking he returns to see if his grist is done. Should the stones run empty for an hour or so, it does no harm.

This is a fair average equipment and capacity of a score of mills that I saw in Tennessee. . . . All the machines of Kentucky and Tennessee are far behind the age. There is scarce a trace of the spirit of speculation and invention so characteristic of the North. . . . Spinning and weaving are done in every one of these mountain cabins wherever the least pretensions are made to thrift and economy. The practice of these ancient arts they deem marks of advancement rather than of backwardness. "There's a place back heah," said my worthy entertainer, "whar there's a mill-house, an' a store-house, an' a still-house, an' a spring-house, an' a blacksmith shop—all in the same yard! Cows too, an' heaps of big gals a-milkin' them."

September 19. Received another solemn warning of dangers through the mountains. Was told by my worthy entertainer of a wondrous gap in the mountains which he advised me to see. "It is called "Track Gap," said he, "from the great number of tracks in the rocks—bird tracks, bar tracks, hoss tracks, men tracks, all in the solid rock as if it had been mud." Bidding farewell to my worthy mountaineer and all his comfortable wonders, I pursued my way to the South.

As I was leaving, he repeated the warnings of danger ahead, saying that there were a good many people living like wild beasts on whatever they could steal, and that murders were sometimes committed for four or five dollars, and even less. While stopping with him I noticed that a man came regularly after dark to the house for his supper. He was armed with a gun, a pistol, and a long knife. My host told me that this man was at feud with one of his neighbors, and that they were prepared to shoot one another at sight. That neither of them could do any regular work or sleep in the same place two nights in succession. That they visited houses only for food, and as soon as the one that I saw had got his supper he went out and slept in the woods, without of course making a fire. His enemy did the same.

My entertainer told me that he was trying to make peace between these two men, because they were both good men, and if they would agree to stop their quarrel, they could then both go to work. Most of the food in this house was coffee without sugar, corn bread, and sometimes bacon. But the coffee was the greatest luxury which these people knew. The only way of obtaining it was by selling skins, or, in particular, "sang," that is ginseng, which found a market in far-off China. . . .

September 20. [At Murphy, North Carolina] All day among the groves and gorges of Murphy with Mr. Beale. Was shown the site of Camp Butler where General Scott had his headquarters when he removed the Cherokee Indians to a new home in the West. . . . Mr. Beale informed me that the paleness of most of the women in his neighborhood, and the mountains in general hereabouts, was caused chiefly by smoking and by what is called "dipping." I had never even heard of dipping. The term simply describes the application of snuff to the gum by means of a small swab.

✔ ✔ ✔

In the preceding chapters are many selections dealing with Negro life in the South. The following will give the reader a chance for a better rounded picture of approximately one third of the inhabitants of the South.

The first, from *DeBow's Review*, New Orleans, Vol. IX, 1850, pp. 325-326, describes the Negro at work.

In this age of canning abolitionism and pseudo philanthropy, we have thought the following sketch from the pen of W. Cullen Bryant, editor of the *New York Evening Post,* worthy of preservation.

I went to . . . a tobacco factory [at Richmond,] the sight of which amused me, though the narcotic fume made me cough. In one room a black man was taking apart the small bundles of leaves of which a hogshead of tobacco is composed, and carefully separating leaf from leaf; others were assorting the leaves according to the quality, and others again were arranging the leaves in layers and sprinkling each layer with the extract of licorice. In another room about eighty negroes, boys they are called, from the age of twelve years up to manhood, who receive the leaves thus prepared, rolled them into long even rolls, and then cut them into plugs of about four inches in length, which were afterwards passed through a press, and thus became ready for market. As we entered the room we heard a murmur of psalmody running through the assembly, which now and then swelled into a strain of very tolerable music.

"Verse sweetens toil—"

says the stanza which Dr. Johnson was so fond of quoting. . . . Verse, it seems, can sweeten the toil of slaves in a tobacco factory.

"We encourage their singing as much as we can," said the brother of the proprietor, himself a diligent masticator of the weed, who attended us, and politely explained to us the process of making plug tobacco; "we encourage it as much as we can, for the boys work better while singing. Sometimes they will sing all day long with great spirit; at other times you will not hear a single note. They must sing wholly of their own accord, it is of no use to bid them to do it.

"What is remarkable," he continued, "their tunes are all psalm tunes. . . . Almost all these persons are church members. . . . Most of them are of the Baptist persuasion; a few are Methodists."

The following description of a corn shucking is also from *DeBow's Review*, New Orleans, Vol. IX, 1850, pp. 326-327.

But you must hear of the corn shucking. The one at which I was present was given on purpose that I might witness the humors of the Carolina negroes. A huge fire of *light wood* was made near the corn-house. *Light wood* is the wood of the long leaved pine, and is so called, not because it is light, for it is almost the heaviest wood in the world, but because it gives more light than other fuel. In clearing land, the pines are girdled and suffered to stand; the outer portion of the wood decays and falls off, the inner part, which is saturated with turpentine, remains upright for years, and constitutes the planter's provision of fuel. When a supply is wanted, one of these dead trunks is felled by the ax. The abundance of *light wood* is one of the boasts of South Carolina. . . .

The *light wood* fire was made, and the negroes dropped in from the neighboring plantations, singing as they came. The driver of the plantation, a colored man, brought out baskets of corn in the husk, and piled it in a heap; and the negroes began to strip the husks from the ears, singing with great glee as they worked, keeping time to the music, and now and then throwing in a joke and an extravagant burst of laughter. The songs were generally of a comic character; but one of them was set to a singularly wild and plaintive air, which some of our musicians would do well to reduce to notation.

These are the words:

Johnny come down de hollow.
                    Oh, hollow!
Johnny come down de hollow.
                    Oh, hollow!
De nigger-trader got he.
                    Oh, hollow!
De speculator bought me.
                    Oh, hollow!
I'm sold for silver dollars.
                    Oh, hollow!
Boys, go catch the poney,
                    Oh, hollow!
Bring him round de corner.
                    Oh, hollow!
I'm going away to Georgia.
                    Oh, hollow!
Boys, good-bye for ever.
                    Oh, hollow!

One of the songs, commonly sung on these occasions, represents the various animals of the woods as belonging to some profession or trade, for example:

"De cooter is de boatman—"

The cooter is the terrapin, and a very expert boatman he is.

De Cooter is de boatman,   De Mocking-bird de lawyer.
    John, John Crow.   John, John Crow.
De red-bird de soger   De alligator, sawyer,
    John, John Crow.   John, John Crow.

When the work of the evening was over, the negroes adjourned to a spacious kitchen. One of them took his place as a musician, whistling and beating time with two sticks upon the floor. Several of the men came forward and executed various dances, capering, prancing and drumming with heel and toe upon the floor with astonishing agility and perseverance, though all of them had performed their daily tasks and had worked all evening, and some had walked from four to seven miles to attend the corn shucking. From the dances a transition was made to a mock military parade, a sort of burlesque of our militia trainings, in which the words of command and the evolutions were extremely ludicrous. It became necessary for the commander to make a speech, and confessing his incapacity for public speaking, he called upon a huge black man named Toby, to address the company in his stead. Toby, a man of powerful frame, six feet high, his face ornamented with a beard of fashionable cut, had hitherto stood leaning against the wall, looking upon the frolic with an air of superiority. He consented, came forward, and demanded a bit of paper to hold in his hand, and harangued the soldiery. It was evident that Toby had listened to stump speeches in his day. He spoke of "de majority of Sous Carolina," "de interests of de State," "de honor of ole Barnwell district," and these phrases he connected by various expletives and sounds, of which we could make nothing. At length he began to falter, when the captain, with admirable presence of mind, came to his relief, and interrupted and closed the harangue with an hurrah from the company. Toby was allowed by all the spectators, black and white, to have made an excellent speech.

The slave trade was criticized by practically all visitors to the South. The following account of a slave auction is from Captain Basil Hall, *Travels in North America, in the Years 1827 and 1828,* Carey, Sea and Carey, 1829, Vol. II, pp. 192-193.

On reaching the Exchange, [in Charleston, South Carolina,] in the Centre of which the Post-office is placed, I heard the sound of several voices in the street, like those of an auctioneer urging an audience to bid for his goods. I walked to the side of the gallery overlooking a court or square, in which a number of people were collected to purchase slaves or other property. One man was selling a horse on which he was mounted, and riding up and down the streets; another, in the same way, was driving about in a curricule, bawling out to the spectators to make an offer for his carriage and horses. But of course my attention was most taken up with the slave market.

A long table was placed in the middle of the street, upon which the negroes were exposed, not one by one, but in families at a time. From this conspicuous station they were shown off by two auctioneers, one at each end of the table, who called out the biddings, and egged on the purchasers by chanting the praises of their bargains.

These parties of slaves varied in number. The first consisted of an old, infirm woman, a stout broad-shouldered man, apparently her son, his wife, and two children. The auctioneer, having told the names of each, and described their qualifications, requested the surrounding gentlemen to bid. One hundred dollars for each member of the family, or 500 for the whole party, was the first offer. This gradually rose to 150, at which they were finally knocked down; that is to say, 750 dollars for the whole. . . . Several other families were then put up in succession, who brought from 250 to 260 dollars each member, including children at the breast, as well as old people quite incapable of work.

The next party was exceedingly interesting. The principal person was a stout well-built man, or, as the auctioneer called him, "a fellow, who was a capital driver." His wife stood by his side—a tall, finely proportioned, and really handsome woman, though black as jet. Her left arm encircled a child about six months old, who rested, in the Oriental fashion, on the hip bone. To preserve the balance, her body was inclined to the right, where two little urchins clung to her knee, one of whom, evidently much frightened, clasped its mother's hand, and never relinquished it during the sale which followed. The husband looked grave and somewhat sad; but there was a manliness in the expression of his countenance, which appeared strange in a person placed in so degraded a situation. What struck me most, however, was an occasional touch of anxiety about his eye as it glanced from bidder to bidder, when new offers were made. It seemed to imply a perfect acquaintance with the character of the different parties competing for him—and his happiness or misery for life, he might think, turned upon a word!

The whole of this pretty group were neatly dressed, and altogether so decorous in their manner, that I felt my interest in them rising at every instant. The two little boys, who appeared to be twins, kept their eyes fixed steadily on their mother's face. At first they were quite terrified, but eventually they became as tranquil as their parents. The struggle amongst the buyers continued for nearly a quarter of an hour, till at length they were knocked down for 290 dollars a-piece, or 1450 dollars for the whole family. . . .

I learnt from a gentleman afterwards that the negroes, independently of the important consideration of being purchased by good masters, have a singular species of pride on these occasions in fetching a high price; holding it, amongst themselves, as disgraceful to be sold for a small sum of money.

✔   ✔   ✔

Negro slaves in Southern towns had a social life of their own, as observed by many travelers. Three of these are quoted below. The first observation is from Timothy Flint, *Recollections of the Last Ten Years,* Boston, 1826, p. 136.

Every year the negroes have two or three holidays, which in New Orleans and the vicinity, are like the "Saturnalia" of the slaves in ancient Rome. The great Congo-dance is performed. Everything is license and revelry. Some hundreds of negroes, male and female, follow the king of the wake, who is conspicuous for his youth, size, the whiteness of his eyes, and the blackness of his visage. For a crown he has a series of oblong, gilt-paper boxes on his head, tapering upwards, like a pyramid. From the ends of these boxes hang two huge tassels, like those on epaulets. He wags his head and makes grimaces. By his thousand mountebank tricks, and contortions of countenance and form, he produces an irresistible effect upon the multitude. All the characters that follow him, of leading estimation, have their own peculiar dress, and their own contortions. They dance, and their streamers fly, and the bells that they have hung about them tinkle.

Never will you see gayer countenances, demonstrations of more forgetfulness of the past and future, and more entire abandonment to the joyous existence of the present moment. I have seen groups of these moody and silent sons of the forest, following these merry bachanalians in their dance, through the streets, scarcely relaxing their grim visages to a smile, in the view of antics that convulsed even the masters of the negroes with laughter.

Frederick Law Olmsted, *A Journey in the Seaboard Slave States,* Dix and Edwards, New York, 1856, p. 554, found the Negroes of Montgomery, Alabama, enjoying activities in imitation of white society.

During the winter, the negroes, in Montgomery, have their "assemblies," or dress balls, which are got up "regardless of the expense," in very grand style. Tickets are advertised to these balls, "admitting one gentleman and two ladies, $1"; and "Ladies are assured that they may rely on the strictest order and propriety being observed." Cards of invitation, finely engraved with handsome vignettes, are sent, not only to the fashionable slaves, but to some of the more esteemed white people, who, however, take no part except as lookers-on. All the fashionable dances are executed; no one is admitted except in full dress: there are the regular masters of ceremonies, floor committees, etc.; and a grand supper always forms part of the entertainment.

❧   ❧   ❧

James S. Buckingham, *The Slave States of America,* Fisher, Son and Company, London, 1842, Vol. II, p. 427, described a Sunday in New Orleans.

On Sundays, when the slaves and servants are all at liberty after dinner, they move about in every public thoroughfare, and are generally more gaily dressed than the whites. The females wear white muslin and light silk gowns, with caps, bonnets, ribbons, and feathers; some carry reticules on the arm, and many are seen with parasols, while nearly all of them carry a white pocket-handkerchief before them in the most fashionable style. The young men, among the slaves, wear white trousers, black stocks, broad-brimmed hats, and carry walking-sticks; and from the bowing, curtseying, and greetings, in the highway, one might almost imagine one's self to be at Hayti, and think that the coloured people had got possession of the town, and held sway, while the whites were living among them by sufferance. This is only the Sunday-aspect, however, but to me it was a very agreeable sight while it lasted; the negroes, of both sexes, seemed so happy in the enjoyment of their holiday and finery, that I wished from my heart I could secure them two Sundays a week instead of one, or, better still, have them happy all the week through. On working days, however, the case is altered, for then they return back to their labor and dirty clothes again. . . .

✔   ✔   ✔

The following illustration of how plantation Negroes frequently sang to lighten their work is from *Blackwood's Edinburgh Magazine*, Vol. 87, 1860, pp. 103-116, *passim*.

Latterly, no doubt, in consequence of a series of revivals, the result of perpetual camp-meetings, the negroes have assumed a certain air of solemn gravity and sobriety, a good deal at variance with the natural vivacity of their dispositions—a characteristic, however, which they never manage effectually to smother. On some plantations in South Carolina they had, at the period of my visit, given up dancing, held constant prayer-meetings, and never sang anything but their own sacred compositions. These chants break with their pleasant melody the calm stillness of the evening, as we glide down the broad bosom of the Wacamaw, and our crew with measured stroke keep time to the music of their own choruses. The words, however, are more original than the music. Here are specimens taken down as they were sung:

> "Oh I takes my text in Matthew,
> And some in Revelation;
> Oh I know you by your garment—
> There's a meeting here to-night."

This is the entire effusion, and is constantly repeated, the last line being the chorus; some, however, are more elaborate:

> "In that morning, true believers,
>   In that morning.
> We will sit aside of Jesus
>   In that morning.
> If you should go fore I go,
>   In that morning.
> You will sit aside of Jesus
>   In that morning.
> True believers, where your tickets
>   In that morning?
> Master Jesus got your tickets
>   In that morning."

And so on, with a number of variations, often extempore, but with the same refrain ever recurring, and joined in by all. Sometimes the metre is less regular, as—

> "I want to sing as the angels sing,
>   Daniel;

> I want to pray as the angels pray,
>> Daniel;
> I want to shout as the angels shout,
>> Daniel.
> Oh Lord, give me the eagle's wing.
> What time of day,   Daniel?
> In the Lions den,   Daniel?
> I want to pray,   Daniel?
> Oh, Lord, give me the eagle's wing."

The sense of the above is more difficult than usual to discover, and affords some notion of the superficial character of their knowledge of the Scripture. Here is one, however, where a definite idea is intended to be conveyed. It is supposed to be sung by a believer on his deathbed, and the air is singularly touching:

> "Master Jesus send for me—
>> Lord, I must go;
> Dem archangels send for me—
>> Lord, I must go.
> Fare de well, my broders—
>> Lord, I must go;
> General Jesus, send for me—
>> Lord, I must go.
> Fare de well, my broders—
>> Lord, I must go;
> General Jesus, send for me—
>> Lord, I must go.
> Fare de well, my sisters—
>> Lord, I must go.
> Weeping Mary, send for me—
>> Lord, I must go;
> Sister Martha, send for me—
>> Lord, I must go."

Generally, indeed, the airs were appropriate to the spirit of the composition; some of them were sung with great vehemence and unction, and from the excitement of tone and manner, the susceptibility of the negro to appeals of this nature to his devotional instincts was evident. The sacred names were generally screamed rather than sung, with an almost ecstatic fervour. The two following were clearly great favourites:

> "The heavenly bell is ringing loud,
> I wish it was ringing for me;

Broders walking to New Jerusalem,
Doubters walking to New Jerusalem.
Oh the heavenly bell is ringing loud,
I wish it was ringing for me;
Sarah's walking to New Jerusalem,
Elias' walking to New Jerusalem,
Heroes walking to New Jerusalem.
Oh the heavenly bell, &c. &c.

And—

"Broders, don't you hear the horn?
Yes, Lord, I hear the horn;
The horn sounds in jubilee.
Sisters, don't you hear the horn?
Yes, Lord, I hear the horn;
The horn sounds from door.
Mourners, don't you hear the horn?
Yes, Lord, I hear the horn;
The horn sounds like broder Tony's horn."

✓   ✓   ✓

Mary Boykin Chesnut, a very intelligent and talented Southern lady, kept an intimate diary for the four years of the Civil War. In it she expressed her doubts concerning the institution of slavery. She frequently referred to miscegenation resulting from the slave system. The following excerpts are from *A Diary from Dixie,* edited by Ben Ames Williams, Houghton Mifflin Company, Boston, 1950, pp. 21, 122, 162.

I wonder if it is a sin to think slavery a curse to any land. Men and women are punished when their masters and mistresses are brutes, not when they do wrong. Under slavery, we live surrounded by prostitutes, yet an abandoned woman is sent out of any decent house. Who thinks any worse of a Negro or mulatto woman for being a thing we can't name? God forgive us, but ours is a monstrous system, a wrong and an iniquity. Like the patriarchs of old, our men live all in one house with their wives and their concubines; and the mulattoes one sees in every family resemble the white children. Any lady is ready to tell you who is the father of all the mulatto children in everybody's household but her own. Those, she seems to think, drop from the clouds. My disgust sometimes is boiling over. Thank God for my country women, but alas for the men! They are probably no worse than men everywhere, but the lower their mistresses, the more degraded they must be. . . . .

I hate slavery. You say there are no more fallen women on a plantation than in London, in proportion to numbers; but what do you say to this? A magnate who runs a hideous black harem with its consequences under the same roof with his lovely white wife, and his beautiful and accomplished daughters. He holds his head as high and poses as the model of all human virtues to these poor women whom God and the laws have given him. From the height of his awful majesty he scolds and thunders at them, as if he never did wrong in his life. Fancy such a man finding his daughter reading "Don Juan." "You with that immoral book!" And he orders her out of his sight. You see, Mrs. Stowe did not hit the sorest spot. She makes Legree a bachelor. . . . .

Martha Adamson is a beautiful mulatress, as good looking as they ever are to me. I have never seen a mule as handsome as a horse, and I know I never will. . . . She is a trained sempstress, and "hired her own time," as they call it; that is, the owner pays the doctor's bills, finds food and clothing, and the slave pays his master five dollars a month, more or less, and makes a dollar a day if he pleases. Martha, to the amazement of everybody, married a coal-black Negro, the son of Dick the Barber, who was set free fifty years ago for faithful services rendered Mr. Chesnut's grandfather. She was asked: How could she? She is so nearly white. How could she marry that horrid Negro? It is positively shocking! She answered that she inherits the taste of her white father, that her mother was black.

8

Education in the Old South

During the colonial period the hope of young Southern gentlemen was to be sent to England to be educated. William Henry Drayton's education was described by his son, John Drayton, in *Memoirs of the American Revolution,* A. E. Miller, Charleston, 1821, Vol. I, p. xii.

WILLIAM HENRY DRAYTON was born in South-Carolina, at Drayton Hall on Ashley River, in September 1742. He was the eldest son of John Drayton, whose father Thomas Drayton was a descendant of the Drayton family of Northhamptonshire in England; and who came to South-Carolina, from the Island of Barbadoes, in the year 1761, with Sir John Yeamans and others.

When William Henry Drayton had arrived at the age of eleven years, his father sent him to England in the year 1753, under the care of Charles Pinckney; who, having resigned the office of Chief Justice of the Province, was then going to England with his family: among whom were his two sons, Charles Cotesworth Pinckney and Thomas Pinckney. With the guidance and protection of this very respectable gentleman, he prosecuted his education at Westminster School in London, until the autumn of 1761; when he was removed to the University of Oxford; where, he matriculated on the 10th day of October in Balliol College. He there continued his studies, for nearly three years; when the call of a parent obliged him to leave his collegiate duties, and to return to Carolina. He did not, however, discontinue the improvements of his mind; but entered upon a course of reading, with great industry; and thereby became well informed in the English, ancient and modern histories, the Law of Nations, and the rights of his own country. His father being a gentleman of large estate, and he the eldest son, he had not been brought up to any profession; but his ardent mind, would not permit him to move in a common sphere: and he therefore turned his attention to law and politics.

ꭴ ꭴ ꭴ

After the American Revolution, young men of well-to-do families were prepared for a classical education in schools such as that attended by John Randolph of

Roanoke, in Williamsburg. The following selection is from William Cabell Bruce, *John Randolph of Roanoke*, G. P. Putnam's Sons, New York, 1922, p. 57.

"My acquaintance with John Randolph," Tazewell says in his manuscript reminiscences of him, which we have had the privilege of perusing, "commenced in the year 1784, when he was about 11 years old, I believe. In that year, he, together with his two older brothers, Richard and Theodorick, entered the grammar school, then recently established by Mr. Walker Maury in the City of Williamsburg, where I resided. Before his removal to Williamsburg, Mr. Maury had conducted a grammar school in the County of Orange and the three young Randolphs had been his pupils there. Their progress therefore was well known to their tutor when they re-entered his school in Williamsburg; in which school I had been a pupil from its commencement in that place. This school was established as an appendage of the College of William and Mary, in which there was no professorship of Humanity existing at that time. It was regulated most judiciously, and was soon attended by more pupils than any other grammar school that had been before established or has since existed in Virginia, I believe. I do not recollect the number of scholars exactly, but it exceeds one hundred, and included boys from every state then in the Union from Georgia to Maryland both inclusive. Such a number of pupils made it necessary that they should be divided into classes. The greater proportion of these classes were consigned by Mr. Maury, the principal, to the superintendency of his assistants, of whom there were four. When the young Randolphs entered the school, the number was not so great as it afterwards became. Richard, the oldest, was placed in the second class under the immediate direction of Mr. Maury himself. Theodorick and John were placed in the fourth class which was the head class consigned to the Superintendency of the chief usher, a Mr. Elliot. To this class I belonged, and when the class was so augmented, it was engaged in reading, and had nearly finished, Eutropius. The book I then used I still possess, and the fact that I have stated is derived from a class-roll written on its fly leaf. [John Randolph was taken away from the school and sent to Bermuda because of ill health.] . . . At the time John Randolph left us, the class was engaged in reading Sallust and Virgil, and had made some progress in learning the Greek and French languages and the elements of Geometry.

In North Carolina the most highly respected preparatory school was that of Dr. David Caldwell (see p. 92). Archibald D. Murphey, great North Carolinian advocate of public education, described the curriculum of Caldwell's school. The following selection is from William Henry Hoyt, Editor, *The Papers of Archibald D. Murphey*, E. M. Uzell and Company, Raleigh, 1914, Vol. II, p. 355.

Before this University [the University of North Carolina] went into operation, in 1795, there were not more than three schools in the State, in which the rudiments of a classical education could be acquired. The most prominent and useful of these schools was kept by Dr. David Caldwell, of Guilford County. He instituted it shortly after the close of the war, and continued it for more than thirty years. The usefulness of Dr. Caldwell to the literature of North Carolina will never be sufficiently appreciated: but the opportunities of instruction in his school were very limited. There was no library attached to it; his students were supplied with a few of the Greek and Latin classics, Euclid's Elements of Mathematics, and Martin's Natural Philosophy. Moral Philosophy was taught from a syllabus of lectures delivered by Dr. Witherspoon in Princeton College. The students had no books on history or miscellaneous literature. There were indeed very few in the State, except in the libraries of lawyers who lived in commercial towns. I well remember, that after completing my course of studies under Dr. Caldwell, I spent nearly two years without finding any books to read, except some old works on theological subjects.

✓   ✓   ✓

Another famous "prep school" was Dr. Moses Waddell's school in Edgefield District, South Carolina. It was described by William John Grayson, *James Louis Pettigru, A Biographical Sketch,* Harper and Brothers, New York, 1866.

The Willington school was a sort of Eton or Rugby of American manufacture, and the doctor at its head the Carolina Dr. Arnold. He had talents for organization and government. His method appealed largely to the honor and moral sense of his pupils. They were not confined with their books unnecessarily in a narrow school-room. The forest was their place of study. They resorted to the old oaks and hickories, and at their feet or among their branches prepared their various lessons. The horn called them at intervals to change of occupation. The sound was repeated from point to point, and the woods echoed with these sonorous signals for recitation or retirement. When cold or wet weather drove the students from their sylvan resorts, log cabins in various quarters afforded the requisite accommodations. At night, with the same sound of the horn, they retired to their lodgings for sleep or farther study. Their food was Spartan in plainness— corn-bread and bacon; and for lights, torches of pine were more in fashion than candles. Monitors regulated the classes and subdivisions of classes, and preserved the order and discipline of the institution with the smallest possible reference to its head. It was a kind of rural republic, with a perpetual dictator. The scholars were enthusiastically attached to their school. After they had become grandfathers they talked of it in raptures.

✓   ✓   ✓

Certain critics have called Richard Malcolm Johnston "The Dean of Southern Writers." His career was divided among three professions: law, teaching, and writing. As a lawyer he rode the circuit, traveling from one county seat to another, in his leisure hours spinning yarns with the other lawyers in small-town hotels and being entertained by townspeople. As a professor at the University of Georgia he developed his philosophy of education. Later he ran a private boarding school, and eventually ceased to be a teacher and wrote stories, Georgia sketches, and a biography of Alexander H. Stephens. He spent the years 1895-1898 as a clerk in the Bureau of Education, during which time he wrote the reports on the Old Field Schools of Georgia from which the following sketches are taken. They are based on his own boyhood experience, when from the age of five he attended "old field schools" for four years. *Education Report, 1894-1895*, U. S. Government, Washington, D. C., pp. 1699ff.

If school keeping in rural districts during colonial and revolutionary periods was conducted within narrow circumstances, it must be more so in new remote settlements. If there had been entirely competent teachers, boys, even girls, could not be spared from domestic work long enough to give—and that in intervals—more than two or three years' attendance at school, for gentlewomen and their daughters, like the rest, cut and sewed upon garments made of flax, wool, and cotton, produced, spun, and woven at home, while their husbands and sons felled the woods, tended the fields, and harvested the crops. In the most genteel families, along with proper morals, children learned good manners and were encouraged to read in the few choice books brought with them from the old homes. . . . But education in school-houses was made, using a homely phrase, to "shift for itself." . . . .

The old field schoolmaster . . . [appeared] during periods in rural communities, bringing in a red-spotted bandanna handkerchief his household goods, and in his tall, whitish-furred, long experienced hat a sheet of foolscap, on which he set down what he called his "school articles." Within some months, seldom completing the year, with the same bandanna and hat, noiselessly as he had come, he went his way. . . .

Now the idea that a native-born citizen competent to instruct children would have been content to undertake such a work was not entertained. Somehow, keeping a school was regarded at the bottom on the list of vocations, fit only for those who were not qualified for any other. . . . Everybody recognized the necessity of children receiving at least rudimentary education. [Yet] in some sections . . . demands on that score were far from being very exacting. . . . .

A place was selected on the edge of a wood and a field turned out to fallow, sufficiently central, hard by a spring of purest fresh water, a log-house was put up, say 30 by 25 feet, with one door and a couple of windows and shelves, with benches along the unceiled walls, and the session began. Most families breakfasted about sunrise, and a brisk walk of three-quarters of an hour brought even the remotest dwellers to the early opening. The one who happened to reach the schoolhouse first on winter mornings kindled a fire. This was before the date of lucifer matches. In winter half-burned logs were so disposed beneath the ashes on the huge fireplaces as to preserve fire through the night, which was quickly rekindled by the aid of pine knots always on hand. . . .

At noon a recess of two hours was allowed for dinner and sports. On days when the sun shone, the hour was made known by its reaching a mark on the floor by the door or one of the window-sills. In cloudy weather it was guessed at. The idea of a schoolmaster owning a watch did not enter anyone's mind. When the day was done, dismissal was out and out. There were no keepings-in at noon or evening tide. Each day had its own history and no more. . . . The master went silently to the house where he boarded, and the pupils, boys and girls, whipped and unwhipped, turned their backs upon everything, journeyed leisurely along, boys anon rallying one another on the day's misadventures, . . . and the girls laughing at them.

✓ ✓ ✓

Thomas Jefferson was the father of much proposed educational legislation. The following extract from a letter which he wrote to John Adams, October 28, 1813, is from Thomas Jefferson, *Works,* Library Edition, Vol. XIII, pp. 399-400.

At the first session of our legislature after the Declaration of Independence, we passed a law abolishing entails. And this was followed by one abolishing the privilege of primogeniture, and dividing the lands of intestates equally among all their children, or other representatives. These laws, drawn by myself, laid the axe to the root of pseudo-aristocracy. And had another, which I proposed, been adopted by the legislature, our work would have been more complete. It was a bill for the more general diffusion of learning. This proposed to divide every county into wards of five or six miles square, like your townships, to establish in each ward a free school for reading, writing, and common arithmetic to provide for the annual selection of the best subjects from these schools, who might receive at public expense a higher degree of education at a district school, and from these district schools to select a certain number of the most promising subjects, to be completed at a university where all the useful sciences should be taught. Worth and genius would thus have been sought out from every condition of life, and completely prepared by education for defeating the competition of wealth and birth for public trusts.

✓ ✓ ✓

In 1809 Jefferson persuaded Governor Tyler of Virginia to send a message to the legislature advocating provision for public education, and a Literary Fund was established as a result. All funds accruing to the state for forfeitures, escheats, and similar sources were to be devoted to public education, for the children of the poor.

Free public education did not make much progress in Virginia, in spite of the existence of the Literary Fund. Free schools were thought of as charity schools and were not popular. For the year ending September 30, 1851, Frederick Law Olmsted quoted educational figures for the following three Virginia counties, in *A Journey in the Seaboard Slave States,* Dix and Edwards, New York, 1856, pp. 292-3.

ALBEMARLE (White population, 11,875; Slave do., 13,338).—"The Board of Commissioners state, that with the present appropriation to the county, they must be dependent upon the schools established by individual enterprise. They can, of course, proffer their assistance only where such schools exist."

"Your Superintendent would bring to your consideration the importance of recommending an increased per diem rate of tuition from four to five cents, as many of the best qualified teachers in the county object to take the indigent children into their schools on account of the reduced price per diem. . . ."

AMELIA (Whites, 2,785; Slaves, 6,819; number of indigent children registered, 120; number of do., who attended school at any time within a year, 68). . . .

CHARLOTTE (White Population, 4,615; Slave, 8,988). "The Superintendent states that in three or four of the districts, school could not be obtained, and in others the children could not be induced to go; that it is utterly impossible to induce the district commissioners to have the accounts and reports made out according to form; the consequence is, that there is a great difficulty in making the returns in due time."

An article in *DeBow's Review,* New Orleans, Vol. IX, 1849, p. 308, described the educational situation in Charleston at that time, with a white population of 14,187 and a Negro population, including both slaves and free colored, of 12,264.

The list of free school pupils is 394, amount expended for them $3,900, average to scholar $10, average attendance five years. These are valuable schools, but they are scarcely adequate to the wants of the city. Private teachers, however, abound. There is an admirable high school, established in 1839, with an average of 130 to 150 scholars. It is endowed with $1,000 per annum, for a hundred years, by council. There are several public libraries in Charleston—the Apprentices, with a fine hall; the Mercantile, and the Charleston Library Society—the last named being the oldest and best.

Parents who could afford to send their children to academies and to college were not likely to support measures to increase taxes to provide free schools. Most of the leadership for public schools came from men who had risen from the common people. Only in North Carolina and Kentucky did the movement result in creditable public school systems before the Civil War. The General Assembly of North Carolina passed a law in 1825 setting aside the dividends from certain state-owned investments to form a Literary Fund for the support of the common schools. Fourteen years later, when money had accumulated in this fund, another law was passed, providing for the creation of common schools. Several subsequent acts were passed during the next two decades, perfecting the common school system, creating the office of State Superintendent of Common Schools, and providing for a compulsory county tax to supplement the income from the Literary Fund.

When the United States Congress in 1836 provided for the deposit with the several states the accumulated surplus in the United States Treasury, the Assembly of Kentucky set aside one million dollars for the support of education in that state. In 1838 an act was passed creating a system of common schools.

The following selections ilustrate two opinions concerning the need of the South for better schools. The first is from "X's Open Letter Against Schools and Internal Improvements," 1829, quoted in Charles L. Coon, *The Beginnings of Public Education in North Carolina,* Edwards and Broughton Printing Co., Raleigh, 1908, p. 431. . . . .

Gentlemen, it appears to me that schools are sufficiently plenty, and that the people have no desire they should be increased. Those now in operation are not all filled, and it is very doubtful if they are productive of much real benefit. Would it not redound as much to the advantage of young persons, and to the honour of the State, if they should pass their days in the cotton patch, or at the plow, or in the cornfield, instead of being mewed up in a schoolhouse, where they are earning nothing? . . . Gentlemen, I hope you do not conceive it at all necessary, that *everybody* should be able to read, write and cipher. If one is to keep a store, or to be a lawyer or physician, such branches may, *perhaps,* be taught him; though I do not look upon them as by any means indispensable: but if he is to be a plain farmer, or mechanic, they are of no manner of use, but rather a detriment. . . . Should schools be established by law, in all parts of the State, as at the North, our taxes must be considerably increased, possibly to the amount of one per cent. and sixpence on a poll; and I will ask any prudent, sane, saving man if he desires his taxes to be higher?

⚹   ⚹   ⚹

The following is from *DeBow's Review*, New Orleans, New Series, Vol. I, 1841, pp. 658-668, *passim*. It is entitled, *"Home Education at the South,"* by the Reverend C. K. Marshall of Mississippi.

One of the first duties we have to perform, in order to the accomplishment of the great work of home education, is the raising up and preparing an army of teachers, thoroughly trained, and fully imbued with their high mission. . . . Teachers are as much a part of a State's wealth and power as her governors, secretaries, judges, ministers, physicians, mechanics, and planters. But, like other professions, there must be a special education with reference to teaching. Youths destined for the army, the navy, for engineering, for mercantile pursuits, for the profession of law or medicine, are placed in institutions prepared to make scholars of them in their several professions. Not one of them all demand more attention, more direct State patronage, or more ample provision and endowment, than normal schools, for the proper education and training of teachers for the active and singularly responsible duties of their profession. . . .

Let each State pass a law providing for the appropriation of at least one hundred dollars for every parish or county in the State where a like sum can be obtained, and let the amount be applied to the education of such young man or woman as would agree to teach at least two years within the State, and let a certain degree of scholarship be requisite as a condition of receiving such aid; then let them be sent to the best schools or colleges in the State, to be educated. By this means the south could raise up for herself an abundance of the best instructors the light of Heaven ever shone upon. Our States abound with the finest material to be found in any country on earth for the great work. Duty requires this work at our hands; *and in its performance is our safety and strength. . . .*

We would still need text books adapted to our ideas, our necessities, or destiny.

At present we have them not. That we have them not is our shame and reproach. Our text books are abolition works. . . . We will refer to . . . "Gilbert's Atlas"—though the real author's name does not appear on the title page. On the title page it is called "Appleton's Complete Guide of the World," published by D. Appleton & Co., New York. This is an elegant and comprehensive volume, endorsed by the Appletons and sent south, containing hidden lessons of the most fiendish and murderous character that enraged fanaticism could conceive or indite. . . . Let us read one of its many sanguinary lessons. Turning to page 184, we find the following language:

"In the southern States, where the culture of cotton and rice is so largely carried on, the field-labor is, for the most part, performed by negro slaves —a race of beings who we understand to be worse treated in the American States than in any other part of the world. They are very numerous, and as they are aware of the establishment of the black government in Hayti, and the emancipation of the black population in Jamaica and the other British colonies, the severe yoke, under the burden of which they have long groaned, must become more and more galling to them every day. Nor is there any doubt that the time is rapidly approaching when they will, by their own bravery, wrest their independence from their American masters, upon the same principle and with the same justice that the Americans wrested their independence from the British government. In the event of a war between Britain and America, the British would greatly accelerate this desirable emancipation by landing a few black regiments from the West Indies, and establish depots for the supply of arms at the places on the coasts of which the black troops had taken possession. There are many facilities for the supply of arms, and if a war should render the measure necessary, the success of it is pretty certain. . . ."

Sir, this book, and many other northern school books scattered over the country, come within the range of the statutes of this State, which provide for the imprisonment for life or the infliction of the death penalty upon any person who shall "publish or distribute" such works; and were I a citizen of New Orleans, this work should not escape the attention of the grand jury.

1   1   1

The first college in the South, and the only one established there during the colonial period, was William and Mary, at Williamsburg, founded in 1693 to provide ministers and to serve as an Indian school. After the Revolutionary War, the states, one by one, established state-supported universities. Georgia was the first to pass such a law, although the University of North Carolina was the first to start such instructional services. In the following selections are descriptions of curricula and college life in three Southern state-supported universities.

The United States Bureau of Education, *Circular of Information,* No. 2, 1888, gives us in "The History of Education in North Carolina, by Charles Lee Smith, Washington, 1888," The University of North Carolina.

North Carolina was one of the first states to make constitutional provision for higher education. To the Scotch-Irish Presbyterians occupying Central and Piedmont Carolina is due the lasting honor of having established the first academies in the Province, and it is said that it was through their influence that the clause providing for a university was inserted in the Constitution of the State. . . .

The writer, while exploiting the manuscript records of the University, came across some correspondence of Prof. Charles W. Harris, . . . which pictures the state of society at Chapel Hill at that time. The letter, from which the following extract is taken, is addressed to Dr. Charles Harris, Cabarrus County, and is dated "University, April 10, 1795. . . ."

"We have begun to introduce, by degrees, the regulations of the University, and as yet have not been disappointed. There is one class in Natural Philosophy and Geography, and four in the Languages.

The Constitution of this college is on a more liberal plan than that of any other in America, and by the amendments which I think it will receive at the next meeting of the trustees, its usefulness will probably be much promoted. The notion that true learning consists rather in exercising the reasoning faculties and laying up a store of useful knowledge, than in over-loading the memory with words of dead languages, is daily becoming more prevalent. . . . Though the laws at present require that the Latin and Greek be understood by a graduate, they will in all probability be mitigated in their effect. . . . At present we find much difficulty in procuring books; the trustees have ordered two hundred dollars to be expended for that purpose, but it is very uncertain when the books will arrive. Dr. Williamson is commissioned to purchase and he is so totally engaged about his own book which he is preparing for the press, that he may forget others of less importance. Col. More presented us with globes; Mr. Beneham with an air pump as soon as it can be procured. We will shortly have an electrical machine and other trifles. Our society is not so good at this place as we could wish. My only resort is to Mr. Kerr, who makes ample amends to me for the want of any other. He is a violent Republican and is continually deprecating the aristocratical principles which have lately prevailed much in our Executive."

On December 9, 1796, the committee appointed by the trustees to prepare and digest a plan of education made its report, which was adopted. The following is an outline of the system introduced:

The students of the institution were "divided into a Preparatory School, and the Professorships of the University."

In the Preparatory School the English language was "taught grammati-cally on the plan of Webster's and South's Grammars." Thorough instruc-tion in arithmetic was provided. Geography was taught on the plan of Guthrie. French and Latin were required, and before the student could enter the University the grammars of these languages had to be mastered and several standard authors in each read. The study of Roman antiquities was required. Greek was optional, but to enter the University class on this, it was necessary that the student should be able to read and translate the Gospels correctly.

Instruction in the University was given in the following schools, called "professorships," viz:

I. Rhetoric and belles-lettres
II. Moral and political philosophy and history
III. Natural philosophy
IV. Mathematics
V. Languages

✓   ✓   ✓

The English lecturer, James S. Buckingham, in *The Slave States of America,* Fisher, Son, and Company, London, 1842, Vol. II, pp. 72-75, described the University of Georgia as it was when he visited Athens, Georgia, in 1839.

It was about forty years ago that this spot was set apart by the State for the foundation of a University, and a tract of land amounting to 50,000 acres was given as an endowment for the same. On this land the sum of 140,000 dollars was raised by way of loan or mortgage; but as a portion of this was in bonds and notes not redeemed when due, the legislature took the whole amount, and gave for it, in money, 100,000 dollars, which, being placed at interest in the State Bank, yields an income of 8,000 dollars annually, as the present permanent revenue of the University. The governor of the state, Milledge, after whom the legislative capital of Georgia is called Milledgeville, made a personal grant, from his own private property, of sufficient land for the buildings and offices of the University, and the State made an advance of 10,000 dollars towards the building-fund. In this manner, the University was first founded. Its subsequent support has been maintained by the annual revenue of 8,000, by the tuition fees, and by occasional grants from the State for the library and other purposes.

Soon after the building of the first college, which is called Franklin College, and which was completed in 1801, families from various parts of the State began to settle here, for the advantage of educating their children; and a Female Academy was soon superadded to the college, for the education of the young women. This has gone on increasing every year, so that there are now at least one hundred good dwelling-houses inhabited by families of easy competency, living on fixed incomes, and about an equal number of smaller dwellings, inhabited by persons in trade. . . .

The board of trustees of the University is formed of twenty-seven of the most eminent men in the State, including the governor, several of the judges, barristers, physicians, and private gentlemen of fortune. The faculty consists of a president, six professors, and two tutors, with a librarian and a secretary. The students, at present 127 in number, are divided into the classes of seniors, juniors, sophomores, and freshmen.

The period for entering college in the freshman class, must not be earlier than fourteen years of age; and the students often remain till they are past twenty-one. The whole expenses of a student for a year do not exceed 180 dollars; and the charge is thus apportioned—tuition in every branch, 50 dollars; board, 114 dollars; washing, 9 dollars; fuel, 7 dollars; so that 36 £. sterling covers the entire cost of board, lodging, washing, attendance, and instruction! There is an annual public examination at "Commencement," as it is called, which occurs on the first week in August, when degrees are conferred, and prizes awarded; and on this occasion, the families and friends of the students repair to Athens from all parts of the country, so that the town is literally full. This lasts for about a week, and is succeeded by a week's vacation. The great vacation is, however, in the winter for ten weeks, from the 1st of November to the 16th of January, as this is the period of the year in which it is safest and best for such of the students as live in the low country, to visit their families and friends.

✓   ✓   ✓

The University of Virginia at Charlottesville was established through the efforts of Thomas Jefferson in 1825. It was unique in that it introduced the elective system. When E. S. Abdy visited the university it had been in operation about eight years. His account is from his *Journal of a Residence and Tour of the United States of America from April, 1833, to October, 1834,* J. Murray, London, 1835, Vol. II, pp. 228, 238.

[I called upon Dr. Patterson,] . . . and he invited me to drink tea with him. . . . It is natural philosophy that Professor Patterson lectures. He has a well-chosen apparatus for the purpose. There is a public examination for the students at the middle and at the end of each session. It is conducted in writing; and the classification, which is determined by marks previously arranged, is into four divisions, according to the answers. The Institution confers three degrees of honor; a certificate of proficiency, the title of graduate in any school or faculty, and the degree of M.A. in the University of Virginia. To obtain the last, the candidate must have graduated in ancient languages, modern languages, mathematics, natural philosophy, chemistry, and moral philosophy. . . .

Charlottesville, which contains about 1500 souls, is a neat, thriving town, surrounded by farms in a good state of cultivation. The University brings a good deal of money to it, without receiving an equivalent in morals. The students reside ten months in the year. Their average age is twenty; considerably higher than it is at Cambridge or Newhaven. Of 201 students, who attended the preceding session, three only were from the free States. The system is in one respect like the German and Scotch; as the professors receive fees, in addition to their salaries, from their pupils, who are allowed to select what "faculty" they will study. . . . .

There are no such public schools here as exist in the north. The expenses of education are defrayed by the State, which has appointed commissioners for the poor, whose children are sent to private establishments, where they are taught with those not under the same necessity: an ingenious method to keep up the most odious features of that distinction which difference of wealth will always make. The consequences of this arrangement are just what might have been expected. Rather than expose them to humiliation, many parents keep their children at home, where they receive little or no education. This feeling in the "lower orders" is imputed to pride; but, if it be pride, it is a feeling very nearly allied to self-respect. These matters are not very equitably estimated. This college draws annually from the public purse 15,000 dollars; while 45,000 are granted for the general pur-

poses of instruction throughout the State; yet the cottager's son is despised
by the rich planter's boy, who is sent to a college, built, endowed, and
supported out of the same fund that is employed for the education of the
former; as parish paupers in "sheep-skins and goat-skins" are objects of
contempt to public paupers in "purple and fine linen."

⟊   ⟊   ⟊

South Carolina College was established in 1805. In the decade of the 1820's,
Dr. Thomas Cooper, an English scientist, was its president. His exercise of academic
freedom was the cause of his forced removal from the presidency in 1834. Dr.
Cooper protested the action of the Trustees in a pamphlet from which the following
extract is taken, *The Case of Thomas Cooper, M.D., President of the South Carolina College;* Submitted to the Legislature and the People of South Carolina,
December, printed at the Times and Gazette Office, Columbia, 1831.

Preface

It seems, that at the ensuing session of the Legislature, Dr. Cooper is to
be denounced for something that is called Infidelity, arising from his
having doubted the necessity of making a trade of religion, and having
doubted also the accuracy of the Geological facts and explanations contained in the book of Genesis. This has been considered as an attack on
Religion, although Dr. Cooper, in each case, appeals to the scripture and to
that alone, in support of the opinions he has advanced. Applications
founded on this accusation, are intended to be made to the Legislature,
to remove him from the Presidency of the College. This denunciation
against the freedom of opinion and the freedom of the press—this attempted prohibition of the free exercise of religious profession, will be
made in South Carolina, at the close of the year, 1831. It will remain on
the pages of history, not a little to the surprise of those who have at heart
the honor of the state, the triumph of truth, and the progress of human
improvement.

This is in fact, a continuation of the warfare that has taken place from
the very earliest period of letters to the present day. . . .

Dr. Cooper's Case

THERE are some preliminary observations bearing upon this question,
that are worthy of remark. WHO, and what description of persons are
they, who exclaim against Dr. Cooper on this occasion? They are, *first,*
the political opponents of the State Rights party, who have on this occasion
called in the aid of the sectarians. It has been over and over declared by
the opponents of Dr. C. and it is well understood, that this attack originated
from his opposition to a favourite candidate and leader among that class
of politicians, who are inclined to extend patience, forbearance, and submission, till resistance to oppression has become powerless and useless.

Secondly. The Clergy and leading members of the Calvinistic persuasion;

all the citizens who are in favour of stopping the Sunday mails; who call for legislative interference in religious questions and controversies; and for penal laws against what they are pleased to call heresy and infidelity.

Thirdly. This is a renewed attempt, so often made, to bring the South Carolina College under Presbyterian influence and controul. An attempt that began with the institution of the College, and has continued ever since. The attack, utterly unprovoked by Dr. C. was commenced on him by a very early remonstrance of a Presbyterian meeting, against his election as President. It was followed up by a pamphlet issued against him, by a member of that persuasion at Charleston; by another of equal violence, published by a Judge of the Federal Bench, resident in that city; by another of the same description, published against him by a reverend gentleman of the Presbyterian Church in York district; by incessant attacks in the newspapers; by the Presentment of two Grand Juries against him for heterodoxy or infidelity. Against this system of persecution kept up for years, who can blame him, if he is tempted, at length, to defend himself by a fair and faithful exposition of the character of the assaults and the assailants, their objects and motives? These gentlemen have as much right to their creed as Dr. C. has to his; but neither of them has an exclusive right.

Fourthly. Dr. C's opinions, known and published long before he came to South Carolina, are unpopular among the orthodox and religious party in this state; who doubtless entertain a conscientious objection to any President, whose sentiments on the subject of religion are widely different from their own. . . .

$\checkmark$ $\checkmark$ $\checkmark$

An interesting experiment in education in the 1830's was a "Manual-Labor School" near Abingdon, Virginia, Emory and Henry. It was visited by James S. Buckingham and described in his *Slave States of America*, Fisher, Son, and Company, London, 1842, Vol. II, p. 276.

The system of manual-labour schools has lately been introduced into this part of Virginia, and a school of this description has been established within about ten miles of Abingdon. It is called the "Amory [sic] and Henry College," the former being the name of a celebrated and popular bishop of Virginia, and the latter the name of their great revolutionary orator, Patrick Henry. There are at present upwards of 100 pupils in the establishment, which is conducted as nearly as practicable on the plan of Mr. Fellenberg's institution at Hoffwyl, in Switzerland. The boys have two hours' study before breakfast, four hours between breakfast and dinner, three hours labour in the field, garden, or workshop after dinner, and the evening is devoted to preparing the lessons for the ensuing day. The sum paid for board and tuition is a dollar and half per week, about a shilling per day, and they are allowed five cents, or about two-pence half-penny an hour, for all labour performed, as a set-off against these charges, so that the cost of educating a boy, who performs his three hours' labour per day regularly, is not more than fifty dollars, or about 10 £. sterling a year, for board and tuition in every branch of useful learning.

✓   ✓   ✓

Many Southerners believed the educational needs of women to be very different from those of men. Schools were founded by religious denominations and by individuals, but they were not colleges. Dr. William A. Webb, President of Randolph Macon Woman's College, summarized the growth of such schools, in a report which he made to the Southern Association of College Women in 1915. The following is from *Proceedings* of the Twelfth Annual Meeting of the Southern Association of College Women, Southern Association of College Women, Raleigh, 1915, p. 25.

The Civil War is a convenient epoch for marking the line of cleavage in the history of the growth and development of separate institutions for women in the United States. In the South, such institutions as Wesleyan Female College, founded in 1837, Greensboro Female College, founded in 1838, and Mary Sharp College, founded in 1851, may be taken as typical ante bellum schools. Measured by modern standards, or even by the standards then prevailing in the best colleges for men, they were in no sense colleges. They were finishing schools and seminaries, whose graduates, in spite of the weakness and poverty of their educational environment, received much that was vital and valuable in intellectual and moral training. From such schools came the women who during the storm and stress of the Civil War gave stability and tone to our Southern civilization and became the mothers of the men and women who are to-day the educational leaders of the South.

✓   ✓   ✓

The following list of educational institutions for women established by the Baptist denomination alone, prior to 1854, will illustrate the great interest shown in such schools. The source of the information is B. F. Riley, *A History of the Baptists in the Southern States East of the Mississippi,* American Baptist Publishing Society, Philadelphia, 1898, p. 361.

Virginia

Hollins Institute, founded in 1842; located at Botetourt Springs; value of property, $150,000; value of library and apparatus, $2,500.
Roanoke Female College, founded 1859, Danville; value of property, $25,-000; value of apparatus, $1,500.

[In other States]

Chowan Female Institute, Murfreesboro, 1848; value of property, $50,000.

Greenville Female College, 1854, Greenville; value of property, $20,000; library and apparatus, $500.

Monroe Female College, Forsyth, Ga., 1840; value of property, $15,000; library and apparatus, $500.

Southern Female College, La Grange, Ga., 1843; value of property not given.

Bethel Female College, Hopkinsville, Ky., 1854; value of property, $30,000; value of library and apparatus, $1,000.

Brownsville Female College, Brownsville, Tenn., 1851; value of property, $20,000; apparatus and library, $500.

Judson Institute, Marion, Ala., 1839; value of property, $61,000; apparatus and library, $20,000.

Hillman College, Clinton, Miss., 1853; value of property, $30,000; library and apparatus, $3,000.

In addition to these, there are many schools of a minor grade such as academies, institutes, and seminaries under the care of denominational local bodies in all the States of the South.

9

Literature of the Old South

In the South writing was an avocation, not a profession. Few of the works of Southern writers have lived as literature. The productions do represent the values of Southern people, and as such a few examples are reproduced here. Two of the selections are from A. B. Meek, of whom Montrose J. Moses, in The Literature of the South, *J. Y. Crowell and Company, New York, 1910, pp. 266-270, said:*

"The career of Meek is an excellent example of the Southern literary existence which was a pleasure and not a necessity, and which was subservient to activity along the lines of civil usefulness. His rank was high as a lawyer, and he filled prominent places, as Attorney-General of Alabama at twenty-two, and as Federal Attorney for the Southern District of Alabama. . . . His political career did not materially affect his literary product, although his influence in Alabama, while residing in Tuscaloosa and in Mobile, afforded him opportunity to enrich his historical studies of the State. . . .

Although literature was a side stream in his life, although he enjoyed to a greater extent both judicial reputation and the distinction of having established Alabama's public school system, Meek by innate taste was a literary man."

This characterization is typical of most Southern writers of the nineteenth century.

The following selection is from an oration delivered by Meek to the Literary Societies of La Grange, Alabama, in 1841. It is quoted from A. B. Meek, *Romantic Passages in Southwestern History,* Goetzel, Mobile, 1857, pp. 147-190, *passim.*

[Speaking of Southern literature] Throughout this broad, green, beautiful land of ours, as it is sometimes rapturously called; from Mason and Dixons', to Hunt and Carroll's line; there is not one native author! Yes,

Stump Speaking, by George Caleb Bingham. Francis Hall wrote in 1816:
". . . the land is literally over-run with orators of all sorts and sizes. . . . Stump
orators [are so called] from their generally choosing to deliver their harangues
from the stump of a tree, or a horse-block. . . . These are the men who undertake
to regulate elections, and to change the votes in the court-yard, before the opening
of the poll."

there is one: one of whom we may be justly proud [William Gilmore Simms]. Solitary and alone, in this barren Patmos he has been struggling for years, to develope and illustrate an indigenous literature. And well, though perhaps unrewarded,—certainly unrewarded by those for whom he has done the most—has he accomplished his exalted mission. His numerous productions have arisen like a line of beautiful hills around the literary horizon of his country. . . . Though his immediate countrymen may not appreciate his efforts; though, like Dante, he may struggle in darkness . . . the time will come when the brow of the author of "Atalantis" and the "Yemasee," of "Mellichampe" and the "History of South Carolina" shall be crowned with garlands of unforgetting love! . . . .

It is in the history of our Periodical Literature that the influence of this iconoclastic spirit is most manifest. Many efforts have been made to establish among us the higher class of periodicals. They have all been ineffectual. The truth has been fully proven that our people do not want, that they are positively unfit for, such intellectual establishments. How sad is the history of the SOUTHERN REVIEW! For profound learning, elegant scholarship, lofty and generous criticism modelled upon the purest standards of taste and philosophy. . . . Fearlessly, eloquently, it defended our peculiar social economy, and better constitutional creed. . . . And yet, —though many of its articles were regularly translated into other languages, and read with rapture by the illuminati of the Continent,—it was permitted, by our all-patriotic population, to die by that most painful of all the processes of decomposition—starvation. Ah! how far below zero, our intellectual thermometer sank, that day those funeral obsequies were performed!

✓ ✓ ✓

From another of Meek's books, *Songs and Poems of the South,* Goetzel, Mobile, 1857, the following stanzas were chosen to illustrate Southern character.

Preface

The poetry of a country should be a faithful expression of its physical and moral characteristics. The imagery, at least, should be drawn from the indigenous objects of the region, and the sentiment be such as naturally [would] arise under the influence of its climate, its institutions, habits of life, and social condition. . . .

These opinions have formed the poetic Faith of the writer of the present volume. He has not attempted to sing in a mere spirit of imitativeness, or in the tropes and metaphors of foreign Art and Precedent. Gazing upon the delightful Land about him—the Land of his birth and affections—he has endeavored to depict its beauties . . . loving at once the Patriotic and the Beautiful.

Stanzas to Illustrate the Credo of the South.

1. [The military cult]

THE FIELDS OF MEXICO

(The American Maiden's Song to her Lover)

Should the God who rules above thee,
   Doom thee to a soldier's grave,
Hearts will break!—but Fame will love thee,
   Canonized among the brave!—
Listen then!—thy country's calling
   On her sons to meet her foe!—
     Rather would I view thee lying
     On the last red field of life,
     'Mid thy country's heroes dying,
     Than to be a dastard's wife!—
Haste then, love! where men are falling
   On the fields of Mexico!

2. THE BELLE

The roses in Spring, their rich fragrance may fling,
   And beauty and song on the senses may steal,
But there's naught in the air, or the earth can compare,
   Young and lovely and fair, with the Belle of Mobile!

. . . .

The East and the West are of fair forms possessed;
   The hills of the Northland proud maidens conceal;
But in beauty and soul, far excelling the whole,
   Is the lovely Creole, the bright Belle of Mobile!

3. THE MOTHER

The Mothers of the South!
   In the lurid morn of Battle,
When, from the cannon's mouth,
   Came the thunder's deadly rattle,—
Their fair and fragile forms
   Shrank not in terror from us,
But,—rainbows on the storms!
   Still gave us freedom's promise!
Then pledge, tonight, their memories bright,
   Our noble Southern mothers!

Who in the strife,—maid, matron, wife,—
Stood by their sons and brothers!

4. THE DEATH OF A CHILD

Why weep for the young and the lovely who die,
In the morning of life, ere the light from the sky,
The pure light of childhood, has flown, or a ray
Of innocence beaming, has vanished away,—
Ere the young, joyous heart, of unkindness hath heard,
Or hope falls exhausted, like a wing-broken bird:—
Ere sin and temptation, the sirocs of life,
Have blasted their beauty—or sorrow or strife,
O'er the morn-dreams of fancy their shadows have flung,
Like pinions of evil;—why weep for the young?

5. COME TO THE SOUTH

Oh, come to the South, sweet, beautiful one,
'Tis the clime of the heart, 'tis the shrine of the sun;
Where the sky ever shines with a passionate glow,
And flowers spread their treasures of crimson and snow;
Where the breeze, o'er bright waters, wafts incense along,
And gay birds are glancing in beauty and song;
Where summer smiles ever o'er mountain and plain,
And the best gifts of Eden, unshadowed, remain.
              Oh, come to the South,
                 The shrine of the sun;
              And dwell in its bowers,
                 Sweet, beautiful one.

6. DO I LOVE THEE?

Do I love thee?—Ask the flowers
    If they love the breath of spring,—
Ask them if the morning hours
    Fragrant dew and freshness bring,—
List their answer! Such to me
Is the love I feel for thee!

7. LAND OF THE SOUTH

Land of the South!—imperial land!—
How proud thy mountains rise!

How sweet thy scenes on every hand!
How fair thy covering skys!
But not for this,—oh, not for these
I love thy fields to roam,—
Thou hast a dear spell to me,—
Thou art my native home!

🙚   🙚   🙚

Among Southern women who might have been successful writers, Octavia Le
Vert may serve as an example. The following is from Mary Forrest, *Women of
the South Distinguished in Literature,* New York, 1860, pp. 16-29, *passim.*

Octavia Walton was born at Belle Vue, near Augusta, Georgia, but her
parents removing soon after to Florida, her first memories are of the
sunshine and flowers of Pensacola: in her own vivid words, "of the orange
and live-oak trees, shading the broad veranda; of the fragrant acacia,
oleander, and Cape jasmin trees, which filled the parterre sloping down
to the sea-beach; of merry races with my brother along the white sands,
while the creamy waves broke over my feet, and the delicious breeze from
the gulf played in my hair; of the pet mocking-birds in the giant oak by
my window, whose songs called me each morning from dreamland."

Pensacola, situated on a noble bay, was the rendezvous of the United
States vessels of the Gulf station. It was a gala time when they returned
from their cruises; balls and parties at the governor's house—splendid
entertainments on board the ships—moonlight excursions upon the bay,
and pic-nics in the magnolia groves. The well-educated and chivalric
officers were a large element in the society to which our author was thus
early accustomed; and yet while a mere child, she had little to learn in
the way of drawing-room ease and elegance.

Amid such scenes, her receptive nature seems to have absorbed the
tropical exuberance of thought, feeling, language, and *presence,* which has
made her name famous. . . .

Before the age of twelve years, she could write and converse in three
languages with facility. So unusual was her talent as a linguist, that it was
the custom of her father to take her to his office to translate from the
French or Spanish the most important letters connected with the affairs of
state. . . .

During her father's administration, as Governor of Florida, he located the
seat of government, and, at the earnest request of his little daughter, Octavia, called it by the Indian name of "Tallahassee." Its signification ("beautiful land") fell musically upon the ear of the imaginative child. . . .

Octavia was never placed within the walls of a schoolroom. Her mother
and grandmother, both women of intellect and cultivation, vied with each
other in developing her earlier mental life, and private tutors were provided to meet the needs of her advance. She and her brother pursued their

studies for years under the eye of an old Scotchman, a fine classic scholar and linguist, who had lived in the family since their birth, as devoted an adherent as was ever Dominie Sampson to the House of Bertram.

Soon after their removal to Mobile, Octavia, in company with her mother and brother, made the tour of the United States; and then commenced the remarkable career as a social genius, which gave to the name of Octavia Walton its world-wide celebrity. Possessing the *entrée* of the most select circles in each city of the Union, she suddenly awoke to the fact that she held also a magic key to human hearts, and could sway at will the moods and emotions of those who surrounded her—a knowledge and position alike dangerous. She was crowned "reigning belle" by acclamation; a title, which, worn as it so often is by the weak and frivolous, or the vain and heartless, has ever done injustice to the high-toned and comprehensive character of our author. That she was more than a mere belle is proved by the fact that her name was never spoken lightly, and of all who then offered her the highest tribute in the gift of man, she has never lost a friend. . . .

During the administration of Jackson, in those memorable times, when, with a daring hand, he removed the deposits, Octavia Walton was each day an earnest listener to the debates in Congress, and transferred at once to her diary the speeches of Calhoun, Clay, and Webster. These three were her warm personal friends, especially Mr. Clay, to whose memory she has since offered a glowing and affectionate testimonial. In 1836 she married Dr. Henry Le Vert of Mobile. . . .

In the summer of 1853, yielding to the solicitations of friends, she accepted an invitation from the Duke of Rutland, and in company with her father and daughter, sailed for England. . . . There probably was never a more signal success in the way of access to foreign society, friendly attentions from royalty, than fell to the share of Madame Le Vert. . . .

In 1854, she returned to America; but after spending one year in the quiet of her own home was persuaded to revisit Europe in company with her husband and daughter. Out of these tours grew the "Souvenirs of Travel," to which we are indebted for such impressions of European life as could have come to us through no other medium.

✓   ✓   ✓

Octavia Walton Le Vert delivered the following address upon laying the cornerstone of a monument to her friend, Henry Clay. It is quoted from Mary Forrest, *Women of the South Distinguished in Literature,* New York, 1860, pp. 29-31.

While the patriotic sons of our country are uniting in a testimonial to the memory of Henry Clay, shall not woman be allowed to place the flowers of gratitude and affection upon the altar of his fame?

To none were the genius and services of the illustrious statesman and orator more dear than to his countrywomen: with all those lofty and commanding qualities which sway senates, and guide the course of empires, he had a heroism of heart, a chivalry of deportment, a deference of demeanor, which while forming the soul and secret of his impassioned eloquence, were irresistible talismans over the minds of the gentler sex.

Great as he was in the "forum of nations," or before multitudes of men, controlling them by his "gleaming finger," as with the wand of an enchanter, it was in the home circle, by the domestic fireside, that his character was seen in its true grace and loveliness; there his voice, that lately rang like a trumpet amid his assembled peers, and whose undying echoes (the richest symphonies of patriotism) are still reverberating from the white hills of New England to the parapets of the Pacific, was attuned to all the softest cadences of social and intellectual intercourse. How delightful it was then to listen to the playful repartee, the genial anecdotes, the sparkling *bonmots,* the vivid reminiscences of European and American society, and the always elevated sentiments of one who had mingled in the most prominent scenes of his time in both hemispheres, without losing in the least the lofty manliness, sincerity, and purity of his nature. . . .

But not alone in this, his more private character, does woman appreciate the excellence of Mr. Clay. His public life, in many of its aspects, had all the romance of chivalry. He stood among the orators and statesmen of his time as Philip Sidney amid his contemporary knights and barons. History had already placed his statue in the pantheon of immortality. . . .

How appropriate then is it that a memorial of this model statesman, patriot and orator, should be erected here in the crescent bend of the Mississippi. . . .

The statue of Themistocles long greeted from a promontory in Greece the home-returning voyager, and fired afresh his love for Attica and Athens. So may the statue of our patriotic orator ever inspire with emulating fervor the citizens of this land of liberty, and especially of this prosperous city of New Orleans.

April 12, 1856.

✦ ✦ ✦

A number of literary magazines were founded in the South from time to time. They were similar in character to such national publications as the *North American Review.* The table of contents of such a magazine, the *Southern Literary Journal,* Charleston, South Carolina, Vol. III, No. 2, February, 1838, is typical of the range of subjects covered.

ORIGINAL PAPERS

Memoir on Slavery.—continued from No. 1, by Chancellor Harper
Old Song
Etchings of Character, sent me by my friend Will Whippoorwill from the

country, to have framed. Number Two, by Wm. Wragg Smith, Esq.
The Cypress Tree. A Ballad. By Mrs. Anna Marie Welles.
Bubbles
I Must Sleep Now
Scenes in a Campaign.—The Old Soldier
Passages from the Life of Joanna I.—The Conspiracy. By Mrs. E. F. Ellet.
"Fair Girl, Whose Joyous Morn of Life"
Notes on Texas. By an Engineer
Stanzas
The Philosophy of Smoking
Fragment
A Dinner in Fifteen Hundred and Three, (translated from the Italian for
    the *Southern Literary Journal*)
"Dinna' Forget."

EDITOR'S PORT FOLIO

The Autobiography of Junius
The Drama.—The New Theatre—Mr. Vandergoff in Damon.—The Forest
    Festival.
Mr. Cooper and the *London Quarterly Review*.
Leila: or the Siege of Grenada

❧   ❧   ❧

A poem from the *Southern Literary Journal*, "I Sigh for the Land of the
Cypress and Pine," is quoted from Vol. III, No. 4, p. 206, April, 1838. It was
"written at the North by a Southern Traveller" (author not given).

> I sigh for the land of the Cypress and Pine!
> Where the Jessamine blooms and the gay Woodbine;
> Where the moss droops low from the green oak tree,—
> Oh! that sun-bright land is the land for me.
>
> The snowy flower of the Orange there
> Sends its sweet fragrance through the air;
> And the Indian Rose delights to twine
> Its branches with the laughing vine.
>
> There the deer leaps light through the open glade,
> Or hides him far in the forest shade,
> When the woods resound in the dewy morn
> With the clang of the merry hunter's horn.
>
> There the humming-bird of rainbow plume
> Hangs o'er the scarlet creeper's bloom;
> While midst the leaves, his varying dyes
> Sparkle like half-seen fairy eyes.

There the echoes ring through the livelong day
With the mock-bird's cheerful roundelay;
And at night when the scene is calm and still
With the moan of the plaintive whip-poor-will.

Oh I sigh for the land of the Cypress and Pine,
Of the Laurel, the Rose, and the gay Woodbine;
Where the long gray moss decks the rugged oak tree—
That sun-bright land is the land for me.

✦   ✦   ✦

The following anecdote is from Shepherd M. Dugger. It, too, illustrates the feeling of Southerners for their homeland. *The Balsam Groves of the Grandfather Mountain,* published by the Author, Banner Elk, North Carolina, 1892, pp. 98-100.

It was in the city of Jackson, West Tennessee, just after the Civil War, that a banquet was given in honor of the Supreme Court judges, federal judges, solicitors, and lawyers. Landon C. Haynes, who lived in Johnson City, Tennessee, was present. About eleven o'clock that night General N. B. Forest, the toastmaster, arose and said: "I know the hour is late, but you would never forgive me unless I introduced to you the Honorable Landon C. Haynes, the silver-tongued orator from the 'God-forsaken' East Tennessee."

Mr. Haynes was sitting in the back of the auditorium, half awake and half asleep. The man sitting beside him shook him saying, "Get up, Landon; they are calling on you for a speech and throwing off on your country."

Mr. Haynes responded as follows:

"Mr. Chairman and Gentlemen: I plead guilty to the soft impeachment. I was born in East Tennessee, on the banks of the Watauga, which in the Indian vernacular means Beautiful River, and beautiful river it is. I have stood upon its banks in my childhood and looked down into its glassy waters and have seen a heaven below, and then looked up and beheld a heaven above, reflecting, like two vast mirrors, each into the other, its moons and planets and trembling stars. Away from its banks of rock and cliff, hemlock and laurel, pine and cedar, stretches back to the distant mountains, a vale more beautiful and exquisite than any in Italy or Switzerland. There stands the great Unaka, the great Roan, the great Black, and the great Smoky Mountains, among the loftiest in North America, on whose summits the clouds gather of their own accord, even on the brightest day. There I have seen the great Spirit of the Storm, after noontide, go and take his evening nap in the pavilion of darkness and of clouds. I have then seen him, aroused at midnight, as a giant refreshed by slumber, cover the heavens with gloom and darkness; I have seen him awake the tempest, let loose the red lightnings that ran along the mountain tops for a thousand miles, swifter than an eagle's flight in heaven; then I have seen them stand up and dance like angels of light in the clouds, to the music of that grand organ of nature whose keys seemed touched by the fingers of Divinity, in the hall of eternity, and responded in notes of thunder, resounding through the universe. Then I have seen the darkness drift away beyond the horizon and the Morn get up from her saffron bed, like a queen, put on her robes of light, come forth from her palace in the sun, and stand tiptoe on the misty mountain top; and while Night fled before her glorious face to his bed chamber at the pole, she lighted, with a smile of sunshine, the green vale and the beautiful river where I was born and played in childhood.

"Oh beautiful land of East Tennessee, with thy sun-kissed hills, how can I ever forget thee!"

✝   ✝   ✝

An article similar in subject matter and style to the writings, opinions, and moralizing of Addison and Steele in *The Spectator*, is "A Thought on Dress," from the *Southern Literary Journal*, Vol. III, April, 1838, p. 274.

A THOUGHT ON DRESS

Simplex Mundicis—Hoc.
"Costly the habit as the purse can buy
But not express'd in fancy; rich not gaudy;
For the apparel oft proclaims the man." *Shakespeare*

As I stood the other day at the door of one of our most fashionable resorts, I could not help remarking the various changes our dress has undergone within the last few years, having a singular zest for the investigation of such small pieces of history.

As little a matter as dress appears to be, I recollected it had given birth to some of the most important events of history. There, I found religion had interfered in the adjustment of its fashion, and had declared heterodox, all those who dared to shave the head; while the trimming of the beard, in the peculiar phraseology of the time, was denounced as "a lie against our faces and an impious attempt to improve the works of the creator." While one nation was torn with faction at the color of its coats, another tottered and trembled to its foundation, in establishing a cockade, or the riband of which it was made . . . from the external appearances of men I could as easily discover their talents or dispositions, as one can infer from the scenery and climate of a country, the peculiar character of its inhabitants, or the phrenologist from the bumps or cavities of the skull, the various quality of the brain underneath. For the first time I felt the excellent "rhyme and reason" of the old English couplet,—

"Dress often, like the horse's skin,
Doth tell what sort of bloods within."

From the mutability which fashion presented, I began seriously to doubt, whether dress would ever be brought to a fixed and proper standard. . . . The true and correct line in manners and dress, lies between the two opposites of the vulgar and affected. . . .

Bachelor B..

✓   ✓   ✓

Oratory played an important part in Southern life; consequently some of the greatest literary work of the section is to be found in orations such as those of John C. Calhoun and Henry Clay. The following selection is Robert Hayne's reply to a resolution offered to the United States Senate in 1829, restricting the sale of public lands to those already in the market; it is part of the so-called "Webster-Hayne Debate," *Gales and Seaton's Register of Debates in Congress,* 1825-1837, 2 Vols., Gales and Seaton, Washington, D. C., Vol. VI, pp. 33-36.

. . . There may be said to be two great parties in this country, who entertain very opposite opinions in relation to the character of the policy which the government has heretofore pursued in relation to the public lands. We find that one party, embracing a very large portion, perhaps at this time a majority of the people of the United States, in all quarters of the Union, entertain the opinion that, in the settlement of the new states and the disposition of the public lands, Congress has pursued not only a highly just and liberal course, but one of extraordinary kindness and indulgence. We are regarded as having acted towards the new states in the spirit of parental weakness, granting to forward children not only everything that was reasonable and proper, but actually robbing ourselves of our property to gratify their insatiable desires. While the other party, embracing the entire West, insist that we have treated them, from the beginning, not like heirs of the estate, but in the spirit of a hard task-master, resolved to promote our selfish interests from the fruit of their labor.

In the creation and settlement of the new states, the plan has been invariably pursued of selling out, from time to time, certain portions of the public lands for the highest price that could possibly be obtained for them in open market, and, until a few years past, on long credits. In this respect, a marked difference is observable between our policy and that of every other nation that has ever attempted to establish colonies or create new states. Without pausing to examine the course pursued in this respect at earlier periods in the history of the world, I will come directly to the measures adopted in the first settlement of the new world, and will confine my observations entirely to North America. The English, the French, and the Spaniards have successively planted their colonies here, and have all adopted the same policy, which, from the very beginning of the world, had always been found necessary in the settlement of new countries, viz.: A free grant of lands, "without money and without price." We all know that the British colonies, at their first settlement here, whether deriving title directly from the crown or the lords proprietors, received grants for considerations merely nominal.

The payment of a "penny," or a "pepper corn," was the stipulated price which our fathers along the whole Atlantic coast, now composing the thirteen states, paid for their lands, and even when conditions seemingly more substantial were annexed to the grants, such, for instance, as "settlement and civilization," these were considered as substantially complied with by the cutting down of a few trees and erecting a log cabin—the work of only a few days. Even these conditions very soon came to be considered as merely nominal, and were never required to be pursued, in order to vest in the grantee the fee simple of the soil.

Now what, let us inquire, was the reason which has induced all nations to adopt this system in the settlement of new countries? Can it be any other than this, that it affords the only certain means of building up in a wilderness great and prosperous communities? Was not that policy founded on the universal belief that the conquest of a new country, the driving out "the savage beasts and still more savage men," cutting down and subduing the forest, and encountering all the hardships and privations necessarily incident to the conversion of the wilderness into cultivated fields, was worth the fee simple of the soil? And was it not believed that the mother country found ample remuneration for the value of the land so granted in the additions to her power and the new sources of commerce and of wealth furnished by prosperous and popular states?

Now, sir, I submit to the candid consideration of gentlemen, whether the policy so diametrically opposite to this, which has been invariably pursued by the United States in the West, has been quite so just and liberal as we have been accustomed to believe. Certain it is that the British colonies to the north of us, and the Spanish and French to the south and west, have been fostered and reared up under a very different system. Lands which had been for fifty or a hundred years open to every settler without any charge beyond the expense of the survey, were, the moment they fell into the hands of the United States, held up for sale at the highest price that a public auction at the most favorable seasons, and not unfrequently a spirit of wildest competition could produce, with a limitation that they should never be sold below a certain minimum price; thus making it, as it would seem, the cardinal point of our policy not to settle the country, and facilitate the formation of new states, but to fill our coffers by coining our lands into gold.

Let us now consider for a moment the effect of these two opposite conditions on the condition of a new state. I will take the state of Missouri by way of example. Here is a large and fertile territory coming into the possession of the United States without any inhabitants but Indians and wild beasts—a territory which is to be converted into a sovereign and independent state. You commence your operations by surveying and selling out a portion of the lands, on long credits, to actual settlers; and, as the population progresses, you go on year after year making additional sales on the same terms; and this operation is to be continued, as gentlemen tell us, for fifty or a hundred years at least, if not for all time to come. The inhabitants of this new state, under such a system, it is most obvious, must have commenced their operations under a load of debt, the annual payment of which must necessarily drain their country of the whole profits of their labor just so long as this system shall last. This debt is due, not from some citizens of the state to others of the same state (in which case the money would remain in the country), but it is due from the whole population of the state to the United States, by whom it is regularly drawn out to be expended abroad. Sir, the amount of this debt has, in every one of the new states, actually constantly exceeded the ability of the people to pay, as is proved by the fact that you have been compelled from time to time, in your great liberality, to extend the credits, and in some instances even to remit portions of the debt, in order to protect some land debtors from bankruptcy and total ruin.

Now, I will submit the question to any candid man whether, under this system, the people of a new state so situated could, by any industry or exertion, ever become rich and prosperous. What has been the consequence, sir? Almost universal poverty; no money; hardly a sufficient circulating medium for the ordinary exchanges of society; paper banks, relief laws, and the other innumerable evils, social, political, and moral, on which it is unnecessary for me to dwell . . . perhaps the present condition of the Southern states has served to impress more deeply on my own mind the grievous oppression of a system by which the wealth of a country is drained off to be expended elsewhere. In that devoted region, sir, in which my lot has been cast, it is our misfortune to stand in that relation to the federal government which subjects us to a taxation which it requires the utmost efforts of our industry to meet. Nearly the whole amount of our contributions is expended abroad; we stand toward the United States in the relation of Ireland to England. The fruits of our labor are drawn from us to enrich other and more favored sections of the Union; while, with one of the finest climates and the richest products in the world, furnishing, with one-third of the population, two-thirds of the whole exports of the country, we exhibit the extraordinary, the wonderful, and painful spectacle of a country enriched by the bounty of God, but blasted by the cruel policy of man. The rank grass grows in our streets; our very fields are scathed by the hand of injustice and oppression. Such, sir, though probably in a less degree, must have been the effects of a kindred policy on the fortunes of the West. It is not in the nature of things that it should have been otherwise. . . .

[It has been suggested] in a report from the Treasury Department, under the late administration, of so regulating the disposition of the public lands as to create and preserve, in certain quarters of the Union, a population suitable for conducting great manufacturing establishments. It is supposed, sir, by the advocates of the American System, that the great obstacle to the progress of manufacturers in this country is the want of that low and degraded population which infests the cities and towns of Europe, who, having no other means of subsistence, will work for the lowest wages, and be satisfied with the smallest possible share of human enjoyment. And this difficulty is proposed to overcome by so regulating and limiting the sales of the public lands as to prevent the drawing off this portion of the population from the manufacturing states. Sir, it is bad enough that the government should presume to regulate the industry of man; it is sufficiently monstrous that they should attempt, by arbitrary legislation, artificially to adjust and balance the various pursuits of society and "to organize the whole labor and capital of the country." But what shall we say to the resort to such means for these purposes! What! create a manufactory of paupers, in order to enable the rich proprietors of woolen and cotton factories to amass wealth? From the bottom of my soul I do abhor and detest the idea that the powers of the federal government should ever be prostituted for such a purpose. Sir, I hope we shall act on a more just and liberal system of policy. The people of America are, and ought to be for a century to come, essentially an agricultural people; and I can conceive of no policy that can possibly be pursued in relation to the public lands, none that would be more "for the common benefit of all the states," than to use them as the means of furnishing a secure asylum to that class of our fellow-citizens who in any portion of the country may find themselves unable to procure a comfortable subsistence by the means immediately within their reach. . . . Giving up the plan of using these lands forever as a fund either for revenue or for distribution, ceasing to hug them as a great treasure, renouncing the idea of administering them with a view to regulate and control the industry and population of the states, or of keeping in subjection and dependence the states, or the people of any portion of the Union, the task will be comparatively easy of striking out a plan for the final adjustment of the land question on just and equitable principles. In short, our whole policy in relation to the public lands may perhaps be summed up in the declaration . . . that they ought now to be kept and be administered chiefly with a view to the creation, within reasonable periods, of great and flourishing communities, to be formed into free and independent states; to be invested in due season with the control of all the lands within their respective limits.

✓   ✓   ✓

The amateur Southern writers created many prototypes which are imitated even today in the cinema, drama, and fiction. Augustus Baldwin Longstreet wrote

Georgia Scenes in 1837 as newspaper sketches for the Augusta *State Rights Sentinel,* of which he was editor. Harper and Brothers, New York, published the sketches in 1840. Typical of Longstreet's characters was Ransy Sniffle. The following characterization is from "The Fight," *Georgia Scenes,* 1875 edition, pp. 54-55.

Now there happened to reside in the county just alluded to a little fellow by the name of Ransy Sniffle: a sprout of Richmond, who, in his earlier days, had fed copiously upon red clay and blackberries. This diet had given to Ransy a complexion that a corpse would have disdained to own, and an abdominal rotundity that was quite unprepossessing. Long spells of the fever and ague, too, in Ransy's youth, had conspired with clay and blackberries to throw him quite out of the order of nature. His shoulders were fleshless and elevated; his head large and flat; his neck slim and translucent; and his arms, hands, fingers, and feet were lengthened out of all proportion to the rest of his frame. His joints were large and his limbs small; and as for flesh, he could not, with propriety, be said to have any. Those parts which nature usually supplies with the most of this article— the calves of the legs, for example—presented in him the appearance of so many well-drawn blisters. His height was just five feet nothing; and his average weight in blackberry season, ninety-five. I have been thus particular in describing him, for the purpose of showing what a great matter a little fire sometimes kindleth. There was nothing on this earth which delighted Ransy so much as a fight. He never seemed fairly alive except when he was witnessing, fomenting, or talking about a fight. Then, indeed, his deep-sunken gray eye assumed something of a living fire, and his tongue acquired a volubility that bordered upon eloquence.

✓   ✓   ✓

Mrs. Caroline Gilman, a resident of Charleston, South Carolina, was a native of New England and a niece of James Russell Lowell. She was editor of the *Southern Rosebud* (later *Southern Rose*), one of the first children's papers in the United States (1832-1839). She wrote to help Northerners to understand the South. Her description of "Mamma" is taken from *Recollections of a Southern Matron,* Harper and Brothers, New York, 1838, pp. 22-30, *passim.*

MAMMA possessed more than "whole *acres* of charms," for though not brilliant, she was good-tempered and sensible. A demure look and a reserved manner concealed a close habit of observation. She would sit in company for hours, making scarcely a remark, and recollect afterwards every fact that had been stated, to the color of a riband or the stripe of a waistcoat. Home was her true sphere; there everything was managed with promptitude and decision, and papa, who was a politician, a candidate for military honors, a commissioner of roads, a churchwarden, a "mighty hunter," and withal an active planter, was glad to find his domestic arrangements quiet and orderly. No one ever managed a plantation better; but there was no appeal from her opinions and I have known her ever eloquent in defending a recipe. She was well entitled to her opinions; for though papa often returned from the city or the chase with unexpected strangers, I never saw her laboring under embarrassment. Her sausages were pronounced to be the best flavored in the neighborhood; her hog's cheese (the English brawn) was delicacy itself; her curds, made in a heart-mould, covered with nutmeg and cream, won the hearts of many a guest; her clabber was turned at that precise moment when a slight acidity tempers the insipidity of milk; her wafers bore the prettiest devices, or were rolled in the thinnest possible consistency; her shrimps, pickled or fresh, were most carefully prepared; her preserved water-melons were carved with the taste of a sculptor; her hommony looked like plates of gathered snow; corn and rice all lent their nice varieties to her breakfast; and her boiled rice answered to Shakespeare's description, "for each particular *grain* did stand on end," or, to use a more expressive term, *crawled*. And all these delicacies were laid on your plate so silently, with a look that seemed to say, "No one will observe you if you do eat this little bit more." An orange leaf, which when crushed in the hand sent out a pleasant odor, was laid on every finger-bowl. A cheerful fire blazed on the bedroom hearths in winter, and flowers orna-mented them in spring, while I was early taught to lay fresh roses on the pillows of strangers.

I recollect mamma most distinctly at the breakfast-table. She entered the room almost invariably followed by her maid Chloe, bearing her small basket of keys. She wore a neat morning-dress, with plaited frills, a tasteful cap, her hands decorated with rings, holding a handkerchief of exquisite fineness, and her gold watch suspended from her belt, with its face outward. Chloe, with a turban of superior height (for there is great ambition in the fold of a negro's turban), stood behind her chair with the basket of keys. Her usual office was to dress and undress her mistress every morning and evening, and perform all offices of personal attendance. To her taste mamma often referred in the choice of a dress for the day, for Chloe's taste was un-questionable.

We sat while papa asked a blessing in a low tone. This is a patriarchal and beautiful custom, connecting, as it does, earthly blessings with the "giver of every good and perfect gift;" but it should either be performed in the Quaker style, in silence, or with distinct and earnest emphasis. My brother John was a bright, observing boy, and yet, at the age of ten years, he said to mamma in a whisper one day, as if fearing he was asking some-thing wrong, "What does papa mean by *tol lol* at the end of the blessing?"

"John," exclaimed she, "is it possible that you do not know that he says 'our Lord?' "

"I always thought it was *tol lol*," said John, blushing to the very eyes.

✓   ✓   ✓

William Gilmore Simms was perhaps the greatest and most prolific of Southern writers before the Civil War. He wrote novels, poetry, short stories, biography and history. His seven novels of the Revolution and his novels about Indian wars and frontier life enable him to rank among the greatest literary portraitists of the epic of America. Many critics feel that Simms was the equal of Cooper as a novelist. He never, however, received the popular acclaim and the financial rewards that Cooper did. In addition to his creative writing Simms worked prodigiously for nine newspapers and magazines and edited the *Southern Literary Gazette*. He was an outspoken defender of slavery and secession and he was a leading advocate of the Southern point of view. Perhaps one of his greatest contributions to Southern literature was the influence and guidance he exerted over Hayne, Timrod, and other lesser-known Charleston and regional writers of his day.

The following paragraphs are from one of Simms' short stories, "How Sharp Snaffles Got His Capital and Wife," *Harper's New Monthly Magazine*, October, 1870, pp. 667-687, *passim*.

Well, we had reached Saturday night. We had hunted day by day from the preceding Monday with considerable success—bagging some game daily, and camping nightly at the foot of the mountains. The season was a fine one. It was early winter, October, and the long ascent to the top of the mountains was through vast fields of green, the bushes still hanging heavy with huckleberries.

From the summits we had looked over into Tennessee, Virginia, Georgia, North and South Carolina. In brief, to use the language of Natty Bumpo, we beheld "Creation." We had crossed the "Blue Ridge"; and the descending water-courses, no longer seeking the Atlantic, were now gushing head-long down the western slopes, and hurrying to lose themselves in the Gulf Stream and the Mississippi. . . .

Saturday night is devoted by the mountaineers engaged in a camp hunt, which sometimes contemplates a course of several weeks, to stories of adventures—"long yarns"—chiefly relating to the objects of their chase, and the wild experiences of their professional life. The hunter who actually inclines to exaggeration is, at such a period, privileged to deal in all the extravagancies of invention; nay, he is *required* to do so! To be literal, or confine himself to the bald and naked truth, is not only discreditable, but a *finable* offense! He is, in such a case, made to swallow a long, strong, and difficult potation! He can not be too extravagant in his incidents; but he is also required to exhibit a certain degree of *art,* in their use; and he thus frequently rises into a certain realm of fiction, the ingenuities of which are made to compensate for exaggerations. . . .

Nearly all our professional hunters assembled on the present occasion were tolerable *raconteurs.* They complimented Jim Fisher, by throwing the raw deer-skin over his shoulders; tying the antlers of the buck with a red hand-kerchief over his forehead; seating him on the biggest boulder which lay at hand; and, sprinkling him with a stoup of whisky, they christened him "The Big Lie," for the occasion. And in this character he complacently presided during the rest of the evening, till the company prepared for sleep, which was not till midnight. He was king of the feast.

It was the duty of the "Big Lie" to regulate proceedings, keep order, appoint the *raconteurs* severally, and admonish them when he found them foregoing their privileges, and narrating bald, naked, and uninteresting truth. They must deal in fiction.

Jim Fisher was seventy years old, and a veteran hunter, the most famous in all the country. He *looked* authority, and promptly began to assert it, which he did with a single word:

"Yaou!"

"YAOU" was the *nom de nique* of one of the hunters, whose proper name was Sam Snaffles, but who, from his special smartness, had obtained the farther sobriquet of "Sharp Snaffles."

. . . he was called "Yaou" from his frequent use of that word, which, in Choctaw dialect, simply means "Yes." . . . He answered to the name.

["Yaou" began his tale, of how he had won his wife and his capital.]   . .

[According to his tale he was sitting in] "the crutch of the tree, which was an almighty big chestnut oak, when, O Lawd! on a suddent the stump I had been a-setting on give way onder me. 'Twas a rotten jint of the tree. It give way, Jedge, as I tell you, and down I went, my legs first and then my whole body—slipping down not on the outside, but into a great hollow of the tree, all the hairt of it being eat out by rot; and afore I knowed whar I waur, I waur some twenty foot down, I reckon; and by the time I touched bottom, I was up to my neck in honey!

"It was an almighty big honey-tree, full of the sweet treacle; and the bees all gone and left it, I reckon, for a hundred years. And I in it up to my neck.

"I could smell it strong. I could taste it sweet. But I could see nothing.

"Lawd! Lawd! From bad to worse; buried alive in a hollow tree with never a chaince to git out! . . .

"Oh, Jedge, you couldn't jedge of my sitivation in that deep hollow, that cave, I may say, of mountain oak! My head waur jest above the honey, and ef I backed it to look up, my long hair at the back of the neck a'most stuch fast, so thick was the honey.

"But I couldn't help looking up. The hollow was a wide one at the top, and I could see when a star was passing over. Thar they shined, bright and beautiful, as ef they waur the very eyes of the angels; and, as I seed them come and go, looking smiling in upon me as they come, I cried out to 'em, one by one:

"Oh, sweet sperrits, blessed angels! ef so be thar's an angel sperrit, as they say, living in all them stars, come down and extricate me from this fix; for, so fur as I kin see, I've got no chaince of help from mortal man or woman.

Hardly onst a year does a human come this way; and ef they did come, how would they know I'm hyar? . . .

"Well, Jedge, suddently, in the midst of my praying, and jest after one bright, big star had gone over me without seeing my sitivation, I hed a fresh skeer. . . .

"All was dark. The stars and sky waur all gone. Something black kivered the hollow, and, in a minit a'ter, I haird something slipping down into the hollow right upon me.

"I could hairdly draw my breath. I begun to fear that I was to be siffocated alive; and as I haird the strange critter slipping down, I shoved out my hands and felt ha'r—course wool—and with one hand I cotched hold of the ha'ry leg of a beast, and with t'other hand I cotched hold of his tail.

" 'Twas a great ba'r, one of the biggest, come to git his honey. He knowed the tree, Jedge, you see, and ef any beast in the world loves honey, 'tis a ba'r beast. He'll go his death on honey, though the hounds are tearing at his very haunches.

"You may be sure, when I onst knowed what he was, and onst got a good gripe on his hindquarters, I warn't gwine to let go in a hurry. I knowed that was my only chaince for gitting out of the hollow, and I do believe them blessed angels in the stars sent the beast, jest at the right time, to give me human help and assistance.

"Now, yer see, Jedge, thar was no chaince for him turning round upon me. He pretty much filled up the hollow. He knowed his way, and slipped down, eend foremost—the latter eend, you know. He could stand up on his hind-legs and eat all he wanted. Then, with his great sharp claws and his mighty muscle, he could work up, holding on to the sides of the tree, and git out a'most as easy as when he come down.

"Now, you see, ef he weighed five hundred pounds, and climb like a cat, he could easy carry up a young fellow that had no flesh to spar', and only weighed a hundred and twenty-five. So i laid my weight on him, eased him off as well as I could, but held on to tail and leg as ef all life and eternity depended upon it.

"Now I reckon, Jedge, that b'ar was pretty much more skeered than I was. He couldn't turn in his shoes, and with something fastened to his ankles, and, as he thought, I reckon some strange beast fastened to his tail, you never seed beast more eager to git away, and git upwards. He knowed the way, and stuck his claws in the rough sides of the hollow, hand over hand, jest as a sailor pulls a rope, and up we went. We hed, howsomdever, more than one slip back; but, Lawd bless you! I never let go. Up we went. . . . I felt myself moving. My nech was out of the honey. My airms were free. I could feel the sticky thing slipping off from me, and a'ter a good quarter of an hour the b'ar was on the great mouth of the hollow; and as I felt that I let go of his tail, still keeping fast hold of his leg, and with one hand I cotched hold of the outside rim of the hollow; I found it fast, held on to it; and jest then the b'ar sat squat on the very edge of the hollow, taking a sort of rest a'ter his labor.

"I don't know what 'twas, Jedge, that made me do it. I warn't a-thinking at all. I was only feeling and drawing a long breath. Jest then the b'ar sort o' looked round, as ef to see what varmint was a-troubling him, when I gin him a mighty push, strong as I could, and he lost his balance and went over outside down cl'ar to the airth, and I could hyar his neck crack, almost as loud as a pistol. . . .

"And thar he lay, jest as quiet as ef he waur a-sleeping, though I knowed his neck was broke. And that b'ar, too, was so much 'capital.' . . ."

[Needless to say, "Sharp Snaffles" made capital of the bear.]

"From the b'ar . . . I made a matter of full one hundred dollars. First, thar waur the hide, $20; then 450 pounds of meat, at 10 cents, was $45; then the grease, 14 pounds, $14; and the tallow, some $6 more; and the biled marrow, $11. . . .

"But I warn't done! Thar was my bee-tree. Don't you think I waur gwine to lose that honey. . . . I brought up all the tight-bound barrels that ever brought whisky to Spartanburg and Greenville, whar they hes the taste for that article strong; and day by day I went off carrying as many barrels as the cart could hold and the mule could draw. I tapped the old tree— which was one of the oldest and biggest chestnut oaks I ever did see, close to the bottom, and drawed off the beautiful treacle. I was more than sixteen days about it, and got something over two thousand gallons of the purest, sweetest, yellowest honey you ever did see. . . . So I got from the honey a matter of fourteen hundred dollars."

10

Social Diversions of the Old South

In an area as predominantly rural as was the nineteenth century South, all occasions when people assembled were of social significance. Militia musters, political rallies, church services, work parties, court weeks, county and state fairs, and shooting-matches were all anticipated with pleasure. A few word pictures of these diversions have been selected as illustrations.

To enable us to imagine the nature of public entertainment in North Carolina in the 1850's we may read between the lines of the following, from the *Public Laws of the State of North Carolina,* 1854-55, pp. 80-81.

[The following types of entertainers are subject to the annual tax stated:] Upon every company of circus riders or equestrian performers, and upon every company or person, who for reward, shall exhibit any collection of animals, commonly known as a menagerie, an annual tax, for each county wherein they may exhibit, of fifty dollars.

Upon every company of stage or theatrical players, slight of hand performers, rope dancers, tumblers, wire dancers, or company exhibiting for reward, artificial curiosities of any kind, (models of useful inventions excepted) and on each one of such persons, when they perform or exhibit alone, an annual tax, for each county wherein they may exhibit, of thirty dollars; and upon every person or company exhibiting any other natural curiosity, not already mentioned, an annual tax, for each county wherein it may be exhibited, of fifteen dollars.

Upon every person or company of singers, dancers, ethiopian serenaders, or performers on musical instruments, who, for the public amusement, shall sing, dance, serenade or play on musical instruments for reward; and upon every other public exhibition for amusement, exhibited for reward, an annual tax of five dollars, unless the reward be wholly devoted to some literary or charitable use in the State.

✦ ✦ ✦

Amos Kendall, as a young man, went to Lexington, Kentucky, to serve as a tutor to the children of Henry Clay. His description of a militia muster is from

THE ALABAMA STATE FAIR—THE TILT.—[FROM A SKETCH BY NIXON.]

The Tilt (tournament) at Alabama State Fair. *Harper's Weekly,* Nov. 27, 1858.

William Stickney, Editor, *Autobiography of Amos Kendall*, Lee and Shepard, Publishers, Boston, 1872, pp. 119-120.

[June] *25th,* [1814]. This day I went with others to give in an invoice of my *rateable property,* and attend a Kentucky training. One rateable poll is the amount of my whole fortune, and even that not without *encumbrances.* I suppose about two thirds of the company appeared, some without muskets, some with muskets without locks, and some with useless pieces,— all without bayonets, uniform, or cartridge-boxes. The business seemed to be electioneering as much as training. After calling the roll, the captain drew up his men in a hollow square, for the accommodation of a Mr. McKinley, who addressed them, offering himself as a candidate for election to the next General Assembly.

He gave a considerable dissertation on the subject of banking, and drew some conclusions which to me seemed incorrect. He was in favor of an extension of the system to an unlimited degree. He then took notice of the Kentucky revenue law, which it seems is rather unpopular, and promised to attempt its repeal. National politics he carefully kept out of view, for it seems he is a Federalist. After he had finished, the company resumed their order, and marched to the whiskey-table under a tree, where, several more candidates arriving, they were dismissed for a short time. I expected more public harangues; but as there were now five or six candidates present, I suppose they had some reluctance to speak in the presence of each other.

Private talk was the only means now used, and after some time most of them departed. The company again paraded and manoeuvred [*sic*] till about six o'clock, when they were dismissed. It was dull business, for they had neither fife, drum, nor whistling. This was the first stump oration I had ever heard. I was not so unpleasantly impressed as I expected. Although a good orator may often mislead the people, the system certainly has a tendency to give them much useful information. It seems to be a sort of primary assembly, where future subjects of legislation are discussed, which are afterwards, in a measure, decided by the choice which the people shall make of their representative. But there seemed to be an indelicacy in a man's saying all this to promote his own election that I could not forgive. It seemed to me that I could have spoken there for a friend, but never for myself.

✓　　✓　　✓

J. S. Buckingham was in Tennessee during a political campaign in 1839. The following extract is from his *The Slave States of America,* Fisher, Son and Company, London, 1842, Vol. II, pp. 239-246, *passim.*

It appeared, on inquiry, that the little town of Greenville had been the scene of great excitement on the previous day. The period was approaching for the election of Governor of the State; and the present occupant of that office, Governor Connor, a Whig, was to be opposed by his rival candidate, Mr. Polk, the present Speaker of the House of Representatives in the General Congress at Washington, a Democrat. As in England, the candidates here patronize different houses, the Whigs made the other hotel their headquarters; and this was the camp of the Democrats. The candidates were on an electioneering tour; and both appeared in the same town at the same time, to address the people at large; but as no room could be found spacious enough to hold the auditors, this was done in the open air. They generally chose some spot in the fields, near the town; had a temporary erection there, where the auditors, ladies as well as gentlemen, gathered round them; and they spoke alternately, in attack and defence, on the measures of the administration, and on such topics as were most likely to win adherents to their respective parties. From all I could learn, the contest was likely to be severe, though Mr. Polk was admitted on all sides to be the best orator; and this weighs much more with the people of America, than higher and more important qualifications. . . .

[At Jonesborough] we found the streets full of horses, saddled and bridled, belonging to the farmers of the neighbourhood, who had come in to attend "the speaking" as it is called, which was going on here today, the rival candidates for the governorship being both here literally "in the field." The place of meeting was in a field above the town, near the skirts of a wood. The audience was said to exceed 3,000 persons; and ladies and children were as numerous as gentlemen. They had been "at it" as our informant said, since breakfast time; and as it was now nearly five in the afternoon, he thought they would soon "give over;" which we found to be the case, as we saw the crowd winding down the hill into the town just as our coach reached the post-office, where the mail was first delivered, and then we repaired to the hotel to change horses. It had been our intention to halt here for the night; but every bed in town was engaged, and the excitement was excessive; we therefore thought it best to proceed onward.

⸎ ⸎ ⸎

Hamilton W. Pierson, an agent for the American Bible Society, described office-seeking in Kentucky. The following selection from his *In the Brush; or Old-Time Social, Political, and Religious Life in the Southwest,* D. Appleton and Company, New York, 1881, pp. 130-155, *passim.*

I have found no class of people in the Southwest so omnipresent as office-seeking politicians. I have visited no neighborhood so remote, no valley so deep, no mountain so high, that the secluded cabins had not been honored by the visits of aspiring politicians, eager to secure the votes of their "sovereign" occupants. In multitudes of such cabins and settlements, their first impressions in regard to me were that I was either a sheriff, collecting the county and State taxes, or a "candidate" soliciting votes. The one vocation was as general and as universally recognized as an honorable employment as the other. If I did not make myself known as a clergyman as soon as I arrived at many of these out-of-the-way cabins, I was frequently greeted with the salutation:

"Howdy, sir. I reckon you are a candidate, stranger!"

Some months preceding each election these aspirants for official honors publicly announced themselves as candidates for the particular office they sought. In those States where the election was held the first Monday in August, these announcements were usually made the preceding spring at the February county or circuit court. On such occasions the court adjourned for the afternoon, and after dinner the crowds in attendance gathered in the court-house, and, one after another, all the aspirants for all the different offices, State and national, came before the assembled people, announced themselves as candidates, and set forth their qualifications for the office sought and their claims upon the suffrages of their fellow-citizens. Sometimes half a dozen or more would announce themselves as candidates for the same office. . . .

In these public speeches, and on all other occasions, both public and private, this pursuit of office was always spoken of as a "race." The most common remarks and inquiries in regard to any political canvass were such as these:

"I intend to make the 'race.' " "It will be a very close 'race.' " "Do you think Jones will make the 'race?' " . . . To "make the race" was to secure an election. . . .

After these public announcements were made, the candidates entered upon their work in dead earnest. They often issued printed handbills, announcing the days on which they would speak at different places. They traveled together, and addressed the same crowds in rotation. These political discussions between candidates for the higher offices, such as governor, member of Congress, etc., were often very able and eloquent. . . . Where they canvassed a State or Congressional district together, they spoke in rotation, an hour each by the watch, and then concluded with half-hour speeches. This gave to each an opportunity to answer the arguments of each other. As both addressed the same audience, and each was applauded and cheered by his own party, they were both stimulated and excited to the highest degree possible. . . . They were like lawyers before a jury, each anxious to secure a verdict in his own favor. I have often thought that this method of conducting a political campaign had many advantages over that which generally prevails in the Northern and Eastern States, where a candidate, with no ability to speak, is nominated by a caucus, and the parties afterward meet in separate mass-meetings, and the speakers convince voters that are already convinced and annihilate opponents that are not there. In this manner neither party has the opportunity to correctly and fairly represent its views to the other.

But public political discussions made but a small part of the labor performed by a great majority of these candidates. They solicited the votes of the people in private, and on all sorts of occasions. Some of them mounted their horses, and went from house to house together as thoroughly as if they were taking the census. A story is told of two opposing candidates who spent a night together at a cabin. Each was anxious to secure the "female influence" of the family in his favor, and one of them took the water-bucket and started for the distant spring to get a pail of water, thinking to make a favorable impression on the hostess by rendering her this aid in preparing the coffee for their supper. His opponent, not to be outdone by this master-stroke of policy, devoted himself to the baby with such success that he won its favor, and succeeded in getting it into his arms. The other candidate returned from his long walk with his well-filled water-bucket, to see his opponent bestowing the most affectionate caresses and kisses upon a baby that very sadly needed a thorough application of the water he had brought, and to hear him pour into the mother's charmed ear abundant and glowing words of praise for her hopeful child. The water-bucket was set down in despair. It is quite unnecessary to say which of the candidates secured the vote from that cabin.

These candidates were always to be found at all large gatherings of the people. They were to be seen at barbecues, shooting-matches, corn-huskings, gander-pullings, basket-meetings, public theological discussions, and all sorts of religious and other gatherings of the people. . . .

The method of private electioneering by going from house to house, or attending such gatherings unattended by an opponent, was called electioneering on the still hunt. In pursuing the wild game of those regions two methods were adopted. Sometimes the hunters went in large parties, with horses, hounds, and horns, and pursued and killed their game by these public and noisy demonstrations. At other times they went alone and quietly through the fields and woods, came upon their game noiselessly, and killed it by stealth. This latter method was called by the people "the *still hunt*." In like manner, the politicians had two methods of electioneering, as already described. . . .

Many of these candidates displayed most wonderful industry and energy in this "still-hunt" method of electioneering. . . . [It] also developed and gave occasion for the display of great tact and skill in influencing every variety of mind and character. . . .

✓ ✓ ✓

Roads were "kept up" by the required labor of every able-bodied man between the ages of eighteen and forty-five. Mary Noailles Murfree (Charles Egbert Craddock, pseud.) depicted in the following brief passage from *In the Tennessee Mountains*, Houghton Mifflin Company, Boston, 1884, p. 81, the social significance of "keeping up the roads."

In the middle of the stony road stood a group of roughly clad mountaineers, each in an attitude of sluggish disinclination to the allotted task of mending the highway, leaning lazily upon a grubbing-hoe or sorry spade,—except, indeed, the overseer, who was upheld by the single crowbar furnished by the county, the only sound implement in use among the party. The provident dispensation of the law, leaving the care of the road to the tender mercies of its able-bodied neighbors over eighteen and under forty-five years of age, was a godsend to the Settlement and to the inhabitants of the tributary region, in that even if it failed of the immediate design of securing a tolerable passway through the woods, it served the far more important purpose of drawing together the diversely scattered settlers, and affording them unwonted conversational facilities. These meetings were well attended, although their results were often sadly inadequate.

✼   ✼   ✼

Several able writers, including James Lane Allen and Irvin S. Cobb, have given us descriptions of court week. The following is from Wilbur G. Zeigler and Ben S. Grosscup, *The Heart of the Alleghanies or Western North Carolina*, Alfred Williams and Company, Raleigh, 1883, p. 286.

In all the mountain towns court-week is the marked event of the year. There is a spring and fall term. As the counties increase in population, the two terms are frequently lengthened into weeks. At such times the village streets are packed with a mass of humanity. The court might well be likened to a magnet, the limit to its attraction being the boundaries of the county; and within the circle, during the periods of its operation, having an irresistible, invisible power to draw every citizen into the county-seat. They are all there at some interval of its proceedings.

As a court-day in any one of the villages is typical of what is seen at such times in all the others, the writer will use as an illustration one which he spent in Waynesville. It was at the time of the fall term; the month being October. On the Sunday preceding the opening Monday, the honorable judge, having closed court in the neighboring county, drove into the village. The usual number of lawyers from scattered villages who go on the circuit soon came straggling in on horse-back not far in his honor's wake. Later in the evening and the next morning others of the profession entered on foot, pursuing this method of traveling as though desirous of saving a little money, or perhaps having none either to save or spend. The days of the circuit are interesting ones for this legal coterie. It has its jovial, crusty, bumptious, bashful, boyish, and baldheaded members; old pettifoggers, young shysters, and the brilliant and erudite real attorney. . . .

Even before all the shop-keepers had opened their doors and swung back their shutters to exhibit newly stocked counters, the farming population began pouring in. Now and then the broad hat of a man on foot would appear above the crest of the hill; then would follow a strong team of horses drawing a white-covered Pennsylvania wagon; next, a slow-moving ox team with hooped and canvassed vehicle. These tents on wheels would disgorge into the street either a whole family or a crowd of men evidently from the same neighborhood. On other occasions they (the wagons), loaded with apples and possibly a barrel of hard cider, would be longer in getting relieved of their contents. The Jerseys of independent valley farmers came rattling in at a later hour. The general way of coming to town, however, is in the saddle. Horses and mules, with good, easy gait, are always in demand through this country, and the number of them ranged along the street fences appears strange to the Northerner. . . .

The call of the crier from an upstairs window announced that court was open. During the course of the morning I went in. Seats arranged on a scale ascending from the lawyers' tables to the rear wall were crowded to overflowing. The single aisle was filled so that one could hardly elbow one's way in. The crowd changed considerably in its make-up during the morning session; for the uninterested auditors were continually sliding out of one of the handy windows and others crawling in to fill the vacancies. Some wormed their way out through the aisle. . . .

At 12 o'clock the court adjourned, and the crier appearing at the front door gave vent in high-strung monotone to the following: "Hear ye! hear ye! This honorable court is now adjourned." Here he took breath and went on again: "The good people of Haywood will take notice that at 2 o'clock the Honorable General Clingman will address them on the issues of the day."

✓   ✓   ✓

From James Lane Allen, *Blue Grass Region of Kentucky*, New York, 1880, pp. 134-150, *passim*, "The Kentucky Fair" was selected.

. . . from the opening of the nineteenth century things grew easier [in Kentucky.] The people, rescued from the necessity of trying to be safe, began to indulge the luxury of wishing to be happy. Life ceased to be a warfare, and became an industry; the hand left off defending, and commenced acquiring; the moulding of bullets was succeeded by the coining of dollars.

It is against the background of . . . a strenuous past that we find the Kentucky fair first projected by the practical and progressive spirit that ruled among the Kentuckians in the year 1816. Nothing could have been conceived with soberer purpose, or worn less the aspect of a great popular pleasure. Picture the scene! A distinguished soldier and honored gentleman, with a taste for agriculture and fine cattle, has announced that on a certain day in July he will hold on his farm a "Grand Cattle Show and Fair, free for everybody." The place is near Lexington, which was then the centre of commerce and seat of learning in the West. The meagre newspapers of the

ime have carried the tidings to every tavern and country cross-roads. It is
novel undertaking; the like has never been known this side of the Al-
eghanies. The summer morning come, you may see a very remarkable
ompany of gentlemen: old pioneers, Revolutionary soldiers, volunteers
f the War of 1812, walking in picturesque twos and threes out of the little
own to the green woods where the fair is to be held; others jogging thither-
ard along the bypaths and newly-opened roads through the forest, clad in
omespun from heel to head, and mindful of the cold lunches and whiskey-
ottles in their coat-pockets and saddle-bags; some, perhaps, drawn thither
n wagons and aristocratic gigs. Once arrived, all stepping around loftily
n the velvet grass, peering curiously into each other's eyes, and offering
heir snuffboxes for a sneeze of convivial astonishment that they could
enture to meet under the clear sky for such an undertaking. The five judges
f the fair, coming from as many different counties, the greatest personages
f their day—one a brilliant judge of the Federal Court; the second, one of
he earliest settlers, with a sword hanging up at home to show how Vir-
inia appreciated his services in the Revolution; the third, a soldier and
lameless gentleman of the old school; the fourth, one of the few early
Kentuckians who brought into the new society the noble style of country-
lace, with park and deer, that would have done credit to an English lord;
nd the fifth, in no respect inferior to the others. These "perform the duties
ssigned them with assiduity," and hand over to their neighbors as many as
ifteen or twenty premium silver cups, costing twelve dollars apiece. After
which, the assemblage variously disperses—part through the woods again,
while part return to town.

Such, then, was the first Kentucky fair. It was a transplantation to Kentucky, not of the English or European fair, but of the English cattle-show.
It resembled the fair only in being a place for buying and selling. And it was
not thought of in the light of a merry-making or great popular amusement.
It seems not even to have taken account of manufactures—then so important an industry—or of agriculture.

Like the first was the second fair held in the same place the year following. Of this, little is and little need be known, save that then was formed
the first State Agricultural Society of Kentucky, which was also first in
the West, and the second in the United States. This society held two or
three annual meetings, and then went to pieces, but not before laying
down the broad lines on which the fair continued to be held for the next
quarter of a century. That is, the fair began as a cattle-show, though stock
of other kinds was exhibited. Then it was extended to embrace agriculture;
and with branches of good husbandry it embraced as well those of good
housewifery. Thus at the early fairs one finds the farmers contesting for
premiums with their wheats and their whiskeys, while their skilful help-
mates displayed their products—the never-surpassed products of their
looms: linens, cassinetts, jeans, and carpetings. . . . .

It was not until about the year 1840 that the fair began to touch the heart of the whole people. Before this time there had been no amphitheatre, no music, no booths, no side-show, no ladies. A fair without ladies! How could the people love it, or ever come to look upon it as their greatest annual occasion for love-making?

An interesting commentary on the social decorum of this period is furnished in the fact that for some twenty years after the institution of the fair no woman put her foot upon the ground. She was thought a bold woman, doing a bold deed, who one day took a friend and, under the escort of gentlemen, drove in her own carriage to witness the showing of her own fat cattle; for she was herself one of the most practical and successful of Kentucky farmers. But where one of the sex has been, may not all the sex—may not all the world—safely follow? From the date of this event, and the appearance of women on the grounds, the tide of popular favor set in steadily towards the fair.

But, as an immediate consequence, seats must be provided. Here one happens upon a curious bit of local history—the evolution of the amphitheatre among the Kentuckians. At the earliest fairs the form of the amphitheatre had been a rope stretched from tree to tree, while the spectators stood around on the outside, or sat on the grass or in their vehicles. The immediate result of the necessity for providing comfortable seats for the now increasing crowd, was to select as a place for holding the fair such a site as the ancient Greeks might have chosen for building a theatre. Sometimes this was the head of a deep ravine, around the sides of which seats were constructed, while the bottom below served as the arena for the exhibition of the stock, which was led in and out through the mouth of the hollow. At other times advantage was taken of the natural sink and semi-circular hill-side. The slope was sodded and terraced with rows of seats, and the spectators looked down upon the circular basin at the bottom. But clearly enough the sun played havoc with the complexions of the ladies, and a sudden drenching shower was still one of the uncomfortable dispensations of Providence. Therefore a roofed wooden structure of temporary seats made its appearance, designed after the fashion of those used by the travelling show, and finally out of this form came the closed circular amphitheatre, modelled on the plan of the Colosseum. . . . By-and-by we shall see this form of amphitheatre torn down and supplanted by another, which recalls the ancient circus or race-course—a modification corresponding with a change in the character of the later fair. . . .

Here were found the hundreds of neat stalls for the different kinds of stock; the gay booths under the colonnade of the amphitheatre for refreshments; the spacious cottages for women and invalids and children; the platforms of the quack-doctors; the floral hall and pagoda-like structure for the musicians and the judges; the tables and seats for private dining; the high swings and turnabouts; the tests of the strength of limb and lung;

he gaudy awnings for the lemonade venders; the huge brown hogsheads
or iced-water, with bright tin cups dangling from the rim; the circus; and
nally, all those tented spectacles of the marvellous, the mysterious, and
nonstrous which were to draw popular attention to the Kentucky fair, as
hey had been the particular delight of the fair-going thousands in England
undreds of years before.

Within the grounds, how rapidly the crowd swells and surges hither and
hither, tasting the pleasures of the place before going to the amphitheatre:
o the stalls, to the booths. . . . Mixed in with the Kentuckians are people
f a different build and complexion. For Kentucky now is one of the great
ummering States for the extreme Southerners, who come up with their
amilies to its watering-places. Others who are scattered over the North
eturn in the autumn by way of Kentucky, remaining till the fair and the
all of the first frost. Nay, is not the State the place for the reunion of
amilies that have Southern members? Back to the old home from the rice
nd sugar and cotton plantations of the swamps and bayous come young
Kentucky wives with Southern husbands, young Kentucky husbands with
outhern wives. All these are at the fair—the Lexington fair. Here, too, are
trangers from wellnigh every Northern state. And, I beg you, do not over-
ook the Negroes—a solid acre of them. They play unconsciously a great
part in the essential history of this scene and festival. Briskly grooming
he stock in the stalls; strolling around with carriage whips in their hands;
unning on distant errands; showering a tumult of blows upon the newly-
rrived "boss" with their nimble, ubiquitous brush-brooms; everywhere,
verywhere, happy, well-dressed, sleek—the fateful background of all this
tage of social history.

1   1   1

The various "Springs" attracted Southerners from Maryland to Alabama, the
Virginia Springs furnishing the model for those of the other states. G. W. Feather-
tonehaugh, in his *Excursion Through the Slave States,* John Murray, London,
1844, Vol. I, pp. 54 ff., was harsh but graphic in his description of life at White
ulphur Springs.

The establishment of the White Sulphur Springs seemed to consist of
a pack of unpromising-looking huts, or cabins, as they are called, surround-
ng an oblong square, with a foot walk in the centre, railed off from a
grassy plot on each side of it. At the entrance into the establishment—
which has very much the air of a permanent Methodist camp meeting—you
have on the left a miserable-looking sort of barrack, badly constructed of
wood, with a dilapidated portico. Nothing can exceed the frowsy appearance
of this building, which contains the grand dining saloon, where daily between three and four hundred persons assemble to a kind of scramble for
breakfast, dinner, and supper. A few of the cabins had a comfortable-looking
appearance, and these were the private property of genteel families residing

in various parts of Virginia, but who have a right to occupy them only in person, and not by proxy. This oblong square descends rather rapidly towards the southwest to the spring, which is surrounded by a small colonnade, with seats around it, generally filled by persons, many of whom are indifferently dressed, and are constantly smoking and spitting. Others are quietly waiting, with emaciated sallow faces, made ghastly with fever and ague, until the time comes to drink another glass of the sulphuretted water, the gaseous effluvium of which extends far around. A few paces from this is another reservoir of the water, surrounded with a curbstone, where the negro servants assemble and drink in imitation of their masters, and out of which water is dipped for the use of the horses in the contiguous stables. From these springs other rows of cabins are visible, of an inferior kind, but all have a very unprepossessing look. . . .

The waters of this region have been frequented by the Virginians during a long period, for relief from the liver complaints and debilitated constitutions occasioned by the annual unhealthiness of all those low parts of Virginia which extend as far as the tide-water penetrates up the Atlantic rivers. The bilious and intermittent fevers general to that flat country, compel almost all the proprietors who can afford to leave their plantations, to fly to the salubrious air of the mountains, where they usually remain from July until the first frosts set in in October. When these waters first became known, and before roads were made, everybody came on horseback, rude huts were constructed for their personal accommodation by those who came, and the game with which the country abounded, venison, partridges, and bear's-meat, supplied their tables. In time roads were opened, and families were enabled to come with greater comfort, and to bring articles of furniture and a few of the luxuries of life with them; this gradually led to settlements, and to a market at the springs for the productions of the settlers. The waters soon acquired a deserved celebrity, and were annually resorted to by many of the most distinguished persons of Virginia. At length this part of the district became private property, and some of the visitors, to ensure themselves of the greatest possible degree of personal comfort, entered into an agreement with the proprietor that he should build for them small wooden cabins, to contain two or three rooms. The expense of erecting each of these cabins, not exceeding 200 dollars, was to be defrayed by the person for whom it was built, the privilege being reserved to him and his family of occupying it whenever he or they came in preference to any body else, he being bound to leave the key with the proprietor when he went away, who then had the right to put other persons into it. These privileged visitors pay the same weekly charge per head for their board that all others do, and some of them bring their cooks and make an arrangement for a private table, so that they, not being obliged to mingle with the heterogenous mass, have a degree of enjoyment that others cannot participate in. At present the increased popu-

tion and wealth of Virginia cause great numbers to resort to these cele-
rated waters. . . .

To a lover of nature the country abounds in attractions, and when the
ay's excursions are over, what with social visits to families backwards and
orwards, agreeable evening walks when the sun has declined, the news by
 regular daily mail, the general and particular intercourse maintained
mongst those who are acquainted with each other, and reunion at night
f the company in the ball-room, this establishment, situated in a romantic
nd plentiful country, might be converted into a refined rural residence,
uring the summer, for a thousand persons. . . .

A beeve and eight sheep are killed every day after dinner, and either
vasted or consumed within the twenty-four hours. Contracts for these are
nade with cattle-drovers, who drive twenty or fifty, as the case may be; the
usual price paid being three cents . . . a pound for the meat when dressed,
he hide and tallow being thrown in. When the lot is brought by the
trover an average animal is selected, killed, dressed, and weighed, and the
vhole lot paid for, per head, at the same rate. The rest are put into a field
f thirty acres, closely fed, and one of them is killed every day. When the
ervants have dined, the butcher, with his attendants, goes to the field,
elects an animal, has it shot with a rifle, and brings away the carcase in
is waggon. . . .

At six in the morning the first bell rings, and a little before seven the
econd bell announces that breakfast is on the table in the dining-hall.
Now the doors of the cabins are thrown open, and the polite and vulgar are
een converging from every quarter to a scene of indescribable confusion
nd filth. On the dirty portico, in front of the hall, all assemble in a dense
rowd as if some extraordinary exhibition was to be presented, and there
re three doors of entrance. Suddenly these doors are opened from within,
nd then it is important for every gentleman to take care of the lady
under his charge. Having forced your way inside after a desperate squeeze,
he next thing is to find your seat. Where three hundred have to sit in a
place which scarce affords room for two hundred, it is better to be first
han last. A single man stands no chance for a place if he is not on the
lert; yet I must do the visitors the justice to say, that although the motto
s of necessity *sauve qui peut, perd qui veut,* yet the claims of a lady
eemed to be always promptly admitted. . . .

Much squeezed as we were at first, there was a sensible relaxation and
nore elbow-room in a very few minutes, in consequence of the great num-
ers who had the talent of bolting their "feed" in five minutes. A gentle-
nan drew my attention to one of these quick feeders, who had been timed
oy himself and others, and who had been observed to bolt the most extraordinary quantities of angular pieces of bacon, beef, and mutton, in the
hort period of two minutes and a half. . . .

The proprietor of this watering-place, in addition to his plan of over-trading, has had recourse to another scheme which deserves the strongest reprobation. He lets one of his houses to a set of sharpers, who keep a public gaming-table, that is open day and night, where faro, roulette, rouge et noir, and other desperate games are played. Thus every direct encouragement is given to vice, and inducements held out to the vilest fellows in the country to flock to the place for the express purpose of preying upon the company who support his establishment. Inconsiderate and ingenuous young men, who accompany their families here, are thus exposed to the worst temptations, and frequently acquire habits that render them miserable for life.

I can speak with more satisfaction of the ballroom, where the company has the opportunity of assembling every evening, and where young persons who love to dance can amuse themselves very well; for the musicians are far above the ordinary rate of those found at American watering-places.

*   *   *

John James Audubon created a monumental work in natural history, his *Birds of America,* together with five volumes of text entitled *Ornithological Biography.* These were published at Edinburgh, 1831-1839. From the text was reprinted *Delineations of American Scenery and Character,* with an introduction by Francis Hobart Herrick, G. A. Baker and Company, New York, 1926. From the latter work, pp. 60-63, the following description of rifle-shooting in Kentucky is extracted.

Having resided some years in Kentucky, and having more than once been witness of rifle sport, I will present you with the results of my observation, leaving you to judge how far rifle-shooting is understood in that State.

Several individuals who conceive themselves expert in the management of the gun, are often seen to meet for the purpose of displaying their skill, and betting a trifling sum, put up a target, in the centre of which a common-sized nail is hammered for about two-thirds of its length. The marksmen make choice of what they consider a proper distance, which may be forty paces. Each man cleans the interior of his tube, which is called *wiping* it, places a ball in the palm of his hand, pouring as much powder from his horn upon it as will cover it. This quantity is supposed to be sufficient for any distance within a hundred yards. A shot which comes very close to the nail is considered as that of an indifferent marksman; the bending of the nail is, of course, somewhat better; but nothing less than hitting it right on the head is satisfactory. Well, kind reader, one out of three shots generally hits the nail, and should the shooters amount to half a dozen, two nails are frequently needed before each can have a shot. Those who drive the nail have a further trial amongst themselves, and the two best shots of these generally settle the affair, when all the sportsmen djourn to some house, and spend an hour or two in friendly intercourse, ppointing, before they part, a day for another trial. This is technically illed *Driving the Nail*.

Barking off Squirrels is delightful sport, and in my opinion requires a reater degree of accuracy than any other. I first witnessed this manner of rocuring squirrels whilst near the town of Frankfort. The performer was ie celebrated Daniel Boon. We walked out together, and followed the ocky margins of the Kentucky River, until we reached a piece of flat ind thickly covered with black walnuts, oaks and hickories. As the general iast was a good one that year, squirrels were seen gambolling on every ree around us. My companion, a stout, hale, and athletic man, dressed in homespun hunting-shirt, bare-legged and moccasined, carried a long and eavy rifle, which, as he was loading it, he said had proved efficient in ll his former undertakings, and which he hoped would not fail on this ccasion, as he felt proud to show me his skill. The gun was wiped, the owder measured, the ball patched with six-hundred-thread linen, and he charge sent home with a hickory rod. We moved not a step from the lace, for the squirrels were so numerous that it was unnecessary to go fter them. Boon pointed to one of these animals which had observed us, nd was crouched on a branch about fifty paces distant, and bade me mark vell the spot where the ball should hit. He raised his piece gradually until he *bead* (that being the name given by the Kentuckians to the *sight*) of the oarrel was brought to a line with the spot which he intended to hit. The vhip-like report resounded through the woods and along the hills in re- oeated echoes. Judge of my surprise, when I perceived that the ball had iit the piece of bark immediately beneath the squirrel, and shivered it nto splinters, the concussion produced by which had killed the animal, ind sent it whirling through the air, as if it had been blown up by the explosion of a powder magazine. Boon kept up his firing, and before nany hours had elapsed, we had procured as many squirrels as we wished; 'or you must know that to load a rifle requires only a moment, and that f it is wiped after each shot, it will do duty for hours. Since that first nterview with our veteran Boon, I have seen many other individuals per- form the same feat. . . .

After what I have said, you may easily imagine with what ease a Kentuckian procures game, . . . more especially when I tell you that every one in the State is accustomed to handle the rifle from the time when he is first able to shoulder it. . . .

11

Sectional Consciousness

Several years before either the North or the South thought of itself as a section having unique interests and needs, the question of states' rights rose. In 1798 Thomas Jefferson and James Madison wrote sets of resolutions denouncing laws which they claimed infringed upon the rights of the states. When sectionalism developed and leaders looked for constitutional principles on which to base their arguments, Thomas Jefferson became their authority. The first of his "Kentucky Resolutions," written in 1798, stated the compact theory of government. The text of this resolution is from *Resolutions of Virginia and Kentucky Penned by Madison and Jefferson*, Robert I. Smith, Richmond, 1835, p. 64.

Resolved, that the several States composing the United States of America are not united on the principle of unlimited submission to their general government; but that by compact under the style and title of a Constitution for the United States and of amendments thereto, they constituted a general government for special purposes, delegated to that government certain definite powers, reserving each State to itself, the residuary mass of right to their own self-government; and that whensoever the general government assumes undelegated powers, its acts are unauthoritative, void, and of no force: That to this compact each State acceded as a State, and is an integral party, its co-States forming, as to itself, the other party: That government created by this compact was not made the exclusive or final judge of the extent of the powers delegated to itself; since that would have made its discretion, and not the Constitution, the measure of its powers; but that as in all other cases the compact among parties having no common judge, each party has an equal right to judge for itself, as well of infractions as of the mode and measure of redress.

✓ ✓ ✓

After the War of 1812 an occasional reference was made in Congressional debates to the differences that existed in the points of view of North and South concerning a protective tariff. While John C. Calhoun, a young Representative from South Carolina, favored a protective tariff in 1816, few Southerners voted in favor of that bill. John Randolph of Virginia opposed it, not on sectional grounds, ut as an agriculturist who believed that the act would benefit only manufacturers. A few years later the tariff became a sectional issue; in 1820 only five Southern Representatives cast their votes in favor of the pending tariff bill while fifty-six voted against it, and in 1824 the vote of Southern Representatives on the tariff was six in favor and seventy against it, and in 1828 the vote of Southern Representatives was six in favor and seventy against it.

John Randolph's speech against the Tariff of 1816, which follows, is taken from *Annals of Congress, 14 Congress, 1 Session,* Gales and Seaton, 1854, pp. 686-687.

What do the principles about which such a contest is maintained amount to, but a system of bounties to manufacturers, in order to encourage them to do that which, if it be advantageous to do at all, they will do, of course, for their own sakes; a largess to men to exercise their own customary callings for their emolument; and Government devising plans, and bestowing premiums out of the pockets of the hard working cultivator of the soil to mould the productive labor of the country into a thousand fantastic shapes; barring up, all the time, for that perverted purpose, the great, deep, rich stream of our prosperous industry. Such a case, sir, I agree with the honorable gentleman, cannot be fairly brought before this House. It eventuates in this: whether you, as a planter, will consent to be taxed in order to hire another man to go to work in a shoemaker's shop, or to set up a spinning jenny. For my part, I will not agree to it, even though they should by way of return, agree to be taxed to help us to plant tobacco; much less will I agree to pay all and receive nothing for it. No, I will buy where I can get manufactures cheapest; I will not agree to lay a duty on the cultivators of the soil to encourage manufactures; because after all we should only get much worse things at a much higher price, and we, the cultivators of the country, would in the end pay for all. Why do not gentlemen ask us to grant a bounty for the encouragement of making flour? —the reason is too plain for me to repeat it; then why pay a man much more than the value for it, to work up our own cotton into clothing, when, by selling my raw material, I can get my clothing much better and cheaper from Dacca? . . . .

The agriculturists bear the whole brunt of the war and taxation, and remain poor while the others run in the ring of pleasure and fatten upon them. The agriculturists not only pay all, but fight all, while the others run. The manufacturer is the citizen of no place, or any place. The agriculturist has his property, his lands, his all, his household goods to defend; and, like that meek drudge, the ox, who does the labor and ploughs the ground, and then, for his reward, takes the refuse of the farm yard, the blighted blades and the mouldy straw, and the mildewed shocks of corn for his support;—while the commercial speculators live in opulence, whirling in coaches and indulging in palaces; to use the words of Dr. Johnson, coaches which fly like meteors, and palaces which rise like exhalations. Even without your aid, the agriculturists are no match for them. Alert, vigilant enterprising and active, the manufacturing interests are collected in masses and ready to associate at a moment's warning, for any purpose of general interest to their body. Do but ring the fire bell, and you can assemble all the manufacturing interests of Philadelphia, in fifteen minutes. Nay, for [the] matter of that, they are always assembled; they are always on the Rialto, and Shylock and Antonio meet there every day, as friends, and compare notes, and lay plans, and possess in trick and intelligence, what in the goodness of God to them, the others can never possess.

✔   ✔   ✔

All was not well in the Old South. John Randolph, in a letter to Josiah Quincy described the poverty of the old Virginia families, the cause of which he believed to be the worn-out soil. This letter is from Edmund Quincy's *Life of Josiah Quincy*, p. 353, quoted from William Cabell Bruce, *John Randolph of Roanoke* G. P. Putnam's Sons, New York, 1922, pp. 606-608.

. . . Before the Revolution, the lower country of Virginia, pierced for more than a hundred miles from the seaboard by numerous bold and navigable rivers, was inhabited by a race of planters of English descent, who dwelt on their principal estates on the borders of these noble streams. The proprietors were generally well educated, some of them at the best schools of the mother country; the rest at William and Mary, then a seminary of *learning* under able classical masters. Their habitations and establishments, for the most part spacious and costly, in some instances displayed taste and elegance. They were the seats of hospitality. The possessors were gentlemen; better-bred men were not to be found in the British dominions. As yet party spirit was not. This fruitful source of mischief had not then poisoned society. Every door was open to those who maintained the appearance of gentlemen. Each planter might be said, almost without exaggeration, to have a harbor at his door. Here he shipped his *crop* (tobacco), mostly on his own account, to London, Bristol, or Glasgow, and from those ports received every article of luxury or necessity (not raised by himself) which his household and even his distant *quarters* required. For these, a regular order was made out twice a year. You may *guess* at the state of things when a bill of exchange on London for half a crown was some times drawn to pay for a dinner at *the Ordinary*. Did a lady want a jewel new-set, or a gentleman his watch cleaned, the trinket was sent *home*. Even now the old folks talk of "going home to England."

Free living, the war, docking entails (by one sweeping act of Assembly), but chiefly the statute of distributions, undermined these old establishments. Bad agriculture, too, contributed its share. The soil of the country in question, except on the margin of the rivers, where it *was* excellent, is (originally) a light, generous loam upon a sand; once exhausted, it is *dead*.

Rice never constituted an object of culture with us. The tide swamps—a mine of wealth in South Carolina—here produce only miasma. You will find some good thoughts on this head, and on the decay of our agriculture generally in our friend J. T.'s (John Taylor of Caroline) whimsical, but sensible, work, *Arator*.

"Unlike you, we had a *church* to pull down, and its destruction contributed to swell the general ruin. The temples of the living God were abandoned, the *glebe* sold, the University pillaged. The old mansions, where they have been spared by fire (the consequence of the poverty and carelessness of their present tenants) are fast falling to decay; the families, with a few exceptions, dispersed from St. Mary's to St. Louis; such as remain here sunk into obscurity. They, whose fathers rode in coaches, and drank the choicest wines now ride on saddle-bags, and drink grog, when they can get it. What enterprise or capital there was in the country retired westward; and in casting your eyes over the map of Virginia, you must look between the North Mountain and a line drawn through Petersburg, Richmond and Alexandria for the population and wealth of the State. The western district is almost a wilderness. The eastern tract, from the falls of the great rivers to the shore of the Chesapeake,—the region above all others in United America the best adapted for commerce— becomes yearly more deserted. Deer and wild turkeys are nowhere so plentiful in Kentucky as near Williamsburg. I say, "the shore of the Chesapeake," because our *Eastern Shore* (the two counties that lie beyond that bay) must be excluded from this description. There, the old Virginian character is yet (I am told) to be found in greatest purity; although before the Revolution it was a poor, despised region. Here are the descendants of those men who gave an asylum to Sir W. Berkeley during Bacon's rebellion. The land, although thin, bears a good price, and is inhabited by a hospitable, unmixed people. On *this,* the western shore, land within two hours' sail of Norfolk, may be bought for one-half the money which the same quality would command one hundred and fifty miles from tide-water.

✔   ✔   ✔

Bad economic conditions made statesmen from Virginia and the Carolinas disapprove of the protective duties which aided the manufacturing interests. John Taylor wrote a series of agricultural essays dealing with this subject. The following selection is from his *Arator, Being a Series of Agricultural Essays,* J. M. Carter, Baltimore, 1817, pp. 7-13.

A PATIENT must know that he is sick, before he will take physick. A collection of a few facts, to ascertain the ill health of agriculture, is necessary to invigorate our efforts towards a cure. One, apparent to the most superficial observer, is, that our land has diminished in fertility.— Arts improve the work of nature—when they injure it, they are not arts, but barbarous customs. It is the office of agriculture, as an art, not to impoverish, but to fertilize the soil and make it more useful than in its natural state. Such is the effect of every species of agriculture, which can aspire to the character of an art.—Its object being to furnish man with articles of the first necessity, whatever defeats that object, is a crime of the first magnitude. Had men a power to obscure or brighten the light of the sun, by obscuring it, they would imitate the morality of diminishing the fertility of the earth. Is one not as criminal as the other? Yet it is a fact, that lands in their natural state, are more valuable, than those which have undergone our habit of agriculture, of which emigrations are complete proofs.

The decay of a multitude of small towns, so situated as to depend for support on unalterable districts, is another proof of the impoverishment of the soil. It is true, that a few large towns have grown up, but this is owing, not to an increased product, but to an increased pasture; whereas, in every case, where the pasture is limited, or isolated by local circumstances, small towns have sprung up, whilst the lands were fresh, and decayed, as they were worn out. . . . .

In collecting the causes which have contributed to the miserable agricultural state of the country, as it is a national calamity of the highest magnitude, we should be careful not to be blinded by partiality for our customs or institutions, nor corrupted by a disposition to flatter ourselves or others. I shall begin with those of a political nature. These are of a secondary providence, which govern unseen the great interests of society; and if agriculture is bad and languishing in a country and climate, where it may be good and prosperous, no doubt remains with me, that political institutions have chiefly perpetrated the evil; just as they decide the fate of commerce.

The device of subjecting it to the payment of bounties to manufacturing, is an institution of this kind. This device is one item in every system for rendering governments too strong for nations. Such an object never was and never can be effected, except by factions legally created at the publick expense. The wealth transferred from the nation to such factions, devotes them to the will of the government, by which it is bestowed. They must render the service for which it was given, or it would be taken away. It is unexceptionably given to support a government against a nation, or one faction against another. Armies, loaning, banking, and an intricate treasury system, endowing a government with the absolute power of applying publick money, under the cover of nominal checks, are other devices of this kind. Whatever strength or wealth a government and its legal factions acquire by law, is taken from a nation; and whatever is taken from a nation, weakens and impoverishes that interest, which composes the majority. There, political oppression in every form must finally fall, however it may oscillate during the period of transit from a good to a bad government; so as sometimes to scratch factions. Agriculture being the interest covering a great majority of the people of the United States, every device for getting money or power, hatched by a fellow-feeling or common interest, between a government and its legal creatures, must of course weaken and impoverish it. . . .

The device of protecting duties, under the pretext of encouraging manufactures, operates like its kindred, by creating a capitalist interest, which instantly seizes upon the bounty taken by law from agriculture; and instead of doing any good to the actual workers in wood, metals, cotton or other substances, it helps to rear up an aristocratical order, at the expense of the workers in earth, to unite with governments in oppressing every species of useful industry.

The products of agriculture and manufacturing, unshackled by law, would seek each for themselves, the best markets through commercial channels, but these markets would hardly ever be the same; protecting duties tie travellers together, whose business and interest lie in different directions. This ligature upon nature, will, like all unnatural ligatures, weaken or kill. The best markets of our agriculture lie in foreign countries, whilst the best markets of our manufactures are at home.—Our agriculture has to cross the ocean, and encounter a competition with foreign agriculture on its own ground. Our manufactures meet at home a competition with foreign manufactures. The disadvantages of the first competition, suffice to excite all the efforts of agriculture to save her own life; the advantages of the second suffice gradually to bestow a sound constitution on manufacturing. But the manufacture of an aristocratical interest, under the pretext of encouraging work of a very different nature, may reduce both manufacturers and husbandmen, . . . to the lowest state of degradation.

This degradation could never have been seen by a friend to either, who could afterwards approve of protecting duties. Let us take the article of wheat to unfold an idea of the disadvantages which have produced it. If wheat is worth 16s. sterling in England the 70lb. the farmers sell it here at about 6s. sterling.—American agriculture then meets English agriculture in a competition, compelling her to sell at little more than one third of the price obtained by her rival. But American manufactures take the field against English on very different terms. These competitors meet in the United States. The American manufactures receive first, a bounty equal to the freight, commission and English taxes, upon their English rivals; and secondly, a bounty equal to our own necessary imposts. Without protecting duties, therefore, the American manufacturer gets for the same article, about 25 per cent. more, and the American agriculturist about 180 per cent. less, than their English rivals. Protecting duties added to these inequalities, may raise up an order of masters for actual manufacturers, to intercept advantages too enormous to escape the vigilance of capital, impoverish husbandmen, and aid in changing a fair to a fraudulent government; but they will never make either of these intrinsically valuable classes richer, wiser or freer.

✓   ✓   ✓

South Carolina's view of the tariffs of 1828 and 1832 were stated by George McDuffie in a Eulogy which he delivered in Charleston in 1840 in memory of Robert Y. Hayne. The following extract is quoted from Edwin L. Green, Editor, *Two Speeches of George McDuffie,* The State Printing Company, Columbia, South Carolina, 1905, pp. 96-114, *passim.*

His memory and his fame are so closely and inseparably identified with the opposition made to the protecting system by himself in Congress, and by South Carolina in the character of a soverign party to the Federal compact, that I should violate the most sacred obligations of friendship and of duty if I did not exhibit, with all the fidelity of history, the part he acted on that memorable question in Congress, in the State convention, and finally as the chief magistrate of the State. . . . His . . . opposition to the tariff of 1828—the fatal consummation of that climax of unequal and oppressive measures which threatened absolute destruction of the great agricultural interests of the exporting States—were in all respects equal to the occasion. . . . He did everything that human reason and human eloquence could do to save the rights and interests of South Carolina and the other planting States from this crowning measure of legislative despotism. But what could human reason and human eloquence avail against a predetermined and infatuated majority, composed of various interests, bound together by a mercenary league to plunder the exporting States of the Union, through the perverted forms of Federal legislation? . . . .

Let us pause for a moment and consider dispassionately the causes which produced our memorable controversy with the Federal government, and the principles involved in that controversy. South Carolina was an exporting State, and her great staple productions derived their value principally from the demand for them in foreign markets, and the free exchange of them for foreign manufactures. Congress possessed the power to regulate commerce with foreign nations, but for the sole purpose of extending and protecting it. In this state of things, when the Federal treasury was full to overflowing, and there was not a shadow of complaint against any foreign power for any imputed violation of our commercial or national rights; that body, securing a majority by bribing various other interests to unite with the manufacturing interest, and by means of certain political combinations connected with the presidential election, passed that most extraordinary compound of heterogeneous and conflicting elements, the tariff of 1828—a measure consistent in nothing but its remorseless wickedness and oppression, and which may be emphatically said to have been "born in sin and brought forth in iniquity". . . . The tariff of 1832 . . . aggravated all the enormities of that of 1828 by increasing its inequality. . . .

We were reduced to the very worst condition of colonial dependencies and tributary vassalage which the world has witnessed since the proconsular despotism of Rome over her conquered provinces, aggravated by the consideration that the free, sovereign, and independent States of a Confederacy of equals was thus degraded and oppressed, in palpable violation of the compact of their political union, and in utter contempt of every principle of that glorious struggle by which they had achieved their common independence, and their common liberties. The colonial restrictions and unconstitutional taxes imposed upon our common ancestors by Great Britain were "trifles light as air" in comparison with those imposed upon us under the perverted forms of a free government.

✓   ✓   ✓

George W. Featherstonehaugh, an English scientist, visited with Dr. Thomas Cooper in Columbia, South Carolina, and with him discussed the Nullification Controversy. The following account of the controversy and of that visit is from Featherstonehaugh, *Excursion Through the Slave States*, John Murray, London, 1844, Vol. II, pp. 332 ff.

I rambled in the afternoon about two or three miles off to call upon Dr. Cooper, whom I had met before in New York. This gentleman, always conspicuous, had made himself particularly so of late, in the agitation of the *Nullification* question, which the tariff law had given birth to, and which had so nearly brought the State of South Carolina into hostile collision with the power of the federal government under the administration of President Jackson. Although the excitement—which at one time threatened such fatal consequences—had been calmed by the judicious conduct of Mr. Clay and Mr. Calhoun in agreeing to the Compromise Act, yet the same question is of such vital consequence to South Carolina, and so important to Northern manufacturers, that it is always liable to be agitated again. The leading planters of South Carolina are generally men who, having inherited large estates with numerous slaves born upon them, and received liberal educations, consider themselves, not without some reason, *the gentlemen of America;* looking down upon the trading communities in the Northern States, where slavery does not exist, with that habitual sense of superiority which men born to command—and above all others slaveholders—always cherish when they are placed in competition with men engaged in mercantile pursuits, whom they consider to be, by the nature of their avocations, incapable of rising to their level; to this feeling, the seeds of which are planted in infancy, is added a distrust sometimes amounting to hatred.

The planter, although his crops of cotton and rice often produce him an annual income far exceeding that of the cultivator of the North and tempt him to live in a style corresponding to the rank he believes himself to hold in society, yet is frequently less independent than the opulent merchant or farmer he undervalues, his annual expenditures being large and certain, whilst his returns are somewhat precarious. He has perhaps to feed and clothe several hundred slaves, and it is not convenient for him to reduce his style of living; so that not unfrequently the merchant at the north, who is his agent, and to whom he consigns his productions for sale, sends him an account current, where, instead of small charges being deducted from large returns, he finds advances made to him in money, the bills for feeding and clothing his slaves, his wines and luxuries, and other charges, swelled to an amount far exceeding the sum-total that his crops have sold for; perceiving himself therefore the debtor and quasi slave of the man he despises, his pride, his interest, and his passions, all combine to rouse his indignation: at such moments the agitated planter is easily led to follow in the wake of any politicians who flatter him with a prospect of redress.

When the politicians and manufacturers of the Northern States combined to enact the tariff of 1828, "for the *protection* of home manufactures," alleging that the productions of the Southern States were admitted without competition into the ports of England, a general feeling of resistance arose in the State of South Carolina: the duties now to be levied upon those articles of British manufacture which the planter was compelled to purchase for the use of his slaves, must necessarily greatly augment his expenditures, and to this was added the apprehension of another evil of still greater magnitude, viz. that Great Britain might lay retaliatory duties upon his exports, and gradually look to other countries to be supplied with them. Politics and interests therefore combined in South Carolina to rouse the people into a resistance to that law, and the government of the State taking the lead, finished by declaring that when the United States government manifestly exceeded its powers—of which fact they held that the suffering State must be the best judge—every single State had a natural constitutional right to "nullify its acts."

Armies were now raised, and everything was prepared for resistance, as much as if a foreign invader was about to enter their territory. Such was the indomitable spirit that appeared to prevail, and the determination not to permit the revenue laws of the United States to be executed in South Carolina, that if President Jackson, as it was believed he was disposed to do, had attempted to execute them by force, there is no doubt that a furious civil war would have raged in the State, of which the consequences—let the questionable result have been either one way or the other—must have been signally fatal; for no one can predict the ultimate consequences of giving military habits to a numerous slave population, which must upon so fatal a contingency have unavoidably taken place. Happily for the country, the wise compromise which took place, the effect of which was to provide for the general reduction of those oppressive tariff duties to an amount limited by the wants of the public revenue, and not by the demands for *protection,* averted this great danger. Mr. Clay, whom the protection-party claimed as their leader, and Mr. Calhoun, the avowed leader of the Nullifying party, patriotically concurred in making sacrifices in favour of peace, by carrying the measure called the Compromise Act through the national legislature. . . .

I found Dr. Cooper in a pleasant little villa, which the ladies of his family had furnished with a great many comforts. He received me very cordially, and although about eighty years old, began to talk with wonderful energy and vivacity upon a variety of subjects. The Compromise Act, however, was uppermost in the Doctor's mind, and I soon saw that he did not like it at all, for it had extinguished all the eloquence, patriotism, and achievement which Nullification might have brought forth at a future day. Upon my congratulating him upon that measure, and the happy consequences which would flow from it, he rose from his easy chair, and although bent double like a hook, he seized the hearth-brush, and with his eyes full of fire, and wielding the brush as if it were a broadsword, denounced the Compromise Act as an ignoble measure which he never could approve of; declared that the Nullifiers were quite in the wrong to make peace with the Union men (their opponents in South Carolina), and that it would have been a much better course for them to have taken the field against General Jackson, and have fought all the power he could have brought against them.

✓   ✓   ✓

Following the War of 1812 a great outburst of national pride resulted in the passage of bills rechartering the Bank of the United States, which had been allowed to die in 1811, and extending the National Turnpike into the Northwest Territory. This legislation was opposed by many Southerners. Nathaniel Macon of North Carolina was alarmed lest Congress might next attempt to abolish slavery. The following letter from Macon to Mr. Bartlett Yancey is quoted from Edwin Mood Wilson, *The Congressional Career of Nathaniel Macon,* James Sprunt Historical Monographs, No. 2, University Press, Chapel Hill, 1900.

WASHINGTON 8 March 1818.
SIR.

This is Sunday. I have just finished my correspondence about business, and cannot I believe do a better act, than to acknowledge the receipt of your acceptable letter of the 22nd ult. . . .

I must ask you to examine the constitution of the U. S.—particularly the following parts, and then tell me if Congress can establish banks, make roads and canals, whether they cannot free all the slaves in the U. S.

The preamble article 1—Section 8—paragraph 1—Same article and paragraph Section 9—article 4 all the Section 2 & 4; with the 9 and 10 amendments. . . .

It takes a long time to produce great events in any nation. The dispute which begun in Great Britain under the reign of Charles the first was not completely settled, until William of Orange was placed on the throne. The American revolution commenced with the Stamp act. How long the French revolution was brewing is more uncertain, but that may be said to have begun when her philosophers first wrote freely on politics. The dispute between Caesar and Pompey did not begin with them, for Marius and Sulla were before them. We have abolition-colonizing bible and peace societies; their intentions cannot be known; but the character and spirit of one may without injustice be considered that of all it is a character and spirit of perseverance, bordering on enthusiasm; and if the general government shall continue to stretch their powers, these societies will un-doubtedly push them to try the question of emancipation. . . .

The states having no slaves may not feel as strongly, as the States hav-ing slaves about stretching the constitution; because no such interest is to be touched by it. Who could have supposed when Mr. Jefferson went out of office that his principles and the principles which brought him into it, would so soon have become unfashionable, and that Mr. Madison the champion against banks, should have signed an act to establish one, con-taining worse principles, than the one he opposed as unconstitutional, and that Mr. Monroe should become apparently the favorite of the federalists, if not so in fact.

The camp that is not always guarded may be surprised; and the people which do not always watch their rulers may be enslaved, too much con-fidence is the ruin of both.

✓   ✓   ✓

Southern writers frequently pointed out the injuries which their section might suffer from the strengthening of the national government. They viewed with alarm proposals for internal improvements at federal expense. Such fears were expressed by Robert James Turnbull in a pamphlet, *The Crisis,* A. E. Miller, Charleston, October, 1827.

It is amongst the invaluable privileges of the citizen, as secured to him by the Constitution, that he has the right, at all times, to address his fellow-citizens, on the subject of their rights, their interests, or their safety. . . .

The subject which ought at this moment, to claim the attention of every South-Carolinian, is the tendency of the government toward a firm *con-solidated* national government. This is no idle speculation. It is not a phantom which exists in the distempered minds of the weak, the timid, or the suspicious. . . . It will be found to exist in the minds of some of our best and wisest men, and daily becomes to our citizens generally, a source of much inquietude. Perceiving that the Congress claims and exercises powers, never contemplated by the framers of the Constitution of the United States, they are *alarmed,* and justly alarmed for the situation of the Southern country, whose safety they feel to consist in the *integrity* and *sovereignty* of the individual States. And well may they be alarmed. Within the last six or seven years, Congress has made more rapid strides toward consolidation, than in the thirty previous years. . . . The subjects of *tariff* and *internal* improvements being earnestly recommended by the President to Congress, and that body having nearly exhausted all the ordinary subjects of legislation, for which the Constitution had provided, and having, in fact, little or nothing to do, being in a state of peace and friendship with all nations, was glad to hear of new subjects on which to exercise its powers, and at length resolved, that it could construct *military* and other national roads, make canals, improve inland navigation, promote manufactures, and appropriate money to *any* extent, for the purpose of promoting, what they would call, the general interests of the States. A new field of power has thus been opened to Congress, as boundless as space itself. All the guards which the framers of the Constitution, and the State Legislatures had cautiously provided, to keep the general government within its prescribed and limited powers, have been discovered to be utterly useless. . . . The more *National,* and the less *Federal,* the government becomes, the more certainly will . . . the interests of the South be depressed and destroyed. . . . [The] interests of the North and West, are diametrically opposed to the interests of the South. . . . .

Amongst all the ends for which the Union was formed, it will hardly be believed, that it was ever intended that Congress should so legislate, as to take from States the advantage given them by nature, and to transfer them to others. And yet, this will be one of the effects of the interference of Congress with this subject. As the States are now situated, New Orleans is destined to be the emporium for the products of the Western country. This is an advantage she possesses by *nature.* It is, however, a part of the design of Providence, that intelligence and art should be made to triumph over certain obstacles of nature, as a means of stimulating the industry of man, and it is certainly fair that Pennsylvania, or New York, or Maryland, should level mountains, and intersect them with fine roads and canals, so as to draw from New Orleans a part of the valuable commerce of the West. This is no more than what New York does to all the cities in the Union. . . . This is all fair in trade.—But I do humbly conceive, that in the *Government* of the United States has not a right so to expend its resources, as to do for Pennsylvania or Maryland, what those States cannot do for themselves. . . . If Congress cannot "by any regulation of revenue, give a preference of one port in the United States over another," without violating the compact, I do not see, why it should be permitted to do so, by national roads or national canals, or by any other regulation of internal improvements.

Let the business of internal improvements be left to the States. . . .

Our ancestors of 1778, foresaw the evils with which we are now afflicted. . . . "You have given to Congress the sword and the purse" exclaims the Virginia Statesman [Patrick Henry,] "and they will take the *rest,* whether you *will it* or not." "Upon my tombstone," concludes the venerable Patriarch of South Carolina, [Rawlins Lowndes] . . . "I desire no other inscription than, that THIS IS THE MAN who opposed the Federal Constitution, because he foresaw that it would finally RUIN THE SOUTHERN COUNTRY."

✓   ✓   ✓

The decades of the eighteen-thirties and forties were a period of reform in Europe and in the United States. Improved penal institutions, insane asylums, educational advancement, were all part of the movement, but the phase which caused the greatest disturbance in America was the agitation for emancipation of the slaves. Colonization societies were supported in the South as well as in the North. Then in 1831 Nat Turner organized an insurrection that brought terror to to South. In that same year Alexis de Toqueville visited the United States and gathered material for his classic work, *Democracy in America.* In the following excerpts from that work he pointed out the complexity of the race problem in the South. The selection is quoted from *Democracy in America,* The Colonial Press, New York, Revised Edition, 1900, Vol. I, pp. 381-385.

The danger of a conflict between the white and black inhabitants of the Southern States of the Union—a danger which, however remote it may be, is inevitable—perpetually haunts the imagination of the Americans. The inhabitants of the North make it a common topic of conversation, although they have no direct injury to fear from the struggle; but they vainly endeavor to devise some means of obviating the misfortunes which they foresee. In the Southern States the subject is not discussed: the planter does not allude to the future in conversing with strangers; the citizen does not communicate his apprehensions to his friends; he seeks to conceal them from himself; but there is something more alarming in the tacit forebodings of the South, than in the more clamorous fears of the Northern States. . . .

In twelve years the Colonization Society has transported 2,500 negroes to Africa; in the same space of time about 700,000 blacks were born in the United States. If the colony of Liberia were so situated as to be able to receive thousands of new inhabitants every year, and if the negroes were in a state to be sent thither with advantage; if the Union were to supply the society with annual subsidies, and to transport the negroes to Africa in the vessels of the State, it would still be unable to counterpoise the natural increase of population amongst the blacks; and as it could not remove as many men in a year as are born upon its territory within the same space of time, it would fail in suspending the growth of the evil which is daily increasing in the States. The negro race will never leave those shores of the American continent, to which it was brought by the passions and vices of the Euroepans; and it will not disappear from the New World as long as it continues to exist. The inhabitants of the United States may retard the calamities which they apprehend, but they cannot now destroy their efficient cause.

I am obliged to confess that I do not regard the abolition of slavery as a means of warding off the struggle of the two races in the United States. The negroes may long remain slaves without complaining; but if they are once raised to the level of free men, they will soon revolt at being deprived of all their civil rights; and as they cannot become the equals of the whites, they will speedily declare themselves as enemies. In the North everything contributed to facilitate the emancipation of the slaves; and slavery was abolished, without placing the free negroes in a position which could become formidable, since their number was too small for them ever to claim the exercise of their rights. But such is not the case in the South. The question of slavery was a question of commerce and manufacture for the slave-owners in the North; for those of the South, it is a question of life and death. God forbid that I should seek to justify the principle of negro slavery, as has been done by some American writers! But I only observe that all the countries which formerly adopted that execrable principle are not equally able to abandon it at the present time.

When I contemplate the condition of the South, I can only discover two alternatives which may be adopted by the white inhabitants of those States; viz., either to emancipate the negroes, and to intermingle with them; or, remaining isolated from them, to keep them in a state of slavery as long as possible. . . . As they are determined not to mingle with the negroes, they refuse to emancipate them. . . .

The legislation of the Southern States with regard to slaves, presents at the present day such unparalleled atrocities as suffice to show how radically the laws of humanity have been perverted, and to betray the desperate position of the community in which the legislation has been promulgated. The Americans of this portion of the Union have not, indeed, augmented the hardships of slavery; they have, on the contrary, bettered the physical condition of the slaves. The only means by which the ancients maintained slavery were fetters and death; the Americans of the South of the Union have discovered more intellectual securities for the duration of their power. They have employed their despotism and their violence against the human mind. In antiquity, precautions were taken to prevent the slave from breaking his chains; at the present day measures are adopted to deprive him even of the desire of freedom. The ancients kept the bodies of their slaves in bondage, but they placed no restraint upon the mind and no check upon education; and they acted consistently with their established principle, since a natural termination of slavery then existed, and one day the slave might be set free, and become the equal of his master. But the Americans of the South, who do not admit that the negroes can ever be commingled with themselves, have forbidden them to be taught to read or write, under severe penalties; and as they will not raise them to their own level, they sink them as nearly as possible to that of the brutes.

✓   ✓   ✓

Among those who opposed slavery and even aided slaves to escape from their masters, were many members of the Society of Friends. Levi Coffin, in his memoirs, *Reminiscences of Levi Coffin, the Reputed President of the Underground Railroad*, R. Clarke and Company, Cincinnati, 1880, pp. 5-17, described the beginning of his career as a liberator.

A while before the Revolutionary War a considerable colony of friends . . . settled at New Garden, in Guilford County, North Carolina, which was then a newly settled country. My grandfather, William Coffin, was among those who migrated. His removal took place in the year 1773. . . . They settled at New Garden . . . and were all members of the religious Society of Friends. My father, Levi Coffin, was the youngest of eight sons and next to the youngest child. [My grandparents] . . . were valuable elders in the Society of Friends, and were highly esteemed in the community. Their house had long been a resort and place of entertainment for Friends who came into the neighborhood to attend religious meetings, and for travelling ministers. They lived on a farm, a short distance from New Garden Meeting-House. My father was brought up as a farmer, but managed to get a fair education, considering the limited advantages of that day, and when a young man, engaged during the winter season in teaching school in the neighborhood. After the marriage of my parents, they settled on a farm in the neighborhood. . . .

Both my parents and grandparents were opposed to slavery, and none of either of the families ever owned slaves; and all were friends of the oppressed, so I claim that I inherited my anti-slavery principles.

I date my conversion to Abolitionism from an incident which occurred when I was about seven years old. It made a deep and lasting impression on my mind, and created that horror of the cruelties of slavery which has been the motive of so many actions of my life. At the time of which I speak, Virginia and Maryland were the principal slave-rearing States, and to a great extent supplied the Southern market. Free negroes in Pennsylvania were frequently kidnaped or decoyed into these States, then hurried away to Georgia, Alabama, or Louisiana, and sold. The gangs were handcuffed and chained together, and driven by a man on horseback, who flourished a long whip, such as is used in driving cattle, and goaded the reluctant and weary when their feet lagged on the journey. One day I was by the roadside where my father was chopping wood, when I saw such a gang approaching along the new Salisbury road. The coffle of slaves came first, chained in couples on each side of a long chain which extended between them; the driver was some distance behind, with the wagon of supplies. My father addressed the slaves pleasantly, and then asked, "Well, boys, why do they chain you?" One of the men, whose countenance betrayed unusual intelligence, and whose expression denoted the deepest sadness replied: "They have taken us away from our wives and children, and they chain us lest we should make our escape and go back to them." My childish sympathy and interest were aroused, and when the dejected procession had passed on, I turned to my father and asked many questions concerning them, why they were taken away from their families, etc. In simple words, suited to my comprehension, my father explained to me the meaning of slavery, and, as I listened, the thought arose in my mind— "How terribly we should feel if father were taken away from us."

This was the first awakening of that sympathy with the oppressed, which, together with a strong hatred of oppression and injustice in every form, where the motives that influenced my whole after life. . . .

The first opportunity for aiding a slave occurred when I was about fifteen years old. It was a custom in North Carolina, at that time, to make a "frolic" of any special work, like corn husking, log-rolling, etc. The neighbors would assemble at the place appointed, and with willing hearts and busy hands soon complete the work. Then followed the supper and merry-making, and the night was in

"The wee sma' hours ayant the twal,"

before the lights were out and the company gone.

At a gathering of this kind, a corn husking at Dr. Caldwell's, I was present. The neighbors assembled about dark, bringing their slaves with them. The negroes were assigned a place at one end of the heap, the white people took their place at the other, and all went to work, enlivening their labor with songs and merry talk.

A slave dealer, named Stephen Holland, had arrived in the neighborhood a short time before, with a coffle of slaves, on his way to the South, and as this was his place of residence, he stopped for a few days before proceeding on his journey. He brought with him his band of slaves to help his neighbor husk corn, and I was much interested in them. When the white people went in to supper I remained behind to talk with the strange negroes, and see if I could render them any service. In conversation I learned that one of the negroes, named Stephen, was born free, but had been kidnapped and sold into slavery. Till he became of age he had been indentured to Edward Lloyd, a Friend, living near Philadelphia. When his apprenticeship was ended, he had been hired by a man to help drive a flock of sheep to Baltimore. After reaching that place he was seized one night as he was asleep in the negro house of a tavern, gagged and bound, then placed in a close carriage, and driven across the line into Virginia, where he was confined the next night in a cellar. He had then been sold for a small sum to Holland, who was taking him to the Southern market, where he expected to realize a large sum for his sale. I became deeply interested in his story, and began to think how I could help him regain his freedom. Remembering Dr. Caldwell's Tom, a trusty negro, whom I knew well, I imparted to him my wishes and desired him, if it could be arranged, to bring Stephen to my father's the next night. They came about midnight, and my father wrote down the particulars of Stephen's case, and took the address of the Lloyd's. The next day he wrote to them, giving an account of Stephen and his whereabouts. In two weeks from that time, Hugh Lloyd, a brother of Edward Lloyd, arrived by stage in Greensboro. Procuring conveyance, he came to my father's, and there learned that Stephen had been taken southward by the slave-dealer Holland. Next day being regular meeting-day at the Friends Meeting-House, at New Garden, the case was laid before the men after meeting, and two of them, Dr. George Swain and Henry Macy, volunteered to accompany Hugh Lloyd in search of Stephen.

A sum of money was made up for the expenses of their journey, and Lloyd was furnished with a horse and saddle and the necessary equipments. The party found Stephen in Georgia, where he had been sold by Holland, who had gone farther South. A suit was instituted to gain possession of him. . . . Lloyd returned North and sent affidavits and free papers giving proof of the case, and in six months Stephen was liberated and returned home. . . .

✓   ✓   ✓

English travelers in America during the 1830's were highly critical of the slave system, slaves in the British Empire having been emancipated in 1834 with compensation to the owners. Typical of such criticism is the following selection from E. S. Abdy, *Journal of a Residence, and Tour of the United States of America from April, 1833 to October, 1834,* J. Murray, London, 1835, Vol. II, pp. 91-99.

It is not sufficient for the national dishonor, that the district marked out for the residence and immediate jurisdiction of the general government should be polluted by slavery. Here, under the eyes of Congress,—in defiance of public opinion,—and as if courting the observation of assembled legislators and ambassadors, a traffic, the most base and revolting, is carried on by a set of ruffians, with whom it would be the greatest injustice to compare our ressurectionmen. They are called slave-traders, and their occupation is to kidnap every colored stranger they can lay their hands on. No matter whether he be free or not, his papers, if he chance to have any they can get at, are taken from him; and he is hurried to gaol, from whence, under pretence that the documents he has in his possession are not satisfactory, or that he is unable to pay the expenses of his arrest and detention, he is sent off to the southern market. Men, women, and children, indiscriminately, who come to Washington in search of employment, or to visit their friends, are liable to be carried off by these land-sharks; one of whom boasted to a man, from whom I had a statement, that he had just made forty dollars by a job. Proprietors of slaves would be ungrateful if they did not connive at the inquities of the kidnapper. The net that is laid for the unfriended free man is pretty sure to catch the runaway. These villians deal with the drivers and agents, and sometimes with the planters themselves. A poor fellow, whose claims to freedom were pronounced defective, was purchased by one of them, not long ago, for a dollar, and sold the next day for four hundred. About the same time, a colored young woman was entering the city from the country, when she was pursued by one of these blood-hounds; and to escape, threw herself into the river, and was drowned. No notice whatever was taken of this horrible occurrence by the public papers, though it was a matter of notoriety. . . . Here, as in most, if not all, slave countries, the presumption is against liberty; and, contrary to every principle of moral and municipal law, a man is pronounced guilty because he cannot prove himself innocent. The onus is thrown upon the accused; and he is declared to be a slave, if he is unable to shew that he is free. . . .

The Benevolent Society of Alexandria stated, in 1827, that they had, in the first nine or ten months of their existence, wrested twelve people of color from the grasp of the slave-traders; and that they had reason to believe there were several others, entitled to their freedom, who had been sold: "If it were not," they added, "for this detestable traffic, those who have a large number of slaves upon poor land," (such is most of the soil near Washington,) "would not long be enabled to hold them; as it generally takes the whole produce of their labor to clothe and support them; and the only profit of the owner is derived from the sale of the young ones."

ʃ ʃ ʃ

The attacks of the abolitionists did not remain unanswered. Southern periodicals were vehicles by which articles in defense of slavery were circulated. The English traveler, James S. Buckingham, in his *The Slave States of America,* Fisher, Son and Company, London, 1842, Vol. I, p. 56, reviewed a few such articles.

In the first volume [of the *Southern Literary Journal*] for 1835, an extract of a letter is given from an anti-abolitionist at the north, in which he says, "I believe that facts will warrant the assertion, that the condition of the slave population in the aggregate is better than that of the free black, who assumes all the cares and responsibilities of self-support." . . .

In the same volume (p. 207) is a brief enumeration of the recent publications on the slave question, which the editor has received for review; and on these, including nine different works by different authors, he has the following remarks: "The Amenability of Northern Incendiaries, as well to Northern as to Southern Laws," is the title of a pamphlet by the senior editor of the Charleston Courier, a gentleman well known in our community as a sound constitutional lawyer, and a successful advocate. The right of South Carolina to demand of the Northern States the *persons* of the incendiaries, for the purpose of punishment, he places on the broad and recognized principles of the law of nations applicable to such cases; the only ground, in law, upon which, in our opinion, the right can be maintained.". . . "Remarks on Slavery, by a Citizen of Georgia," is described as "an able and successful attempt to prove that slavery is upheld and countenanced by the writers of the Old and New Testaments"; and another work, entitled "Two Sermons on the Subject of Slavery, by Simon Doggett," is said to "sustain ably the scriptural argument in *favour* of slavery, from the classical pen of a venerable clergyman of Massachusetts, who passed the last winter among us (in the South)". . . . Dr. Cooper, the president of Columbia College, in the capital of South Carolina, says, in an article on slavery in the same volume, p. 188— "I do not know a more bold, a more impudent, a more unprincipled, unblushing falsehood, than to say that *slavery is inconsistent with the laws of God,* if the Bible be assumed as the repository of those laws. I do not wish to go over the ground again, already trodden for the hundredth time; but I claim the right of appealing to your readers who read the Bible, whether, from the time of the Apostle Paul, there be not the most ample proof of domestic slavery being ordained, practiced, and approved by the Jews in the Old, and by the Christians in the New Testament, without one contradictory or commendatory passage or precept?"

✦   ✦   ✦

William Harper of South Carolina delivered an oration before the South Carolina Society for the Advancement of Learning, December ninth, 1835, his subject being "Domestic Slavery." In the *Southern Literary Journal,* Charleston, Vol. II, July, 1836, pp. 375-392, *passim,* appeared the following: "Reflections Elicited by Judge Harper's Anniversary Oration."

Judge Harper in the discourse before us, regards the institution of *Domestic Slavery* as a feature which, more than any other, gives a marked and distinctive character to the social condition of the Southern States of the American confederacy, and he accordingly invites the attention of the members of the recently formed Literary Association to this topic, as one of primary and paramount importance. . . .

"I believe," he says, "that no one who has the slightest acquaintance with the subject . . . imagines it to be possible that slavery should cease to exist among us in our day, or for generations to come. Our proudest and most deeply cherished feelings—which others, if they will, may call prejudices—our most essential interests—our humanity and consideration for the slaves themselves—nay, almost physical impossibility, forbid that this should be done by our own act, and thank God, we, the slave-holding communities of the South, are too strong, and on this subject too united, to admit the thought that it can be effected by external force. . . ."

But although the entire moral force of the South is enlisted in defence of her cherished institutions—although the most perfect unanimity exists and ever will continue to exist among her citizens in reference to these vital interests which constitute a rallying point for the enlightened exertions of the greatest and purest minds among us—although, in consequence, the distinguishing feature referred to can never be eradicated from the moral face of our society, without utterly annihilating the South itself, and sweeping its citizens from existence, still the institution of slavery is attacked, and will continue to be assailed from various quarters, and much (which must be met) is to be apprehended from the wild spirit of fanaticism, its disorganizing attempts, and its direct tendency to implicate and perchance sever the relations which subsist between the South and the other parts of the Union . . . formidable associations even now exist,—even already have planted themselves firmly, and extended their roots deeply into the very heart of the country,—composed of men, who under the garb of friendship and patriotism, carry the dagger of the assassin, and who are ready, with the first opportunity that offers, to aim a fatal blow at our happiness and quiet. . . . Their minds, their pens, their presses are never idle, but constantly employed in sending forth, from all quarters, the most inflammatory doctrines . . . ; those who cannot read, have revolting pictures spread before them to awaken indignation for imaginary ills; the public mails, established for the common benefit, are prostituted to the extensive dissemination of the mischief; bold and desperate emissaries are bribed to go through the country, with instructions to excite servile insurrections, and no expedients, which the fertile imagination of the projectors of these evil measures can suggest, are left unattempted, which are calculated to disturb the public peace, and finally to involve the citizens of a republic, united by many enduring ties, in all the horrors of a civil convulsion. . . .

✦   ✦   ✦

Among the first institutions to be disrupted by this North-South controversy over slavery were the churches. Northern church officials expressed disapproval of the slave system, while in the South such officials became apologetic, and eventually there was disunion in the churches, years before the rupture in the federal government took place. John C. Calhoun, in his speech read before the United States Senate in March, 1850, described the disunion in the churches. The following excerpt is quoted from *The Congressional Globe,* 31st Congress, Vol. XXI, Part I, p. 453.

The cords that bind the States together are not only many, but various in character. Some are spiritual or ecclesiastical; some political; others social.

. . . The strongest of those of a spiritual and ecclesiastical nature, consisted in the unity of the great religious denominations, all of which originally embraced the whole Union. All these denominations, with the exception, perhaps, of the Catholics, were organized very much upon the principle of our political institutions. Beginning with smaller meetings, corresponding with the political divisions of the country, their organization terminated in one great central assemblage, corresponding very much with the character of Congress. At these meetings the principal clergymen and lay members of the respective denominations, from all parts of the Union, met to transact business relating to their common concerns. It was not confined to what appertained to the doctrines and discipline of the respective denominations, but extended to plans for disseminating the Bible—establishing missions, distributing tracts—and of establishing presses for the publication of tracts, newspapers, and periodicals, with a view of diffusing religious information—and for the support of their respective doctrines and creeds. All this combined greatly to strengthen the bonds of the Union. The ties which held each denomination together formed a strong cord to hold the whole Union together; but, powerful as they were, they have not been able to resist the explosive effect of slavery agitation.

The first of these cords which snapped, under its explosive force, was that of the powerful Methodist Episcopal Church. The numerous and strong ties which held it together, are all broken, and its unity gone. They now form separate churches; and, instead of that feeling of attachment and devotion to the interests of the whole church which was formerly felt, they are now arrayed into two hostile bodies, engaged in litigation about what was formerly their common property.

The next cord that snapped was that of the Baptists—one of the largest and most respectable of the denominations. That of the Presbyterian is not entirely snapped, but some of its strands have given way. That of the Episcopal Church is the only one of the four great Protestant denominations which remains unbroken and entire.

✓　　✓　　✓

This separation of the Northern and Southern Baptists was described, with quotations from original documents, by B. F. Riley in *A History of the Baptists in the Southern States East of the Mississippi*, American Baptist Publishing Society, Philadelphia, 1898, pp. 199-214, *passim*.

The Southern Baptist Convention was one of the direct effects of the agitation of the question of African slavery. Many years before the separation took place between Northern and Southern Baptists, the question of slavery had been warmly discussed in Baptist circles and councils. Many of the largest owners of slaves in the South were Baptists who were eminent in denominational ranks. They were as pronounced and sincere in the defence of slavery as were the Baptists of the North in its denunciation.

The countersentiment of the two sections grew commensurately during the last quarter preceding the outbreak of the Civil War. . . .

It was claimed by the pro-slavery advocates in the Baptist denomination in the South that . . . the Board of Foreign Missions procured the retirement from its service of Rev. John Bushyhead, a highly respected Indian Baptist preacher, because he was an owner of slaves. This created an impression throughout the South that slaveholders would not henceforth be admitted to appointment under the Board. . . . The matter was brought to the attention of the Alabama State Convention by a query from the Tuscaloosa Church. . . . "Is it proper for us, at the South, to send any more money to our brethren at the North, for missionary and other benevolent purposes, before the subject of slavery be rightly understood by both parties! . . .

The reply of the Foreign Mission Board . . . says: "In the thirty years in which the Board has existed, no slaveholder, to our knowledge, has applied to be a missionary taking slaves with him; were it morally right, it could not, in accordance with all our past arrangements or present plans, possibly occur. If, however, any one should offer himself as a missionary, having slaves, and should insist on retaining them as his property, we should not appoint him. One thing is certain, we can never be a party to any arrangement which would imply approbation of slavery." . . . . .

The hour for dissolution had come. One by one the Conventions of the Southern States began to withdraw. Along with them went the auxiliary missionary societies. . . .

May 8, 1845, marks a memorable epoch in the history of Southern Baptists. In response to the call made for the assemblage of Baptist representatives from the South, three hundred and seventy-seven delegates met at the time named, in the city of Augusta, Georgia, for the purpose of forming the Southern Baptist Convention. . . .

An elaborate address was prepared, and appealed "to the brethren of the United States; to the congregations connected with the respective churches; and to all candid men." The address opens with the frank statement:

"A painful division has taken place in the missionary operations of the American Baptists. We would explain why . . . that division . . . became necessary. Let not the extent of this disunion be exaggerated. At the present time it involves only the Foreign and Domestic Missions of the denomination. Northern and Southern Baptists are still brethren. They differ in no article of the faith. They are guided by the same principles of gospel order. Fanatical attempts have indeed been made, in some quarters, to exclude us of the South from Christian fellowship. . . . Our Christian fellowship is not, as we feel, a matter to be obtruded upon by any one. . . . We do not regard the rupture as extending to foundation principles, nor can we think that the great body of our Northern brethren will so regard it. Disunion, however, had proceeded deplorably far. The first part of our duty is to show that its entire *origin* is with others. . . .

In parting with our beloved brethren and coadjutors in this cause we could weep, and have wept, for ourselves and for them; but the season as well of weeping as of vain jangling is, we are constrained to believe, just now past. For years the pressure of men's hands have been upon us far too heavily. Our brethren have pressed upon every inch of our privileges and our sacred rights, but this shall only urge our gushing souls to yield proportionately of their renewed efforts to the Lord, to the church universal, and to a dying world. . . .

⚹   ⚹   ⚹

Henry Clay, the "great compromiser," in a speech before the United States Senate in February, 1839, pled with the abolitionists to cease their activities which threatened to disrupt the Union. The following extract from his address is from Calvin Colton, Editor, *The Works of Henry Clay,* G. P. Putnam's Sons, New York, 1904, Vol. I, pp. 227-229.

. . . Abolition should no longer be regarded as an imaginary danger. The abolitionists, let me suppose, succeed in their present aim of uniting the inhabitants of the free states, as one man, against the inhabitants of the slave states. Union on one side will beget union on the other. And this process of reciprocal consolidation will be attended with all the violent prejudices, embittered passions, and implacable animosities, which ever degraded or deformed human nature. A virtual dissolution of the Union will have taken place, while the forms of its existence remain. The most valuable element of union, mutual kindness, the feelings of sympathy, the fraternal bonds, which now happily unite us, will have been extinguished for ever. One section will stand in menacing and hostile array against the other. The collison of opinion will be quickly followed by the clash of arms. I will not attempt to describe scenes which now happily lie concealed from our view. Abolitionists themselves would shrink back in dismay and horror at the contemplation of desolated fields, conflagrated cities, murdered inhabitants, and the overthrow of the fairest fabric of human government that ever rose to animate the hopes of civilized man. Nor should these abolitionists flatter themselves that, if they can succeed in their object of uniting the people of the free states, they will enter the contest with a numerical superiority that must insure victory. All history and experience proves the hazard and uncertainty of war. And we are admonished by Holy Writ, that the race is not to the swift, nor the battle to the strong. But if they were to conquer, whom would they conquer? A foreign foe— one who had insulted our flag, invaded our shores, and laid our country waste? No, sir; no, sir. It would be a conquest without laurels, without glory; a self, a suicidal conquest; a conquest of brothers over brothers, achieved by one over another portion of the descendants of common ancestors, who, nobly pledging their lives, their fortunes, and their sacred honor, had fought and bled, side by side, in many a hard battle on land and ocean, severed our country from the British crown, and established our national independence.

The inhabitants of the slave states are sometimes accused by their northern brethren with displaying too much rashness and sensibility to the operations and proceedings of abolitionists. But before they can be rightly judged, there should be a reversal of conditions. Let me suppose that the people of the slave states were to form societies, subsidize presses, make large pecuniary contributions, send forth numerous missionaries throughout all their own borders, and enter into machinations to burn the beautiful capitals, destroy the productive manufactories, and sink in the ocean the gallant ships of the northern states. Would these incendiary proceedings be regarded as neighborly and friendly, and consistent with the fraternal sentiments which should ever be cherished by one portion of the Union toward another? Would they excite no emotion? occasion no manifestations of dissatisfaction? nor lead to any acts of retaliatory violence? But the supposed case falls far short of the actual one in a most essential circumstance. In no contingency could these capitals, manufactories, and ships, rise in rebellion, and massacre inhabitants of the northern states. Mr. Clay concludes this speech as follows:—

If one dark spot exists on our political horizon, is it not obscured by the bright, and effulgent, and cheering light that beams all around us? Was ever a people before so blessed as we are, if true to ourselves? Did ever any other nation contain within its bosom so many elements of prosperity, of greatness, and of glory? Our only real danger lies ahead, conspicuous, elevated and visible. It was clearly discerned at the commencement, and distinctly seen throughout our whole career. Shall we wantonly run upon it, and destroy all the glorious anticipation of the high destiny that awaits us? I beseech the abolitionists themselves, solemnly to pause in their mad and fatal course. Amid the infinite variety of objects of humanity and benevolence which invite the employment of their energies, let them select some one more harmless, that does not threaten to deluge our country in blood. I call upon that small portion of the clergy, which has lent itself to these wild and ruinous schemes, not to forget the holy nature of the divine mission of the founder of our religion, and to profit by his peaceful example. I entreat that portion of my countrywomen, who have given their countenance to abolition, to remember, that they are ever most loved and honored when moving in their own appropriate and delightful sphere; and to reflect that the ink which they shed in subscribing with their fair hands abolition petitions, may prove but the prelude to the shedding of the blood of their brethren. I adjure all the inhabitants of the free states to rebuke and discountenance, by their opinion and their example, measures which must inevitably lead to the most calamitous consequences. And let us all, as countrymen, as friends, and as brothers, cherish, in unfading memory, the motto which bore our ancestors triumphantly through all the trials of the revolution, as, if adhered to, it will conduct their posterity through all that may, in the dispensations of Providence, be reserved for them.

✓   ✓   ✓

Abolitionist literature pictured American history as being directed by a Southern slavocracy conspiracy. This conspiracy was believed to have originated with the writing of the Constitution. The following selection illustrates this point of view:

Quincy, Josiah, "Address Illustrative of the Nature and Power of the Slave States, and the Duties of the Free States, Delivered at the Request of the Inhabitants of the Town of Quincy, Massachusetts, on Thursday, June 5, 1856. Boston: Ticknor and Fields, 1856.

Dedicated
to
THE PEOPLE OF THE FREE STATES, WHO ARE ENTREATED TO CONSIDER THE VIEWS AND STATEMENTS IT PRESENTS.

The question to be decided, at the ensuing Presidential election is, Who shall henceforth rule this nation,—the Slave States, or the Free States? All the aspects of our political atmosphere indicate an approaching hurricane. Whether it shall sweep this Union from its foundations, or whether it shall be prosperously weathered; depends, under Heaven, on the man whom the people shall choose to pilot them through the coming storm. In my judgment, that man is John Charles Fremont. . . .

.   .   .   .

The *art* by which, for more than fifty years, the Slave States have subjugated the Free States, and vested in their own hands all of the powers of the Union, they call *policy*. Its proper name is *cunning;* that "left-handed wisdom," as Lord Bacon calls it, which the Devil practised in the garden of Eden,—"divide and conquer." By this, they established the seat of national government in a slave country, and thus surrounded Congress with an atmosphere of slavery, and subjected the Free States to its influences, in the place where the councils of the nation are held, and where the whole public sentiment is hostile to the principles of the Free States; and where, in case of collisions resulting in actions at law and indictments, slaveholders are judges, jurors, and executioners. This location of the seat of government has been one of the most potent causes of that dominion over the nation which they have acquired.

Again: by *cunning,* they inserted Louisiana into the Union, not only without the concurrence of the Free States, but without so much as asking it,—a measure which has been the Pandora's box of all our evils.

Another of their arts is *arrogance,* or an insolent assumption of superiority. This, though a result of their condition as masters of slaves, is of great power. . . . In Slave States, slaveholders are sovereigns, and deem themselves entitled to govern everywhere. In them, with few inconsiderable exceptions, they are proprietors of all the lands; which few persons can afford to hold, except owners of slaves. As the rate of wages is regulated by the expense of supporting slaves, it is, of course, the least possible. Of consequence, slaves are the successful rivals of the *white poor;* being more obedient, and the expense of supporting them being less. Thus the *white poor,* in the Slave States, are reduced to a state of extreme degradation; in some respects, lower than the negro. They cannot dig; for field labor to a white person is there a disgrace. To beg, they are ashamed; and they have no master to whom they can look for support. Having no land, they have no political power: the value of their labor is below that of the slave; and their actual condition comparatively that of extreme wretchedness. One-half of the white population of the Slave States are said to be in that condition.

Fifty years ago, there were two classes of slaveholders in Congress; the one, generous in spirit, polished in manners, true to the principles of Liberty and the Constitution, uniting heart and hand with the representatives of the Free States in objects and policy; of the same type and character as George Washington, John Marshall, William Pinckney, Henry W. Dessaussure, John Stanley, Nicholas Vandyke, . . . and a host of others, too numerous to be recapitulated, in principle and views coincident with the Constitution, destitute of all desire to establish the supremacy of slaveholders. They spoke of slavery, like Patrick Henry, as "a curse," which blighted the prospects and weakened the strength of the Slave States,—with him deplored the necessity of holding men in bondage, declaring their belief that the time would come when "an opportunity will be afforded *to abolish* this lamentable evil;" . . .

In 1810, John Randolph, in whose mind Virginia included all the South, said to me, "Virginia is no longer what it once was. The spirit of the old planters is departed or gradually wearing away; we are overrun by time-servers, office-hunters, and political blacklegs." In a letter to me, dated "Richmond, 22d March, 1814, after giving a melancholy description of a visit he had just made to "the seat of his ancestors, in the maternal line, at the confluence of the James and Appomattox Rivers," he adds, *"The curse of slavery, however, an evil daily magnifying, great as it already is, imbitters many a moment of the Virginian landowner, who is now duller than the clod under his feet."* And, recurring to the then-existing state of Virginia, in the same letter he adds, "In your country, the state of society is not changed, the whole fabric uprooted, as it is with us. Here the rich vulgar are everybody and every thing. You can almost smell the rum and cheese and loaf and lump-sugar out of which their mushroom fortunes have sprung, much more offensive to my nostrils than 'muck and merinos.' These fellows . . . make up in ostentation for other deficiencies of which they are always conscious, and sometimes ashamed."

Slaveholders have been for fifty years, a few only excepted, the political masters of these States. Rampant with long-possessed authority, in the natural spirit of the class, they have now put on the lash, and are getting ready for use their fetters and manacles.

Let the Free States understand that the crisis has come. Their own fate and that of their posterity depend upon the fact, whether, in this crisis, they are true or false to themselves. The extension of slavery has been, from the days of Jefferson, the undeviating pursuit of the slaveholders. . . . It is well known that the Free States cannot, from their state of society, always send their best men to Congress. They are often compelled, from the circumstances in which Heaven has placed them, to labor, in their respective vocations, for the support of themselves and their families. They have no negroes to make work for them when they are away, none that they can sell to make up the deficiencies of their income while they are absent. The Slave States, on the contrary, can always command their best men,—best not from morals, not from virtues, nor yet from talents, but best for their purposes. The slaveholders form a class of slaveholding aristocratic land-holders, who take up the trade of democracy in order to get possession of and victimize the leaders of the democracies of the Free States. . . . These men never trouble themselves what services the slaveholders will require. They are ready to vote for them in order to make new Slave States in the old-acquired territories; or to fight for them in order to conquer new territories in which to extend the area of slavery; or to assist them in breaking down the barrier, erected by compromise, to prevent its farther extension; and, to maintain the slaveholders' triumph, do not hesitate to dip their hands in the blood of their brethren of the Free States.

The slaveholders' mode of operation in extending their power is well worthy of analysis. Having no necessity nor inclination to labor, those of them who have, from their great wealth, more idle time than the generality, devote themselves to politics; which, in their vocabulary, means how to govern their slaves and how to control the Free States. . . . This is the topic of discussion at their homes, in their court-houses, their caucuses, and in their senate-chambers. In their plantations, they live in a species of lordly solitude. Though thus, mostly, they think and reason and write apart, yet, from the identity of their interests and fears, their thoughts and reasonings result in the same line of policy, which, at their general meetings, they agree upon and settle. Though widely separate, the chiefs sit as spiders in the centre of their respective webs, throwing out filaments to every State in the Union, in every one of which the threads of some of them find points of attachment and reciprocation, in custom-houses, post-offices, those of contracting printers, and many others, from each of which ready sympathetic responses are returned, as sure and as quick as by the wires of the telegraph. These responses are collected at Washington, in which the character and qualification of each member of Congress is as well known as at his own home.

How to secure and manage those members of Congress who are likely to take a lead in debate, or exert any influence in either branch, never fails to be a special study of the slaveholders, which is greatly facilitated by the location of Congress in the city of Washington. Such men from the Free States soon become objects of attention of men well versed in the arts of governing slaves, and of winning white men to their purposes; and while the new member is, perhaps, wondering what makes him such a special object of kindness, and is thinking only of how to reciprocate, they are examining him as an article in the market,—whether he can be bought at all; whether he is worth buying; whether, if bought, he has sufficient influence at home to carry his whole district with him. These questions settled to the satisfaction of the slaveholders, and the certainty established that there will be no flinching, however hard the service they may exact, the price at which he may be had being ascertained, will in due time be paid, whether it be by a place in the customs, or in the post-office, or in the cabinet, or an embassy in Europe or in China, and mayhap, if he stand trial in the hardest service, by even the President's chair.

Let the people look into the history of the Union ever since the days of Andrew Jackson, and they can trace the services to the slaveholders, by which men from the Free States have attained their offices, and see the humbleness of the servility with which they have executed all the orders of the slaveholders. . . .

✓   ✓   ✓

Hinton Rowan Helper, of North Carolina, made a violent attack against slavery in his book, *The Impending Crisis,* A. B. Burdick, New York, 1857. He introduced many statistics to prove that the North had surpassed the South in every area of economic life, and advocated abolition of slavery to enable the South to enter upon a period of prosperity. He enjoined the nonslaveholding whites of the South to rise up against slavery and against the ruling oligarchies of their states. The following selection is from pp. 355-358 of that work.

Reader! would you understand how abjectly slaveholders themselves are enslaved to the products of Northern industry? If you would, fix your mind on a Southern "gentleman"—a slave-breeder and human-flesh monger, who professes to be a Christian! Observe the routine of his daily life. See him rise in the morning from a Northern bed, and clothe himself in Northern apparel; see him walk across the floor on a Northern carpet, and perform his ablutions out of a Northern ewer and basin. See him uncover a box of Northern powders, and cleanse his teeth with a Northern brush; see his reflecting his physiognomy in a Northern mirror, and arranging his hair with a Northern comb. See him dosing himself with the mendicaments of

Northern quacks, and perfuming his handkerchief with Northern cologne. See him referring to the time in a Northern watch, and glancing at the news in a Northern gazette. See him and his family sitting in Northern chairs, and singing and praying out of Northern books. See him at the breakfast table, saying grace over a Northern plate, eating with Northern cutlery, and drinking from Northern utensils. See him charmed with the melody of a Northern piano, or musing over the pages of a Northern novel. See him riding to his neighbor's in a Northern carriage, or furrowing his lands with a Northern plow. See him lighting his segar with a Northern match, and flogging his negroes with a Northern lash. See him with Northern pen and ink, writing letters on Northern paper, and sending them away in Northern envelopes, sealed with Northern wax, and impressed with a Northern stamp. Perhaps our Southern "gentleman" is a merchant; if so, see him at his store, making an unpatriotic use of his time in the miserable traffic of Northern gimcracks and haberdashery; see him when you will, where you will, he is ever surrounded with the industrial products of those whom, in the criminal inconsistency of his heart, he execrates as enemies, yet treats as friends. His labors, his talents, his influence, are all for the North, and not for the South; for the stability of slavery, and for the sake of his own personal aggrandizement, he is willing to sacrifice the dearest interests of his country.

As we see our ruinous system of commerce exemplified in the family of our Southern "gentleman," so we may see it exemplified, to a greater or less degree, in almost every other family throughout the length and breadth of the slaveholding States. We are all constantly buying, and selling, and wearing, and using Northern merchandise, at a double expense to both ourselves and our neighbors. . . .

We must begin to feed on a more substantial diet than that of pro-slavery politics; we should leave off our siestas and post-meridian naps, and employ our time in profitable vocations. Before us there is a vast work to be accomplished . . . that of infusing the spirit of liberty into all our systems of commerce, agriculture, manufactures, government, literature, and religion. Oligarchal despotism must be overthrown; slavery must be abolished. . . .

✓ ✓ ✓

The Republican Party advertised that they wished to publish speeches and documents suitable for use in the coming election, and would mail them in quantities of one hundred for a dollar (documents of 8 pages) to such post offices or names as may be desired. The above document, Hinton Rowan Helper's *Impending Crisis*, A. B. Burdick, New York, 1857, was so distributed by the Republican Party. Another such publication was a pamphlet entitled *The Poor Whites of the South*, by George M. Weston, D. C. Buell and Blanchard, Washington, 1856. Weston was for some time editor of *The Age*, the leading Democratic newspaper of Maine. After giving statistics concerning the number of slave owners in the South, he drew the following conclusions.

Upon the whole, it may safely be concluded that at least seven tenths of the whites in the slave States, are not slave owners, either in their own right or by family relation. . . .

The non-slaveholding whites of the South, being not less than seven tenths of the whole number of whites, would seem to be entitled to some inquiry into their actual condition; and especially, as they have no real political weight or consideration in the country, and little opportunity to speak for themselves. I have been for twenty years a reader of Southern newspapers, and a reader and hearer of Congressional debates; but, in all that time, I do not recollect ever to have seen or heard these non-slave-holding whites referred to by Southern gentlemen, as constituting any part of what they call "the South." When the rights of the South, or its wrongs, or its policy, or its interests, or its institutions, are spoken of, reference is always intended to the rights, wrongs, policy, interests, and institutions, of the three hundred and forty seven thousand slaveholders. Nobody gets into Congress but by their direction; nobody speaks at Washington for any Southern interest except theirs. Yet there is, at the South, quite another interest than theirs; embracing from two to three times as many white people; and, as we shall presently see, entitled to the deepest sympathy and commiseration, in view of the material, intellectual, and moral privations to which it has been subjected, the degradation to which it has already been reduced, and the still more fearful degradation with which it is threatened by the inevitable operation of existing causes and influences. . . .

It is for the people of this country to determine whether the further spread of a system, of which the worst fruits are not seen in wasted resources and in impoverished fields, but in a neglected and outcast people, shall be left to the accidents of latitude, of proximity, of border violence, or of doubtful assent of embryo communities; or whether, on the other hand, it shall be stayed by an interdiction, as universal as the superiority of Good to Evil, as perpetual as the rightful authority of reason in the affairs of men, and as resistless as the embodied will of the nation.

✓   ✓   ✓

Slaveholders reacted to the tirades of the abolitionists with arguments supporting slavery as a "positive good." Such arguments were compiled in the book, *Cotton Is King, and Pro Slavery Arguments*, edited by E. N. Elliott, Pritchard, Abbott and Loomis, Atlanta, Georgia, 1860. This book was published and sold entirely by subscription and contained the writings of seven men. The following selections are from the Introduction, pp. iv-v, viii, x-xi, xiv-xv, and from the section "Liberty and Slavery," by Albert Taylor Bledsoe, pp. 411-417, *passim*.

Geographical partisan government and legislation . . . had its origin in the Missouri contest, and is now beginning to produce its legitimate fruits: witness the growing distrust with which the people of the North and South begin to regard each other; the diminution of Southern travel, either for business or pleasure, in the Northern States; the efforts of each section to develop its own resources, so as virtually to render it independent of the other; the enactment of "unfriendly legislation," in several of the States, towards other States of the Union, or their citizens; the contest for the exclusive possession of the territories, the common property of the States; the anarchy and bloodshed in Kansas; the exasperation of parties throughout the Union; the attempt to nullify, by popular clamor, the decision of the supreme tribunal of our country; the existence of the "underground railroad," and of a party in the North organized for the express purpose of robbing the citizens of the Southern States of their property; the almost daily occurrence of fugitive slave mobs; the total insecurity of slave property in the border States; the attempt to circulate incendiary documents among the slaves in the Southern States, and the flooding of the whole country with the most false and malicious misrepresentations of the state of society in the slave States; the attempt to produce division among us, and to array one portion of our citizens in deadly hostility to the other; and finally, the recent attempt to excite, at Harper's Ferry, and throughout the South, an insurrection, and a civil and servile war, with all its attendant horrors.

All these facts go to prove that there is a great wrong somewhere, and that a part, or the whole, of the American people are demented, and hurrying down to swift destruction. . . .

The present slave States had little or no agency in the first introduction of Africans into this country; this was achieved by the Northern commercial States and by Great Britain. Wherever the climate suited the negro constitution, slavery was profitable and flourished; where the climate was unsuitable, slavery was unprofitable, and died out. Most of the slaves in the Northern States were sent southward to a more congenial clime. Upon the introduction into Congress of the first abolition discussions, by John Quincy Adams, and Joshua Giddings, Southern men altogether refused to engage in debate, or even to receive petitions on the subject. They averred that no good could grow out of it, but only unmitigated evil.

The agitation of the abolition question had commenced in France during the horrors of her first revolution, under the auspices of the Red Republicans; it had pervaded England until it achieved the ruin of her West India colonies, and by anti-slavery missionaries it had been introduced into our Northern States. During all this agitation the Southern States had been quietly minding their own business, regardless of all the turmoil abroad. They had never investigated the subject theoretically, but they were well acquainted with all its practical workings. They had received from Africa a few hundred thousand pagan savages, and had developed them into millions of civilized Christians, happy in themselves, and useful to the world. They had never made the inquiry whether the system were fundamentally wrong, but they judged it by its fruits, which were beneficent to all. When therefore they were charged with upholding a moral, social, and political evil; and its immediate abolition was demanded, as a matter not only of policy, but also of justice and right, their reply was, we have never investigated the subject. Our fathers left it to us a legacy, we have grown up with it; it has grown with our growth, and strengthened with our strength, until now it is incorporated with every fibre of our social and political existence. . . .

The Apostle, in the Epistle to Timothy, has not only explicitly laid down the law on the subject of slavery, but has, with prophetic vision, drawn the exact portrait of our modern abolitionists.

"Let as many servants as are under the yoke count their own masters worthy of all honor, that the name of God and his doctrine be not blasphemed. And they that have believing masters, let them not despise them, because they are brethren; but rather do them service, because they are faithful and beloved, partakers of the benefit. These things teach and exhort. If any man teach otherwise, and consent not to wholesome words, even the words of our Lord Jesus Christ, and to the doctrine which is according to godliness, he is proud, knowing nothing, but doting about questions and strifes of words, whereof come envy, strife, railings, evil surmisings, perverse disputings, of men of corrupt minds and destitute of the truth, supposing that gain is godliness; from such withdraw thyself."

Can any words more accurately and vividly portray the character and conduct of the abolitionists, or more plainly point out the results of their efforts? . . . Envy, the root of the evil; strife, see the divisions in our churches, and in our political communities; railings, their calling slave-holders robbers, thieves, murderers, outlaws; evil surmisings, can any good thing come out of Nazareth, or from the Slave States? Perverse disputings of men of corrupt minds, their wresting the Scriptures from their plain and obvious meaning to compel them to teach abolitionism. Finally; the duty of all Christians: from such withdraw thyself. . . . .

"Our patriarchal scheme of domestic servitude," says Governor Hammond, "is indeed well calculated to awaken the higher and finer feelings of our nature. It is not wanting in its enthusiasm and its poetry. The relations of the most beloved and honored chiefs, and the most faithful and admiring subjects, which, from the time of Homer, have been the theme of song, are frigid and unfelt, compared with those existing between the master and his slaves; who served his father, and rocked his cradle, or have been born in his household, and look forward to serve his children; who have been through life the props of his fortune, and the objects of his care; who have partaken of his griefs, and looked to him for comfort in their own; whose sickness he has so frequently watched over and relieved; whose holidays he has so often made joyous by his bounties and his presence; for whose welfare, when absent, his anxious solicitude never ceases, and whose hearty and affectionate greetings never fail to welcome him home. In this cold, calculating, ambitious world of ours, there are few ties more heart-felt, or of more benignant influence, than those which mutually bind the master and the slave, under our ancient system, handed down from the father of Israel." . . .

The abolitionists, with the most singular unanimity, perseveringly assert that Southern slavery degrades its subjects "into brutes." This assertion fills us with amazement. If it were possible, we would suppose, in a judgment of charity, that its authors knew nothing of the history of Africa or of the condition of our slaves. But such ignorance is not possible. . . .

The native African could not be degraded. Of the fifty millions of inhabitants of the continent of Africa, it is estimated that forty million were slaves. The master had the power of life and death over the slave; and, in fact, his slaves were often fed, and killed, and eaten, just as we do with oxen and sheep in this country. Nay, the hind and fore-quarters of men, women, and children, might be seen hung on the shambles and exposed for sale! Their women were beasts of burden; and, when young, they were regarded as a great delicacy by the palate of their pampered masters. A warrior would sometimes take a score of young females along with him, in order to enrich his feasts and regale his appetite. He delighted in such delicacies. As to his religion, it was even worse than his morals; or rather, his religion was a mass of the most disgusting immoralities. His notion of a God, and the obscene acts by which that notion was worshipped, are too shocking to be mentioned. The vilest slave that ever breathed the air of a Christian land could not begin to conceive the horrid iniquities of such a life. And yet, in the face of all this, we are told—yea, we are perseveringly and eternally told—that "the African has been degraded into a brute" by American slavery! . . .

No fact is plainer than that the blacks have been elevated and improved by their servitude in this country. We cannot possibly conceive, indeed, how Divine Providence could have placed them in a better school of correction. . . . [If the abolitionists] will show us on the continent of Africa, or elsewhere, three millions of blacks in as good a condition—physically and morally—as our slaves, then will we most cheerfully admit that all other Christian nations, combined, have accomplished as much for the African race, as has been done by the Southern States of the Union.

✶   ✶   ✶

Between the years 1854 and 1860 the breach between the North and South widened. Events such as Charles Sumner's Senate address entitled "The Crime Against Kansas" and John Brown's raid aroused Southern ire, while the fugitive slave law of 1850 and the Dred Scott decision were deplored and nullified by actions of some of the Northern states. After the creation of the new territories, Kansas and Nebraska, in 1854, both of which were open to slaveholding, the new Republican Party was formed to fight the extension of slavery into the territories. "Fire-eaters," whose wish in 1850 to take the Southern states from the Union had been thwarted by the adoption of the Compromise of 1850, renewed their demands for secession. Henry K. Burgwyn, of North Carolina, wrote a pamphlet entitled *Considerations Relative to a Southern Confederacy with Letters to the North by a Citizen of North Carolina,* "Standard Office" print., Raleigh, 1860.

He who now denies that "there is danger to the State"—that a dissolution of the Confederacy established by our fathers is threatening and imminently so, is blind to what is passing around him, is regardless of the continuing progress and increasing aggressions of the abolitionists and their affiliators, the black Republicans, and closes his reason to the teaching of history— that of the Puritans in particular—who have always been exhibited as fanatics and despotically aggressive from the time of John Knox and Oliver Cromwell to those of Gerritt Smith and Wendall Phillips.

In this state of trouble and danger, it is eminently proper for us to consider what we, the citizens of the State shall do, first for our self preservation, next, for the preservation of law and good order among ourselves, and (if consistent with these) our present Union. . . .

What in 1830 and '35 was the denunciation of Arthur Tappan and his satellites, in 1859 became the raid of John Brown, encouraged and supported by thousands of men, public and private, and aided by money enough to arm and equip thousands of insurrectionary negroes! What, at the former period, were the muttered vaporings of a few fanatics and the revilings of a few obscure prints, is now disseminated broadcast through the land by the press, by the pulpit . . . , and by orators and lecturers, and is even forced upon *us*, by vile, false, and incendiary documents. "An irrepressible conflict" is loudly proclaimed by one of the great leaders of the North, who declares that "they can and will' exterminate slavery from the land; they "will follow it in Virginia, in the Carolinas, aye, even into Texas." And to effect this, calls to his aid a "higher law" than the constitution *he has solemnly sworn to support.* . . .

Again: what but a few years back was an attempt at various conciliations, is at this moment an attempt at one of the most gratuitous insults ever put by one nation upon another! The John Brown raid was bad enough, but the encouragement of efforts to produce insurrection and treason among us, ten times more numerous and a hundred times more horrible, is *far beyond* the John Brown raid, in atrocity; what then can we think of those who have banded together for months, with unanimity unparalleled in our political history, for the purpose of electing as the governing officer over Southern men that man whose homes and households and whose property he had been encouraging others to destroy! The animus which governed sixty-eight Representatives to the North, to encourage the attempts recommended in Helper's book to create insurrection and treason among us, and the unanimous support of these men by the black Republican party, must be looked on by candid minds as out-weighing for all the good effect of all the Union meetings at the North, *unaccompanied* as they have been by any rebuke to these men, New Jersey alone standing out in view as having done so.

Such being the state of things in our country, it is time to ponder them well; it *is* time to look out for self-preservation. Now the question comes up, shall we be any better off in a Southern Confederacy than in one with such discordant elements in it as the present one with the North, and especially with the puritan people of New England? . . .

A Southern Confederacy would present to Europe a nation that produces all those great staples, Cotton, Sugar, Tobacco, Naval Stores, &c., &c., which are not only in great demand, but of absolute *necessity* to the maintenance of *millions* of her inhabitants, either for consumption, manufacture, or revenue. The destruction or even the material diminution of these products of the *South,* would be attended by a total change in the course of trade, manufacture, and commerce of the civilized world. Its destruction would be followed immediately by bankruptcies and ruin of thousands in England, France and Germany, such as were not witnessed even during the wars of Napoleon. It would throw out of employment and upon the public support, the millions—five in Great Britain alone—who now support themselves by the manufacture, &c., of our products alone. . . .

Further: the southern part of the United States manufactures but a very inconsiderable portion of her consumption, either of her own products or those of other countries; . . . the fact that the profitable employment of her labor in agriculture, and the indisposition of her capitalists towards manufacturing, gives promise that she is not likely for many years to interrupt these supplies from Europe, by high tariffs or engaging in rival manufactories. Thus, a confederacy of the slave States would offer to the friendship and alliances of Europe the "material interests" of a doubly profitable trade—that of a supply of raw products, and a demand for manufactures and other goods. What other nation on the face of the globe can offer such a temptation to England, France and Germany? . . . . . .

I will now consider some of the more prominint [sic] points of the position that would be presented to the North by a confederacy of the Southern States, in case such were to occur. Massachusetts, Vermont, Wisconsin, and several of the other Northern States having already repudiated the contract between us, i.e., the constitution, by passing laws contrary to the provision of that contract, in those particulars that do not *please them,* and thereby "voiding the whole contract," let us suppose that the fifteen Southern States were to "accept the annulment," and call a convention among themselves "to form a more perfect Union" under a new confederation. Let us suppose further that in the interval between the election of a black Republican President and the time of his inauguration in March, *a period of four months,* this convention had met, organized, agreed upon a contract or constitution which had been accepted by the States in their Legislative assemblies; had elected and inaugurated a President; had called home her sons from the army and navy, and put the country on her defence, a defence not only of political rights—not only of property, nor even of life! but of that which is far more dear, of the defence of their wives and families from the horrors of another St. Domingo war! and think you, Mr. Editor, would not the North pause before attempting to "whip in" such a people armed for defence of such a cause? . . . For the purpose of an argument, however, let us consider this question of an attack of the North upon the South, either for the purpose of "whipping" us back into forced Union, or of conquest. The States of Virginia, Maryland, Kentucky, Tennessee, and North Carolina possess a militia of over 500,000 able bodied men, badly armed, it is true, but quite as well as their fathers of the revolution. Of this body 200,000 could always be kept ready for action, meanwhile living in their own country and among friends at little expense. Now, to *attack* an enemy's country, an army must be well armed and thoroughly equipped, provisioned, &c. This, by the estimate of our engineer corps, cannot be done under a cost of $1,000 per head, so that to form and bring into the field, ready for attack, in any enemy's country, an army of 100,000 men, which would be the least any military man would think of beginning an attack with, would cost not less than 100 millions of dollars. Where is this sum to come from? . . . the bankers of England, France and Germany will hardly be willing to loan money to their *rivals* to crush their friends, whose products are necessary to them, while the South can offer any security upon the pledge of her products. . . . In short, if the North were united in an attempt to force the South back into a Union, it would soon be driven off in disgrace by the power which the South possesses of raising, not only by her own forces *in defence*, but by the control she has of the material interest of the civilized world as against a mad attack of this kind upon her. . . .

Bear in mind that the *border* country in New Jersey, Pennsylvania, Ohio, Illinois and Indiana, are friendly, and oft times connected by marriage, property, &c. with their Southern neighbors; it is only the more northern countries of those States that supply the John Brown raid, the slave stealers, &c. This gives us great assurance of exemption from smaller raids upon the border, and these could be completely prevented by a cordon of border police, armed and mounted—ready to act at a moment's warning—and keeping close watch on all suspicious persons crossing the border. This could be effected for *one quarter part of the amount of the present losses* by slave stealers, and would only be necessary till the relation between the two countries could be decided. . . . .

We are in many respects a different people from those of New England, and more homogenous. This difference first arose from the different "stock" from which we sprung. This is too well known to every one familiar with the early history of his own country, for me to do more than refer to it at present. It is sufficient to say there has been, at different periods, antagonism between the two ever since the times of Queen Mary, of Scotland, and Charles the 1st, of England, and our own.

This difference of origin has not been obliterated; indeed, the difference of early education, of domestic institutions, of general religious training, and of occupation, (we being chiefly engaged in agriculture and they trade and manufactures) has continued the marked difference between the men of the Southern and those of the Northern and New England States especially.

12

Secession and Civil War

On January 21, when Jefferson Davis, Senator from Mississippi, retired from the United States Senate he made the following speech. The text is from *Jefferson Davis, Constitutionalist. His Letters, Papers, and Speeches,* Collected and Edited by Dunbar Rowland, Mississippi Department of Archives, Jackson, Mississippi, 1923, Vol. V, pp. 40-45.

I rise, Mr. President, for the purpose of announcing to the Senate that I have satisfactory evidence that the State of Mississippi, by a solemn ordinance of her people in convention assembled, has declared her separation from the United States. Under these circumstances, of course my functions are terminated here. It has seemed to me proper, however, that I should appear in the Senate to announce that fact to my associates, and I will say but very little more. The occasion does not invite me to go into argument; and my physical condition would not permit me to do so if it were otherwise; and yet it seems to become me to say something on the part of the State I here represent, on an occasion so solemn as this.

It is known to Senators who have served with me here, that I have for many years advocated, as an essential attribute of State sovereignty, the right of a State to secede from the Union. Therefore, if I had not believed there was justifiable cause; if I had thought that Mississippi was acting without sufficient provocation, or without an existing necessity, I should still, under my theory of the Government, because of my allegiance to the State of which I am a citizen, have been bound by her action. I, however, may be permitted to say that I do think she has justifiable cause, and I approve of her act. I conferred with her people before that act was taken, counseled them then that if the state of things which they apprehended should exist when the convention met, they should take the action which they have now adopted.

I hope none who hear me will confound this expression of mine with the advocacy of a State to remain in the Union, and to disregard its constitutional obligations by the nullification of the law. Such is not my theory. Nullification and secession, so often confounded, are indeed antagonistic principles. Nullification is a remedy which it is sought to apply within the Union, and against the agent of the States. It is only to be justified when the agent has violated his constitutional obligation, and a State, assuming to judge for itself, denies the right of the agent thus to act, and appeals to the other States of the Union for a decision; but when the States themselves, and when the people of the States, have so acted as to convince us that they will not regard our constitutional rights, then, and then for the first time, arises the doctrine of secession in its practical application.

A great man who now reposes with his fathers, and who has been often arraigned for a want of fealty to the Union, advocated the doctrine of nullification, because it preserved the Union. It was because of his deep-seated attachment to the Union, his determination to find some remedy for existing ills short of a severance of the ties which bound South Carolina to the other States, that Mr. Calhoun advocated the doctrine of nullification, which he proclaimed to be peaceful, to be within the limits of State power, not to disturb the Union, but only to be a means of bringing the agent before the tribunal of the States for their judgment.

Secession belongs to a different class of remedies. It is to be justified upon the basis that the States are sovereign. There was a time when none denied it. I hope the time may come again, when a better comprehension of the theory of our Government, and the inalienable rights of the people of the States, will prevent anyone from denying that each State is a sovereign, and thus may reclaim the grants which it has made to any agent whomsoever.

I therefore say I concur in the action of the people of Mississippi, believing it to be necessary and proper, and should have been bound by their action if my belief had been otherwise; and this brings me to the important point which I wish on this last occasion to present to the Senate. It is by this confounding of nullification and secession that the name of a great man, whose ashes now mingle with his mother earth, has been invoked to justify coercion against a seceded State. The phrase "to execute the laws" was an expression which General Jackson applied to the case of a State refusing to obey the laws while yet a member of the Union. This is not the case which is now presented. The laws are to be executed over the United States, and upon the people of the United States. They have no relation to any foreign country. It is a perversion of terms, at least it is a great misapprehension of the case, which cites that expression for application to a State which has withdrawn from the Union. You may make war on a foreign State. If it be the purpose of gentlemen, they may make war against a State which has withdrawn from the Union; but there are no laws of the United States to be executed within the limits of a seceded State. A State finding herself in the condition in which Mississippi has judged she is, in which her safety requires that she should provide for the maintenance of

From a collection of Battle Scenes, University of North Carolina Library.
The Battle of Richmond, 1865.

Constitution was formed, the same idea was rendered more palpable, for there we find provision made for that very class of persons as property; they were not put upon the footing of equality with white men—not even upon that of paupers and convicts; but, so far as representation was concerned, were discriminated against as a lower caste, only to be represented in the numerical proportion of three fifths.

Then, Senators, we recur to the compact that binds us together; we recur to the principles upon which our Government was founded; and when you deny them, and when you deny to us the right to withdraw from a Government which thus perverted threatens to be destructive of our rights, we but tread in the path of our fathers when we proclaim our independence, and take the hazard. This is done, not in hostility to others, not to injure any section of the country, not even for our own pecuniary benefit; but from the high and solemn motive of defending and protecting the rights we inherited, and which it is our sacred duty to transmit unshorn to our children.

I find in myself, perhaps, a type of the general feeling of my constituents toward yours. I am sure I feel no hostility to you, Senators from the North. I am sure there is not one of you, whatever sharp discussion there may have been between us, to whom I cannot say now, in the presence of my God, I wish you well; and such, I am sure, is the feeling of the people whom I represent towards those whom you represent. I therefore feel that I but express their desire when I say I hope, and they hope, for peaceful relations with you, though we must part. They may be mutually beneficial to us in the future, as they have been in the past, if you so will it. The reverse may bring disaster on every portion of the country; and if you will have it thus, we will invoke the God of our fathers, who delivered us from the power of the lion, to protect us from the ravages of the bear; and thus, putting our trust in God, and in our own firm hearts and strong arms, we will vindicate the right as best we may.

In the course of my service here, associated at different times with a great variety of Senators, I see now around me some with whom I have served long; there have been some points of collision; but whatever of offense there has been to me, I leave here; I carry with me no hostile remembrance. Whatever offense I have given which has not been redressed, or for which satisfaction has not been demanded, I have, Senators, in this hour of our parting, to offer you my apology for any pain which, in heat of discussion, I have inflicted. I go hence unencumbered of the remembrance of any injury received, and having discharged the duty of making the only reparation in my power for any injury offered.

Mr. President, and Senators, having made the announcement which the occasion seemed to me to require, it only remains for me to bid you a final adieu.

her rights out of the Union, surrenders all the benefits, (and they are know
to be many,) deprives herself of the advantages, (they are known to be grea
severs all ties of affection, (and they are close and enduring,) which ha
bound her to the Union; and thus divesting herself of every benefit, takin
upon herself every burden, she claims to be exempt from any power t
execute the laws of the United States within her limits.

I well remember an occasion when Massachusetts was arraigned befor
the bar of the Senate, and when the doctrine of coercion was rife and t
be applied against her because of the rescue of a fugitive slave in Boston
My opinion was then the same that it is now. Not in a spirit of egotism
but to show that I am not influenced in my opinion because the case i
my own, I refer to that time and that occasion as containing the opinior
which I then entertained, and on which my present conduct is based. I
then said, if Massachusetts, following her through a stated line of conduct,
chooses to take the last step which separates her from the Union, it is her
right to go, and I will neither vote one dollar nor one man to coerce her
back; but will say to her, God speed, in memory of the kind associations
which once existed between her and the other States.

It has been a conviction of pressing necessity, it has been a belief that
we are to be deprived in the Union of the rights which our fathers bequeathed to us, which has brought Mississippi to her present decision. She
has heard proclaimed the theory that all men are created free and equal,
and this made the basis of an attack upon her social institutions; and the
sacred Declaration of Independence has been invoked to maintain the
position of the equality of the races. That Declaration of Independence is
to be construed by the circumstances and purposes for which it was made.
The communities were declaring their independence; the people of those
communities were asserting that no man was born—to use the language of
Mr. Jefferson—booted and spurred to ride over the rest of mankind; that
men were created equal—meaning the men of the political community;
that there was no divine right to rule; that no man inherited the right to
govern; that there were no classes by which power and place descended to
families, but that all stations were equally within the grasp of each member
of the body politic. These were the great principles they announced; these
were the purposes for which they made their declaration; these were the
ends to which their enunciation was directed. They made no reference to
the slave; else, how happened it that among the items of arraignment made
against George III was that he endeavored to do just what the North has
been endeavoring of late to do—to stir up insurrection among our slaves?
Had the Declaration announced that the negroes were free and equal, how
was the Prince to be arraigned for stirring up insurrection among them?
And how was this to be enumerated among the high crimes which caused
the colonies to sever their connection with the mother country? When our

✓   ✓   ✓

A foreign correspondent summed up the reasons for secession in an article which appeared in *Blackwood's Edinburgh Magazine,* Vol. 89, 1861, p. 58, and Vol. 91, 1862, p. 526.

The perfect unanimity throughout the whole South in the belief that their cause is just, strikes the stranger as one of the most formidable symptoms which the Union has to fear. Without pretending to form an opinion as to whether this universal conviction is rightly or wrongly arrived at, we simply assert the fact. The same story is told in the trains, in the hotels, on the plantations, in the drawing-rooms, in the camps, and in the newspapers, by young and old, rich and poor, men and women, with a uniformity that would be monotonous, were it not for the fire generally thrown into its narration.

They say that the North began the conflict years ago, in the irritating and unprovoked agitation of the slavery question, and have continued it from the time of the Missouri controversy to the 4th of last March, when the President announced that the platform was "a law unto him," and that party had declared there was an "irrepressible conflict" between the two sections of the Union. If we remarked that slavery was an evil about which we considered all American statesmen must feel anxiety, they replied, The President was sworn to defend it. It is an institution which feeds and clothes the world, which protects the negro against the vicissitudes of old age, sickness, and infancy, and keeps him in the only position where he can be useful to society, and harmless to himself. That the sun fixed the boundaries between white and black labour, in spite of arms and laws; and so sure as one flourished in Massachusetts, the other would prosper in Georgia. That when the North abolished slavery, and sold their slaves to the South, they then turned round, broke faith, and endeavored to disquiet a title emanating from themselves.

That the tariff laws were ruinous to the South. That in raising their revenue by heavy duties on foreign goods, which came back in return for Southern produce, the North were making the South pay the great bulk of the expense of government.

That by prohibiting trade in foreign ships, the South were obliged to take Northern to the exclusion of foreign goods.

That, by monopolizing the European trade, the North obtained great profits in brokerage and in freights upon Southern produce to Europe as well as upon European goods brought back in return for that produce, from all of which the South reaped little benefit.

✓   ✓   ✓

Again in *Blackwood's Edinburgh Magazine,* Vol. 91, 1862, p. 526, we read an explanation of the difference between the North and the South.

It is clear . . . that the difference between North and South is sectional and geographical—not moral. That differences of feeling, of interest, of manners, of origin, of occupation, of society, and of soil and climate, do exist, is a fact too familiar to be enlarged on here. And it being assumed as proved, that this wide and deep division is politically, and not morally, coincident with slavery, it only remains to show how this political pre-ponderance has been turned to the disadvantage of the South. . . .

Circumstances of soil, race, and climate, have caused the South to become almost entirely agricultural, while the manufacturing interests predominate in the North; and, this being the case, the North have used their political power to protect their own—that is, the manufacturing—interests. This they have effected by duties levied on foreign manufactures. And though certain Southern products are also protected, yet that does not prevent the South from being the chief sufferers by the system. . . . The Southerners have been compelled to pay, on such manufactures as are necessary to them, a tribute which is calculated to be as high as 25 per cent, for the benefit of Northern interests. Against this they have struggled for thirty years. And that it is a grievance capable of producing the most bitter feelings and most serious consequences, must be admitted on consideration of the two facts,— that it was a tax on imports, and a very insignificant one, that produced the American rebellion against England; and that it was the refusal to permit the South to share in the benefit of a surplus revenue by the remission of a vexatious tariff, which drove South Carolina to revolt in 1832.

In his inaugural address Abraham Lincoln made it clear that the govern-ment could not and would not agree to its own dissolution by recognizing secession. He stated that the federal government would "hold, occupy, and possess the property and places belonging to the government," meaning the federal forts and property in the seceded states. While he affirmed that the two sections of the country could not separate he declared that he had "no purpose, directly or indirectly to interfere with the institution of slavery where it exists." He solemnly indicated that he would "preserve, protect, and defend" the Union.

Many Southerners did not believe in his sincerity. They did not believe his statement that he would not interfere with slavery in the Southern states. To them the Republican Party was the party of abolition, of extremists like Charles Sumner and William Lloyd Garrison, of attitudes like those in Helper's Impending Crisis, of fanaticism and slave insurrections as ex-emplified by John Brown. Lincoln's election seemed a challenge to the Southern social and economic system, to their whole way of life.

After his inauguration the two most crucial problems confronting Lin-

coln were to conciliate the Upper South in order to halt the secession movement and what to do about Fort Sumter.

Most Union arsenals and forts in the Southern states had been easily and
peaceably surrendered to those states. Fort Pickens at Pensacola was still
in Union hands, and in Charleston Major Anderson had moved his force
from Fort Moultrie to Fort Sumter. President Buchanan had refused to
evacuate Fort Sumter and had unsuccessfully attempted to reinforce it.
Such strong feeling and tension had arisen over the issue that aggressive
action by either side could have started a war.

Lincoln decided that reinforcements should be sent to Fort Pickens and
to Fort Sumter. The purpose of the expedition was to supply food to Fort
Sumter and reinforcements were to be landed only in case of attack.

On April 11 General G. T. Beauregard who was in charge of Confederate troops
in Charleston sent the following ultimatum to Major Anderson, commander at
Fort Sumter. The text is from *The War of the Rebellion, A Compilation of the
Official Records of the Union and Confederate Armies,* Government Printing Office,
Washington, 1880, Series I, Vol. I, 13.

Charleston, S.C., April 11, 1861.

SIR: The Government of the Confederate States has hitherto forborne
from any hostile demonstration against Fort Sumter, in the hope that the
Government of the United States, with a view to the amicable adjustment
of all questions between the two Governments, and to avert the calamities of
war, would voluntarily evacuate it.

There was reason at one time to believe that such would be the course
pursued by the Government of the United States, and under that impression my Government has refrained from making any demand for the surrender of the fort. But the Confederate States can no longer delay assuming
actual possession of a fortification commanding the entrance of one of
their harbors, and necessary to its defense and security.

I am ordered by the Government of the Confederate States to demand
the evacuation of Fort Sumter. My aides, Colonel Chesnut and Captain
Lee, are authorized to make such demand of you. All proper facilities will
be afforded for the removal of yourself and command, together with company arms and property, and all private property, to any post in the
United States which you may select. The flag which you have upheld so
long and with so much fortitude, under the most trying circumstances, may
be saluted by you on taking it down.

Colonel Chesnut and Captain Lee will, for a reasonable time, await
your answer.

I am, sir, very respectfully, your obedient servant,
G. T. Beauregard,
Brigadier-General, Commanding.

The following reply was sent by Anderson.

FORT SUMTER, S.C., *April* 11, 1861

GENERAL: I have the honor to acknowledge the receipt of your communication demanding the evacuation of this fort, and to say, in reply thereto, that it is a demand with which I regret that my sense of honor, and of my obligations to my Government, prevent my compliance. Thanking you for the fair, manly, and courteous terms proposed, and for the high compliment paid me,

I am, general, very respectfully, your obedient servant,

ROBERT ANDERSON,

Major, First Artillery, Commanding.

✓   ✓   ✓

The Confederate bombardment of Fort Sumter began on April 12 at 4:30 A.M. and lasted until 8 P.M. of the 13th. At 4 o'clock on the afternoon of the 14th the troops of the United States garrison were transferred by the steamer Isabel to the United States vessels which had arrived off the harbor. Major Anderson sent the following terse report to Secretary of War Cameron. The text is from the *Official Records,* Series I., Vol. 1, p. 12.

STEAMSHIP BALTIC, OFF SANDY HOOK,

April 18, 1861—10:30 a.m.—via NEW YORK

Having defended Fort Sumter for thirty-four hours, until the quarters were entirely burned, the main gates destroyed by fire, the gorge walls seriously injured, the magazine surrounded by flames, and its door closed from the effects of heat, four barrels and three cartridges of powder only being available, and no provisions remaining but pork, I accepted terms of evacuation offered by General Beauregard, being the same offered by him on the 11th instant, prior to the commencement of hostilities, and marched out of the fort Sunday afternoon, the 14th instant, with colors flying and drums beating, bringing away company and private property, and saluting my flag with fifty guns.

ROBERT ANDERSON,

Major, First Artillery, Commanding.

On April 15 Lincoln issued a proclamation calling forth "the militia of the several states of the Union to the number of 75,000 . . ." to put down an insurrection in seven states. He also called a special session of Congress to meet on July 4. The secession of Virginia, Tennessee, Arkansas, and North Carolina followed this proclamation. The result for these states was indeed tragic. They were strongly unionist in sympathy and were opposed to secession. They wished to stay in the Union if possible, but they were resolved that if the South were "coerced" they would go to the aid of sister states. They feared that if war came their territory would be invaded.

They resented both secession and abolition. They deplored Lincoln's April policy, feeling that he should have been more conciliatory and that he should have avoided a crisis at Fort Sumter. It was not the attack on Fort Sumter, however, but the proclamation which impelled the states of the Upper South to secede.

When the division of the states was finally made there were twenty-three states in the North, eleven in the South. Also there were twenty-two million people in the North, nine million in the South, and of these nine million, three and a half million were slaves. In wealth, manufacturing, transportation, banking, and finance, iron and steel resources, the North had an overwhelming superiority. The South had the psychological advantage of fighting for independence and in defense of homes and a cherished way of life. The North seemed an oppressor or subjugator.

A planter of Pine Bluff, Arkansas, S. R. Cockrell, wrote the following letter to General LeRoy Pope Walker, Confederate Secretary of War, assuring him of Arkansas' support. The letter is quoted from the *Official Records,* Series 1, Vol. I, p. 686.

Nashville, *April* 21, 1861.

General Walker, *Montgomery:*

. . . The legislature meets next Thursday, and the plan is to pass the ordinance of secession and let the people ratify it, arm the State, and stand ready to march South or North.

Arkansas will go out 6th of May before breakfast. The Indians come next. Companies are forming rapidly, and I expect both my sons to go whenever the insolent invader shall tread a hostile foot upon our soil. The slave States [as] a unit are omnipotent in defense.

Arkansas and Tennessee are wild with indignation at the insolence and usurpation of the buffoon at Washington City. They are ready for the fight, every man, white and black. The blacks in Arkansas would be entirely reliable, if necessary, in defense. I know the fact is so. They are more obedient and loyal than ever before. When the fight is over, a separation of the free blacks from the slaves is the true plan to protect and guard the institution. It is one of the domestic relations that I have studied with much care.

I indorse without a proviso every act in the cotton States, done separately or together, by President, Congress, and Cabinet, and am ready to aid in all that may be necessary to accomplish what has been undertaken.

The stores for troops at Fort Smith were seized as they went up the Arkansas River and stored in Pine Bluff, one mile from my plantation. Flour and bacon chiefly. I think Arkansas, Virginia, and Tennessee will be represented in your next Congress, called for the 29th instant.

I don't think there is any danger of an overflow. The Mississippi is level full, but not against the levee above Napoleon. The Arkansas has a 10-foot bank, and falling, when I came out a few days ago. The prospect for a corn crop fine. I planted one hundred acres for your army. The cotton crop is just coming up and promises well.

With streamers gay push forward with sanguine cheer. The God of Battles must and will be with you. Success to the arm which strikes for our rights.

Very truly, your friend,
S. R. COCKRELL.

✓ ✓ ✓

Another British correspondent, William H. Russell, described the excitement in the Carolinas immediately after the surrender of Fort Sumter. The selection is from his *My Diary North and South,* Bradbury and Evans, London, 1863, Vol. I, pp. 41-43.

At Goldsborough, which is the first place of importance on the line, the wave of the secession tide struck us in full career. The station, the hotels, the street through which the rail ran was filled with an excited mob, all carrying arms, with signs here and there of a desire to get some kind of uniform—flushed faces, wild eyes, screaming mouths, hurrahing for "Jeff Davis" and the "Southern Confederacy," so that the yells overpowered the discordant bands which were busy with "Dixie's Land." Here was the true revolutionary furor in full sway. The men hectored, swore, cheered, and slapped each other on the backs; the women, in their best, waved handkerchiefs, and flung down garlands from the windows. All was noise, dust, and patriotism.

It was a strange sight and a wonderful event at which we were assisting. These men were a levy of the people of North Carolina called out by the governor of the State for the purpose of seizing forts Caswell and Macon, belonging to the Federal government, and left unprotected and undefended. The enthusiasm of the "citizens" was unbounded, nor was it quite free from a taint of alcohol. Many of the volunteers had flint firelocks, only a few had rifles. All kinds of head-dress were visible, and caps, belts, and pouches of infinite variety. . . . .

At nightfall the train stopped at Wilmington, and I was shot out on a platform under a shed, to do the best I could. . . . Early the next morning, soon after dawn, I crossed the Cape Fear River, on which Wilmington is situated, by a steam ferry-boat. On the quay lay quantities of shot and shell. "How came these here?" I inquired. "They're anti-abolition pills, said my neighbor; "they've been waiting here for two months back, but now that Sumter's taken, I guess they won't be wanted." . . . From the small glance I had of Wilmington, with its fleet of schooners and brigs crowding the broad and rapid river, I should think it was a thriving place. Confederate flags waved over the public buildings, and I was informed that the forts had been seized without opposition or difficulty. . . .

The Carolinians are capable of turning out a fair force of cavalry. At each stopping-place I observed saddle-horses tethered under the trees, and light driving vehicles, drawn by wiry, muscular animals, not remarkable for size, but strong-looking and active. Some farmers in blue jackets, and yellow braid and facings, handed round their swords to be admired by the company. . . . I inquired of a fine, tall, fair-haired fellow whom they expected to fight. "That's more than I can tell," quoth he. "The Yankees ain't such cussed fools as to think they can come here and whip us, let alone the British." "Why, what have the British got to do with it?" "They are bound to take our part; if they don't, we'll just give them a hint about cotton, and that will set matters right." This was said very much with the air of a man who knows what he is talking about, and who was quite satisfied "he had you there". . . .

The streets of Charleston present some such aspect as those of Paris in the last revolution. Crowds of armed men singing and promenading the streets. The battle-blood running through their veins—that hot oxygen which is called "the flush of victory" on the cheek; restaurants full, revelling in bar-rooms, club-rooms crowded, orgies and carousings in taverns or private house, in tap-room, from cabaret—down narrow alleys, in the broad highway. Sumter has sent them distraught; never was such a victory; never such brave lads; never such a fight. There are pamphlets already full of the incident. It is a bloodless Waterloo or Solferino.

The North sought to hold Missouri, Kentucky, Maryland, and Delaware, to gain the mastery of the Mississippi River, to blockade the Southern coasts, and to capture Richmond. Shortly after Virginia seceded the capital of the Confederacy was moved from Montgomery to Richmond.

In the early days of the war Washington was virtually undefended, and perhaps Beauregard missed a golden opportunity when he did not advance northward after Sumter and seize Washington.

By July, 1861, General McDowell guarded Washington from Centerville, about twenty miles from the capital, while the main Confederate army under Beauregard was based at Manassas. McDowell planned to defeat Beauregard and drive on to Richmond. His plan involved an understanding that General Patterson would engage Joseph E. Johnston's Confederate force at Winchester and prevent that force from joining Beauregard. Patterson failed to do this and part of Johnston's force joined Beauregard on July 20. The following day McDowell attacked and was at first successful: However, after hard fighting the Confederates turned possible defeat to victory and McDowell was forced to retreat. This retreat, at first orderly, was impeded by spectators and Congressmen and soon turned into a rout and the army fled in panic to Washington. Both armies were largely composed of untried civilians in uniform; and although Bull Run seemed a serious defeat for the North, the Confederates were not sufficiently organized to follow up the victory and capture Washington. Indeed, the result stimulated war preparation in the North and caused complacency in the South, so that perhaps the ultimate advantage was with the Union forces.

After the first battle of Bull Run there was a lull in the fighting on the eastern front. Lincoln appointed McClellan in command of the armies of the United States. McClellan devoted months to organizing the Army of the Potomac. During this period the Confederate army under Johnston was at Manassas. A reporter for *Blackwood's Edinburgh Magazine,* Vol. 90, 1861, pp. 768-779, described these two forces at the close of the year.

With regard, in the first place, to the main Federal army of the Potomac, there can be no doubt that, for its size, it is one of the best equipped which any nation has set on foot. Its transport is superb; its artillery numerous, well appointed, and of the best description; the *physique* of its men unsurpassed. It is moreover, at the disposal of a Government virtually drawing at will upon the accumulated capital and the entire credit of the nation. For practical purposes, the President and his ministers are all-powerful. Such as the army is, and in so far as they can depend upon its good conduct, it is at their absolute disposal; and upon the use they are able to make of it depends the solution of the great question at issue. . . .

. . . We cannot leave unnoticed the action of causes of weakness to the North. . . . The strife of parties in the North is reviving. Republicans and Democrats are charging each other with culpability in the origin of the war, and differ widely as to its objects and limits. The former, avowedly or secretly, desire the subjugation, or at least the permanent restraint, of the Slave States; the latter, that the war shall be prosecuted only so long as may be necessary to induce the seceded States to accept the terms of compromise. . . . We must not forget that the rank and file of [the Federal army] . . . is little more experienced than it was at the battle of the 21st July—that its officers are taken from the same class as they were on that day, and elected in the same manner—and that of all the causes to which the rout of Manassas has been attributed, none is better proved than the incapacity of the regimental officers. The unfitness of the great mass of the general officers for their position is a necessity. Moreover, a large, and we believe the most trustworthy part of the Federal army is composed of foreigners; and although the Germans are valuable for their aptitude for drill, and the Irish for their courage, their services cannot be the offspring of a patriotic spirit, which might compensate for a defective discipline. They are just such troops as high pay will attract to any service in the world; but the time essential to their military education has been wanting. . . .

It is evident, too, . . . that the confidence expressed by the Northern newspapers in the invincible character of the army . . . is hardly shared by its commanders. Their measures within their lines on the right bank of the Potomac are rather calculated for defence, or for a secure retreat, than for the advance of an eager and "imposing army." Every road is commanded by powerful batteries and breastworks—every hillock crowned with a redoubt—every mile to which the retreating enemy encourages the advance of their outposts is marked by fresh fieldworks of the strongest description.

The Northern army may probably consist . . . of about 360,000 men. . . . Many of the 360,000 must be as yet very little drilled, and few have seen four months service. . . .

[The Southern army] is inferior to that of the North in equipment, in military material, in the command of European supplies. . . . It is not uniformly clad; its *train* is less regular and splendid; its field artillery probably less numerous; and the supply of rifled ordnance and gunpowder must necessarily be difficult.

But the spirit which has created and maintained hitherto the Southern Confederacy, has also found means to supply many of its wants. Formerly neglectful of manufacturers, even of the simplest kind, the blockade has called forth many which were before hardly known in the South. At Nashville a factory has been established, from which half a million of copper caps are turned out daily. The Navy Yard at Norfolk furnished numerous heavy guns, which are supplemented by factories at Richmond and elsewhere. It is worthy of note that the Federal officers failed to destroy the valuable machinery at Norfolk before they retreated, though they dealt fire and destruction upon the wooden sheds. The arms found in the Federal arsenals, or purchased by the several States, amounted, by the report of the Secretary of War in July, to 707,000 stand; since which large quantities of the superior kinds or rifles have been introduced through Kentucky, or by running the blockade. . . . And it must be remembered that in the South almost every man was possessed of arms, generally a rifle—that skill as a marksman was highly esteemed—and that in a war *wherein bayonets are never crossed,* and a "battle" is a volley in the bush, such arms cannot be ignored in the enumeration of the national armament. . . .

The Southern force is possessed of elements of strength which might compensate for greater numerical disparity. It is commanded beyond all question by the most talented officers of the late United States Army. Few without actual military experience hold the command even of brigades,— and very young "West Point officers" hold considerable commands which, but for the jealousy of the Southern public of civilian commanders, might have been given, as in the North, to influential politicians. While General M'Clellan himself, great as his abilities are admitted to be, never held a command, and had, before the separation of the States, retired to a civil appointment, at least twenty of the Confederate generals were brigadiers or field-officers of the little United States' army, and eight or ten others commanded brigades in the Mexican war. . . .

The army itself, to be understood, must be seen and inspected. Roughly, irregularly, often quaintly clothed, . . . but with something like a soldierly appearance—with bright and generally well-carried arms, alert on duty, very rapid on the march—they do not look like men to be readily subdued. The cavalry consists of men accustomed to constant horsemanship; they generally bring their own horses into the service, and their aptitude is proved by the rapidity and accuracy of the movements of strong squadrons quite lately formed . . .

The moveability of the army deserves notice. Each brigade can strike its camp and pack its baggage on its carts in twenty minutes; change of camp by some of the brigades is often made—so that, concealed by the partially-cleared forest, its enemy knows not from day to day how far its flanks extend. . . .

But the most interesting feature in this army is its composition. In the first place, it is composed almost entirely of Americans. In its ranks, as subalterns and even as privates, are to be found many men of wealth and good social position serving from a sense of necessity for united national exertion, and cheerfully performing every duty. A rough-looking sentry, or an orderly with an officer's horse, often proves to be a man with land and property of his own, whom you might have met a few months since in the ball-room or opera.

There are many companies, troops, and batteries, in whose ranks stand the men at whose expense they have been formed, and horsed, and armed—free gifts to the State—men of great wealth, whose life has been of ease, accepting the lowest posts in the service of their State. Mothers sending every son whose age enables him to bear arms to the war, without regret or a pang—whole families side by side. . . .

Again, the clothing of the army causes but a slight drain upon the treasury. States, counties, cities, associations, individuals, clothe their own brigades, regiments, and companies. Everywhere ladies are working in the common cause. Those who last year were crowding the Northern watering-places, and scattering their gold broadcast, have this summer and autumn been working in vast establishments, spinning thread, weaving cloth, cutting out and fashioning rough soldiers' clothing, organising hospitals, and tending the sick and wounded.

As to money matters, there is more gold in the treasury and in the banks than when the struggle commenced; the latter are within their issues of paper, although cash payments are suspended, as this year no money is going abroad. . . . So far from there being any anxiety for the sale of the cotton crop, its export is prohibited by the States, or by the order of

the governors, with the entire approval of the public. . . . Recognition of
their independence and close commercial relations with England, without
restrictions upon trade, are earnestly desired by the people of the South;
and there may be a little impatience that their nationality is as yet ignored
by the civilised world. A more correct view appears, however, to be taken
by the heads of the Government. "Our separation from the North," said
President Davis lately, "is as complete as if it had been accomplished fifty
years. But I am far from complaining of the tardy recognition of European
governments. It is better for us that we should work out our own independence, and the rest will come in good time."

*Early in 1862 McClellan made plans for an advance on Richmond. Presi-
dent Lincoln expected a direct attack, but McClellan decided to attack
Richmond by an advance up the Peninsula between the York and James
rivers, and by May 1, 1862, he was safely on the Peninsula with an army of
112,000 and a strong base at Fort Monroe. McClellan captured Yorktown
after a month's siege. Then in the battle of Williamsburg on May 5, Longstreet commanding the Confederate vanguard fought off large Union forces
and prevented McClellan from attacking the main Confederate army under Joseph Johnston. Norfolk was captured and the James River was
opened to land-and-water operations by the Union forces. McClellan
established his headquarters at White House Landing and urged that his
army be reinforced by the army of 40,000 men under McDowell which was
defending Washington. Lincoln and Stanton, fearful for the safety of
Washington, withheld these forces. They did order McDowell to advance
in a direct line from Washington to Richmond. This advance was disrupted by Stonewall Jackson's Valley campaign. Jackson with 16,000 men
faced 45,000 Federal troops in the Valley. Following the hit-and-run
strategy of attacking Union commanders consecutively before they could
unite, by marching and countermarching, he struck successive blows against
Shields, Milroy, Banks, and Fremont in five different battles. He mystified
Union forces and Northern newspapers and authorities; their fear that
Washington was in danger caused the recall of McDowell's corps. This
valley campaign of Jackson's is one of the most brilliant in the history of
military tactics. Jackson, having kept Union forces away from Richmond,
joined Lee in time to help defend Richmond against McClellan.*

*In June, 1862, the Confederates had about 85,000 men to defend Rich-
mond against approximately 100,000 under McClellan. The first main
battle of the Peninsular campaign occurred at Seven Pines or Fair Oaks on
May 31-June 1. Johnston's forces were driven back, Johnston was wounded,
and Robert E. Lee became the commander of the Confederate forces. In
the "Seven Days" (June 25-July 1) the two armies fought at Beaver Dam
Creek, Gaines Mill, and Fraser's Farm, and finally at Malvern Hill. This
last was in a sense a Union victory, but McClellan was unable to take*

Richmond and retreated down the Peninsula. Lincoln and the North were disappointed with McClellan and he was soon removed from the command of all the Union forces, though he retained command of the army of the Potomac.

The Shenandoah Valley was an important artery for the movement of troops. Participating in Stonewall Jackson's Valley campaign in 1862 was Richard Taylor, son of President Zachary Taylor. In the following selection he described the valley, showing the significance of its location and character. The extract is quoted from his *Destruction and Reconstruction,* D. Appleton and Company, New York, 1879, pp. 44-45, *passim.*

The great Valley of Virginia was before us in all its beauty. Fields of wheat spread far and wide, interspersed with woodlands, bright in their robes of tender green. Wherever appropriate sites existed, quaint old mills, with turning wheels, were busily grinding the previous year's harvest; and grove and eminence showed comfortable homesteads. The soft vernal influence shed a languid grace over the scene. The theatre of war in this region was from Staunton to the Potomac, one hundred and twenty miles, with an average width of some twenty-five miles; and the Blue Ridge and Alleghanies bounded it east and west. Drained by the Shenandoah with its numerous affluents, the surface was nowhere flat, but a succession of graceful swells, occasionally rising into abrupt hills. Resting on limestone, the soil was productive, especially of wheat, and the underlying rock furnished abundant metal for the construction of roads. Railway communication was limited to the Virginia Central, which entered the Valley by a tunnel east of Staunton and passed westward through that town; to the Manassas Gap, which traversed the Blue Ridge at the pass of that name and ended a Strasburg; and to the Winchester and Harper's Ferry, thirty miles long. The first extended to Richmond by Charlottesville and Gordonsville, crossing at the former place the line from Washington and Alexandria to Lynchburg; the second connected Strasburg and Front Royal, in the Valley, with the same line at Manassas Junction; and the last united with the Baltimore and Ohio at Harper's Ferry. Frequent passes or gaps in the mountains, through which wagon roads had been constructed, afforded easy access from east and west; and pikes were excellent, though unmetaled roads became heavy after rains.

But the glory of the Valley is Massanutten. Rising abruptly from the plain near Harrisonburg, twenty-five miles north of Staunton, this lovely mountain extends fifty miles, and as suddenly ends near Strasburg. Parallel with the Blue Ridge, and of equal height, its sharp peaks have a bolder and more picturesque aspect, while the abruptness of its slopes gives the appearance of greater altitude. Midway of Massanutten, a gap with good road affords communication between Newmarket and Luray. The eastern or Luray Valley, much narrower than the one west of Massanutten, is drained by the east branch of the Shenandoah, which is joined at Front Royal, near the northern end of the mountain, by its western affluent, whence the united waters flow north, at the base of the Blue Ridge, to meet the Potomac at Harper's Ferry.

The inhabitants of this favored region were worthy of its inheritance. The north and south were peopled by scions of old colonial families, and the proud names of the "Old Dominion" abounded. In the central counties of Rockingham and Shenandoah were many descendants of German settlers. These were thrifty, substantial farmers, and, like their kinsmen of Pennsylvania, expressed their opulence in huge barns and fat cattle. The devotion of all to the Southern cause was wonderful. Jackson, a Valley man by reason of his residence at Lexington, south of Staunton, was their hero and idol. The women sent husbands, sons, lovers, to battle as cheerfully as to marriage feasts. No oppression, no destitution could abate their zeal. Upon a march I was accosted by two elderly sisters, who told me they had secreted a large quantity of bacon in a well on their estate, hard by. Federals had been in possession of the country, and, fearing the indiscretion of their slaves, they had done the work with their own hands, and now desired to *give* the meat to their people. Wives and daughters of millers, whose husbands and brothers were in arms, worked the mills night and day to furnish flour to their soldiers. To the last, women would go distances to carry the modicum of food between themselves and starvation to a suffering Confederate. . . . The command (Taylor's) was in superb condition, and a four-gun battery from Bedford county, Virginia, had recently been added to it. The four regiments, 6th, 7th, 8th, and 9th Louisiana, would average above eight hundred bayonets. . . . The 6th, Colonel Seymour, recruited in New Orleans, was composed of Irishmen, stout, hardy, fellows, turbulent in camp and requiring a strong hand, but responding to kindness and justice, and ready to follow their officers to the death. The 9th, Colonel Stafford, was from North Louisiana. Planters or sons of planters, many of them of fortune, soldiering was a hard task to which they only became reconciled by reflecting that it was "niddering" in gentlemen to assume voluntarily the discharge of duties and then shirk. The 8th, Colonel Kelly, was from the Attakapas—"Acadians," the race of which Longfellow sings in "Evangeline." A home-loving, simple people, few spoke English, fewer still had ever before moved ten miles from their natal *cabanas;* and the war to them was "a liberal education," and was the society of the lady of quality to honest Dick Steele. They had all the light gayety of the Gaul, and, after the manner of their ancestors, were born cooks. A capital regimental band accompanied them, and whenever weather and ground permitted, even after long marches, they would waltz and "polk" in couples with as much zest as if their arms encircled the supple waists of the Celestines and Melazies of their native Teche. The Valley soldiers were largely of Presbyterian Faith, and of a solemn, pious demeanor, and looked askant at the caperings of my Creoles, holding them to be "devices and snares."

Off . . . [one] morning, my command still in advance, and Jackson riding with me. The road led north between the east bank of the river and the western base of the Blue Ridge. Rain had fallen and softened it, so as to delay the wagon trains in rear. Past midday we reached a wood extending from the mountain to the river, when a mounted officer from the rear called Jackson's attention, who rode back with him. A moment later, there rushed out of the wood to meet us a young, rather well-looking woman, afterward widely known as Belle Boyd. Breathless with speed and agitation, some time elapsed before she found her voice. Then, with much volubility, she said we were near Front Royal, beyond the wood; that the town was filled with Federals, whose camp was on the west side of the river, where they had guns in position to cover the wagon bridge, but none bearing on the railway bridge below the former; that they believed Jackson to be west of Massanutten, near Harrisonburg; that General Banks, the Federal commander, was at Winchester, twenty miles northwest of Front Royal, where he was slowly concentrating his widely scattered forces to meet Jackson's advance, which was expected some days later. All this she told with the precision of a staff officer making a report, and it was true to the letter. Jackson was possessed of these facts before he left Newmarket, and based his movements upon them; but, as he never told anything, it was news to me, and gave me an idea of the strategic value of Massanutten—pointed out, indeed, by Washington before the Revolution. . . .

On another occasion Jackson leading the way, my brigade, a small body of horse, and a section of the Rockbridge (Virginia) artillery forming the column. Major Wheat, with his battalion of "Tigers," was directed to keep close to the guns. Sturdy marchers, they trotted along with the horse and artillery at Jackson's heels, and after several hours were some distance in advance of the brigade, with which I remained.

A volley in front, followed by wild cheers, stirred us up to a "double," and we speedily came upon a moving spectacle. Jackson had struck the Valley pike at Middletown, twelve miles south of Winchester, along which a large body of Federal horse, with many wagons, was hastening north. He attacked at once with his handful of men, overwhelmed resistance, and captured prisoners and wagons. The gentle Tigers were looting right merrily, diving in and out of wagons with the activity of rabbits in a warren; but this occupation was abandoned on my approach, and in a moment they were in line, looking as solemn and virtuous as deacons at a funeral. Prisoners and spoil were promptly secured. The horse was from New England, a section in which horsemanship was an unknown art, and some of the riders were strapped to their steeds. Ordered to dismount, they explained their condition, and were given time to unbuckle. Many breast-plates and other protective devices were seen here, and later at Winchester.

We did not know whether the Federals had organized cuirassiers, or were recurring to the customs of Gustavus Adolphus. I saw a poor fellow lying dead on the pike, pierced through breastplate and body by a rifle ball. Iron-clad men are of small account before modern weapons.

✓   ✓   ✓

From *Blackwood's Edinburgh Magazine*, Vol. 93, 1863, p. 14 ff., is quoted a description of the Shenandoah Valley just a few months later, following the continuous Virginia campaigns of 1862. It illustrates some of the life behind the lines in the Confederate Army.

Staunton, a town containing about 4000 inhabitants, is now in a forlorn condition; no business doing there, and many shops closed altogether from the owners having sold off their entire stock, and being unable to lay in fresh supplies. . . . Being at the end of the railway and the commencement of the turnpike road line of communication with the army, it has necessarily become an entrepot for stores, waggons, and ambulances, &c. &c. Most of the best houses have been converted into hospitals, from which sick and wounded men seem to be constantly coming and going, some from the front, others being sent off to the rear by railway. Throughout the war it has been the practice to send all sick and wounded men who require some time to recover to their own friends, where, of course, they receive the kindest treatment; and in this manner the regular hospitals have been greatly relieved, and the service in every way benefitted. . . . A regular stage, drawn by four horses, runs between Staunton and Winchester. But as there are daily crowds of men going up along the road to join the army, many of whom have what is called "transportation" found them by order of the Quartermaster's Department, and all being very properly allowed a preference over civilians, we were informed that it was hopeless attempting to get seats unless we were content to wait several days for that purpose. As time was a great object to me, . . . we were determined, if the worst came to the worst, to walk the ninety-two miles. . . . We were most fortunate . . . in getting an ambulance cart, one of a large number going up to carry back sick and wounded men. It was four-wheeled, covered over with a tarpaulin-hood, and drawn by two horses, the body of the cart being made to carry two men on stretchers, with room for another man beside the driver. It was mounted on very tolerable springs, but being one of a batch lately made in Richmond after the Yankee pattern, and having been hastily put together by unskilled workmen, its construction was so bad, and the wheels so weak, that I feel convinced the whole affair must have tumbled to pieces in one day's march over the ordinary country roads of Virginia. Very fortunately, however, the road down the Shenandoah valley is macadamized, being, I believe, the [only] regularly metalled road in the State. There were thirteen ambulance-carts in the train with which we travelled, all under the charge of an officer of the Quartermaster's Department. We had not proceeded more than about six miles when two or three of the carts had to halt at a smith's shop for the purpose of having the wheel-tires cut and reduced in size, the dry weather having so affected the new wood, that the spokes in some of the wheels were rattling loosely about like lucifer-matches in a box. This delayed us some two hours, so that we did not make more than five-and-twenty miles the first day, halting for the night in a field a few miles short of Harrisonburg. . . . This valley of the Shenandoah and its tributaries is about the most fertile portion of the State, and by many called the garden of Virginia. The farms are extensive, with larger fields than in most of the other counties I had passed through; and in a number of places well-built walls of loose stone had been substituted for the usual snake and rail fences. Happy men those were whose fathers had thus enclosed their farms, for all the stone walls remained in perfect order, whereas many of the wooden posts and rails had disappeared altogether. Wherever a column had halted for the night, these posts had been used for firing; for with every desire to protect private property, it is idle to suppose that men will see fine logs, cut regularly so as to burn well, around them, and yet go without a fire—the soldier's only solace and comfort in a bivouac. For all such injuries done to their property the farmers are well paid, particularly where men of Union sympathies are concerned, the Government are cheated by having to pay several times over for the same farms. As, since the commencement of hostilities, this valley has been the theatre of operations, it is now almost exhausted of supplies, and it is so difficult to purchase even bread there, that I fear the residents will suffer severely this winter. . . .

Every day during our journey to Winchester we passed batches of convalescents marching to join the army, many of whom were totally unfit for work. This, of course, spoke very highly for the men; but it evinced a great want of judgment on the part of the medical officers, for such men would be an incubus to any army, and would . . . reduce its power of movement and action immensely. Each day we also passed batches of sick and wounded going to the rear; those totally unable to march being conveyed in ambulances, or the empty waggons returning to Staunton for more supplies. It was an extremely painful sight to see such numbers of weakly men struggling slowly home, many of them without boots or shoes, and all indifferently clad; but posts were established every seventeen miles along the road, containing commissariat supplies, for provisioning them. We also encountered several long trains of guns and ammunition-waggons proceeding to the rear, amongst which were most of the guns taken at Harper's Ferry. It was amusing to see "U. S." marked upon almost all ambulance-carts we passed. The North have not only clothed and equipped the millions of men whom they boast of having had at various times enrolled, but they have also similarly supplied the Southern armies.

Into whatever camp you go, you are sure to see tents, carts, horses, and guns all marked with the "U. S." Officers have declared to me, that they have seen whole regiments go into action with smooth-bore muskets and without great-coats, and known them in the evening to be well provided with everything—having changed their old muskets for rifles. The Northern troops have been so liberally supplied with all, and, indeed, I may say, *more* than a soldier wants in the field, that they do not value their knapsacks or blankets, and in action invariably throw them away before they "skedaddle;" knowing that if they succeed by swiftness in living to "fight another day," their Government will provide them with a new kit, rifle, and all.

Following the Peninsular campaign Lee and Jackson slashed at Pope's army until they soundly defeated him at Second Manassas. Lee then invaded Maryland to "liberate that state for the South." Jackson captured Harper's Ferry with its garrison of 11,000 men, and Lee and McClellan fought a bloody but indecisive battle at Antietam. McClellan had vastly superior forces, but he allowed Lee's army to escape across the Potomac without pursuit. For the second time Stuart rode completely around McClellan's army. McClellan was replaced by Burnside who was disastrously defeated at Fredericksburg. In January, 1863, Lincoln removed Burnside and placed Hooker in command of the army of the Potomac. Hooker divided his army, and Lee sent Jackson to attack the right wing under Howard. Jackson defeated Howard badly at Chancellorsville, but on returning from reconnaissance he was mortally wounded by his own men, and Lee had lost his "right arm." Lee had to decide whether to fight south of the Potomac, to invade the North, or to send part of his troops west to relieve Pemberton and Bragg and try to save Vicksburg from Grant. He decided to invade the North and the historic battle of Gettysburg followed.

Gideon Welles, Lincoln's Secretary of the Navy, showed in his *Diary* how poorly informed the President and other officials in Washington were concerning Lee's second invasion of the North. The following is quoted from *Atlantic Monthly*, Boston, Vol. 103, 1909, pp. 756-770, passim.

Sunday, June 14, 1863. . . . Scary rumors abroad of army operations and a threatened movement of Lee upon Pennsylvania. . . .

Monday, June 15. . . . Something of a panic pervades the City. Singular rumors reach us of rebel advances in Maryland. It is said they have reached Hagerstown, and some of them have penetrated as far as Chambersburg in Pennsylvania. . . .

I have a panic telegraph from Gov. Curtin, who is excitable and easily alarmed, entreating that guns and gunners may be sent from the Navy

Yard at Philadelphia to Harrisburg without delay. We have not a gunner that we can spare. Commodore Stribling can spare men, temporarily, from the Navy Yard. . . . .

Wednesday, June 17, 1863. Had a telegraph at ten last night from Mr. Felton, President of the Philadelphia and Baltimore Railroad, requesting that a gun-boat might be sent to Havre de Grace to protect the Company's ferry-boat property. Says he has information that the rebels intend going down the river to seize it.

I went forthwith to the War Department to ascertain whether there was really any such alarming necessity, for it seemed to me, from all I had been able to learn, that it was a panic invocation. Found the President and Stanton at the War Department, jubilant over intelligence just received that no rebels had reached Carlisle as had been reported, and it was believed had not even entered Pennsylvania. Stanton threw off his reserve, and sneered and laughed at Felton's call for a gun-boat. . . .

Sunday, June 28, 1863. . . . the President drew from his pocket a telegram from General Hooker, asking to be relieved. The President said he had, for several days, as the conflict became imminent, observed in Hooker the same failings that were witnessed in McClellan after the battle of Antietam—a want of alacrity to obey, and a greedy call for more troops which could not, and ought not to be taken from other points. . . . . .

Some discussion followed, in regard to a successor. . . . The President finally remarked, he supposed General Halleck had issued the orders. . . . Stanton replied affirmatively, that Hooker had been ordered to Baltimore and Meade to succeed him. We were consulted after the fact. . . . Of Meade I know very little. He is not great. His brother officers speak well of him, but he is considered rather a "smooth bore" than a rifle. . . . .

Tuesday, June 30, 1863. . . . Lee and his army are well advanced into Pennsylvania, and they should not be permitted to fall back and recross the Potomac. Halleck is bent on driving them back, not on intercepting their retreat; is full of zeal to drive them out of Pennsylvania. . . . This movement of Lee and the rebel forces into Pennsylvania is to me incomprehensible, nor do I get any light from military men or others in regard to it. Should they cross the Susquehannah, as our General-in-Chief and Governor Curtin fear, they will never recross it without being first captured. . . .

Thursday, July 2, 1863. Met Stanton and went with him to the War Department. The President was there, and we read the despatches received from General Meade. There was a smart fight, but without results, near Gettysburg yesterday. . . .

Friday, July 3, 1863. . . . A despatch from General Meade, dated 3 P.M. yesterday, is very poor in tone. . . . They were concentrating for a fight, and unless Meade is greatly deceived, there will be a battle in the neighborhood of Gettysburg.

Saturday, July 4, 1863. I was called up at midnight precisely by a messenger with telegram from Byington, dated at Hanover Station, stating that the most terrific battle of the war was being fought at or near Gettysburg. . . . Byington is the editor and proprietor of a weekly paper in Norwalk, Connecticut. . . . Later in the day despatches from Haupt and others state that Lee with his army commenced a retreat this A.M. at 3 o'clock. Our army is waiting for supplies to come up before following—a little of the old lagging infirmity. . . .

Two intercepted despatches were received, captured by Captain Dahlgren. One was from Jeff Davis, the other from Adjutant General Cooper, both addressed to General Lee. They disclose trouble and differences among the rebel leaders. Lee, it seems, had an understanding with Cooper that Beauregard should concentrate a force of forty thousand at Culpepper for a demonstration, or something more, on Washington, when the place became uncovered by the withdrawal of the Army of the Potomac in pursuit of Lee. Davis appears not to have been informed of this military arrangement, nor satisfied with the programme when informed of it. Lee is told of the difficulty of defending Richmond and other places, and that he must defend his own lines, instead of relying upon its being done from Richmond.

Tuesday, July 7, 1863. The President said this morning, with a countenance indicating sadness and despondency, that Meade still lingered at Gettysburg, when he should have been at Hagerstown or near the Potomac, to cut off the retreating army of Lee.

In the West combined land and flotilla attacks and the able and determined leadership of Grant enabled the Union forces to capture Forts Henry and Donelson early in 1862. Grant then advanced farther into Tennessee and fought the bloody and indecisive battle at Shiloh in which the Confederate general, Albert Sidney Johnston, was killed and the Confederates were forced to withdraw. The Union army under Pope was also successful on the Mississippi and captured a force of 5000 Confederates on Island Number Ten. Admiral Farragut captured New Orleans in April, 1862. Following these victories, the Federal forces in the West suffered various delays before winning further victories at Vicksburg and Chattanooga in 1863. Late in 1862 Grant sought unsuccessfully to capture Vicksburg by way of the Yazoo. Then he boldly marched south on the Louisiana side, waited for the fleet to run the Vicksburg batteries and in twenty days mastered the Vicksburg area and laid siege to Vicksburg. After a siege of

*six weeks Pemberton surrendered Vicksburg and his whole force of 30,000
men to Grant on July 4, 1863.*

In the flowering of Southern literature after the Civil War, some excellent
reconstructions of scenes of the war were produced, two of which are used here.
From *The Cable Story Book,* edited by Mary E. Burt and Lucy L. Cable, C. Scribner's Sons, New York, 1899, pp. 106-123, is the following narrative of the surrender
of New Orleans. The story was edited for young readers by Miss Burt with the
approval of the author, George Washington Cable.

In the spring of 1862 we boys of New Orleans had no game. Nothing was
"in"; none of the old playground sports that commonly fill the school-boy's
calendar. We were even tired of drilling. Not one of us between seven and
seventeen but could beat the drum, knew every bugle-call, and could go
through the manual of arms and facings like a drill-sergeant. We were
blasé old soldiers—military critics.

Who could tell us anything? I recall but one trivial admission of ignorance on the part of any lad. On a certain day of grand review, when the
city's entire defensive force was marching through Canal Street, there
came along a stately body of tall, stalwart Germans, clad from head to
foot in velveteen of a peculiarly loud smell, and a boy, spelling out their
name upon their banner, said:

"H-u-s-a-r-s; what's them?"

"Aw, you fool!" cried a dozen urchins at once, "them's the Hoosiers;
don't you smell 'em?"

But now the day of grand reviews was past. Hussars, Zouaves, and
numberless other bodies of outlandish name had gone to the front in
Tennessee and Virginia. Our cultivated eyes were satisfied now with one
uniform that we saw daily. Every afternoon found us around in Coliseum
Place, standing or lying on the grass, watching the dress parade of the
"Confederate Guards." Most of us had fathers or uncles in the long, spot-
less, gray, white-gloved ranks that stretched down the hard, harsh turf
of our old ball-ground.

This was the flower of the home guard. The merchants, bankers, under-
writers, judges, real-estate owners, and capitalists, of the Anglo-American
part of the city, were "all present or accounted for" in that long line. Gray
heads, hoar heads, high heads, bald heads. Hands flashed to the breast
and waist with rigid precision at the command of "Present arms,"—
hands that had ruled by the pen—the pen and the dollar—since long before any of us young spectators was born, and had done no harder muscular
work than carve roasts and turkeys these twenty, thirty, forty years. Here
and there among them were individuals who, unaided, had clothed and
armed companies, squadrons, battalions, and sent them to the Cumberland
and the Potomac. A good three-fourths of them had sons on distant battle-
grounds, some living, some dead.

We boys saw nothing pathetic in this array of old men. To us there was only rich enjoyment in the scene. If there was anything solemn about it, why did the band play polkas? . . . Away down to the far end of the line and back again, the short, stout German drum major, holding his gaudy office in this case by virtue of his girth, not height, flourished his big stick majestically, bursting with rage at us for carelessly repeating at short intervals in his hearing that "He kot it mit his size."

In those beautiful spring afternoons there was scarcely a man to be found anywhere, out of uniform. Down on the steamboat landing, our famous Levee, a superb body of Creoles drilled and paraded in dark-blue. The orders were given in French; the movements were quick, short, nervy. The "about march" was four sharp stamps of their neatly shod feet—one, two, three, four—that brought them face about and sent them back, tramp, tramp, tramp, over the smooth, white pavement of powdered oyster-shells. Ah! the nakedness of that once crowded and roaring marketplace.

And there was a "Foreign Legion." Of course, the city had always been full of foreigners; but now it was a subject of amazement, not unmixed with satire, to see how many, whom everyone had supposed to be Americans or "citizens of Louisiana," bloomed out as British, or French, or Spanish subjects. But even so, the tremendous pressure of popular sentiment crowded them into the ranks and forced them to make every show of readiness to "hurl back the foe," as we used to call it. And they really served for much. Merely as a police force they relieved just as many Confederate soldiers of police duty in a city under martial law, and enabled them to man forts and breast-works at short notice, whenever that call should come.

That call, the gray heads knew, was coming. They confessed the conviction softly to one another in the counting-rooms and idle store-fronts when they thought no one was listening. I used to hear them—standing with my back turned, pretending to be looking at something down street, but with both ears turned backward and stretched wide. They said under their breath that there was not a single measure of defense that was not behindhand. And they spoke truly. In family councils a new domestic art began to be studied and discussed—the art of hiding valuables.

There had come a great silence upon trade. Long ago the custom warehouses had first begun to show a growing roominess, then emptiness, and then had remained shut, and the iron bolts and cross-bars of their doors were gray with cobwebs. One of them, where I had earned my first wages as a self-supporting lad, had been turned into a sword-bayonet factory, and I had been turned out. For sometime later the Levee had kept busy; but its stir and noise had gradually declined, faltered, turned into the commerce of war and the clatter of calkers and ship-carpenters, and faded out. Both receipts and orders from the interior country had shrunk and shrunk, and the brave, steady fellows, who, at entry and shipping and cash and account desks, could no longer keep a show of occupation, had laid down the pen, taken up the sword and musket, and followed after the earlier and more eager volunteers. There had been one new, tremendous sport for moneyed men for a while, with spoils to make it interesting. The seagoing tow-boats of New Orleans were long, slender side-wheelers, all naked power and speed, without either freight or passenger room, each with a single, tall slim chimney and hurrying walking-beam, their low, taper hulls trailing behind, scarcely above the water, perpetually drenched with the yeast of the wheels. Some merchants of more audacious sort, restless under the strange new quiet of their streets, had got letters of mark and reprisal (the right, that is, to capture an enemy's ships), and let slip these sharp-nosed deerhounds upon the tardy, unsuspecting ships that came sailing right up the Passes, unaware of any declaration of war. But that game, too, was up. The blockade had closed in like a prison gate; the lighter tow-boats, draped with tarpaulins, were huddled together under Slaughterhouse Point, with their cold boilers and motionless machinery yielding to rust; the more powerful ones had been moored at the long wharf vacated by Morgan's Texas steamships; there had been a great hammering, and making of chips, and clatter of railroad iron, turning these tow-boats into iron-clad cotton gun-boats, and these had crawled away, some up and some down the river, to be seen in that harbor no more. At length, only the foundries, the dry-docks across the river, and the shipyard in suburb Jefferson, where the great ram *Mississippi* was being too slowly built, were active, and the queen of Southern commerce, the city that had once believed it was to be the greatest in the world, was absolutely out of employment.

There was, true, some movement of the sugar and rice crops into the hands of merchants who had advanced the money to grow them; and the cotton presses and cotton-yards were full of cotton, but there it all stuck; and when one counts in a feeble exchange of city for country supplies, there was nothing more. Except—yes—that the merchants had turned upon each other, and were now engaged in a mere passing back and forth among themselves in speculation the daily diminishing supply of goods and food. Some were too noble to take part in this, and dealt only with customers. I remember one odd little old man, an extensive wholesale grocer, who used to get tipsy all by himself every day, and go home so, but who would not speculate on the food of a distressed city. He had not got down to that.

Gold and silver had long ago disappeared. Confederate money was the currency; and not merely was the price of food and raiment raising, the value of money was going down. The State, too, had a paper issue, and the city had another. Yet with all these there was first a famine of small change, and then a deluge of private paper money, called "shinplasters." Pah! What a mess it was! The boss butchers and the keepers of drinking houses actually took the lead in issuing "money." The current joke was that you could pass the label of an olive oil bottle, because it was greasy, smelt bad, and bore an autograph. I did my first work as a cashier in those days, and I can remember the smell of my cash drawer yet. Instead of five-cent pieces we had car-tickets. How the grimy little things used to stick together! They would pass and pass until they were so soft and illegible with grocers' and butchers' handling that you could tell only by some faint show of their original color what company had issued them. Rogues did a lively business in "split tickets," literally splitting them and making one ticket serve for two.

Decay had come in. In that warm moist climate it is always hungry, and, wherever it is allowed to feed, eats with a greed that is strange to see. With the wharves, always expensive and difficult to maintain, it made havoc. The occasional idle, weather-stained ship moored beside them, and resting on the water almost as light and void as an empty peascod, could hardly find a place to fasten to. The streets fell into sad neglect, but the litter of commerce was not in them, and some of their round pavement-stones, after a shower, would have the melancholy cleanness of weather-bleached bones. How quiet and lonely the harbor grew. . . . .

I shall not try to describe the day the alarm bells told us the city was in danger and called every man to his mustering-point. The children poured out from the school gates and ran crying to their homes, meeting their sobbing mothers at their thresholds. The men fell into ranks. I was left entirely alone in charge of the store where I was employed. Late in the afternoon, receiving orders to close it, I did so, and went home. But I did not stay. I went to the river-side. There, until far into the night, I saw hundreds of drays carrying cotton out of the presses and yards to the wharves, where it was fired. The glare of those serpentine miles of flame set men and women weeping and wailing thirty miles away on the farther shore of Lake Pontchartrain. But the next day was the day of horrors. During the night fear, wrath and sense of betrayal had run through the people as the fire had run through the cotton. You have seen, perhaps, a family fleeing with lamentations and wringing of hands out of a burning house; multiply it by thousands upon thousands; that was New Orleans, though the houses were not burning. The firemen were out; but they had cast fire on the waters, putting the torch to the empty ships and cutting them loose to float down the river.

Whoever could go was going. The great mass, that had no place to go or no means to go with, was beside itself. "Betrayed! betrayed!" it cried, and ran in throngs from street to street, seeking some vent, some victim for its wrath. I saw a crowd catch a poor fellow at the corner of Magazine and Common Streets, whose crime was that he looked like a stranger and might be a spy. He was the palest living man I ever saw. They swung him to a neighboring lamp-post, but the Foreign Legion was patrolling the town in strong squads, and one of its lieutenants, all green and gold, leaped

with drawn sword, cut the rope, and saved the man. This was one occurrence; there were many like it. I stood in the rear door of our store, Canal
Street, soon after reopening it. The junior of the firm was within. I called
him to look toward the river. The masts of the cutter *Washington* were
slowly tipping, declining, sinking—down she went. The gunboat moored
next her began to smoke all over and then to blaze. My employers lifted
up their heels and left the city—left their goods and their affairs in the
hands of a mere lad—no stranger would have thought I had reached fourteen—and one big German porter. I closed the doors, sent the porter to
his place in the Foreign Legion, and ran to the Levee to see the sights.

What a gathering! The riff-raff of the wharves, the town, the gutters.
Such women—such wrecks of women! And all the juvenile ragtag. The
lower steamboat landing, well covered with sugar, rice and mollasses, was
being rifled. The men smashed; the women scooped up the smashings. The
river was overflowing the top of the Levee. A rainstorm began to threaten.
"Are the Yankee ships in sight?" I asked of an idler. He pointed out the
tops of their naked masts as they showed up across the huge bend of the
river. They were engaging the batteries at Camp Chalmette—the old field
of Jackson's renown. Presently that was over. Ah, me! I see them now as
they come slowly round Slaughterhouse Point into full view, silent, grim
and terrible, black with men, heavy with deadly portent, the long-banished
Stars and Stripes flying against the frowning sky. Oh, for the *Mississippi!*
the *Mississippi!* Just then here she came down upon them. But how? Drift-
ing helplessly, a mass of flames.

The crowds on the Levee howled and screamed with rage. The swarming
decks answered never a word; but every old tar on the *Hartford,* standing
with lanyard in hand beside a great pivot-gun, so plain to view that you
could see him smile, silently patted its big black breech and blandly
grinned.

And now the rain came down in torrents. About one or two o'clock in
the afternoon came a roar of shoutings and imprecations and crowding
feet down Common Street. "Hurrah for Jeff Davis! Shoot them! Kill them!
Hang them!" I locked the door on the outside and ran to the front of the
mob, bawling with the rest, "Hurrah for Jeff Davis!" About every third
man there had a weapon out. Two officers of the United States Navy
were walking abreast, unguarded and alone, looking not to right or left,
never frowning, never flinching, while the mob screamed in their ears,
cursed and crowded and gnashed upon them. So, through the gates of
death, these two men walked to the City Hall to demand the town's surrender. It was one of the bravest deeds I ever saw done.

Later events, except one, I leave to other pens. An officer from the
fleet stood on the City Hall roof about to lower the flag of Louisiana. In
the street beneath gleamed the bayonets of a body of marines. A howitzer
pointed up, and another down, the street. All around swarmed the mob.

Just then Mayor Monroe—lest the officer above should be fired upon and the howitzers open upon the crowd—came out alone and stood just before one of the howitzers, tall, slender, and with folded arms, eyeing the gunner. Down sank the flag. Captain Bell, tall and stiff, marched off with the flag rolled under his arms and the howitzers clinking behind. Then cheer after cheer rang out for Monroe. And now, I daresay, everyone is well pleased that, after all, New Orleans never lowered her colors with her own hands.

✓   ✓   ✓

Mark Twain revisited the Mississippi River in 1882; he traveled on the river from St. Louis to New Orleans and then up again to St. Paul. One thing that interested him was the change in the river towns he had known as a steamboat pilot before the Civil War. He included the following account in *Life on the Mississippi*, 1874, De Luxe Edition, The American Publishing Company, Hartford, 1899, pp. 277-281.

Signs and scars still remain, as reminders of Vicksburg's tremendous war experiences; earthworks, trees crippled by cannon-balls, cave refuges in the clay precipices, etc. The caves did good service during the six weeks bombardment of the city—May 18 to July 4, 1863. They were used by the non-combatants—mainly by the women and children; not to live in constantly, but to fly to for safety on occasion. They were mere holes, tunnels driven into the perpendicular clay-bank, then branched Y-shape, within the hill. Life in Vicksburg during the six weeks was perhaps—but wait; here are some materials out of which to reproduce it:

Population, twenty-seven thousand soldiers and three thousand non-combatants; the city utterly cut off from the world—walled solidly in, the frontage by gunboats, the rear by soldiers and batteries; hence, no buying and selling with the outside; no passing to and fro; no godspeeding a parting guest, no welcoming a coming one; no printed acres of world-wide news to be read at breakfast, mornings—a tedious dull absence of such matter, instead; hence, also, no running to see steamboats smoking into view in the distance up or down, and plowing toward the town—for none came, the river lay vacant and undisturbed; no rush and turmoil around the railway station, no struggling over bewildered swarms of passengers by noisy mobs of hackmen—all quiet there; flour two hundred dollars a barrel, sugar thirty, corn ten dollars a bushel, bacon five dollars a pound, rum a hundred dollars a gallon, other things in proportion; consequently, no roar and racket of drays and carriages tearing along the streets; nothing for them to do, among that handful of non-combatants of exhausted means; at three o'clock in the morning, silence—silence so dead that the measured tramp of a sentinel can be heard a seemingly impossible distance; out of the hearing of this lonely sound, perhaps the stillness is absolute; all in a moment come ground-shaking thunder-crashes of artillery, the sky is cobwebbed with the crisscrossing red lines streaming from soaring bombshells, and a rain of iron fragments descends upon the city, descends upon the empty streets—streets that are not empty a moment later, but mottled with dim figures of frantic women and children scurrying from home and bed toward the cave dungeons—encouraged by the . . . grim soldiery, who shout, "Rats, to your holes!" and laugh.

The cannon-thunder rages, shells scream and crash overhead, the iron rain pours down, one hour, two hours, three, possibly six, then stops; silence follows, but the streets are still empty; the silence continues; by and by. a head projects from a cave here and there and yonder, and reconnoitres cautiously; the silence still continuing, bodies follow heads, and jaded, half-smothered creatures group themselves, stretch their cramped limbs, draw in deep draughts of the grateful fresh air, gossip with neighbors from the next cave; maybe straggle off home presently, or take a lounge again, by and by, when the war-tempest breaks forth once more. . . . . . .

Years ago I talked with a couple of the Vicksburg non-combatants—a man and his wife. . . . What the man said was to this effect:

It got to be Sunday all the time. Seven Sundays in the week—to us, anyway. We hadn't anything to do, and the time hung heavy. Seven Sundays, and all of them broken up at one time or another, in the day or in the night, by a few hours of the awful storm of fire and thunder and iron. At first we used to shin for the holes a good deal faster than we did afterward. The first time I forgot the children, and Maris fetched them both along. When she was all safe in the cave she fainted. Two or three weeks afterward, when she was running for the holes, one morning, through a shell-shower, a big shell burst near her and covered her all over with dirt, and a piece of iron carried away her game-bag of false hair from the back of her head. Well, she stopped to get that game-bag before she shoved along again! Was getting used to things already, you see. We all got so that we could tell a good deal about shells; and after that we didn't always go under shelter if it was a light shower. Us men would loaf around and talk; and a man would say, "There she goes!" and name the kind of shell it was from the sound of it. If a shell was bursting close over us, we stopped talking and stood still; uncomfortable, yes, but it wasn't safe to move. When it let go, we went on talking again, if nobody was hurt—maybe saying, "That was a ripper!" or some such commonplace comment before we resumed. . . . Often and often I saw gangs of ladies promenading the streets, looking as cheerful as you please, and keeping an eye canted up watching the shells; and I've seen them stop still when they were uncertain about what a shell was going to do, and wait and make certain; and after that they s'antered along again, or lit out for shelter, according to the verdict. Streets in some towns have a litter of pieces of paper, and odds and ends of one sort or another lying around. Ours hadn't; they had iron litter. . . . No glass left; glass couldn't stand such a bombardment; it was all shivered out. Windows of the houses vacant—looked like eyeholes in a skull. *Whole* panes were as scarce as news. . . .

Sometimes the caves were desperately crowded, and always hot and close. Sometimes a cave had twenty or twenty-five people packed into it; no turning-room for anybody; air so foul, sometimes, you couldn't have made a candle burn in it. A child was born in one of those caves one night. Think of that; why, it was like having it born in a trunk.

The treatment given prisoners of war was a subject of items in newspapers of both North and South. Actually neither North nor South should be held guilty of atrocities. They were not prepared to house and feed the thousands of soldiers whom they were required to hold as prisoners. In 1862 an agreement for the exchange of prisoners shortened the detention and lightened the burdens of both governments. Prisoners taken by either side were paroled and sent to their own army to be detained until their exchange could be arranged. When the Union discarded that plan in 1863 the number of prisoners became so large that the problem became almost insurmountable.

A newspaper, the *Daily Richmond Examiner,* June 24, 1863, gave the following description of a Yankee prison.

A member of General Bragg's army gives the Memphis *Appeal* some account of his experience in the Federal prison at Alton, Illinois. . . .

The Alton penitentiary was, some three or four years ago, condemned by the State authorities as totally unfit for criminals even. Yet thirteen hundred officers and privates, two hundred of which had the small pox, were confined in the basement, five feet below the ground, almost shut off from daylight, sunshine and air—stone floor covered with water, trickling from the walls on either side, and mid winter as it was, the only provisions for a fire was a small stove to eight men. The berths were after the fashion of horse stalls, one above the other, with a passage so narrow as barely to admit of one person passing a time, and soon there was an average of more than every other berth occupied by some unfortunate Confederate with small pox, and as soon as they died others from St. Louis prisons supplied their places. During January the average of deaths reached for a time eight, and eventually thirteen per day; and in February the mortality became so great, and burying Confederates became such a tax to the Government, and so lucrative to the undertaker, that the commander of the prison advertised in one of the Alton papers: "Proposals for burying the Confederates will be received and let to the lowest bidder." This same enterprising undertaker was detected by one of our number, who suspected him, and privately marked one of the coffins, in the work of "Yankee swindling," by closing the coffins in the "dead room" and on arriving at the cemetery would dump the corpse in the grave and return the same coffin for another subject until nine had been thus buried, and he of course receiving pay for nine coffins, when he had really supplied but one.

The quality of rations supplied was altogether unfit for the sick. Well men (I've seen it) would go to the sweepings of the prison dining room and gather up scraps of bread and meat and eat them with perfect relish; and of the sick, those of them that were fortunate enough to recover, were supplied by their fellow prisoners with rats which they killed and prepared with their own hands.

*   *   *

Bad as were the conditions at this Alton prison, they could not compare with the horrors of some of the prisons in the last two years of the war. Union strategy was to refuse to exchange prisoners, thus depriving the Confederate Army of badly needed soldiers. Lack of medicine, food, and shelter for the many thousands of prisoners taken by the Confederates forced them to resort to the use of prison pens such as the one at Andersonville, Georgia. John W. Urban, a soldier in the Union Army and three times a prisoner of war, described conditions at Anderson-ville in his *Battle Field and Prison Pen,* Hubbard Brothers, Philadelphia, 1882, pp. 309-436, *passim.*

We arrived at Andersonville at two o'clock P.M., June 16th, and as the train stopped we looked around anxiously to see what kind of a place it was. We were somewhat surprised to find that it was only a small way station, with few houses in sight. Directly after our arrival we were ordered to get out of the cars and form in line for the purpose of marching to the prison, which was about one mile from the station. It was raining very fast at the time, and as we were in a country almost entirely covered with timber, we expected to find some kind of shelter in our new prison; but as we marched from the station, and caught a sight of the prison, our hearts sank within us, for inside of the large inclosure we saw a living mass of prisoners, the most of them being wholly without shelter, standing around in the rain and mud, presenting an appearance no words can describe. It was so crowded that we could not at first believe it possible for them to put all of us into the inclosure. As we came near the gate we noticed that a regiment of rebel soldiers were drawn up in a line to the right of us, and were kept in that position until we were inside the prison. . . . The entire prison was inclosed with a high stockade made of pine logs. These logs were about sixteen feet long, and were put into the ground about four feet, thus making a fence twelve feet high. As some of the prisoners succeeded in tunneling out, the rebels built a second stock-ade a short distance from the first, and the intervening space they kept lit up during the night with large fires, to prevent the prisoners who might succeed in getting out from escaping. Sentinel boxes were built on top of the stockade; these were about fifty feet apart, and were reached by steps from the ground on the outside. On the inside, about thirty or thirty-five feet from the stockade, was a small railing, fastened on stakes about two feet high. This was called the "Dead Line," and woe to the poor prisoner, whether ignorant of its terrible meaning or not, who crossed, or even reached under it, for instant death was sure.

The rebels, in building this terrible prison, cut down all the trees in the inside with the exception of two, which stood in the northeast corner of the prison, and in such a position that the shade fell on the *outside* of the inclosure. The earth, with the exception of the swamp, was of hard, red clay, with a slight covering of soil almost as light as sand. Lying and starving on this unmerciful, unyielding earth dying from exposure, hunger and thirst; the sun beating on them until in many cases the hands and neck were burned to blisters—what would not these suffering and dying men have given for the tempering shade of the trees, which the rebels so cruelly and ruthlessly cut away? . . .

Inside of this enclosure, thirteen thousand two hundred and fifty-three Union soldiers perished, averaging more than one thousand deaths every month that the prison existed. . . . Some of . . . [the men] were almost naked, and were all covered with dirt and vermin, presenting an appearance that made our hearts sink within us as we looked upon them; and the terrible thought would continually force itself into my mind, How can I ever expect to live in this horrible place. . . .

The rain had been pouring down in torrents, and as it had been raining several days before our arrival, the mud was almost ankle deep, and we could not even see a place to sit down without getting right into it. . . . One of my comrades, with a groan of despair, exclaimed, "My God, can this be hell?"

✓   ✓   ✓

Conditions were equally bad in a prison camp kept by the Union Army at Point Lookout in Virginia, as described by Randolph Abbott Shotwell, *The Papers of Randolph Abbott Shotwell*, edited by J. G. De Roulhac Hamilton, North Carolina Department of Archives and History, Raleigh, 1931, Vol. II, pp. 118-123, 126. Shotwell was detained in this camp in the spring of 1864.

Point Lookout is the southernmost tip of a sandy peninsula pointing like a finger down between the bay and the river, which is itself an inland sea, seven miles in width for a long distance above the Point.

The peninsula is less than half a mile in width, low, level, and covered with light white sand which the slightest breeze stirs into dense clouds, than which nothing could be more distressing to man or beast.

Northward from the Point is a vast stretch of wooded wilderness; abounding in swamps, and traversed by a narrow road, without a traveller, or a habitation for miles on miles. The peculiarly isolated and uncomfortable features of the Point recommend it to the Federals as a Prison Camp; while its location midway between Fortress Monroe and both Baltimore and Washington make it convenient as a supply station for military and naval stores, forage, coal, etc.

Accordingly about a mile of the sandy tongue was seized, and cut off from the interior by a high stockade of logs running across from river to bay, and leaving a deep ditch cut just outside. Sentries were posted along this fence day and night, altho there was never any real necessity therefor.

At the southern end of the Point was a lighthouse tower, half a dozen wharves; a double row of frame hospitals, officers' barracks, etc.; and a large colony of negro women and children stolen from Southern plantations and held here at government expense; virtually prisoners, as they could not escape from the limits of the Point. But the striking feature of the place has yet to be mentioned. The newcomer, looking up the stretch of sandy beach, saw two large parallelograms; one comprising perhaps 4 acres; the other somewhat larger; both enclosed by a high plank fence, full thirty feet above the surface, surmounted by a narrow platform or walkway, upon which a number of negroes in Yankee uniform could be seen lazily promenading to and fro.

These were the *"Rebel Prison Pens!"* The smaller known as the "Officers' Pen," the other, the "Privates' Pen." Both were filled to overflowing and a continual hum of voices rose from within as if they were human bee hives. Nearly ten thousand privates occupied the larger stockade, and perhaps eight hundred officers the smaller.

Cruelty's own self must have melted at the spectacle of the half suffocated, half dead Southerners disembarking after a day and a night of horror in the "Black Hole" of the vessel. All were weary, begrimed, sleepy and miserable beyond description; while none of us had eaten anything for nearly forty-eight hours.

The officers were marched through the sand to Provost Marshal Brady's office, where every prisoner was forced to surrender every article of value or interest that he possessed, no matter how harmless or how useful. The robberies embraced all money, watches, rings, keepsakes, lockets, gold pencils, knives, trinkets, etc.; everything in short that cupidity could covet, or petty malice delight in depriving us of the enjoyment of using. It is scarcely necessary to say that these articles were never returned. There may have been exceptional cases of officers of high rank, who by means of influential Northern friends, or "old army" acquaintances were enabled to recover their watches, money, etc., but the vast majority of the prisoners never again laid eyes upon their property.

And now we were marched into the four-acre pen, and told to "Scratch into some hole or other!"—meaning, to find shelter as best we could.

The lower portion of the Pen was occupied by rows of small tents or pretense of tents, they being a lot of condemned canvas, ruined by salt water and mildewed so that they afforded less protection than the same number of fly-nets.

Yet, even of these there were so few that from seven to ten men were huddled in each tent like a sweltering nest of pigs. It would have been better to have allowed us, like the Yankee prisoners at Andersonville to construct small shelters of our own.

In rainy weather the rotten canvas served to gather and pour down upon us steady streams of water, more annoying than the universal shower; while within an hour after the rain ceased, great clouds of dry sand began their tireless whirling, like another simoon amid the great Sahara. No pen nor tongue can portray the plague of this fine sand eternally filling the air, inflaming the eyes, penetrating the hair, the beard, the ears, nose and clothing; covering blankets, towels, paper, etc. with a thick coat of grit within an hour's time after brushing them off; and filtering through the canvas so that at morn each sleeper seems peppered with white powder.

It was of course out of the question to keep clean; particularly as there were neither tubs nor boilers for washing, and not enough water for drinking purposes. Moreover, few of the prisoners had any clothing, except that upon their persons when captured, hence were obliged to remain partially nude while cleansing, or trying to cleanse their soiled garments.

I made a practice of arising at daybreak to secure a canteen of water, for my morning ablutions, ere the continual pumping converted it into red paste.

And now I must speak of the fearful effects of this much coveted fluid. Horrified at seeing a cart filled with dead bodies, I enquired, what had occasioned this surprising mortality. *"Oh, it is the water!"* was the reply— *"that well is rank poison! It is killing us all by inches."*

The well had been dug deep enough to reach a substratum of reddish earth, with a vein of mineral, either iron or copper or both. The water left a reddish sediment; had a brackish, ironish taste; and was sufficiently powerful in coloring matter to color an egg a bright red within an hour! Far more fearful proof of its fatal potency was the aspect of the human corpses of those who had used it, which became *hideously black* simultaneously with death! Almost as apparent was the effect of the deadly draught upon the living. Every cupful acted as a powerful diuretic, reducing hale hearty men to staggering weakness, and causing the weak and sickly to look like skeletons.

Hundreds of poor fellows, suffering from wounds, or debilitated by fevers and lack of proper food, succumbed in a few days. The camp was full of haggard, half-clad men, whose sunken eyes, and tottering gait bespoke them already doomed to the "Death Cart." The food allowed the prisoners consisted of a cup of rice-water (called soup) and three crackers at 9:00 a.m.; and the same, with a morsel of rancid bacon at 3:00 p.m.

It was just sufficient to maintain life; yet leaving everyone in a continual state of yearning hunger. True, the soup was always luke-warm, and garnished with white worms half an inch long; while the food was gritty with sand and dirt. Hunger, however, can overlook trifles of taste, and during the long summer days when the system appeared about to collapse from gnawing emptiness, men could be seen gazing wolfishly at their own old shoes.

It is perhaps needless to say that our captors took measures to draw profit from the famishing condition of the prisoners. Many of them had Northern relations and friends who hastened to supply them with money, clothes, and boxes of provisions. A few boxes were allowed to come in, from time to time, to encourage the prisoners to send for more; but everything of value or luxury was stolen from them, and the odds were as three to five that the box would never be heard from, notwithstanding that the express companies reported its delivery at the prison door.

One scheme called the "Wholesale Steal" was to make proclamation that all boxes would be admitted without stoppage. Instantly each starving prisoner began to ransack his memory for the name of some one to whom he could apply for food and clothes. Many of the Southerners had sisters or brothers, or old mercantile customers at the North; hence were quickly furnished with what they asked. Nay—the articles were started, and duly arrived at the prison; *but never reached the prisoner.*

As soon as a large number of boxes came to hand, a fresh proclamation was issued confiscating the *whole* lot. Correspondence was also shut off for a time so that the prisoners could not warn their friends to withhold their kindness; consequently the official thieves revelled for weeks upon the food sent to the poor starving wretches who were being hauled out daily by cart loads. . . . .

There was not a tree upon the Point, or any green thing to lessen the glare of the July sun on the hot sand and glassy waters; the sieve-like tents afforded no shelter; the high fence cut off every whiff of breeze, and the "Pen" seemed like the bottom of a great gravepit glowing at a white heat!

✓ ✓ ✓

Lincoln's proclamation of April 19, 1861, created a blockade of the ports of the Southern states. By subsequent proclamations the blockade was extended. Vessels and cargoes belonging to citizens of the seceded states found at sea or in a port of the United States were to be confiscated. In defiance of this blockade a class of professional blockade runners developed. The Confederate Government regulated blockade-running by specifying that vessels were to carry first, arms and ammunition; second, clothing; third, drugs and chemicals which were sorely needed. Materials thus imported that were not taken by the government were auctioned to dealers from all over the Confederacy. "A Visit to the Cities and Camps of the Confederate States, 1863-64," *Blackwood's Edinburgh Magazine,* Vol. 97, 1865, p. 153, carried the following description of blockade-running.

Wilmington is at present the most important port of entry in the South, and the custom-house receipts, both here and at Charleston, last year, far exceeded anything they had ever been during a similar period before the war. There were about a dozen blockade-running steamers lying at the wharves, loading cotton, and unloading all manner of stores brought from Bermuda and Nassau. Besides cotton, the chief exports are tobacco and rosin. One great treat we had here was to find English newspapers in abundance, and of dates little more than a month old.

A day or two after our arrival we went down to Fort Fisher, at the mouth of the Cape Fear river, the Commandant, Colonel Lamb, taking us down in his boat. Going down we met three steamers coming up the river, having successfully run the blockade, the Hansa, the Lucy, and the Bendigo. We exchanged cheers as they passed us; but the great sight is when they come up to the wharves. They all dress up with flags as if for a victory; and as the ships which belong to the same company do the same, the spectacle is very gay. The cheering, too, is vociferous, and all those who have any interest in the vessel must, no doubt, feel extremely comfortable, as every successful trip brings an enormous profit. The moon is the blockade-runner's greatest enemy; but these vessels to-day had come in, notwithstanding the moon, which did not set till three o'clock in the morning. . . .

In the far distance we could see two Federal men-of-war keeping up a nominal blockade. They always remain at a respectful distance, for if they come within three or four miles, Colonel Lamb is apt to make targets of them, and his gun practice is very accurate. They seldom catch a blockade-runner going in or out, but if on the high seas they can capture a ship laden with suspicious cargo, they condemn her as a prize without more ado, and as the vessels all sail under the supposed protection of the British flag, the owners never have any redress.

Sometimes a vessel gets "beached," as in a dark night it is very difficult exactly to hit the point for which they are steering. This accident happened to the Ceres, a noble double screw steamer, that was making her first voyage. The Yankees coming up in the morning, the ship had to be set on fire; her mail and a small portion of passengers' luggage was saved, but the cargo was lost. Some of the passengers had a narrow escape, the ebbing tide having carried their boat far out to sea, but eventually all got safe to land.

The Daily Richmond Examiner, June 24, 1863, carried the following item.

Some days since a blockade runner, named Edward N. Brown, took into his financial confidence a partner, loaded a vessel in Baltimore with goods for Richmond. While Brown was elsewhere his partner left with the vessel and cargo, and, rushing the goods to Richmond, sold them at an enormous sacrifice, in advance of Brown's arrival, and started off further South with the funds. On Brown's arrival, several days since, he instituted a search among the auction and commission houses, and succeeded in recognizing and laying claim to a portion of his goods. As an instance of the sacrifice the partner had made in his haste to get rid of the goods, Irish linen, that would have readily commanded six dollars per yard, was sold for seventy-five cents.

Brown, once on the track, traced his unfaithful partner to Atlanta, Georgia, where he found and laid violent hands on him and recovered eighteen hundred dollars. . . . Brown estimates the value of his goods in the Richmond market at between thirty and forty thousand dollars. . . .

On the same page the following advertisements appeared.

LARGE AND ATTRACTIVE SALE OF DRY GOODS AT AUCTION —On Wednesday, 24th instant, commencing at 10 o'clock, we will sell a large and very desirable assortment of

FRESH DRY GOODS

Many of which have been received direct from Nassau, and will be closed without reserve. . . .

Kent, Paine and Co., Auctioneers.

By Ellett, Bell & Co.—EXTENSIVE SALE OF DRY GOODS AT AUCTION.—On Tuesday, 30th June, we will sell a very large and attractive assortment of NEWLY IMPORTED DRY GOODS. . . .

The sale will commence promptly at 10 o'clock.

✓   ✓   ✓

An editorial in the same issue of the *Daily Richmond Examiner* revealed disapproval of blockade-running.

Gold is now worth seven dollars premium in Richmond, says the Columbus, Ga., *Sun,* and has been sold as high as seven and a half and eight dollars in Charleston. . . . The cause of this unparalleled premium on gold and silver is well understood. . . . The cause does not lie in the depreciation of Confederate notes; it is occasioned by the scarcity of gold and silver within the Confederate lines, and this scarcity has been occasioned by blockade-running. Confederate notes will not purchase goods at the North; they will not even pay tavern bills there; nor yet defray travelling expenses after leaving the Confederate ports. To run the blockade requires gold and silver, or cotton, or the equivalent either in "greenbacks" or in Sterling exchange. Hence, large premiums are offered for it, and every steamer going out from a "Confederate port" contributes to the comparative depreciation of our paper currency just in proportion to the amount of specie which she carries out.

Not only does this system of blockade running drain us of all our gold and silver currency, but it drains us of the great basis of our national currency also. Congress having done nothing to regulate this matter, large quantities of cotton are daily finding a foreign market. The drain may be comparatively slow but it is *constant*. There has been very little or no cotton raised in the Confederacy since the war began. Indeed, such is the state of public sentiment that he who would now raise cotton in preference to provision crops, must first make up his mind to receive the almost universal execrations of his fellow citizens. Whilst, therefore, our cotton is constantly finding its way out, there is none coming in to supply the future demand. More cotton has left the port of Charleston, alone, for foreign markets, within the last four months, than has been raised in the whole Confederacy during the last two years. . . .

What is the necessity for such trade? What good is to result from it?

The Confederate Army of Tennessee was soon to face a Northern army led by General William Tecumseh Sherman. Sherman was one of the first advocates of total war. He knew that war was bloody, inhumane, ruthless, and that it must be fought to the uttermost. For a long time he had been dedicated to General Scott's plan of capturing the Mississippi and cutting the South lengthwise into two dissevered parts. Now he was to lead an invasion of the deeper South through Georgia, thus bisecting the South laterally as well. He planned to destroy all means of transportation, all supplies, all the war potential of the country through which he passed. His was not a mere raid but an invasion sweeping like a scythe through Georgia and up through the Carolinas and carrying in its sweep total destruction. Therefore he wrote to Lincoln in 1863:

"I would banish all minor questions, assert the broad doctrine that a nation has the right, and also the physical power to penetrate to every part of our national domain, and that we will do it—that we will remove and destroy every obstacle, if need be, take every life, every acre of land . . . that we will not cease till the end is attained. . . . The South has done her worst and now is the time for us to pile on blows thick and fast."

After the defeat of Bragg at Lookout Mountain and Missionary Ridge the Confederate Army now commanded by General Joseph E. Johnston was forced to retreat into northern Georgia, where Sherman, Commander of the Union forces of the Military Division of this Mississippi pursued him to Atlanta. Johnston's retreating tactics were condemned by the people of Georgia and he was replaced by General John B. Hood. After fierce fighting around Atlanta, Hood evacuated the city and marched into Tennessee. Sherman, instead of pursuing Hood, marched eastward through Georgia. By piecing together some of the Confederate correspondence and portions from the reports of General Sherman and Captain Poe, Chief Engineer, of the Military Division of the Mississippi we have the following narrative of the Union troops "Marching through Georgia." The following are quoted from the War of the Rebellion *Official Records,* Government

Printing Office, Washington, 1890-1901, 70 volumes in 128, Series I, Vol. XLIV, pp. 858-967, *passim*.

Griffin, November 15, 1864.

General S. Cooper:

The enemy has burned Atlanta and destroyed railroad to Allatoona, burning bridge over Chattahoochee. He moved out of Atlanta with very large force in direction of Macon by Jonesborough and McDonough. We have no force to hinder him and must fall back to Macon, where re-en-forcements should be sent at once to meet him successfully.

HOWELL COBB,
Major-General, Commanding.

• •

LOVEJOY'S, [*November*] *16, 1864—11 a.m.*
(Via Barnesville)

General BRAGG:

Scouts from enemy's rear report that Sherman left Atlanta yesterday morning with Fifteenth, Seventeenth, Twentieth Corps in two columns—one on Jonesborough, and one on the McDonough road; cavalry on his flanks. Many houses been burned in Rome, Marietta, and Atlanta, and rail-road bridge over Chattahoocheee Destroyed by the enemy. Enemy advancing this morning.

Jos. Wheeler,
Major-General.

• •

Macon, Georgia, [November 17,] 1864

President DAVIS,
Richmond, Va.:

Sherman's move upon this place is formidable, and the most dangerous of the war. His policy is universal destruction. If by concentration of all forces that can be brought together Sherman's army could be crushed, he having cut loose from his communications, it would be the greatest result of the war. The only mode I see for making defense and destroying Sherman is to order garrisons of Charleston, Savannah, and Wilmington here at once. If not beaten here he will either march to Charleston or Savannah.

HOWELL COBB
Major-General

• •

Macon, *Thursday Morning, November 17, 1864.*
[Governor J. E. BROWN:]

DEAR GOVERNOR: Things are very bad here. Sherman in person is leading, say 30,000 men against us. We are retreating as rapidly as possible, consistent with good order and efficiency. The militia are retreating in admirable order and discipline, as General Cobb reports. I will meet them between this and Forsyth this evening. I believe the Legislature will grant you large and liberal powers. Tell them the country is in danger. Let all her sons come to her rescue.

Yours Faithfully.
R. TOOMBS

. . . .

RICHMOND, VA., *November 18, 1864.*
General H. COBB,
Macon, Georgia.:
In addition to the troops of a kinds you should endeavor to get out every man who can render any service, even for a short period, and employ negroes in obstructing roads, by every practicable means. Colonel Rains, at Augusta, can furnish you with shells prepared to explode by pressure, and these will be effective to check an advance. General Hardee has, I hope, brought some re-enforcements, and General Taylor will probably join you with some further aid. You have a difficult task, but will realize the necessity for the greatest exertion.

JEFFN. DAVIS.

. . . .

RICHMOND, *November 18, 1864.*
TO THE PEOPLE OF GEORGIA:
You have now the best opportunity ever presented to destroy the enemy. Put everything at the disposal of our generals; remove all provisions from the path of the invader, and put all obstructions in his path. Every citizen with his gun, and every negro with his spade and axe, can do the work of a soldier. You can destroy the enemy by retarding his march. Georgians, be firm! Act promptly, and fear not!

B. H. HILL,
Senator.

. . . .

CORINTH, *November 18, 1864.*
TO THE PEOPLE OF GEORGIA:
Arise for the defense of your native soil! Rally round your patriotic Governor and gallant soldiers! Obstruct and destroy all roads in Sherman's front, flank, and rear, and his army will soon starve in your midst! Be confident and resolute! Trust in an overruling Providence, and success will crown your efforts. I hasten to join you in defense of your homes and firesides.

G. T. BEAUREGARD.

. . . .

MACON, *November 19, 1864.*

Hon. JAMES A. SEDDON,
   Secretary of War:
   There is a great scarcity of arms in Georgia and South Carolina to meet
the enemy. It is necessary to have additional arms to put into the hands of
the levy en masse ordered by the Legislature of Georgia, and the reserve
militia of South Carolina now called out by Governor Bonham. Please have
all spare arms sent to Charleston, S.C., subject to my orders.

W. J. HARDEE,
Lieutenant-General.

. . . .

AUGUSTA, *November, 19, 1864-11 a.m.*

General S. COOPER:
   Enemy advancing toward Macon; also a strong column of all arms along
the railroad from Atlanta to Augusta; where at Social Circle yesterday.
General Hardee passed last evening on his way to Macon.

B. D. FRY
Brigadier-General

. . . .

AUGUSTA, *November 25, 1864*

Col JOHN B. SALE,
   Military Secretary, Richmond:
   Arrived late last night, and take command this morning. We learn from
General Wayne, who holds the Oconee railroad bridge, that the enemy has
not crossed the river in any force. He has concentrated at Milledgeville, and
seems to be tending south. Our Cavalry, under Wheeler, is in his front, and
has been ordered to destroy every vestige of subsistence and forage as it
retires, to hand upon his flanks, and retard his progress by every possible
means. . . .

BRAXTON BRAGG,
General.

[Later the same day]
   The enemy has crossed the Oconee; was met this evening in force at
Buffalo Creek, near Sandersville. His movements from that point will
determine whether he designs attacking here or on Savannah.

BRAXTON BRAGG

. . . .

AUGUSTA, *November 26, 1864.*

Col. JOHN B. SALE,
   Military Secretary, Richmond:
   So far we have failed to open communication with Macon, the enemy

having interposed his whole force between us—seems to have neglected that point . . . No offensive movement can be undertaken, but a temporary defense of our scattered posts. If no more means can be had our only policy is to make sacrifices and concentrate. The country is being utterly devastated wherever the enemy move.

BRAXTON BRAGG.

✓   ✓   ✓

Once the Confederate generals had confirmed their belief that Savannah was Sherman's destination they began concentrating their forces in that area. Messages sent on December 2 illustrate this movement.

GRAHAMVILLE, December 2, 1864.

General SAMUEL JONES:
    Troops coming from Augusta must not stop in Charleston, but be hurried forward to Savannah. I leave for Savannah this afternoon.

W. J. HARDEE,
Lieutenant-General

. . . .

AUGUSTA, December 2, 1864

General SAMUEL JONES:
    Thirteen hundred South Carolina militia, under Colonel De Saussure, will leave here for Savannah at 6 P.M. Provide transportation to Savannah on their arrival. . . .

M. B. McMicken,
Lieutenant-Colonel and Chief Quartermaster

✓   ✓   ✓

The following circular issued by Major-General Wheeler of the Confederate Cavalry indicates that all of the devastation suffered in Georgia was not caused by the United States troops.

IN THE FIELD, December 10, 1864.

CIRCULAR.
    Soldiers! While you have been engaged gallantly fighting the enemy a band of thieves and stragglers have spread over the country robbing and insulting the wives and children of your brother soldiers who are opposing the invaders upon other fields. These soldiers expect protection from you, and I appeal to every officer and soldier of this command to assist in arresting and bringing to justice these depredators, who claim to belong to the command, and by their conduct are bringing disgrace upon you and distress upon citizens, the families of comrades in arms.

JOS. WHEELER,
Major-General.

✔   ✔   ✔

The preceding messages illustrate the inability of the Confederate army to defend Georgia and the bewilderment that its officers experienced when Sherman began his march. They could not determine whether he planned to attack Macon, Augusta, Savannah, or Charleston. Sherman placed his army between Macon and Augusta to divide his enemy's forces in order to defend all four of the above-named cities. The march to the sea was made in four columns, sometimes at a distance of fifteen or twenty miles from each other, but all traveling in the general direction of Savannah.

The railroads which ran into Atlanta and all of the other railroads in Central Georgia were destroyed. Chief Engineer Poe's account of the treatment given Atlanta is an example of this policy. It is quoted from the *Official Records,* Series I, Vol. XLIV, p. 56.

General Sherman directed me to destroy with engineer troops all railroads and property belonging thereto; all storehouses, machine shops, mills, factories, &c., within the lines of the enemy's defenses at Atlanta. The work of destruction was thoroughly done, under my personal supervision, by the Michigan Engineers and Missouri Engineers. About ten miles of track were destroyed by burning the wood-work and twisting each rail, the latter operation being performed by a very simple machine designed by myself. The designated buildings were first burned and the walls afterwards razed to the ground. For military purposes the city of Atlanta has ceased to exist, there being no railroad either to or from it.

✔   ✔   ✔

On December 17 General Sherman sent to General Hardee in Savannah, by flag of truce, a formal demand for the surrender of the place; General Hardee refused and Sherman prepared for assault, but during the night of December 20 the Confederates evacuated Savannah to save their men from capture. The following paragraphs from Sherman's report to General Grant, Commander of the Armies of the United States, complete our picture of the march through Georgia. The report is from the *Official Records,* Series I, Vol. XLIV, pp. 12-13.

I was very much disappointed that Hardee had escaped with his garrison, and had to content myself with the material fruits of victory without the cost of life which would have attended a general assault. The substantial results will be more clearly set forth in the tabular statements of heavy ordnance and other public property acquired. And it will suffice here to state that the important city of Savannah, with its valuable harbor and river, was the chief object of the campaign. With it we acquire all the forts and heavy ordnance in its vicinity, with large stores of ammunition, shot and shells, cotton, rice, and other valuable products of the country. We also gain locomotives and cars, which, though of little use to us in the present condition of the railroads, are a serious loss to the enemy; as well as four steam-boats gained, and the loss to the enemy of the iron-clad Savannah, one ram, and three transports, blown up or burned by them the night before.

Formal demand having been made for the surrender, and having been refused, I contend that everything within the line of intrenchments belongs to the United States, and I shall not hesitate to use it, if necessary, for public purposes. But inasmuch as the inhabitants generally have manifested a friendly disposition, I shall disturb them as little as possible consistently with the military rights of present and future military commanders, without remitting in the least our just rights as captors. . . .

Our base of supplies will be established in Savannah as soon as the very difficult obstructions placed in the river can be partially removed. These obstructions at present offer a very serious impediment to the commerce of Savannah, consisting of crib-work of logs and timber heavily bolted together, and filled with the cobble stones which formerly paved the streets of Savannah. All the channels below the city were found more or less filled with torpedoes, which have been removed by order of Admiral Dahlgren. So that Savannah already fulfills the important part it was designed in our plans for the future. . . .

[We have broken up] the Georgia State Railroad . . . from Fairburn Station to Madison and the Oconee, and the Central Railroad, from Gordon clear to Savannah, with numerous breaks on the latter road from Gordon to Eatonton and from Millen to Augusta, and the Savannah Gulf Railroad. We have also consumed the corn and fodder in the region of country thirty miles on either side of a line from Atlanta to Savannah, as also the sweet potatoes, cattle, hogs, sheep and poultry, and have carried away more than 10,000 horses and mules, as well as a countless number of slaves. I estimate the damage done to the State of Georgia and its military resources at $100,000,000; at least $20,000,000 of which has inured to our advantage, and the remainder is simple waste and destruction. This may seem a hard species of warfare, but it brings the sad realities of war home to those who have been directly or indirectly instrumental in involving us in its attendant calamities.

✗   ✗   ✗

Savannah having been occupied, Sherman advanced through South Carolina carrying even greater destruction than in Georgia. Many towns were burned, including Columbia, the capital. Authorities disagreed about who started the blaze, Sherman claiming that retreating Confederates were responsible. Two points of view concerning the treatment of the city are the subjects of the two following letters. They are quoted from the *Official Records,* Series I, Vol. XLVII, pp. 457, 596-7.

Columbia, S.C., February 17, 1865.

Maj. MAX. WOODHULL,
   Assistant Adjutant-General, Fifteenth Army Corps:

MAJOR: I respectfully report that at 3 o'clock this morning I began crossing the Third Brigade of my division (Colonel Stone commanding)

over the Broad River, using three pontoon boats for the purpose. The process was so difficult that it was 7 o'clock before the brigade reached the opposite shore. Passing through the swamps, with skirmishers well thrown
forward, the brigade soon reached the high land, and at once took position
on a range of hills looking toward the city. The opposition was but slight.
The city soon surrendering, Colonel Stone moved forward and occupied
the place, the remainder of my division following as soon as the pontoon
bridge was laid. . . . The troops first entering Columbia were met on the
roadside by citizens of every grade, who most unwisely furnished them with
great quantities of intoxicating liquors, bringing it out in buckets, cups,
and vessels of all description. As a result the confusion prevailing throughout the town was increased tenfold, and at night, in obedience to the direction of the corps commander, the brigade on duty as guards in the town
was relieved by the First Brigade, commanded by Brevet Brigadier-General
Woods, and every practicable measure was promptly adopted to prevent the
spreading of the conflagration that was rapidly extending over the entire
town and to arrest the countless villains of every command that were roam-
ing over the streets. As strong patrols as could be furnished by the brigade
were distributed throughout the town. . . .

I am, major, very respectfully, your obedient servant,

C. R. WOODS,
Brevet Major-General.

HEADQUARTERS,
In the Field, February 27, 1865.

Maj. Gen. W. T. SHERMAN, U.S. Army:

GENERAL: Your communication of the 24th instant reached me to-day.
In it you state that it has been officially reported that your foraging parties
are "murdered" after capture. You go on to say that you have "ordered a
similar number of prisoners in our hands to be disposed of in like manner;"
that is to say, you have ordered a number of Confederate soldiers to be
"murdered." You characterize your order in proper terms, for the public
voice, even in your own country, where it seldom dares to express itself in
vindication of truth, honor, or justice, will surely agree with you in pronouncing you guilty of murder if your order is carried out. Before dismiss-
ing this portion of your letter, I beg to assure you that for every soldier of
mine "murdered" by you, I shall have executed at once two of yours, giving
in all cases preference to any officers who may be in my hands.

In reference to the statement you make regarding the death of your
foragers, I have only to say that I know nothing of it; that no orders given
by me authorize the killing of prisoners after capture, and that I do not
believe my men killed any of yours, except under circumstances in which
it was perfectly legitimate and proper that they should kill them. It is a
part of the system of the thieves whom you designate as your foragers to

fire the dwellings of those citizens whom they have robbed. To check this inhuman system, which is justly execrated by every civilized nation, I have directed my men to shoot down all of your men who are caught burning houses. This order shall remain in force so long as you disgrace the profession of arms by allowing your men to destroy private dwellings. . . .

You are particular in defining and claiming "war rights." May I ask if you enumerate among these the right to fire upon a defenseless city without notice; to burn that city to the ground after it had been surrendered by the inhabitants who claimed, though in vain, that protection which is always accorded in civilized warfare to non-combatants; to fire the dwelling houses of citizens after robbing them; and to perpetrate even darker crimes than these crimes too black to be mentioned?

You have permitted, if you have not ordered, the commission of these offenses against humanity and the rules of war; you fired into the city of Columbia without a word of warning; after its surrender by the mayor, who demanded protection to private property, you laid the whole city in ashes, leaving amidst its ruins thousands of old men and helpless women and children, who are likely to perish of starvation and exposure. Your line of march can be traced by the lurid light of burning houses, and in more than one household there is now an agony far more bitter than that of death. The Indian scalped his victim regardless of age or sex, but with all his barbarity he always respected the persons of his female captives. Your soldiers, more savage than the Indian, insult those whose natural protectors are absent.

In conclusion, I have only to request that whenever you have any of my men "murdered" or "disposed of," for the terms appear to be synonymous with you, you will let me hear of it, that I may know what action to take in the matter. In the meantime I shall hold fifty-six of your men as hostages for those whom you have ordered to be executed.

I am yours, &c.,

WADE HAMPTON
Lieutenant-General

✓   ✓   ✓

Desertion from the Confederate army became common as the morale of the Southern people fell. In February, 1865, General Robert E. Lee wrote the following letter to Governor Zebulon Vance of North Carolina. It is quoted from the *Official Records*, Series I, Vol. XLVII, pp. 1270-71:

GOVERNOR: The state of despondency that now prevails among our people is producing a bad effect upon the troops. Desertions are becoming very frequent and there is good reason to believe that they are occasioned to a considerable extent by letters written to the soldiers by their friends at home. In the last two weeks several hundred have deserted from Hill's corps, and as the division from which the greatest numbers of desertions have taken place are composed chiefly of troops from North Carolina they furnish a corresponding proportion of deserters. I think some good can be accomplished by the efforts of influential citizens to change public sentiment and cheer the spirits of the people. It has been discovered that despondent persons represent to their friends in the army that our cause is hopeless, and that they had better provide for themselves. They state that the number of deserters is so large in the several counties that there is no danger to be apprehended from the home guards. The deserters generally take their arms with them. The greater number are from regiments from the western part of the State. So far as the despondency of the people occasions this sad condition of affairs, I know of no other means of removing it than by the counsel and exhortation of prominent citizens. . . . Trusting that you will do all in your power to help us in this great emergency,

I remain, very respectfully, your obedient servant,

R. E. LEE,
General

✓   ✓   ✓

Ten days before General Lee wrote the above letter Governor Vance had issued a proclamation to the people of North Carolina entreating them to rally in support of the army; in it he made the following statement concerning desertions. The proclamation is in *Official Records,* Series I, Vol. XLVII, pp. 1191-2.

All things may be supplied if we were but possessed of that bold and manly spirit of resistance to tyranny of which liberty and independence are born. . . . Are our men all slain? Over 400,000 names yet stand upon the muster-rolls of the Confederacy, to say nothing of the many thousands who shirk. Where are they? Thousands upon thousands, absent without leave, are lurking in the woods and swamps of the South. Are our provisions all gone? Hundreds of thousands of bushels of grain now rot at the various depots of the South for want of transportation; and this transportation cannot be protected because these absent soldiers are not at the post of duty. Oh, my countrymen, if you would but rise to entreat, to shame, to drive them back to their country's standard! Has our territory been overrun? It has, but how much of it has been held? . . . The cities they garrison, the land their armies actually stand upon, and the waters ridden by their fleets, are all that they really hold, or ever can hold except by our ignoble consent. Let the balance of our cities go, Mobile, Charleston, Wilmington, Richmond, all, and if we are determined to be free our subjugation is quite as distant as ever. . . . Therefore, my countrymen, . . . I now appeal to you by everything held sacred among men to bear yourselves as becomes your high lineage and future hopes. I implore you to lay down all party bitterness, and to be reconciled to your neighbor for the sake of your country; to use every possible exertion to restore absentees to the army; to divide of your abundance freely with the poor and suffering; to strengthen the arms of your rulers, and to sustain your soldiers and their generals. . . .

On March 9, 1864, Grant was made a lieutenant-general and given general command of the Union armies. He almost immediately began his war of attrition in Virginia and Sherman began his invasion of Georgia. In May, 1864, Grant moved across the Rapidan. The bloody Battle of the Wilderness followed. In spite of 18,000 casualties Grant attacked again, flanked Lee at Spottsylvania, attacked the strongly entrenched Lee at Cold Harbor and had 12,000 casualties in a very brief time. Grant swung around behind Richmond and attacked it from the rear. The Southerners massed in front of Petersburg and the long siege began. Meanwhile Sheridan's cavalry raid nearly captured Richmond as Early's cavalry raid threatened Washington. Grant detached Sheridan to destroy Early and devastate the Shenandoah Valley. With Lee contained and faced by vastly superior forces, with Sherman sweeping up from the South, the end was certain. On April 2, 1865, Lee escaped from Petersburg with most of his artillery and sought to retreat via Lynchburg to join Johnston in North Carolina. Grant cut off the escape, trapped Lee's army, and on April 9, Lee surrendered to Grant at Appomattox Courthouse.

The following narrative is W. J. Holdsclaw's account of the trip from Petersburg to Appomattox with the wagon train. It is an appendix in *A True History of Company I, 49th Regiment, North Carolina Troops, in the Great Civil War, Between the North and the South,* by W. A. Day, a member of Company I, printed at Enterprise Job Office, Newton, North Carolina, 1893.

I had been on detail with the wagon train for some time and when we left Petersburg we moved out to some old winter quarters about ten miles from the city where we remained until about the 3rd of April, 1865. We then broke up camp and moved to the South Side railroad. The next morning the wagon train from Petersburg arrived. We fell in with it and moved towards the Appomattox river. The roads were very muddy and the wagons heavily loaded. Before reaching the river we had a creek to cross, there being but one ford, the wagons kept stalling in the creek, so we did not travel more than three miles the whole night. We crossed the river on a bridge about sun up, and fell in with the wagon train from Richmond, which made the train about five miles long.

About twelve o'clock that day the train was cut in two by the enemy and 150 wagons cut down and burned. While our troops were fighting the enemy back from the wagons, General Lee rode up and said, "Boys stick to me a few days longer and I will send you all home." That was the last time I saw General Lee. When the train was cut in two the foremost wagons moved on up the road and the others turned and started back. The returning wagons were stopped and turned into line and all moved on to near Appomattox Court House, reaching there late in the evening. We drove into camp and took out the mules and fed them, and heard for the first time that General Lee had surrendered. The next day we moved nearer the Court-House and delivered the wagons to the Federals and remained with them all night.

The next day we were ordered to report to our commands, received our paroles and started home. I saw the place where General Lee surrendered, but the apple tree was gone; it had been cut down and every chip and twig carried away. The Federals sent a four horse wagon loaded with rations with us to go as far as Greensboro, North Carolina. Our squad was in charge of Captain J. H. Sherrill. Arriving at a fork in the road, we divided into two parts, some taking the left in the direction of Salem. We camped one night in the woods, and it rained all night. I made my bed of two rails to keep out of the water. . . .

[The next day] we traveled about a mile and stopped at a house and got a good breakfast. Harwell and I traveled on, faring very well in the way of rations until we fell in with General Johnston's men from Greensboro. The people seemed to be afraid of them, as they were in the habit of capturing horses along the road. We were locked up in a house one night by two ladies for fear we would steal their horses. The next morning they let us out and gave us a good breakfast.

🖋   🖋   🖋

W. A. Day, in *A True History of Company I, 49th Regiment, North Carolina Troops, in the Great Civil War, Between the North and the South,* Newton, North Carolina, 1893, printed at Enterprise Job Office, described the activities at Point Lookout where he was a prisoner, when Lee surrendered.

On the 10th of April, a paper was tacked on the bulletin board, announcing the surrender of General Lee. That was a day of general rejoicing among the Federal troops stationed on the Point. They fired two hundred and twenty rounds from their batteries.

On the 15th came the news of President Lincoln's assassination, and their rejoicing was then turned to sorrow. The flags were lowered to half mast, the soldiers wore badges of mourning, and all the houses were draped in black. The infantry Regiments were marched out and fired all day by platoons, and the artillery fired three days. On the 16th a cannon was fired every minute from sunrise to sunset. They were called minute guns. It was several days before everything quieted down. . . .

On the 19th the guns boomed for the surrender of General Joseph E. Johnston, but the United States authorities not being pleased with the terms agreed upon by Generals Johnston and Sherman, the surrender did not take place until the 26th of April, 1865. The last to surrender was General E. Kirby Smith in Texas, on the 26th of May, 1865.

13

Reconstruction

Words can hardly describe the social and economic situation of the South at the close of the war: the hunger of the people; the discouragement that came with the realization that for millions of people of both races a way of life had ended and a new way of life must be worked out; the destruction and devastation that had undone the efforts of generations in both cities and countryside. An English traveler, Robert Somers, observed the South in 1870. He described the ruin that had existed in Charleston, which had been bombarded from Union ships for five years. The description is from Robert Somers, *The Southern States Since the War,* Macmillan and Company, London and New York, 1871, pp. 37-38.

Never had a completer ruin fallen upon any city than fell upon Charleston. . . . Her planters were reduced from affluence to poverty—her merchants were scattered to the four winds of heaven—her shopkeepers closed their doors, or contrived to support a precarious existence on contraband of war—her young men went to die on the battlefields or in the military prisons of the North—her women and children, who could, fled to the country. The Federal Government kept Charleston under close blockade, and added to its miseries by occasional bombardments. When this process in five years had reached the last stage of exhaustion, and the military surrender gave practical effect to emancipation, the negroes in the country parts, following up the childlike instinct of former days that Charleston was the El Dorado of the world, flocked into the ruined town, and made its aspect of misery and desolation more complete. . . . The houses had not only lost all their bright paint without, but were mostly tenantless within; . . . and the demand for labour and the supply of provisions were at the lowest point. Seldom . . . has there been a more hopeless chaos out of which to construct a new order of things than Charleston presented in those days. Yet the process of amelioration has year by year been steadily going forward. . . . Some of the old planters have also survived, and are seen, though diminished in numbers and with saddened countenances, yet with the steady fire of Anglo-Saxon courage in their eyes, attending to affairs like men determined to conquer fortune even in the depths of ruin and in the brink of the grave. . . .

✓   ✓   ✓

Thousands of white people and hundreds of thousands of Negroes were destitute after the war. The Freedman's Bureau, created by Congress in March, 1865, undertook the relief of all the needy and for a time and in some areas furnished the only food and shelter available. In the following accounts the needs of both races are described. The texts are requoted from Walter Lynnwood Fleming, *Documentary History of Reconstruction*, 2 vols., Columbia University Press, New York, 1906-7. The first is quoted from *Senate Executive Document* No. 27, Congress, 1 Session, pp. 68, 73, 77. The second, from the Report of Carl Schurz to the President, is quoted from *Senate Executive Document* No. 2, 39 Congress, 1 Session, pp. 15, 31.

(1) Two months ago women and children and broken down men came thirty and forty miles to beg a little food . . .

Much destitution also exists among the families of the late rebels, for the soldiery, . . . consumed their substance when the means of the Union people were all exhausted . . . The general destitution has rendered many kindly disposed people unable to do anything for the negroes who were formerly their slaves, and who might be supposed to have some claims upon them for temporary assistance on that account, and there is much suffering among the aged and infirm, the sick and helpless, of this class of people . . . It is a common, and everyday sight in Randolph County, that of women and children, most of whom were formerly in good circumstances, begging for bread from door to door. Meat of any kind has been a stranger to many of their mouths for months. The drought cut off what little crops they hoped to save, and they must have immediate help or perish. . . .

By far the greater suffering exists among the whites. Their scanty supplies have been exhausted, and now they look to the government alone for support. Some are without homes of any description. This seems strange and almost unaccountable. Yet on one road leading to Talladega I visited four families, within fifteen minutes' ride of the town, who were living in the woods, with no shelter but pine boughs, and this in mid-winter. Captain Dean, who accompanied me, assured me that upon the other roads leading into town were other families similarly situated. These people have no homes. They were widows, with large families of small children. Other families, as their provisions fail, will wander in for supplies, and I am fearful the result will be a camp of widows and orphans. If possible, it should be prevented; and yet I saw about thirty persons for whom shelter must be provided, or death will speedily follow their present exposure and suffering. . . .

(2) When the war came to a close, the labor system of the South was already much disturbed. During the progress of military operations large numbers of slaves had left their masters and followed the columns of our armies; others had taken refuge in our camps; many thousands had enlisted in the service of the national government. Extensive settlements of negroes

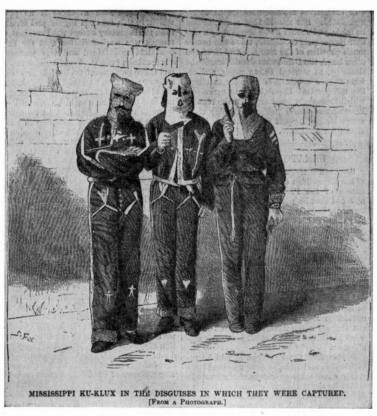

MISSISSIPPI KU-KLUX IN THE DISGUISES IN WHICH THEY WERE CAPTURED.
[FROM A PHOTOGRAPH.]

From *Harper's Weekly,* Jan. 27, 1872.

had been formed along the seaboard and the banks of the Mississippi, under the supervision of army officers and treasury agents, and the government was feeding the colored refugees, who could not be advantageously employed, in the contraband camps. Many slaves had been removed by their masters, as our armies penetrated the country, either to Texas or to the interior of Georgia and Alabama. Thus a considerable portion of the laboring force had been withdrawn from its former employments. But a majority of the slaves remained on the plantations to which they belonged, especially in those parts of the country which were not touched by the war, and where, consequently, the emancipation proclamation was not enforced by the military power. When . . . the report went . . . out that their liberation was . . . a fixed fact, large numbers of colored people left the plantations; many flocked to our military posts and camps to obtain the certainty of their freedom, and others walked away merely for the purpose of leaving the place on which they had been held in slavery, and because they could now go with impunity. Still others, and their number was by no means inconsiderable, remained with their former masters and continued their work on the field, but under new and as yet unsettled conditions, and under the agitating influence of a feeling of restlessness. . . . The country found itself thrown into that confusion which is naturally inseparable from a change so great and so sudden . . .

✓   ✓   ✓

Some of the problems of peace were faced by Frances Butler Leigh, whose work has already been quoted. The daughter of the English actress, Fanny Kemble, and her American Senator-husband, Pierce Butler, Mrs. Leigh went South, with her father the year after the end of the war. There for the next ten years she worked, aided by her father and her husband, to restore their sea island plantation. Her description of travel in the South and of the revolution which the South had undergone is from her book, *Ten Years on a Georgia Plantation After the War*, R. Bentley and Son, London, 1883, pp. 1-12, 45, 275, *passim*.

The year after the war between the North and the South, I went to the South with my father to look after our property in Georgia and see what could be done with it.

The whole country had of course undergone a complete revolution. The changes that a four years' war must bring about in any country would alone have been enough to give a different aspect to everything; but at the South, besides the changes brought about by the war, our slaves had been freed; the white population was conquered, ruined, and disheartened, unable for the moment to see anything but ruin before as well as behind, too wedded to the fancied prosperity of the old system to believe in any possible success under the new. And even had the people desired to begin at once to rebuild their fortunes, it would have been in most cases impossible, for in many families the young men had perished in the war, and the old men, if not too old for the labour and effort it required to set the machinery of peace going again, were beggared, and had not even money enough to buy food for themselves and their families, let alone their negroes, to whom they now had to pay wages as well as feed them. . . .

On March 22, 1866, my father and myself left the North. The Southern railroads were many of them destroyed for miles, not having been rebuilt since the war, and it was very questionable how we were to get as far as Savannah, a matter we did accomplish however, in a week's time . . . [We reached] Richmond at four o'clock on Sunday morning. I notice that it is a peculiarity of Southern railroads that they always either arrive, or start, at four o'clock in the morning. That day we spent quietly there, and sad enough it was, for besides all the associations with the place which crowded thick and fast upon one's memory, half the town was a heap of burnt ruins, showing how heavily the desolation of war had fallen upon it. . . . We traveled all day on the train, reaching Greensborough that night at eight o'clock. Not having been able to get any information about our route further on, we thought it best to stop where we were until we did find out. This difficulty was one that met us at every fresh stopping place along the whole journey; no one could tell us whether the road ahead were open or not, and, if open, whether there were any means of getting over it. So we crawled on, dreading at each fresh stage to find ourselves stranded in the middle of the pine woods, with no means of progressing further . . . At four in the morning . . . we started for the train, driving two miles in an old army ambulance. From that time until eight in the evening we did not leave the cars, and then left them to get into an old broken-down coach, which was originally intended to hold six people, but into which on this occasion they put nine, and thus cramped and crowded, we drove for five hours over as rough a road as can well be imagined, reaching Columbia at three o'clock A.M., by which time I could hardly move. Our next train started at six, but I was so stiff and exhausted that I begged my father to wait over one day to rest, to which he consented. At this place we struck General Sherman's track, and here the ruin and desolation was complete. Hardly any of the town remained; street after street was merely one long line of blackened ruins, which showed from their size and beautifully laid out gardens, how handsome some of the houses had been. It was too horrible!

On Thursday, at six A.M., we again set off, going about thirty miles in a cattle van which brought us to the Columbia River, the bridge over which Sherman had destroyed. This we crossed on a pontoon bridge, after which we walked a mile, sat two hours in the woods, and were then picked up by a rickety old car which was backed down to where we were, and where the rails began again, at the rate of five miles an hour, we travelled until four in the afternoon, when we were again deposited in the woods, the line this time being torn up in front of us. Here, after another wait, we were packed into a rough army waggon, with loose boards put across for seats, and in which we were jolted and banged about over a road composed entirely of ruts and roots for four more hours, until I thought I should not have a whole bone left in my body. . . .

Between nine and ten in the evening we arrived at a log cabin, where, until three A.M. we sat on the floor round a huge wood fire. The train then arrived and we started again, and did not stop for twenty-four hours; at least, when I say I did not stop, I mean, did not leave the cars, for we really seemed to do little else but stop every few minutes. This brought us, at three A.M., to Augusta, where we were allowed to go to bed for three hours, starting again at six and travelling all day, until at seven in the evening we at last reached Savannah. Fortunately we started from the North with a large basket of provisions, that being our only luggage, the trunks having been sent by sea; and had it not been for this, I think we certainly should have starved, as we were not able to get anything to eat on the road, except at Columbia and Augusta.

With respect to the attitude of people in the South, Mrs. Leigh wrote:

I can hardly give a true idea of how crushed and sad the people are. You hear no bitterness towards the North; they are too sad to be bitter; their grief is overwhelming. Nothing can make any difference to them now; the women live in the past, and the men only in the daily present, trying, in a listless sort of way, to repair their ruined fortunes. They are like so many foreigners, whose only interest in the country is their own individual business. Politics are never mentioned, and they know and care less about what is going on in Washington than in London. . . .

[We met Mr. James Hamilton Cooper before, in Sir Charles Lyell's description of Hopeton Plantation and his visit there. We may compare the fortunes of the Cooper family before and after the war.] Mr. James Hamilton Cooper died last week, and was buried at the little church on the island here yesterday. The whole thing was sad in the extreme, and a fit illustration of this people and country. Three years ago he was smitten with paralysis, the result of grief at the loss of his son, loss of his property, and the ruin of all his hopes and prospects; since which his life has been one of great suffering, until a few days ago, when death released him. Hearing from his son of his death, and the time fixed for his funeral, my father and I drove down in the old mule cart, our only conveyance, nine miles to the church. Here a most terrible scene of desolation met us. The steps of the church were broken down, so we had to walk up a plank to get in, the roof was fallen in, so that the sun streamed down on our heads; while the seats were all cut up and marked with the names of Northern soldiers, who had been quartered there during the war. The graveyard was so overgrown with weeds and bushes, and tangled with cobweb like grey moss, that we had difficulty in making our way through to the freshly dug grave.

In about half an hour the funeral party arrived. The coffin was in a cart drawn by one miserable horse, and was followed by the Cooper family on foot, having come this way from the landing, two miles off. From the cart to the grave the coffin was carried by four old family negroes, faithful to the end. Standing there I said to myself, 'Some day justice will be done, and the Truth shall be heard above the political din of slander and lies, and the Northern people shall see things as they are, and not through the dark veil of envy, hatred, and malice.

[St. Simon's Island, one of Georgia's famous sea islands, had almost reverted to a state of nature.] St. Simon's was the resort of many wealthy families, who had fine houses, beautiful grounds, and flourishing cotton plantations, where the famous Sea Island cotton was raised to perfection. Fine hard shell roads were made from one end of the island to the other (a distance of about twelve miles), and the gentlemen used to meet at their clubhouse to play at quoits and billiards, &c., or to arrange for a deer hunt or a fishing excursion.

Great hospitality was shown, and open house was kept for all comers, whilst picnics and regattas were constantly taking place. The late disastrous civil war changed all this. The fine houses have fallen to decay or been burnt down; the grounds neglected and grown over with weeds; the plantations left, with a few exceptions, to the negroes; olive groves choked up with undergrowth; stately date-palms ruthlessly burnt down by negroes to make room for a small patch of corn, where there were hundreds of acres, untilled, close at hand; a few solitary men eking out an existence by growing fruit trees and cabbages, by planting small patches of cotton or corn, by hunting deer, or by selling whiskey to the negroes.

✔   ✔   ✔

To the average yeoman farmer the Civil War did not bring as great changes as those we have observed among the planter class. Robert Lee Stowe, Sr., in his book, *Early History of Belmont and Gaston County, North Carolina*, Belmont, 1952, privately published, p. 13, generalized on this subject.

This community was not left in as bad condition after the Civil War as were some of the wealthier parts of the country where there had been a lot of slaves. The people here had been accustomed to working themselves and they knew how to do it. The per capita wealth was no more in 1890 than it was in 1860. The cotton mill business was the first thing that ever put life into the people of this comunity. From the time the first settlers arrived here until after the Civil War, the country gradually improved, but conveniences were few and people could not turn to the outside world for many of their needs, and so they had to do the best they could with what they had at home. All their farm tools were homemade, as were their clothes and shoes. The cooking was done at an open fireplace on the hearth. . . . The wool from the sheep was carded and spun by hand and woven by hand looms. The yarn when spun and twisted was dyed and made into cloth and knit into socks and stockings.

✓   ✓   ✓

While the word reconstruction implies social and economic rebuilding, in actual practice it was confined to political changes planned in the nation's capital to be applied in the Southern states. On December 8, 1863, with his third annual message President Lincoln outlined his plan for restoring the Southern states to the Union, usually known as the "ten per cent plan." The text of the plan is from James D. Richardson, *A Compilation of the Messages and Papers of the Presidents, 1789-1902,* Washington, published by Authority of Congress, 1902, Vol. VI, pp. 213-215, *passim.*

. . . I, Abraham Lincoln, President of the United States, do proclaim, declare, and make known to all persons who have, directly or by implication, participated in the existing rebellion, except as hereinafter excepted, that a full pardon is hereby granted to them and each of them, with restoration of all rights of property, except as to slaves and in property cases where rights of third persons have intervened, and upon the condition that every such person shall take and subscribe an oath and thenceforward keep and maintain said oath inviolate, and which oath shall be registered for permanent preservation and shall be of the tenor and effect following, to wit:

I, _____ _____, do solemnly swear, in presence of Almighty God, that I will henceforth faithfully support, protect, and defend the Constitution of the United States and the Union of the States thereunder; and that I will in like manner abide by and faithfully support all acts of Congress passed during the existing rebellion with reference to slaves, so long and so far as not repealed, modified, or held void by Congress or by decision of the Supreme Court; and that I will in like manner abide by and faithfully support all proclamations of the President made during the existing rebellion having reference to slaves, so long and so far as not modified or declared void by decision of the Supreme Court. So help me God.

The persons excepted from the benefits of the foregoing provisions are all who are or shall have been civil or diplomatic officers or agents of the so-called Confederate Government; all who have left judicial stations under the United States to aid in the rebellion; all who are or shall have been military or naval officers of the so-called Confederate Government above the rank of colonel in the army or of lieutenant in the navy; all who left seats in the United States Congress to aid the rebellion; all who resigned commissions in the Army or Navy of the United States and afterwards aided the rebellion; and all who have engaged in any way in treating colored persons, or white persons in charge of such, otherwise than lawfully as prisoners of war, and which persons may have been found in the United States service as soldiers, seamen, or in any other capacity.

And I do further proclaim, declare, and make known that whenever, in any of the States of Arkansas, Texas, Louisiana, Mississippi, Tennessee, Alabama, Georgia, Florida, South Carolina, and North Carolina, a number of persons, not less than one-tenth in number of the votes cast in such State at the Presidential election of the year A.D. 1860, each having taken the oath aforesaid, and not having since violated it, and being a qualified voter by the election law of the State existing immediately before the so-called act of secession, and excluding all others, shall reestablish a State government which shall be republican . . . , such shall be recognized as the true government of the State. . . .

And I do further proclaim . . . that any provision which may be adopted by such State government in relation to the freed people of such State which shall recognize and declare their permanent freedom, provide for their education, and which may yet be consistent as a temporary arrangement with their present condition as a laboring, landless, and homeless class, will not be objected to by the National Executive.

. . . It may be proper to say . . . that whether members sent to Congress from any State shall be admitted to seats constitutionally rests exclusively with the respective Houses, and not to any extent with the Executive. . . .

Given under my hand at the city of Washington, the 8th day of December, A.D., 1863. . . .

ABRAHAM LINCOLN

✓   ✓   ✓

Lincoln's second inaugural message, brief and devoted entirely to the war, indicates that his intention to restore the Southern states quickly and without recrimination had not changed. The text is from James D. Richardson, *A Compilation of the Messages and Papers of the Presidents, 1789-1902,* published by Authority of Congress, Washington, 1902, Vol. VI, pp. 276-7.

FELLOW-COUNTRYMEN: At this second appearing to take the oath of the Presidential office there is less occasion for an extended address than there was at the first. Then a statement somewhat in detail of a course to be pursued seemed fitting and proper. Now, at the expiration of four years, during which public declarations have been constantly called forth on every point and phase of the great contest which still absorbs the attention and engrosses the energies of the nation, little that is new could be presented. The progress of our arms, upon which all else chiefly depends, is as well known to the public as to myself, and it is, I trust, reasonably satisfactory and encouraging to all. With high hope for the future, no prediction in regard to it is ventured.

On the occasion corresponding to this four years ago all thoughts were anxiously directed to an impending civil war. All dreaded it, all sought to avert it. While the inaugural address was being delivered from this place, devoted altogether to *saving* the Union without war, insurgent agents were in the city seeking to *destroy* it without war—seeking to dissolve the Union and divide effects by negotiation. Both parties deprecated war, and the other would *accept* war rather than let it perish, and the war came.

One-eighth of the whole population were colored slaves, not distributed generally over the Union, but localized in the southern part of it. These slaves constituted a peculiar and powerful interest. All knew that this interest was somehow the cause of the war. To strengthen, perpetuate, and extend this interest was the object for which the insurgents would rend the Union even by war, while the Government claimed no right to do more than to restrict the territorial enlargement of it. Neither party expected for the war the magnitude or the duration which it has already attained. Neither anticipated that the *cause* of the conflict might cease with or even before the conflict itself should cease. Each looked for an easier triumph, and a result less fundamental and astounding. Both read the same Bible and pray to the same God, and each invokes His aid against the other. It may seem strange that any men should dare to ask a just God's assistance in wringing their bread from the sweat of other men's faces, but let us judge not that we be not judged. The prayers of both could not be answered. That of neither has been answered fully. The Almighty has his own purposes. "Woe unto the world because of offenses; for it must needs be that offenses come, but woe to that man by whom the offense cometh." If we shall suppose that American slavery is one of those offenses which, in the providence of God, must needs come, but which, having continued through His appointed time, He now wills to remove, and that He gives to both North and South this terrible war as the woe due to those by whom the offense came, shall we discern therein any departure from those divine attributes which the believers in a living God always ascribe to Him? Fondly do we hope, fervently do we pray, that this mighty scourge of war may speedily pass away. Yet, if God wills that it continue until all the wealth piled by the bondsman's two hundred and fifty years of unrequited toil shall be sunk, and until every drop of blood drawn with the lash shall be paid by another drawn with the sword, as was said three thousand years ago, so still it must be said "the judgments of the Lord are true and righteous altogether."

With malice toward none, with charity for all, with firmness in the right as God gives us to see the right, let us strive on to finish the work we are in, to bind up the nation's wounds, to care for him who shall have borne the battle and for his widow and orphan, to do all which may achieve and cherish a just and lasting peace among ourselves and with all nations.

❧   ❧   ❧

On the night of April 14, 1865, President Lincoln was mortally wounded by an assassin and lived only a few hours. Upon the shoulders of Andrew Johnson, a Democrat who had been inaugurated just six weeks earlier, fell the guidance of Congress and the states in the restoration of the Union. In his inaugural address on April 15 he admitted: "I feel incompetent to perform duties so important and responsible as those which have been so unexpectedly thrown upon me. As to an indication of any policy which may be pursued by me in the administration of the Government, I have to say that that must be left for development as the administration progresses." Eight months were to pass before Congress would convene, and during that period Johnson's policy did develop, along lines similar to those outlined by President Lincoln. Johnson reported that policy in his first annual message, December 4, 1865. The text of the message is from James D. Richardson, *A Compilation of the Messages and Papers of the Presidents, 1789-1902*, published by Authority of Congress, Washington, 1902, Vol. VI, pp. 353-371, *passim*.

I found the States suffering from the effects of a civil war. Resistance to the General Government appeared to have exhausted itself. The United States had recovered possession of their forts and arsenals, and their armies were in the occupation of every State which had attempted to secede. Whether the territory within the limits of those States should be held conquered territory, under military authority emanating from the President as the head of the Army, was the first question that presented itself for decision.

Now military governments, established for an indefinite period, would have offered no security for the early suppression of discontent, would have divided the people into the vanquishers and the vanquished, and would have envenomed hatred rather than have restored affection. Once established, no precise limit to their continuance was conceivable. They would have occasioned an incalculable expense. . . .

Besides, the policy of military rule over a conquered territory would have implied that the States whose inhabitants may have taken part in the rebellion had by the act of those inhabitants ceased to exist. But the true theory is that all pretended acts of secession were from the beginning null and void. The States cannot commit treason nor screen the individual citizens who may have committed treason any more than they can make valid treaties or engage in lawful commerce with any foreign power. The States attempting to secede placed themselves in a condition where their vitality was impaired, but not extinguished; their functions suspended, but not destroyed.

. . . I have . . . gradually and quietly, and by almost imperceptible steps, sought to restore the rightful energy of the General Government and of the States. To that end provisional governors have been appointed for the States, conventions called, governors elected, legislatures assembled, and Senators and Representatives chosen to the Congress of the United States.

At the same time the courts of the United States may be enforced through their agency. The blockade has been removed and the custom-houses re-established in ports of entry, so that the revenue of the United States may be collected. . . . Is it not a sure promise of harmony and renewed attach-ment to the Union that after all that has happened the return of the General Government is known only as a beneficence? . . .

The next step which I have taken to restore the constitutional relations of the States has been an invitation to them to participate in the high office of amending the Constitution. . . . The evidence of sincerity in the future maintenance of the Union shall be put beyond any doubt by the ratification of the proposed amendment to the Constitution, which provides for the abolition of slavery forever within the limits of our country. . . .

The amendment to the Constitution being adopted, it would remain for the States whose powers have been so long in abeyance to resume their places in the two branches of the National Legislature, and thereby complete the work of restoration. Here it is for you, fellow-citizens of the Senate, and for you, fellow-citizens of the House of Representatives, to judge, each of you for yourselves, of the elections, returns, and qualifications of your own members . . .

The relations of the General Government toward the 4,000,000 inhabi-tants whom the war has called into freedom have engaged my most serious consideration. . . . When at the first movement toward independence, the Congress of the United States instructed the several States to institute governments of their own, they left each State to decide for itself the conditions for the enjoyment of the elective franchise. . . . After the forma-tion of the Constitution it remained, as before, the uniform usage for each State to enlarge the body of its electors, until now universal suffrage, or something very near it, is the general rule. So fixed was this reservation of power in the habits of the people and so unquestioned has been the inter-pretation of the Constitution that during the civil war the late President never harbored the purpose—certainly never avowed the purpose—of dis-regarding it; and in the acts of Congress during that period nothing can be found which . . . would have sanctioned any departure by the Executive from a policy which has so uniformly obtained. . . .

Every danger of conflict is avoided when the settlement of the question is referred to the several States. They can, each for itself, decide on the meas-ure, and whether it is to be adopted at once and absolutely or introduced gradually and with conditions. . . .

Good faith requires the security of the freedmen in their liberty and their property, their right to labor, and their right to claim the just return for their labor. . . . The country is in need of labor, and the freed-men are in need of employment, culture, and protection. . . . Let us en-courage them to honorable and useful industry, where it may be beneficial to themselves and to the country. . . . The public interest will be best

promoted if the several States will provide adequate protection and remedies
for the freedmen. . . .

✓   ✓   ✓

Johnson's mild policy of amnesty and resumption of normal conditions was not
to prevail. During Lincoln's Presidency a radical group within the Republican
party in Congress had attempted to control the government and the conduct of
the war. This group wished to inflict severe terms on the South. While President
Johnson was directing the formation of new state governments in the South, Thad-
deus Stevens, veteran Congressman from Pennsylvania, was carrying on a correspondence with Senator Charles Sumner of Massachusetts, planning to arrest the
President's policy. In September, 1865, in Lancaster, Pennsylvania, Stevens made
a speech in the courthouse square in which he asked for confiscation of property in
the South and redistribution of the wealth in the interests of the freedmen. Stevens'
speech was printed in a pamphlet, Lancaster, 1865, and is quoted from Richard
Nelson Current's *Old Thad Stevens,* University of Wisconsin Press, Madison, 1942,
pp. 214-216.

. . . Four years of bloody and expensive war waged against the United
States by eleven States, under a government called the "Confederate States
of America" to which they acknowledged allegiance, have overthrown all
governments within those States, which could be acknowledged as legitimate
by the Union. The armies of the Confederate States having been conquered
and subdued, and their territories possessed by the United States, it becomes
necessary to establish governements therein, which shall be republican in
"form and principles, and form a more perfect union" with the parent
government. . . . We hold it to be the duty of the Government to inflict
condign punishment on the rebel belligerents, and so weaken their hands
that they can never again endanger the Union; and so reform their municipal institutions as to make them republican in spirit as well as in name.

We especially insist that the property of the chief rebels should be seized
and appropriated to the payment of the National debt, caused by the unjust and wicked war which they instigated.

How can such punishments be inflicted and such forfeitures produced
without doing violence to established principles.

Two positions have been suggested.

1st—To treat those States as never having been out of the Union. . . .

2nd—To accept the position in which they placed themselves as severed
from the Union; an independent government *de facto,* and an enemy alien
to be dealt with according to the laws of war. . . .

In reconstruction . . . no reform can be effected in the Southern States
if they have never left the Union. But reformation *must* be effected; the
foundation of their institutions, both political, municipal and social *must*
be broken up and *relaid,* or all our blood and treasure have been spent in
vain. This can only be done by treating and holding them as a conquered
people. Then all things which we can desire to do, follow with logical and

legitimate authority. As conquered territory Congress would have full power to legislate for them. . . . They would be held in a territorial condition until they are fit to form State Constitutions, republican in fact not in form only, and ask admission into the Union as new States. . . .

We propose to confiscate all the estate of every rebel belligerent whose estate was worth $10,000, or whose land exceeded two hundred acres in quantity. Policy if not justice would require that the poor, the ignorant, and the coerced should be forgiven. They followed the example of their wealthy and intelligent neighbors. The rebellion would never have origi- nated with them. Fortunately those who would thus escape form a large majority of the people, though possessing but a small portion of the wealth. The proportion of those exempt compared with the punished would be I believe about nine tenths.

There are about six millions of freemen in the South. The number of acres of land is 465,000,000. Of this those who own above two hundred acres each, number about 70,000 persons, holding in the aggregate (to- gether with the States) about 394,000,000 acres, leaving for all others below 200 each about 71,000,000 of acres. By thus forfeiting the estates of the leading rebels, the Government would have 394,000,000 of acres. . . . , yet nine tenths of the people would remain untouched. Divide this land into convenient farms. Give if you please forty acres to each adult male freed man. . . .

The whole fabric of southern society *must* be changed, and never can it be done if this opportunity is lost. Without this, this Government can never be, as it never has been, a true republic. Heretofore it has had more the features of aristocracy than of democracy. . . .

Let us forget all parties, and build on the broad platform of reconstruct- ing the Government out of the conquered territory, converted into new and free states, and admitted into the Union by the sovereign power of Congress, with another plank,—*the property of the rebels shall pay our national debt, and indemnify freed-men and loyal sufferers.* . . .

Let all who approve of these principles tarry with us. Let all others go with Copperheads and rebels. Those will be the opposing parties. Young men, this duty devolves on you. Would to God, if only for that, that I were still in the prime of life, that I might aid you to fight through this last and greatest battle of Freedom.

✓   ✓   ✓

When the thirty-ninth Congress met in December, 1865, the radical group prevented the admission of Congressmen from the Southern states by the creation of a joint committee composed of six senators and nine representatives "to inquire into the condition of the states which formed the so-called Confederate States of America, and report whether they, or any of them, are entitled to be represented in either house of Congress." Subcommittees were appointed to hold hearings and testimony taken served two purposes: it was printed for campaign use in the election of 1866; with this testimony the radicals were able to convince Congress that the Constitution must be amended to protect the civil rights of the Negroes, guarantee the payment of the national debt while repudiating that of the Confederacy and the several Southern states, and disfranchise the Southern leaders. Examples of the testimony which follow are quoted from Benjamin B. Kendrick, *The Journal of the Joint Committee of Fifteen on Reconstruction,* Columbia University, New York, 1915, pp. 274-291, *passim.*

Major General Edward Hatch, who had been stationed in Mississippi and Alabama after the close of the war, gave the following testimony:

Question. What is the disposition of the people there towards the colored population?

Answer. The poorer classes of the white people have an intense dislike towards them. So far as any love, or regard or care for the negro, or the slave, I have never seen any of it, and do not believe it ever existed, except so far as his former money value may have caused care for him. There are men in Mississippi who are willing to accept the state of affairs as they are now, and to employ the negro and pay him a fair reward for his services. But a great portion of the people of Mississippi are not of large enough views to understand this matter. They wish to control the negro and his labor in such a way that he will be compelled to remain with them for never less than a year, and upon their own terms.

Question. According to your observation, what is the disposition of the negroes in reference to working, if they can be assured of pay for their work?

Answer. We have always found them very ready to work. I have seen no instance where they were not willing to work when they have been assured of their rights. The superintendent, who by the way was a northern man, of the work of opening the Mobile and Ohio railroad, told me that the negro men whom he had to work for eight dollars a month and army rations worked as well as any men; that men never worked better. We issued the rations to those negroes working on that road. We issued no rations to indigent negroes, though we issued a large amount of rations to indigent whites; also a large amount of Confederate corn that we had taken, and I run one or two mills to grind corn to feed them. We never issued a ration to an indigent negro while I was there.

Question. Why not.

Answer. They never asked for any. I stopped issuing to the whites, but they made so many complaints that I was ordered to commence issuing again. They were in a starving condition, as the armies, the Confederate as well as our own, had gone over the country and nearly eaten it up. I have always found the negro ready to work when he was assured that he would be paid according to his contract.

Question. As a general thing, would northern men be kindly received who might go to Mississippi to live?

Answer. No, sir; there is a very intense antipathy towards northern men in all Mississippi, with perhaps an occasional exception. I have heard them say that no northern man should come there and work their plantations and live among them, unless he was an overseer under them, or something of that kind; that he could not come there and expect to own a plantation. There is no doubt at all that there is an intense hatred felt toward northern men.

Judge John C. Underwood, of New York, whom Lincoln made a federal judge of the district court in Virginia:

Question. Let me put a hypothetical case to you. Suppose that by means of a combination with the so-called Democratic party, *alias* copperhead party, *alias* conservative party, they, the rebels, should again obtain political power in Congress, and in the executive department; suppose this to be the result of a combination between the ex-rebel party in the South and this so-called Democratic party in the North; what would be the effect of that ascendancy upon the rebel states? What measures would they resort to?

Answer. They would attempt either to accomplish a repudiation of the National debt, or an acknowledgement of the Confederate debt, and compensation for their negroes. I think these would be their leading measures, their leading demands; and I think if either the rebel debt could be placed upon an equality with the National debt, or both could be alike repudiated, they would be satisfied. But the leading spirits would expect to get it by such a combination.

Homer A. Cooke, a former quartermaster in the United States Army, who had been stationed in North Carolina:

Question: How do the ex-rebels feel about the payment of the Federal war debt? If it was left to them to vote *yes* or *no* on the question of paying it, what way would they vote generally?

Answer. They would vote *no,* without doubt.

Question. It would not be a very close struggle?

Answer. It would be about as unanimous as the vote in this district on the question of negro suffrage.

Question. Suppose the question were referred to them whether or not they would pay the rebel war debt, how would they vote there generally, *yes* or *no?*

Answer. I think their vote would be in the affirmative, to pay it; because the mass of voters are under the influence of a few men, and those men are directly interested in the debt, as they hold the bonds.

J. W. Alvord, an agent of the Freedmen's Bureau, testified in regard to his experience in Virginia and other southern states.

Question. Now state what, among the rebel people, is the general feeling toward the Government of the United States?

Answer. It is hostile, as it seems to me, in the great majority of the southern people; I mean that part of them who were engaged in the rebellion. There is evidently no regret for the rebellion, but rather a defence of it, and only a submission to the circumstances of the case as a conquered people. They everywhere defend the principles on which the rebellion commenced.

Question. They still insist that those principles were right?

Answer. Yes, sir; they seem to feel that peace was brought about by an arrangement which allowed them the equal condition of belligerents, and [to remain] in possession of all they previously had had of government privileges. They everywhere insist upon the immediate restoration of such privileges, and that they shall be readmitted as states into the Union. They complain bitterly of the treatment they are receiving in being kept out.

The Joint Committee of Fifteen formulated the fourteenth amendment and made it a condition of restoration of the Southern states to the Union. When, after nine months, only Tennessee of the former Confederate states had ratified it, Congress passed, over the President's veto, a reconstruction act dividing the South into military districts subject to martial law. The new regime would last until such time as the Southern states should have held constitutional conventions, established new state governments, and have been readmitted to the Union by act of Congress. Although President Johnson had objected to the law he enforced it scrupulously. Voters who could qualify under the proposed fourteenth amendment were registered by the military governments. In some of the states Negro voters outnumbered the white ones. These Negroes participated in writing the new constitutions, in operating the state governments, and in patrolling the South as United States troops. However, leadership came from white men known as carpetbaggers and scalawags, the former being Northerners who came South to exert their influence, and the latter, Southern whites who allied themselves with the radicals. By mid-summer of 1868 seven states were readmitted to the Union (Tennessee had been accepted upon her ratification of the fourteenth amendment in 1866). Mississippi, Texas, and Virginia were required to ratify the fifteenth amendment, and when it had been accepted by three-fourths of the states and had become part of the Constitution in 1870, all were restored. However, to protect the civil rights of the Negroes, federal troops were retained in different parts of the South until the last ones were withdrawn by President Hayes in April, 1877.

On June 23, 1867, Frances Butler Leigh wrote a letter which is a commentary on the Congressional Reconstruction Policy which had just been decided upon. The text is from Leigh, *Ten Years on a Georgia Plantation After the War*, R. Bentley and Son, London, 1883, pp. 66-70.

We are, I am afraid, going to have terrible trouble by-and-by with the negroes, and I see nothing but gloomy prospects for us ahead. The unlimited power that the war has put into the hands of the present Government at Washington seems to have turned the heads of the party now in office, and they don't know where to stop. The whole South is settled and quiet, and the people too ruined and crushed to do anything against the government, even if they felt so inclined, and all are returning to their former peaceful pursuits, trying to rebuild their fortunes, and thinking of nothing else. Yet the treatment we receive from the Government becomes more and more severe every day, the last act being to divide the South into five military districts, putting each under the command of a United States General, doing away with all civil courts and law. Even D——, who you know is a Northern republican, says it is most unjustifiable, not being in any way authorized by the existing state of things, which he confesses he finds very different from what he expected before he came. If they would frankly say they intend to keep us down, it would be fairer than making a pretense of readmitting us to equal rights, and then trumping up stories of violence to give a show of justice to treating us as conquered foes of the most despotic Government on earth, and by exciting the negroes to every kind of insolent lawlessness, to goad the people into acts of rebellion and resistance. . . .

The true reason is the desire and intention of the Government to control the elections of the South, which under the constitution of the country they could not legally do. So they have determined to make an excuse for setting aside the laws, and in order to do this more fully,—[they have disfranchised] the whole white population, while the negroes are allowed to vote *en masse*. . . . Meanwhile, in order to prepare the negroes to vote properly, stump speakers from the North are going all through the South, holding political meetings for the negroes, saying things like this to them: 'My friends, you will have your rights, won't you ('Yes,' from the negroes.) 'Shall I not go back to Massachusetts and tell your brothers there that you are going to ride in the street car with the white ladies if you please?' ('Yes, yes,' from the crowd.) 'That if you pay your money to go to the theatre you will sit where you please, in the best boxes if you like?' ('Yes,' and applause.) This I copy verbatim from a speech made at Richmond the other day, since which there have been two serious negro riots there, and the General commanding had to call out the military to suppress them.

⚡   ⚡   ⚡

The two following accounts illustrate the motives which actuated both North and South during the reconstruction period, and were written by extreme partisans. James G. Blaine, author of the first, was a member of the House of Representatives, and from 1869-76 was a Speaker of the House and an ardent Radical who "waved the bloody shirt" repeatedly in political campaigns. In 1884 he wrote *Twenty Years of Congress,* The Henry Bill Publishing Co., Norwich, Connecticut, 1884, from which the first selection is taken. The text is from Volume II, pp. 447-471, *passim.*

As soon as the war had closed there was a considerable influx of Northern men in the States of the late Confederacy. The original motive which induced the migration was financial and speculative. A belief was prevalent in the North that great profit might be derived from the cotton-culture, and that with the assured sympathy of the colored men they would be able to command the requisite labor more readily than the old slave masters. As a mere business enterprise cotton-growing at that period, except in a very few instances, proved to be unprofitable. The complete disorganization of labor throughout the South, consequent upon emancipation; had embarrassed production and added largely to its cost. . . .

It soon became apparent that, under the protection of the National power and with the numerical superiority of the negroes in several States (certain Southern leaders being under political disabilities), it would be easy for the loyal white men to obtain control of the local governments. Out of these circumstances there came into political power the class of men known as "Carpet-baggers"—so described from the insulting presumption that the entire worldly estate of each one of the class was carried in a carpet-bag, enabling him to fly at any moment of danger from the State whose domestic policy he sought to control. The prospect of the success of the new movement induced a number of former rebels to join in it, and to them the epithet of "Scalawag" was applied. This combination was not without disadvantages to the negro . . . It increased the hatred and desperation of the ruling element among the whites, and demonstrated that the negro could secure the rights conferred upon him by the Constitution and laws, only through violence and bloodshed.

Many of those denounced under the epithet of Carpet-bagger and Scalawag were honorable and true men; but a majority of these were unobtrusive and not brought strongly into popular view: while many of those who became entrusted with the power of State governments and found themselves unexpectedly in possession of great authority were not morally equal to its responsibility. The consequence was that some of the States had wretched governments, officered by bad men, who misled the negro and engaged in riotous corruption. Their transgressions were made so conspicuous that the Republican leaders of other Southern States, who were really trying to act their part worthily and honorably, were obscured from view, and did not obtain a fair hearing at the bar of public opinion. The government of South Carolina, under its series of Republican administrations, was of such character as brought shame upon the Republican party, exposed the negro voters to unmerited obloquy, and thus wrought for the cause of free government and equal suffrage in the South incalculable harm. . . .

The assignments of Army officers to the Southern districts were made early in the spring of 1867. From that time onward it was hoped that the preservation of order would be secured in the South, and that the rights of all classes would be adequately protected in the novel experiment. . . .

of allowing loyal men regardless of race or color to share in the suffrage and to participate in the administration of the Government. . . . Conventions were held successively in all the States, the elections being conducted in good order, while every man entitled to vote was fully secured in his suffrage. The conventions were duly assembled, constitutions formed, submitted . . . and approved by popular vote. State governments were promptly organized under these organic laws, Legislatures were elected, and the Fourteenth Amendment ratified in each of the States with as hearty a unanimity as in the preceding winter it had been rejected by the same communities . . .

Eight of the eleven Confederate States, at the close of June, 1868, had their senators and representatives in Congress. Three—Virginia, Mississippi, and Texas—were prevented by self-imposed obstacles from enjoying the same privilege . . . Of the representatives on the floor of the Fortieth Congress from the eight States lately in rebellion, only two were Democrats . . .

The senators first admitted from the reconstructed States were about equally divided between native Southerners and those who had gone from the North at the close of the war; but all were Republicans except one in Virginia and one in Georgia. . . .

Though the Reconstruction measures were all perfected before General Grant's election to the Presidency, the necessary Acts prescribed by them had not been completed by all the States . . . Virginia, Mississippi, and Texas had by the spring of 1870 fully complied with all the requirements and were therefore admitted to all the privileges which had been accorded to the other States of the South. . . .

The reconstruction of Georgia, supposed to have been completed the preceding year by the admission of her representatives to the House, was taken up for review at the opening of the Forty-first Congress. . . . Her Legislature, after complying with every condition of reconstruction, . . . decided that colored men were not entitled to serve as legislators or to hold any office in Georgia. They were therefore expelled from their seats, while white men, not eligible to hold office under the Fourteenth Amendment, were retained. . . .

Congress . . . passed a . . . bill declaring "that the exclusion of persons from the Legislature upon the ground of race, color, or previous condition of servitude, would be illegal and revolutionary, and is hereby prohibited." In order to make the prohibition effective, Georgia was required, before her senators and representatives could be seated, to ratify the Fifteenth Amendment. . . . The course pursued by Georgia made her the last State to be reconstructed. The final act for her re-admission to the right of representation in Congress was passed on the 15th of July, 1870. . . .

The action of Georgia in expelling colored men from the Legislature after her reconstruction was supposed to be complete, roused the country

to the knowledge of what was intended by the leading men of the South.
. . . On the 30th of March Secretary Fish issued a proclamation making
known to the people of the United States that the Fifteenth Amendment
had been ratified by the Legislatures of thirty states and was therefore a
part of the Constitution of the United States. . . .

As the Reconstruction of each State was completed, the Military Government that was instituted in 1867 was withdrawn. . . . But it was soon disclosed that on the part of the large mass of those who had participated in the
rebellion, properly speaking, indeed, on the part of the vast majority of
the white men of the South, there was really no intention to acquiesce in
the legislation of Congress, no purpose to abide by the Constitutional
Amendments in good faith. . . . They regarded themselves justified in opposing, repudiating, and if possible destroying, the governments that had
grown up under the protection of the Reconstruction Laws. . . . It was
not . . . the purpose of the Southern Democrats to be fettered and embarrassed by . . . restraints. By means lawful or unlawful they determined
to uproot and overthrow the State governments that had been established.
. . . They were resolved that the Negro should not be a political power in
their local governments; that he should not, so far as their interposition
could prevent it, exert any influence over elections, either State or
national; and that his suffrage, if permitted to exist at all, should be only
in the innocent form of a minority. Seeing this determination, the National
Government interposed its strong arm, and a detail of soldiers at the principal points throughout the South gave a certain protection to those whose
rights were otherwise in danger of being utterly trodden down. . . .

Between the effort, therefore, of President Grant's administration to protect free suffrage in the South, and the protest of the Democratic party
against protecting it by the military arm of the Government, a physical
contest ensued in the Southern States and a political contest throughout the
Union. It was perfectly understood . . . that the withdrawal of the protection of the National Government from the States lately in rebellion
meant the end of suffrage to the colored man, or at least its . . . impair-
ment. . . . Vicious organizations, of which the most notable were the
Ku-Klux-Klans, were formed throughout the South for the express purpose
of depriving the negro of the political rights conferred upon him by law.
To effect this purpose they resorted to a series of outrages calculated to
inspire the negroes with terror if they attempted to resist the will of white
men.

In prosecuting their purposes these clans and organizations hesitated at
no cruelty, were deterred by no considerations of law or of humanity.
They rode by night, were disguised with masks, were armed as freebooters.
They whipped, maimed, or murdered the victims of their wrath. White men
who were co-operating with the colored population politically were visited
with punishments of excessive cruelty. It was difficult to arrest the authors

of these flagrant wrongs. Aside from their disguises, they were protected against inculpating testimony by the fear inspired in the minds of those who might be witnesses; and they were protected even by that portion of the white race who were not willing to join in their excesses. . . .

Congress did its utmost to strengthen the hands of the President in a contest with these desperate elements. By the Act of April 20, 1871, "to inforce the provisions of the Fourteenth Amendment . . ." (commonly known as the Ku-Klux Act, or the Enforcement Act), the President was empowered to go the extreme of suspending the writ of *habeas corpus* where peace and order could not otherwise be restored. . . .

✓   ✓   ✓

The process of congressional reconstruction as a Southerner saw it "was one of the mistakes that constitute what in the life of a nation is worse than a national crime,—a national blunder." Thomas Nelson Page, descended from two aristocratic Virginia families and educated in the tradition of a Southern gentleman, received the LL.B. degree from the University of Virginia in 1874. Having grown up during the reconstruction period, he was well qualified to explain the period from the Southern point of view. The following account is from his article, "The Southern People During Reconstruction," *Atlantic Monthly,* Vol. 88, September, 1901, pp. 289-304, *passim.*

The terms had been equally honorable to both the victors and the vanquished; and the troops returned home fully prepared to abide by those terms in every particular. They were sustained by the consciousness of having been animated by the highest of motives,—love of country and of home,—of having made an unsurpassed struggle, and of being able to meet and endure every fortune that could befall. . . .

The worst that the people of the South anticipated was being brought back into the union with their property gone and their wounds yet smarting. The sense of defeat, together with the loss of property by force of arms, which left them almost universally impoverished, and the disruption of their social system, was no little burden for them to bear; but it was assumed bravely enough, and they went to work with energy and courage, and even with a certain high-heartedness. They started in on the plantations, where by reason of the disorganization of all labor they were needed, as wagoners or ploughmen or blacksmiths. They went to the cities, and became brakemen or street-car drivers, or watchmen or porters. Or they sought employment on public works in any capacity; men who had been generals even taking places as axemen or teamsters till they could rise to be superintendents and presidents. But they had peace and hope.

On the 18th of December, 1865, General Grant, who had been sent through the South by the President to inspect and make a report on its condition, in his report said:—

"I am satisfied the mass of thinking men in the South accept the present situation of affairs in good faith. The questions which have hitherto divided the sentiment of the people of the two sections—slavery and state rights, or the right of the state to secede from the Union—they regard as having been settled forever by the highest tribunal, that of arms, that man can resort to."

He also made the wise suggestion that negro troops should not be employed in garrisoning the Southern states, as they tended to excite the people and intensify their animosity. . . .

It was the South's misfortune that the new problems could not be worked out on their own merits. . . . The institution known as the Freedmen's Bureau, and its work in the South, played a not inconsiderable part in the trouble that arose. The motive for its origin was, no doubt, a good one, and, no doubt, a part of its work was beneficial to one of the races. It had the "supervision and management of all abandoned lands, and the control of all subjects relating to refugees and freedmen." It issued rations to freedmen; regulated all matters of labor and contract in which freedmen were interested; administered justice wherever they were concerned; and had power to take charge of all "abandoned lands" and parcel them out to negroes as homes, and generally to administrate the negro and his affairs. Incident to these duties was the power to arrest and imprison. The Bureau began its work with an idea which was fatal to its success: that the negro was a poor oppressed creature who was to be treated as the nation's ward, and that the white was a hardened tyrant who had to be restrained.

The officials of the Bureau were of various kinds: honest men, hopelessly prejudiced and bigoted; and men without honesty, wisdom, or any other qualification. . . . Unhappily, the largest, or at least the most active element among the officials were the last class . . . refuse of a great army, who had no sooner found the dangers of war over than they had begun to look about them to see what spoil they could appropriate, and, recognizing in the newly freed negroes the most promising instrument at hand for their purposes, had ingratiated themselves with the Freedmen's Bureau. One of the first evidences of their malign influence was the idea disseminated among the negroes, which grew out of the provision relating to abandoned lands, that every freedman was to be given by the government, out of the lands of his old master, forty acres and a mule,—a teaching which was productive of much danger to the whites, and of much evil to the blacks. Among other things, it prevented the former from settling the negroes on the old plantations, as they would otherwise have done very generally.

The Freedmen's Bureau and its work soon had the whole South in a ferment. The distribution of rations relieved the slaves, but misled them into thinking that the government would support them, whether they worked or not. The officials began their inquisitorial investigations. They summoned the best and the most stately of the old gentry before them, as if they had been schoolboys. . . .

The negroes in some places began to hold night meetings, and parcel out the lands of their former masters. . . .

A dispassionate reading of the records shows that the army officers in the South endeavored, in the main, to perform their duties with wisdom, equity, and moderation. Conditions, however, were to grow worse. . . . The legislatures of the various states, assuming that, after a successful war to preserve the Union, the Union still existed, and unable to recognize the completeness of their overthrow, began to pass labor laws directed at the negro, some of which were calculated to impair his freedom of action. Similar laws existed in some of the Northern states, such as Maine, Rhode Island, and Connecticut. But these new statutes were frankly aimed to control the newly emancipated slaves. An impression of profound distrust was created throughout the North, the people of which, with their sympathies quickened for an entire race turned adrift, without homes or property, had almost begun to consider that the war had been fought for the emancipation of the blacks. Unhappily, at the same time state representatives were chosen whose votes might have a decisive influence on the fortunes of those leaders who now esteemed themselves the saviors of the country. It was determined by these leaders to perpetuate their power at every hazard, even if it were found necessary to overthrow the white race altogether, and put the black over them. The South was intractable and uncompromising. The North was blinded by passion, and led by partisan leaders bent on domination and without scruple in their exercise of power. . . . Those who had been the masters, and had given proof by their works that they were behind no people in the highest fruits of civilization,—who had just shown by their constancy, if by no other virtue, that they were worthy of being treated with consideration,—were disfranchised and shut out from participation in the government, while their former slaves were put over them. . . . Later on, when "ironclad oaths" had been devised, and the full work of disfranchisement had been effected, no whites but those who had had the disabilities specially removed could hold office or vote. For a time, only the negroes, the carpet-baggers, and those who disregarded perjury voted.

The white race . . . were not allowed the franchise again until they had assented to giving the black race absolute equality in all matters of civil right. This the leaders of the other side vainly imagined would perpetuate their power, and for a time it almost promised to do so.

The result of the new regime thus established in the South was such a riot of rapine and rascality as had never been known in the history of this country, and hardly ever in the history of the world. . . . The states were given over to pillage at the hands of former slaves, led largely by adventurers whose only aim was to gratify their vengeance or their cupidity.

. . . The true measure of injury to the people of the South was the humiliation to which they were subjected during the progress of this system of rapine. Some states were subjected to greater damage, and if possible, deeper humiliation than others. The people of South Carolina, Mississippi, Louisiana, and Arkansas, perhaps suffered the most. . . . Virginia escaped in a measure some of the most extreme consequences. For instance, there were no continued incitements to riot and no wholesale arrests of an entire community, as took place in South Carolina; there was no general subjection to an armed and insolent militia of former slaves who terrorized the country, as happened in the more southerly states. Virginia never had a governor, as Arkansas had, who issued to his adjutant general proscription lists of leading citizens, accompanied by a notification that he had marked with asterisks the names of the most obnoxious persons, and that if they could be tried by court-martial and executed while the writ of habeas corpus was suspended, the finding would be approved by the governor. The Ku Klux Klan, with its swath of outrage and terrorism, never obtained the footing in Virginia that it had in states farther south, where life had been made more unendurable. . . . Unhappily the credulity and ignorance of the negroes threw them into the hands of the worst element among the adventurers who were vying to become their leaders. The man who was bold enough to bid the highest outstripped the others. . . .

Unable to resist openly the power of the National government that stood behind the carpet-bag governments of the states, the people of the South resorted to other means which proved for a time more or less effective. Secret societies were formed, which, under such titles as the "Ku Klux Klan," the "Knights of the White Camellia," the "White Brotherhood," etc., played a potent and, at first, it would seem, a beneficial part in restraining the excesses of the newly exalted leaders and their excited levies.

Wherever masked and ghostly riders appeared, the frightened negroes kept under cover. The idea spread with rapidity over nearly all the South, and the secret organizations, known among themselves as the "Invisible Empire," were found to be so dangerous to the continued power of the carpet-bag governments, and in places so menacing to their representatives personally, that the aid of the National government was called in to suppress them.

In a short time every power of the government was in motion, or ready to be set in motion, against them. "Ku Klux Acts" were passed; presidential proclamations were issued; the entire machinery of the United States courts was put in operation; the writ of habeas corpus was suspended in those sections where the Ku Klux were most in evidence, and Federal troops were employed. . . .

With Congress passing penal acts against all connected with the secret societies, the army of the United States at hand to put them down, and the United States courts ready to push through the convictions of all participants in their work, the constituency and purposes of the secret societies soon changed. The more law-abiding and self-respecting element dropped out, and such organizations as remained were composed only of the most disorderly and reckless element. Under conduct of such a class, the societies, whatever their original design, soon degenerated into mere bands of masked ruffians, who used their organization and their disguises for the private purposes of robbery and revenge. Eventually reconstruction . . . began to be known at the North for what it really was, and the people of the North began to revolt against its continuance. The indorsement of the government leaders at Washington became more and more half-hearted; and as this was recognized, the white people of the South began to be reanimated with hope. . . .

In the last stages of their existence, these governments were sustained solely by the bayonet. As soon as the United States troops were removed they melted away. As an illustration: In South Carolina, in 1876, after the extraordinary Wade Hampton/campaign, in which the whites won a signal victory, two distinct state governments performed their functions in the State House; a small guard of United States soldiers marched their beats back and forth, representing the power that alone sustained one of those governments. An order was issued by the President of the United States removing the troops, and in twenty-four hours, without a drop of blood shed, without a single clash, the government of the carpet-bagger and the negro had disappeared, and the government of the native South Carolinian and the white man had quietly, after a lapse of years, resumed control. But during those years the people of the South had seen their most cherished traditions traversed, their civilization overthrown. . . .

✦ ✦ ✦

The following letter written by J. W. Leigh, husband of Frances Butler Leigh, described the effect of the franchise on the Negroes. The text is from Frances Butler Leigh, *Ten Years on a Georgia Plantation After the War,* R. Bentley and Son, London, 1883, pp. 285-293.

It is indeed easy enough for a traveller passing rapidly through the Southern States . . . to write a lot of nonsense about the intelligence of the coloured man, the mixture of the races, miscegenation, &c. But most travellers see nothing of the inner life and character of these people, and an American might just as well get his opinion of a Dorsetshire labourer from what he saw of a waiter at the Langham Hotel, as a traveller in the United States form his opinion of plantation negroes from what he saw of . . . intelligent and civil waiters at large hotels. To know and understand the negro in his present position, you must see him and hear him on the floor of the State Legislature, and transact business with him on a plantation, as well as chat familiarly with him on a pleasure excursion, or be waited on by him in a hotel. I have done all this, and therefore have some authority in speaking, and yet I can scarcely say that I know the emancipated African thoroughly yet.

The fact is that the poor negro has since the war been placed in an entirely false position, and is therefore not to be blamed for many of the absurdities he has committed, seeing that he has been urged on by Northern 'carpet-baggers' and Southern 'scalawags,' who have used him as a tool to further their own nefarious ends.

The great mistake committed by the North was giving the negroes the franchise so soon after their emancipation, when they were not the least prepared for it. In 1865 Slavery was abolished, and no one even among the Southerners, I venture to say, would wish it back. In 1868 they were declared citizens of the United States, and in 1870 they had the right of voting given them, and at the same time the persons concerned in the rebellion were excluded from public trusts by what was called the 'iron-clad' oath; and as if this was not enough, last year the Civil Rights Bill was passed, by which negroes were to be placed on a perfect equality with the whites, who were to be compelled to send their children to the same schools. The consequence of all this is that where there is a majority of negroes, as is the case in the States of Louisiana, Mississippi, and South Carolina, these States are placed completely under negro rule, and scenes occur in the State Legislatures which baffle description. I recollect at the beginning of 1870 being at Montgomery, the capital of Alabama, and paying a visit to the State House there when a discussion was going on with respect to a large grant which was to be made for the building of the Alabama and Chattanooga Railway, the real object of which was to put money into the pockets of certain carpetbaggers, who, in order to gain their object had bribed all the negroes to vote for the passing of the Bill. The scene was an exciting one. Several negro members were present, with their legs stuck up on the desks in front of them, and spitting all about them in free and independent fashion. One gentleman having spoken for some time against the bill, and having reiterated his condemnation of it as a fraudulent speculation, a stout negro member from Mobile sprung up and said, Mister Speaker, when yesterday I spoke, I was not allowed to go on because you said I spoke twice on the same subject. Now what is sauce for the goose is sauce for the gander. Dis Member is saying over and over again de same thing; why don't you tell him to sit down? for what is sauce for '&c. To which the Speaker said, 'Sit down yourself, sir.' Another member (a carpet-bagger) . . . shook his fist in the speaking member's face, and told him he was a liar, and if he would come outside he would give him satisfaction.

This is nothing, however, to what has been going on in South Carolina this last session. Poor South Carolina, formerly the proudest State in America, boasting of her ancient families, remarkable for her wealth, culture, and refinement, now prostrate in the dust, ruled over by her former slaves, an old aristocratic society replaced by the most ignorant democracy that mankind ever saw invested with the functions of government. Of the one hundred and four [124] representatives, there are but twenty-three representatives of her old civilization, and these few can only look on at the squabbling crowd amongst whom they sit as silent enforced auditors. Of the 101 remaining, 94 are colored, and 7 their white allies. The few honest amongst them see plundering and corruption going on on all sides, and can do nothing. . . . The negroes have it all their own way, and rob and plunder as they please. The Governor of South Carolina lives in luxury, and treats his soldiers to champagne, while miserable planters have to pay taxes amounting to half their income, and if they fail to pay, their property is confiscated.

Louisiana and Mississippi are not much better off. The former has a negro barber for its Lieutenant-Governor, and the latter has just selected a negro steamboat porter as its United States Senator, filling the place once occupied by Jefferson Davis. . . . Georgia, I am happy to say, owing to the prudent policy of her people and the energies of the population in possession of a State rich in resources of every kind—industrial, commercial, and mineral—has been able to shake off the carpet-bag and negro yoke, and is in a fair way to recover her independence. Still even in Georgia, and especially in our immediate neighbourhood, a very bad influence has been exercised over the negroes, which has caused us no small difficulty in one's dealings with them.

✓   ✓   ✓

Randolph Abbott Shotwell was the son of a minister who accepted a charge in North Carolina at about the beginning of the Civil War. Young Shotwell fought in the Confederate army and then went to Rutherfordton, North Carolina, to settle while recovering from fever and ague. Purchasing the fragments of a printing office, he published the weekly *Western Vindicator*. During those years he became an ardent defender of those whom he called "decent white men," against the persecution of the Scalawags and Carpetbaggers. In his autobiographical account of experiences of "Three Years in Battle and Three in Federal Prisons," he justified the work of the Ku Klux Klan. The text is from J. G. de Roulhac Hamilton, Editor, *The Papers of Randolph Abbott Shotwell,* The North Carolina Department of Archives and History, Raleigh, 1931, Vol. II, pp. 287-297, *passim*.

It is well known that the mountain population of East Tennessee, and Western North Carolina, were at no time cordial supporters of the Confederate government. They were for a year, or more, swept away in the flood of enthusiasm and uninterrupted success, which marked the first epoch of our sad struggle for Independence. But they were—(I speak of the poorer classes . . .)—never cordial in their feelings towards the other portions of their states whom they looked upon as "rich and aristocratic",

and whom they first denominated—"the Secesh," or "fire eaters," etc. There
were also other causes of long-standing jealousies, and uncongeniality between them.

But as the War drew on, and reports of defeat came from all quarters . . . ; the pressure of scarcity and depletion began to be felt; and
worst of all, the call of the "conscript officer" was heard through the mountains—then, the half-smothered ill-wind towards "Jeff Davis Secession Aristocracy"—meaning the government, and the War-Party—broke forth into
full flame. . . .

Gradually the hardships of the War, a gloom of a long succession of
failures, the steady contraction of the Southern lines, with the daily increasing strenuousness of the call to arms—and a large amount of suffering
and privation among soldiers' families—so swelled the number of "union-
ists" or "Skulkers"—(for they had no special love for the Union)—that the
"woods were full of them," so to speak, and the local demagogues in the
several counties began to court their favor. . . . Thus arose the "Peace
Party" of the West. And now the mal-contents became so strong that they
aspired to elect members to Congress from the Western Districts and to
even shape the policy of the State Government. To accomplish this . . . a
secret, oath-bound League was fashioned. . . . The organizations spread
rapidly, and took the colloquial epithet of "Red-Strings," from the secret
sign of a crimson cord, which when worn at the button hole, or suspended
from the door latch, was the emblem of recognition among the membership; its significance being based upon the scriptural story of Rahab, the
harlot, who in recompense for her concealment of Joshua's spies during
their sojourn in Jerico, was given a scarlet cord to hang upon her door-
lintel as a token of deliverance when the victorious host should sack the
city! The Red String was to perform the same service when the hosts of
Grant and Sherman were carrying fire and sword through the homes of the
"Secessionists." Furthermore the "sign" was for the benefit of the deserters
and escaped prisoners, who were now swarming to the mountains. . . . The
League . . . was now . . . all-powerful throughout the greatest portion of
Western Carolina. . . . It was dominant, and domineering, almost to the
extent of driving all open opposition from the field.

Tongue nor pen can describe the condition of things when in 1867-8,
I first went to Rutherfordton to reside. . . . Politically there was but one
class—*the Red Strings!* For the Democrats and decent people were so hopelessly in the minority that few of them even took the trouble to go to the
polls, while at least 250 of the wealthiest citizens (being required to go a
full day's journey to Morganton and take the oath of allegiance before an
insolent Freedman's Bureau officer) *had never registered.*

On the first Saturday after my return to Rutherfordton I was surprised at
seeing long processions of countrymen entering the village by the various
roads, mounted and afoot, whites and blacks marching together, and in

frequent instances arm-in-arm, a sight to disgust even a decent negro. These proved to be members of the Red String League, which had gradually enlisted in its ranks a large majority of the small farmers, tenants, laborers, and rougher classes of the region. There were local meetings at the school houses, and other places, in different townships, but the county conclave convened at the Courthouse once or twice a month, besides called meetings. These meetings were strictly secret, and were conducted behind closed doors, with armed guards posted outside to prevent approach by any save the Elect. All that could be learned by casual passersby was that the negroes, and low-whites, often became worked up to a frenzy of fury as the shrewd wire pullers, for whose benefit the Leagues were devised appealed to their passions and prejudices by inflammatory declarations as to their wrongs at the hands of the "White Aristocracy," and by declaring that the Democrats were plotting to re-enslave the Freedmen, and renew the Rebellion, etc. . . . .

The Ku Klux Klan originated among the returned Confederate "Refugees" of East Tennessee, who in consequence of deadly feuds with their more numerous "Tory" neighbors were forced to adopt some such plan of secret association for mutual defense. . . . The teachings of the Radical agents, the Freedmen's Bureau officials, the cunning carpetbaggers, and even more corrupt native renegades, speedily paved the way for the spread of the Klan to every section of the Southern States. With four and a half millions of rude Africans, ignorant in mind, and brutal by instinct, suddenly set free, and virtually vested with superior political privileges over their late masters; with vile political adventurers swarming into every Southern community, unblushingly bent upon the acquisition of public plunder, by means of negro majorities; with the petty military minions of the Government, clothed with absolute and autocratic powers, by virtue of *"The Freedmen's Bureau Agency"*—holding daily courts in every city, town and county in the South, and losing no occasion to instill the most arrogant and unprincipled ideas into the minds of the ex-slaves in relation to their former masters; and, finally, with these ignorant, credulous, and inflammable, Africans secretly organized into dark-lantern mid-night "Leagues" bound by blood-curdling oaths; and between their prejudices, and their superstitious fears, held in utter mental bondage to their unscrupulous white leaders, by whom they were incited to nightly deeds of murder, arson, rape, rapine, and outrage, against which the honest conservative citizens could neither find protection, nor redress, because those same Mongrel White wire-pullers of the *"Leagues"* also held every executive office of the laws, both Federal and State, and allowed perfect immunity to their secret agents in crime, rendering the laws a nullity, and the pretended administration of the laws *a bitter farce*. With such a state of things prevailing everywhere throughout the Reconstructed Provinces, is it surprising that such an association as we have shown the Klan to be, became disseminated in those localities where Radicalism, and Leaguery were most rampant? For it is well to note the fact that in these states, and those portions of states, where the laws were faithfully administered—where Radicalism and carpet-baggism took least root, and where, as a natural sequence, the crimes and violence of the mid-night Leagues were unknown—there the Klan never came, or if it came, never manifested its existence by any sign. In short, all the mass testimony shows that the Ku Klux Klan sprang into life, and continued to spread, as a "Counter-irritant" and corrective of "Loyal League" lawlessness, and abuse of law. . . .

The Klan under the name of the "Constitutional Union Guard," or "White Brotherhood," spread . . . through Tennessee, propagated by the hourly outrages of "Gov." Brownlow's armed cut-throat State Troops whereby the respectable White Conservatives were harried like outlaws. . . . Lieut.-General Nathan B. Forrest was elected to be the head of the order. It expanded . . . to Georgia (where such men as U. S. Senator John B. Gordon, were connected with it) to the Carolinas (where thousands of the first citizens were its members); and eventually to all parts of the South. The field was ripe for its propagation, because almost everywhere the same terrible state of negro insolence and outrage, Radical scheming and maladministration of the laws, and universal disquiet among the better class of citizens, was in existence. The field was ripe, and the idea flew, and took root, and sprang up, like certain seeds that are wafted by the winds, far and near.

It erupted . . . in Eastern North Carolina, where mid-night assassinations by the League were of appalling frequency. When reprisals had been made, and a wholesale check given to the lawlessness, the Klan disbanded, or relapsed into somnolency. A year later the schemes of the carpet-baggers and negroes forced the "mobilization" (to use a military phrase) of the Klan in Central Carolina. Then followed the Holden-Kirk War, wherein many of the worthiest citizens of the State were imprisoned, maltreated, bullied, badgered, hung up by the thumbs, and actually *by the neck,* until three times unconscious, in a vain attempt to manufacture evidence to criminate innocent persons . . . ; all of which eventually resulted in the impeachment, and expulsion from the state of the so called Governor, together with his infamous tools. Meanwhile, the organization, in some one, or other of its different branches, had spread to nearly every county in the Carolinas. . . . Large numbers of farmers and waggoners in their frequent trips to market were sworn into the Order, and eventually organized lodges in their own neighborhoods. These scattered "camps" or "Dens" were irregular; that is, had no "charter," constitution or by-laws, and were really subject to no superior; each acting as it saw fit, somewhat as the Baptist churches are organized, tho' having the same oath, and acting under a kind of general understanding and "Common Law". . . . So the Klan did its work, and bloody, and irregular though it was, no one can deny that *justice* was done, and a great terror laid upon evildoers. . . .

✓   ✓   ✓

At the request of President Johnson, Carl Schurz, a former anti-slavery man and an organizer of the Republican party, went to the South to make a survey of the Johnson governments. The unfavorable report submitted by Schurz was used by the Joint Committee of Fifteen as evidence that the President's plan of reconstruction would not effect the social revolution which they insisted upon accomplishing. The following letters written by Schurz were reprinted, "Carl Schurz's Letters from the South," edited by Joseph H. Mahaffey, *Collections of the Georgia Historical Society,* Savannah, Vol. XXXV, No. 3, September, 1951, pp. 244-247, *passim.*

THE UNCONQUERED

But there is another class of people here, mostly younger men, who are still in the swearing mood. You can overhear their conversations as you pass them on the streets or even sit near them on the stoop of a hotel. They are "not conquered but only overpowered." They are only smothered for a time. They want to fight the war over again and they are sure in five years they are going to have a war bigger than any we have seen yet. They are meaning to get rid of this d—d military despotism. They will show us what stuff Southern men are made of. They will send their own men to Congress and show us that we cannot violate the Constitution with impunity. They have a rope ready for this and that Union man when the Yankee bayonets are gone. They will show the Northern interlopers that have set-tled down here to live on their substance the way home. They will deal largely in tar and feathers. They have been in the country and visited this and that place where a fine business is done in the way of killing negroes. They will let the negro know what freedom is, only let the Yankee soldiers be withdrawn. Such is their talk. You can hear it every day if you have your ears open. You see their sullen frowning faces at every street corner. Now, there may be much of the old Southern braggadocio in this, and I do not believe that such men will again resort to open insurrection; but they will practice private vengeance whenever they can do it with impunity, and I have heard sober-minded Union people express their apprehensions of it. This spirit is certainly no evidence of true loyalty.

It was this spirit which was active in an occurrence which disgraced this city on the 4th of July. Perhaps you have heard of it. The colored firemen of this city desired to parade their engine on the anniversary of our inde-pendence. If nobody else would, they felt like celebrating that day. A number will deny that it was a legitimate desire. At first the engineer of the fire department, who is a citizen of this town, refused his permission. Finally, by an interposition of an officer of the "Freedmen's Bureau," he was prevailed upon to give his consent, and the parade took place. In the principal street of the city the procession was attacked with clubs and stones by a mob opposed to the element above described, and by a crowd of boys all swearing at the d—d niggers. The colored firemen were knocked down, some of them severely injured, their engine was taken away from them, and the peaceable procession disbursed. Down with the d—d niggers. A Northern gentleman who loudly expressed his indignation at the proceeding was in danger of being mobbed, and had to seek safety in a house. You ask where was the militia. Alas, a number of Northern soldiers joined the roughs in the attack. Northern soldiers, stationed in the south, do not always abstain from showing some of their old Five Points spirit, when the negro is the victim. Witness the 165th New York Duryea's Zouaves, who knocked down negroes in the streets of Charleston and drove them out of the market-house merely for a pastime, and were then by the praiseworthy energy of Generals Quincy A. Gillmore and John P. Hatch, disarmed, deprived of their colors, and shut up in Fort Sumter to spend their time in meditation until they shall be dishonorably mustered out.

To return to the "unconquered" in Savannah—the occurrence of the Fourth of July shows what they are capable of doing even while the Yankee bayonets are still here. If from this we infer what they will be capable of doing when the Yankee bayonets are withdrawn, the prospect is not altogether pleasant and Union people, white and black, in this city and neighborhood may well entertain serious apprehensions. How numerous this "unconquered" element is, I am not able to say; perhaps not numerous enough to organize rows on a grand scale beyond the limits of a city or a neighborhood. But it is certainly strong enough to interrupt the peaceful development of things, to render it dangerous for a Union man to live here, to prevent immigration from the North, and to bring about serious conflict between the whites and blacks.

THE VEIL QUESTION

Unfortunately, this spirit receives much encouragement from the fair sex. We have heard so much of the bitter resentment of the Southern ladies that the tale becomes stale by frequent repetition, but when inquiring into the feelings of the people, this element must not be omitted. There are certainly a good many sensible women in the South who have arrived at a just appreciation of the circumstances with which they are surrounded. But there is a large number of Southern women who are as vindictive and defiant as ever, and whose temper does not permit them to lay their tongues under any restraint. You can see them in every hotel, and they will treat you to the most ridiculous exhibitions whenever an occasion offers. A day or two ago a Union officer, yielding to an impulse of politeness, handed a dish of pickles to a Southern lady at the dinner-table of a hotel in this city. A look of unspeakable scorn and indignation met him. "So you think," said the lady, "a Southern woman will take a dish of pickles from a hand that is dripping with the blood of her countrymen?"

It is remarkable upon what trifling material this female wrath is feeding and growing fat. In a certain district in South Carolina, the ladies were some time ago, and perhaps are now, dreadfully exercised about the veil question. You may ask me what the veil question is. Formerly, under the old order of things, negro women were not permitted to wear veils. Now, under the new order of things, a great many are wearing veils. This is an outrage which cannot be submitted to; the white ladies of that neighborhood agree in being indignant beyond measure. Some of them declare that whenever they meet a colored woman wearing a veil that they will tear the veil from her face. Others, mindful of the consequences which such an act of violence might draw after it, under this same new order of things, declare their resolve never to wear veils themselves as long as colored women wear veils. This is the veil question, and this is the way it stands at present.

Such things may seem trifling and ridiculous. But it is a well-known fact that a silly woman is sometimes able to exercise a powerful influence over a man not half as silly, and the class of "unconquered" above described is undoubtedly in a great measure composed of individuals that are apt to be influenced by silly women. It has frequently been said that had it not been for the spirit of the Southern women, the rebellion would have broken down long ago, and there is, no doubt, a grain of truth in it.

$$\text{✓}\qquad\text{✓}\qquad\text{✓}$$

An English traveler, Sir George Campbell, toured the Southern states to obtain information regarding the relation of the black and white races, which he felt might help the British to deal with masses of the black race in South Africa. His report, "Black and White in the Southern States," was published in *The Fortnightly Review*, Vol. XXV, New Series, March, 1879, pp. 449-468, April 1879, pp. 588-607, from which the following text is taken.

In the course of my tour I have had opportunities of conversing with many men of many classes (and quite as much on one side of politics as the other) who have had the greatest experience of the blacks in various aspects—educational, industrial, political, and other. . . . I have visited not only the towns but the rural districts of four of the principal States formerly slave-holding, viz. Virginia, North Carolina, South Carolina, and Georgia; and it so happened that I was in South Carolina (the *ne plus ultra* of Southernism) on the day of the late general election. I have seen and conversed with the Negroes in their homes, and in their fields, in factories in churches, and in political meetings, and I think I have been able to learn something of a very prominent part of the population—the Negresses. . . .

The prominent position taken by the Negro women is a feature in which they are distinguished from some Oriental races. No doubt this has some advantages, but also I shall have to note some attendant disadvantages—

social, industrial, and political. In matters matrimonial the women are somewhat too independent and light-hearted; and the men also being on this subject given to a rather loose philosophy, the marital tie is not so binding and indissoluble as it might be. . . . Under slavery the family could not be introduced—it was impossible that there could be much permanency of marital arrangements when the parties were constantly liable to be, and frequently were, sold away like cattle; and the relation between parent and child was especially weakened or rather not created. The parents were not really responsible for the children; on the contrary, the women were sent to work, and the children were carefully tended by persons appointed by the masters for the purpose, like calves or lambs or any other valuable stock. Parents had little affection for children thus reared, and children owed no respect or obedience to parents. The family as we know it is, in fact, a novelty to the Negro since emancipation, and such institutions are not perfected in a day. . . .

At the time of emancipation the Negroes were destitute of education to an excessive degree. Not only were the means of education wanting to them, but after some local troubles which alarmed the masters, most of the Southern States passed laws making it highly penal to educate a Negro. These laws endured to the last, and under them the generation upon whom emancipation came grew up entirely without instruction. The only educated persons of the race were the few blacks who had obtained instruction in the North, and a very few domestic slaves whom their mistresses had to some degree educated, the penal laws notwithstanding. Since emancipation a great deal has been done to educate the Negro. Many schools in which a superior education is afforded have been maintained by benevolent Northerners, and the State Governments have set up, and continue to maintain, several colleges in which the more ambitious and aspiring young blacks are educated. For the education of the masses a public school system has been started in all the States, of which the blacks have a fair share. Owing, however, to financial difficulties these schools are extremely imperfect, being open but a small portion of each year—in some States as little as two months, and in none, I believe, more than about four months on an average. However, this is better than nothing. . . .

Since the North has insisted that the blacks should be admitted to political equality, neither North or South has made any movement whatever toward admitting them to social equality; in fact, the movement has been rather the other way. A certain friendly familiarity and association was possible and common, more especially in the South, when the parties met on acknowledged terms of superiority and inferiority. Now the whites assert their superiority by social exclusion, and the blacks themselves, unwilling to accept the old situation in social matters, have much withdrawn themselves from association with the whites on occasions which formerly brought the two races together. This is particularly noticeable in the churches. I am told that in former days almost every church had a recognized black quarter; now the black churches are almost entirely separate from the white churches.

✓ ✓ ✓

Several agencies were interested in the education of Negroes after the war. Churches and religious organizations, the Freedmen's Bureau, the reconstruction State governments, and many individuals, including philanthropists and teachers, contributed toward the establishment of schools for the children of the ex-slaves. Booker T. Washington, the nation's greatest Negro educational leader, looking backward in 1902 to the reconstruction period, wrote the following comment in an article entitled "The Fruits of Industrial Training," in the *Atlantic Monthly,* Vol. 92, September, 1903, pp. 453-462.

I want to call attention here to a phase of Reconstruction policy which is often overlooked. All now agree that there was much in Reconstruction which was unwise and unfortunate. However we may regard that policy, and much as we may regret mistakes, the fact is too often overlooked that it was during this Reconstruction period that a public school system for the education of all the people of the South was first established in most of the states. Much that was done by those in charge of Reconstruction legislation has been overturned, but the public school system still remains. True, it has been modified and improved, but the system remains, and is every day growing in popularity and strength.

✓ ✓ ✓

American periodicals displayed a great interest in the South after the Civil War, and consequently they afford a wealth of comment on social, economic and political trends in that section. Among the articles dealing with the education of Negroes is the following one, "The Hampton Normal and Agricultural Institute," by Helen W. Ludlow, *Harper's New Monthly Magazine,* XLVII, October, 1873, pp. 672-685.

The ten years that separate us from the Proclamation of Emancipation have wrought some natural but curious changes in public sentiment, both North and South. . . . One of the most important questions that the years have settled is that of negro education. The best thinkers of the North and South, however distant their stand-points, are no longer apart in the conclusion that it is of vital importance to the nation. This conviction is shown at the South by the action taken by most of the reconstructed States in embodying some provision for the negroes in their free-school system, and quite as remarkably by the increasing favor, or tolerance, to say the least, extended to the schools and colleges for freedmen established in them by Northern benevolence. . . . It is a curious fact that the only institution south of the national capital which . . . offers to destitute youth an opportunity to earn at once a solid English education and a valuable industrial training, is a college for negroes. The Normal and Agricultural Institute of Hampton, Virginia, and its rapid growth and success, prove the adaptation of its system to the public needs.

Another demand of the South, which may be expected to continue and increase for some time, is that of colored teachers for its colored schools. . . . The colored teacher . . . is called upon not only to teach in the schoolhouse, but in the cabin; to advise the people how to build better houses, and raise better crops, and be better citizens. He is to be a little centre of civilization among them, and help, in his proper degree, to elevate his race by the power of his own life. His education should not unfit him to dwell among them; a poor man himself, he should be able at any time to enter the workshops or the fields, and make up the deficiencies of his often ill-paid salary. . . .

The practical working of this principle has been attended by a remarkable degree of success. For the first three years, at the end of which the school numbered eighty-six, the young men were boarded, lodged, and clothed mainly from the avails of their own labor. . . . In March, 1872, the General Assembly of Virginia passed an act appropriating one-third of the interest accruing from the proceeds of the State college land scrip to this institution as an endowment for its agricultural and mechanical departments. This gift, from which it will secure five per cent on $95,000, will enable it to extend the opportunities it alone of all colleges for freedmen offers of industrial training and self-help. . . .

In 1867 General S. C. Armstrong was stationed at Hampton as superintendent of a department of the Freedmen's Bureau. His experience during and after the war gave him a quick sense of . . . [the Negroes'] needs. . . . General Armstrong induced the American Missionary Society to buy the "Wood Farm," which was the bureau station, for the establishment of a normal and agricultural school. The position of its superintendent was given, entirely unsought, to himself, and he has been ever since its inspirer and prime mover. As far as any great work of the kind can be ascribed to one man's agency, this is the result of his enthusiasm and foresight and almost unlimited executive abilities. . . .

In June, 1870, the institute was incorporated by the act of the General Assembly, a board of trustees created, including men of character and influence both of the North and South. And to this board the American Missionary Association deeded the entire property of the school.

✓   ✓   ✓

Conditions in Negro schools were described in an unsigned report in the *Atlantic Monthly*, Vol. 50, 1882, pp. 478-479.

Many of the negro schools are maintained under great disadvantages and inconveniences. . . . Here is an instance: I saw two colored men at work in one room with a school in which the average daily attendance for the winter was one hundred and twenty-six. They had to conduct recitations at the same time in opposite corners of the room. The house was open and very cold. The teachers were obliged to furnish fuel, and to provide desks, brooms, blackboards, and all other appliances at their own expense. The school was free to the pupils, the salaries of the teachers being paid for out of the public school fund. The house in which the school was maintained was owned by some Northern missionary or aid society, and was held by colored trustees, living in the town in which it was situated. They were too poor to repair or improve the building, and the (white) public school officers would not (perhaps could not under the law) appropriate anything for repairs to the house, unless the colored people would surrender their title to the property, which they declined to do. . . .

It is very interesting to listen to the singing in the colored schools. I several times heard many hundred children singing together the old plantation and revival melodies, and other songs of their race. Some of these are very peculiar and wonderful. One hears everywhere a few rich and powerful voices, and the negro churches in the larger towns have fine choirs. But the old negro music will soon disappear. All the educated negro ministers discourage or forbid the use of it among their people, and the strange, wild songs, whether religious or not, are coming to be regarded as relics and badges of the old condition of slavery and heathenism, and the young men and women are ashamed to sing them.

✓   ✓   ✓

Southerners came to look upon the missionaries and religious leaders from the North with hostility and hatred, because many of these visiting leaders gave actual support to the carpetbag governments, some actually occupying seats in the reconstruction legislatures. The Northern churches hoped to effect a reunion of their denominations, which they believed could be accomplished only by political and social reform of the South in the direction of New England ideas. Hunter Dickinson Farish, in *The Circuit Rider Dismounts*, the Dietz Press, Richmond, Virginia, 1938, pp. 108-162, *passim*, shows how a malicious verbal warfare was carried on between the Northern and Southern branches of the Methodist Church during the period following the Civil War, in the various church publications. The following sentiments will illustrate this warfare.

The Central Christian Advocate, in 1867, warned:

The real business of the Protestant Churches of the North is to bear down upon the South with all their forces. We inform the *St. Louis Advocate* that we are going to map out, and then spread over the South, bearing with us free schools, equal rights, free speech and a thoroughly Christian civilization. We expect to put down by the free ballot and the true Gospel every form of barbarism including all the untold villainies of slavery. We intend to keep right on, and when there are enough school teachers, radical voters and Yankee notions all over the South, we expect Wendell Phillips, William

Lloyd Garrison, and other fanatics, to swing round that circle through Arkansas, Texas, Mississippi and South Carolina and talk *just as they please* without the slightest molestation. You must really grin and bear it. We will not stop for 'line upon line,' leaving out the 'n' if you like. We will leave 'whining' to your ancient friends, the bloodhounds, now out of office with the slaveholders, and whimpering to the chagrined rebels, who have been suppressed but not taught.

✓   ✓   ✓

Dr. Daniel Curry, editor of the *New York Christian Advocate,* filled his columns with advice concerning the punishment of the South. In the May 23, 1867, issue of the *Advocate,* Dr. Curry wrote regarding the trial of Jefferson Davis:

Meanwhile hundreds of thousands of the best sons of Northern families sleep on unavenged in their patriotic graves throughout rebel territory. Some assassins, some prison-keepers, have been brought to justice in vindication of the laws; not one of the leaders of the great crime, not one really responsible man, has been brought to condign punishment. The politicians, the administrators of the country have these matters in hand; the people look on and ponder them; eyes dim with weeping for their dead read the facts, and continue to weep. The great heart and head of the people remember and reason and are beginning to demand what is the significance and what the moral consequence of this unheard-of policy.

✓   ✓   ✓

A secular journal, the Cartersville, Georgia, *Express,* addressed an editorial to the Reverend E. Q. Fuller, advising:

Go home, Doctor Fuller, and let the poor Negroes alone. They will improve slowly and behave themselves if your sort will cease to put mischief into their heads. Go home, and preach the Gospel to those who may be willing to hear you, and cease to vex your righteous (?) soul about the sins of the Southern people. . . . Go home, and may joy go with you, and peace be left behind you.

✓   ✓   ✓

Missionaries and ministers aided in the establishment of the Union League and in the indoctrination of the Negro to vote the Republican ticket. The following comment from the *New Orleans Christian Advocate,* August 11, 1866, dealt with such political activity.

The churchmen of the Presbyterian and Methodist Churches in the North are largely identified with this attempt of violent revolution. In fact

Quoted from *Central Christian Advocate* in the *Southern Christian Advocate,* May 24, 1867.

these godly gentlemen who are scattered throughout the South, taking ecclesiastical guardianship of hundreds of thousands of the freedmen of the South, have a very large interest in this new order of things which is to be precipitated. . . . They are on hand to open conventions with prayer which are avowedly to subvert the reigning government of the States; to take a 'guardianship' of the Negro, which ends in madness, riot and blood. These gentlemen constitute no mean part of the extensive machinery in motion to fan the worst passions of the Negro and to inflame anew the half-extinct coals of civil strife. The Lord judge between us and them.

✓   ✓   ✓

In a series of articles which were published in *Harper's New Monthly Magazine* in 1874, Edwin De Leon, a native Southerner, described "The New South." The following article on agriculture appeared in Vol. 48, January, 1874, pp. 270-280.

The situation of the South immediately after the four years' struggle was very exceptional, and great changes took place successively during the years which followed. When the war ended, the belief was generally entertained at the South that reunion, oblivion, and amnesty would quickly follow the cessation of hostilities. It was thought that the whole Southern people, with the exception of a few obnoxious leaders, would be at once restored to their former status after ratifying changes wrought by the war, faithfully accepting the situation. The first effect of this belief, equally entertained at the North and South, was to give a new impulse to the agricultural and industrial development of the latter. Northern energy and capital immediately poured in to avail themselves of the opportunity; plantations were purchased or worked by Northern money, with or without the aid of former owners; sawmills and cotton factories absorbed Northern energy and capital; and the South, even under her political disabilities, seemed awakening to a new birth and unparalleled prosperity. But the almost universal loss and failure attendant on the well-meant but unskillful essays of these new allies in a field and a business they did not understand, under the disorganization of the only available labor, drove them away and caused a strong ebb tide of Northern sentiment to set in within the first two years, against which the South has been slowly making headway. For the past six years her people have been staggering under burdens, financial, industrial, and political, which have retarded her progress, impoverished her population, crippled her resources, and repelled all outside aid. . . . For the past two years they have been slowly but surely struggling up to a better position, and the prospects of the South to-day are more promising than they ever have been since she essayed her most disastrous experiment. . . .

The great planters and slave-owners, whose names had become historical in the South and the Union, collapsed, and their plantations fell into the hands of men who had accumulated capital, were worked for the benefit of their creditors, or on shares with the freedmen.

Several plans of planting on shares with the freedmen have been adopted by the Southern planters, and are now in active operation—the object being to secure his labor, and make it more reliable, by interesting him in its results. In some instances the landed proprietor still pays regular wages, but the system of planting on shares is more common, in which the laborer gets, in lieu of wages, a stipulated portion of the profits out of the proceeds of the crop, varying from one-half to one-third.

There is a third plan also resorted to, whereby the proprietor of the land takes no interest in the crop further than holding a lien over it for the payment of a stipulated sum, at which he leases it absolutely, with mules, implements, etc., to a body of laborers, represented by one selected as head of the gang. In some instances different parts of the same plantation are thus leased out to several separate gangs. . . .

The white proprietors of small portions of land who themselves work their farms, . . . in Georgia, Alabama, South Carolina, and other Southern States, have gone into the use of the cultivators and phosphates, working thoroughly small patches, instead of planting a greater breadth with less care and labor.

To a class as generally impoverished and pressed for money as the cotton planters, the great expense of these cultivators or fertilizers is an insuperable drawback, for they are cash commodities. Hence the Southern planter, ever slow to adopt novelties, has not materially varied his old slovenly system of cotton planting to any very marked extent . . . only the accustomed eye can recognize returning prosperity in what presents an outward aspect of dilapidation, neglect, and ruin. Throughout the Southern cotton belt in Mississippi, Alabama, and the Gulf States generally, tumble-down houses and out-buildings, falling fences, ghostly-looking dead pine-trees stretching their naked arms over the falling fields, or stumps erecting their unsightly shapes, meet the eye of the traveler where he expects to see fields smiling with fertility. Yet in these very fields the practiced eye can see the plentiful cotton blooms whitening the surface; and although the plant generally looks small, and the pod also, yet the abundance of the yield compensates for all. With the exception of the fortunate few whose means were not destroyed by the war and its results, or who have since recuperated, and are able to control and work their own plantations as formerly, only hiring their labor instead of owning it, the system of *planting on shares* has been generally adopted by the cotton planters on the larger tracts or plantations, but with modifications which vary almost as much as the separate contracts, dependent on what the laborer can bring into the partnership, and his capacity.

↗   ↗   ↗

The Atlantic Monthly published a series of "Studies in the South," Vol. 51, pp. 90-91, 1883, the authorship of which was not disclosed. The following description of the Southern storekeeper appeared in the series.

One of the worst features of the condition of things in the South I found in the character and methods of a large number of men, who were selling goods in the smaller towns and villages, and at the "cross-roads" and landings almost everywhere. They were mostly foreigners or Northern men, but in some parts of the country a few native Southerners were taking up the same kind of business, as good Southern citizens now and then confessed to me with shame. These merchants, or "store-keepers," were commonly as rapacious as pirates, wholly destitute of principle, conscience, and honesty. I do not mean that all the "small merchants" or dealers in the country places in the South are of this character; but the class is a very large one, and has its representatives in every State. These men are growing rich faster than any other class in the Southern States. They sell goods to the negroes and poor whites at two hundred to three hundred per cent. profit, and very often they simply take all that a man has. A large part of their business is conducted in the following way: a dealer of this class makes an agreement during the winter with a negro or white laborer to "run" him for the season. That is, the merchant furnishes the "small planter" with all his provisions and supplies of every kind for the spring, summer, and autumn, agricultural implements, and everything needed, on credit; all these things to be paid for out of the crop, when it is matured and gathered.

Each merchant may thus supply, or "run," a dozen, twenty, or fifty men. During the summer, and all the time the crop is growing, the dealer rides about the country and inspects each man's fields, or sends some competent man to do it, so that he can estimate the probable product. An experienced judge can do this very accurately. When the cotton is ready to be picked, the merchant knows almost exactly how much has been produced by each man that he has "run." All along through the season he has of course entered on his books each article furnished to the planters; and now he goes over his books, and sets down the price, the amount the customer is to be required to pay for it; and the prices are so arranged that the aggregate charged for the season's supplies will exactly take the planter's whole crop. The laborer is thus left, at the end of the season, absolutely penniless.

There are often stormy scenes on "settling-day." Such a merchant will submit without resistance to the bitterest cursing a wronged, disappointed, and enraged negro can utter. Often there would be violence, but that the merchant is armed and his dupe is cowed. The end or result of it all is, usually, that the dealer makes the man a cheap, showy present, and arranges to "run" him again next year. But sometimes, when a negro is concerned, the outcome is different. The merchant buys cotton. In many cases he has a gin of his own, or a cotton-press. This gives the wronged, helpless negro an opportunity for revenge. The gin or press is fired, some dark night; there is a deduction from the dealer's profits for the year; the negroes exult among themselves; and there is a new "political outrage"—or there was, when these were useful—for the newspapers and politicians.

14

Bourbon Rule

James G. Blaine reported in *Twenty Years of Congress,* The Henry Bill Publishing Co., Norwich, Connecticut, 1884, Vol. II, pp. 638-644, that in 1879 when President Hayes called the Forty-Sixth Congress to meet in extra session the Democratic ascendency in the South had become so complete that out of one hundred and six Congressional districts the opposition had been able to elect only four representatives. The Senate also had received several Southerners of ante-bellum importance, of whom he commented as follows:

Southern men of note were rapidly filling the Democratic side of the Senate chamber: Wade Hampton had taken a very conspicuous part in the Rebellion, had assisted in its beginning when South Carolina was hurried out of the Union. He immediately joined the Confederate Army, where he remained in high command until the close of the war, after which he took an active part in the politics of his State and was elected to the Governorship in 1876. An extreme Southern man in his political views, he was in all private relations kindly and generous. His grandfather Wade Hampton was engaged in two wars for the Union which the grandson fought to destroy. He was with the men of Sumter and Marion during the Revolutionary war, and was a major-general in the war of 1812, commanding in Northern New York. At his death in 1835 he was believed to be the largest slave-holder in the United States, owning it was said three thousand slaves. . . .

Zebulon B. Vance was born and reared in Buncombe County, North Carolina. He belongs originally to that conservative class of Southern Whigs whose devotion to the Union was considered steadfast and immovable. He was a representative during Mr. Buchanan's Administration, adhering to the remnant of the Whig party, which went under the name of "American" in the South. He joined the Confederate Army immediately after the war began, and a year later was elected Governor of his State. He became extensively known through the North, first by the rumors of his disagreements with Jefferson Davis during the war, and afterwards by Horace Greeley's repeated reference, in the campaign of 1872, to his "political disabilities" as an illustration of Republican bigotry. He has been noted as a stump-speaker and as an advocate. Since the war he has been so pronounced a partisan as in some degree to lessen the genial humor which had always been one of his leading personal traits.

John S. Williams of Kentucky succeeded Thomas C. McCreery in the Senate. He had gained much credit when only twenty-seven years of age as Colonel of a Kentucky regiment in the Mexican war; but when the rebellion broke out he joined the Confederates and served as Brigadier-General in the army of General Joseph E. Johnston. It was said of him, as of many other Southern men of character and bravery, that they had gallantly borne the flag of the Union in foreign lands and the flag of Disunion at home. The genial nature of General Williams won for him in Congress many friends beyond the line of his own party. . . .

For the first time since the Congress that was chosen with Mr. Buchanan in 1856, the Democratic party was in control of both branches. . . .

Blaine pointed out that once again Southern influence was felt in that session in the passage of the Army Bill.

The main point of difference which had caused the failure of the Army Bill in the previous Congress was an amendment insisted upon by the Democratic majority in the House concerning "the use of troops at the polls," as the issue was popularly termed. It would be unjust to the Republicans to say that they demanded military aid with the remotest intention of controlling any man's vote. It was solely with the purpose of preventing votes from being controlled, and especially of preventing voters from being driven by violence from the polls. But as has been already set forth in these pages, public opinion in the United States is hostile to any thing that even in appearance indicates a Government control at elections, and most of all a control by the use of the military arm. The majority of Representatives seemed to prefer that voters by the thousand should be deprived by violence of the right of suffrage, rather than that their rights should be protected by even the semblance of National authority in the person of a soldier.

It was demonstrated in the debate that it was only the semblance of National authority which was present in the South. The number of troops scattered at various points through the Southern States was not so large as the number of troops in the Northern States, and, as was readily shown, did not amount on an average to one soldier in each county of the States that had been in rebellion. But this fact seemed to have no weight; and the Democrats, having a majority in both Senate and House, now appended to the Army Appropriation Bill the amendment upon which the House had insisted the previous session: "that no money appropriated in this act is appropriated or shall be paid for the subsistence, equipment, transportation, or compensation of any portion of the Army of the United States to be used

REMEMBER THE

These degenerate sons of the white race who control the republican machine in this county, or those whose positions made them influential in putting negro rule on the whites, will suffer the penalty of their responsibility for any disturbance consequent on the determination of the white men of this county to carry the election at any cost.

REMEMBER THE

A poster used to intimidate Negroes and white Republicans in a Southern election.

as a police force to keep peace at the polls at any election held within any State." As this enactment was in general harmony with the Southern policy indicated by President Hayes upon his inauguration, he approved the bill; and the elections in several of the Southern States were thenceforth left, not to the majority of the voters, but to the party which had the hardihood and the physical resources to decree any desired result. But it was well known to all familiar with political struggles in the South that the white men were not required to use force after the protection of the National Government was withdrawn. Colored voters were not equal to the physical contest necessary to assert their civil rights, and thenceforward personal outrages in large degree ceased. The peace which followed was the peace of forced submission and not the peace of contentment. Even that form of peace was occasionally broken by startling assassinations for the purpose of monition and discipline to the colored race.

✓   ✓   ✓

No longer were the leading Southern statesmen emphasizing sectionalism and states' rights. When Charles Sumner, who had been pre-eminent in the Senate in securing the passage of the Reconstruction Laws, died in 1874, L. Q. C. Lamar, Representative from Mississippi, delivered a eulogy which might be said to typify the new attitude which was to prevail in the South, that of conciliation of the North. The following comment on Lamar's eulogy was written by James G. Blaine, *Twenty Years of Congress,* The Henry Bill Publishing Company, Norwich, Connecticut, 1884, Vol. II, pp. 546.

A singular interest was added to the formal eulogies of Mr. Sumner by the speech of Mr. Lamar of Mississippi, who had just returned to the House of Representatives which he had left thirteen years before to join his State in secession. It was a mark of positive genius in a Southern representative to pronounce a fervid and discriminating eulogy upon Mr. Sumner, and skilfully to interweave with it a defense of that which Mr. Sumner like John Wesley believed to be the sum of all villainies. Only a man of Mr. Lamar's peculiar mental type could have accomplished the task. He pleased the radical anti-slavery sentiment of New England; he did not displease the radical pro-slavery sentiment of the South. . . . His reason, his faith, his hope, all led him to believe in the necessity of preserving the Union of the States; but he persuaded himself that fidelity to a constituency which had honored him, personal ties with friends from whom he could not part, the maintenance of an institution which he was pledged to defend, called upon him to stand with the secession leaders in the revolt of 1861. . . .

✓   ✓   ✓

The men who regained control of the State governments of the South at this time were persons of prominence and had been leaders before the war. Their opponents called them "Bourbons," thus comparing them to the French royal family which was restored to power after the defeat of Napoleon. *The Atlantic*

Monthly's editor who made studies in the South in 1881, *op. cit.,* Vol. 49, 1882, p. 191, explained the identity of the Bourbons as follows:

As used in the North, this word "Bourbon" designates a class of white men, composed chiefly of leading citizens of the Southern States. The Bourbons are the principal business men, lawyers, physicians, teachers, clergymen, merchants, and farmers of the South. They are everywhere the leaders of society, in the best sense of the word. They sustain the churches, and give such efficiency to the moral activities and discipline of the local communities as they have thus far attained. Taken broadly or generally, the class includes the best people of the South, or most of them. They are Bourbons because in politics they are democrats, and act in opposition to the principles, policy, or methods of the republican party, which has administered the national government since the time of our civil war. . . .

✓   ✓   ✓

Booker T. Washington summed up the political change which came with the presidency of Hayes, in "The Fruits of Industrial Training," *Atlantic Monthly,* Vol. 92, September, 1902, pp. 453-462, *passim.*

Beginning with the year 1877, the Negro in the South lost practically all political control; that is to say, as early as 1885 the Negro had scarcely any members of his race in the national Congress or state legislatures, and long before this date had ceased to hold state offices. This was true, notwithstanding the protests and fervent oratory of such strong race leaders as Frederick Douglass, B. K. Bruce, John R. Lynch, P. B. S. Pinchback, and John H. Langston, with a host of others. When Frederick Douglass, the greatest man that the race has produced, died in 1895, it is safe to say that the Negro in the Southern states, with here and there a few exceptions, had practically no political control or political influence, except in sending delegates to national conventions, or in holding a few Federal positions by appointment.

✓   ✓   ✓

Sir George Campbell, *The Fortnightly Review,* London, Vol. 25, New Series, 1879, pp. 590-593, explained the process by which the Bourbons acquired possession of the governments.

[After the days of black reconstruction] . . . In most States the white leaders soon came to their senses, and perceived, what might have been seen from the first, that a population which had half the numbers, and all the property, influence, and education, must prevail over the black half possessed of none of these advantages, and in many respects dependent on the propertied classes. They therefore very early returned to the electoral charge, and by no very unfair means regained possession of most of the

State Governments and the control of the State Legislatures. Fortunately, taught by adversity, the white leaders so restored to power took a reasonable and moderate course, honestly accepting the situation and the great constitutional amendments. In these States it is a great gain that, in order to introduce certain amendments of a moderate character, the people, under white leadership, have recently passed revised editions of their State constitutions (embodying the war amendments), which no one can gainsay as not being real and voluntary; whereas the first constitutions imposed after the war were certainly the work of very one-sided conventions, acting under the protection of United States bayonets. Besides the management of their own States, the white party have been more and more gaining the great majority of the Southern seats in the United States Congress, and things have been more and more tending to that democratic "Solid South" of which we have lately heard so much. . . .

When I left the States, several of the recent elections were still disputed; but I believe there is no doubt that in Virginia and North Carolina two or three Republican members have been returned for the districts in which the black vote is in a very overwhelming majority, which is as much as could be expected under the circumstances. In Georgia no Republican Congressmen were elected; but several "independent" Democrats have been returned under circumstances which tend much to insure fair dealing toward the blacks, inasmuch as, the whites being divided, the black vote has been important. The Independents justify their separation from the regulars of the party by denouncing the evils and jobbery of the "caucus" system; and they go on to say that it was a sort of bargain with the blacks that if they quietly yielded the reins of power to the whites, they should be fairly treated, and their right to vote should be honestly recognized; whereas if the whole thing is settled in white caucus, from which the blacks are excluded, they are practically disfranchised.

As regards, then, what I may call the moderate States, I see no ground for taking a gloomy view of the situation. . . . My only doubt is as regards one constitutional amendment which most of these States have adopted. I do not seriously quarrel with that which, as with us, deprives of the franchise those who have not paid their taxes. But it must be fairly worked. There is generally a direct poll tax, justified by its application to popular education of which the masses are so much in need; and there is a question of a tax on dogs, the slaves of ex-slaves. If any laxity is shown in the collection of taxes from poor and ignorant people about election time, or the date of payment is put near election day, very many may be disfranchised, who must soon pay the money nevertheless. The provision in the new constitution which I most fear is that which permanently disfranchises all who are convicted of crime, unless the governor remits the sentence. In principle exception can hardly be taken to this; but I have some doubt whether, in the matter of justice, the Negroes are quite secure of fair play; and it is somewhat dangerous if a nearly balanced constituency may be affected by a rigorous administration of the criminal laws. It is certain that the prison populations are composed of blacks in a proportion greater than the general population to an overwhelming degree. . . . The magistrates and judges are either elected or nominated by the white rulers. . . . Very few blacks are admitted on juries; in Virginia, I believe, none at all.

Then as regards punishment, flogging is very freely used in Virginia; but further South the system of *chain-gangs, i.e., extra-mural labour,* is universal. The convicts are not only employed on public works, railways, and the like, but are usually let out to private speculators, and they are made a source of profit instead of an expense. It comes simply to this, that the punishment for crime is reduction to the old state of slavery in a form not very widely differing from the old form. I am told that the people most often convicted and sent to the chain-gang are the undisciplined young Negroes who have grown up since the days of slavery. I have often heard it said by reliable men that they employ no man so readily as one who has come out of the chain-gang, because he has there learnt discipline. . . .

On the whole I am inclined to think that there is some foundation for the assertion sometimes put forward by friends of the blacks, that a much harder justice is dealt to one class than to another; that in the outrages and murders committed by the whites in the troubled years after the war, very little condign punishment has been executed, while justice and something more is done on the blacks. One thing did astonish me during my tour, and that is, to find how much Judge Lynch survives, especially when the accused are blacks. I imagined he was a thing of the past, but I found that several lynching cases of great atrocity occurred before I had been many weeks in the States; that is, hanging by popular movement without the intervention of judge and jury. This is generally the case when there is any alleged assault of any kind by a black on a white woman. The blacks are popularly said to be prone to that kind of crime; with what justice I cannot say. An experienced judge told me he has known many accused and many hanged, but none convicted on trial. The mere suggestion that a black man would like to do something of the kind if he could, seems enough to hang him.

✶   ✶   ✶

In describing politics in the South during the 1870's and 80's observers frequently referred to the "Solid South." A closer examination would have revealed differences that were developing to destroy the unity of the Democratic party. *The Atlantic Monthly,* "Studies in the South" July, 1882, Vol. 50, p. 109, commented on the "old Whigs who hate the name of Democrat."

These men . . . say that they do not care at all for the democratic party; that they do not care what party controls the South, if . . . property and industry can be made secure; that anybody is welcome to hold offices and govern their States who will do so honestly. "We simply want such state governments as you usually have in the North." This was said to me many times in the States of which I am writing. I was somewhat surprised to find large numbers of men who are leaders in the democratic party in the South who said, as they said to me repeatedly, "We are no democrats." In meeting men of this class I constantly heard such utterances as this: "I am no democrat. For my part, my political education was that of a whig. My father was a whig, and I grew up with his ideas and sentiments regarding political matters. I despise the very name of democrat. There is not a principle or tradition belonging to the organization which I approve. I wish to God we might have an administration party, a republican party, in our State, that a gentleman could belong to without the sacrifice of all honesty and self-respect. What in the name of Heaven is the reason that the republican party in the South is left in the hands of such men as its local managers usually are?"

They go on to say, as in Alabama, in Mississippi, and in Louisiana many of them said to me, that it is a misfortune to the South and to the nation to have the South solid; that the South does not wish to be solid, but that it really seems to be the interest of most of the local republican politicians in the Southern States to keep the South solid as long as possible. . . .

[The Negroes] have the "right" to vote under the law, but they have no real power or ability to vote. They do not and cannot choose; they have no knowledge of what is involved on one side or the other. They have no materials for an opinion or judgment, nor any ability to form a preference or decision regarding political matters. They know nothing of the position, doctrines, history, traditions, or aims of either party, and they have no idea or notion whatever of their respective merits or principles. They simply vote as they are told to vote by the local republican managers, and that is the whole matter. So far as I can learn, it seems probable that they would vote for anything or any man bearing the republican name. They attribute whatever is good or desirable in their present condition to the influence and agency of the republican party, and hope for impossible things from the same source in the future.

✓ ✓ ✓

The Republican party, which had controlled elections in the South from 1867 until 1876, suddenly accepted the fact that the Democrats had taken oven the Southern state governments. Two factors may explain their acceptance of this change. First, many influential Republicans were interested in business opportunities in the South. They needed the support of conservative, careful state legislatures to guard their investments, and they desired the good will of the real Southern leaders. The second factor is that the reform element in the Republican party disapproved of the further coercion of the South. Edwin L. Godkin, editor of the *Nation* and of the New York *Evening Post,* in 1888 explained why the Republicans could no longer supervise elections in the South. The following article,

"The Republican Party and the Negro," appeared in the *Forum,* Vol. VII, May, 1888, pp. 246-256.

The party is not considered bound to do or say anything, as a party, for the protection of the Negro's political or social rights at the North, even when they are occasionally violated, as in the matter of equality in the public schools, or in public vehicles, or in hotels, or in theatres. With the advancement of the Negro at the North, in fact, the Republican Party does not specially, as an organization, concern itself. It lets him work his own way and fight his own battles. It is the southern Negro whom it considers its special care; and the reason for this is obvious. The southern Negroes owe to it their existence as freemen and citizens. But for the Republican Party they would enjoy neither political rights nor the common rights of humanity. . . . For ten years after the war was over, it kept garrisons at the South to protect the Negroes in the enjoyment of all the rights, privileges, and emoluments which their votes gave them, and in some States their votes gave them the entire control of the local government. When it was found that public opinion would no longer tolerate the continuance of this protection, federal interference at the South ceased, and the troops were withdrawn by President Hayes. The reason public opinion would no longer tolerate it was very simple, namely, that the spectacle of State governments kept in order or protected for an indefinite period by federal military force was calculated to bring popular government into contempt, or at all events diminish popular respect for constitutional forms, all over the Union. It was felt that the experiment of making citizens of the Negroes could not be tried by halves without serious injury to the whole country; that although the United States might hold large communities in subjection and administer them as conquered territory, there was no place under our system for communities partly free and partly subject, partly able to manage their own affairs and partly fit for military supervision. The results of the Negro government, too, in some States, as for instance, South Carolina and Mississippi, showed clearly the mischief of giving the freedmen power without responsibility, that is, of enabling the Negro legislatures to waste the property of the State through taxation and jobbery, and then of protecting them by troops against the just indignation of the owners. . . .

Nothing in the opinions of southerners is better known than that their State governments are, for reasons partly social, partly political, partly historical, by far their greatest concern, and that no denunciations by the northern newspapers or orators on this point make any impression on them. . . . The Supreme Court in the Yarborough case, allows Congress has the power to protect Negroes, as all other citizens, in the exercise of suffrage at the elections of federal officers, and that a conspiracy to threaten, intimidate, or hinder a Negro or any citizen on such occasions, would be indictable and punishable in the federal courts. The court held that in all such elections "Congress has the power to protect the act of voting, the place where it is done, and the man who votes from personal violence and intimidation, and the election itself from corruption and fraud. . . ."

We may take it as settled, therefore, beyond question, that what the Republican Party can do for the Negro at the South, and all it can do, is to take charge by legislation of the election of members of Congress and of the presidential electors, and of the State legislatures as the electors of Senators. But such legislation would have to be uniform. It would have to apply to northern as well as to southern States. The president would have to execute the law in every part of the country. He could not, as some have suggested, single out particular States for a "special policy," that is, supervise the election in South Carolina or Mississippi, and leave it to the local authorities in Massachusetts or Maine. What Republicans who contemplate the passage of such a law have to ask themselves, therefore, is whether it is the least likely they could get a Republican majority to enact what would be justly considered a very serious step toward a complete centralization and whether, if it were enacted, they could reasonably expect to be able to enforce and maintain it in the northern States without great disaster to the party. There is no reason to suppose that any State at the North would be willing for the sake of the southern Negro, to commit the election of its State legislature to the charge of federal officers. Any party which seriously proposed such a thing would probably be driven from power. But . . . it is only at the election of State officers that there is any strong and steady disposition at the South to practice intimidation and fraud on the Negro. It is in the State offices only that the southern whites fear Negro supremacy, and consequently it is at State elections only that federal protection would really do the Negro any good. . . . . .

Very few of us, when discussing the suppression of the Negro vote, ask ourselves what would be the effect on southern society of *not* suppressing the Negro vote, and yet this question, to every rational mind, forms at least one-half—and not the least important half—of the whole subject. Southern society does not exist for the purpose of enabling ignorant Negroes to cast ballots; civilized society does not exist anywhere in order to afford ignorant men an opportunity of going through the forms of government. It exists in order that "peace and happiness, truth and justice, religion and piety may be established among us to all generations." . . . But not only does the ignorance with which the South has to contend surpass the ignorance with which any other popular government has had to contend, but it is ignorance which has already tried its hand at governing a civilized community; so that we have an unprecedented knowledge about the consequences of its complete predominance. No such experiment as was tried in South Carolina and Mississippi under the Reconstruction Acts was ever tried before, within historic times at least. The machinery of no highly-civilized society was ever before put into the hands of persons such as the Negro voters of the South between 1868 and 1872. So that in resisting a repetition of the experiment the southerners are resisting with full knowledge of the probable consequence of failure. They are not resisting simply under the influence of that vague fear of "mob rule" which plays so large a part in the conservative gospel of other countries. They are resisting the restoration of a *regime* which they intelligently believe would not only prevent industrial progress, but put their civilization itself in some peril. . . .

The recovery of the South from two hundred years of Negro slavery cannot be accomplished in twenty years, or perhaps in fifty. Providence does not allow diseases of such malignity to be cured in a day by acts of Congress. Complete restoration of the South to the American political system cannot be effected by any legislation. If we had soldiers at all the polls in the South at every election, to see that the intelligent portion of the community did not defraud the ignorant of their political rights, it would create an unAmerican government. . . . Laws evolved by ignorance under the protection of bayonets, would not be American laws. American laws are evolved from persuasion exerted by intelligence on intelligence. There is no democratic country in which the ignorant voter is not cheated at the polls, that is, in which he is not in some manner made to cast his vote in some other person's way instead of his own. The priest cheats him, or the landlord, or the corner grocer, or the saloon-keeper, or his employer, or his political boss; and from this all the laws in the world can not save him. Nothing can save a voter's independence except his own character and understanding. Nothing but education will make the southern Negro a free voter in the American sense of the term. The one question, we have to ask ourselves about his political prospects, is whether the whites who control the State governments are making reasonable provision for raising him in point of intelligence to the white man's level. . . . Taking everything into account, it may be said that they are doing more in this field than the northern States, to make the corrupton and intimidation of voters difficult or impossible.

✓　　✓　　✓

The Whiggish characteristics of the Democratic party in the South may be attributed in part to the influence of Northern business men who were acquiring financial interests in the South. Edwin De Leon, in "The New South," *Harper's New Monthly Magazine,* Vol. 48, January, 1874, p. 414, reported such a trend in the lumbering industry.

Next in importance to cotton manufacture is the lumber business which . . . is being rapidly transferred to the South—the pine region of Georgia, Alabama, Mississippi, and Florida furnishing immense supplies for a universal and increasing want. Years ago the hardy Maine lumbermen were in the habit of making annual winter raids on the South Atlantic coast in Georgia, penetrating somewhat into the interior; but since the war Northern energy and capital have poured into Alabama and Florida, and great mills, with all the modern improved machinery, have been erected, and the somewhat harsh music of the saw now sends its echoes through the sylvan solitudes which but recently resounded only to the cries of wild beasts. Florida has become one of the great centres of this new development, and both in her eastern portion, bordering on the Atlantic, and in her western, on the Gulf, sends forth annually immense quantities of hewn and sawed timber to the North and to Europe. . . .

Some shrewd experienced mill owners from Michigan, commanding large capital, having exhausted their own field, came down South to find new mill sites to which to transfer their works. After securing the site they coveted on the Perdido, a year ago, they went over to Alabama, and there purchased from the governor of that State 250,000 acres of "unreclaimed swamp lands," as they were termed, which he was invested by the legislature to sell, for which they paid *ten cents* an acre, thus purchasing a principality on the opposite side of the Perdido, splendidly wooded, and just suited to their purpose, for a mere song, comparatively. The company now value their purchase at twenty times what it cost them, and will reap a rich harvest in coming years, making Alabama's loss their gain, and that of Florida as well. [Their headquarters were in Florida.] It certainly was a sharp move to make the lumber region of Alabama thus tributary to an enterprise whose seat was in Florida, and whose benefits would accrue to her people and the adventurous strangers within her borders. Yet in Alabama they console themselves with the reflection that whereas those lands hitherto brought in no revenue to the State, now they are taxed, and the proprietors must pay the very small amount the State calls for in this shape. A better illustration of "penny wise and pound foolish" has seldom been offered than this; but both parties seem pleased, and there is now a certainty that someone will benefit by these long-neglected sources of wealth, of which many millions of acres still remain neglected in the South.

✓   ✓   ✓

Another example of absentee ownership is furnished by M. B. Hillyard, *The New South,* The Manufacturers' Record Company, Baltimore, 1887, p. 37.

Although the mineral resources of the South and her vast forests have attracted much consideration and large investment, in no regard has she so much enlisted the attention of the nation or of Europe as in building railroads. This is the most commanding theatre of capital, and strikes the eye of the world not only for its colossal combinations of money, but the prestige of its participants. Some of the most sagacious and celebrated railroad men of this continent are largely interested in Southern railroads. Nor is the participation in the South's progress in this respect confined to the United States. The Erlanger syndicate, headed by Baron Erlanger, of Paris, and other rich foreign corporations, have invested during late years many millions of dollars in building new railroads and improving old ones throughout the South. These gentlemen and a number of others who represent capital in Europe and the United States have added untold and incomputable momentum to the progress of the South. . . .

It were a vain task to attempt to keep pace with the Southern railroad projects. It seems as though almost every day brings a revelation of some new railroad scheme. It is quite certain that railroads are projected, surveys being made, "ground" being "broke," under the auspices of such wealthy corporations as to confirm public confidence in the seriousness and good faith of their operations and intentions.

✓   ✓   ✓

Thus Southern businessmen became agents for these Northern and foreign capitalists, and many members of the legislatures were attorneys representing these business interests. Henry L. Nelson pointed out this trend in "Industrial Daybreak in the South," *International Review,* Vol. 12, January, 1882, pp. 77-85, *passim.*

The North is beginning to have a direct pecuniary interest in the South, and that means the end of such sectional strife as the Union has known almost from its foundation. Northern capital is going at last into Southern railways and farms and factories and mines. It is trusting itself to the care of the local legislation of the Southern States. Northern money lenders are forming companies to loan money to cotton growers at a rate of interest that is high in New York, but very low in Georgia and Mississippi, where men who ought to be prosperous have been kept in poverty by being compelled to pay as much as twenty per cent. a year on the loans on their lands. Northern spinners are cooperating with Southern farmers, with a view to benefiting both by securing better cultivation and better crops.

✓   ✓   ✓

The term "Bourbon rule" is misleading, because it implies that the planters had once again gained control of the South. This was only partially true. The politicians were in many cases "brigadiers" of the war and members of the old planter oligarchy, but now the businessmen furnished the money and dominated the state governments. Business prosperity was the new theme. This development is summed up by John Spencer Bassett, a professor of history, editor of the *South Atlantic Quarterly,* "Industrial Decay of Southern Planters," Durham, North Carolina, Vol. II, April, 1903, p. 107.

The rise of the middle class has been the most notable thing connected with the white population since the war. These men have begun life on a natural basis. They have done much work with their hands, and their spirits have not chafed against their fate as they worked. They have not been so much oppressed with a sense of their gentility that they have hesitated to do the unpleasant things connected with honest labor. They have not had so many physical wants that they have had to ignore the behests of economy and saving. They have been, for those reasons, steady gainers in the struggle for existence. They have accumulated property. They have acquired political and social influence. They bid fair to build in a few generations a new class of rich men, out of which a new and somewhat different civilization will develop. At the present time this class has absorbed a large part of the agricultural business in the South. Everywhere the small farm is gaining, and in the northern tier of Southern States it is prevalent. Everywhere trade and manufacturing is almost entirely in the hands of men who are sprung from the non-planter class, and with the growth of popular education the professions seem to be going the same way.

✔   ✔   ✔

The "New South" interests of the Bourbons furnished the theme of many lectures and editorials during the 1880's. Henry W. Grady was one of the leading apostles of industrialism. Typical of his addresses is the following one which was delivered at the Texas State Fair in Dallas on October 26, 1887. It is quoted from Henry Woodfin Grady, *The New South and Other Addresses,* edited by Edna Henry Lee Turpin, Maynard Merrill and Co., New York, 1904.

There is a figure with which history has dealt lightly, but that, standing pathetic and heroic in the genesis of our new growth, has interested me greatly—our soldier farmer of '65. What chance had he for the future as he wandered amid his empty barns, his stock, labor, and implements gone —gathered up the fragments of his wreck—urging kindly his borrowed mule—paying sixty per cent. for all that he bought, and buying all on credit—his crop mortgaged before it was planted—his children in want, his neighborhood in chaos—working under new conditions and retrieving every error by a costly year—plodding all day down the furrow, hopeless and adrift, save when at night he went back to his broken home, where his wife, cheerful even then, renewed his courage, while she ministered to him in loving tenderness. Who would have thought as during those lonely and terrible days he walked behind the plow, locking the sunshine in the glory of his harvest and spreading the showers in the verdure of his field —no friend near save nature that smiled at his earnest touch, and God that sent him the message of good cheer through the passing breeze and the whispering leaves—that he would in twenty years, having carried these burdens uncomplainingly, make a crop of $800,000,000. Yet this he has done, and from his bounty the South has rebuilt her cities, and recouped her losses. While we exult in his splendid achievement, let us take account of his standing.

Whence this enormous growth? For ten years the world has been at peace. The pioneer has now replaced the soldier. Commerce has whitened new seas, and the merchant has occupied new areas. Steam has made of the earth a chessboard, on which men play for markets. Our western wheat-grower competes in London with the Russian and the East Indian. The Ohio wool grower watches the Australian shepherd, and the bleat of the now historic sheep of Vermont is answered from the steppes of Asia. The herds that emerge from the dust of your amazing prairies might hear in their pauses the hoofbeats of the antipodian herds marching to meet them. Under Holland's dykes, the cheese and butter makers fight American dairies. The hen cackles around the world. California challenges vine-clad France. The dark continent is disclosed through meshes of light. There is competition everywhere. The husbandman, driven from his market, balances price against starvation and undercuts his rival. This conflict often runs to panic, and profit vanishes. The Iowa farmer burning his corn for fuel is not an unusual type.

Amid this universal conflict, where stands the South? While the producer of everything we eat or wear, in every land, is fighting through glutted markets for bare existence, what of the Southern farmer? In his industrial as in his political problem he is set apart—not in doubt, but in assured independence. Cotton makes him king. Not the fleeces that Jason sought can rival the richness of this plant, as it unfurls its banners in our fields. It is gold from the instant it puts forth its tiny shoot. The shower that whispers to it is heard around the world. The trespass of a worm on its green leaves means more to England than the advance of the Russians on her Asiatic outposts. When its fibre, current in every bank, is marketed, it renders back to the South $350,000,000 every year. Its seeds will yield $60,000,000 worth of oil to the press and $40,000,000 in food for soil and beast, making the stupendous total of $450,000,000 annual income from this crop. And now, under the Tomkins patent, from its stalk newspaper is to be made at two cents per pound. . . .

Since 1880 cotton consumption in Europe has increased 28 per cent., wool only 4 per cent., and flax has decreased 11 per cent. As for new areas, the uttermost missionary woos the heathen with a cotton shirt in one hand and a Bible in the other, and no savage I believe has ever been converted to one without adopting the other. To summarize: Our American fibre has increased its product nearly three-fold, while it has seen the product of its rival decrease one-third. It has enlarged its dominion in the old centers of population, supplanting flax and wool, and it peeps from the satchel of every business and religious evangelist that trots the globe. In three years the American crop has increased 1,400,000 bales, and yet there is less cotton in the world today than at any time for twenty years. The dominion of our king is established; this princely revenue assured, not for a year, but for all time. It is the heritage that God gave us when he arched our skies, established our mountains, girt us about with the ocean, tempered the sunshine, and measured the rain—ours and our children's forever.

Not alone in cotton, but in iron, does the South excel. . . . Having ores and coal stored in exhaustless quantity, in such richness and in such adjustment that iron can be made and manufacturing done cheaper than elsewhere on this continent, is to now command, and at last control, the world's market for iron. The South now sells iron, through Pittsburgh, in New York. She has driven Scotch iron first from the interior, and finally from American ports. Within our lives she will cross the Atlantic. . . . In 1880 the South made 212,000 tons of iron. In 1887, 845,000 tons. She is now actually building, or has finished this year, furnaces that will produce more iron in 1889 than the entire South produced in 1887.

Our coal supply is exhaustless, Texas alone having 6,000 square miles. In marble and granite we have no rivals, as to quantity or quality. In lumber our riches are even vaster. More than fifty per cent. of our entire area is in forests, making the South the best timbered region in the world. We have enough merchantable yellow pine to bring in money, $2,500,000. . . . Back of this are our forests of hard woods and measureless swamps of cypress and gum. Think of it. In cotton a monopoly. In iron and coal establishing a swift mastery. In granite and marble developing equal advantage and resource. In yellow pine and hard woods the world's treasury. Surely the basis of the South's wealth and power is laid by the hand of Almighty God, and its prosperity has been established by divine law which works in eternal justice and not by taxes levied on its neighbors through human statutes. Paying tribute for fifty years that under artificial conditions other sections might reach a prosperity impossible under natural laws, it has grown apace —and its growth shall endure. . . .

I see a South, a home of fifty millions of people, who rise up every day to call her blessed; her cities, vast hives of industry and thrift; her countrysides the treasures from which their resources are drawn; her streams vocal with whirring spindles; her valleys tranquil in the white and gold of the harvest; her mountains showering down the music of bells, as her slow-moving flocks and herds go forth from their folds; her rulers honest and her people loving, and her homes happy and their hearthstones bright, and their waters still, and their pastures green, and her conscience clear; her wealth diffused and poor-houses empty, her churches earnest and all creeds lost in the gospel; . . . her two races walking together in peace and contentment; sunshine everywhere and all the time.

15

Progress in Industry and Agriculture

At least fifteen years before the Civil War there was a textile industry in the South. In Gaston County, North Carolina, two cotton mills for the manufacture of coarse cloth for use for shirts, sheets, and towels, as well as a coarse yarn which was packaged in five pound lots and sold for knitting purposes and hand weaving, were started in 1845. In 1852 Frederick Law Olmsted made his first tour of the Southern states. The following description of the textile industry of Columbus, Georgia, is from his *A Journey in the Seaboard Slave States,* Dix and Edwards, New York, 1856, p. 547.

At Columbus, I spent several days. It is the largest manufacturing town, south of Richmond, in the Slave States. It is situated at the falls, and the head of steamboat navigation of the Chatahooche, the western boundary of Georgia. The waterpower is sufficient to drive two hundred thousand spindles, with a proportionate number of looms. There are, probably, at present from fifteen to twenty thousand spindles running. The operatives in the cotton-mills are said to be mainly "Cracker girls" (poor whites from the country), who earn, in good times, by piece-work, from $8 to $12 a month. There are, besides the cotton-mills, one woolen-mill, one paper-mill, a foundry, a cotton-gin factory, a machine-shop, etc. The laborers in all these are mainly whites, and they are in such a condition that, if temporarily thrown out of employment, great numbers of them are at once reduced to a state of destitution, and are dependent upon credit or charity for their daily food. Public entertainments were being held at the time of my visit, the profits to be applied to the relief of the operatives in the mills which had been stopped by the effects of a late flood of the river.

✓   ✓   ✓

In 1838 a Southern commercial convention was held in Augusta; and from time to time thereafter other meetings, chiefly economic in nature, were assembled in various Southern cities. At these meetings were set forth the South's need for commerce, manufactures, and capital. An article by T. B. Thorpe, which appeared in *Harper's New Monthly Magazine,* New York, Vol. 8, March, 1854, p. 463, entitled "Cotton and Its Cultivation," pointed out the growing interest in manufacturing in the South.

Within the last few years the cotton planters have had their "conventions," and we have in these "signs of the times"—whatever may have been the result—an evidence of a growing community of feeling, that is bound to increase until the cotton-growing states understand and practice what is to their true interests.

Georgia has set an example of wisdom, and very soon she will possess within herself so completely all the elements of empire, that she might be forever separated from the surrounding world, and yet flourish with unexampled prosperity. Upon her hilltops begin to smoke the wealth-achieving furnace; the buzz of the cotton spindle mingles with the whisperings of her clear blue streams; the "iron horse" is far and wide circulating her products; her heretofore isolated population is beginning to feel that a market is created for "home industry," and that Georgia could, if the demand was made, make her shipments of unginned cotton as obsolete as is now the shipment of cotton in the seed. What cares such a state whether a foreign country enriches itself by spinning her cotton? The staple is produced by the wearing labor of the muscles of men, defiant of malaria, and regardless of fever-breeding heat—the easier, and *quadruply* more profitable work of manufacturing, by the never-tiring engine, and the sinews of the spindle and loom, is at her command. Georgia has but to grasp the sceptre, and she is commercially free.

Will her sister states, so rich in agricultural products, and which are equally interested with her in the cultivation of the "great staple," imitate her example? If they do so, "the South" will become, in the natural course of things, the most independent portion of our extending empire, and thus forever hold the benefits of a great cotton monopoly in her hands.

✔   ✔   ✔

James S. Buckingham, the English traveler, visited a cotton mill at Athens, Georgia, in 1839. His comments on the employment of Negro workers alongside white ones is interesting in comparison with later practice of using only white textile workers. The following selection is from his *The Slave States of America,* Fisher, Son and Company, London, 1842, Vol. II, pp. 111-112.

On the banks of the Oconee river—one fork of which runs close by the town of Athens, [Georgia,] in a deep valley, the town itself being on a hill, and the other forks at a distance for a few miles only—are three cotton factories, all worked by water power, and used for spinning yarn, and weaving cloth of coarse qualities for local consumption only. I visited one of these, and ascertained that the other two were very similar to it in size and operations. In each of them there are employed from 80 to 100 persons, and about an equal number of white and black. In one of them, the blacks are the property of the mill-owner, but in the other two they are the slaves of planters, hired out at monthly wages to work in the factory.

There is no difficulty among them on account of colour, the white girls working in the same room and at the same loom with the black girls; and boys
of each colour, as well as men and women, working together without apparent repugnance or objection. This is only one of the many proofs I
had witnessed of the fact, that the prejudice of colour is not nearly so
strong in the South as in the North. Here, it is not at all uncommon to see
the black slaves of both sexes, shake hands with white people when they
meet, and interchange friendly personal inquiries; but at the North I do
not remember to have witnessed this once; and neither in Boston, New
York, or Philadelphia would white persons generally like to be seen shaking
hands and talking familiarly with blacks in the streets.

✓ ✓ ✓

D. R. Hundley reported in 1860 that the manufacturing interest was rapidly
advancing in the South, particularly the manufacture of coarse cotton and woolen
stuffs. The following comment is from his *Social Relations in our Southern States*,
H. B. Price, New York, 1860, p. 118.

Manufactories of this kind are springing up everywhere in the cotton
states of late years; but they are most numerous in the State of Georgia . . .
and in this State they are owned not infrequently, at least in part, by persons from the North; what is more, these manufactories are generally
profitable investments—more so, in truth, than those of Massachusetts or
other Northern States. . . .

From a late digest of the statistics of manufacturers, which has just been
completed in accordance with an act of Congress, and transmitted to that
body by the President, we learn that the total value of manufacturers in
the South for the year ending June 1, 1858, amounted to one hundred and
sixty-two millions one hundred and twelve thousand three hundred and
twenty-four dollars. The number of establishments is about thirty thousand;
the number of hands employed about one hundred and sixty thousand;
the amount of capital invested ninety-one millions two hundred and eighty
thousand nine hundred and sixty-four dollars. This is certainly no mean
showing for what has been considered an almost exclusively agricultural
community.

✓ ✓ ✓

Much of the South's manufacturing capacity was destroyed by the Civil War, as
was a large proportion of her railroad systems, which had never kept pace with
the rapid growth of mileage in the North and Middle West. Scarcity of capital
delayed the economic rehabilitation of the South, but an exception in the case of
the railroads was made possible by investments of northern capitalists, encouraged
by aid from the reconstruction state governments. Railroads played a part in the
politics of most of the Southern states during reconstruction, and succeeded in
winning various favors. Robert Somers, in *The Southern States Since the War*,

Macmillan and Company, London and New York, 1871, pp. 165-166, described the rapid growth of railroads.

Every strategic point in railway construction is searched out in all this old Southern country with a keenness seldom equalled. The old lines may be tolerably serviceable, and may not have traffic more than to make them moderately prosperous; but these considerations do not damp the ardour with which new lines are devised, if two or three hundred miles of distance are to be saved to the Atlantic seaboard, and new and fertile tracts to be opened up by the way. The point of departure may be Vicksburg, a small place rising into commercial importance on the Mississippi, and the point of arrival Brunswick, trying to become a seaport, one hundred and thirty miles south of Savannah, because it has three or four feet deeper water than any port, save perhaps Norfolk, on the Atlantic coast; but all this poverty of present resource is scarcely deemed a rational impediment, and though the difficulty of raising the necessary loans is great, and the difficulty of obtaining a respectable subscription of capital is greater, yet the idea of an "air-line" as direct as birds can fly seizes on the general mind, and gathering up all the interests at either end, and piecing itself on to existing roads with the rarest ingenuity, gets itself lobby-rolled through the Legislature into a legal shape, and forthwith becomes more or less an accomplished fact. In a few years hence every salient point on the Mississippi will be connected by direct "air-lines" with the Atlantic seaboard, and the great draught of steam and capital to New York of late years, which would speedily become suffocating to the American continent, will be gradually modified and counteracted by railway enterprise, and by the desire of British and Continental manufacturers, in the natural course of commerce, to get into the most immediate relation with the producers of their raw material. On any narrower hypothesis the present railway making in the South would seem quite unjustifiable. But the interior and local interest of the new railway projects at the same time is very manifest. The great difficulty of the United States is country roads, and the want of stone and rock. The constant tendency to drop into ruts and puddles both wide and deep wherever wheeled vehicles can pretend to go, is observable from the suburbs of Philadelphia to this point. [Written at Selma, Alabama.] It is only by the iron track, liberally distributed, that the produce of the Southern States can hope to get to the market; and over-numerous as the great lines of communication, made and projected, seem to be, they all pass through wide interior regions of country, thinly peopled indeed, but settled and in working order, and capable of much development.

✓   ✓   ✓

By 1874 the manufacture of cotton was experiencing a revival which was described by Edwin De Leon in *Harper's New Monthly Magazine*, Vol. 48, January, 1874, pp. 406-422, *passim*.

Of the young and growing Lowells of the new South—at Graniteville, in South Carolina, at Augusta and Columbus, at the eastern and western extremes of Georgia, at or near Montgomery, in Alabama—little has been said or written, and less generally known as yet; but these are indeed most promising pioneers in this mighty industrial movement, and the rapid though steady progress they have made in the past three years recalls the similar march to success and wealth made in Massachusetts, and throughout New England, during the early part of this century.

In the South, as in the North, the incipiency as well as the progress of this great industry is due to individual effort. . . . As in the history of cities it seldom happens that the pioneer or his children own or occupy the valuable town lots into which his "clearing" extends, so in industrial enterprises the same old story is apt to be repeated. The pioneer must do the rough work, cut down the forest trees and brush-wood, make the clearing; then succeeds the settler, improving the town lots; and finally the speculator and capitalist step in, who, profiting by the labor of their predecessors, make paying investments, and reap rich rewards. This is the usual division of labor; whether equitable or not it were useless to grumble about, for the main matter ever must be "the greatest good of the greatest number"— that is, of the community.

The pioneers of manufacturing at the South prior to the war have proved no exception to this rule; yet they "builded wiser than they knew," and their work has survived them. But the actual progress made is the main point of interest today. . . . In the term of [the last] four years [there has been] an increase of almost double the quantity of cotton consumed in Southern mills—that is, from thirty-six and a half millions of pounds in 1870 (or rather 1869, when estimates must have been made) to sixty and a half millions of pounds in 1873. . . . The number of cotton-mills in the South, already considerable, promises to increase in certain quarters. Three new and large mills are contemplated on the Chatahooche River, near Columbus, Georgia (where there are five already), and part of the capital to build these has already been subscribed by people in the vicinity and other parts of the State. Nothing could more substantially establish the success and profits of the existing mills than this anxiety of the people on the spot to invest in new ones, especially when money, North and South, is in such demand. . . .

Anyone who visits the Southern mills must arrive at the conclusion that Georgia, South Carolina, and Alabama will become the great centres of the cotton manufacture of the South. . . .

The following was the substance of answers made to queries addressed to the manager of the Eagle and Phenix Mill, which . . . is one of the largest and most prosperous of the Southern factories. . . .

"We employ about 800 operatives, all of whom are white, except the yard laborers, ten in number, who are negro men. We have secured most of our labor from the poorer white population of Alabama and Georgia, and find them ready and willing to learn. . . . It is very difficult to procure skilled labor in Georgia; and the easiest and most practicable way to do it is to take the people of the country and educate them to labor. The labor here is cheaper than at the North, but less experienced; so that while we enjoy the benefit of cheaper labor per capita, its cost is increased in this way. There is no difficulty in obtaining operatives if a mill will take unskilled labor to teach. . . ."

The company makes a great variety of goods, most of the cotton goods being dyed, consisting of checks, stripes, tickings, ginghams, and kindred goods. The woolen goods are kerseys and jeans. . . .

The profits of this company are estimated at eighteen per cent. per annum; larger could be realized but for the quantity of unavailable capital lying idle . . . [in water lots], together with the unskilled character of the labor. To render this idle water-power available and productive, the company will commence next spring to build a third mill on one of their sites, and will continue to put its surplus (as reserved) into additional mills, until most of their idle lots are utilized.

In answer to a query the following response was made, which conveys the opinion of all the experts and mill-owners: "We do not think the negroes adapted to the labor of the cotton-mills. Their lack of quickness, sensitiveness of touch, and general sleepy characteristics disqualify them for work which needs requisites they lack. Being far better fitted for out-door labor, they will no doubt always be kept so employed."

It is only necessary to add to this clear statement . . . that the great majority of the workers in the mills (in many almost exclusively) are women and children. The Eagle and Phenix employs more men than others, in consequence of the great variety of fabrics it turns out. . . .

With reference to the general appearance of these factory hands, personal observation convinces me that the popular prejudice as to the unhealthiness of this kind of labor, under proper restrictions and with proper surroundings, is erroneous. The women and boys, though certainly not as florid and fresh-looking as the lads and lasses who spend all their time in the open air . . . look strong and healthy, and are quite jolly when they leave the mills at six o'clock in the afternoon. Their hours of work are usually from 7 A.M. to 6 P.M., with an interval at mid-day of half an hour for dinner. Attached to some of the mills are residences for the operatives, but in the majority of instances they board themselves, thus avoiding some of the supposed demoralizing effects of colonization. . . . The additional comforts provided for the family by the utilization of the formerly idle hands of the women and children can be readily appreciated. Nor is the education of the latter neglected, as night schools supply the loss of daily tuition: and their labor is so light in the factories as not to incapacitate them from attending night school, when sufficiently ambitious to aspire to improvement. The rate of wages, though less than the Northern, in consequence of superior cheapness of living South, is more remunerative. Women can earn an average of thirty dollars per month, and children about half as much, which is more than sufficient for a support. For experts higher wages are given. . . .

✦   ✦   ✦

An *Atlantic Monthly* article, Vol. 49, June, 1882, pp. 747-749, described "Life and Its Conditions" in the cotton mills of the South.

. . . the relation between the factory people and their employers is plainly different in the South from anything I have observed in New England; it is more "patriarchal" and less democratic. The control, authority, or influence of the owners and managers over the working people is more absolute than in the North. I am obliged to say that it seems to be a just and beneficent control. The employers appear to feel a real interest in the welfare and prosperity of the people whom they employ. I have not been able to detect, on either side, any feeling of antagonism, any notion that the interests of the manufacturers and those of the laborers are opposed, or even distinct. Almost universally, perhaps in all cases, the operatives are paid in full, in money, and at short intervals. In many places the corporations own most of the houses occupied by the operatives. The rent is usually much lower than the prevailing rates in the same town. The houses are carefully kept in repair by the mill owners. At some of the largest mills, each family among the operatives has a garden and keeps a cow. The laborers in the mill go to church on Sundays, and are members of churches, far more generally than in the North. There is much less drinking, and there is beyond all comparison less of the licentiousness, among them than in their class in New England. The women and girls who work in Southern mills are, I am convinced, almost all of good character. . . .

An observer who is familiar with the appearance of the laborers in the Northern cotton-mills can see at once that Southern operatives are less intelligent; that they are not so "well-informed about what is going on in the world," in the New England sense of these expressions. They are more placid, contented, and industrious, and less restless, than people of the same class in New England; they are more domestic, settled, and regular in their habits and character. There is far less moving about from place to place, and from one mill to another, than in the North. All, or very nearly all, the hands in Southern factories are Southerners, natives of the region near the mill in which they work, and they all belong to a more primitive, simple, and old-fashioned order of things than is now anywhere in existence in connection with factory life in New England. Southern operatives read less than Northern; they have not so many ideas, and they have not been affected in any considerable degree by the "reforming and progressive" sentiments and influences of the time. They are, in consequence, happier, less liable to discontent, and far more useful and agreeable to their employers. . .).

Some of the principal Southern cotton-mills have savings-banks connected with them, belonging to the corporation; that is, the corporation receives the savings of their own operatives who wish to deposit them, and pays interest on them, the same as any other savings-bank. . . .

The owners and managers of Southern mills and factories whom I have met appear to me to be gentlemen of high character; . . . the principal mills have good schools connected with them, and nearly all the children of the operatives attend Sunday-schools. The Methodist and Baptist churches appear to be doing the most for the moral and social welfare and guidance of the working people, as they are the principal churches in most places in the South, but other religious organizations are doing their part. The operatives are not regarded in the South as constituting a class so separate or distinct as in New England. They belong more fully and vitally to the body of the people.

✓ ✓ ✓

The development of the cotton industry in North Carolina was very rapid during the decade of the 1880's and even more so in the 1890's, so that by 1900 the state ranked third in the nation in this product. In contrast with South Carolina and Alabama, where the industry was financed largely by outside capital, in North Carolina ninety per cent of the capital was furnished by local residents. In Holland Thompson's *From Cotton Field to Cotton Mill,* The Macmillan Company, New York, 1906, pp. 81-85, the method of finance is described.

The industry is distinctly a home enterprise, founded and fostered by natives of the state. During the ten years just past, several large mills have been built with foreign capital, but they have not greatly changed the proportion. A larger amount of such capital has been invested in mills already in operation, or has enabled a successful manager to enlarge his plant. The ownership of the mills is widely distributed. . . . While there are many in which a single man, or a single family group, owns the whole, or a controlling interest, as, for example, the Holt family in Alamance and Davidson counties, which owns more than a dozen mills, the stock in the majority is widely distributed, owing to the method of building, which has often been an installment plan, on the following order:—

The subscription to the shares (usually of a par value of $100) is made payable in weekly installments either of 50 cents or $1 the share, without interest. Occasionally a mill has been built with a 25 cent installment. Experience has shown, however, that this requires too long a period, as nearly eight years is required to pay the stock in full as against four or two years for the larger sums. Those having ready money may pay the whole amount at once less 6 per cent. discount for the average time, making the stock cost $89.60 in cash. Usually nearly or quite a year is required to construct the buildings. The installments more than suffice to pay the expenses, as real estate and buildings rarely cost more than 20 per cent. of the capital stock. The installments and the amount paid by those who have taken advantage of the discount is placed in some bank, which is thus put under obligations to the mill, and besides has a lively anticipation of business to come. Often the directors of the mill are also stockholders or directors of the bank. Machinery may be bought on long credit, six, twelve, or even eighteen months, with interest at 6 per cent. after delivery. Sometimes the makers of the machinery have taken a part of the cost of the machinery in stock, and in a few instances the commission houses have also subscribed in order to control the product. There has seldom been any bonded indebtedness intended to be permanent.

Profits in the past have been so large that often before the last payment on the stock is due, a sum sufficient to pay all obligations has been accumulated. One especially successful mill of this class, organized with a capital of $100,000, secured the buildings of an unsuccessful wood-working establishment, which with alterations and additions were adequate for the purpose. The installment was fifty cents the week on each share. When $35 a share had been paid in, in seventy weeks, a dividend of 4 per cent. on the capitalization was declared, and it has never failed to pay either 4 or 5 per cent. each half year since. . . .

At first the stock is widely distributed. Bankers, merchants, physicians, clerks, lawyers, teachers, mechanics, and even operatives in other mills subscribe. When difficulty is experienced in securing the desired amount, subscriptions of one share may be accepted. The average holding is seldom above $1000. This widest distribution does not last, of course. Some subscribers find difficulty in keeping up with their installments and transfer their subscriptions to others; some grow tired of waiting for dividends, which seem slow in coming. Some, who have used their subscriptions as a savings bank, sell in order to buy a home, or to start a business for themselves. The stock tends to become concentrated in fewer hands, though a small body of men seldom secures control of a successful mill of this class.

✦   ✦   ✦

One characteristic of modern industry is the utilization of by-products. In the following account M. B. Hillyard implied that the utilization of cotton seeds was a new trend in the 1880's, but experiments in the use of the seeds in the ante-bellum period led to their use as fertilizer, as cattle feed, and to furnish oil used in lamps and as a cure for colic, as well as for lubricating purposes. Mills were established to manufacture the seed into these various products. By the time Mr. Hillyard made his observations, this was a flourishing industry. His account is from *The New South,* The Manufacturers' Record Company, Baltimore, 1887, p. 34.

Another phase of development in the South since the war is that of manipulation of cotton seed, mainly for its oil, but also as a food for stock and fertilizer. It is one of the most wonderful oversights of the South that cotton seed should have remained so long undiscovered, so to speak. They used to be regarded as a nuisance by planters, and were dumped into the rivers and bayous to be got rid of. It is only within a very few years that one could go on any plantation where there was a cotton gin, and not find large piles of the seed utterly unregarded. Now there is a demand for all that can be produced. This change has been brought about within three or four years for most of the South. . . .

At the present time all interest in this business is centered in the American Cotton Oil Trust, an organization very similar to the Standard Oil Company. The Trust has succeeded in obtaining control of a large majority of the Oil mills of the South, and there is much speculation as to the future of its operations. Many of the leading papers of the South have taken very strong ground against it, believing that it will work serious injury to the planters. Having the control of most of the mills, the Trust can dictate the prices of cotton seed throughout the greater part of the South. There has been some talk of the planters combining against this organization, but it hardly seems probable that this will be done. . . .

Cotton-seed has entered so largely into so many articles, that it will be likely to enter more. It will, probably, largely supplant lard some day (when better refined) at the South, and possibly in other parts of the world. People are beginning to understand that they have been largely using it, while supposing that they were using olive oil—the former being exported from the United States to Italy, and brought back labeled olive oil. So they have learned its merits, and can have a chance to be patriotic, at less cost, by its use under its true name.

✓   ✓   ✓

Among other new industries of the South after the war was the manufacture of ice, a commodity which had heretofore been imported from the North, where it had been cut from lakes and rivers, and stored. One writer says that the price of ice was reduced from forty to fifteen dollars a ton when Southern factories were built. Mark Twain, in *Life on the Mississippi,* expressed surprise at the quantity of ice manufactured. 1874, De Luxe Edition, The American Publishing Company, Hartford, 1899, pp. 302-303.

Natchez, like her near and far river neighbors, has railways now, and is adding to them—pushing them hither and thither into all rich outlying regions that are naturally tributary to her. And like Vicksburg and New Orleans, she has her ice factory; she makes thirty tons of ice a day. In

Vicksburg and Natchez, in my time, ice was jewelry, none but the rich could wear it. But anybody and everybody can have it now. I visited one of the ice factories in New Orleans, to see what the polar regions might look like when lugged into the edge of the tropics. But there was nothing striking in the aspect of the place. It was merely a spacious house, with some innocent steam machinery in one end of it and some big porcelain pipes running here and there. No, not porcelain—they merely seemed to be; they were iron, but the ammonia which had breathed through them had coated them to the thickness of your hand with solid milk-white ice. It ought to have melted; for one did not require winter clothing in that atmosphere; but it did not melt; the inside of the pipe was too cold. . . .

✔   ✔   ✔

During the Civil War a phenomenal development in industry took place in the North. Railroads and factories, and technological improvements such as the Bessemer process for making steel, superseded later by the "open-hearth process," created a new demand for pig iron. During the 1880's northern Alabama and eastern Tennessee, with resources of iron ore and coal, entered this field and spurted to second place in the Union in pig-iron production; and the area was also making large quantities of steel. James Kitson, "Iron and Steel Industries of America," *The Contemporary Review*, Vol. LIX, May, 1891, pp. 635-637, is the source of the following account.

[A party of Englishmen had been visiting the iron and steel industries in the North.] Our party, which, with American friends, numbered over a thousand, divided at Chicago, one section going North to visit the iron ore districts of Michigan, Wisconsin and Minnesota, . . . the other proceeding southwards to visit Alabama and other Southern States which are fast being opened up to new industries and becoming industrial rivals of the Northern States. I accompanied the Southern contingent. . . . Birmingham is a conspicuous example of rapid development. In the course of a few years it has grown into a town of 50,000 inhabitants with eight trunk lines of railway converging on it, seventy miles of street railways, excellent hotels, parks, many beautiful buildings, and an opera house. The social surroundings give evidence of the spread of education and material advancement. The progress of the town of Birmingham has been contemporaneous with the general development of the State of Alabama. The rapid growth of the iron trade in this State is attributable to the close proximity and abundance of coal and iron ore rather than to any excellence in methods of mining or manufacture. Owing to these geological conditions, it is claimed, . . . that the cheapest pig iron in the United States is produced here. . . . As illustrating the vast and rapid expansion of the Southern States—a phenomenon which will have an important bearing on the commercial policy and future of the republic—it may be interesting to note that Alabama produced 62,000 tons of iron in 1880, and 1,789,000 tons in 1890.

The colored population are largely employed as miners and labourers about blast-furnaces and ironworks. They are cheap and slow. To cope with their irregularities it is necessary to keep twice the staff for the same work. They are sluggish, and are quite content to earn a livelihood by working continually half-time. Their social wants are few. They live cheaply, often herding together in unsanitary conditions. They do not act as foremen, nor are they placed in responsible positions. White men must superintend and direct them. It is very noticeable how the white and coloured population of the South keep absolutely distinct. There is no intermingling or social intercourse between them. The groups of women and children seen in the streets and at the railway stand entirely apart. The white people apparently hold no communication with the blacks. . . .

[Next] we were on our way to study . . . the town of Middlesborough in Kentucky. This new town, with a good English name, was all the more interesting to us because it is being developed by English capital. It is "run" by an English company, and is a model of systematic development on regular American methods. The town has been planned and laid out to accommodate a population of 200,000. All the institutions for a commercial centre are being established. Middlesborough is already surrounded by a belt of railway, with sidings from which roads will be continued to serve the different industries which it is understood are to spring up within and around the town. The first thing done in the foundation of an American town is to build a hotel; and here in Middlesborough we have a splendid hotel, capable of accommodating 200 guests, with all the requirements of a first-class house. . . . Lines of streets in the usual chess-board style are marked out, and house sites and corner lots bring high prices. A population of 7000 are busy building houses for the industrial population of the future. At the same time blast furnaces, rolling mills, and steel works are being erected. . . .

✓   ✓   ✓

Urban centers in the North and West were experiencing rapid growth between 1865 and 1900. While the South did not share in the growth of large cities, her towns and smaller cities grew and multiplied. The following material was compiled for the *Manufacturers' Record* and appeared in that paper on December 21, 1889. It was reissued in pamphlet form, Richard H. Edmonds, *The South's Redemption,* Manufacturers' Record, Baltimore, 1890, pp. 5-12.

So rapid has been the industrial advancement of that section during the last eight or nine years, and more especially during the last four, that the business world is now seeking information about every phase of Southern growth, and of the South's resources. Capitalists in Europe and America are looking to the South as the field for investment; manufacturers of iron, cotton and lumber, realizing that the South is destined to control all of these and allied industries, are directing their attention to this section. The cry is no longer "Go West, young man," but "Go South." . . . . .

The history of many Southern towns during the last five years reads almost like a romance. While Birmingham, Chattanooga, Anniston, Roanoke, Dallas, Fort Worth and many of the most widely advertised industrial centers have grown with a rapidity that is almost beyond belief, other towns and cities all through the South have kept well up in the march of progress. Louisville, Atlanta, Nashville, Richmond, Charleston, Savannah, Columbus, Knoxville, Memphis, Macon, Augusta, and others, have not fallen much behind the most rapidly growing places. In 1880 Knoxville had 9,000 inhabitants, and the assessed value of its property was $3,485,000; now its population is estimated at 42,000 and the value of its property is $9,500,000. Louisville has increased its population from 123,000 to 227,000, and the capital invested in manufactures from $21,900,000 to $35,000,000. Nashville had a population of 46,000 in 1880, and now has about 110,-000. . . .

In the newer, or what is known as the booming towns, the gain in population and capital employed in manufacturing has been astonishing. Birmingham and Chattanooga are so well known that it is almost needless to mention their history. Anniston, Ala., which in 1880 had probably 1,200 inhabitants, has now about 12,000. Bessemer, in the same State, which had no existence prior to 1887, now has several million dollars invested in furnaces, rolling mills, and kindred enterprises, with 4,000 or 5,000 people living where a forest stood in 1887. Bessemer already has five completed furnaces and two more under construction; . . . Sheffield was a cotton field in 1885; its five furnaces alone can furnish nearly as much freight in tons to the railroads as the cotton crop of the entire South. . . . Roanoke, with its 17,000 people, was Big Lick with 300 inhabitants eight years ago. Heretofore Alabama had led in iron development, but now Virginia is going to enter the race, and new furnaces and other iron enterprises are to be built at Buena Vista, Waynesboro, Salem, Radford, Pulaski, Max Meadows, Graham, Richlands and other points. The whole country tributary to the Norfolk & Western Railroad, which includes the valley of Virginia down to Bristol, Tenn., is moving rapidly.

Two years ago Florence, Ala., was one of the most attractive towns in the South as a place of residence; visitors grew enthusiastic over it, and its inhabitants, who numbered about 2,000, thought no place in America equalled it for attractiveness; but it was simply a beautiful town, and few then looked upon it as destined to be a great city. Its history for eighteen months tells the story of the South's possibilities. A year and a half ago a few energetic Southerners, charmed with it as a place of residence, and realizing its unsurpassed advantages for the manufacture of iron, cotton and wood, undertook the work of building a manufacturing city. In the short time that has elapsed they have secured the establishment of thirty or more new enterprises, which have an aggregate cash value of several million dollars. . . . There are two furnaces (one now in blast), a $100,000 wagon factory, a $300,000 hardware factory, and two cotton mills (one in operation and one of 53,000 spindles under construction), and other factories large and small, are to be built at once. These enterprises will employ over 6,000 hands. This has all been done without any real estate speculation; there has been no unhealthy "booming," but simply energetic work on the part of a few people, and from 2,000 its population has increased to probably 10,000 with still more rapid growth in the future assured. . . .

Six months ago the name of Middlesborough, Ky., could not have been found upon even the latest railroad maps. It was known to a comparatively few as the place which the English capitalists, including many of the foremost iron and steel makers of Great Britain, had selected as the site for building a city on a very broad basis, backed by an apparently unlimited supply of money. Of its advantageous location at Cumberland Gap, where railroads must of necessity meet, and where minerals and timber are in sufficient quantity to supply the most extensive demands of the future, it is needless to speak. . . . Suffice it to say, that for several years these English capitalists had been quietly, but vigorously, at work. Their experts had thoroughly explored the mineral and timber resources of the surrounding country, and over 60,000 acres of picked lands had been purchased. Every arrangement had been made for the establishment of gigantic enterprises before a railroad had reached the place, and before much publicity had been made of their plans regarding the building of a city. Where less than twenty-five people were half a year ago, there are now, it is estimated, fully 4,000, and Middlesborough is growing as few towns have ever grown. . . . Over $18,000,000 have already been invested or contracted for investment in the building of railroads, and in the establishment of many and varied industries. . . .

✓   ✓   ✓

Coal had become increasingly important because of the substitution of coal for charcoal in the iron industry. The Southern coal fields developed concurrently with the Alabama and Tennessee iron region. The following excerpt is from Richard H. Edmonds, *The South's Redemption,* Manufacturers' Record, Baltimore, 1890, pp. 24-26.

The magnitude of the wealth of the South in coal is beyond computation. The entire coal area of Great Britain covers 11,900 square miles, while West Virginia alone has 16,000 square miles of coal fields; Alabama, 8,660 square miles; Kentucky, nearly 13,000; Tennessee, 5,100, Arkansas, over 9,000, and other Southern States considerable coal areas. Moreover, the coal is easily and cheaply mined, and it, as to much of it, of the best quality. . . . Nowhere else, so far as is known, are the coal fields so admirably located in relation to iron ore, to the best markets and as regards ease and cheapness of mining, as in the South. The wide mineral belt, which extends from Wheeling and Harper's Ferry, W. Va., to Northern Alabama, has greater undeveloped wealth and a greater combination of advantages and possibilities of development than any other area of equal extent in the world. This belt includes a large part of the two Virginias, the Carolinas, Kentucky, Tennessee, Georgia, and Alabama. . . .

The American Association, Limited, which owns about 60,000 acres of coal lands in the neighborhood of the new town of Middlesborough, Ky., has within the last twelve months made leases of coal properties for mining to fourteen different operators. . . .

✓   ✓   ✓

Farming continued to be the occupation of most Southerners, and few improvements were introduced by the generation of farmers following the Civil War. The more ambitious youth left the land to earn success in the professions or in industry. Walter Hines Page, "The Rebuilding of Old Commonwealths," *Atlantic Monthly,* Vol. 89, New York, May, 1902, p. 653, pointed out the static condition of life in areas remote from towns in the South.

A few months ago I rode for a hundred miles or more on . . . a railway . . . in the company of a man who had gradually amassed a fortune by the good management of a cotton mill. As we passed a dozen . . . towns, he said that he had always believed in the success of "our people." "They are as capable as any people under the sun, and are better neighbors than most; and I had no idea that I should ever live to see such a degree of financial prosperity as they have already reached." Then, after a long talk about the growth of these communities, he remarked, "Schools, schools, schools of the right sort—that is what we need."

But in the country, only a few miles from almost any of these towns, men and women live and think as men and women did fifty years ago, or eighty years, or even a hundred. The farmers have more money than their grandfathers had, but the general structure of their life is the same—a dull succession of the seasons where agriculture is practiced in old-fashioned ways, where weary housewives show resignation rather than contentment, and where ignorance has become satisfied with itself. The country is somewhat more densely populated than it was twenty years ago, but the growth of population suggests only a denser stagnation.

These men and women are not poor, that is, they do not feel poor. They have a civilization of their own of which they are proud. They have for a hundred years been told to be proud of it. The politicians have told them that they are the best people on earth, that the state they live in is the most important in the Union, that the ideas they stand for are the bulwark of our liberties. Do they not own the land? Are they not independent? What more could men ask? One in five is illiterate. But what matter? Some of the illiterate are more successful than some others that can read. What does it profit a man, then, to read? They have a self-satisfied personal dignity that prevents near approach. If you propose to change a law or custom, or are suspected of such a wish, or if you come with a new idea, the burden of proving its value rests on you. What they are they regard as the normal state of human society. If you would change it or them, you are under suspicion as a disorganizer of social life. There was talk in one household, I recall, about the possibility that the son of one of the more prosperous men in the neighborhood might go away to study medicine. "I don't see the use," said the father. "We've got two doctors nigh enough, and there ain't no room for a third." The preacher, too, has hardened their self-contentment, especially the self-contentment of the women. A profession of faith after "conversion" prepares them for the life to come, and breeds an indifference to the transitory inconveniences of the life that is.

A country schoolmaster in this region told me last year (truly enough) that the ability to read was not a good test even of a man's intelligence, to say nothing of his character. "Why, do you know," said he, "how many of the Confederate soldiers were illiterate? Yet they were the best soldiers that ever went to war."

"Suppose they had all been trained,—trained to some useful occupation,— some as geologists, some as miners, some as machinists, some as shipwrights, some as gun-makers. The iron in Alabama, the wood and coal near by, would these not have been utilized in war?"

"Utilized? We'd 'ave whipped the Yankees—shore!"

"What would you think of schools where men should now be trained to occupations, schools here in this neighborhood, to make ploughs, wagons, furniture, everything useful?"

"That'd be a mighty good thing; but it ain't education."

There is a considerable variety of social conditions in these rural communities, as everywhere else. Near one home, where both children and grandchildren are illegitimate, is the residence of a man who holds his land by direct descent in his family from a colonial grant, and whose sons are successful lawyers and preachers and physicians in four states. A good many youths go to the towns and find wider opportunities. From this same neighborhood a youth went to New York, and he is now a rich merchant; another went to college by his own exertions, and he is now an electrical engineer in a great manufacturing city; another is a partner in a factory in New England; another is a judge in Oregon. The most ambitious are those who go away; and the general level of life seems as low as it was generations ago. The emigration from the older Southern States has been enormous.

Three influences have held the social structure stationary: first slavery, which pickled Southern life and left it just as it found it; then the politician, and the preacher. One has for a hundred years proclaimed the present social state as the ideal condition; and, if any has doubted this declaration, the other has told him that this life counts for little at best. Thus gagged and bound, Southern rural society has remained stationary longer than English-speaking people have remained stationary anywhere else in the world. It is a stage of life that keeps permanently the qualities of the frontier civilization long after the frontier has receded and been forgotten. The feeling that you bring away with you is a feeling that something has intervened to hold these people back from their natural development. They have a capacity that far outruns their achievement. They are citizens of an earlier time and of a narrower world, who have not had the development that a democracy implies. The clue to a proper understanding of them is the historic fact that they are a capable people whose growth, when democracy began to develop men, was interrupted.

✓ ✓ ✓

At the Atlanta Cotton Exposition, Edward Atkinson met two grandsons of John C. Calhoun who had removed to Mississippi. With them he discussed the problems of the tenant farmers and of the land owners of that state. The following is the summary of that conversation. It is quoted from Edward Atkinson, "Significant Aspects of the Atlanta Cotton Exposition," *Century Magazine,* Vol. XXIII, February, 1882, pp. 563, *passim.*

The slave emerged from slavery without a dollar, and at first the planter had to borrow the money to supply him with the necessities of life. At the high prices of provisions, this was no small item. In spite, however, of all the obstacles, the planter found no difficulty in obtaining advances at high rates of interest, and with the high price of cotton and an average season, he was able to make a large sum of money. The result was, that he continued to spend and borrow, and that 1874 found him poorer than 1865. If the merchants had demanded payment for their claims, it is safe to assert that nearly the entire planting system would have been found bankrupt, and that the majority of the property would have passed into the hands of the creditors. But it was not the interest of the merchant to foreclose. He could not personally attend to the growing of cotton, and it was better for him to carry the planter at high rates and secure control of his cotton. If, in order to protect himself, he was forced to foreclose, he willingly sold again on credit. Thus, the planter became, in all but name, the manager of the merchant. His debts, as a rule, were only carried from year to year. What was left after paying the merchant back the special advance for the year, with the interest, went to the interest on the old debt, and the remainder, after defraying the expenses of the planter's family, which seemed to have a wonderful way of adapting themselves to the largest crops, went to the principal of the old debt. Thus it happens that every year the planter has had to borrow to run his places. It would be safe to assert that even now, after several years of closer economy than the planter ever practiced, and after reducing the balance against him. it would be cheaper for him to let his land go to pay his debts, and borrow money at a legitimate interest with which to buy and run it. The interest he now pays for yearly advances alone, not counting the interest on older debts, would more than pay the interest at six per centum on the present value of his plantations and the money it would take to run them.

But I do not wish to be understood as condemning the merchants. But for them the planter could not have planted at all, and they have probably been as liberal as any capitalists who had the borrower completely at their mercy. From nowhere else could the planter borrow. Again, the capital of the merchant was, and is, limited. By advancing upon cotton and sugar, and receiving and selling the articles advanced upon during the same month, for a large part of the year, he is able to make five per cent. commissions in one month, besides interest.

The secret is, that the merchant is not simply a money-lender. Money is to him the lever with which to obtain commissions. No wonder, then, that the commission merchant should be willing to advance to the planter at such high rates, or should be willing to sell places which have fallen into his hands, and which rent for eighteen and twenty per cent. on their present value. These latter it necessarily takes some attention to manage, and, lying, as they do, hundreds of miles from him, are the sources of annoyance.

Another of the great evils of this system is, that the planter cannot protect his laborers from the extortions of the store-keepers who supply them, or, if he provides for them himself, he, from force of circumstances, becomes an extortioner himself. Borowing money at a high and ruinous rate, he takes the risk of loaning to the laborer. Many of these are responsible; many are not. The practice is to make the hardworking, the industrious, the frugal, pay for the deficits of the idle. The result of the whole is, to speak in the language of one of the most intelligent merchants of America, to make paupers of the planters and tramps of the negroes.

Add to this vicious system of business the disturbed state of that section incident to the total overthrow of the former social status, and you have a complete picture of the obstacles under which the planter has labored.

✵   ✵   ✵

In an address delivered by the well-known Benjamin H. Hill of Georgia at an agricultural fair, the South was admonished to diversify its farming. The speech was quoted by Edwin De Leon in "The New South," *Harper's New Monthly Magazine,* Vol. 48, January, 1874, pp. 279-80.

We of the South are very poor. With individual exceptions we are all poor. I fear we do not know how poor we are. I am confident we do not imagine how poor we are going to be. As a people the agricultural population of the South are poorer today than they have ever been, and they are getting poorer every day. . . . Now let me ask you this question, How

much will you make this year? I will answer for you. A large majority of
the planters of Georgia will be poorer on the last day of December next
than they were on the first day of January, last. I admit that large profits
will be made by some people on this year's cotton crop in the South, but
what I affirm is that (with individual exceptions) these profits will not be
reaped by the planters of this cotton. Who will get the profits, then? you
will ask. I will tell you. Wall Street will get millions of your profits; the
manufacturers in New England will get many millions; the lien merchants
around you will get millions; the corn growers and hop-raisers in the
West will get many millions; the brokers and cotton factors and commission
merchants will get still other millions; guano men, life-insurance companies,
and many other artful contrivances will get the remaining millions of your
profits; and the great majority of the farmers may go home and be thankful
if they have food and clothing, and have settled up their bills, and preserved credit enough to go through the per cent. mill another year. . . .
I wish I had the time to show you how all the commercial, manufacturing,
speculating world have formed their schemes, shaped the laws, and united
in harmonious shrewdness to gather the profits of cotton planting in the
South. . . .

But you ask, How can . . . [a] better destiny be secured? I will tell you.
First, *make cotton your surplus crop.* . . . Make your own fertilizer by
resting, cropping, grassing and manuring your lands—thus you become independent of guano merchants. Your cheapest and safest line of transportation runs from your own fields and hog-pens to your own barns and
meat-houses. With no debts for supplies, you will need *no accommodation
credits at two per cent. per month* thus you become independent of brokers
and cotton factors and lien merchants. You can then sell your own cotton
at your own time, to your own chosen buyers and for your own price, and
will get your own money. None of these things can a planter do who plants
on credit, and borrows money to buy his provisions. Go on as you are now
going, making cotton your chief crop, and slavery is the doom of your
children and your children's children forever. A people that depend on
other people for food and clothing are and must be slaves.

✓   ✓   ✓

Many farmers in the South who were near systems of transportation changed
from one-crop production to truck farming. In 1887 M. B. Hillyard observed this
trend. The following is quoted from his *The New South,* The Manufacturers'
Record Company, Baltimore, 1887, pp. 15-16.

Fruit raising as a vocation was hardly known South until after the war.
Before the war many had their orchards of one fruit and another; but it
would have been considered utterly petty and contemptible to have raised
fruit and sold it as beneath any gentleman! Thirty-five years ago this was

precisely the view in Delaware. But immediately after the war, fruit raising began as a business in the South. The influence wave broke across the narrow boundry of sea between the peninsula on which Delaware and the Eastern Shores of Maryland and Virginia are situated, and Norfolk, Virginia, and deluged the latter locality with a fruit-raising settlement. Small fruit was "set" in large quantities, and soon grew to large proportions. Before the war some other fruit had been planted; and one gentleman had secured both wealth and eminence from a pear orchard of his planting that had an almost national reputation. Delaware and Maryland soon felt the influence of the competition of Norfolk in the decreased prices brought by their fruit. (The writer, then living in Dover, Delaware, and raising fruit largely well remembers this.) Very quickly, wide-awake Delawareans strove to get ahead of Norfolk, and moved further South—even as far down as Wilmington, North Carolina—and "set" strawberries. So the spirit grew.

About the close of the war, possibly in the fall of 1865, Dr. Clayton A. Cowgill, of Dover, Delaware, moved on the Saint John's River, in Florida, and went at once largely into the business of orange raising. It is stated that while numberless persons had raised oranges for fruit and as a pastime, he was the first who did it as a scheme for money-making. About the same time, Mrs. Harriet Beecher Stowe went down on the Saint John's River in Florida, and began writing those letters in its praise which set the whole North in a blaze of enthusiasm, and soon drew thither the capital and immigration with an ever-swelling flood since. Except Mr. Charles Nordhoff's letters and book on Southern California, there has been no approximation, in the building up of a State by a single pen, to the influence of Mrs. Stowe's literary work in behalf of Florida. Who shall tell of the development of Florida in fruit culture? Who can fix its boundaries? Who can depict the transformation scenes of the trackless pine woods into orange bowers, citron groves, pineapple plantations, banana farms, and what not? . . .

But while Florida is great, not only on account of the magnitude of her business in fruit culture, and especially in the magnitude of a fruit culture possible to only a limited area of the country, she is by no means the only State far South which is conspicuous by fruit culture. Georgia, greatly through the influence of her celebrated citizen, Mr. P. J. Berckmans, is raising a great deal of fruit, pears especially, and a goodly quantity of peaches and apples and small fruits, and is a leader among the Southern States. Along the Jackson Railroad, (Southern Branch of the Illinois Central,) in the pine woods of Mississippi, and about and above Canton, there is a very considerably developed fruit-raising interest; and Southwestern Tennessee is well advanced, too. But it is impossible to particularize in full. It may be stated in brief, that there is no Southern State in which fruit raising is not more or less prosecuted as a vocation; that in some States it is a very particular interest and quite a source of revenue, and that all fruit raising South as a Vocation or with a view to money-making has obtained since the war. . . .

Vegetable raising or "trucking" is an immense business South, and it stretches from Norfolk to the Gulf of Mexico, well down into Florida. A very long and interesting chapter might be written on its growth, and figures might be given to prove its magnitude. At Norfolk, Virginia, it takes a large steamer per day to transport what that vicinity sends to New York City alone. All along the Atlantic coast to and in Florida, trains and steamers are well laden for months with early vegetables. From New Orleans, La., go great quantities. Mississippi, along the Illinois Central Railroad, sends considerable quantities, as does Southwestern Tennessee. Mobile, Ala., has become the most considerable vegetable raising area in the South, with, perhaps, one or two exceptions. . . . Mobile used to import cabbages, because it was supposed that they could not be raised there. Now she sends off every year to Western markets from one to three hundred or more car-loads of early cabbages. What a revolution in ideas and business! . . . Suffice it to say, that all this business of raising vegetables for the early market North and West is a new thing to the South—as to anything considerable, the growth of the last decade.

✓ ✓ ✓

Sidney Lanier wrote an article for *Scribner's Magazine,* entitled "The New South," pp. 840-51. He commented on the tendency in Georgia for farmers to do just what Benjamin Hill had advised in 1874. The following extract is from Lanier's article, "The New South," Centennial Edition, *Sidney Lanier,* Johns Hopkins Press, Baltimore, 1945, Vol. V, pp. 338-343.

The phrase "small farming," used of the South, crops out in directions curious enough to one unacquainted with the special economics and relations of existence in that part of our country. While large farming in the South means exclusive cotton-growing,—as it means in the West exclusive wheat-growing or exclusive corn-growing—small farming means *diversified farm-products;* and a special result of the Southern conditions of agriculture has brought about a still more special sense of the word, so that in Georgia, for example, the term "small farmer" brings up to every native mind the idea of a farmer who, besides his cotton crop, raises corn enough to "do" him. But again, the incidents hinging upon this apparently simple matter of making corn enough to do him are so numerous as, in turn, to render *them* the distinctive feature of small farming. Small farming means, in short, meat and bread for which there are no notes in bank; pigs fed with home-made corn, and growing of themselves while the corn and cotton were being tended; yarn spun, stockings knit, butter made and sold (instead of bought); eggs, chickens, peaches, water-melons, the four extra sheep and a little wool, two calves and a beef,—all to sell every year, besides a colt who is now suddenly become, all of himself, a good, serviceable horse; the four oxen, who are as good as gifts made by the grass; and a hundred other items, all representing income from a hundred sources to the small farmer, which equally represent outgo to the large farmer,—items, too, scarcely appearing at all on the expense side of the strictest account-book, because they are either products of odd moments which, if not so applied, would not have been at all applied, or products of natural animal growth, and grass at nothing a ton. All these ideas are inseparably connected with that of the small farmer in the South.

The extent of this diversity of product possible upon a single small farm in Georgia, for instance, and the certain process by which we find these diversified products presently creating demands for the village library, the neighborhood farmers'-club, the amateur Thespian society, the improvement of the public schools, the village orchestra, all manner of betterments and gentilities and openings out into the universe: show significantly, and even picturesquely, in a mass of clippings which I began to make a couple of years ago, from a number of country papers in Georgia, upon the idea that these unconsidered trifles of mere farmers' neighborhood news, with no politics behind them and no argumentative coloring in front of them, would form the best possible picture of actual small-farm life in the South—that is, of the New South.

To read these simple and homely scraps is indeed much like a drive among the farms themselves with the ideal automaton guide, who confines himself to telling you that this field is sugar-cane, that one yonder is cotton, the other is rice, and so on, without troubling you for responsive exclamations or other burdensome commentary.

Rambling among these cuttings, one sees growing side by side, possibly upon a single small farm, corn, wheat, rice, sugar-cane, cotton, peaches, plums, apples, pears, figs, water-melons, cantaloupes, musk-melons, cherries, strawberries, raspberries, blackberries, Catawba grapes, Isabellas, Scuppernongs, peas, snap-beans, butter-beans, okra, squash, beets, oyster-plant, mustard, cress, cabbage, turnips, tomatoes, cauliflower, asparagus, potatoes, onions; one does not fail, too, to catch a glimpse of pigs sauntering about, chickens singing, colts flinging their heels at you and off down the pasture, calves likewise, cows caring not for these things, sheep on the rising ground, geese and turkeys *passim,* perhaps the green-gray moss—surely designed by nature to pack vegetables in and send them "North,"—a very bed of dew for many days after cutting, and the roses and morning-glories everywhere for a benison. . . .

And so, looking along through this batch of items,—which surely never dreamed of finding themselves together,—one gathers a great number of circumstances illustrating the small farm of Georgia from various points of view. One hears, for instance, how the people of Thomas County (southern Georgia) are now busy gathering, packing and forwarding the sand pear to Boston and New York (the sand pear, or Le Conte pear, is a luscious variety which has recently been pushed with great success among the sandy lands of lower Georgia; the entire stock is said to have come from one tree on the Le Conte plantation in Liberty County—the same farm which sent out a further notable product in the persons of two illustrious professors John and Joseph Le Conte, now of the University of California); how last week thirty bushels of pears were obtained from the old tree mentioned in the preceding clause; how southern Georgia is making sugarcane a leading crop; how Mr. Anthony (in Bibb County, middle Georgia) has twenty-eight varieties of grapes growing on a few acres, and has just introduced a new variety; how Bartow County (above Atlanta) shipped 225,000 pounds of dried apples and peaches last season; how over 15,000 pounds of wool have been received during the last four days at one warehouse in Albany (south-west Georgia) while in Quitman (same portion) our streets are constantly thronged with carts laden with wool from Colquitt and Berrien and Lowndes counties—this wool being, it should be added, the product of small farmers who "raise" many other things; how the common sheep is an extremely profitable beast, it being but a sorry specimen which will not furnish one lamb and two and a half pounds of wool per annum, which lamb will sell for two dollars while the wool will bring nearly another dollar, and all for no tendance except a litle rice-straw and cotton-seed during the weaning season, together with careful folding at night; how—and here the connection with small farming is only apparently remote—a library society is being organized in Milledgeville, while in another town the *Advertiser* is making a vigorous call for a library, and in a third the library has recently received many additions of books, and in a county an amateur Thespian corps has just been formed, consisting of five ladies and fourteen gentlemen, whose first performance is to be early in July; how there are curious correlations between sheep, whiskey, public schools and dogs—the State school commissioner vigorously advocating the Moffett bell-punch system of tax on liquor and a tax on dogs (of which, I find from another slip, there are 99,414 in the State, destroying annually 28,625 of the small farmers' sheep), for the purpose of increasing the school fund to a million dollars annually; how, at Atlanta University for colored people, which is endowed by the State, the progress of the pupils, the clearness of their recitations, their excellent behavior, and the remarkable neatness of their schoolrooms altogether convince "your committee that the colored race . . . are capable of receiving the education usually given at such institutions"; how last Thursday a neighboring club of small farmers, on Walnut Creek (near Macon), celebrated the fifth anniversary of the club by meeting under the trees, with their wives and children, recounting in turn how many acres each had in cotton, how many in corn, how many in potatoes, how many in peas, etc., . . . and a barbecue. . . . [The] last few years have witnessed a very decided improvement in Georgia farming: moon-planting and other vulgar superstitions are exploding, the intelligent farmer is deriving more assistance from the philosopher, the naturalist and the chemist, and he who is succeeding best is he who has plenty of horses, cattle, sheep, hogs, and poultry of his own raising, together with good-sized barns and meat-houses filled from his own fields instead of from the West,—in short, the small farmer. . . .

16

The Farmers' Revolt

During the first sixty years of the nineteenth century there were numerous farm clubs and organizations in the South, and many agricultural journals were published. These were read in the homes of the more literate farmers. County and state fairs encouraged more scientific farm methods. These efforts were completely divorced from politics and were not designed to create a solid front to influence legislation.

After the Civil War a national organization, the Patrons of Husbandry, or the Grange, was started in 1867, and by 1871 it was well established in the South. By that time the prices of farm products had declined and unrest among the farmers was creating a class consciousness; farmers felt that railroads, corporations, and banking interests were exploiting them. The founders of the Grange had hoped to encourage cultural interests and self-improvement, but the members soon turned to discussion of economic issues; they began to engage in the co-operative buying of farm machinery and farm supplies. In some states the Grange attempted to operate manufacturing plants. These efforts failed. Agitation for railroad legislation was one of the most successful activities of the Grange; however, the states of the Middle West were more active in this respect than were those in the South.

Among other farmers' clubs in the South after the Civil War was the Agricultural Wheel, originally known as the Wattensas Farmers' Club. It became strongest in Arkansas, and in 1887 it had a national membership of 500,000, with separate divisions for white and colored farmers. It opposed national banks, trusts, mortgages on agricultural crops and livestock, and a protective tariff, while it favored graduated income taxes and participation of farmers in legislative bodies.

About May, 1874, the Alliance movement appeared in Texas, in opposition to "land sharks." It used about the same methods as the Grange, dabbled in politics, drew up a declaration of principles, and then died down to be revived later. In 1887 the Farmers' Alliance of Texas and the Farmer's Union of Louisiana consolidated, and in 1888 the Agricultural

Wheel joined them. In 1889 the name the National Farmers' Alliance and Industrial Union was adopted. This is usually known as the Southern or Southwestern Alliance. There was also a Northern Alliance. Eight of the Southern state Alliances were completely autonomous. In addition an Alliance of Colored Farmers of Texas was fostered and it spread to ten other states with 1,200,000 members.

A farm magazine published in North Carolina, and a mouthpiece of the Southern Farmers' Alliance, *The Progressive Farmer,* published on May 15, 1888, and July 31, 1888, reviewed the work accomplished by the Alliances.

The order originated in Texas only a few years ago, and has grown and spread with astonishing rapidity until now it is an established institution in nearly all the Southern States. It promises to supersede all other farmers' organizations in the South . . . In Texas . . . where its membership approximates three hundred thousand farmers, it has over 200 cotton yards under and belonging to it, nearly 50 patent roller flouring mills, with a capacity of from 50 to 500 barrels of flour per day, the largest woolen mill in all the South or the Southwest, a number of cotton factories in process of construction, and a property on which factories, an Alliance Female University and a great city is soon to be built, a State Business Exchange for selling the produce of the farmers and for buying their supplies, machinery, &c., in bulk and at wholesale prices. This exchange is on a perfectly solid financial basis, having as its support in the commercial world about five hundred thousand dollars in cash as a guarantee fund. It has besides all this the largest implement, machinery and hardware house in the South or Southwest, and which did a business of over two hundred thousand dollars during last month. These are the more prominent features of the business system of the order in the State of Texas, to say nothing of hundreds of smaller enterprises now being prosecuted.

In the other States the order is catching the spirit of their brethren in the "Lone Star" State and are preparing to move along the same line as fast as they become able to do so. . . . .

The colored Farmers' Alliance is a separate and distinct organization from the white Alliance. It is regularly chartered, and according to its Constitution is composed of colored members alone. Its principal objects are: To educate the colored race, to make them more industrious, more frugal, more reliable, more thoughtful, more faithful, better people, better citizens, and to better their condition financially. This order originated in Texas on the 10th day of December 1886, by 16 colored men and citizens of Texas. They set forth their declaration of purposes and assigned reasons why they desired to incorporate and organize for themselves. Among other reasons, they assign the following: "A great many organizations have been fixed up for us by *our friends?* both North and South, and have proved mere frauds and deceptions."

"That there are organizations now in existence that take in both white and colored people as members, thereby imperiling, if not destroying the harmony and good of the order."

"That our churches and schools thrive better entirely separate."

"That though we are organizing separate and apart from the Farmers' Alliance now existing in Texas, composed of white members, we believe it will be to our interest to work in harmony with that organization. That we ask the members of the white Alliance throughout the United States to aid us in perfecting our organization."

It is true that the colored Alliance is spreading rapidly, now being in ten different States, with a General Superintendent in each State. . . .

✔   ✔   ✔

Women attended the Alliance meetings with their husbands. It is probable that the wives influenced their husbands to back the movement, as is suggested by Mollie Hall, the writer of the following article from the *Mercury,* publication of the National Alliance, which was reprinted in *The Progressive Farmer,* January 19, 1888.

The first question is, "What were we created for?" We are to be the helpmate to man, and we must all try to do our part in the battle. We can be a great help to our husbands, or we can be a great drawback to them. These hard times our husbands need encouragement and all the help they can get. I don't believe in a woman going to the field to plow or hoe, for that is not her work. If a woman does all of her housework and washing and ironing and her sewing for her family she will do a very good part. We must raise our chickens and supply our table with chickens and eggs, and milk our cows and supply our table with milk and butter, and all have a few stands of bees and tend to them ourselves. We bought two stands of bees six years ago. Now we have twenty-three stands, and have sold several stands of bees and have some honey to sell every year, so that is a great help. We Alliance people must raise what we eat at home. It won't do for poor farmers to live at home and board at the store. We must live as saving as we can until we all get out of debt. We must not run our husbands into debt for fine dressing. We must make our own dresses and trim them over, and they will look as well as new. We must trim over our hats, for a poor farmer cannot afford to buy his wife a new hat or bonnet every season of the year. When a woman tries to help her husband and saves all she can, that encourages him to work and try to make a living for her, but if a woman don't try to help and save, and always runs her husband into debt, he soon becomes discouraged, and he very often takes to drinking and his course is soon run. A word to all Alliance women: We must encourage our husbands in their great and noble cause and go with them to their meetings. That is a great encouragement to them. I have missed but one meeting since I joined it. It has been eleven months since I joined. Who can do better than that? If the women go, that encourages the men to go, for they would not like to see their wives go and they stay at home.

✓   ✓   ✓

Reform governors were elected in 1890 in North Carolina, South Carolina, and Georgia. The Platform of the Farmers' Alliance of Virginia adopted at Lynchburg, August 21, 1890, will illustrate the beliefs of Southern Alliance members. It is quoted from William DuBose Sheldon, *Populism in the Old Dominion, Virginia Farm Politics,* 1885-1900, Princeton University Press, Princeton, 1935, pp. 163-165, Appendix A.

The Virginia State Farmers' Alliance, in annual session assembled, declares its allegiance to the national organization and reiterates its adherence to those principles upon which our order was founded—of unity in all things essential; equal rights to all and special privileges to none.

Whereas the depressed condition of the agricultural and laboring classes of our country cries aloud for help, and the statistics of our government show that in the advancement of our country in the last twenty-five years the agricultural and laboring classes—the wealth producers—have been left far behind, and that the wealth of the country is rapidly concentrating in the hands of a favored few to the detriment of the many, so that now more than half of the wealth of the country is held by less than 25,000 of its 64,000,000 people:

And whereas we believe the legislation of the Congress of the United States for the last twenty-five years has been greatly to the prejudice of a large majority of the people and in the interest of the favored few; that the monetary system as administered under the national banking laws, its demonetization of silver and contraction of the currency, has so reduced the value of our lands and their products as to materially lessen their farm values, while at the same time the bonds and holdings of capitalists and monopolists have been greatly enhanced in value:

And whereas unjust and onerous burdens of taxation have been imposed upon the farmer and the laborer through our internal-revenue and tariff laws framed in the interests of monopolists and trusts; these laws while professing to protect the farmer and laborer tax with a heavy hand almost every article necessary for their daily wants, and at the same time close the markets of the world to their products; and recognizing the facts that to accomplish the reforms we demand, we must select and vote for candidates in accord with our views; yet we believe that this may be accomplished inside the two great parties now existing by demanding and exacting pledges from those seeking our suffrage to give us and our interests fair and equitable treatment, refusing to support in either party those who refuse us support; and whereas it is proper that we should set forth what we believe may give relief to our depressed people, therefore be it

Resolved, 1. That we favor the free and unlimited coinage of silver.

2. The repeal of the national banking laws, and the substitution of legal-tender Treasury notes in lieu of national bank notes and in sufficient quantity to do the business of the country.

3. That Congress issue a sufficient amount of fractional paper currency to facilitate exchange through the medium of the United States mails.

4. Such a revision of our tariff laws as shall reduce the burdens of taxation upon the necessities of life, placing upon luxuries the burden they should bear, reducing the tariff taxation to the necessities of government economically administered and so adjusted as to promote rather than suppress our commercial intercourse with the nations of the world.

5. We demand that Congress shall pass such laws as shall effectually prevent the dealing in futures of all agricultural and mechanical products.

6. The destruction of trusts and the withdrawal of all favors in the shape of subsidies and bounties.

7. The abrogation of all partisan and class legislation.

8. Equal distribution of the burdens of taxation, that capitalists' bonds &c. shall be required to bear a just share of taxes and the enactment of such laws as will insure this end.

9. We oppose the alien ownership of land and all land grants to railroads, corporations, and syndicates, and demand the forfeiture of all unearned land grants and that all land held by railroads and other corporations in excess of such as are actually used and needed by them for their legitimate purposes be reclaimed by the government and held by actual settlers only.

10. We demand a railroad commission consisting of three persons to which shall be given the full power to protect the rights and interests of the people; to have power to regulate and correct all discriminations in freights and other charges and to adjust a schedule of tariffs favorable to the people and just to the railroads, making rates uniform per mile as far as possible, allowing for loading and unloading.

11. We will not support for office the representatives or paid attorneys of railroads, transportation companies, and other corporations. We demand pledges from all candidates for office that they will not accept free passes upon railroads or other transportation lines, and we condemn the use of free passes by the judiciary.

The farmers and their leaders had several explanations for their distress. Some thought that national legislation worked to their disadvantage; others believed that the railroads, which had gained a dominant position in farm economic life, discriminated against farmers; lack of credit at reasonable rates of interest was a third factor in farm discontent, and a fourth was the marketing system which allowed middlemen to become wealthy while the farmers did not even receive enough from their crops to cover the cost of production.

The following selection from Charles H. Otken, *The Ills of the South*, G. P. Putnam Sons, New York, 1894, pp. 33ff., outlines the history of lien laws in the Southern states.

It is history today, that farms of every dimension, all over the South, and the livestock, with the products raised on these farms, have barely enabled the occupants to live. In other words, in many instances the farms, horses, mules, and cattle, personal labor of the owners, and the general products raised, were required to pay the expense bill. Ten years made these men homeless.

A still larger number, whose condition is not so bad, are toiling year after year, but can not reach the point to buy supplies for cash. They are always a year behind. Every year they are contending with risks. Storms, a drought, a rainy season, a bad crop year generally, inefficient labor, low price of cotton, high prices incident to this method of doing business, extravagance in buying, are all ugly contingencies. Many a sorrowful experience will recognize these elements in the business problem. To secure supplies next year, security may be demanded in the view of the risk to be taken. The following year, affairs on the farm may be worse still. . . .

The inefficient and unmanageable negro labor, soon after the war, involved Southern farmers deeper in debt than they were involved in 1865. Lien laws were enacted in all the Southern States to help this class of men, as well as the negroes. The humane intent of these laws was to furnish a basis of credit. The man who had land could give a lien on that. Those who had live stock only could get their years' supplies on this security. Those who had neither land nor live stock could rent land and a mule, and could give a lien on the prospective crop to secure the landowner, and the merchant for the goods bought. This last lien enabled the negroes to be independent of the white man's supervision.

No legislator could foresee the practical operation of these laws. One of the first effects was to derange negro labor. He was desirous to be to himself; to get away from his former master; to feel that all the old relations of a former condition were destroyed forever. This was natural. Whether it was wise in the negro to be his own manager, and to act upon his own responsibility, is another question. The negroes had everything to learn, and the disposition to learn and be directed was wanting. The truth is, the old master was the negro's best friend and safest adviser. Unfortunately, the negroes as a class were far more disposed to listen to the stranger than to the old master.

Prior to the enactment of these laws, some negroes worked on the wage plan. The number that worked in this way, as far as our observations and inquiries extend, was small at any time since the war. It never met with much favor among the negroes. It involved too much regularity as to the hours of work, and too much direction on the part of the employer as to how to do the work. . . . The wages were graded according to general efficiency and industry. It was difficult to make them understand why one negro's work was worth eight dollars a month, and another's ten dollars. The employer furnished everything under this plan, and assumed all responsibility for supplies bought of the merchant.

The share plan was a favorite with the negroes. They were their own managers. The employer furnished the land, the mule, and necessary farm tools. He was responsible to the merchant for the supplies furnished the share worker. He generally received half the cotton and corn made by the negro. The corn was in many cases less than the quantity furnished by the employer and consumed by the plow animal during the year.

How did this plan work? Generally speaking, it neither benefited the negro nor the white farmer. The reason is plain. As soon as the negro became his own manager, his industrial qualities declined in value. Besides, he generally managed affairs badly. We speak of them as a class, and not of the exceptional good and successful negro farmers—a small number at best. The negro under this plan gave little attention to the corn crop. He raised no meat. The result of the year's work proved that half of the cotton was not sufficient to pay the store account. The balance due was paid by the employer. The employer, already in debt, and unable to pay his annual store account, in time lost part or all of his land.

In various localities in every State, merchants came into possession of many farms. Some merchants had a strong hankering to become large land-owners. It exalted them in the estimation of the world to be the possessors of 50,000, 100,000, and 500,000 acres of land. By indirect means, the aim was to get possession of land. . . . Some merchants took land because they could not help themselves. Other merchants so conducted their business that the necessity to take land was firmly registered.

Before the lien laws were enacted, and before they were used as a basis of credit, thousands of farmers in every Southern State had already increased their debt obligations to merchants. At that period in Southern history, had no lien laws been enacted, and had all credit business been reduced to one-tenth of what it was annually, the whole South would now be solvent and prosperous. It would have entailed some suffering, but no one would have starved. Such an economic policy would have been of untold value to the negroes.

Under the operations of this system of business and these laws, merchants in various localities became large landowners. . . . On general principles it was a mistake. Whenever this was done, bitter rivalry between the resident farmer and the merchant farmer of the town ensued. . . .

The practical working of this new plan may be profitably illustrated.

Mr. A., a merchant, owns one hundred farms. He proposes to cultivate these places on the share or rent plan. In no case, under these circumstances, does he employ hands for wages. The risk is too great, and supervision is impossible. In some instances land is sold, mostly to negroes; here and there to white men. He does a flourishing business. He provides them with plow stock and farming implements, if necessary; also with bread and meat and clothing. This will be severely allowanced by the crop prospect. And this bread and meat supply, it is claimed by those who have the opportunity to know the facts, is less, in many instances, than the necessity of hunger demanded. The merchant is not to be blamed for refusing to furnish a man more than he is able to pay. The method of working farms in certain localities is under consideration, and not men. The purposes of men may be fair, yet the principles upon which they act may prove disastrous to the general welfare. Liens of one sort or another bind these people to him. What they make on these farms is practically his. . . . It is a common opinion, that the tenants on the places of the merchant farmers fare worse, upon the whole, than those working for resident farmers. The attraction of the negro tenant for these places is, that he is lord of all he surveys on his farm. He is the sole master of his time, work and management. . . .

Under the treacherous operation of these laws, farmers involved themselves in debt, gave security on their estates when cotton was selling at 30, 25, 15, and 10 cents a pound. They bought land, horses, and merchandise when the great Southern staple brought a high price. Everything else was high. Interest accumulated year by year. A steady pressure was kept on cotton production. Grain growing and meat raising were neglected. The increase of the cotton crop pressed down its price. Now, when cotton is down to 7 cents, the attempt to pay old debts incurred when the price of cotton ruled at 15, 12, and 10 cents, is an herculean task. . . .

The debts of the people, incident to the credit system of the Southern States, have been no small factor in bringing about the over-production of the great staple crop. Men in debt, want money. Farmers know that cotton is the only crop that will bring money. In their opinion there is no time for anything else. . . .

For years a class of merchants encouraged their credit customers to raise cotton exclusively, or very largely. They reasoned very naturally and very logically, that, the more goods sold to farmers, the greater their sales and the greater their aggregate profits. Corn, bacon, and pickled pork are just as good commodities on which to make money as molasses, calico, and brogans. Mr. Henry W. Grady in his second article in the *New York Ledger,* 1889, writing on "The Era of Speculation in the South," states how this class of dealers viewed the matter of cotton raising: "When he (the farmer) saw the wisdom of raising his own corn, bacon, grasses, and stock, he was NOTIFIED that reducing his cotton acreage was reducing *his line of credit*. He was thus helpless. . . . The debts of the farmer bound him to cotton.

✔   ✔   ✔

Among the complaints made by the farmers were many against the trusts. The following appeared in *The Progressive Farmer,* February 2, 1888, p. 1.

The "Trust" must go. It is narrow in its principles. It is unscrupulous in its methods. It is conducted for the purpose of beating everybody out of the last cent possible. Is it felt in the South? Of course it is. Look at the "Cotton Seed Oil Trust." Louisiana had tried to drive this monopolist out of that State. Why? Because, as Attorney-General Cunningham says, it was formed to acquire and control all the cotton seed oil mills in the South, and that it is an illegal, invalid, immoral and corrupt association.

There are some North Carolinians who have felt, directly, the evil consequences of the "Trust." In the New York *Herald* of Sunday, we find Mr. Frederick Oliver of Charlotte, saying: "We owned two mills, at Charlotte and at Columbia and turned our stock over to the trust, and we received trust certificates in exchange. But when we tried to find out something about the business of the concern whose paper we held we could learn absolutely nothing. The business is entirely in the hands of the trustees, who manage everything for themselves. They are at liberty to vote themselves any salary they please, sell themselves seed if they wish and absorb all the profits of the business if they so incline. In addition, we discovered that there was an immense issue of trust certificates representing now, I believe, $50,000 00 [Does this mean $50,000.00 or $500,000 or $5,000,-000? I. V. N.]

In so far as the State of North Carolina is concerned, and it has some interest at stake, according to Mr. Oliver, we trust that it will follow the example of Louisiana. But it should go farther. It should put every trust under a ban. So, also, should every other Southern State. Furthermore, so, also, should every other State in the Union. Food, fuel, light and clothing should not be in the ownership of a few monopolies.—*Wilmington Messenger*.

✔   ✔   ✔

The Progressive Farmer printed a series of three articles from the Scotland Neck *Democrat* on August 2, and September 10 and 17, 1889; these contained arguments favoring a state railroad commission.

NO. 1

During the session of our Legislature last winter there was a feeling of intense excitement over the proposed passage of an act creating a railroad commission. As a rule the Republicans and a few Democrats, some of whom were known to be in the employment of some railroad company, and the great army of railroad lobbyists persistently, earnestly, and bitterly denouncing the measure; and everybody else, with almost equal earnestness, advocates it. During the discussion in the Senate of the bill creating the commission, which had passed the House . . . , the lobby was crowded with farmers, business men, lawyers, editors, politicians, railroad men and railroad lobbyists. There were many ladies in the gallery, among whom could be seen the excellent wife of a distinguished railroad president, pencil and paper in hand ready to keep the count of the vote, and who, as was apparent to the most casual observer, was deeply, intensely interested in the discussion. . . .

But why this intense excitement? . . .

I went to one of the many railroad lobbyists, hired to influence legislators as to measures pertaining to railroads, whose business it was to hang around the legislative lobbies, the hotels, the boarding houses and everywhere else a legislator might happen to be, and, by hook or crook, get control of him. . . . [I] asked him please to explain to me why this excitement, why this unusual and, of course, expensive fight on the part of the railroads against the creation of a railroad commission, and his answer came, prompt and fluent:

"A lot of politicians, desiring fat places for themselves and friends, and others wishing to reward party leaders, are playing upon the credulity of the honest plain people of the country and seeking to place our properties" (one of these big capitalists never speaks of "his property" but always says "his properties") in the hands of three inexperienced, perhaps ignorant men to say how much we shall charge on a barrel of apples from Waynesville to Raleigh. We have invested our capital in purchasing, repairing and building railroads in North Carolina, in engines, cars, etc., for the transportation of passengers and produce. We have given our time, thought, experience and money, to the development of the material interests of North Carolina and now this farmer legislature proposes to rob us of our properties by putting men in office with power to say to us where we shall build our depots, how fast our trains shall run, and what we shall charge for the transportation of passengers and produce. The Legislature has no more right to say how we shall manage our properties, and how much income we shall receive for the use of our capital than it has to declare how often the farmer shall plow his cotton or what he shall receive for it when it is ready for market. The farmers have been organized, talked to about hard times, duped and excited by designing politicians pretending to be their disinterested friends, until they are wild, and imagine that if they can only have a railroad commission with power to regulate freights, the cotton and the corn will flourish and grow while the farmer loafs at the neighboring village, and with the end of the harvest will come heavily laden barns and gin houses and big prices. Such legislation will put an end to railroad building in North Carolina and utterly bankrupt and destroy those roads now in operation."

From one to another of these lobbyists and railroad men I went seeking information, and from one and all I received substantially the same answer. . . .

I next turned my attention to certain legislators who were pronounced advocates of a railroad commission. . . . I gathered but little from them except that the railroad presidents had been dictating the nomination of State officers, in perhaps the conventions of both political parties, to such an extent that no man, however deserving and popular, could possibly hope for political promotion without first bending the knee to the railroad presidents of the State. . . . that the charges of the different railroads were unequal and unjust and that these corporations, creatures of the State, had become so powerful and dictatorial that they had already, or were about to take charge of and become the master of their creator, the State. . . .

NO. 2

For what purpose do the railroad managers issue free passes to our Congressmen, our Legislators, our Judges, our Solicitors and our State officers? Is it because these persons are any more entitled to free transportation than the humblest and poorest citizen who helps to pay taxes to support the convicts that build and repair these railroads? Don't you know, my reader, that these passes are given to these public officers for the purpose of obtaining their assistance in the performance of their official duties? Do you suppose, or are you so blind as to believe that these passes are given because of any personal regard? . . .

NO. 3

Some of our judges apparently recognizing the impropriety of accepting free passes from railroads, undertake to excuse it by saying that, under our rotating system, they have to travel so much that if they had to pay for their transportation there would not be enough left of their salary of $2,000 to support the wife and children. The answer to this is if the State is too niggardly to pay you a decent salary do not accept the office. . . .

Why is it that whenever a plain, hard-working farmer, or country lawyer, merchant, mechanic or doctor is elected to the General Assembly he suddenly becomes a man of such vast learning and importance in the eyes of the railroad in the State . . . [is] he tendered a free pass over every railroad in the State and is treated with such distinguished consideration by the various railroad presidents and lobbyists? . . . unlike the judge he is paid by the State ten cents per mile both while coming to the seat of government and while returning, a sum much more than sufficient to defray his actual travelling expenses, and there can be no excuse or necessity for accepting the free pass.

In 1891 leaders of the Northern Alliance, plus a few Southerners, met in Cincinnati and made plans for a People's Party. A convention held at St. Louis in 1892 and another at Omaha in that year completed the organization. Thus the Alliance movement gave way to the People's Party. Southern Democrats began to counteract the efforts of the new party by reviving the white man's fear of Negro rule in the South, saying that "every vote cast for the third party will be a Republican vote by proxy, tending to encourage the Negro to another effort for supremacy." Democrats reminded the voters of the Force Bill which the Republicans in Congress attempted to pass in 1890 calling for the federal supervision of elections. In addition the Democrats endorsed many of the farmers' demands, thus making it seem unnecessary to have a new farmers' party. Thus the Democrats controlled the new movement. An exception was in North Carolina, where a fusion Populist-Republican ticket won the governorship and control of the legislature in 1894 plus one full term and one short term in the United States Senate.

The activities of the Populist or People's Party led to a Senatorial investigation of the problems of cotton farmers. The following report to the United States Senate reveals several theories concerning farm problems. The text is from *Reports of Committee of the Senate of the United States,* 3rd Session, 1894-95, No. 986, Part I.

On April 19, 1892, the Senate passed a resolution providing for the study of agriculture, price of agricultural products, causes of depressed prices, etc. The following excerpts are from the report on Cotton Production and Consumption and Prices and the Remedy. First, circulars were sent to a large number of farmers in each of the cotton states, and other businessmen having dealings with farmers. The answers were summarized as follows:

First: That generally the financial condition of the farmers is bad, a very large percentage insolvent, and that very few indeed are substantially increasing in the possession of property. That the few who are actually solvent and making some increase in their estates are those who raise their own supplies, meat, corn, plow stock, producing cotton only as surplus. Whilst it can not be said that these are prosperous, yet as compared with their neighbors, who rely mainly on cotton, their condition is better. . . .

Second: That with the prices prevailing in the years 1891-92-93 in nearly every part of the cotton-producing region the cost of production equaled, if it did not exceed, the value of the cotton raised. This applies also to those small farmers who raise their crops by the labor of themselves and their families, if only the low agricultural wages prevailing were allowed for their labor and a fair rent for their land. This labor is by no means compensated, as it is in more prosperous communities, yet it suffices to prevent actual pecuniary loss. . . .

Absolute destitution is rarely the fate of any human being in the cotton-growing States. The mild climate, requiring the minimum of expenditure in clothing and fuel and in dwellings, and the generous soil yielding food with abundance, and open-hearted charity everywhere characteristic of the people prevent destitution even in the most unfortunate.

Yet, while there is no destitution, there is but little accumulation. The energy and enterprise of the people fail, under these adverse conditions, to make that steady and sure progress to which people have been accustomed and which up to now has been the concomitant and effect of free institutions.

The result has been to produce widespread discontent among cotton producers, and a disposition to discredit their old-time conservative methods and to induce a too ready acceptance of plausible theories for relief.

Progress, steady and rapid progress, has been the rule in Anglo-Saxon development. Immobility, or even that slow advance which is perceptible to laborious statisticians only, and is unfelt and unseen by the masses, produces discouragement and discontent.

We proceed now to inquire into the causes of the low prices. It is admitted that the obvious, apparent, and proximate cause is overproduction. . . . Overproduction in the sense that more cotton has been produced than can find an effective demand at fair prices, in the present condition of the finance and trade of the world, is undeniably true. Overproduction in the sense that the needs of the world for cotton and cotton manufacturers have been more than met is denied. . . .

Our tariff policy has so operated as to increase the cost of cotton goods, and thereby to diminish the consumption. This tariff policy has helped to produce that overproduction complained of. Another potential stimulus in this direction has been our general tariff policy, which by impeding, and in many instances by prohibiting, the introduction of the goods of other nations, has diminished their power to consume our products. In the effort to secure a home market for our products, we have, so far as cotton is concerned, not only impaired foreign markets, but have so arranged as to diminish the purchasing power of the laboring classes of our people. . . .

Another cause has contributed to the low price. This is the enormous extent to which dealings in "futures" has attained in late years. A great deal of valuable testimony has been taken on this point. Whilst there is a difference between commercial men as to the effect of these dealings, yet we think the arguments advanced and the facts stated by those who oppose these dealings carry the greater weight, and are entitled to our approbation. . . .

In the first place, let it be noted, that only in, and through, and under the regulations of the two cotton exchanges in New York and New Orleans can this business be transacted. The Cotton Exchange in New York is a corporation under the laws of that State. It is composed of less than 500 members, and the number can not be increased beyond that number. The initiation fee is $10,000, and the new members are elected by the old. No man can deal directly in futures unless he is a member. The corporation has absolute power over the dealings. All disputes and controversies are settled by a court established by the corporation itself, in what is called arbitration proceedings. Neither party is allowed to call in a Federal or State court. It fixes all grades of cotton, designates the warehouses in which it shall be stored, fixes the fees and charges for storage, weighing, and all other work done in relation to cotton. It fixes the quotations of prices which are to be published to the world, and these quotations are thus fixed under its rule for months for which there are no actual sales.

It and its members have such wealth that it is claimed, in a published letter of one of the principal members made in response to arguments made on the floor of this body, that the exchange can absolutely dominate and fix prices, as against all others, by flooding the market with offers of an un-limited supply of futures when at other places prices are, in its opinion, too high, when it deems prices are too low at other places, may immediately buy all that can be offered.

The New Orleans Cotton Exchange, though located in the largest spot-cotton market this side of the Atlantic, is a mere annex to and a subordinate of the New York Cotton Exchange, and so need not to be described further than by saying if it had the will to do good it has not the power. . . .

These exchanges are, in fact, an oligarchy of wealth, self-created and self-perpetuated, which hold in subjection to their will the interests of the people of at least ten States in the Union.

In all these they assume and exercise a power of regulating interstate and foreign commerce in cotton, which is vested by the Constitution in Congress alone. . . . . A few quotations from the replies submitted by in-dividual farmers to the circulars sent out by the Senate Committee:

In my opinion the greatest cause of financial distress among the cotton raisers is due more to the acts of Congress than to any other cause. The demonetization of silver, the national-banking system, the high tax for pro-tection, and the dealings in futures have all conspired to paralyze this great industry. The first has enabled the money power to contract the currency to such an extent as to leave us almost without currency; the second virtually destroys our credit, for we can not obtain money on the faith of our estate, and our State is powerless to offer us a hand in the way of a State currency; the third has gradually drained us of our substance by not only forcing us to pay too high for what we consume, but it places a heavier burden upon us than it does upon those better able to pay; the fourth puts millions of cotton upon the market never produced, thus adding to our already de-pressed market. These are the reasons why I charge that Congress is more responsible for our poverty and want than are the other causes stated. . .

The price of cotton will remain low as long as more than enough to sup-ply the world's demand is raised, and this is true of every other product of the farm.

National lesiglation has militated against agriculture in every section of the country, and especially in the cotton-growing States. I believe in special favors to none, but equal and just laws for all. Why should the Government pay a bounty to the producer of sugar and not to the producer of cotton? The tax on oleomargarine is unjust and class legislation of the very worst kind. I would have Congress repeal the Sherman bullion purchase act. There is no more reason for buying and storing bullion by the act of Government than there is for buying and storing cotton. Both are commodities. I would have the Government coin the bullion on hand as fast as possible. Let them stop issuing bills of a less denomination than $10. This would force a very large amount of silver into actual circulation. . . . If Congress should find it necessary to raise more money. . . . I would raise it by a tax on incomes. For the last thirty years the poor people, and especially the agricultural classes, have borne an undue proportion of the burdens of indirect taxation, and it is nothing but right that those who have been enabled to accumulate colossal fortunes under the burdensome and unjust system that has prevailed in the past should now be made to bear their due proportion of supporting the Government that has so long protected them.

Discourage in every way all combinations in restraint of trade. Prohibit by law all gambling in the necessaries of life or any product of the farm. . . .

The avowed purpose of the capitalistic class was and is to enslave labor and reap the rewards to themselves which justly belong to labor, and they have been aided in the fulfillment of their plans by our legislative bodies at Washington. We find it in the recommendations of the London bankers to their prototypes in the United States, and in their relations to one another. . . .

Improper management of their financial business is one great cause. The mortgage system has been a disadvantage to 50% of those who give mortgages, for when a man gives a mortgage he can not trade anywhere else on credit, and he has to pay the highest credit price, and probably 50% of what he buys could be done without. The per cent charged on goods sold on a mortgage or credit is ruinous, for it is an undeniable fact that the merchants and loan associations are getting possession of a large per cent of the land in this country. There is not money enough in the Southern States to do the business of the country.

✓   ✓   ✓

In the twentieth century the farmers made another effort to organize, this time in the Farmers' Union, which rose, as the Alliance did, in Texas. While Dr. Seaman A. Knapp was demonstrating how to produce more cotton per acre, the Farmers' Union was planning to reduce acreage and thus force prices to rise. John L. Mathews, "The Farmers' Union and the Tobacco Pool," *Atlantic Monthly,* Vol. 102, October 1908, pp. 482-491, gives a survey of one phase of the organization's work in 1908.

Kentucky has been having an experience unique, costly, tragic and probably to some extent valuable, with the farmers engaged in the chief agricultural industry of the state—growing tobacco. Some 80,000 of them, representing probably 400,000 of the population of the state, have been engaged in a union demonstrating for the purpose of securing higher pay. . . . Educated, more or less wisely, by the cheaper magazines and the newspapers, to the methods and aggressions of the so-called trusts, awakened to a knowledge of the skill and impunity with which some capitalists break both civil and moral law, he the farmer is apparently becoming less devoted to his old ideal of the law, and more inclined to try these new ventures for himself. We have a multitude of indications of this on every hand. The new constitutions, such as that of Oklahoma, are designed to allow him wide latitude. In Texas, in Illinois, and in many other states, he has passed anti-trust laws which specifically exempt the farmer from their terms. In Montana, Idaho, and Utah, the wool-growers have combined to raise the price of their wares, with considerable success. In the South, the cotton-growers, under the able leadership of Mr. Harvie Jordan, have held together for higher prices and for reduced acreage. They have pointed out clearly to the farmer, if it costs him 7 cents a pound to raise cotton, and he raises ten bales to sell at 10 cents, he will make 3 cents a pound, or $150 cash whereas if he raises only five bales, and the price goes to 15 cents, he will have a profit of 8 cents a pound, or $200 cash profit; he will only have done half as much work, and will have half his land left on which to grow other things. This sound reasoning holds many acres out of the cotton crop—until cotton goes so high that every farmer hastily plants all his acreage in the hope of getting the extra profit on his whole farm. Then comes the big drop, the price about equals the price of production, the "pool" has failed, and the work is all to do again.

The farmers'-union movement has reached the point of establishing regular warehouses captalized by farmers, in which the union man may hold his goods, drawing cash against them at the bank, refusing to sell at the cheap prices which prevail at harvest, and holding them until the later, higher price comes on. And there has grown up out of all this a still stronger movement, which has its headquarters now at Indianapolis, called the equity movement, intended to unite the farmers of the entire nation in a movement for more equitable living, in which the chief element is to secure a higher price for farm products. This equity movement—the American Society of Equity is its official style—has developed the method of "pooling crops" to the highest point that it has yet attained.

This method of pooling has now arrived at a test of a peculiar character, in which there has been pooled a crop which is by nature limited to a small area of production, and which is by financial manipulation limited to a small market for sale. That is, a trust having arisen in New York which was able to control the output, and therefore to make prices to suit itself, the farmers have answered this trust by forming under the equity society a union of their own, and going on strike for higher prices. Combining the methods of labor union and capitalistic organization, they have chosen, not to fight the trust under the laws of the state, nor to attempt to build up its commercial rivals, but to battle with it in the open, fight it to a standstill, and compel it to dicker with their organization as an equal. . . .

Almost all tobacco in Kentucky is grown upon the share-tenant system, and is the "money crop" of those who grow it. That is, instead of working a whole farm as a business proposition, conserving the soil, practicing advanced methods of rotation, and studying the markets to discover what may be grown on the land to return the highest value, the farmer sets aside his tobacco-land to raise his money, and uses the rest of the land for running support. A few acres of corn, a little rye, a little wheat,—the traditional crops,—and a more or less thin stand of blue grass,—these make up in the hill counties the burden of the poorly-tilled soil. Out of 300 acres, perhaps 90 acres will be suited for tobacco. The tobacco so drains this that it can be used for the crop only once in six years, and during the other five generally lies idle, or is set in clover. Thus a 300-acre farm has, in a given year, 15 acres of tobacco, which will keep entirely employed the families of two tenants. To them the landlord furnishes houses, stock, and tobacco-barns, corn-land, gardens, pasturage, money-advance for living, and the tools to work the crop. In return, he takes half the produce of the corn-land—which is very little—and half the tobacco.

There is land in the hill counties that produces 1000 pounds to the acre of Burley. The average, however, is not over 800 pounds. The crop is the hardest of all crops to grow, requiring about 123 days' labor from the tenant, and in busy times the assistance of all his family and some hired help. One man can grow only about four acres, and then requires help for "worming," "suckering," topping, and harvesting.

The crop is begun with a forcing-bed in early spring, and often is not marketed for sixteen months. At 10 cents a pound it returns to the landlord, in the hill counties, $40 to the acre, or $600 as the money return from a 300-acre farm in a year. Out of this he pays interest, taxes, insurance, and upkeep on two tenant houses, several tobacco-barns (worth about $800 each), and the tenants' stock-barns; pays taxes and interest on his idle 75 acres of tobacco-land; pays interest on perhaps $500 which he has advanced to his tenant; renews tools, and meets certain other expenses. The tenant requires help, works in the field himself, and at the end of the year has raised his own corn and hogs, has worked hard and continuously, has paid out perhaps $250 for help, insurance, paris green for spraying, and other necessities, and has at the end $300, or a cash profit of $50, for his years' work. Sometimes he has not this, but remains in debt to his landlord. At 6.5 cents a pound Burley cannot be grown under decent living conditions in such counties as Mason, which produces now 7,000,000 pounds a year.

In the Blue Grass there is no such sad tale. At 10 cents a pound, on land producing 2000 pounds to the acre, so easily tilled that a tenant can handle twice as much as on the hills, the return to the landlord may amount to $100 an acre, on land which may bear tobacco every fourth year and which in the intervening years bears abundant crops of clover, grass or rye. The tenant who handles ten acres may receive $1000, out of which he may have $500 clear. And, at that, many tenants have bought the costly Blue Grass land for themselves. The price of 6.5 cents just about meets the cost of production in this region, and means beggary for the hills.

Pooling tobacco in Kentucky started down in the Black Patch, the southwestern corner, or received its greatest impetus there. The . . . buyers combined, or were formed into a combination by their superiors, and the Patch was districted, each man being given an exclusive territory, and no farmer being allowed to sell to any one but his own buyer. In this way a set price as low as four cents was made, and the farmer had no option but to take it; no option, at least, that was open to the farmer not rich enough to ship his crop to Bremen and seek European competition.

In this situation a group of canny planters formed a tight little corporation of $200 capital, for the avowed purpose of holding, handling, buying, and selling tobacco. They induced about a thousand of their neighbors— there are at least forty thousand dark-tobacco growers in the Patch—to pledge their crops with them, and they planned to hold this much off the market and compel the . . . buyers to pay a higher price for it. This proving popular, they soon had five thousand pledges. Then they—or interests closely allied with them—organized a band of Ku-Klux, called Night Riders, who, first by so-called "peace armies," and then by raiding by night all who resisted, frightened or forced—during the next three years—all the forty thousand to sign.

The tight little corporation thus had a monopoly of the dark tobacco. It forced the . . . buyers to pay a price raised by slow degrees to 11 cents a pound, exacted large commissions and profits,—as much as 1500 per cent a year on the capital,—and now controls the Black Patch absolutely. All its pledges expire in January, 1909, and the situation will then become anarchistic. The success of this Black Patch plan was entirely due to the employment of Night Riders, who correspond to the professional "sluggers" of a labor union, or the hired assassins of a Black-Hand league. Both Kentucky and Tennessee were at the time suffering from weak state administrations, neither Governor Beckham nor Governor Patterson caring to endanger his political fences by risking the enmity of the Night Riders and their friends. So, with a series of horrors such as no city union has ever equaled, these Ku-Klux swept over the Patch, burning cities, destroying homes, burning barns, shooting men and women, until from very terror the great majority of planters, unable to secure state protection, joined the association and pledged their tobacco to the little corporation. In this way it came to handle nearly 100,000,000 pounds in a year, and, absolutely controlling the market, forced the price up step by step until it has now reached 11 cents. This is a very high price for dark tobacco. It can be maintained only so long as the association is held together. As this is not a voluntary association, but a private trust, into alliance with which the individuals have been herded by an army, there is no doubt that the expiration of 40,000 pledges in January next will see the Patch plunged into trouble and both association and Night Riders fighting for life. . . .

The partial success of the Black-Patch combination stirred up the Burley planters to form a pool of their own. It is remarkable in this, that while it was the hard-driven hill-country men who began the agitation, it was the prosperous landlords of the Blue Grass who took the lead and carried out the plans; for these owners of rich plantations have been more bitter over the decimation of their abundance than the others over the passing of their livelihood.

The movement of the Burley Pool took shape in the formation of the Burley Tobacco Society, an organization allied with the American Society of Equity, and working under its general plan. J. Campbell Cantrill, state president of the Equity Society, took the lead in directing the organizations; and Clarence Lebus, a speculator in tobacco, became president of the new concern. The two societies worked in common. A plan was devised by which the Burley Society in each county should make a pool of all the 1906 crop, and should hold it off the market until the price went up so high that it could be sold at a round price of 15 cents per pound. The Equity Society aided this, not only by agitation but by organizing local warehouses in which the pool crops could be stored, so that money could be raised on them. (bout 50,000,000 pounds, perhaps a third of the 1906 crop, was thus pledged and held. Some of this was held in common. That is, in some counties all the tobacco was entered at the round price of 15 cents, and thereafter, whenever any was sold, the money was divided pro rata among the whole county membership. In other counties, individual lots were held separately, but all for the same round price.

The headquarters of the pool were established at Winchester, Kentucky, and there in a big warehouse were gathered the samples or types, one sample representing each hogshead in the pool—45,000 or 50,000 in all. . . .

The agitation by the Equity Society and the Burley Society was kept up, until one after another the farmers came under the shelter of the association, and about 115,000,000 or possibly 125,000,000 pounds were pledged.

Meanwhile the Equity Society had been playing at politics. In order to strengthen its position, it had gone into the legislature and secured several new laws. It is a curious commentary on the hopes of the farmers, that these were not directed toward destroying the American Tobacco Company, or intended to hurt any other trust. They were, on the contrary, *trust-em-powering*, designed to provide for the development of a secure trust in agricultural products which would be as safe within the law as the Tobacco Company without it. The constitution of Kentucky makes it mandatory upon the legislature to enact laws making it an offense for any person or corporation to combine or pool any objects to enhance their price. The legislature, however, being strongly affected by the agricultural population, passed a bill providing that persons "engaged in agriculture" might combine or pool "products of agriculture grown by themselves, in order to secure a better price for them."

It provided further that such persons might pledge their crops to an agent, or to the pool as an agent, and that it should be an offense for any person to persuade any pledged member to withdraw from the pool or to buy pledged or pooled tobacco except through the regular officers of the pool. Securely intrenched in these unconstitutional statutes, the Burley Society continued its campaign. It made no attack on the trust, nor the trust on it, for by a peculiar working it was certain that neither had any real cause to oppose the other. . . .

*   *   *

Tom Watson of Georgia was one Alliance leader who joined the Populist Party and remained a Populist. In 1896 he ran for Vice-President, published the *People's Party Paper,* after 1892, and after the election of 1896 dropped out of politics for eight years. In the elections of 1904 and 1908 he ran for President on the Populist ticket. In 1905 he began his new publication, *Tom Watson's Magazine.* The following extract from that magazine, Vol. I, 1905, pp. 135-136, illustrates his point of view.

J. P. Morgan is the absolute king of the railroads of Georgia. He makes the Governor, controls the Legislature, overrides the Commission and tramples the Constitution of the State under his feet.

The Georgia Outlaw made the Constitution for the good of the people; the Wall Street Outlaw violates it for the good of the Wall Street plutocrats.

In violating the Constitution, J. P. Morgan has the aid of the worst men in Georgia, and they dare not submit their work to a free vote of the people.

The party machinery of the Democratic party is prostituted to the vile uses of the corporation lobbyists, and the negro vote is held in reserve to be used as a club to beat down any organized opposition. . . . A Republican Wall Street outlaw uses the machinery of the Democratic party in Georgia to trample upon the Constitution and plunder the people.

What is the secret of this astonishing situation?

Bribery—direct and indirect bribery.

Daily and weekly newspapers subsidized; rebates given to certain ship-

pers; favors granted where they will do the most good; campaign funds
supplied to needy candidates; free passes dealt out by the bushel, princely
salaries paid to plausible lobbyists.

Bribery, *bribery,* BRIBERY!

✔   ✔   ✔

Two indirect outcomes of the farmers' revolt are the more permanent disfran-
chisment of the Negro and the wave of prohibition in the South. The Democrats, in
their efforts to defeat populism, encouraged greater participation of the masses
of white people in elections and encouraged these masses to eliminate completely
Negro suffrage. The different states used various methods to accomplish this purpose. The following digest of an article by a talented Negro writer is a protest
against the new trend in suffrage requirements. It is from Charles W. Chesnutt,
"The Disfranchisement of the Negro," *The Negro Problem,* a series of articles by
representative American Negroes of today, James Pott and Company, New York,
1903, pp. 79-124, *passim.*

The right of American citizens of African descent, commonly called
Negroes, to vote upon the same terms as other citizens of the United States,
is plainly declared and firmly fixed by the Constitution. No such person is
called upon to present reasons why he should possess this right; that question is foreclosed by the Constitution. The object of the elective franchise
is to give representation. So long as the Constitution retains its present form,
and State Constitution, or statute, which seeks, by juggling the ballot, to
deny the colored race fair representation, is a clear violation of the fundamental law of the land, and a corresponding injustice to those thus deprived
of this right.

For thirty-five years this has been the law. As long as it was measurably
respected, the colored people made rapid strides in education, wealth,
character, and self-respect. This the census proves, all statements to the
contrary notwithstanding. A generation has grown to manhood and woman-
hood under the great, inspiring freedom conferred by the Constitution and
protected by the right of suffrage—protected in large degree by the mere
naked right, even when its exercise was hindered or denied by unlawful
means. They have developed, in every Southern community, good citizens,
who, if sustained and encouraged by just laws and liberal institutions,
would greatly augment their number with the passing years, and soon wipe
out the reproach of ignorance, unthrift, low morals and social inefficiency,
thrown at them indiscriminately and therefore unjustly, and made the excuse for the equally undiscriminating contempt of their persons and their
rights. They have reduced their illiteracy nearly 50 per cent. Excluded from
the institutions of higher learning in their own States, their young men hold
their own, and occasionally carry away honors, in the universities of the
North. They have accumulated three hundred million dollars worth of
real and personal property. Individuals among them have acquired substantial wealth, and several have attained to something like national dis-

tinction in art, letters and educational leadership. They are numerously represented in the learned professions. Heavily handicapped, they have made such rapid progress that the suspicion is justified that their advancement, rather than any stagnation or retrogression, is the true secret of the virulent Southern hostility to their rights, which has so influenced Northern opinion that it stands mute, and leaves the colored people, upon whom the North conferred liberty, to the tender mercies of those who have always denied their fitness for it.

It may be said, in passing, that the word "Negro," where used in this paper, is used solely for convenience. By the census of 1890 there were 1,000,000 colored people in the country who were half, or more than half, white, and logically there must be, as in fact there are, so many who share the white blood in some degree, as to justify the assertion that the race problem in the United States concerns the welfare and the status of a mixed race. Their rights are not one whit the more sacred because of this fact; but in an argument where injustice is sought to be excused because of fundamental differences of race, it is well enough to bear in mind that the race whose rights and liberties are endangered all over this country by disfranchisement at the South, are the colored people who live in the United States to-day, and not the low-browed, man-eating savage whom the Southern white likes to set upon a block and contrast with Shakespeare and Milton and Washington and Lincoln.

Despite and in defiance of the Federal Constitution, to-day in the six Southern States of Mississippi, Louisiana, Alabama, North Carolina, South Carolina and Virginia, containing an aggregate colored population of about 6,000,000, these have been to all intents and purposes, denied, so far as the States can effect it, the right to vote. This disfranchisement is accomplished by various methods, devised with much transparent ingenuity, the effort being in each instance to violate the spirit of the Federal Constitution by disfranchising the Negro, while seeming to respect its letter by avoiding the mention of race or color.

These restrictions fall into three groups. The first comprises a property qualification—the ownership of $300 worth or more of real or personal property (Alabama, Louisiana, Virginia and South Carolina); the payment of a poll tax (Mississippi, North Carolina, Virginia); an educational qualification—the ability to read and write (Alabama, Louisiana, North Carolina). Thus far, those who believe in a restricted suffrage elsewhere, could perhaps find no reasonable fault with any one of these qualifications, applied either separately or together.

But the Negro has made such progress that these restrictions alone would perhaps not deprive him of effective representation. Hence the second group. This comprises an "understanding" clause—the applicant must be able "to read, or understand when read to him, any clause in the Constitution" (Mississippi), or to read and explain or to understand and explain

when read to him, any section of the Constitution (Virginia); an employment qualification—the voter must be regularly employed in some lawful
occupation (Alabama); a character qualification—the voter must be a
person of good character and who "understands the duties and obligations
of citizens under a republican(!) form of government" (Alabama). The
qualifications under the first group it will be seen, are capable of exact
demonstration; those under the second group are left to the discretion and
judgment of the registering officer—for in most instances these are all requirements for registration, which must precede voting.

But the first group, by its own force, and the second group, under imaginable conditions, might exclude not only the Negro vote, but a large part of
the white vote. Hence, the third group, which comprises a military service
qualification—any man who went to war, willingly or unwillingly, in a
good cause or a bad, is entitled to register (Ala., Va.); a prescriptive qualification, under which are included all male persons who were entitled to
vote on January 1, 1867, at which date the Negro had not yet been given the
right to vote; a hereditary qualification, (the so-called "grandfather" clause),
whereby any son (Va.), or descendant (Ala.) of a soldier, and (N.C.) the descendant of any person who had the right to vote on January 1, 1867,
inherits that right. If the voter wish to take advantage of these last provisions, which are in the nature of exceptions to a general rule, he must
register within a stated time, whereupon he becomes a member of a privileged class of permanently enrolled voters not subject to any of the other
restrictions.

It will be seen that these restrictions are variously combined in the different States, and it is apparent that if combined to their declared end, practically every Negro may, under color of law, be denied the right to vote,
and practically every white man accorded that right. The effectiveness of
these provisions to exclude the Negro vote is proved by the Alabama registration under the new State Constitution. Out of a total, by the census of
1900, of 181,471 Negro "males of voting age," less than 3,000 are registered;
in Montgomery county alone, the seat of the State capital, where there are
7,000 Negro males of voting age, only 47 have been allowed to register, while
in several counties not one single Negro is permitted to exercise the franchise. . . .

Under the Southern program it is sought to exclude colored men from
every grade of the public service; not only from the higher administrative
functions, to which few of them would in any event, for a long time aspire,
but from the lowest as well. A Negro may not be a constable or a policeman.
He is subjected by law to many degrading discriminations. He is required to
be separated from white people on railroads and street cars, and, by custom,
debarred from inns and places of public entertainment. His equal right to
a free public education is constantly threatened and is nowhere equitably
recognized. . . .

The Negro is subjected to taxation without representation, which the forefathers of this Republic made the basis of a bloody revolution.

✓   ✓   ✓

William Archer, in *Through Afro-America,* Chapman and Hall, London, 1910, pp. 146-155, *passim,* described the effects of prohibition as he saw them in the South.

Everyone agrees that the most remarkable phenomenon in the recent history of the South is the "wave of prohibition" which has passed, and is passing, over the country. "There are 20,000,000 people in the fourteen Southern States, 17,000,000 of whom are under prohibitory law in some form. . . ."

Georgia led the way in "State-wide" prohibition, by a law which came into force on January 1, 1908. This law nominally affected only fifteen counties, since 135 out of the 150 counties in the State had already "gone dry" under local option. But its importance is not to be measured by the mere number of the counties affected; it lies in the stoppage of the "jug trade" between "wet" counties and "dry."

Alabama and Mississippi both passed State-wide prohibition laws which came into force in January 1909. A strong fight is being made for State-wide prohibition in Tennessee, though "all but five of the ninety-six counties in the State are now 'dry' and only three cities—Memphis, Nashville, and Chattanooga—remain 'wet'." Though Kentucky has over $30,000,000 invested in distilleries, the saloon has been expelled from 94 out of 119 counties, and from the great majority of its towns and cities. All over the South, in fact, the same tale is being told—even where State-wide prohibition cannot as yet be carried, local option is riddling the defenses of the whisky trade.

Of course I made it my business to inquire into the effects of this great movement, and, of course, I received many conflicting answers to my inquiries.

Many people told me, just as they would in England, that "You can't make a man sober by Act of Parliament." They enlarged on the evils of the "blind tiger," or illicit saloon. They sang to me the refrain:

> "Hush, little grog-shop, don't you cry:
> You'll be a drug-store by-and-by!"

They told me of the "clubs" where each member can keep his private locker full of alcohol, and get drunk at his leisure. As for drink and the negro (they said), what is the use of keeping whisky out of his way, when in ten cents' worth of a "patent medicine" he can find enough cocaine to make him more dangerous than could a gallon of whisky?

On the other hand, I was told of a State in which the gaol-keepers, who (strange to say) made their living out of catering for the prisoners under

their charge, applied for a special "grant-in-aid" on the ground that prohibition had so depopulated their preserves that they could no longer keep
body and soul together.

This, though I believe it to be true, sounded a little like a fairy-tale; so
I thought I would go to headquarters for exact information. Atlanta was
the only city I visited where prohibition was actually in force; so I betook
me to Decatur Street Police-court, in the middle of its lowest quarters. I
arrived at a fortunate moment; it happened to be the first of May, and Mr.
Preston, the Clerk of the Court, was just making up his statistics for April.
He took the trouble of looking up the records of the previous year for me,
and gave me the following figures:

Number of cases tried in the first four months of 1907 (before prohibition), 6056.

Number of cases tried in the first four months of 1908 (after prohibition), 3139.

Convictions for drunkenness before prohibition, 1955.

Convictions for drunkenness after prohibition, 471.

"Take it all round," said Mr. Preston, "Our work has been reduced by
just about one-half. . . ."

Of the negroes to whom I spoke of prohibition, all but one were strongly
in its favour. That one, Dr. Oberman of Memphis, thought that more real
good would be done by a "high licence." Mr. Millard, of Montgomery, was
emphatic in his approval. "I believe we're the ones that are going to get the
biggest part of the bargain," he said. "My people are going to have better
homes and look after their families better—to pay for their schooling and
pay their bills." It is only fair to point out, however, that this was pure
prophecy, since in Montgomery prohibition had not then come into force.

Being myself but a small consumer of alcohol, I was not irresistibly impelled to study the various methods of liquor laws. One mild evasion of
them I did come across at one of the "Country Clubs" which are such a
delightful adjunct to American city life. Here each member could by law
have his locker; but it was found an intolerable nuisance to carry the system
literally into effect. So, as a matter of fact, drinks did not come from any
individual locker; they were supplied from the club cellar in the ordinary
way; only the club must not be paid for them, since that would be a confession that the member ordering them had not stored them for his own
use. What, then, was the method adopted? Members bought of the club
books of ten-cent coupons, and with these coupons they paid the waiters
who brought the drinks—not for the drinks, but for their services in bringing them! It appeared to me a complex and rather childish fiction, but
probably it was no one's business to look into its seams.

It was at this club that a Senator from an adjoining State, who had been
very active in the prohibition campaign, was found one day seated before
a "high-ball" of imposing dimensions. On being reproached for inconsistency,

he replied; "Prohibition is for the masses, not for the classes." A most un-American sentiment, some will say; but to my thinking characteristically American.

In Savannah, Georgia, 147 "locker clubs" were organized the day after prohibition came into force, one of them, a negro club numbering 1700 members. But it will not be long before this evasion is dealt with. It is held by able jurists that, even under the present law, such clubs are illegal. In the mean time, I suppose they exist in Atlanta no less than in Savannah; yet, as we have seen, the work of the police court has been reduced by one-half.

As for the "blind tigers," there is no doubt that they follow in the track of prohibition laws, and that it is fairly easy, for those who know how, to procure bad liquor at high prices. But in the first place you have got to "know how;" in the second place, even for those who know how, it costs more time, trouble, and money than it did of old, to attain the requisite exhilaration; in the third place, "blind tigers" can, and do, have their claws pared now and then. Most of the people I spoke to, at all events, admitted that the evils of the "blind tigers" are not to be compared with the constant temptations offered by the open saloon. . . .

The agrarian revolt aroused in the common man a new realization of his power as a voter. Politicians found it necessary to appeal to the average voter in terms of his own problems, and as farmers outnumbered all other occupational groups, office-seekers devoted much attention to farm problems. The twentieth century produced in the South what observers called a "new breed of Demagogues." Jeff Davis, Governor and then Senator from Arkansas, may serve as an example of this type of political leader. The following extract from one of his campaign speeches is from *Jeff Davis, Governor and United States Senator. His Life and Speeches,* L. S. Dunaway, Little Rock, 1913, Chapter VI. Governor Davis's Speech at Bentonville, 1905.

DAVIS VS. BERRY

. . . . You will remember, my friends, when I was chosen Governor, five years ago, almost the entire press of the State said that if Jeff Davis was elected Governor the State would go to the bad; the State would go to the bow-wows; that it would be ruined. Now, let us see if this prediction has proven true; let us see if this statement can be borne out by the records; let the books be opened; let the records speak.

My fellow-citizens, when I became your Governor, five years ago, how much was the State of Arkansas indebted? How much did you owe in valid out-standing indebtedness? You owed $64,000. How much do you owe today? Ah, my fellow-citizens, I am proud to say that you do not owe one dollar; that you do not owe one penny; that the entire debt of the State, during my administration, has been wiped out. This has been my highest aspiration; it has been one of my highest ambitions, that when I leave the Governor's office I shall leave my State absolutely free from indebtedness. But, you may say, Governor, how much money have you in the State treasury? Gentlemen, I want to say to you today that we have in the State treasury, in money and securities, convertible into cash, $3,855,000.

But you say, Governor, this is Populism, that it is rot. I do not know whether there are any Populists here today, and I do not care. I used to hate the Populists worse than any man in the State. I used to fight them. In 1888 I was chosen by the Democracy of this State, a freckled-faced, red-headed boy, as one of their presidential electors, and nothing gave me more pleasure than to fight the Pops of our State. You will remember, my fellow-citizens, that in 1888 Grover Cleveland tried to turn over to the gold bugs the Government of the United States and that 30,000 true and brave souls in this State rebelled and established the Populist Party. You will also remember that in 1896, when we nominated the grandest and truest man that man ever knew—William Jennings Bryan—for President, we stole all the Populists had: we stole their platform, we stole their candidate, we stole them out lock, stock and barrel, and today these same men have come back into the Democratic Party and are voting the Democratic ticket as bravely and loyally as any men that ever cast an honest ballot.

Populists—why, I used to hate them; but I did not know as much then as I do now; I did not have as much sense then as I do now. These old Populists twenty years ago saw what we are seeing today. Bryan today is advocating just what the Populists advocated twenty years ago; that is, the public ownership of public franchises; . . . if it does not soon own public carriers, that the public carriers will own this Government. I came very nearly getting mixed up with "Cyclone" Davis one time, the Populist leader of Texas. I had been invited to make a speech in Batesville in 1888 while I was a mere boy. They telegraphed for "Cyclone," who was in St. Louis. When I discovered this, I was almost scared to death, knowing what a mighty man he was, but the old Pops received a wire from him saying that he could not come. Someone had slipped into his room the night before and stolen his pants and his money, and the train left so early that he could not get out and get more, and I have thanked God ever since that "Cyclone" lost his breeches.

Ah, my fellow-citizens, this old Populist Party advocated some of the grandest doctrines that the world ever knew. Among them was this: that you could legislate prosperity into a country. I used to believe that this was a fool idea, but I had not been tangled up with the Arkansas Legislature as I have since. I thought at that time you might as well say that a man could take himself by his bootstraps and lift himself over the fence. In a town where he was preaching, Sam Jones once found this sign, "Vote as you pray." In his sermon that night he said: "Yes, brethren and sisters, vote as you pray, but be careful that you have no foolish praying around the house;" and I say to you here that you can legislate prosperity into a country if you have the right kind of men to do the legislating.

You remember the Hatch Bill. You remember that about fifteen years ago a fellow by the name of Hatch broke into Congress of the United States. The other fellows looked at him in amazement and said: "Old Hayseed, why are you here?" He said: "I came from a Democratic county in Missouri and I am loaded." Loaded with what? "Loaded with a bill to prevent the gamblers from gambling in the products of the soil of the Southland."

Ah, my fellow-citizens, whether you be growers of corn, wheat, hogs or cotton, do you control the price of your products? I say no. Who does control it? Not the merchant, because he gives you only prices quoted in the market. Who controls these quotations? Not you, nor the merchant. You growers of the products of the soil are as helpless as an unborn babe; you do not control the prices of your hogs, your wheat, your corn, your cotton. Who does control it, then, you say, Governor? I will tell you. There is a crowd of gamblers in New York City, called the Board of Exchange, that controls these prices. Did any of you ever visit the Board of Exchange in New York? I presume not. I was there about two years ago. I visited New York with Governor Clarke to try a lawsuit, and while there we visited this gambling house. You say, Governor, you should not call it a gambling house; it is a Board of Exchange. I say to you that it is a gambling house. The poor boy in this audience that steals a pig is sent to the penitentiary for larceny. The man that steals a million dollars or a railroad of this country is called a financier and sent to Congress. That is the difference.

As I say, we went to this gambling house. Let me describe it to you. . . . How many men comprise this institution called the Board of Exchange? Four hundred—no more, no less. How much does it cost to be a member? Forty thousand dollars. . . . These men were sitting there tearing open telegrams and going yow, yow, yow. I could not understand what they said, but in less than five minutes Clarke said, "Jeff, look there!" A price had been posted; they had changed the price of cotton the world over $5 a bale. Did they ever own a bale of cotton, my fellow-citizens? Did they ever see a cotton field ripening under a Southern sun? Do they ever expect to own a bale? No. What were they doing? Gambling in the products of the South. As I came up White River the other day that stream, more beautiful than the Hudson, out of the car window I saw little children, girls and boys, thinly clad on a cold frosty morning, children just as dear to their parents as yours or mine are to us, picking the cotton, pulling it from the bolls, with their little hands almost frozen.

When I saw this sight, my fellow-citizens, my mind turned back to that other scene in New York City where the gamblers of Wall Street sat around the gambling table gambling, not only in the products of the soil of the South, but gambling in the flesh and blood and bones of the children of the South, and my heart cried aloud: "My God! Is there no help in Israel? Is there no help for the children of the South?" Then the old Populist doctrine announced twenty years ago came ringing back into my ears, like the voice of one crying in the wilderness: "Yes, organization at home; obtain friendly legislation in Congress." . . .

Did you know, my fellow-citizens, that these gamblers sold 75,000,000 bales of cotton last year against 13,000,000 crop? And yet you tell me that they do not control the price of cotton? . . . .

Senator Berry says there is too much politics. He has not seen any politics yet. I have not got started. It is like an old man that lived in Thayer, Mo., who had never seen a railroad train. (You know this is only three miles from the Arkansas line on the north.) He said to his son, Bill, one morning: "Take me down there and let me see that thing." A freight train was running through the mountains, whizzing around the curves at about thirty miles an hour. Bill said, "Father, what do you think of it?" and the latter replied, "Stop it, Bill; stop it. It will kill someone in the country." His son answered, "Why father, it has been running here for two months and has not hurt anyone yet." He said, "Yes, Bill, but the durned thing is running endways now; wait till it turns sideways and it will kill everything in the country." So I say to Senator Berry that this senatorial race has hardly started yet; wait until the senatorial race turns sideways and he will see some politics.

✓   ✓   ✓

A generation later Huey Long became one of the most talked-about figures on our national scene. His rise to ascendency in Louisiana and his part in shaping public opinion to demand "Share Our Wealth" policies in national government are described in *The Fortnightly,* Vol. CXXXVII, New Series, London, January-June, 1935, "The New American Demagogues," pp. 676-678.

Senator Huey Long, of Louisiana, is unique as a portent and a personality. His life-story might seem to belong to the America of one hundred years ago. It could just as well be cited as a proof that the United States is still a land of opportunity, producing as of old the most amazing progeny. Huey Long belongs entirely to the Deep South. He began life on a Louisiana farm, suffering all the hardships of a poor rural community, made the more intolerable by the tyranny of fundamentalism in the Southern Baptist Church. This discipline, however, furnished him with at least one weapon of value; he can quote the Bible for every personal and political purpose. He spent some years as a traveling salesman; then made his way through a law school, and as an obscure small-town attorney devoted himself to the frustration of the mighty Standard Oil Company in his home State. He has practiced before the Supreme Court in Washington and earned emphatic praises from that august Bench. He has been Governor of Louisiana, and intends to vacate the Senate next year in order to take the governorship again. He is today the dictator of Louisiana, with no man and no organization in a position to say him nay. He controls all the functions of government. He commands the entire administration and owns the political machine. There is not a person in the State who can hold a public office of any kind against the word of Huey Long. His unscrupulous methods, his rowdy despotism, his lurid profanity, his habit of holding court in a bedroom dressed in pajamas—these have been described by thousands of American pens within the past year, for it must be borne in mind that Huey Long is a fount of newspaper copy, and that as a national figure he did not emerge before the spring of 1934.

Farcical State governors are common enough in present-day America, as the exploits of Ma Ferguson in Texas and Alfalfa Bill Murray have recently shown. If Huey Long had chosen to keep within his own region he might not have come much nearer than those local worthies came to a position in national politics. But he was not content to remain a local celebrity. He was elected to the United States Senate, and enjoyed in Washington a special repute because he had done more than any Southern politician to ensure the election of Mr. Roosevelt. The Senate is still the finest arena in America, and Senator Long was clever enough to exploit all its opportunities without slackening his hold on Louisiana. That Legislature continues to do his bidding in the extravagant State capitol built during his governorship, while from Washington or New Orleans, whenever the fancy takes him, he harangues the immense radio audience, employing a technique of his own invention. Huey Long is an incomparable showman, but it is now generally admitted that the Press made a mistake in treating him as though, outside the State over which he ruled, there was nothing else in him save his preposterous foolery. There is, of course, much more. He has great shrewdness and an uncanny political talent. He is fully aware that clowning and invective by themselves do not carry very far; the demagogue of these days must be provided also with a slogan and a platform. Huey Long's slogan is "Share Our Wealth." It may prove to be a very effective war-cry—and yet, curiously enough the phrase is commonly printed incorrectly in American newspapers. Stimulated by the news-reels as well as by the radio, Share-Our-Wealth clubs are springing up through the country, while Huey Long, with the untiring energy of his kind, descants upon the eight points of his American charter. Here they are:—

(1) Poverty to be abolished by endowing every deserving family with an income of not less than $5,000 free of debt.

(2) Fortunes to be limited in such a degree (say, to $4,000,000) as will allow an equitable sharing of the national wealth.

(3) A restricted working day, to prevent over-production and permit the sharing and recreation.

(4) Old age pensions of $30 a month, at sixty.

(5) Balanced agricultural production (according to the divine law).

(6) Care for war veterans.

(7) Taxation, to start with the reduction of large fortunes, with ample public works for unemployment.

(8) Free education, including maintenance for all young persons up to maturity.

Until the radio provided him with his popular following Huey Long was more or less regular in national politics, a Democrat not too vexatious. He has become a vitriolic foe of the administration, almost as abusive where the President is concerned as he is when railing at those members of the Cabinet whom he particularly denounces. His performances are a favorite turn in the Washington merry-go-round. The Senate galleries are crowded for him as for no other, but he is no longer allowed to rage with impunity. He is at last provoking the reprisals which in a normal debating chamber would have been his portion from the start.

17

The Southern Negro

There is probably no more important factor in Southern life than the existence of a subculture, that of the Negro. Problems of labor supply, education, and law enforcement are closely associated with the quality of the cultural level enjoyed by the whole population.

In the 1870's the Southern Negro was reduced to political impotence. During the 1880's a Supreme Court decision gave acquiescence to segregation. The Negro was put in a niche from which he was not allowed to emerge. Jobs were limited to farming and menial work in industry. James Bryce of Great Britain, later to become Ambassador to the United States, was one of the most accurate observers of American life. In the *North American Review,* Vol. 153, December, 1891, pp. 641-660, "Thoughts on the Negro Problem," he pointed out the Negro's lack of opportunity.

Both in the middle Southern and in the semi-tropical States, and alike in the cities and rural districts, the colored people form the lower stratum of the population. In the lower and hotter parts of the Gulf States and of South Carolina they do all the field work; in the cities and in the mining and manufacturing regions their labor is almost entirely (though less so from year to year) unskilled labor. Very different descriptions of their condition, especially in the agricultural districts, are given by different observers. But two facts stand out. The one is that few, in proportion to the total number, have acquired wealth by commerce, or have risen to any sort of eminence in the professions. The other is that, unlike the negroes of the West India islands, they are generally industrious, working pretty steadily, whether as hired laborers or as the tenants of small farms, and that they are, though no doubt by slow degrees, learning thrift and self-control.

When it is remembered that the grandparents or great-grandparents of many of them were African savages,—for the importation of slaves was not forbidden till 1808,—we must not be surprised that large masses, especially in Louisiana and Mississippi, remain at a low level of intelligence and morality, with rudimentary notions of comfort and still dominated by gross superstitions. Still less is it strange, considering that only twenty-five years have passed since they were slaves,—slaves to whom it was an offence to teach reading,—that the great majority should lack even the elements of an education. So far from finding these facts discouraging, he who travels through the South now is surprised at the progress that has been made since 1865. . . . The best proof of progress is the fact that the negroes have begun to help themselves; that they are supporting their own churches and schools more liberally, organizing charitable societies for their own benefit, showing an increased desire for education, and profiting by it. . . .

One thing, however, freedom has not done. It has not brought colored people any nearer to the whites. Social intercourse is strictly confined to business, unless where the negro is a domestic servant; and is far less frequent and easy than in the days of slavery. Then in the home establishment and on the best plantations—plantations like the Dabney estate in Mississippi of which so pleasing a picture was lately given in Mrs. Smedes's book— even the field hands were on familiar terms with the master and mistress, while the children of both colors played together. This has entirely ceased. In some States the negro is allowed to enter the same street-cars or railroad cars; in some he is less rigidly than in others kept apart in places of public resort. But everywhere in the South he is confined to schools and colleges for his own race; he worships in his own churches; he mingles in none of the amusements, he is admitted to none of the social or industrial organizations, which white people, even the humblest of them, enjoy or form. Most significant of all, his blood is never mixed with theirs. The intermarriage of the races is forbidden by law in all or nearly all the Southern States, as well as in some Western States; but legal prohibition was scarcely needed, for public sentiment is universally opposed to such unions. Those illicit relations of white men with colored women which were not uncommon in the days of slavery have almost wholly disappeared; and it is now a rare thing for a child to be born with parents of different colors. No intermediate race grows up to link the other two together; for, though there are mulattoes and quadroons, born under the old state of things, they are all reckoned with the negroes.

This social separation does not spring from nor imply any enmity between the races. The attitude of the richer and more educated whites in the South is distinctly friendly to the negro. They like him for his amiable qualities; and they remember that, when during the Civil War all the men fit to bear arms had gone off to fight the North, the white women and children, left unprotected behind upon the plantations, dwelt in perfect safety, with not an insulting word to fear. The lower class of whites have somewhat less kindly feelings. The negroes used formerly to despise those whom they called "poor white trash"; and the poor whites, in their turn, were all the more proud of their skin because they had little else to be proud of. In the cities and mining districts the white laborer feels some jealousy of the negro, and is anxious to assert his superiority. Yet, even in these humbler ranks, it would be incorrect to speak of hostility. There is

From an oil painting, "Mending Socks," by Archibald Motley, Jr., a Negro artist. Owned by the University of North Carolina Library.

a strong feeling of separation, but there is also a desire to live peaceably and amicably together. Negroes are sometimes lynched or shot by individual whites whom they have offended. But in the wilder parts of the South and West whites also are lynched, and though less frequently than negroes, yet sometimes with circumstances of barbarity. Allowing for the lawlessness which prevails in the more backward districts, for the tendency to cruelty which the sense of power creates, and for the habits formed in Ku Klux days, the negro fares better than might have been expected. But race prejudice is very strong—far stronger than in the British or Spanish West Indies. It shows no signs of declining; it is unaffected by the merits of the individual. A negro who gains wealth or wins for himself a good position in the profession of medicine or law or teaching is no nearer to social equality than a negro blacking boots in the street; and this remark applies to the Northern as well as to the Southern States.

As regards civil rights, those rights of the citizen which the law gives and protects, equality is complete in the public as well as in the private sphere. The negro has not only the suffrage on the same terms as the whites, but he has the same eligibility to every kind of office, State office equally with federal office. But although this equality has existed on paper for more than twenty years, the benefits which it has actually secured to the colored people have been so small that one may doubt whether they have substantially gained by those famous amendments of the federal constitution which secure these active civil rights. Since the carpet-bag governments fell, during the years between 1870 and 1876, few indeed have been the negroes who have been elected or appointed to any but the very humblest offices. Although they form in some States one-third, in others one-half or more, of the population, they are seldom elected to a State legislature, or to any post of consequence in State or city government.

*   *   *

Given freedom of his person which he had never before known, the Negro found obedience to law difficult, and no doubt the courts were more severe with Negroes than they were with white people. Such was the conclusion of T. Thomas Fortune, *Black and White*, Fords, Howard and Hulbert, New York, 1884, pp. 30-31. The author was commenting on a paragraph from a newspaper.

Speare, Mitchell Co., N.C., March 19, 1884.—Col. J. M. English, a farmer and prominent citizen living at Plumtree, Mitchell County, N.C., shot and killed a mulatto named Jack Mathis at that place Saturday, March 1. There had been difficulty between them for several months.

Mathis last summer worked in one of Col. English's mica mines. Evidence pointed to him as being implicated in the systematic stealing of mica from the mine. Still it was not direct enough to convict him, but he was discharged by English. Mathis was also a tenant of one of English's houses and lots. In resentment he damaged the property by destroying fences, tearing off weather-boards from the house, and injuring the fruit trees. For this Col. English prosecuted the negro, and Feb. 9, before a local Justice, ex-Sheriff Wiseman, he got a judgment for $100. On the date stated, during a casual meeting, hot words grew into an altercation, and Col. English shot the negro. Mathis was a powerful man. English is a cripple, being lame in the leg from a wound received in the Mexican war.

A trial was had before a preliminary court recently, Col. S. C. Vance appearing for Col. English. After a hearing of all the testimony the court reached a decision of justifiable homicide and English was released. . . .

My knowledge of such affairs in the South is, that the black and white have an altercation over some trivial thing, and the white to end the argument shoots the black man down. The negro is always a *"powerful fellow"* and the white man a "weak sickly man." The law and public opinion always side with the white man.

✓ ✓ ✓

For the more serious deviations from law observance, the Negroes were never given trial. Mob executions were customary where the crime was rape of a white woman or murder of a white man. Andrew Sledd, in "The Negro: Another View," *Atlantic Monthly,* Vol. 90, 1902, pp. 65-73, *passim,* held the illiterate whites responsible for the high rate of lynchings in the Southern states.

The Negro is made, in Southern phrase, "to know and keep his place." . . . The black man, *because of his blackness,* is put in this lowest place in public esteem and treatment.

In the last decade of the last century of Christian grace and civilization, more men met their death by violence at the hands of lynchers than were executed by due process of law. And this holds true, with possibly one exception, for each year in the decade. The total number thus hurried untried and unshriven into eternity during these ten unholy years approximated seventeen hundred souls.

The lynching habit is largely sectional. Seventy to eighty per cent of all these lynchings occur in the Southern states.

The lynchings are largely racial. About three quarters of those thus done to death are negroes.

The lynching penalty does not attend any particular crime, which, by its peculiar nature and heinousness, seems to demand such violent and lawless punishment. But murder, rape, arson, barn-burning, theft,—or suspicion of any of these,—may and do furnish the ground for mob violence. . . .

One adult man in the South in every six or eight can neither read nor write; and if the standard be put above the level of the most rudimentary literacy the disproportion rapidly increases. . . . Wholly ignorant, absolutely without culture, apparently without even the capacity to appreciate the nicer feelings or higher sense, yet conceited on account of the white skin which they continually dishonor, they make up, when aroused, as wild and brutal a mob as ever disgraced the face of the earth. For them, lynch-ing is not "justice," however rude; it is a wild and diabolic carnival of blood. . . .

As for the law's delay or inefficiency, the lyncher does not wait to see what the law will do; and yet it is a well-known fact in the South that in the case of a negro, where violent rape is proven, the punishment of the law is both swift and sure. And in other negro crimes as well, it is known that the negro will receive at the hands of the constituted authorities the same, perhaps even a little sharper justice than is meted out to the white man.

ʹ   ʹ   ʹ

Most of the inmates in Southern prisons were Negroes. The excessive cost of feeding, lodging, and guarding convicts led the debt-ridden Southern states, and some Northern ones, to pass laws providing for convict labor. The following digests illustrating the convict-lease laws are quoted from the *Second Annual Report of the Commissioner of Labor,* 1886, Washington, 49th Congress, 2d Session, House of Representatives, Ex. Doc. 1, Part 5, 528, 557, 579, 200.

Georgia Code, 1882.

The governor of the state is hereby authorized and required to farm or lease said convicts . . . for the space of time not less than twenty years, to one or more companies. . . . Said lease or hiring for said term shall be upon such terms and considerations as shall be agreed upon with said company by the governor. . . . No lease or hiring may be made which shall not relieve the state of all expense, except the salary of the principal keeper, physician, and chaplain.

Mississippi, Revised Code, 1880.

The board of supervisors of each county shall advertise, as they advertise for bidders for any public work to be done . . . for proposals for the custody and service of prisoners committed to the jails of their respective counties, and at the time fixed for the purpose, shall make a contract with such persons as will undertake the duties arising from such contract. . . .

Such contractor shall have the right to require said prisoners to labor on a farm, or at any manual labor, and may adopt such appliances and safe-guards against escape by such prisoners as are lawful and customary in secur-ing prisoners in penitentiaries, jails, or workhouses, from escape.

North Carolina Code, 1883.

The board of directors is authorized and directed to farm out to railroad companies or other public corporations, or private corporations, or any individual or company, every able-bodied convict who cannot be employed to advantage within the penitentiary. . . .

The following is condensed.

In the following states—number of convicts leased.

Alabama	—State Penitentiary—	564	County control —1535
Arkansas	" "	— 518	
Florida	" "	— 181	
Georgia	" "	—1,560	
Kentucky	" "	— 872	City workers —60
Louisiana	" "	— 798	
Maryland	" "	— 788	
Mississippi	" "	— 787	County workers—1323
Tennessee	" "	—1,274	

COMPARISON OF PRICE OF LABOR PER DAY

State	Ave. daily price of Convict Labor	Free Labor
Alabama	$0.32 to .40	$1.25
Arkansas	.14½	2.12—2.62½
Georgia	.05½	.61½—1.00
Kentucky	.02⅔	1.00—2.40
Louisiana	.07½	1.25—1.50
Maryland	.10—.57½	.67—1.75
Mississippi	.16—.23½	.70—1.50
N. Car.	.40	1.00
S. Car.	.48—.50	1.00
Virginia	.25	1.50

✓   ✓   ✓

George Washington Cable, who had become one of the nation's leading white advocates of Negro rights, condemned the system of convict leasing in his book, *The Silent South,* Scribners, New York, 1907, pp. 31-33, 142-169, *passim.*

In studying, about a year ago, the practice of letting out public convicts to private lessees to serve out their sentences under private management, I found that it does not belong to all our once slave States nor to all our once seceded States. Only it is no longer in practice outside of them. Under our present condition in the South, it is beyond possibility that the individual black should behave mischievously without offensively rearousing the old sentiments of the still dominant white man. As we have seen too, the white man virtually monopolizes the jury-box. Add another fact: the Southern States have entered upon a new era of development. Now, if with these conditions in force the public mind has been captivated by glowing pictures of the remunerative economy of the convict-lease system, and by the seductive spectacle of mines and railways, turnpikes and levees, that everybody

wants and nobody wants to pay for, growing apace by convict labor that
seems to cost nothing, we may almost assert beforehand that the popular
mind will—not so maliciously as unreflectingly—yield to the tremendous
temptation to hustle the misbehaving black man into the State prison under
extravagant sentence, and sell his labor to the highest bidder who will use
him in the construction of public works. For ignorance of the awful condition of these penitentiaries is extreme and general, and the hasty half-conscious assumption naturally is, that the culprit will survive this term of
sentence, and its fierce discipline "teach him to behave himself."

But we need not argue from cause to effect only. Nor need I repeat one
of the many painful rumors that poured in upon me the moment I began
to investigate this point. The official testimony of the prisons themselves
is before the world to establish the conjectures that spring from our reasoning . . . ; what is to account for the fact that in 1881 there were committed
to the State prison at Columbia, South Carolina, 406 colored persons and
but 25 whites? The proportion of blacks sentenced to the whole black population was one to every 1488; that of the whites to the white population was
but one to every 15,644. In Georgia the white inhabitants decidedly out-
number the blacks; yet in the State penitentiary, October 20, 1880, there
were 115 whites and 1071 colored. . . . Yet of 52 pardons granted in the
two years then closing, 22 were to whites and only 30 to blacks. . . .

[In North Carolina in 1879-80] were scattered about in companies under
lessees, [about eight hundred prisoners who] . . . were at different times
at work on six different railways and one wagon road. What their experiences were at these places can be gathered, by one at a distance, only from
one or two incidental remarks dropped by the prison officers in their reports and from the tabulated records of the convict movement. There is
no hospital record given concerning them, nor any physician's account of
their sickness. When they drop off they are simply scored as dead. The
warden says of them that many had "taken their regular shifts for several
years in the Swannanoa and other tunnels on the Western North Carolina
Railroad, and were finally returned to the prison with shattered constitutions and their physical strength entirely gone, so that, with the most skillful medical treatment and the best nursing, it was impossible for them to
recuperate."

But such remarks convey but a faint idea of the dreadful lot of these
unfortunate creatures. The prison physician, apologizing for the high death-
rate within the walls, instances twenty-one deaths of men "who had returned
from the railroads completely broken down and hopelessly diseased." And
when *these deaths are left out* of the count, the number of deaths *inside*
the walls, not attributable to *outside* hardships, amounted in 1880, to just
the number of those in the prisons of Auburn and Sing-Sing in a population
eight times as large. Ten-elevenths of the deaths for 1879 and 1880 were
from lingering diseases, principally consumption. Yet, year in and year

out, the good citizens of Raleigh were visiting the place weekly, teaching Sunday-school, preaching the gospel, and staring these facts in the face.

Now, what was the death-rate among the convicts working at railroad construction? The average number of prisoners so engaged in 1879 and 1880 was 776. The deaths, including the 21 sent back to die in prison, were 178, an annual death-rate of nearly eleven and a half per cent., and therefore greater than the year's death-rate in New Orleans in 1853, the year of the Great Epidemic. But the dark fact that eclipses everything else is that not a word is given to account for the deaths of 158 of these men, except that 11 were shot down in trying to escape from this heartless butchery. . . .

It only remains to be asked, For what enormous money consideration did the State set its seal upon this hideous mistake? The statement would be incredible were it attempted to give other than a literal quotation. "Therefore it will be seen," says the warden at the bottom of his resumé of accounts, "that the convicts have earned $678.78 more than the prison department has cost for two years ending October 31, 1880. . . .

The convict force of Georgia . . . presents the Lease System under some other peculiarly vicious aspects. . . . From the "General Notice to Lessees" the following is taken, with no liberties except to italicize:

"In all cases of *severe illness* the *shackles* must be promptly removed." "The convicts shall be turned off *the chain* on the Sabbath and allowed to recreate in and about the stockade." Elsewhere the principal keeper says, "When a convict is sick, the chains are to be taken off of him."

A new warden in the Alabama state penitentiary described conditions which prevailed when he assumed his duties:

"I found the convicts confined at fourteen different prisons controlled by as many persons or companies, and situated at as many different places. . . . They [the prisons] were as filthy, as a rule, as dirt could make them, and both prisons and prisoners were infested with vermin. . . . Convicts were excessively and, in some instances, cruelly punished. . . . They were poorly clothed and fed. . . . The sick were neglected, insomuch that no hospital had been provided, they being confined in the cells with the well convicts. . . . Our system is a better training school for criminals than any of the dens of iniquity that exist in our large cities. . . . The system is a disgrace. . . .

✓   ✓   ✓

The philosopher and educator, W. E. Burghardt DuBois, Northern born and educated Negro, devoted his life to the education of his race. His article, "Of the Training of Black Men," appeared in the *Atlantic Monthly*, Vol. 90, September, 1902, pp. 289-297.

From the shimmering swirl of waters where many, many thoughts ago the slave-ship first saw the square tower of Jamestown have flowed down to our day three streams of thinking: one from the larger world here and overseas, saying, the multiplying of human wants in culture lands calls for the world-wide cooperation of men in satisfying them. Hence arises a new human unity, pulling the ends of earth nearer, and all men, black, yellow, and white. The larger humanity strives to feel in this contact of living nations and sleeping hordes a thrill of new life in the world, crying, If the contact of Life and Sleep be Death, shame on such life. To be sure, behind this thought lurks the afterthought of force and dominion,—the making of brown men to delve when the temptation of beads and red calico cloys.

The second thought streaming from the death-ship and the curving river is the thought of the older South: the sincere and passionate belief that somewhere between men and cattle God created a *tertium quid,* and called it a Negro,—a clownish, simple creature, at times even lovable within its limitations, but straitly fore-ordained to walk within the Veil. To be sure, behind the thought lurks the afterthought,—some of them with favoring chance might become men, but in sheer self-defense we dare not let them, and build about them walls so high, and hang between them and the light a veil so thick, that they shall not even think of breaking through.

And last of all there trickles down that third and darker thought, the thought of the things themselves, the confused half-conscious mutter of men who are black and whitened, crying Liberty, Freedom, Opportunity— vouchsafe to us, O boastful World, the chance of living men! To be sure, behind the thought lurks the afterthought: suppose, after all, the World is right and we are less than men? Suppose this mad impulse within us is all wrong, some mock mirage from the untrue?

So here we stand among thoughts of human unity, even through conquest and slavery; the inferiority of black men, even if forced by fraud; a shriek in the night for the freedom of men who themselves are not yet sure of their right to demand it. This is the tangle of thought and afterthought wherein we are called to solve the problem of training men for life. . . .

We may decry the color prejudice of the South, yet it remains a heavy fact. Such curious kinks of the human mind exist and must be reckoned with soberly. They cannot be laughed away, nor always successfully stormed at, nor easily abolished by act of legislature. And yet they cannot be encouraged by being let alone. They must be recognized as facts, but unpleasant facts; things that stand in the way of civilization. . . . They can be met . . . [only] by the breadth and broadening of human reason, by catholicity of taste and culture. And so, too, the native ambition and aspiration of men, even though they be black, backward, and ungraceful, must not be lightly dealt with. To stimulate wildly weak and untrained minds is to play with mighty fires; to flout their striving idly is to welcome a harvest of brutish crime and shameless lethargy in our very laps. The guiding of thought and the deft coördination of deed is at once the path of honor and humanity.

And so, in this great question of reconciling three vast and partially contradictory streams of thought, the one panacea of Education leaps to the lips of all; such human training as will best use the labor of all men without enslaving or brutalizing; such training as will give us poise to encourage the prejudices that bulwark society, and stamp out those that in sheer barbarity deafen us to the wail of the prisoned souls within the Veil, and the mounting fury of shackled men.

But when we have vaguely said Education will set this tangle straight, what have we uttered but a truism? Training for life teaches living; but what training for the profitable living together of black men and white? Two hundred years ago our task would have seemed easier. Then Dr. Johnson blandly assured us that education was needful solely for the embellishments of life, and was useless for ordinary vermin. To-day we have climbed to the heights where we would open at least the outer courts of knowledge to all, display its treasures to the many, and select the few to whom its mystery of Truth is revealed, not wholly by truth or the accidents of the stock market, but at least in part according to deftness and aim, talent and character. This programme, however, we are sorely puzzled in carrying out through that part of the land where the blight of slavery fell hardest, and where we are dealing with two backward peoples. To make here in human education that ever necessary combination of the permanent and the contingent—of the ideal and the practical in workable equilibrium —has been there, as it ever must in every age and place, a matter of infinite experiment and frequent mistakes.

In rough approximation we may point out four varying decades of work in Southern education since the Civil War. From the close of the war until 1876 was the period of uncertain groping and temporary relief. There were army schools, mission schools, and schools of the Freedman's Bureau in chaotic disarrangement, seeking system and cooperation. Then followed ten years of constructive definite effort toward the building of complete school systems in the South. Normal schools and colleges were founded for the freedmen, and teachers trained there to man the public school. . . . Meantime, starting in this decade yet especially developing from 1885 to 1895, began the industrial revolution of the South. . . .

The industrial school springing to notice in this decade, but coming to full recognition in the decade beginning with 1895, was the proffered answer to this combined educational and economic . . . [situation]. From the very first in nearly all the schools some attention had been given to training in handiwork, but now was this training first raised to a dignity that brought it in direct touch with the South's magnificent industrial development, and given an emphasis which reminded black folk that before the Temple of Knowledge swing the Gates of Toil.

Yet after all they are but gates, and when turning our eyes from the temporary and contingent in the Negro problem to the broader question of the permanent uplifting and civilization of black men in America, we have a right to inquire, as this enthusiasm for material advancement mounts to its height, if after all the industrial school is the final and sufficient answer in the training of the Negro race; and to ask gently, but in all sincerity, the ever recurring query of the ages, Is not life more than meat, and the body more than raiment? And men ask this to-day all the more eagerly because of sinister signs in recent educational movements. The tendency is here, born of slavery and quickened to renewed life by the crazy imperialism of the day, to regard human beings as among the material resources of a land to be trained with an eye to future dividends. Race prejudices, which keep brown and black men in their "places," we are coming to regard as useful allies with such a theory, no matter how much they may dull the ambition and sicken the hearts of struggling human beings. And above all, we daily hear that an education that encourages aspiration, that sets the loftiest of ideals and seeks as an end culture and character rather than bread-winning, is the privilege of the white man and the danger and delusion of black. . . .

There stand in the South two separate worlds: separate not simply in the higher realms of social intercourse, but also in church and school, on railway and in street car, in hotels and theatres, in streets and city sections, in books and newspapers, in asylums and jails, in hospitals and graveyards. There is still enough of contact for large economic and group cooperation, but the separation is so thorough and deep, that it absolutely precludes for the present between the races anything like that sympathetic and effective group training and leadership of the one by the other, such as the American Negro and all backward peoples must have for effectual progress.

And finally, above all this, it must develop men: . . . there must come a loftier respect for the sovereign human soul that seeks to know itself and the world about it; that seeks a freedom for expansion and self-development; that will love and hate and labor in its own way, untrammeled alike by old and new. Such souls aforetime have inspired and guided worlds, and if we be not wholly bewitched by our Rhine-gold, they shall again. Herein the longing of black men must have respect; the rich and bitter depth of their experience, the unknown treasures of their inner life, the strange rendings of nature they have seen, may give the world new points of view and make their loving, living, and doing precious to all human hearts. And to themselves, in these days that try their souls the chance to soar in the dim blue air above the smoke is to their finer spirits boon and guerdon for what they lose on earth by being black.

I sit with Shakespeare and he winces not. Across the color line I move arm in arm with Balzac and Dumas, where smiling men and welcoming women glide in gilded halls. From out the caves of Evening that swing between the strong-limbed earth and the tracery of the stars, I summon Aristotle and Aurelius and what soul I will, and they come all graciously with no scorn and no condescension. So, wed with Truth, I dwell above the Veil. Is this the life you grudge us, O knightly America? Is this the life you long to change into the dull red hideousness of Georgia? Are you so afraid lest peering from this high Pisgah, between Philistine and Amalekite, we sight the Promised Land?

✔ ✔ ✔

In 1909 the National Association for the Advancement of Colored People (NAACP) was organized with W. E. B. DuBois as a leading figure. It has carried on an aggressive campaign for Negro rights, boasting of influential white members as well as Negroes. A Negro press became very active, publishing several powerful weekly newspapers and some magazines. The Negro press does not confine its efforts to bettering the economic and social position of that race. It also condemns the provincial character of Southern economic life, which it claims is dominated by Northern corporations. The following article by Victor Bernstein which appeared in the short-lived New York Newspaper, *P.M.,* was reprinted in a Negro newspaper, *The Afro-American,* Baltimore, September 19, 1942.

. . . today damyankee carpetbaggers still control Southern economy and to a great extent its political life.

Here is a list of some of the bigger corporations now operating in Georgia and Alabama:

United States Steel	Ford Motor Co.
Republic Steel	Armour and Co.
Piggly Wiggly	Swift and Co.
Commonwealth and Southern	Metropolitan Life
F. W. Woolworth	Equitable Life
Sears Roebuck	Standard Oil
General Motors	Texas Oil
U. S. Rubber	Pure Oil
Goodyear Rubber	Greyhound Lines

This is, of course, an extremely sketchy list. I don't smell any magnolia blossoms in it, do you? And, after all, the offices of the National Association of Manufacturers are not on Peachtree Street in Atlanta or in downtown Birmingham, but at 14 W. 49th Street, New York City.

Let's see how this set-up works.

In Birmingham, people talk of Alabama's Gov. Dixon as a Big Mule man. The Big Mules, to the Alabamian, mean the coal and iron dynasty— Tennessee Coal and Iron (United States Steel owned), captive Republic Steel mines, the powerful and independent Woodward Iron Co., and others.

The Big Mules also include Alabama Power Co. which belongs to Commonwealth and Southern (fifteen directors, of which only four are from the South).

As I say, people talk of Gov. Dixon as a Big Mule man. I wouldn't know. All I know is that I never heard any one down South deny that. And I know that Dixon's staunchest supporter is the magazine *Alabama,* which frankly speaks for the Associated Industries of Alabama, which is the State organization of industrial management.

✦   ✦   ✦

After forty-five years of endeavor the influence of organized Negroes led to a change in the status of the race. This change was gradual, and the South felt that it was coping with the problem sensibly without upsetting the harmony that had been cultivated between the races (see p. 481). In the Charlotte *Observer,* September 11, 1944, was reprinted an article by Thurman Sensing, "The South Has No Race Problem," from the *Manufacturers Record,* which expresses the attitude of many Southerners toward the race problem.

The South has no problem in connection with its race relations. The South has a race situation but no race problem. To say that the South has a problem would indicate that the South has not yet decided the best way to handle its relationship with the Negro. This is not the case. There has never been any question in the mind of the South as to the best way to handle it. . . .

The South has been accused of being unjust to the Negro and discriminating against him whereas the rest of the country was not doing so. Why, then, haven't the Negroes during the past eighty years left that part of the country where they have been so badly treated and gone to those other parts of the country where they are received on "equal terms?" . . .

Taking the South as a whole approximately 33⅓ per cent of its population are Negro whereas for the nation as a whole only 10 per cent are Negro and and for the area outside the South only 3½ per cent are Negro. These percentages have remained so nearly constant over all these years that we may consider invalid any claim by anyone, white or black, that the Negro receives better treatment outside of the South than he does in the South.

How does the South treat the Negroes? By the only way under natural laws they can be treated—by segregation. The Negro race did not come to America of its own free will. The Negroes did not come here as immigrants. If no Negroes were in this country at the present time, it is to be doubted that under our present immigration laws any would be allowed to enter. . . . Segregation is best for both peoples. It permits the development of pride of race, without which no people can hope to progress. This principle does not apply to the Negro race alone. It would apply to any race. . . .

Let us assume for a moment the attitude of the people outside the South toward the Negro. . . . As a matter of fact they . . . segregate the Negro in many places, such as hotels, restaurants, and so on, but not in the schools and churches and on the trains and in public conveyances as is done down South. But are the Negroes really welcome in these places? They are not. Their presence is resented. Their association is endured.

The Negro children struggle along in school seated beside the white children where their presence is usually resented or at best tolerated. After they finally secure their diplomas these Negros, regardless of their qualifications, are relegated as a rule to unimportant, undesirable work. The training of these Negroes has been such that they are not acceptable in the South for the filling of such positions among the Negroes of the South. Their attitudes are such that they just do not fit in.

On the other hand in the South, through the practice of segregation, Negroes are trained for the professions in their own schools and they have their own organizations in which to practice their professions or trades after the training is finished. They are able to rise in their professions and thus they are able to maintain a self-respect and racial integrity that they cannot have in the North. . . .

Southerners as a people probably have a higher regard for the Negroes as a race and get along better with them than could any other group. . . . The people of the South are thoroughly acquainted with the situation and know how to handle it. It is the agitators outside the South who don't understand the situation . . . to whom it therefore appears a problem. These people would do well to let the South alone.

✓   ✓   ✓

A number of cases testing the constitutionality of the segregation laws were reviewed by the United States Supreme Court in 1954. Benjamin Fine, education editor of the *New York Times,* commented on the Supreme Court's possible ruling setting aside the said laws and showed that, regardless of the outcome of the cases then pending, great steps had been taken to eliminate the barrier between the races in higher education. The following summary appeared in the *New York Times,* March 15, 1954.

The color line is slowly giving way in many Southern colleges and universities.

More than 2,000 Negro students—most of them on the professional or graduate levels—are attending white institutions of higher learning . . . in the seventeen Southern states and in the District of Columbia where educational segregation is mandatory. The number of Negroes in the colleges ranges from one at William and Mary in Virginia to 275 at the University of Louisville in Kentucky.

The growth of Negro enrollment in what were until recent years all-white colleges has taken place without any disorders or major disturbances of any kind. The Negroes eat in the same cafeterias with white students, go to athletic contests, and to a lesser extent to social functions.

For the most part, it was found, the students and faculty have accepted the presence of the Negro students without opposition. They just seem to take them for granted, after the novelty has worn off. But here and there, reports indicate, parents, college trustees and community residents raise more than eyebrows. In some instances they have raised a row over this breaking down of a tradition that long has been taken for granted. . . .

Of course in terms of numbers, the 2,000 or so Negro students in Southern white colleges is only a minute percentage of the total. There are more than 100,000 Negro youths in colleges, most of them in the 105 Negro colleges and universities in the South.

ィ   ィ   ィ

In May, 1954, the Supreme Court announced its decision in the segregation cases, and on May 23 the opinion was reviewed in a *New York Times* article.

Last week the Supreme Court cut through to the heart of the segregation problem and issued a historic judgment for racial equality. Unanimously the nine high court Justices ruled that enforced segregation of Negro children in public schools violated the Constitution. . . .

World War II launched a new era in the battle over the status of the Negro. Industrialization of the South had already given impetus to the demands for better Negro education. The assignment of Negro draftees to racial units in the armed forces sharpened their resentment against segregation. The courts were flooded with suits attacking the validity of various segregation laws. . . . Negroes won many decisions—against the all-white primary; against the restrictive covenants forbidding the sale of property to Negroes; against segregation in public carriers in interstate commerce; against segregated state university graduate schools on the ground that even if a Negro graduate school had "equal" physical facilities it could not offer its students "equal" professional contacts and prestige. . . .

In many respects the decision was unusual. It was unanimous, and on important issues the court frequently is split. It was short—only 1,500 words. It was couched in layman's English, without resort to legalisms, and it emphasized moral and sociological factors more than legal arguments.

ィ   ィ   ィ

The letting-down of racial barriers continued to be news all through the year 1954. The following instances were mentioned in the *New York Times.*

November 26, 1954. New Orleans, Nov. 25. Loyola University of the South dropped today all segregation barriers—among both players and spectators—at its basketball games.

The Jesuit institution has scheduled three home contests with teams listing Negroes on their rosters, La Salle College, Philadelphia, the University of Illinois, and Keesler Air Force Base, Biloxi, Miss.

The La Salle game Dec. 5 will . . . be the first New Orleans collegiate basketball game participated in by both Negroes and whites.

While school officials made no official announcement, it is known that there will be no special section set aside for Negroes in the field house. All seating and other facilities will be on the same basis.

November 26, 1954. Danville, Va., Nov. 25. The First Baptist Church was filled to overflowing today at the city's first bi-racial Thanksgiving service at which the Rev. L. W. Chase, a Negro, preached the sermon. The worshippers appeared to be about evenly divided between the races.

November 26, 1955. Atlanta, Nov. 25. The order to end segregation of passengers in interstate travel apparently will have its biggest impact on public waiting rooms. In many places in the South they are segregated by state or city law. Actual operation of the waiting rooms is maintained by the railroads and bus lines themselves, or affiliated companies, but the operators conform to local regulations. . . .

Washington. The Interstate Commerce Commission decreed today that racial segregation on trains and buses that cross state lines must end by Jan. 10. The decision applied also to public waiting rooms in railway and bus terminals.

The ruling was patterned after the Supreme Court's decision of May 17, outlawing segregation in public schools. . . . The Court already has applied its decision to public parks, beaches, and playgrounds. . . .

✓   ✓   ✓

In most Southern towns where there is a significant proportion of Negroes a distinct culture exists, apart from that of the white people. Hylan Lewis, *Blackways of Kent,* University of North Carolina Press, Chapel Hill, 1955, is an intimate account of Negro life in Piedmont, South Carolina. Kent is a pseudonym for a typical cotton-mill town of 4000 people. It has three social elements: the old settlers, descendants of Scotch-Irish Presbyterians who settled there more than two hundred years ago; the mill people who moved in from rural areas to work in the textile mills, from 1896-1907; and the Negroes. The following excerpts are from *Blackways of Kent,* pp. 233-256, *passim.*

RESPECTABLES AND NONRESPECTABLES

. . . In general, the respectable persons are defined by what they do not do. They are people who are careful of their public conduct and reputation: they don't drink whisky in public or get drunk in public; they don't frequent the taverns; they don't get in trouble; and they are proud of their lack of contact with the law and the courts. The respectables are not clustered in any particular section of the town, nor does any of the churches have a monopoly on them. Although the category is not composed exclusively of the persons with the best jobs, the most property, or the highest incomes, these features are positively associated with the status. The reason is that respectability—or conventionally-moral conduct—is an expected accompaniment of education and a good or responsible job. People with education and economic advantage are looked upon as persons who have achieved, and they are people who have a standard of public demeanor to maintain; they are people the nonrespectables tend to *want* to look up to. In other words, being differentiated by education or economic status not only involves the voluntary assumption of different behavior standards but it also means having imposed upon one a definite role: since they are people who are going somewhere—or aspiring to—they should act like it. For example, a local businessman insisted on getting drunk publicly while under an emotional strain related to a domestic crisis: a nonrespectable friend chastised him: "Man, don't drink. Let me do it, not you. Let somebody do it who don't matter and who they don't expect no better of." . . .

Family status and name are not determinants of personal respectability. The family of Mrs. Robinson, the insurance agent, consists of herself, her husband, three sons, and one daughter; the only respectable members of the family, however, are the mother and daughter. "Miss Phoebe" Thorpe has one son, two sons-in-law, a brother, a nephew, and two brothers-in-law who are considered nonrespectable. On the other hand, there are families with a majority of their members in the nonrespectable category that have a member or members referred to as "the best of the lot" and who are looked upon as respectables. . . .

The categories respectable and nonrespectable cut across all segments, levels, or groups in the Negro population—occupational, educational, kinship, religious. It is difficult to describe the persons in these categories in terms of precise numbers or proportions because the line between the two categories cannot be sharply drawn; there are some people who are considered more nonrespectable than others, and similarly there are some people who adhere more rigidly to respectable standards of conduct than others who nevertheless would be considered—and consider themselves—nonrespectable persons. . . .

Concretely, these are among the types of people who are considered respectable:

(1) A number of three-or-four generation families having relatively clear lineage, particularly in recent generations and having relative security and a tradition of success or achievement. . . . The Roberts family . . . has most of these characteristics; it is headed by Mr. Sam Roberts, a gruff, hard-bitten, active, elderly man who owns considerable real estate and has been farmer, carpenter, and store owner. He is probably the most influential and best known of the older men. It has been said that whenever Mr. Sam is connected with anything and the Negroes want to pick a leader or spokesman, they appoint Mr. Sam. He heads the local NAACP (National Association for the Advancement of Colored People), the Kent County Colored Fair Association, and is a prominent church and fraternal leader. Both the Thorpes and

the Roberts are pillars of the Methodist church. One of the sons of Sam Roberts married a Thorpe; yet there is no intimate, clique-like social contact between the families. The two families combined have furnished the bulk of local college graduates, the majority of native school teachers, and much of the leadership in the Negro community. Although there are many other stable family groups with significant pride, no other family matches them for dominance, extent of influence, and over-all prestige.

(2) The secure widow: a person whose husband left her relatively "well-fixed" by way of property and insurance; or a person who by her own energies and thrift has achieved a measure of security. An example of the latter is Mrs. Louise Todd, the "flower woman" and faithful church worker:

Mrs. Louise Todd is a widow; her husband died 42 years ago and left her with "three children and one coming." She worked a "hoe farm" (worker furnishes labor and shares in proceeds to the extent of one-third) and did domestic work for five years. She never failed to show a profit. She decided to move to town so that her children might get better schooling. She is very profuse in attributing her success to the Lord and her prayers; the Lord blessed her and made her a strong woman who could and would work. Her twin passions are the Lord and her flowers.

When Mrs. Todd came to Kent, she raised vegetables for sale and did domestic work for awhile. She didn't like domestic work. One day while looking at a small bouquet of flowers she had made, she said to herself that someone would like that. She began to grow and experiment with flowers; she ordered and read a great variety of seed catalogues. She has been selling flowers on the streets and in the local stores and offices for over twenty-five years. Every available space in her yard is planted with flowers. She knows the names of all and can indicate genus and species. Her prize exhibit is a rock wall that she built herself. She tells proudly how she found and carried each rock and mixed the mortar.

(3) The successful farm owner or operator: a high status type by virtue of land ownership or control and independence. The successful farm operators maintain an above-average standard of living—good housing and equipment, diet, automobiles, clothing. There is a marked contrast between them and the poorer tenants; they are generally appreciated as symbols of success and enterprise among a people whose lives are colored to so large an extent by agricultural activities and who themselves are not far removed from a rural background. The high level farm incomes of recent years have added to their stature. The fact that most of the prominent ones of the area are using modern methods—mechanization, crop rotation and diversification, and soil conservation—increases their recognition as intelligent and serious economic operators. They are among the most solid citizens of the community. To say that a person is a farmer or has a big farm carries a significant connotation locally.

(4) The successful artisan: he is the energetic and reliable worker who

possesses a skill such as brick-laying, carpentry, and painting. Reliability and personal reputation are important earmarks of success. The few successful artisans are in considerable demand among the whites. They are concrete examples of "people who can do something." "When a man can do something he's in demand." . . .

(5) The principal of the school and the school teacher. . . .

(6) The undertaker: the size of the community, the lack of a Negro professional group, the limited roles played by teachers and preachers in the local community are factors that help define the role of the Negro undertaker and impose a variety of functions in relation to the Negro community. The local undertaker has to be a friend and trouble shooter in life and death; he combines many of the conventional functions of the lawyer, doctor, preacher, banker, credit agency, confidential agent, taxi driver. Not untypical were the following events that took place at the undertaking establishment in the course of a single afternoon: a man came by to have an appointment made with a dentist in a nearby city; a woman came by to borrow fifteen dollars to get her husband out of jail; two youths got assistance with their draft cards; a man sought to get a house built for him; the pastor arrived to discuss church finances; a call from a rural region fifteen miles away to pick up a patient and deliver her to a hospital that is fifteen miles away in the other direction; a lady acquaintance asked to be driven home; Western Union called to inquire about the address of a local resident. The undertaker must be a diplomat in handling preacher, friends, family, and insurance companies. The position as the most important Negro business-profession in the community and the necessity of frequent contact with white businessmen, professionals, and public officials means that he must be skilled and restrained in public relations with whites. Leadership and liaison functions are imposed or taken-for-granted by both the white and Negro communities.

(7) The preacher: the religious and social functions of the church automatically make the preacher's role an important one. It is probable that local whites still think of the minister as the most influential and important person in the Negro community; the "preacher" or the "professor"—as any Negro who deviates from the over-all pattern is likely to be called by whites —gets a kind of patronizing respect from whites. The Negro community looks upon the preacher in quite a different way. The functions of the office—preaching and presiding over significant ceremonies such as the burial rites—are important; the individual minister is highly expendable locally and his prestige as a person may be low. He comes to be a sort of part-time expert presiding with more or less satisfaction over traditional and necessary rites. In actual practice, he has a rather tenuous hold on his job, and his leadership functions are made difficult by the limited expectations of the congregation, chronic financial problems, limitations related to training or personal characteristics, and a factionalism in the church that is inherent

in the gap between young and old, traditionalists and progressives. His lack of financial independence doesn't help his prestige or his self-confidence. . . . The ministers are ranked informally as to ability as pulpit orators, training, courage, and interest in community affairs, money-raising abilities, and the propensity to extramarital sex play. In practice, both office and person tend to be stripped of much of the sacred and spiritual quality, leadership and control are diminished, and the prestige of the individual minister cannot be taken for granted.

(8) The person with a "good" or relatively rare job; a "good" job is a stable job under good working conditions or an attachment to a white person of power or prestige. Among the "good" jobs of Kent would be some of the cooking positions, chauffeur for rich whites, clerk-porter in the drugstore. On the one hand, it is probable that selection operates to pick the more stable and responsible persons for such jobs. On the other hand, the vary stability of the jobs makes that person "lucky" in this setting of limited economic opportunity, and the reflected prestige of attachment to someone important reinforces individual prestige and influence in the Negro community. . . .

In general, with the exception of teaching, the best job for the woman is that of cook for a person of prestige or wealth; those who are "good" employers represent premium jobs. . . . The woman who doesn't have to work or who has "never worked for white folks" is a fortunate and envied person.

(9) The businessman: the status of the businessman tends to be marginal and not too well defined, although there is some respect for the enterpriser, particularly if he appears to be doing well, and there is appreciation for the businessman's design for independence and "making some money." . . . Attempts are made to tap or recruit persons with businesses for leadership or support functions, particularly in the church; a number of them are active church officers.

(10) The "good" or "nice" woman: this is a type about which there is a consensus; it is about the greatest compliment that can be given a woman. It does not represent an emphasis upon morality as such, although good personal reputation is an important ingredient. The emphasis is upon general manner and disposition. The women who are called "good" women or "wonderful persons" are above reproach and gossip; they are cheerfully cooperative; they are active and dependable in community and church affairs; and their range of congenial association is interdenominational. Marital status is not important. . . . The male counterpart, the "good man," has, in general, the same traits, but he is much rarer in this community. . . .

Turning now to the nonrespectables . . . among the types included . . . are the following:

(1) The drunk or excessive drinker: the person who is a regular drinker or who gets "booted" often and is seen in public drinking or drunk. . . .

(2) The person who has served time for a criminal offense: there are several distinctions made: (a) Those who have been on the chain gang or served time at the county prison camp; (b) those who have been to the state penitentiary; (c) those who have been arrested and even jailed for minor offenses but have never been to the "big jail" (county jail) or to court (county court); the inference is that those in the latter group are the victims of common minor vices such as drinking or fighting, but that they are not criminals. . . .

(3) The person who has brutally assaulted or killed another person: these are not necessarily persons who are feared or ostracized; they are rather persons with distinctive negative reputations—curiosities in part and persons to be careful of in part. . . .

(4) The stool pigeon or procurer for whites: the term "pimp" is used locally to describe both types of group betrayal—carrying tales and getting Negro girls for whites. These are probably the worst things that a Negro can do so far as the Negro community is concerned.

(5) The woman who goes with white men: this type of woman shares low status honors with the procurer and stool pigeon. If known, she is thoroughly ostracized and her movements are carefully checked. . . .

(6) The "bad woman" or "no good woman": this type of woman is not defined solely in terms of sex morality; she rather tends to be a person who is extremely indiscreet, loose, and unethical. In one instance, she is a person who has had higher status and is expected to act differently by virtue of certain advantages of education or income. The "bad woman" is the woman whom nobody respects; she is usually a heavy-drinking woman also. . . .

(7) The bootleggers and numbers agents: these are something of an elite among the nonrespectables; they provide a desired service; they are conceded to be shrewd, clever and lucky, as is anybody who lives "by his wits." As a type they seem to be money-conscious, hard-dealing, and a little suspicious and aloof.

(8) The "slick cat": this type is rare in this small community and is the result of two things: (a) contact with the urban prototype of the "hep cat" and (b) dissatisfaction with local status coupled with a certain disdain for local people and ways. In dress and manner, he is blatantly deviate; in conversation, he tries to impress with his cosmopolitan background and experience; he is prone to brag of his cleverness and superiority. . . .

(9) The town derelicts: these are slow-thinking, good-natured persons who are defenseless against the jibes and derision that come their way. They are obsequious among whites for whom they do odd jobs or from whom they cadge small favors, and they are timid among Negroes who assault their egos without fear of retaliation of reply in kind.

18

Education in the New South

Following the reconstruction period the public schools of the South did not receive enthusiastic support. The states were in debt and the Bourbon administrations were frugal in appropriations for education. Many of the political leaders still believed that parents should be responsible for their children's schooling. Private schools and academies continued to train the children of the upper classes.

The following selection from Russell Bowie, *Sunrise in the South,* The Wm. Byrd Press, Inc., Richmond, 1942, pp. 18-39, *passim,* reveals the education of Mary-Cooke Branch, a young lady of the upper class in Richmond shortly after the Civil War.

She was not quite four years old when her father was killed, and the next year Gran'pa Patteson died. The family went into mourning; and the house on Broad Street would not seem the same again. In 1871 Martha Branch moved with the children to a house with a wide old garden which she rented from Dr. Barney on Main Street, between Fourth and Fifth; and a few years later, she moved again, to a house which she bought for her own at First and Franklin Streets.

Richmond was still not much more than a large old town, growing slowly westward. Opposite the house at First and Franklin Streets were the dignified but simple brick fronts and white porches of Linden Row, shaded in their shallow front yards by magnolia trees. One block to the west, diagonally across the street, stood the fine old stuccoed house of the Kents. Beyond that, up Franklin Street, were other square-roomed houses in big yards, but not many. At a comparatively short distance to the west the fringes of the city melted into open fields. The unpaved streets were muddy or dusty according to the seasons and the weather. In the summer watering carts sprinkled ineffectively in front of the houses that paid for the watering, while the dust from the houses that didn't blew impartially up and down. Market carts from Hanover County, covered barrel-like with canvas, came by, each with a slow-moving mule and a black driver who called out in a kind of chanting cadence, "Watermelun-n-ns, watermelu-n-n-ns, sweet an' fine."

Down at Broad and Sixth Streets, and running through to Marshall, was the Market, a shed-like structure inside which were stalls for meat and fish, but outside which on the sidewalks and crowding out in to the street were the more picturesque piles of vegetables and fruit and bunches of flowers—or at Christmas-tide the holly and mistletoe—which the cheerful and chattering Negro men and women whom everybody knew had brought in from the country to their particular pavement spots. From time out of mind in Richmond it had been the custom for the ladies of the household, or for their husbands, to go to market; it was not only the method of getting the freshest food, but it was the social rendezvous where everybody met everybody else. Mrs. James Branch drove down every morning in her carriage, with the market basket to be taken about from stall to stall, and the children too young to be in school might go with her. In general of course the children liked this; but Mary-Cooke was sometimes disposed to imitate a small acquaintance of hers, Roberta Wellford, who habitually would try to hide herself under the skirts of the long fur cape her grandmother wore, in order to escape the attentions of unwelcome demonstrative ladies among her grandmother's friends.

When Mary-Cooke was old enough to graduate from going to market, she started to school at Mr. Merill's, on Cary Street. According to the standards of the times as to what well-brought-up young girls should learn and not learn, it was a good school. Mr. Merill was strict to see that his pupils should study their lessons and know what the lesson-books taught; they must read well, spell correctly, and be accurate in arithmetic, and understand French, and know geography and a good deal of history, especially the history of Virginia and the Confederacy and the Civil War. But there was no thought that the school should be preparatory to any advanced studies, nor, particularly, to anything so unheard-of for a southern girl, as college. Later, an independent and resolute little woman, Virginia Ellett, starting a fine school in Richmond which was to grow into a large and influential one, set in motion a new influence. Combining oddly an inherited conservatism with courageous ideas of her own, "Miss Jennie"—as she was known to two generations of Richmond girls—not only gave her girls all the culture she could give them, but fired in them the ambition to stretch their own wings for wider flights. In Mary-Cooke Branch's day, however, both at school and in the social circles to which her mother and her mother's friends belonged, anything adventurous in a girl's education was regarded with surprise and hostility. The community mind was like that which has been pictured brilliantly by Ellen Glasgow in her description of "Dinwiddie Academy for Young Ladies": "Education was founded upon the simple theory that the less a girl knew about life, the better she would be to contend with it. . . . She was taught that a natural curiosity about the universe was the beginning of infidelity . . . to solidify the forces of mind into the inherited mould of fixed beliefs was to achieve the definite end of education."

There was not only the "mould of fixed beliefs" that a girl had to reckon with, but the softer mould of social custom. Mrs. James Branch wanted her daughter to shine in the sort of graces which matrons who set the tone of Richmond society admired, and she had her share of a mother's vanity over a beautiful child. Mary-Cooke was early taught to dance, and was often called upon to give her solo dances in the old ball-rooms of the Blue Ridge Springs and the Allegheny Springs, to the good-humored applause of the ladies and gentlemen who went there with their families in the summer. As she grew toward her early teens, she used to take the leading part every spring in a "May Festival" which she organized among the children of her age in Richmond. Her mother, who had a quick wit and inventiveness, used to devise the parts which the children played and write the lines which they recited; and her assumption that Mary-Cooke should play the leading part was deftly furthered by an ice cream party which she would give to all the small girls concerned if there appeared to be any hesitation in their assent as to who should have the stellar role. So Mary-Cooke, partly through her own natural leadership and partly through custom which the other children took as a matter of course, was the Queen of the May. . . .

The years went by, and Mary-Cooke Branch was growing up. Mostly her life and her experience were like those of other Richmond girls. In the compact society of the old city, there was not much incentive to be different. Girls finished school, and then "came out," and usually they married early. Mary-Cooke's three sisters were married at twenty-one, eighteen, and twenty. But she did not seem to be inclined that way. She went the social round that her mother would have felt it highly unfitting that any of her daughters should ignore; the calls on the family friends, the sessions at the dress-maker's, the parties at home and in the other familiar houses which for the most part opened on Franklin Street or no far from it, the climactic winter dances which went by the name of "Richmond Germans" and to be invited to lead which was regarded as a crowning distinction for a Richmond belle, and in summer the visits to White Sulphur Springs and other resort hotels where the young people danced again and flirted on the long porches or on the cottage walks. Such were the interests which a girl who had grown up among the "best families" was supposed to like, and outwardly at least Mary-Cooke Branch was part of the general pattern. . . . There was nothing to keep her from being what would have been approvingly called a "social success," and young men admirers were plentiful. But something within her was restless and aloof. . . . She was conscious that she wanted something different from what most of the girls she knew, and nearly all their mothers' generation, were content with. They played and danced and fell in love and got married and had babies; and then many of them settled down to interests and ideas which did not go beyond the nursery. They were supposed to think that their husbands, being men, were creatures of superior wisdom, whose opinions should be authoritative in the larger matters "outside a woman's sphere." Some of them never addressed their husbands by their first names, but called them "Mister McAdams" and Doctor Cabell," as even her two admired and vigorous older sisters did to their husbands' dying day. There were still curious strains of old-world feudalism that lingered in Richmond life, particularly as applied to women. . . .

New ideas . . . were not popular in Richmond among "the best people." There was much wonderment and considerable shaking of heads when it was learned that Mary-Cooke Branch, and some of the other girls of her group, had established a club for working girls in two rooms which they had rented in a little house on Main Street. She did this because of her sense of responsibility for girls who had fewer advantages than she had, and because of her spontaneous desire to widen her own sympathy and understanding through knowing them. Such books and magazines as the founders of the club could get hold of were put in the club; and the girls met there to play games and talk and discuss. The Y.W.C.A. had not come to Richmond then, and the little club on Main Street was the first venture in the city in the direction of equal contact between girls of different social ranks. But what did these girls discuss? the elders were asking, and what upsetting motions might be in their heads? . . .

But as to Mary-Cooke Branch, the chief cause for consternation among her acquaintances was not the founding of the club for working girls, but something further. She wanted to go to college. That was being "strong minded" to a degree that made Richmond society gasp. To go to college was something that simply was not done by southern women; ergo, it ought not to be done. There might be women's colleges somewhere, but they could be disposed of as "only a Yankee notion." Mary-Cooke did go, it was true, in her older girlhood to a school in New York City—Miss Peeble's school; this excursus outside the region of the late Confederacy was very doubtfully regarded by her mother, but was consented to for the double reason that it was a school of impeccably correct standing, and that her cousin, Effie Branch, was going there. But when the idea of going to college was suggested, Mrs. James Branch was shocked. She could not believe a daughter of hers wanted to do anything so unfeminine. If Mary-Cooke went, it would be over her shamed and indignant protest.

Here was a crisis in the girl's life which tested her character more than almost anything else she was ever called upon to face. She wanted to go to college with a consuming intellectual eagerness. . . . She knew she could go if she determined to; from her father's will enough income had come to make her financially independent. But she saw that her going would make an emotional breach with her mother which might never be healed. . . .

Fundamentally, her mother should have understood and shared her longing. Her mother's mind was quick and keen, as hers was. . . . But she had been born into a time which wove its restrictions upon women into the closest fabric of its family affections. . . . So she (Mary-Cooke) deliberately gave up the one ambition which she most passionately cherished.

✓   ✓   ✓

Dr. William A. Webb, whose comments on colleges for women in the ante-bellum South have already been quoted (see p. 200), continued to evaluate women's colleges following the Civil War. This excerpt is from *Proceedings* of the Twelfth Annual Meeting of the Southern Association of College Women, Raleigh, 1915, p. 25.

The quarter of the century following the close of the Civil War saw the organization of the five great [women's] colleges of the North. . . .

Conditions in the South, so far as separate institutions for the higher education of women were concerned, remained very much as they had been before the war. It is true that more than one hundred of the so-called female colleges were in operation, but in not a single one of these institutions could a Southern girl secure a real college training. In 1888, Goucher College, formerly known as the Woman's College of Baltimore, opened its doors and gave to the young women of its vicinity the privileges and opportunities of a genuine college. Five years later, in 1893, Randolph-Macon Woman's College . . . gave to young women of the South their first opportunity to obtain in a distinctly Southern College an education equal to that given in the best colleges for young men. . . . Agnes Scott, organized in 1888, was chartered as a college in 1905; and Converse College, organized in 1889, was reorganized and opened as a college in 1902. These institutions are the only separate colleges for women so far admitted into membership in the Association of Colleges and Secondary Schools of the Southern States. . . .

⚹ ⚹ ⚹

At the time that the Farmers' Alliances were flourishing, the movement for the industrial education of women culminated in the establishment of such schools as Winthrop College in South Carolina and the State Normal and Industrial School for Women in North Carolina. Elizabeth Avery Colton addressed the Thirteenth Annual Meeting of the Southern Association of College Women on the subject, "The Changing Emphasis in the Education of Women in the South." The following excerpt from her address is quoted from the *Proceedings* of the Thirteenth Annual Meeting, Southern Association of College Women, Raleigh, 1916.

During the whole of the nineteenth century our numerous so-called Colleges for women in the South were far more interested in providing girls with parlor accomplishments than with kitchen skill. The girls, as a rule, "specialized" as they called it, in music, art, literature, history, or elocution; this "specializing," however, consisted merely in dropping Latin and Mathematics, or any other study which they did not like. The few who took the regular course and received a nominal A.B. degree discovered if they went to a northern college for further study that their training had not thoroughly prepared them even for the freshman work of a real college. Some, however, by private reading and study, by association, and by travel attained a high degree of culture; and many even of the "accomplishment specializers" acquired in the school of experience a high degree of efficiency in directing the affairs of the home. In other words, our southern women who became cultured and efficient, in the majority of cases became so in spite of, rather than on account of, the education provided for them in our southern schools. . . .

And the majority of Colleges for women in the South are still largely of the finishing school type; but the education of women has for the past ten or twelve years been developing in a new direction, due largely to the increasing emphasis on vocational training all over the country. Not only are our normal schools emphasizing training in industrial and household arts; but three even of our six standard separate colleges for women have introduced into their curriculum courses in cooking, sewing, and household management; and within the past ten years practically all southern co-educational state universities have also added departments of home economics. . . . Consequently the Southern Association of College Women is making every effort not so much to change the present tendency to emphasize vocational training for women as to differentiate technical training of all kinds from college training. . . . We are . . . encouraging our six standard colleges to leave to normal schools, to State universities and to conservatories of music technical training in vocational subjects and in fine arts, and to devote themselves to the distinctive work of liberal education. . . . Professor Trent . . . reflects that women need "not only the sciences to aid them in advancing the race physically, but especially the classics and the great modern literatures to enable them to instill into their children the ideals that preserve and advance the race spiritually."

In the 1890's the Southern educational revival began. Walter Hines Page, North Carolina journalist and editor, was one of the evangelists. From "The Forgotten Man," an address delivered at the State Normal and Industrial School for Women at Greensboro, North Carolina, June, 1897, the following selection describes the educational needs of that day. It is quoted from his *The Rebuilding of Old Commonwealths*, Atlantic Monthly, Vol. 89, May, 1902, pp. 1-28, *passim*.

. . . We have often reminded ourselves and informed other people that we have incalculable undeveloped resources in North Carolina, in our streams, our forests, our mines, our quarries, our soil—that Nature has been most bountiful; so that our undeveloped resources invite men under the pleasantest conditions to productive industry. And so they do. But there is one undeveloped resource more valuable than all these, and that is the people themselves. It is about the development of men that I shall speak, more particularly about the development of forgotten and neglected men. . . .

The common people is the class most to be considered in the structure of civilization. Moreover, in proportion as any community in the organization of its society or in the development of its institutions lays emphasis on its few rich men, or its few cultivated men, it is likely to forget and to neglect its very foundations. It is not those small classes that really make the community what it is, that determine the condition of its health, the soundness of its social structure, its economic value and its level of life. The security and the soundness of the whole body are measured at last by the condition of its weakest part. . . .

In the days of our fathers the social structure of North Carolina was to a slight extent aristocratic, but it was much less aristocratic than the social structure was, for example, in Virginia or in South Carolina. The mass of the people were common people; they lived directly out of the soil and they had the manners and virtues and the limitations of a simple agricultural population, which was much the same in the early part of the century in all countries where a livelihood was easily obtained. They were nearly all of English and Scotch, and Scotch-Irish stock. Most of them were sprung from peasants of sturdy qualities; a very few from gentlemen; and some were descended from forced and hired immigrants. Taken all together they were a common people, capable of as sound development as the population of any other State. But they were ignorant, as the common people in all lands were a hundred years ago.

The dominant idea of education was that it was a luxury for the rich, or a privilege of the well-born—if a necessity at all, a necessity only for the ruling class. This class-feeling in education was perceptible even within my recollection. When I was a pupil at the most famous school for boys in the State, a lad whose father had not had a military or political career, was at a certain disadvantage. . . .

The first conception of education was the aristocratic conception, and the first system of teaching was controlled by those who held political power; it was the old system of class education. It did not touch the masses. They had no part in it. They grew up with the idea that education was a special privilege; they did not aspire to it, did not believe it was attainable, and at last they came to believe that it was not desirable, certainly that it was not necessary. They remained illiterate, neglected, forgotten. There was no substantial progress in broadening educational opportunities in North Carolina from the time of the colony till the beginning of the civil war, except the noteworthy and noble work that was done just before the war to develop a public school system. This notable and noteworthy effort gives us good reason to hold those who made it, chief among whom was Calvin H. Wiley, in grateful remembrance. . . .

Later than the aristocratic system of education and overlapping it, came the ecclesiastical system. In establishing and developing this, the preachers did valiant service. . . . The churches established, besides preparatory schools for boys and girls, three schools for men which grew into colleges. At first they were established for the education of preachers, but they broadened their field of labour and became schools of general culture, and most admirable service they have done. The denominational educational movement was broader in its benefits than the old aristocratic educational movement had been, for these colleges were open to the common people and they proclaimed the desirability of general education. Still they were class institutions; each was a school of a sect. Universal education, universal free education, was not on their programme. . . .

In 1890, twenty-six per cent. of the white persons of the State were unable to read and write. One in every four was wholly forgotten. But illiteracy was not the worst of it; the worst of it was that the stationary social condition indicated by generations of illiteracy had long been the general condition. The forgotten man was content to be forgotten. . . .

But now the story brightens. These old educational systems having failed here, as they have failed in other States, the public-spirited, far-sighted and energetic young men, chief among them your own President and the President of the University, who came into activity ten years or more ago, began seriously to develop a public school system, first of course in the towns. . . . One town followed another, levying a local tax to supplement the State tax. . . . The level of life has been moved further upward in these ten years than it was moved in any preceding fifty years. . . .

In my judgment there has been no other event in North Carolina since the formation of the American Union that is comparable in importance to this new educational progress.

✓ ✓ ✓

Mary-Cooke Branch (see p. 456) became Mrs. B. B. Munford, and both she and her husband were affiliated with the educational reform movement in the South. The following selection is a condensation of an address which she made, "The Southern Woman's Work for Education; a Record and an Interpretation," *Proceedings,* Conference for Education in the South, Raleigh, 1909, pp. 133-139.

In studying the history of the school movement in the South it is significant that the first School Improvement Association was formed in Richmond in May, 1900, by five women, and the first State organization was born in 1902 at the suggestion of Dr. McIver at a woman's industrial college. . . . He wrote, "It is plain that the State and Society, for the sake of their future educational interests, ought to decree that for every dollar spent by the Government, State or Federal, and by philanthropists in the training of men, at least another dollar should be invested in the work of educating womankind. . . ."

Southern woman has set herself with determination to the task of public education. . . . Each State as she has fallen into line has seemed to make some contribution all her own to the common store of knowledge which is slowly gathering around this movement for the consecration of the school to the purposes of democracy. . . .

Mrs. Munford cited for each of the Southern states some educational accomplishment initiated by women. A few are quoted in the following paragraphs:

Miss Pettit's work in *Kentucky* stands for the possibilities of a school based on first hand knowledge of conditions, to minister to and remold the life of our mountain people. The women of that State have shown initiative in raising funds to carry on campaign work and have had a very special share in shaping the legislative acts in reference to education. They are eligible as school trustees, and one woman is a member of the State Education Commission. They have laid special emphasis upon teachers' and farmers' institutes as places where they might preach the gospel of the common school.

In *Tennessee* we have the Farragut School, one of the best developed model public rural schools in the South. Seven schools for mountain children have been started by the woman's clubs, and attention is invited to the work of the "Lookout Committee" in Knoxville to increase school attendance.

Mississippi has the honor of having one of her women as the mother of the idea of her State Industrial School and College for White Girls, the first State institution of its kind in the United States.

In *Alabama* . . . the work for kindergartens among the mill children has been beautifully developed by Miss Lindsay. . . .

We cannot think of *Georgia* without a picture of Miss Berry and her boys for whom she has made a "chance in life" a real and tangible thing. Four model rural schools and the library work are under the care of the Federation of Women's Clubs. The presence of a goodly number of college women in the State seems to bring into prominence the scientific study of educational and social problems. And at the other end of the scale Mrs. Hill, with her band of farmers' wives, is journeying up to the State University at Athens that they too may share in some of the good things now abroad in the land—so far as I know—the first attempt in a Southern State of a conference for farmers' wives under the aegis of a leading State educational institution. . . .

✓ ✓ ✓

Many men and women devoted their lives to bringing educational opportunities to rural and mountain districts. Typical of these was Martha Berry who founded the Berry School. The following brief account is the foreword from Tracy Byers, *Martha Berry, the Sunday Lady of Possum Trot*, G. P. Putnam's Sons, New York, 1932.

There are estimated to be a million illiterate or semi-literate white people in the mountains of Southern Appalachia, of the purest Anglo-Saxon stock which America can boast, who in their poverty and pride have been allowed to retire, both physically and mentally, into their mountain fastnesses. This tragic human waste still continues. Nothing was ever done about it until Martha Berry started the Berry School and, by her method of training mind and hand together, turned thousands of these people into useful citizens. . . .

She went forth into the hills in search of the raw material of human greatness. She found it. . . . The mountains began to appear at her door-way. A youngster comes down the "big road" toting his entire earthly possessions in a paper sack. He says simply, "Here I am, ma'am, come ter git larnin!" and sure enough, here he is, and he gets it.

In the past thirty-five years Martha Berry has educated some ten thousand boys and girls in her school at Mt. Berry, Georgia, a state in which fifty per cent of its children never finish the fourth grade. A thousand students are enrolled now, studying anything from primers to college texts for degrees, including the art of gracious living. She has exalted the dignity of manual labor among a people whose retrogression has been due in part to the fact that they have always been too proud to compete with the Negroes. She has created a paradise on what is now the largest campus in the world; twenty-five thousand acres of farm and woodland.

And she has accomplished this in the face of a century-old tradition of inactivity on the part of the people for whom she is working, and against the constant opposition of her own kind in the South. She has been alone save for the unquestioning loyalty of her boys and girls, who were as eager to learn as she was to teach. . . .

There is little in her background to explain her, save that she must have inherited forcefulness and integrity from her father, courage and beauty of character from her mother. Her training was that of any wealthy and highly-bred Southern girl who was pretty but had no outstanding talent. She had private governesses at home and was "finished" at a select school for young ladies. Her life was one of cultured ease and frivolous enjoyment.

There was poverty, distress, and illiteracy hidden in the hills, but every one of her own class viewed these things with equanimity. To the mountain people themselves, their lot, though hard, was part of the established order of things and they were resigned.

Martha Berry alone stepped out of her environment. She found herself in the grip of an idea; something must be done, and since no one else was making it his business, she must make it hers. It is amazing enough that this idea should obsess her to the extent of making her sacrifice her entire life for it, but even more amazing is the fact that, with no preparation, she should be able to carry the idea to a successful conclusion. . . . She has always borne the entire responsibility for the school and time after time has had to take over the jobs of others who, unfired by the light that burned within her, flickered and expired in the face of many difficulties.

✓ ✓ ✓

North Carolina supported the educational revival with enthusiasm. J. Y. Joyner, State Superintendent of Schools, delivered the following address "The Public Schools and the Future," at the dinner of the North Carolina Society of New York, December 7, 1908.

. . . North Carolina was the first Southern State to give serious attention to the problem of providing a system of public schools for the education of all her children. When the war began she had the best system of public education in all the South, and one which had attracted attention and commendation throughout the Nation. . . .

It should never be forgotten that North Carolina was compelled by inexorable fate to wander forty years in a wilderness of poverty; and that in 1890, according to the United States census, she was only thirty-four million dollars richer in taxable property than she was in 1860.

With the increased prosperity of the past decade has come a correspondingly rapid increase in educational progress.

During the past five years, our people have built and equipped two thousand new public school houses, more than one a day for every day in the year, Sundays included. These houses have been built in accordance with plans approved by the State Superintendent of Public Instruction, prepared by the most competent architects, according to the most modern principles of school architecture, as to convenience, beauty, light, ventilation, heat, and the general laws of sanitation. At this rate we may reasonably hope to have within the next few years a comfortable, modern public school house within reasonable reach of every school child of the state. . . .

During the last five years at least twelve hundred little, unnecessary school districts have been abolished by consolidation into larger and stronger school districts with longer terms, better houses, more and better teachers.

Teachers' salaries have been increased, though not in proportion to the increase in salaries of those in other professions and callings. County supervision of schools has been greatly improved. The salary of the county superintendent has been more than doubled in the last five years; in most counties he is now no longer a mere clerk to the county board of education, and a mere examiner of teachers, but a real supervisor and director of the county school system, giving his entire time, thought, and attention to the discharge of his duties. . . .

The state is now supporting a State University, a State Normal and Industrial College for white women, three normal schools for white men and women, three normal and industrial schools for colored men and women, an Agricultural and Mechanical College for white men, and one for colored men and women. All of these institutions, as well as the excellent denominational colleges for white and colored men and women, are filled to overflowing with students and taxed to the limit of their capacity. Not less than three thousand five hundred young white men and women are enrolled in our state institutions of higher learning and our first-class denominational colleges.

The appropriations for the schools for the blind and the deaf and dumb of both races have been nearly doubled. . . .

It may interest you to know that, based upon the total school fund and the total valuation of taxable property as officially recorded in the respective states, North Carolina is raising annually for school purposes eighty-two cents for every hundred dollars of taxable property, Massachusetts forty-one cents, and New York sixty-one cents. In other words, North Carolina, in proportion to her wealth, is bearing twice as heavy a burden as Massachusetts for the education of her children, and one and one-third as heavy a burden as New York. But the assessed taxable property for each child of school age in Massachusetts is about ten times as great and that of New York about seven times as great as that of North Carolina. . . .

Under an act of the General Assembly of 1907, making a special state appropriation therefor, and requiring the county and districts in which they are established each to duplicate the amount provided by the state for their maintenance, one hundred and fifty-nine rural public high schools have been established in eighty-four countries, enrolling during the first year four thousand country boys and girls. Through the development of these schools and the establishment of others, high school instruction for preparation for college or for life ought soon to be placed within reasonable reach, at small cost, of every country boy or girl.

This progress has been made in spite of scant wealth, sparse population, 82 per cent. of which is rural, and the burden of maintaining a double system of schools for the education of two races that must be separated forever, one of which has been able to contribute but little in taxation for the support of its schools.

✓ ✓ ✓

Seventeen years progress in Negro education was surveyed in an article in the *Atlantic Monthly*, Vol. 50, 1882, p. 349. The article was unsigned.

The various churches and religious organizations in the Southern States all appeared to be deeply interested in the work of popular education, and their leading men were evidently studying the problems and difficulties connected with the subject with serious attention. Most of these religious bodies have schools and colleges of various grades under their supervision. . . . Education is not so general in the South as in New England, but it is regarded with more respect, and its possession confers greater distinction.

The educational work already accomplished in the South by the American Missionary Society is of a high character, and it deserves all possible recognition and assistance. The best Southern people everywhere spoke of it gratefully and enthusiastically. At the Normal and Agricultural Institute, Hampton, Virginia, Talladega College, in Alabama; Tugaloo University, Mississippi; Tillotson Normal School, Austin, Texas, and at several other colleges and normal schools which I saw, though the money and en-dowments are scanty compared with the amounts which are needed, the endowments in personal qualities and character, as represented by the teachers, are of a remarkable high order. This is necessary, for the work of educating the colored people of the South requires the best teachers that can be obtained.

In many of these institutions the boys learn something of various trades or mechanical occupations, and of farming; and the girls are taught sewing, cooking, and the care of a house. I examined a great number of the negro common and high schools, which are taught by graduates and students of the colleges and normal schools which I have named, and I think it wonderful that so many of these negro teachers are successful. They have to struggle against many disadvantages, but nearly all whom I saw had the confidence and respect of the leading white citizens where they were at work. There were a few fools among them, of course, but a great majority appeared to be serious and sensible young men and women. . . .

The State of Kentucky appropriates the taxes received from colored persons and the fines collected from them to the support of the colored schools, not considering it just to tax white people for the education of negro children. As there is comparatively little wealth in the possession of the colored people of Kentucky, their school fund is by no means adequate to their needs. . . .

Among the most important features of the educational work now going on in the South is one which, from its nature, can have little public recognition. I refer to the personal missionary efforts of the women of the leading white families for the improvement of the common people of both races in their own communities. In many places, where the men are discouraged and depressed by the greatness of the work which needs to be done for the people around them, the feebleness of their resources, and the unfavorable conditions under which such efforts must be made, there are a few women who feel that something must be done, and who are circulating every scrap of reading matter that they can obtain; are advising, instructing, and encouraging the colored girls whenever they can obtain any hold upon them; are trying to inspire and strengthen the young men of both races to resist the evil influences about them; and are, in short, reconstructing society by the old, slow, best method of personal effort and influence. . . .

In several towns and country neighborhoods these women are forming reading circles and clubs, and trying to prepare the way for the establishment of small public libraries.

✦   ✦   ✦

The best-known Negro educator of the 19th century was Booker T. Washington, who was invited to found a Negro industrial school at Tuskegee, Alabama. The following extract is from his book, *My Larger Education,* Doubleday, Page and Company, Garden City, 1911, pp. 21-35.

One of the first questions that I had to answer for myself after beginning my work at Tuskegee was how I was to deal with public opinion on the race question.

It may seem strange that a man who had started out with the humble purpose of establishing a little Negro industrial school in a small Southern country town should find himself, to any great extent, either helped or hindered in his work by what the general public was thinking and saying about any of the large social or educational problems of the day. But such was the case at that time in Alabama; and so it was that I had not gone very far in my work before I found myself trying to formulate clear and definite answers to some very fundamental questions.

The questions came to me in this way: coloured people wanted to know why I proposed to teach their children to work. They said that they and their parents had been compelled to work for two hundred and fifty years, and now they wanted their children to go to school so that they might be free and live like the white folks—without working. That was the way in which the average coloured man looked at the matter.

Some of the Southern white people, on the contrary, were opposed to any kind of education of the Negro. Others inquired whether I was merely going to train preachers and teachers, or whether I proposed to furnish them with trained servants.

Some of the people in the North understood that I proposed to train the Negro to be a mere "hewer of wood and drawer of water," and feared that my school would make no effort to prepare him to take his place in the community as a man and a citizen.

Of course all these different views about the kind of education that the Negro ought or ought not to have were tinged with racial and sectional feelings. The rule of the "carpet-bag" government had just come to an end in Alabama. The masses of the white people were very bitter against the Negroes as a result of the excitement and agitation of the Reconstruction period.

On the other hand, the coloured people—who had recently lost, to a very large extent, their place in the politics of the State—were greatly discouraged and disheartened. Many of them feared that they were going to be drawn back into slavery. At this time also there was still a great deal of bitterness between the North and South in regard to anything that concerned political matters.

I found myself, as it were, at the angle where these opposing forces met. I saw that, in carrying out the work I had planned, I was likely to be opposed or criticized at some point by each of these parties. On the other hand, I saw just as clearly that in order to succeed I must in some way secure the support and sympathy of each of them.

I knew, for example, that the South was poor and the North was rich. I knew that Northern people believed, as the South at that time did not believe, in the power of education to inspire, to uplift, and to regenerate the masses of the people. I knew that the North was eager to go forward and complete, with the aid of education, the work of liberation which had begun with the sword, and that Northern people would be willing and glad to give their support to any school or other agency that proposed to do this work in a really fundamental way.

It was, at the same time, plain to me that no effort put forth in behalf of the members of my own race who were in the South was going to succeed unless it finally won the sympathy and support of the best white people in the South. I also knew—what many Northern people did not know or understand—that however much they might doubt the wisdom of educating the Negro, deep down in their hearts the Southern white people had a feeling of gratitude toward the Negro race. . . . I felt confident that, if I were actually on the right track in the kind of education that I proposed to give them and at the same time remained honest and sincere in all my dealings with them, I was bound to win their support, not only for the school that I had started, but for all that I had in my mind to do for them. . . . .

First, that I should at all times be perfectly frank and honest in dealing with each of the three classes of people that I have mentioned;

Second, that I should not depend upon any "short-cuts" or expedients merely for the sake of gaining temporary popularity or advantage, whether for the time being such action brought me popularity or the reverse. With these two points clear before me as my creed, I began going forward.

One thing which gave me faith at the outset, and increased my confidence as I went on, was the insight which I early gained into the actual relations of the races in the South. I observed, in the first place, that as a result of two hundred and fifty years of slavery the two races had become bound together in intimate ways that people outside the South could not understand, and of which the white people and coloured people themselves were perhaps not fully conscious. More than that, I perceived that the two races needed each other and that for many years to come no other labouring class of people would be able to fill the place occupied by the Negro in the life of the Southern white man. . . . .

I determined, first of all, that as far as possible, I would try to gain the active support and cooperation, in all that I undertook, of the masses of my own race. With this in view, before I began my work at Tuskegee, I spent several weeks travelling about the rural communities of Macon County, of which Tuskegee is the county seat. During all this time I had an opportunity to meet and talk individually with a large number of people representing the rural classes, which constitute 80 per cent. of the Negro population in the South. I slept in their cabins, ate their food, talked to them in their churches, and discussed with them in their own homes their difficulties and their needs. In this way I gained a kind of knowledge which has been of great value to me in all my work since.

As years went on, I extended these visits to the adjoining counties and adjoining states. Then, as the school at Tuskegee became better known, I took advantage of the invitations that came to me to visit the more distant parts of the country, where I had an opportunity to learn still more about the actual life of the people and the nature of the difficulties with which they were struggling. . . . .

In Macon County, Ala., where I live, the coloured people have a kind of church-service that is called an "all-day meeting." The ideal season for such meetings is about the middle of May. The church-house that I have in mind is located about ten miles from town. To get the most out of the "all-day meeting" one should make an early start, say eight o'clock. During the drive one drinks in the fresh fragrance of forests and wild flowers. The church building is located near a stream of water, not far from a large, cool spring, and in the midst of a grove or primitive forest. Here the coloured people begin to come together by nine or ten o'clock in the morning. Some of them walk; most of them drive. A large number come in buggies, but many use the more primitive wagons or carts, drawn my mules, horses, or oxen. In these conveyances a whole family, from the youngest to the eldest, make the journey together. All bring baskets of food, for the "all-day meeting" is a kind of Sunday picnic or festival. Preaching, preceded by much singing, begins at about eleven o'clock. If the building is not large enough, the services are held out under the trees. Sometimes there is but one sermon; sometimes there are two or three sermons, if visiting ministers are present. The sermon over, there is more plantation singing. A collection is taken —sometimes two collections—then comes recess for dinner and recreation.

Sometimes I have seen at these "all-day meetings" as many as three thousand people present. No one goes away hungry. Large baskets, filled with the most tempting spring chicken or fresh pork, fresh vegetables, and all kinds of pies and cakes, are then opened. The people scatter in groups. . . . Here old acquaintances are renewed; relatives meet members of the family whom they have not seen for months. Strangers, visitors, every one must be invited by some one else to dinner. . . . The animals are fed and watered, and then at about three o'clock there is another sermon or two, with plenty of singing thrown in; then another collection, or perhaps two. In between these sermons I am invited to speak, and am very glad to accept the invitation. At about five o'clock the benediction is pronounced and the thousands quietly scatter to their homes with many good-bys and well-wishes. This, as

I have said, is the kind of church-service that I like best. In the opportunities which I have to speak to such gatherings I feel that I have done some of my best work.

In carrying out the policy which I formed early, of making use of every opportunity to speak to the masses of the people, I have not only visited country churches and spoken at such "all-day meetings" as I have just described, but for years I have made it a practice to attend, whenever it has been possible for me to do so, every important ministers' meeting. I have also made it a practice to visit town and city churches and in this way to get acquainted with the ministers and meet the people.

✓   ✓   ✓

Booker T. Washington's plan for industrial education at Tuskegee set an example for many Southern Negro schools. In the *Atlantic Monthly,* Vol. 92, 1903, pp. 454-456, he defended this plan.

From its first inception the white people of the South had faith in the theory of industrial education, because they had noted, what was not unnatural, that a large element of the colored people at first interpreted freedom to mean freedom from work with the hands. . . . The white people saw in the movement to teach the Negro youth the dignity, beauty, and civilizing power of all honorable work with the hands something new that would lead the Negro into his new life of freedom gradually and sensibly, and prevent his going from one extreme of life to the other too suddenly. Furthermore, industrial education appealed directly to the individual and community interest of the white people. They saw at once that intelligence coupled with skill would add wealth to the community and to the state, in which both races would have an added share. . . .

One of the most interesting and valuable instances of the kind that I know of is presented in the case of Mr. George W. Carver, one of our instructors of agriculture at Tuskegee Institute. For some time it has been his custom to prepare articles containing information concerning the conditions of local crops, and warning the farmers against the ravages of certain insects and diseases. The local white papers are always glad to publish these articles, and they are read by white and colored farmers.

Some months ago a white land-holder in Montgomery county asked Mr. Carver to go through his farm with him for the purpose of inspecting it. While doing so Mr. Carver discovered traces of what he thought was a valuable mineral deposit, used in making a certain kind of paint. The interests of the land-owner and the agricultural instructor at once became mutual. Specimens of the deposits were taken to the laboratories at the Tuskegee Institute and analyzed by Mr. Carver. In due time the land-owner received a report of the analysis, together with a statement showing the commercial value and application of the mineral. I shall not go through the whole interesting story, except to say that a stock company, composed of some of the best white people in Alabama, has been organized, and is now preparing to build a factory for the purpose of putting their product on the market. I hardly need to add that Mr. Carver has been freely consulted at every step, and his services generously recognized in the organization of the concern. . . . .

I want to call attention here to a phase of Reconstruction policy which is often overlooked. All now agree that there was much in Reconstruction which was unwise and unfortunate. However we may regard that policy, and much as we may regret mistakes, the fact is too often overlooked that it was during this Reconstruction period that a public school system for the education of all the people of the South was first established in most of the states. Much that was done by those in charge of Reconstruction legislation has been overturned, but the public school system still remains. True, it has been modified and improved but the system remains, and is every day growing in popularity and strength.

✓   ✓   ✓

J. L. M. Curry was the Secretary of the fund established by George Peabody, Northern philanthropist, for the advancement of education in the South. He encouraged the establishment of normal schools for both races, and he was well acquainted with the educational problems of the section. In his pamphlet, *Difficulties, Complications, and Limitations Connected with the Education of the Negro*, Trustees of the John F. Slater Fund, Baltimore, 1895, he outlined some of the errors that had been made in Negro education.

Much of the aid lavished upon the negro has been misapplied charity, and like much other alms-giving hurtful to the recipient. Northern philanthropy, "disastrously kind," has often responded with liberality to appeals worse than worthless. Vagabond mendicants have been pampered; schools which were established without any serious need for them have been helped; public school systems, upon which the great mass of children, white and colored, must rely for their education, have been underrated and injured, and schools, of real merit and good work, which deserve confidence and contributions, have had assistance, legitimately their due, diverted into improper channels. Reluctantly and by constraint of conscience, this matter is mentioned and this voice of warning raised. Dr. A. D. Mayo, of Boston, an astute and thoughtful observer, a tried friend of the black man, an eloquent advocate of his elevation, who for fifteen years has traversed the South in the interests of universal education, than whom no one has a better acquaintance with the schools of that section, bears cogent and trustworthy testimony, to which I give my emphatic endorsement:

"It is high time that our heedless, undiscriminating, all-out-doors habit of giving money and supplies to the great invading army of southern solicitors should come to an end. Whatever of good has come from it is of the same nature as the habit of miscellaneous alms giving, which our system of associated charities is everywhere working to break up. It is high time that we understood that the one agency on which the negroes and nine-tenths of the white people in the South must rely for elementary instruction is the American common school. The attempt to educate 2,000,000 of colored and 3,000,000 of white American children in the South by passing around the hat in the North; sending driblets of money and barrels of supplies to encourage anybody and everybody to open a little useless private school; to draw on our Protestant Sunday schools in the North to build up among these people the church parochial system of elementary schools, which the clergy of these churches are denouncing; all this, and a great deal more that is still going on among us, with of course the usual exceptions, has had its day and done its work. The only reliable method of directly helping the elementary department of southern education is that our churches and benevolent people put themselves in touch with the common school authorities in all the dark places, urging even their poorer people to do more, as they can do more, than at present. The thousand dollars from Boston that keeps alive a little private or denominational school in a southern neighborhood, if properly applied would give two additional months, better teaching and housing to all the children, and unite their people as in no other way. Let the great northern schools in the South established for the negroes be reasonably endowed and worked in co-operation with the public school system of the State, with the idea that in due time they will all pass into the hands of the southern people, each dependent on its own constituency for its permanent support. I believe, in many instances, it would be the best policy to endow or aid southern schools that have grown up at home and have established themselves in the confidence of the people. While more money should every year be given in the North for southern education, it should not be scattered abroad, but concentrated on strategic points for the uplifting of both races."

✓   ✓   ✓

Many white leaders believed that the Negro child needed a type of education different from that of the white child. Booker T. Washington belonged to this group, as did Thomas Nelson Page, from whose book, *The Negro: The Southerner's Problem*, Charles Scribner's Sons, New York, 1904, pp. 303-310, the following is quoted.

Now, as to the form of education which will be of most value to the Negroes and of most value to the South—for the two, instead of being opposed to each other, as according to our self-righteous critics, we appear to believe, are bound up in one.

Unhappily, the system of education heretofore pursued with the Negroes has been so futile in its results that a considerable proportion of Southerners, knowing the facts against all the assertion of Negro leaders, and all the clamor of those outside the South who are ignorant of the facts, believe sincerely that the educated are more worthless and dangerous to the welfare and peace of the community in which they live than the uneducated. . . .

It is, undoubtedly, true that the apparent result of the effort to educate the Negro has been disappointing. There are a few thousand professional men, a considerable number of college or high school graduates, but, for the greater part, there is discernible little apparent breadth of view, no growth in ability, or tendency to consider great questions reasonably. There is, indeed, rather a tendency to racial solidarity in opposition to the whites on all questions whatsoever; continued failure to distinguish soundly between outward gifts and character; a general inclination to deny crime and side with criminals against the whites, no matter how flagrant the crime may be. There is, moreover, a not rare belief among the whites that the preachers and leaders contribute to increase these tendencies and teach hostility rather than try to uplift the race morally. This view is held by a considerable section of the well-informed whites of the South. . . .

There are only two ways to solve the Negro problem in the South. One is to remove him; the other is to elevate him. The former is apparently out of the question. The only method, then, is to improve him.

In suggesting the method of education that will prove of greatest service, it is easier to criticize than to reform. Hitherto, the idea has been to educate the Negro race just as the white race is educated; that is, to give him book education and "turn him loose." There was, it is true, no field except the curious politics of the time in which the Negro could exercise his powers, based on such an education. The whites did not want this; the Negroes could not use it; but this made no difference with those who had the matter in charge. Education was understood to be ability to show book-learning. With this meagre equipment, the "educated Negro" rushed into politics, or into the pulpit, which mainly was but another name for the same thing. Sentiment, however, demanded that the Negro should be placed on an equality with the whites, and other conditions were left out of the account, with disheartening results. It is axiomatic to say that the education given to the Negro should be of the kind which will benefit him most. A few plain principles may be stated: He should be taught that one of the strongest elements in racial development is purity of family life; he should be taught that the duties of citizenship are much more than the ability to cast a ballot, or even to hold an office; that elevation to superiority among the people of his own race is of far greater moment to him at this time than external equality with another race, and that true superiority is founded on character. He should be taught to become self-sustaining, self-reliant, and self-respecting. A people, like a class, to advance must be either strong enough to make its way against all hostility, or must secure the friendship of others, particularly of those nearest it. If the Negro race in the South proposes, and is powerful enough to overcome the white race, let it try this method—it will soon find out its error; if not, it must secure the friendship of that race. Owing to conditions, the friendship and the sympathy of the Southern section of that race are almost as much more important to the Negro race than is that of the North, as the friendship of the latter is more important than that of the yet more distant Canadian section of the white race.

The best way—perhaps the only way—for the Negro race to progress steadily is to secure the sympathy and aid of the Southern whites. It will never do this until the race solidarity of the Negroes is broken and the Negroes divide on the same grounds on which the whites divide; until they unite with the whites and act with them on questions which concern the good of the section in which they both have their most vital interests. . . .

✓   ✓   ✓

William E. Burghardt DuBois was a militant adherent of Negro equality. A great Negro scholar, Northern born and educated, he devoted his life to the advancement of his race. In 1903 he wrote "The Talented Tenth," an essay in the collection entitled *The Negro Problem,* James Pott and Company, New York (A Series of Articles by Representative American Negroes of Today).

The Negro race, like all races, is going to be saved by its exceptional men. The problem of education, then, among Negroes must first of all deal with the Talented Tenth; it is the problem of developing the Best of this race that may guide the Mass away from the contamination and death of the Worst, in their own and other races. Now the training of men is a difficult and intricate task. Its technique is a matter for educational experts, but its object is for the vision of seers. If we make money the object of man-training, we shall develop money-makers but not necessarily men; if we make technical skill the object of education, we may possess artisans but not, in nature, men. Men we shall have only as we make manhood the object of the work of the schools—intelligence, broad sympathy, knowledge of the world that was and is, and of the relation of men to it—this is the curriculum of that Higher Education which must underlie true life. On this foundation we may build bread winning, skill of hand and quickness of brain, with never a fear lest the child and man mistake the means of living for the object of life. . . .

How then shall the leaders of a struggling people be trained and the hands of the risen few strengthened? There can be but one answer: The best and most capable of their youth must be schooled in the colleges and universities of the land. We will not quarrel as to just what the university of the Negro should teach or how it should teach it—I willingly admit that each soul and each race-soul needs its own peculiar curriculum. But this is true: A university is a human invention for the transmission of knowledge and culture from generation to generation, through the training of quick minds and pure hearts, and for this work no other human invention will suffice, not even trade and industrial schools. All men cannot go to college but some men must; every isolated group or nation must have its yeast, must have for the talented few centers of training where men are not so mystified and befuddled by the hard and necessary toil of earning a living, as to have no aims higher than their bellies and no God greater than Gold. This is true training, and thus in the beginning were the favored sons of the freed-men trained. Out of the colleges of the North came, after the blood of war, Ware, Cravath, Chase, Andrews, Bumstead and Spence to build the foundations of knowledge and civilization in the black South. Where ought they to have begun to build? At the bottom, of course, quibbles the mole with his eyes in the earth. Aye! truly at the bottom, the very bottom; at the bottom of knowledge, down in the very depths of knowledge there where the roots of justice strike into the lowest soil of Truth. And so they did begin; they founded colleges, and up from the colleges shot normal schools, and out from the normal schools went teachers, and around the normal schools clustered other teachers to teach the public schools; the college trained in Greek and Latin and mathematics, 2,000 men; and these men trained 50,000 others in morals and manners, and they in turn taught thrift and the alphabet to nine millions of men, who to-day hold $300,000,000 of property. It was a miracle—most wonderful peace-battle of the 19th century, and yet to-day men smile at it, and in fine superiority tell us that it was all a strange mistake; that a proper way to found a system of education is first to gather the children and buy them spelling books and hoes; afterward men may look about for teachers, if haply they may find them; or again they would teach men Work, but as for Life—why, what has Work to do with Life, they ask vacantly? . . .

The college-bred Negro is, as he ought to be, the group leader, the man who sets the ideals of the community where he lives, directs its thoughts and heads its social movements. It need hardly be argued that the Negro people need social leadership more than most groups; they have no traditions to fall back upon, no long established customs, no strong family ties, no well defined social classes. All these things must be slowly and painfully evolved. The preacher was, even before the war, the group leader of the Negroes, and the church their greatest institution. Naturally this preacher was ignorant and often immoral, and the problem of replacing the older type by better educated men has been a difficult one. Both by direct work and by direct influence on other preachers, and on congregations, the college-bred preacher has an opportunity for reformatory work and moral inspiration, the value of which cannot be overestimated.

It has, however, been in the furnishing of teachers that the Negro college has found its peculiar function. Few persons realize how vast a work, how mighty a revolution has been accomplished. To furnish five millions and more of ignorant people with teachers of their own race and blood, in one generation, was not only a very difficult undertaking, but a very important one, in that, it placed before the eyes of almost every Negro child an attainable ideal. It brought the masses of the blacks in contact with modern civilization, made black men the leaders of their communities and trainers of the new generation. In this work college-bred Negroes were first teachers, and then teachers of teachers. And here it is that the broad culture of college work has been of peculiar value. Knowledge of life and its wider meaning, has been the point of the Negro's deepest ignorance, and the sending out of teachers whose training has not been simply for bread winning, but also for human culture, has been of inestimable value in the training of these men.

✓   ✓   ✓

The following description of a typical Negro school in a rural section early in the twentieth century illustrates the shallowness of this educational process at that time. It is from Thomas Pearce Bailey, *Race Orthodoxy in the South,* Neale Publishing Company, New York, 1914, pp. 273ff. The author was a professor of education, superintendent of schools in Memphis, Dean of the Department of Education at the University of Mississippi, etc. This report describes a Negro rural school in Mississippi.

We started, the County Superintendent and I, at halfpast eight in the morning on a hot day in August. The school was four miles distant from the county seat. On the way we met negro children of various sizes and complexions wending their leisurely way to school. When we were returning, at about ten-thirty a.m., some of the pupils were still unconcernedly straggling to school. At the schoolhouse I saw several groups come in. None showed the slightest embarrassment. All said, Good Morning. Their coming in and their greeting produced no effect whatever on either teacher or pupils. The county superintendent did not seem to think it in the realm of possibility to bring about any improvement in punctuality. The parents are "free American citizens." If hurried or harried on the subject of punctuality, they usually, it is said, prefer having their children quit school to having themselves or their children hurried. . . .

The schoolhouse is in a pleasant grove, close by a negro church. . . . The church and the schoolhouse were apparently substantial buildings. Although the windows of the schoolhouse were not higher than a tall man's chin, they extended to the floor, and with the aid of front and back doors, gave fairly good ventilation. There were no desks. The children sat on wooden benches, some of which were grouped in the rear of the room and some placed along the windows. The children "lined up" to recite. Each had a "number" given him or her. The reason for this could not be discovered, for no reference was made to the numbers after they had been assigned, except that the teacher became rather severe in his language if a pupil could not give his number when called upon for it. Perhaps he was trying to teach attention and obedience to command.

I have already intimated that the range of ages in the three or four grades of the school was between four and eighteen. The teacher said that sixty were in attendance; I suppose he meant that there were sixty "a-comin' and a-gwyne!"

Some of the children were atrociously filthy and ragged; others were fairly neat and clean. Most of them were African in color and feature. However, practically none of them looked like the pictures of the lower African type that one sees in popular books on ethnology. Not a few had fairly pleasing, regular features, though of the higher African type. No difference in mental brightness could be detected between the pure negroes and the mixed types. The most intelligent face I saw was that of an apparently full-blooded little negro girl. There was not a harsh voice in the room; the tones were soft and musical. The children seemed to pay little attention to the presence of white strangers. Sometimes a child would "study out loud," but seemingly without disturbing the work of the others. The children moved about freely, but noiselessly, without asking permission. In fact, they were un-conventionally easy in their manners. Apparently not a ripple of interest was excited when a boy came in with a bundle of able-bodied switches which he handed to the teacher, who selected one and used it as a pointer. I could detect no mischievous talking and laughing. Perhaps there had been a letting-off of steam before we entered. And perhaps our presence and the timely appearance of the switches produced the effect of salutary peace.

One of the most noticeable phenomena I observed, one which is con-stantly to be noted, was the unhurried flow of the children's movements, without sign of articulate sharpness or angularity or self-conscious awkward-ness. The thought came to me, How impossible it is to decide how much of the negro's assumed lack of resentment is due to his easy, smooth "Brer Rabbit" manners! How easy it is for us to misunderstand an alien people! There is such a quality as tactful and astute childlikeness.

The teacher was very methodical as to ritual, and absolutely without intel-lectual method. He lined up the children; he numbered them; he was punctilious in placing the reciter in front of the class and in requiring the rhythmic following of the leader as he sang: "Twenty, twenty-one, twenty-two, etc.; thirty-one, etc.; forty, forty-one, etc. No attempt was made to count by tens; most of the time was wasted in going over the digits, with which all were familiar. About half the class would make absurd mistakes with the sequence of tens. One put ninety after twenty. Another went back to forty after having reached sixty. The class repeated the errors in chorus, after which the teacher allowed corrections. By means of some intuition which I do not understand, the teacher would announce from time to time to the reciter: "That's as far as you can go; that will do." I did not see any blackboard work. There was a very small piece of blackboard of some description in one corner of the room. Here, as in other respects educational, the negro gets his minimum—"good enough for the niggers." If the white men of the county were asked whether the schools of the negroes had enough blackboard space, they would be likely to reply—as some have replied: "Enough for the kind of pupils and teachers that use them."

The reading of a "third reader" class was instructive—to me. The seven children had one and a part books. To all appearances, there was not a third enough books to use in the school. The teacher said that "the books had not *come.*" I don't believe that the books had any intention of coming. . . .

The teacher spent most of the reading period in having the children spell out the new words from the reader as the book was passed from hand to hand. If the teacher himself had a reader, he did not use it, but stood behind each pupil as the child tried to read. However, the children *could* read a little. I wonder why! And the superintendent says that this teacher who, with great difficulty, after several trials, succeeds in getting the lowest (third-grade) certificate, teaches about as well as the holders of first-grade certificates. I was told that the teacher was a reputable, excellent fellow,—and he looked the part. I want to find out from him how he can dress so well on less than one hundred and twenty dollars a year. His shining laundered collar and cuffs, glistening alpaca coat, striped trousers, well-blacked shoes, would have passed muster anywhere. Although he came out to meet us as we arrived, and accompanied us to the buggy as we were leaving, the superintendent did not present him to me; nor was any word of farewell uttered.

In some Southern cities the negro principals are called "Mr." and are duly introduced to strangers; but my friend, the county superintendent, was natural and logical in making no pretense of departing from the social *facts* of the case; who should blame him? And who can blame him for spending on the negro schools proportionately only from one-tenth to one-twentieth of his time? His chances for reelection would be faint indeed if he "wasted his time on niggers." He is a compassionate, Christian man; but facts are facts, "niggers are niggers," and the belief of the average Southerner in the literary education of the negro is less than half-hearted. Most Southerners are perfectly willing to be "shown" that the negro should be educated; but attempts to prove this by pointing out the absence of a select class of negroes from the penitentiary does not convince them. The alleged existence of a higher percentage of bare literacy in the penitentiary of South Carolina, for instance, than exists outside in that state, more than offsets what one might urge in favor of a crude smattering of literary education for the negroes.

I think that this rural school is fairly typical; in some respects (building, for instance) it is superior to most of the negro country schools that I have seen. Now, if you ask me frankly whether the kind of education I see in a school like this is really worth anything, I find it hard to reply, although I believe in the education of every human being to the limit of his capacity.

Surely it would be worth while to prove to the Southerner that the education of the negro masses is worth while, and that it would pay the South and the country at large to spend vastly more than we do in training negro rural teachers and in equipping negro rural schools. But I confess that the proof is neither self-evident nor easy.

✓   ✓   ✓

Great changes have taken place in Negro schools since Thomas Pearce Bailey wrote the above account. Don C. Shoemaker, editor of the Asheville *Citizen*, in a nationally syndicated article, substituting for Robert S. Allen, discussed the Negro schools of the state of North Carolina. The following extract is from the Asheville *Citizen*, September 22, 1953.

The [North Carolina] Constitution sets forth: "Religion, morality and knowledge being necessary to good government and the happiness of mankind, schools and the means of education shall forever be encouraged."

As for segregation, it is embedded in the same Constitution, but the segregation clause is followed by another which says: "There shall be no discrimination in favor of, or to the prejudice of, either race. . . ."

Negro school teachers, of whom there are 7,872 in North Carolina, actually are paid more—$80 a year on the average classroom level—than white teachers.

This is because 98 per cent of the Negro elementary teachers . . . hold Class A certificates. But one question both Negroes and whites ask is, "If segregation is abolished, what would happen to those 7,872 well-paying jobs? . . . .

Ex-Governor W. Kerr Scott appointed a Negro, Dr. Harold Trigg, to the State Board of Education, where he still sits—in what is probably the highest ranking post of its kind held by a Negro in the South.

Educational opportunity has also improved for Negro college students, who now may enter some specialized schools, such as the law school at the formerly all-white (though it had Negro students during Reconstruction days!) University of North Carolina. The State maintains five teacher, technical, and liberal arts colleges for Negroes. Thirty years ago there were 295 Negroes enrolled in public and private colleges. By 1949-50 there were 8,898. . . .

Moreover, Negro participation in the public schools at the all-important high school level is nigh onto phenomenal. There was a 75.8 per cent increase in Negro high schools in the last seven years against a white increase of 43 per cent. In fact, for all schools, elementary and secondary, the Negro's proportion of nearly 30 per cent of the total enrollment is in excess of his population ratio. . . .

Spending or planning to spend perhaps 45 to 50 per cent of State building funds for a Negro minority of 26 per cent, North Carolina thinks it is doing right well on its own to meet the problem within its own accustomed social system.

✐   ✐   ✐

Mr. J. B. Frizell, Director of Education, Edinburgh, Scotland, made a tour of America on an intensive study of education in this country. He wrote a series of articles for *The Scotsman of Edinburgh,* from which the following was quoted in the Raleigh *News and Observer,* March 1, 1954.

Not all the States affected by the segregation cases then under consideration [by the Supreme Court] are as generous as Tennessee or as enlightened as the city of Chattanooga, where the provision for Negro children is so praiseworthy and where every effort is made to blend together the principals and staffs of schools for whites and schools for Negroes into a team, for the advancement of the education of all children and where the standard of work and modern progressive methods are so admirable in both systems.

As an earnest of their determination to provide equal facilities the Board of Education in that city are erecting a great new Negro high school standing on some 40 acres of land and costing 2,800,000 dollars, which will provide for children from the first grade to college preparatory level. When it is completed there will be few schools to equal it in the whole country. The utmost care and thought in professional and lay circles has gone into its design.

19

Religion

Orthodox religion is characteristic of the South in the twentieth century just as it was at the start of the nineteenth century. One of the valuable studies of Southern life is *Culture in the South,* edited by W. T. Couch, University of North Carolina Press, 1934. The following excerpts from that book are quoted from the chapter, "Religion of the South," by Edwin McNeill Poteat, Jr., pp. 250ff.

The South had been solid politically for a long time. So strong is this traditional solidarity in the nation that there is seldom any question as to how the South will vote in national elections. . . . The South is religiously solid in much the same way. As the South is solid, the North and West are fluid. Political and religious heresy in other sections . . . may be regarded as enlightenment or liberalism. In the South heresy is still heresy with the vast majority of people. That is to say that the religious South exhibits a more homogeneous quality than other sections. . . . People still go to church, support church enterprises, make much of their ministers. They still in the main submit readily to demagogy in the pulpit, and enjoy the thrill of denominational competition.

How account for this . . . difference? There is the much advertised southern temperament. It is notably hospitable, it is emotional and romantic; it is lazy. If climate has induced these qualities, an easy excuse is at hand for the defections it has caused. The cause, however, seems to lie further back. It is striking to observe that the first settlers of the southern states were more of a type, racially and religiously, than was the case with New England, for example. Racially they were mainly from the stock of England. . . . There were a few Huguenots, Moravians, Salzburgers, and others in North and South Carolina and Georgia, a few early Spanish in Florida and French in the Mississippi delta. Their influence has dominated some localities, but in considering the whole region, they have been relatively unimportortant. . . .

[The] record of considerable conflict in the religious life of the North has found its way into our histories. . . .

The South, a vaster area in which communities were smaller and more scattered, escaped much of this conflict and seems to have created little of its own. . . . Episcopal influence was strongest in the South and there were no clergymen in that fellowship who could match the fervor of Jonathan Edwards or stir revolt against Calvinist extremes through the passion of pulpit utterance. . . . Perhaps the languid climate helped to hush debate; perhaps it was easier to move into uninhibiated spaces and establish a new settlement than to stay at home and quarrel about theology. . . .

The South, moreover, was agrarian, and its one staple crop was cotton. The consequences of this fact were—and still are—far reaching. Cotton created an aristocracy and demanded slavery. It became the arbiter of fashion and the register of wealth. It gave to religion a weird and haunting ardor through the Negroes' sharing its worship and interpretation.

With the coming of the Civil War every northern and southern interest was cleft sharply. The bitterness of that strife left the South suspicious of northern culture, politics, and religion and intensified its loyalty to what it had come to feel was uniquely its own. The preachers who thundered abolition from Yankee pulpits were apostates. There heresy was met by an elaborate and furious defense of slavery from the Holy Scriptures. . . . After the war missionaries from the North to southern Negroes found themselves socially outcast among the whites. The Ku Klux Klan enlisted under its sheets many a Baptist and Methodist parson who could boast of its saving grace among the carpetbaggers and their followers. During the stormy days when white supremacy was a political issue, its enthusiasm spilled over into religious attitudes and finally created a situation which often found white Christians acting like pagans toward their black brethren.

It was inevitable that religion should have shared the "backwardness" of the South in the post-bellum decades. A zeal for the old orthodoxy was a part of the reluctance of the southerners to lose the old aristocratic tradition in society. . . .

[The protestant minister in the South] is withal a good sort. He is agreeable company, he exercises a genial and beneficent influence where he goes. Once in a while he becomes pompous and affects an artificial tone of voice. But he is all right. He comprehends baseball; he can cast a fly for bass; his fund of good clean stories is well-nigh inexhaustible. He can enliven nearly any gathering with an exhortation or an anecdote. He is welcomed in homes; he is offered a place on the platform on almost every occasion; he invokes divine blessing on barbecue and ballot; he is a valued customer in the shops; he complains little and praises much; his generosity is proverbial and his demands a minimum. He can ill be dispensed with for all his declining importance in modern life. . . .

A study of the denominational press of the South and the doctrinal statements of the various denominations recalls a marked accord in the fundamental tenets which they preach. In spite of considerable ecclesiastical differences the theology of the South is the same in its broad essentials among all the religious groups. Whether one meets in a Quaker Meeting House in Guilford County, North Carolina, or in a Methodist Church in Savannah, or in St. Louis Cathedral in New Orleans, the basal religious philosophy is the same. Scratch any sectarian skin and the same orthodox blood flows. . . . [The] unorthodox theological sects exist in quite as unimportant numbers as do the unorthodox denominational or federated churches. . . . Only seven per cent of the Unitarian Churches in the country are in the South—25 out 353. And of the Christian Science churches in the United States totaling 1,913 only 259 are in the South, or a ratio of approximately 13 per cent.

Another feature of this fidelity to traditional doctrine is the distrust of the "social gospel" and the almost exclusive concern for individual salvation as opposed to social reform. This has resulted in extraordinary restriction of the social vision of the ministry. . . . The impact of Christianity has either been feeble or its contact cushioned as it has touched race relationships, industry, business, politics, and the like; and there is a pretty general feeling among Christians that preachers had far better let social fires alone and keep to the business of saving individual brands from burning.

✠   ✠   ✠

As more of the Southern population moved to mill towns, villages, and cities, their devotion to religion was even more apparent than it was in rural areas. In this respect urban centers in the South exhibited a tendency opposite to that in other regions. Holland Thompson, *From Cotton Field to Mill Town,* The Macmillan Company, New York, 1906, pp. 174-178, described the religious life of the mill towns.

The churches are, next to the mill itself, the chief centers of community life. The largest in membership are the Methodist and the Baptist. The Presbyterians and the Lutherans have organizations at some mills. The Episcopal church has never had a hold upon the rural population of the middle and western sections of the state, and prejudice against it has been assiduously cultivated. The number of Roman Catholics is negligible.

The power of the church is perhaps greatest in those communities where a large proportion of the operatives is fresh from the country. Often the manager may act as superintendent of the Sunday school, and use his powerful influence to aid the organization. At some mills the corporation itself acts as collecting agent and deducts from the wages the subscriptions which have been made for the support of the work. As a result of this policy, the ministers, who are often men of ability, receive their salaries promptly.

The idea of an institutional church has gained no ground. The church authorities are conservative. The methods used in the country have not been changed to meet the new conditions. Two sermons on Sunday, a weekly prayer meeting, and the Sunday school are universal. Perhaps there is a missionary society among the women or a "Parsonage Aid Society," and some organization of the young people. These, however, meet with opposition among some of the older members who hold that no organization within the church itself is justified. Some of the Sunday schools have small libraries. The books are usually bought in bulk, however, and are more distinguished for ethical and doctrinal soundness than for literary value.

Old-fashioned orthodox sermons are the rule. The terrors of a literal burning hell, the joys of the righteous hereafter, are expounded with fervor. The emphasis is laid upon the life to come, and upon renunciation of the world, rather than upon a broader, fuller life upon the earth. One minister in charge of a cotton mill church in a burst of impatience exclaimed to me that the mill managers did not wish the thinking powers of their operatives developed, but did wish them to be very religious. This statement is not entirely justified, but undoubtedly the value of religion as an aid to discipline is fully recognized.

Frequent "revivals" are held by the Methodists and Baptists. The churches are filled every night for a week or more, and the services often last until a very late hour. A strange mixture of methods prevails. The "mourner's bench" at which those "convicted of sin" may kneel, and the invitation to shake the hand of the minister as a token of conversion, are both used. The Moody and Sankey hymns, and the old tunes full of haunting minor chords which have done duty at camp-meetings for a century, are heard. Members kneel beside their young friends or move about exhorting them to "come to the altar." The air is electric with emotion, and the old-fashioned type of "shouting Methodist" is not yet extinct.

The pastors of these churches are earnest men, who work faithfully for their charges; but the task is discouraging. Pastoral visiting is unsatisfactory, as often the whole family is never together except on Sunday, and the mother is busy when the call is made. If one family receives a disproportionate share of pastoral attention, the others are jealous. Infinite tact is required, and many ministers avoid so far as possible the care of factory churches.

In spite of all the efforts, the testimony is universal that they are losing their hold upon the mill population. The migratory families neglect to bring letters of dismissal from their former churches, and gradually lose interest in church work. With the increased incidental opportunities for association with their fellows the church services are no longer so important from a social standpoint. In the country, the monthly or semi-monthly services afforded an excellent opportunity to meet acquaintances and friends, who were seldom seen elsewhere. Then, too, the workers are tired on Sunday, and the day is more and more devoted to rest and recreation.

✓ ✓ ✓

William Archer, an Englishman who toured the South, reported in 1910 the fundamentals of the Southern theology. The following portion is from his *Through Afro-America,* Chapman and Hall, London, 1910, pp. 73-75.

The South is by a long way the most simply and sincerely religious country that I was ever in. It is not, like Ireland, a priest-ridden country; it is not, like England, a country in which the strength of religion lies in its social prestige; it is not like Scotland, a country steeped in theology. But it is a country in which religion is a very large factor in life, and God is very real and personal. In other countries men are apt to make a private matter of their religion, in so far as it is not merely formal; but the Southerner wears his upon his sleeve. There is a simple sincerity in his appeal to religious principle which I have often found really touching. I have often, too, been reminded of that saying of my Pennsylvanian friend: "The South may be living in the twentieth century, but it has skipped the nineteenth." The Southerner goes to the Gospels for his rule of life, and has never heard of Nietzsche; yet I am wholly unable to discover how the system of race-discriminations is reconcilable with the fundamental precepts of Christianity. It is far easier to find in the Old Testament the justification of slavery than in the New Testament the justification of the Jim Crow car, the white and black school, and the white and black church. This is not necessarily a condemnation of the Southerner's attitude; I do not think that the colour problem was foreseen in the New Testament. Christianity is one thing, sociology another, and the Southerner's logical error, perhaps, lies in not keeping the distinction clear. But I am sure there are many sincere and earnest Christians in the South who will scarce be at ease in heaven unless they enter it, like a Southern railway station, through a gateway marked "For Whites."

✓   ✓   ✓

Similar observations were written by Maurice Evans, *Black and White in the Southern States,* a study of the race problem in the United States from a South African point of view, Longmans, Green and Company, London, 1915. The following selection is from pp. 66-67.

All through the South one sees evidence of religious observance. William Archer in "Afro-America" goes so far as to say it is the most simply and sincerely religious community he ever was in. In the towns churches are numerous, and often large and well built in proportion to the population. In the country one passes little frame churches at frequent intervals. Several times I met on the trains bands of young people wearing badges and rosettes, who belonged to religious organizations, Sunday School Unions, and the like, who had been attending Conferences. I attended many Church services, mostly of those belonging to denominations holding Evangelical views, which form the majority in the South. In England and the Colonies at the present day one seldom hears sermons and addresses which denote an absolute acceptance of the Evangelical doctrine of our fathers, preached in its entirety, with full stress laid on punishment as on reward. Modern criticism and latter day tolerance have modified it, and even if the creed or catechism be nominally accepted, the emphasis is not where it was when I was a boy. I found the South had not departed so far from the pure doctrine, and heard sermons there such as I remember long ago, pressing home future punishment in materialistic detail; the wrath to come, the danger of delay. The attendance was generally good, with a great proportion of women, but with a larger number of men than one usually sees in England and the Colonies in these days. Once when attending such a service and looking round at the staid and devout worshippers, I remembered the facts of a lynching that had taken place in the neighborhood, and could not help wondering whether any of those I saw with bowed heads had been present, and what their views on such an occurrence would be. I felt the discords and antagonisms that everywhere go to make up our human nature. But the contrast is not often forcibly brought home to one. I never saw a Negro in these churches, they have their separate organizations, managed entirely by themselves. . . .

Before Emancipation the white churches in the South supported the institution of slavery, and numerous clerical writers could be cited who attempted to prove from Scripture that it was of Divine origin and had the Divine sanction. To-day there are their descendants, Christian ministers who condone if they do not approve lynching, and who turn to the Scripture to prove that the Negro is, and always will be, an inferior, and attempt thus to justify discrimination and repression. To the Negrophilist and humanitarian of Western Europe this sounds the rankest hypocrisy. But the Southerner is not the only man who clips his religion to suit his peculiar sins and environment.

✓   ✓   ✓

That the church is one of the most important forces in Southern rural life was concluded by S. H. Hobbs, Jr., in his book, *Church and Community in the South*. This study of 71 rural communities was prepared by the Institute for Research in Social Science of the University of North Carolina and published in mimeographed form by the Presbyterian Committee of Publication, John Knox Press, Richmond, 1949. The following extracts are quoted from Chapter 3, and are used by permission of the publisher.

In order to get a picture of the rural church situation in the South, let us look at a few communities. The following material is taken from digests of rural social surveys.

The trend in the South as elsewhere was for the opening of more churches in villages with a decline in the number of open-country churches. The average membership of both village and country churches increased, resulting in part from elimination of some of the smaller churches. The South also had the highest percentage of inactive members of village and country Protestant churches. Four-fifths of all the rural churches in the United States with buildings worth less than $1,500 are in the South.

The church is the principal social organization in the rural southern community. Churches are numerous in most rural areas of the region; in fact, they are usually too numerous, although competition and conflict among the rural churches have declined considerably in recent years. The large number of churches and the lack of resident ministers prevent their providing moral leadership in many communities. Indeed, the inefficient and unorganized programs of the church are often the source of low community morale. The church should emphasize a better social and economic life for the community through better farming, soil conservation, and improved recreational facilities. Ministers should be better prepared including a knowledge of agriculture techniques, and their salaries should be supported by the parent church when necessary. This will enable the church to get a good man as minister.

Coffee County, Alabama, has 118 churches, 86 for whites, and 32 for Negroes. Thirteen are in urban areas and the remainder in the open country or smaller communities. Recently there has been a considerable development of newer denominations, like the Holiness and Pentecostal church, etc. Only a small proportion of the total population goes to church. The average congregation has about sixty persons at each service with some having as few as twenty. It appears that about one-fifth of the rural white population goes to church regularly. Church attendance has declined. It is claimed that in addition to the effect of a declining population and the attraction of the urban church the rural churches of Coffee county are declining. . . .

The churches of Covington County, Mississippi, function chiefly on a neighborhood basis. There is a church to every seven square miles, and one for every 182 persons over ten years of age. 58 of the 76 churches in the county are in the open country. Church buildings were in bad repair. There was only one resident minister in the whole county. . . .

Among white residents Harmony Baptist Church (Georgia) is by far the most important institution in the country next to the family and most families are members of it. Services were held one Sunday each month and revival services once a year. The pastor was non-resident and untrained. The church had three organizations—a Sunday School, a Young People's Union, and a Woman's Missionary Union. Most members agreed that the influence of the church had declined. The Jefferson Baptist Church was in the forefront among the institutions for Negroes in the community. Preaching services were held once a month. Prayer meetings were held every Saturday and Sunday school was scheduled once a week. Members were required to attend services regularly but their interests had waned. . . .

In Beaverdam community, Virginia, next to the general store, the church was the most characteristic neighborhood institution. Churches were to be found in six neighborhoods. Approximately four out of every five white families in the community had one or more members attending church. Most of those families not participating in church attendance were from the lowest income classes. Church participation in the area had a tendency to be grouped by social caste and class. . . .

Of the 61 religious groups, that is, churches and related organizations studied in Cumberland County, Tennessee, over a third were Baptist. Church worship was held weekly by 12 per cent of the population; every two weeks by 40 per cent; monthly by 24 per cent of the churches; and intermittently by the remainder. All churches, with the exception of 5 per cent, had a Sunday school: only 5 per cent of the churches considered social activities a major function of the church. . . .

In the rural areas of Kentucky, all preachers are poorly prepared to do effective work. The funeral meeting, in which itinerant preachers hold service for all who have died since the last meeting, is the social event of the year. The meetings are held in the spring and fall of the year. . . .

The Catholic Church (south Louisiana) is the nucleus of the entire community. Practically the entire community goes to church services. The church provides weekly religious instruction to children between six and twelve years of age. . . .

In four counties in South Louisiana ninety per cent of the marsh dwellers are Catholic, at least nominally. Every locality has church services at least once a week, but attendance varies from place to place. A common characteristic is that the men consider religion something for women and children. . . .

Rural life conditions have undergone tremendous changes in the United States in the last few decades. Perhaps no institution has changed as little as the country church. Improved roads, the automobile, and other means of communication and transportation have annihilated distance. The mechanization of agriculture and agricultural education have transformed farming. The farm population has declined by approximately one-fourth since 1910. Rural needs have given us a type heretofore unknown, namely, the village which is the service station to the farmer. . . . The consolidated school has largely replaced the one-teacher school. Everywhere in rural America horizons are enlarging. This applies to everything except the country church. . . . If all . . . rural churches were thrown into a hopper and assorted according to size, the most numerous group would be those churches with one or two rooms supported by a slowly declining number of active members served by a non-resident minister, having but two organizations—an ungraded Sunday School and a ladies' aid society competing for new members with several other churches, some of which would be aided in the struggle by home mission grants. The above describes the average situation which practically all the denominations cling to tenaciously, and under which there can be no progress.

✓   ✓   ✓

To many of the colored people especially the church is an important force seven days a week. Maurice Evans, *Black and White in the Southern States,* Longmans,

Green and Company, London, 1915, pp. 114-120, gave a well-rounded picture of
this institution, the Negro church, as a social center.

Around the Church as a centre are aggregated all that goes to make up the
social life of the Negro, and social life means more to him than it does
to the more self-centered white man.

Until quite recently all the Negro people, men and women alike, were
Church members, and the great majority took an active part in religious
observance. Even those who were not regular in their attendance, or who
were backsliders, were not antagonistic, and might always be won back
to an ideal they had never abandoned.

To-day I heard from the older Negroes who had grown up in the faith,
and whose lives were closely knit to Church associations, many laments that
the younger ones were lax, indifferent and fond of pleasure, and too often
put pleasure first, and religious observance second. This note of disappointment is not of course peculiar to this generation, it was no doubt the plaint
of the elders in the days of the Ark of the Covenant, but it is probably truer
to-day than ever before. With the decay of old custom, with the invasion
of the South by modern ideas and practices which is bound to come, will
also come indifferentism, love of pleasure, and the chaffing at control, which
are so peculiarly characteristic of the present day.

Anything of the nature of philosophic doubt seems foreign to the Negro
character. I asked an intelligent mulatto who dwelt on the tendency to
forsake religion whether it is due in part to this cause, and his reply was
in the negative. They did not, he said, think enough to become atheists or
agnostics in the usual acceptance of the term. It is reported that a similar
question was put to an old-time Negro and he answered: "Golly no, it takes
some sense to be an atheist and niggers hasn't enough sense."

The common charge against Negro manifestations of religious feeling is
that it begins and ends in emotion, and that this emotion is a sensuous kind
begotten of his love of rhythmic, musical sound, and worked up to fervour
by the contagion of the crowd. His nervous force being thus drawn upon,
it exhausts itself, and there is little left for the works that should go with
the faith. It is charged against him, that even among the elect, a high
standard of morality does not accompany emotional fervour, and that even
gross immorality is frequent, and too often condoned.

Notwithstanding many theological colleges, the standard of learning and
conduct demanded by the congregations from their ministers is not high,
and lapses in one who may be other-wise acceptable, are looked upon lightly.
It is not difficult to find in the writings of Negroes themselves these weak-
nesses emphasized much more strongly than I have done, indeed some charge
the admittedly low standard among the people as a whole, to the absence
of high moral ideals among those holding the most influential positions
in Negro religious life.

Granting all this, I have no doubt but that the Negro Church has been an enormous power for good among the people, and has probably been the one force that has kept the race from utter stupefaction and degradation. Unable to find their satisfactions in the usual secular channels, finding little but hardship and restriction in their everyday life, and yet bursting with emotionalism, they grasped at the compensations of a life to come, when all toil and sorrow should be done away with, and everlasting joy, of a kind they could understand, would be the portion of all believers. No wonder the songs that dwelt on the golden streets, the harp and crown, and eternal rest, appealed to them, and that their prayers are full of yearning for this glorious hereafter.

Not only for his religious emotions, but for his social satisfactions has the Church been the solace of the Negro. I attended many services, and found in Sunday school and church, as well as the many other activities which clustered around them, an obvious satisfaction at the mere pleasure of being together; chatting conversations, a purring satisfaction in moving among their fellows, a personal importance in occupying recognized official positions, were obviously very pleasant to them. I found that debating societies, tea-parties, guilds, class-meetings, benevolent societies, and similar activities, filled up the week, while almost the whole of Sunday was taken up with services, the necessary intervals being largely occupied with sociability,—in meeting, walking, and talking.

Poor and naked indeed would the Negro have been had he not had his Church to fill in his life. While as compared with the nervous force he puts into his praise, prayer, and exhortations, the moral side is weak and often stumbling, still the Church does stand for morality, and the doctrine is preached that works should accompany faith. It cannot be doubted but that the Church has been in all respects a force for the uplifting of the Afro-American people. Unsatisfactory as are the results in many ways, still the imagination is shocked, when one thinks what this people might have been and become, had they not known, or been bereft of, this forcement and satisfaction.

The principal denominations favoured by the Negroes are of the Protestant Evangelical type, Baptists and Methodists of various kinds being in the ascendant. Some of these are nominally the same as the Northern bodies of the same name, Congregationalists, Wesleyan-Methodists, Presbyterians and others. These, however, include only a small portion of the total Negro worshippers; the majority belong to independent organizations, of which the principal are the Baptists, with about two and three-quarter million communicants, and the African Methodist Episcopal Church with over half a million members.

It is noteworthy that neither the Episcopal Church, as we understand it in England, nor the Roman Catholic communion has attracted the Negro. One would have thought that the more elaborate ritual, especially that of the latter, would have specially appealed to him, but such is not the case. In 1906 there were only 38,235 Negro Roman Catholics in the United States. In that year there were 3,685,067 Christian communicants of all sects, and the value of Church property owned by all the Negro Churches was $56,636,159.

Practically the whole of this vast organization is in the hands of the Negro people, and it is altogether managed by them, the whites evincing no interest in it. Probably the Negroes would resent interference with the management, although they would doubtless accept monetary assistance. This yielding to the black man in the domain of religion, is in marked contrast to the demand for white supremacy in all spheres of secular activity. A Negro says: "In politics, education, business, the white man manages and controls the Negroes' interests, it is only in the Church that the field is undisputed." It seems to me this is an illustration of the practical and material nature of the white temperament, the white man takes all that leads to power and wealth, and leaves to the black man the culture and control of his materially unfruitful emotions. . . .

My experience of Negro churches was chiefly in the towns, though I did visit religious gatherings in the country. Many of the churches in the cities are very large and well-built edifices. They are, naturally enough, copies of those belonging to similar denominations among the whites. I found that architecture, furniture, order of service, and all that went to make up the church organization were copies. I noticed the preponderance of women over men, which is so apparent in English and Colonial churches to-day, was not so marked in the Negro churches. Considering their positions in life, the congregations were remarkably well dressed, both men and women often attired in the extreme fashion. I have little doubt but that the love of display enters largely into the attractiveness of church attendance.

In these large Negro city churches the emotional displays, common in smaller and less conventional gatherings, were subdued, though interjections were much more frequent than in the white churches. The singing was a special feature, and when the congregation warmed up to it, was distinguished by power and rhythm. In one church the choir wore surplices and college caps.

Most of the discourses I heard were conventional, and did not bear the impress of deep thought, or even feeling; personal feeling, and in one case personal grievance at an alleged slight at Convocation, were introduced. One sermon, however, stands out as an exception. It was a powerful, restrained address on the duty of the race. It contained rebuke of apathy, and a plea for higher morality, and expecially denounced prevalent drinking habits, and the supine toleration by the coloured people of the evils inflicted on them by the whisky dealers, and the lack of public spirit when an attempt was made to obtain prohibition. It was delivered by a striking personality, a light-coloured mulatto, and was admirable in matter, delivery and earnestness. . . .

The Negro gives generously of his substance to build up and support his Church. The spirit of personal emulation is brought into play, and offerings are made in public. Members of the congregation come forward bearing their gifts, and as the warmth and emulation waxes, they often reappear or increase their donations. I met a man, a Southerner engaged in Evangelical work and the distribution of religious books, who contrasted their open-handedness with the niggardliness of the whites among whom he travelled. In one small town I find that, although the real and personal property of the Negroes only amounted to some $80,000, the Church property belonging to them cost nearly $28,000! I should think that of all people on earth professing the Christian religion they give more of their substance to Church work than any other, not even excluding the Roman Catholic population of Ireland.

✓   ✓   ✓

An interesting study of the sermons of Negro ministers in Macon County, Georgia, was made by a summer-session class of students in a Negro Teachers College. Macon County was chosen because the "Black Belt" was believed to have clung closely to the conditions of the days of slavery, and the county offered good examples of old-fashioned Negro preaching. The source of the following introduction is William H. Pipes, *Say Amen, Brother. Old-time Negro Preaching: A Study in American Frustration,* The William Frederick Press, New York, 1951, p. 1.

". . . the Negro church is the one institution where the colored people of the community are in full control. It is their own." (Quoted from Hortense Powdermaker, *After Freedom,* Viking Press, New York, 1939.) Also, in addition to the profoundly important religious urge, Negroes cling to the church because it serves a social purpose by being a center where friends meet. Whether a Christian or a sinner, the Negro attends church because it is often a substitute for the clubhouse, the amusement park, and the theatre. Negroes, "whether they derive any particular joy therefrom or not, . . . must go to church, to see their friends, as they are barred from social centers open to whites. They must attend church, moreover, to find out what is going on" (from C. G. Woodson, *History of the Negro Church,* Associated Publishers, Washington, D. C., 2nd edition, 1921, pp. 267-68). Many young Negroes, Christian or not, go to church partly to meet their sweethearts, to impress them, and to woo them in marriage. Many farmers go to church partly to learn of developments in the outside world.

"The old-time Negro preacher has not yet been given the niche in which he properly belongs. He has been portrayed only as a semi-comic figure. He had, it is true, his comic aspects, but on the whole he was an important figure, and at bottom a vital factor. . . . It was also he who instilled into the Negro the narcotic doctrine epitomized in the Spiritual, 'You May Have All Dis World, But Give Me Jesus.' This power of the old-time preacher, somewhat lessened and changed in his successors, is still a vital force; in fact, *it is still the greatest influence among the colored people of the United States*. The Negro today, is, perhaps, the most priest-governed group in the country."

✓   ✓   ✓

The author of the above-quoted book, *Say Amen, Brother*, made recordings of seven sermons as they were delivered in Negro churches in Macon County. The following is an excerpt from an impromptu sermon delivered at an all-day meeting where none of the ministers present knew which three would be chosen to deliver sermons. The minister in this case was blind, had finished the third grade in school, and had preached 28 years. At the time he delivered this sermon he was serving as pastor of four churches, pp. 37-38.

"WHY WE COME TO CHURCH"

I'm glad we could come together again to pray and thank God, observing His will. Praise His name. The reason we come together is to sing, pray and talk about God. We come to this fer de purpose of singing, praying and knowing that God is the Keeper. Yer hear His word; His word is good. You satisfy ter enjoy home and here, wherever God puts yer.

Yer know, I'm dis way. I believe in doing everything where it ought to be done at. I believe when you have a car, don't put no gas in no-no radiator; it don't belong dere. Put de water in de radiator; and the gas in the tank whar it belong, and it'll do good. Put things where dey don't belong, won't do no good; it'll do harm. Put everything in its own place.

And so as we assemble together, we couldn't honor a better man, greater man than He is. Greatest hero ever sat on the throne. He has great power throughout all ages. And the sweetness of His disposition in the hearts of many have caused us to have hope. He's the only man. . . . Only one fer us.

And whatever fer you all this morning, just hold yer cups, and whatever fer yer all, yer get it. Kinda like a mailcarrier or post-office: give yer whatever fer you. So jest keep everything waiting and we'll see what's gwine to come ter you.

Now *Rev.* ————, follow and gwine *Continue* the service fer you. The Lord say, "Open yer mouth and I'll speak fer you." See what the Spirit gwine do. Tryin' to preach the Word of God. Pray His will be done.   .   .   .

Following the delivery of the other two sermons, the first minister continued preaching.

Yer know, when us git hooked up here together, it's like a city and a town—ain't it?—when yer turn on de light. It's down in de corner stores and all behin' 'em and all over the house. It shine everwhar. Child of God'll shine anywhar you put it. Yer may git 'im bowed down, but he gon' shine anyhow! Ain't got no bread, but he'll shine anyhow! Ain't got no clothes, but he'll shine anyhow! Don't care how much yer talk 'bout 'im, he'll shine right on! Lay down at night; yer may . . . , but he'll shine right on! Git up in de mornin' he'll shine everwhar he go! Ever time yer look at 'im, he's shinin'! Ain't dat right?

. . . Now, we on our way home.

20

Literature of the New South

This chapter does not seek to cover the literature of the South since the Civil War. It merely presents a few excerpts which illustrate trends in Southern writing, traits of Southern character, and certain fictional types of character that are found in Southern literature, or that originated in Southern fiction. Several examples have been used in other parts of the present work. They may be located by reference to the index.

At the end of the Civil War the local color school of writing was popular. Southern authors of this group included George Washington Cable, who has been referred to (see p. 296), and James Lane Allen (see p. 228).

Among the group who wrote nostalgically of the Old South was Thomas Nelson Page, whose sentimental books in Negro dialect followed the pattern portrayed by Kennedy in the 1830's (see p. 156) and by Margaret Mitchell in the 1930's. The following extract is from "Marse Chan. A Tale of Old Virginia," which appeared first in *Century Magazine*, and then in his collection of tales, *In Ole Virginia*, Charles Scribner's Sons, New York, 1887, pp. 1-12, *passim*. In it he "viewed the feudal South in sentimental retrospect."

One afternoon, in the autumn of 1872, I was riding leisurely down the sandy road that winds along the top of the water-shed between two of the smaller rivers of eastern Virginia. The road I was travelling, following the "ridge" for miles, had just struck me as most significant of the character of the race whose only avenue of communication with the outside world it had formerly been. Their once splendid mansions, now fast falling to decay, appeared to view from time to time, set far back from the road, in proud seclusion, among groves of oak and hickory, now scarlet and gold with the early frost. Distance was nothing to this people; time was of no consequence to them. They desired but a level path in life, and that they had, though the way was longer, and the outer world strode by them as they dreamed.

I was aroused from my reflections by hearing someone ahead of me calling, "Heah! heah-whoo-oop, heah!"

Turning the curve in the road, I saw just before me a negro standing with a hoe and watering-pot in his hand. He had evidently just gotten over the "worm-fence" into the road, out of the path that led zigzag across the "old field" and was lost to sight in the dense growth of sassafras. When I rode up, he was looking anxiously back down this path for his dog. So engrossed was he that he did not even hear my horse, and I reined in to wait until he should turn around and satisfy my curiosity as to the handsome old place half a mile off from the road.

The numerous out-buildings and the large barns and stables told that it had once been the seat of wealth, and the wild waste of sassafras that covered the broad fields gave it an air of desolation that greatly excited my interest.

. . . .

[The traveller engaged the Negro in conversation about the place and its former occupants.]

"Marse Chan," said the darky, "he's Marse Channin'—my young marster; an' dem places—dis one's Weall's, an' de one back dyar wid de rock gate-pos's is ole Cun'l Chahmb'lin's. Dey don' nobody live dyar now, 'cep niggars. Arfter de war some one or nurr bought our place, but his name done kind o' slipped me. I nuver hearn on 'im befo'; I think dey's half-strainers. I don' ax none on 'em no odds. I lives down de road heah, a little piece, an' I jes' steps down of a evenin' and looks arfter de graves."

"Well, where is Marse Chan?" I asked.

"Hi! don' you know? Marse Chan, he went in de army. I was wid im. Yo' know he wanr' gwine an' lef' Sam.

"Will you tell me all about it?" I said, dismounting.

Instantly, and as if by instinct, the darky stepped forward and took my bridle. I demurred a little; but with a bow that would have honored Old Sir Roger, he shortened the reins, and taking my horse from me, led him along.

"Now tell me about Marse Chan," I said.

"Lawd, marster, hit's so long ago, I'd a'most forgit all about it, ef I hedn' been wid him ever sence he wuz born. Ez 'tis, I remembers it jes' like 'twuz yistiddy. Yo' know Marse Chan an' me—we wuz boys togerr. I wuz older'n he wuz, jes' de same ez he wuz whiter'n me. I wuz born plantin' corn time, de spring arfter big Jim an' de six steers got washed away at de upper ford right down dyar b'low de quarters ez he wuz a bringin' de Chris'mas things home; an Marse Chan, he warn' born tell mos' to de harves' . . . 'bout eight years arfterwoods.

"Well, when Marse Chan wuz born, dey wuz de grettes' doin's at home you ever did see. De folks all hed holiday, jes' like in de Chris'mas. Ole marster (we didn' call 'im *Ole* marster tell arfter Marse Chan wuz born—befo' dat he wuz jes' de marster, so)—well, ole marster, his face fayr shine wid pleasure, an' all de folks wuz mighty glad, too, 'cause dey all loved ole marster, an aldo' dey did step aroun' right peart when ole marster was lookin' at 'em, dyar warn' yar han' on de place but what, ef he wanted anythin', would walk up to de back poach, and say he warn' to see de marster. An' ev'body wuz talkin' 'bout de young marster, an' de maids an' de wimmens 'bout de kitchen wuz sayin' how 'twuz de purties chile dey ever see; an' at dinnertime de mens (all on 'em hed holiday) come roun' de poach an' ax how de missis an' de young marster wuz, an' ole marster come out on de poach an' smile wus'n a 'possum, an' sez, 'Thankee!' . . . .

"Well, you nuver see a chile grow so. Pres'n'y he growed up right big, an' ole marster sez he must have some edication. So he sont 'im to school to ole Miss Lawry down dyar, dis side o' Cun'l Chahmb'lin's, an' I use' to go 'long wid 'im an' tote he books an' we all's snacks; an' when he larnt to read an' spell right good, an' got 'bout so-o big, ole Miss Lawry she died, an' ole marster said he mus' have a man to teach 'im an' trounce 'im. So we all went to Mr. Hall, whar kep' de school-house beyant de creek, an dyar we went ev'y day, 'cept Sat'd'ys of co'se, an' sich days ez Marse Chan din warn' go, an' ole missis begger 'im off. . . . .

Dem wuz good ole times, marster—de bes' Sam ever see! Dey wuz, in fac'! Niggers didn' hed nothin' 't all to do—jes' hed to 'ten' to de feedin' an' cleanin' de hosses, an' doin' what de marster tell 'em to do; an' when dey wuz sick, dey had things sont 'em out de house, an' de same doctor come to see 'em what 'ten' to de white folks when dey wuz po'ly. Dyar warn' no trouble nor nothin'.

"Well, things tuk a change arfter dat. Marse Chan he went to de bo'din' school, whar he use' to read me de latters. . . .

"Den ole Marster he run for Congress, an' ole Cun'l Chahmb'lin he wuz put up to run 'g'indt ole marster by de Dimicrats; but ole marster he beat 'im. Yo' know he wuz gwine do dat! Dat made old Cun'l Chahmb'lin he sort o' got in debt, an' sell some o' he niggers, an' dat's de way de fuss begun. Dat's whar de lawsuit cum from. Ole marster he didn't like nobody to sell niggers, an' knowin' dat Cun'l Chahmb'lin was sellin' o' his, he writ an' offered to buy his M'ria an' all her chil'en, 'cause she hed married our Zeek'yel. An' don' yo' think, Cun'l Chahmb'lin axed old marster mo' 'n th'ee niggers wuz wuth fur M'ria! Befo' ole marster bought her, dough, de sheriff cum and levelled on M'ria an' a whole parecel o' urr niggers. Ole marster he went to de sale, an' bid for 'em; but Cun'l Chahmb'lin he got some one to bid 'g'inst ole marster. De wuz knocked out to ole marster dough, an den dey had a big lawsuit, an' ole marster was agwine to co't, aff an' on, fur some years, till at lars' de co't decided dat M'ria belonged to ole marster. Ole Cun'l Chahmb'lin den wuz so mad he sued ole marster for a little strip o' lan' down dyar on de line fence, whar he said belonged to 'im. Evy'body knowed hit belonged to ole marster. Ef yo' go down dyar now, I kin show it to yo', indiside de line fence, whar it hed done bin ever since long befo'

Cun'l Chahmb'lin wuz born. But Cun'l Chahmb'lin wuz a mons'us perseverin' man, an' ole marster he wouldn' let nobody run over 'im. No, dat he wouldn'! So dey wuz agwine down to co't about dat, fur I don' know how long, till ole marster beat 'im.

"All dis time, yo' know, Marse Chan wuz agoin' back'ads an' for'ads to college, an' wuz growed up a ve'y fine young man. He wuz a ve'y likely gent'man!

✓   ✓   ✓

Joel Chandler Harris wrote animal tales in the Negro dialect of Uncle Remus, the eighty-year-old story-teller and philosopher. Harris wrote in his introduction to *Uncle Remus,* D. Appleton Company, New York, 1886, pp. 1, 12.

My purpose has been to preserve the legends themselves in their original simplicity, and to wed them permanently to the quaint dialect—if, indeed, it can be called a dialect—through the medium of which they have become a part of the domestic history of every Southern family; and I have endeavored to give the whole a genuine flavor of the old plantation. . . . .

If the reader not familiar with plantation life will imagine that the myth-stories of Uncle Remus are told night after night to a little boy by an old negro who appears to be venerable enough to have lived during the period which he describes—who has nothing but pleasant memories of the discipline of slavery—and who has all the prejudices of caste and family that were the natural results of the system; if the reader can imagine all this, he will find little difficulty in appreciating and sympathizing with the air of affectionate superiority which Uncle Remus assumes as he proceeds to unfold the mysteries of plantation lore to a little child who is a product of that practical reconstruction which has been going on to some extent since the war in spite of the politicians. . . .

✓   ✓   ✓

Perhaps the best-known of the Uncle Remus stories is "The Wonderful Tar-Baby Story." It is quoted from the edition published by D. Appleton Company, New York, 1886, pp. 23-25.

"Didn't the fox *never* catch the rabbit, Uncle Remus," asked the little boy the next evening.

"He come mighty nigh it, honey, sho's you bawn—Brer Fox did. One day atter Brer Rabbit fool 'im wid dat calamus root, Brer Fox went ter wuk an got 'im some tar, en mix it wid some turkentime, en fix up a contrapshun wat he call a Tar-Baby, en he tuck dish yer Tar-Baby en he sot 'er in de big road, en he lay off in de bushes fer ter see wat de news waz gwinter be. En he didn't hatter wait long, nudder, kaze bimeby here come Brer Rabbit pacin' down de road—lippity-clippity-lippity, dez ez sassy ez a jay-bird. Brer

Fox, he lay low. Brer Rabbit come prancin' 'long twel he syp de Tar-Baby, en den he fotch up on his behime legs like he wuz 'stonished. De Tar-Baby, she sot dar, she did, en Brer Fox, he lay low.

" 'Mawnin'!' sez Brer Rabbit, sezee—'nice wedder dis mawnin',' sezee.

"Tar-baby ain't sayin' nuthin', en Brer Fox, he lay low.

" 'How duz yo' sym'tums seem ter segashuate?' sez Brer Rabbit, sezee.

"Brer Fox, he wink his eye slow, en lay low, en de Tar-Baby, she ain't sayin' nuthin'.

" 'How you come on, den? Is you deaf?' sez Brer Rabbit, sezee. 'Kaze if you is, I kin holler louder,' sezee.

"Tar-Baby stay still, en Brer Fox, he lay low.

" 'Youer stuck up, dat's w'at you is,' says Brer Rabbit, sezee, ' 'en I'm gwinter kyore you, dat's w'at I'm a gwinter do,' sezee.

"Brer Fox, he sorter chuckle in his stummuck, he did, but Tar-Baby ain't sayin' nuthin'.

" 'I'm gwinter larn you howter talk ter 'specttubble fokes ef hit's de las' ack,' sez Brer Rabbit, sezee. 'Ef you don't take off dat hat en tell me howdy, I'm gwinter bus' you wide open,' sezee.

"Tar-Baby stay still, an Brer Fox, he lay low.

"Brer Rabbit keep on axin' 'im, en de Tar-Baby, she keep on sayin' nuthin', twel present'y Brer Rabbit draw back wid his fis', he did, en blip he tuck 'er side er de head. Right dar's whar he broke his merlasses jug. His fis' stuck, en he can't pull loose. De tar hilt 'im. But Tar-Baby, she stay still, en Brer Fox, he lay low.

" 'Ef you don't lemme loose, I'll knock you agin,' sez Brer Rabbit, sezee, en wid dat he fotch 'er a wipe wid de udder han', en dat stuck. Tar-Baby, she ain't sayin' nuthin', en Brer Fox, he lay low.

" 'Tu'n me loose, fo' I kick de natal stuffin' outen you,' sez Brer Rabbit, sezee, but de Tar-Baby, she ain't sayin' nuthin'. She des hilt on, en den Brer Rabbit lose de use er his feet in de same way. Brer Fox, he lay low. Den Brer Rabbit squall out dat ef de Tar-Baby don't tu'n 'im loose he butt 'er cranksided. En den he butted, en his head got stuck. Den Brer Fox, he sa'ntered fort', lookin' des es innercent ez wunner yo' mammy's mockin'-birds.

" 'Howdy, Brer Rabbit,' sez Brer Fox, sezee. 'You look sorter stuck up dis mawnin',' sezee, en den he rolled on de groun', en laft en laft twel he couldn't laff no mo'. 'I speck you'll take dinner wid me dis time, Brer Rabbit. I done laid in some calamus root, en I ain't gwinter take no skuse,' sez Brer Fox, sezee.

Here Uncle Remus paused, and drew a two-pound yam out of the ashes.

"Did the fox eat the rabbit?" asked the little boy to whom the story had been told.

"Dat's all de fur de tale goes," replied the old man. "He mout, en den agin he moutent. Some say Jedge B'ar come 'long en loosed 'im—some say he didn't. I hear Miss Sally callin'. You better run 'long."

Southern people have always loved to sing, and this is especially true of the mountain folk of North Carolina, Virginia, Kentucky and Tennessee. Specialists in folklore have shown great interest in this region, because they found people there singing the same ballads, or ballads similar to those, that their English ancestors had sung. Cecil J. Sharp, the English folk-song specialist, spent a year in the mountain country, which resulted in a volume of 122 ballads and songs of the mountain people. He said that in that region he found singing almost as universal a practice as speaking. Children learned to sing as early as they learned to talk, and so the songs were handed down from generation to generation, varying slightly, as they became integrated with the life of the people. Ballads often grew with current events as their inspiration.

The ballad, "Barbara Allen" is widely known and sung in England and America. It is believed to date back to the seventeenth century. The following version, one of many, was recorded as sung by Mrs. Julia Grogan of Zionville, North Carolina, to C. A. Smith in 1914. It is quoted from the Frank C. Brown, *Collections of North Carolina Folklore*, Duke University Press, Durham, Vol. II, 1952, pp. 121-123.

Early, early in the spring,
When the flower buds were a-swellin',
Sweet Willie he was taken sick
For the love of Barbara Allen.

He sent his servant to the town
Where Barbara was a-dwellin':
'My master said for you to come
If your name be Barbara Allen.'

Slowly, slowly she came up
And slowly she went near him,
And all she said when she got there,
'Young man, I think you are dyin'.'

'Oh yes, oh yes, I am very low,
And death is in me dwellin';
No better will I ever be
Till I get Barbara Allen.'

'Oh yes, you are very low,
And death is in you dwellin'.
No better will you ever be
By getting Barbara Allen.

'Don't you remember in yonder town
Where you were all a-drinkin',
You drank to the health of the ladies round
And you slighted Barbara Allen.'

'Oh, yes, I remember in yonder town
Where we were all a-drinkin',
I drank a health to the ladies round
And my love to Barbara Allen.'

Slowly, slowly she rose up
And slowly she went from him.
'It's if you die, and die you must,
You'll never get Barbara Allen.'

She had not got a mile away
Till she heard the death bells tollin'.
And every stroke they seemed to say
'Hard-hearted Barbara Allen.'

She looked to the east, she looked to the west,
And saw the corpse a-comin'.
'Oh, lay him down, oh, lay him down
So I may look upon him!'

The more she looked, the more she sighed
Until she burst out cryin'.
And she cried until the day she died
For the love of Willie Harrell.

'Oh, mother, make my dying bed,
And make it soft and narrow.
Sweet Willie died for me today,
I will die for him tomorrow.'

Sweet Willie was buried in the new churchyard
And Barbara buried beside him.
Out of his grave grew a red rose bush
And out of hers a brier.

They grew till they reached the church top,
And there they could grow no higher.
And there they entwined in a true love knot,
The rose bush and the brier.

✔   ✔   ✔

Ellen Glasgow's novels comprise a social history of Virginia from the Civil War until the 1920's; they deal chiefly with the problems of adapting the ideals and customs of an outmoded past to the realities of the present. *Barren Ground* is considered her greatest novel. In it Dorinda Oakley, the central character, is in love with the land. Through her efforts the worn-out land is returned to fertility. The following excerpts are from Ellen Glasgow, *Barren Ground,* copyright, 1925, 1933, 1938. Reprinted by permission of Harcourt, Brace and Company, Inc.

Early in the nineteenth century, John Calvin Abernethy, a retired missionary from India and Ceylon, came from the upper Valley into the region of the Shenandoah, with a neat Scotch-Irish inheritance in his pocket. . . . Since there was no canny bargain to be driven, at the moment, in the Shenandoah Valley, John Abernethy regretfully left the highlands for the flat country, where he picked up presently, at a Dutch auction, the thousand acres of land and fifty slaves which had belonged to one William Golden Penner. One may charitably infer that the fifty slaves constituted a nice point in theology; but with ingenious Presbyterian logic and circumscribed Presbyterian imagination, John Calvin reconciled divine grace with a peculiar institution. The fifty slaves he sold farther south, and the price of black flesh he devoted to the redemption of black souls in the Congo. . . .

In his long white house, encircled by the few cultivated fields in the midst of his still-virgin acres, John Calvin Abernethy lived with learning, prudence, and piety until he was not far from a hundred. He had but one son, for unlike the Scotch-Irish of the Valley, his race did not multiply. The son died in middle age, struck down by an oak he was felling, and his only child, a daughter, was reared patiently but sternly by her grandfather. When, in after years, this granddaughter, whose name was Eudora, fell a victim to one of those natural instincts which Presbyterian theology has damned but never wholly exterminated, and married a member of the "poor white" class, who had nothing more to recommend him than the eyes of a dumb poet and the head of a youthful John the Baptist, old Abernethy blessed the marriage and avoided, as far as possible, the connection. . . . When he was dead, his granddaughter's husband, young Joshua Oakley, worked hard, after the manner of his class, to lose everything that was left. He was a good man and a tireless laborer; but that destiny which dogs the footsteps of ineffectual spirits pursued him from the hour of his birth. . . .

Of this union . . . three children survived. Two of these were sons, Josiah and Rufus; the other was a daughter, Dorinda. . . .

"Ebenezer Green?"

"Dat's me."

"Peter Plumtree?"

"Dat's me."

"Toby Jackson?"

"Dat's me, Miss D'rindy."

"Rapidan Finley?"

"Dat's me."

She was calling the names of the field-hands, and while she went over the list, her mind was busily assorting and grouping the faces before her. Yes, she knew them all. Ever since she could remember they had been a part of the country; she had passed them in the road every week, or seen them in the vegetable patches in front of their cabins. Like her mother, she was endowed with an intuitive understanding of the negroes; she would always know how to keep on friendly terms with that immature but not un-generous race. Slavery in Queen Elizabeth County had rested more lightly than elsewhere. The religion that made people hard to themselves, her mother had often pointed out, made them impartially just to their dependents; and like most generalizations, this one was elastic enough to cover the particular instance. It was true that the colored people about Pedlar's Mill were as industrious and as prosperous as any in the South, and that, within what their white neighbors called reasonable bounds, there was, at the end of the nineteenth century, little prejudice against them. Here and there a thriftless farmer, such as Ike Pryde or Adam Snead, would display a fitful jealousy of Micajah Green, who had turned a few barren acres into a flourishing farm; but the better class of farmers preferred the intelligent coloured neighbor to the ignorant white one. Both were social inferiors; but where the matter was one solely of farming, the advantages would usually fall to the more diligent. As for the negroes themselves, they lived contentedly enough as inferiors though not dependents. In spite of the influence of Aunt Mehitable Green, they had not yet learned to think as a race, and the individual negro still attached himself instinctively to the superior powers.

"I remember you well, Ebenezer," she said; "you have a sister, Mary Joe. I want her to help look after my hen-house." She laughed as she spoke because she knew that the negroes would work twice as well for an employer who laughed easily; but she wondered if they detected the hollowness of the sound. It occurred to her, as she looked at the doomed broomsedge across the road, that farming, like love, might prove presently to be no laughing matter.

Turning back toward the house, she met her mother, who was coming out with a basin of cornmeal dough for the chickens. The sun had just risen, and there was a sparkling freshness over the earth and in the luminous globe of the sky. She had slept well, and with the morning weakness had vanished. The wild part of her had perished like burned grass; out of nothing, into nothing, that was the way of it. Now, armoured in reason, she was ready to meet life on its own terms.

"Do you know where Rufus is?" she asked. "I want him to see that the hands start work in the eighteen-acre field."

Mrs. Oakley shook her head. "I don't know. I thought he was going to finish ploughing the tobacco-field, but I saw him start off right after breakfast with Ike Pryde. It seems they found honey in a big oak over by Hoot Owl Woods, and they've set off with an axe to cut down the tree."

"Oh, the fool, the fool!" Dorinda exclaimed, and determined that she would expect nothing more from Rufus.

"Well, you know how men are," returned her mother, with unpolemical wisdom. "They'll seize any excuse to stop work and cut down a tree."

"I do know. But to cut down a big oak, and for honey!"

The old woman scattered dough on the ground with an impartial hand. "Rufus has got a mighty sweet tooth," she remarked.

"So has Pa, but you never found him making an excuse to stop work."

"I know. Your Pa always put his wishes aside. There ain't many men you can say that of." Though she sighed over the fact, she accepted it as one of the natural or acquired privileges of the male; and she felt that these were too numerous to justify a special grievance against a particular one. Even acquiescence with a sigh is easier than argument when one is worn out with neuralgia and worse things. A frost had blighted her impulse of opposition, and this seemed to Dorinda one of the surest signs that her mother was failing. There were moments when it would have been a relief to be contradicted.

"Well, I'll have to do it myself. Because I am a woman the hands will expect me to shirk, and I must show them that I know what I am about."

"I'll help you all I can, daughter."

"I know you will." Dorinda's conscience reproached her for her impatience. "You will be wonderful with the hens, and I'll get Ebenezer's sister Mary Joe to help you. She must be fourteen or fifteen."

"Yes, she's a real bright girl," Mrs. Oakley remarked without enthusiasm. She had scarcely closed her eyes all night, and bright coloured girls, even when they helped in the hen-house, left her indifferent. "I'm going down in the garden to see if I can find a mess of turnip salad," she added after a pause, in which she scooped the last remnant of dough out of the basin and flung it into the midst of the brood of chickens. . . . .

[After dinner Dorinda drove to the Ellgoods' in the buggy.] Dan travelled slowly, and the Ellgoods lived three miles on the other side of Pedlar's Mill. Green Acres was the largest stock farm in the county; but what impressed Dorinda more than the size was the general air of thrift which hovered over the pastures, the deep green meadows, and the white buildings clustering about the red brick house.

"I couldn't have anything like this in a hundred years," she thought cheerlessly. Her scheme, which had appeared so promising when she surveyed it from Central Park, presented, at a closer view, innumerable obstacles. There was not one chance in a thousand, she told herself now, that the venture would lead anywhere except into a bog. "But I'm in it now, and I must see it through," she concluded, with less audacity than determination. "I'll not give up as long as there is breath left in my body." Rolling in mud-caked wheels up the neat drive to the house, she resolved stubbornly that no one, least of all James Ellgood, should suspect that she had lost heart in her enterprise.

James Ellgood was at Queen Elizabeth Court-House for the day; but Bob, his son, who had recently brought home a dissatisfied and delicate wife from a hospital in Baltimore, was on the front porch awaiting his visitor. When she appeared in sight, he threw away the match he was striking on his boot, and after thrusting his old brier pipe into his pocket, descended the steps and came across the drive to the buggy. Nathan would have smoked, or still worse have chewed, Dorinda knew, while he received her; but inconsistently enough, she did not like him the less for his boorishness. Utility, not punctilio, was what she required of men at this turning-point in her career.

While Bob Ellgood held out his hand, she could see her reflection in his large, placid eyes as clearly as if her features were mirrored in the old mill-pond. It gave her pleasure to feel that she was more distinguished, if less desirable, than she had been two years ago; but her pleasure was as impersonal as her errand. She had no wish to attract this heavy, masterful farmer, who reminded her of a sleek, mild-mannered jersey bull; no wish, at least, to attract him beyond the point where his admiration might help her to drive a bargain in cows. Gazing critically at his handsome face, she remembered the Sunday mornings when she had watched him in church and had wished with all her heart that he would turn his eyes in her direction. Then he had not so much as glanced at her over his hymn-book, his slow mind was probably revolving round his engagement; but now she felt instinctively that he was ready to catch fire from a look or a word. The absurd twist of an idea jerked into her mind. "He would have suited me better than Jason, and I should have suited him better than the woman he married." Well, that was the way the eternal purpose worked, she supposed, but it seemed to her a cumbersome and blundering method.

"Nathan told me you wanted to buy some cows," he was saying, for he was as single-minded as other successful men, only more so. "I picked out seven fine ones this morning and had them brought up to the small pasture. They'll be at the bars now, and you can look them over. There isn't a better breed than the Jersey, that's what we think, and these young cows are as good as any you'll find."

At the bars of the pasture, where a weeping willow dipped over the watering-trough, the Jerseys were standing in a row, satin-coated, fawn-eyed, with breath like new-mown hay. What beauties they were, thought Dorinda.

. . . Even the price, which seemed to her excessively high, could not spoil her delight. A hundred dollars for each cow, Bob explained, was a third less than they would bring at the fair next autumn. . . .

A little later, as she drove across the railway tracks and down the long slope in the direction of Old Farm, she reflected dispassionately upon the crookedness of human affairs. Why had that honest farmer, robust, handsome, without an idea above bulls and clover, mated with a woman who was afraid of a grasshopper? And why had she, in whom life burned so strong and bright, wasted her vital energy on the mere husk of a man? Why, above all, should Nature move so unintelligently in the matter of instinct? Did this circle of reasoning lead back inevitably, she wondered, to the steadfast doctrine of original sin? "The truth is we always want what is bad for us, I suppose," she concluded, and gave up the riddle. . . . .

When she looked back on the year that followed her mother's death, Dorinda could remember nothing but work. Out of the fog of recollection there protruded bare outlines which she recognized as milestones of her prosperity. She saw clearly the autumn she had turned the eighteen-acre field into pasture; the failure of her first experiment with ensilage; the building of the new dairy and cow-barns; the gradual increase of her seven cows into a herd. Certain dates stood out in her farm calendar. The year the blight had fallen on her corn-field and she had had to buy fodder from James Ellgood; the year she had first planted alfalfa; the year she had lost a number of her cows from contagious abortion; the year she had reclaimed the fields beyond Poplar Spring; the year her first prize bull had won three blue ribbons. With the slow return of fertility to the soil, she had passed, by an unconscious process, into mute acquiescence with the inevitable. . . . She had worked relentlessly through the years; but it was work that she enjoyed, and above all it was work that had created anew the surroundings amid which she lived. . . .

At thirty-three, the perspective of the last ten years was incredibly shortened. All the cold starry mornings when she had awakened before day and crept out to the barn by lantern light to attend to the milking, appeared to her now as a solitary frozen dawn. All the bleak winters, all the scorching summers, were a single day; all the evenings, when she had dreamed half asleep in the firelit dusk, were a single night. She could not separate these years into seasons. In her long retrospect they were crystallized into one flawless pattern.

Through those ten years, while she struggled to free the farm from debt, she had scrimped and saved like a miser. . . . And only Fluvanna, who lived in the house with her now, knew the hours she spent beside her lamp counting the pounds of butter and the number of eggs she had sent to market. If only she could save enough to pay off the mortgage. . . .

*   *   *

DuBose Heyward was born in Charleston, South Carolina. He was obliged to earn his living at an early age, and various occupations made him familiar with the Negro life of the water front. The following selection is from *Porgy:* a novel, by DuBose Heyward. Copyright 1925 by Doubleday & Company, Inc. It depicts a colorful all-day Negro excursion, and is quoted from pp. 111-113.

It was the day set for the grand parade and picnic of "The Sons and Daughters of Repent Ye Saith the Lord," and, with the first light of morning, Catfish Row had burst into a fever of preparation. Across the narrow street, the wharf, from which the party was to leave, bustled and seethed with life. A wagon rattled out to the pier-head and discharged an entire load of watermelons. Under the vigilant eyes of a committee a dozen volunteers lifted the precious freight from the vehicle, and piled it ready for the steamer.

From behind the next pier, with a frenzied threshing of its immense stern paddle, came the excursion boat. Tall open exhaust funnels flanked the walking-beam, and coughed great salmon-colored plumes of steam into the faint young sunlight. A fierce torrent of wood-smoke gushed from the funnel and went tumbling away across the harbor. Painters were hurled, missed, coiled, and hurled again. Then, amid a babblement of advice and encouragement, the craft was finally moored in readiness for the Lodge.

The first horizontal rays of the sun were painting the wall a warm claret, when Porgy opened the door, to find Peter . . . perched upon the back of his gaily blanketed horse. He wore a sky-blue coat, white pants which were thrust into high black leggings, and a visored cap, from beneath which he scowled fiercely down upon the turmoil around the feet of his mount. Across his breast, from right shoulder to left hip, was a broad scarlet sash, upon which was emblazoned, "Repent Ye Saith the Lord!" and from his left breast fluttered a white ribbon bearing the word "MARSHAL." From time to time, he would issue orders in hoarse, menacing gutturals, which no one heeded; and twice, in the space of half an hour, he rode out to the pier-head, counted the watermelons, and returned to report the number to an important official who had arrived in a carriage to supervise the arrangements.

Momently the confusion increased, until at eight o'clock it culminated in a general exodus toward the rendezvous for the parade.

The drowsy old city had scarcely commenced its day when down through King Charles Street, the procession took its way. Superbly unselfconscious of the effect that it produced, it crashed through the slow, restrained rhythm of the city's life like a wild, barbaric chord. All the stately mansions along the way were servantless that day, and the aristocratic matrons broke the ultimate canon of the social code and peered through front windows at the procession as it swept flamboyantly across the town.

First came an infinitesimal negro boy, scarlet-coated, and aglitter with brass buttons. Upon his head was balanced an enormous shako; and while he marched with left hand on hip and shoulders back, his right hand twirled a heavy gold-headed baton. Then the band, two score boys attired in several variations of the band master's costume, strode by. Bare, splay feet padded upon the cobbles; heads were thrown back, with lips to instruments that glittered in the sunshine, launching daring and independent excursions into the realm of sound. Yet these improvisations returned always to the eternal boom, boom, boom of an underlying rhythm, and met with others in the sudden weaving and ravelling of amazing chords. An ecstasy of wild young bodies beat living into the blasts that shook the windows of the solemn houses. Broad, dusty, blue-black feet shuffled and danced on the many-colored cobbles and the grass between them. The sun lifted suddenly over the housetops and flashed like a torrent of warm, white wine between the staid buildings, to break on flashing teeth and laughing eyes.

After the band came the men members of the lodge, stepping it out to the urge of the marshals who rode beside them, reinforcing the marching rhythm with a series of staccato grunts, shot with crisp, military precision from under their visored caps. Breasts cross-slashed with the emblems of their lodge, they passed.

Then came the carriages, and suddenly the narrow street hummed and bloomed like a tropic garden. Six to a carriage sat the sisters. The effect produced by the colors was strangely like that wrought in the music; scarlet, purple, orange, flamingo, emerald wild, clashing, unbelievable discords; yet in their steady flow before the eye, possessing a strange, dominant rhythm that reconciled them to each other and made them unalterably right. The senses reached blindly out for a reason. There was none. They intoxicated, they maddened, and finally they passed, seeming to pull every ray of color from the dun buildings, leaving the sunlight sane, flat, dead.

For its one brief moment out of the year the pageant had lasted. Out of its fetters of civilization this people had risen, suddenly, amazingly. Exotic as the Congo, and still able to abandon themselves utterly to the wild joy of fantastic play, they had taken the reticent old Ango-Saxon town and stamped their mood swiftly and indelibly into its heart. Then they passed, leaving behind them a wistful envy among those who had watched them go—those whom the ages had rendered old and wise. . . .

ʃ   ʃ   ʃ

Rainbow Round My Shoulder, by Howard Odum, copyright 1928, 1955, used by special permission of the publishers, the Bobbs-Merrill Company, Inc., is a tale of a wandering Negro. The late Dr. Odum was a professor of sociology at the University of North Carolina. In the following excerpts Ulysses' background is presented, followed by a few typical experiences from his wanderings. The selection is quoted from pp. 67-75.

"The story of Negro childhood and youth in the South one of early disorganization and nomadic trends. Parents working out. One or both par-

ents dead. Children with relatives. Children at work at all so
Large families and high mortality. High rates of irregularity in
marriages. Quick shifting scenes in homes and communities. Prii
for expression and survival. Quests for utopias. "Ramblin' minds. *Impulse*
and circumstances rather than planning and judgment the guiding forces.

"Examples and examples. Now a youngster of eight years, with parents
dead, off to Texas to stay with an uncle. Then "po' mistreated boy" back to
Louisiana and Mississippi and Georgia, across South Carolina and back
home to North Carolina. Then to Washington to stay with an aunt who
mistreats "po' boy" workin' him instead of letting him go to school. Then
to Philadelphia and Pittsburgh and uttermost parts of Pennsylvania and
Ohio. Then to Chicago and across to Harlem and back South again. And
the years have intervened to work their processes.

"Another in Georgia, a child, number ten, of eighteen children. Another,
both parents "widowers" in Mississippi. Another, an uncharted ward of the
race. The "leaving" age uncommonly common at from ten to fourteen years.
Youth and adolescents on the road and without anchor during formative
stages. Case studies of criminals and roustabouts and good "ole citerzens"
abounding in the same formula. How the Negro survives a problem story
of great variety and reach. Black Ulysses starting as no more than an "average" nomad, reflects a rare cumulative Odyssey."

When I was 'bout twelve years old my peoples still very poor an' I wanted
clothes an' things an' wanted to run roun' like other boys an' so I ran away
from home first time. Went to farm of Mr. Triers 'bout six miles from old
Atkins plantation few miles below our home on ol' Watkins road. I worked
fer him for dollar day an' plowed mules.

> *Captain, call me early in mornin',*
> *Call me to shake six-hoss plow.*
> *I told my captain, Lawd,*
> *Captain, I can't shake this plow.*

> *Some o' these days, Lawd,—*
> *It won't be long,*
> *Captain gonna call me,*
> *An' I'll be gone.*

So I got tired o' that soon an' stayed only one week 'cause too much work.
I wanted to make more money an' jes' naturally wanted to ramble roun'. I
heard other boys tell 'bout makin' big money. So I sets out to find loggin'
camp I heard 'em tell 'bout twenty miles over near big Tigue swamp. I
worked there, but didn't git mo' 'n dollar day an' I sho' got in worse place

than I ever been in an' stayed 'bout two weeks, an' only reason I stay that long couldn't get 'way no sooner. My business was to cut wood to fire donkey engine.

That camp was what we call sort of outlaw camp. Folks very mean an' rough an' rowdy, stealin' an' gamblin' an' drinkin' an' one man got killed while I was there. Outlaw camp place where ain't no rules much an' no law, an' captain hard on boys, won't let 'em get away. Onliest way to leave is slip off but boys say if you tell on 'em they kill you an' bury you sho'. Boys claim they seed heaps o' graves.

Some niggers in these camps powerful mean. . . . Well, cos'n I didn't know this was no outlaw camp else I never would tried to find it, but when I got in had to stay. Way it was, I was looking' fer job an' jes' walked into this place. Nex' time I know better.

Then one night 'bout 'leven o'clock I slipped off an' walked 'bout ten miles, seem to me, an' nex' mornin' I started walkin' again an' finally come to sawmill camp of C. M. McHenry Company on railroad sidin', an' so started to workin' there. I stayed there nearly month, workin' on green ends an' rollin' good lumber an' slabs. Then I decided to leave there, work was so hard an' I wasn't gittin' enough pay. An' so I come back to town an' had 'bout ten dollars an' got with some boys said they was goin' to Greensboro to work on big job where they paid big money. They seemed to be good friends an' so I loaned them part of what I had lef', 'bout five dollars. An' so we start out walkin' to save money, an' walk 'bout ten miles an' we decided to hobo rest o' way. So there was a freight train called fohty-seven hundred goin' through. I didn't know how to swing it, so they let me try first so if I missed it they stay with me. I jes' couldn't swing on fast runnin' cars, so I got skinned up an' one boy stayed with me but others rode dat freight an' took my money. Nex' night I missed first try, then caught third car from las' an' other boy caught caboose. Then we stop at station called Gibson-ville an' brakeman caught us an' tole us to git off. We tole him we won't gwine to git off. So he pulls gun on us an' put us off. . . . So we tramped other sixteen miles.

When we got to Greensboro found they didn't need no workers an' we stayed an' spent our money, sleepin' outdoors while until we found old lady stayed by herself an' give us room till we could git job. So we couldn't find no job an' she puts us out an' 'bout that time we was gittin' mighty hungry. We would eat anything we could find round back doors o' restaurants an' hotels. Clothes all dirty an' wo' out.

> Pity po' boy, stray 'way from home.
> If I ever gits back sho' never mo' to roam.
> If I had listened to what mommer said,
> I'd be at home in mommer's bed.

Finally I found some o' my people, uncle I heard of, an' told him condition I was in. They give me some clothes an' money an' so come back, but I wouldn't go home 'cause I didn't have no money an' scared an' 'shamed to come back home. So I went to Wilson on train bes' I could. I didn't know nobody there but jes' wanted to ramble an' thought Wilson be good place 'cause I heard of road an' bridge force. They didn't need no help an' so I found a place to stay with lady kinder rough. Eve'body comin' an' goin' an' drinkin' an' gamblin' an' eve'ything. An' so I stayed there a few days, then started back home. I walked 'bout three days an' two nights gittin' in 'bout fifteen miles o' home, feets tired an' sore, clothes all dirty an' wo' out again, hungry an' tired.

So I took up with farmer who offered me fifteen dollars a month an' board, an' begun to work on Thursday an' work till Sat'day at dinner. Farmer wanted me to work Sat'day evenin', an' so I wouldn't work an' went over to 'nuther house where I seen colored fellow. I come back Monday mornin' an' farmer say if I work for him I got to work Sat'day evenin'. I told him I did not work on Sat'day evenin' for nobody. He said I had to quit then an' I said it suited me an' fer him to pay me off. He refused to pay me 'cause month wasn't up an' I told him he was gonna pay me or pay doctor, one. So he gave me dollar an' half.

His son was friendly an' ast me if I ever worked roun' liquor still. I told him no but I was a fellow would try anything, an' so I come back that night an' we started makin' liquor at night. That was 'fo' days of prohibition but lots of stills eve'ywhere. One night officers run us in but missed us. So I was scared to come back an' so I stayed in woods, hungry an' sleepin' out. I got mighty tired an' sore.

> *Ain't had nothin' to eat,*
> *Ain't had nowhere to sleep.*
> *Freezin' ground was my foldin' bed.*
> *I'm on my way, Lawd, I'm on my way.*

Finally I come back in an' the young white man got me somethin' to eat an' tole me I could stay an' try again. So I told him I'd better go an' maybe I could find it better somewhere else as I was feller never to give up an' always believe in findin' somethin' better. So I didn't go home 'cause I didn't have no money an' I hadn't written home tellin' how I was farin'. So I come to Zeb Atkin's, runnin' 'nuther sawmill camp, an' he ast me if I would work an' I say yes. Then I ast him how much he was payin' an' he say dollar seventy-five an' camp, so feller could batchellor alone. So I worked 'bout two weeks an' save 'bout twenty-five dollars an' got some clothes an' look like folks.

An' so I come home but didn't tell 'em what hard time I been in, neither did I tell 'em 'bout hoboin' an' gittin' hurt an' run in by officers. So my mother was mighty glad to see me but I never tole her 'bout my troubles.

I stayed home 'bout a week an' rested up eatin' mama's good cookin' an' then I told her I had learned I could do better somewhere else, so I lef' an' went on to Nelson's, contractors' camp, drivin' a wheeler, big scoop on wheels. Folks mighty rough there an' we git keerless an' roustabout. Foreman tole me not to ride these wheelers but we would do so. So after workin' there 'bout two weeks I got my leg and kneecap busted an' Mr. Teer kep' me an' sent me home. Then I decided to stay home till I come to be a man to take keer o' myself. An' so I was in bed an' walkin' on crutches from fifth of August to middle o' September. My mama sho' treated me right.

> *Lawd, I wonder, huh,*
> *Lawd, I wonder, huh,*
> *Will I ever git back home?*

> *Well, cuckoo keep on hollerin', huh,*
> *Lawd, cuckoo keep on hollerin'.*
> *Mus' be day, Lawd, mus' be day.*

> *Well, whistle keep on blowin', huh,*
> *Lawd, whistle keep on blowin'.*
> *Time ain't long, huh, time ain't long.*

✦　　✦　　✦

Look Homeward, Angel by Thomas Wolfe, Charles Scribner's Sons, New York, was published in 1929. It is the story of a boy who tried to escape from the domination of his family, a drunken father and a self-centered and greedy mother. Yet it is an expression of the appreciation of living. The following paragraphs, pp. 84-86, will convey to the reader the richness of Wolfe's boyhood experiences in spite of their sordidness and ugliness. His home in Asheville, North Carolina, might easily have been in any other town of similar size in Southern United States.

He had heard already the ringing of remote church bells over a countryside on Sunday night; had listened to the earth steeped in the brooding symphony of dark, and the million-noted little night things; and he had heard thus the far retreating wail of a whistle in the distant valley, and faint thunder on the rails; and he felt the infinite depth and width of the golden world in the brief seductions of a thousand multiplex and mixed mysterious odors and sensations, weaving, with a blinding interplay of aural explosions, one into the other.

He remembered yet the East India Tea House at the Fair, the sandalwood, the turbans, and the robes, the cool interior and the smell of India tea; and he had felt now the nostalgic thrill of dew-wet mornings in Spring, the cherry scent, the cool clarion earth, the wet loaminess of the garden, the pungent breakfast smells and the floating snow of blossoms. He knew the inchoate sharp excitement of hot dandelions in young Spring grass at noon; the smell of cellars, cobwebs, and built-on secret earth; in July, of watermelons bedded in sweet hay, inside a farmer's covered wagon; of cantaloupe and crated peaches; and the scent of orange rind, bittersweet, before a fire of coals. He knew the good male smell of his father's sitting-room; of the smooth worn leather sofa, with the gaping horse-hair rent; of the blistered varnished wood upon the hearth; of the heated calf-skin bindings; of the flat moist plug of apple tobacco, stuck with a red flag; of woodsmoke and burnt leaves in October; of the tired brown autumn earth; of honey-suckle at night; of warm nasturtiums; of a clean ruddy farmer who comes weekly with printed butter, eggs and milk; of fat limp underdone bacon and of coffee; of a bakery-oven in the wind; of large deep-hued stringbeans smoking-hot and seasoned well with salt and butter; of a room of old pine boards in which books and carpet have been stored, long closed; of Concord grapes in their long white baskets. . . . .

Yes, and of a hardware store, but mostly the good smell of nails; the developing chemicals in a photographer's darkroom; and the young-life smell of paint and turpentine; of buckwheat batter and black sorghum; of a negro and his horse, together: of boiling fudge; the brine smell of pickling vats; and the lush undergrowth smell of southern hills; of a slimy oyster can, of chilled gutted fish; of a hot kitchen negress; of kerosene and linoleum; of sarsaparilla and guavas; and of ripe autumn persimmons; and the smell of the wind and the rain; and of the acrid thunder; of cold starlight, and the brittle-bladed frozen grass; of fog and the misted winter sun; of seed-time, bloom, and mellow dropping harvest.

✓ ✓ ✓

The close ties of kinship among mountain people as well as the depth of love of a mountain mother for her children are illustrated by the following selection from James Still, *River of Earth,* The Viking Press, New York, 1941, pp. 6-11. Seasonal layoffs in the mines of Kentucky intensified the suffering of the miners. Brack Baldridge, his wife and four children, along with numerous relatives at different times, lived fairly well when Brack had work in the coal mines, but the mines were closed down several months each year, and then they had very little to eat. Mother told Father his relatives would have to go, but Father said: "I can't turn my kin out." He would say no more. On one occasion when the food supply was exhausted and Father's two cousins and an uncle paid no attention to Mother's hints that they go home, a crisis occurred. The following incident is told in the words of Brack's seven-year-old son. Reprinted by permission of The Viking Press, Inc., New York.

Mother and Father took a lamp and went out to the smokehouse. We followed, finding them bent over the meat box. Father dug into the salt with a plow blade, Mother holding the light above him. He uncovered three curled rinds of pork. We stayed in the smokehouse a long time, feeling contented and together. The room was large, and we jumped around like savages and swung head-down from the rafters.

Father crawled around on his hands and knees with the baby on his back. Mother sat on a sack of black walnuts and watched us. "Hit's the first time we've been alone in two months," she said. "If we lived in here, there wouldn't be room for anybody else. And it would be healthier than that leaky shack we stay in." Father kept crawling with the baby, kicking up his feet like a spoiled nag. Fletch hurt his leg. . . . Father rubbed the bruise and made it feel better. . . . Mother said, "I'd rather live in this smokehouse than stay down there with them. A big house draws kinfolks like a horse draws nit-flies."

It was late when we went to the house. The sky was overcast and starless. During the night, rain came suddenly, draining through the rotten shingles. Father got up in the dark and pushed the beds about. He bumped against a footboard and wakened me. I heard Uncle Samp snoring in the next room; and low and indistinct through the sound of water on the roof came the quiver of laughter. Harl and Tibb [the cousins] were awake in the next room. They were mightily tickled about something. They laughed in long, choking spasms. The sound came to me though afar off, and I reckon they had their heads under the covers so as not to waken Uncle Samp. I listened and wondered how it was possible to laugh with all the dark and rain.

Morning was bright and rain-fresh. The sharp sunlight fell slantwise upon the worn limestone earth of the hills, and our house squatted weathered and dark on the bald slope. Yellow-bellied sapsuckers drilled their oblong holes in the black birch by the house, now leafing from tight-curled buds. Fletch and I had climbed into the tree before breakfast, and when Mother called us in we were hungry for our boiled wheat.

We were alone at the table, Harl and Tibb having left at daylight for Blackjack. They had left without their breakfast, and this haste seemed strange to Mother. "This is the first meal they've missed," she said.

Uncle Samp slept on in the next room, his head buried under a quilt to keep the light out of his face. Mother fed the baby at her breast, standing by Father at the table. We ate our wheat without sugar, and when we had finished, Mother said to Father, "We have enough bran for three more pans of bread. If the children eat it by themselves, it might last a week. It won't last us all more than three meals. Your kin will have to go today."

Father put his spoon down with a clatter. "My folks eat when we eat," he said, "and as long as we eat." The corners of his mouth were drawn tight into his face. His eyes burned, but there was no anger in them. "I'll get some meal at the store," he said.

Mother leaned against the wall, clutching the baby. Her voice was like ice. "They won't let you have it on credit. You've tried before. We've got to live small. We've got to start over again, hand to mouth, the way we began." She laid her hand upon the air, marking the words with nervous fin-

gers. "We've got to tie ourselves up in such a knot nobody else can get in."
Father got his hat and stalked to the door. "We've got to do hit today," she
called. But Father was gone, out of the house and over the hill toward
Blackjack.

Mother put the baby in the empty woodbox while she washed dishes.
Euly helped her, clearing the table and setting out a bowl of boiled wheat
for Uncle Samp. I went outside with Fletch, and we were driving the sapsuckers from the birch when Uncle Samp shouted in the house. His voice
crashed through the wall, pouring between the seamy timbers in blasts of
anger. Fletch was up in the tree, near the tiptop, so I ran ahead of him into
the shedroom. Mother stood in the middle of the floor listening. Baby Green
jumped up and down in the woodbox. Euly ran behind the stove.

I ran into the room where Uncle Samp was and saw him stride from the
looking glass to the bed. His mouth was slack. A fierce growl flowed out of
him. He stopped when he saw me, drawing himself up in his wrath. Then
I saw his face, and I was frightened. I was suddenly paralyzed with fear. His
face was fiery, the red web of veins straining in his flesh, and his mustache,
which had been cut off within an inch of his lips, sticking out like two small
gray horns. He rushed upon me, caught me up in his arms, and flung me
against the wall. I fell upon the floor, breathless, not uttering a sound.
Mother was beside me in a moment, her hands weak and palsied as she
lifted me.

I was only frightened, and not hurt. Mother cried a little, making a dry
sniffling sound through her nose; then she got up and walked outside and
around the house. Uncle Samp was not in sight. She came back and gave
Fletch the key to the smokehouse. "We're going to move up there," she said.
"Go unlock the door." I helped Euly carry the baby out in the woodbox.
We set him on the shady side of the woodpile. We began to move the
furniture, putting the smaller things in the smokehouse, but leaving the
chairs, beds, and tables on the ground halfway between. The stove was heaviest of all, and still hot. The rusty legs broke off on one side, and the other
two bent under it. We managed to slide it into the yard. Mother carried
the clock and the rio lamp to the smokehouse. The clock rattled with four
pennies Fletch kept inside it.

After everything had been taken out we waited in the backyard while
Mother went around the house again, looking off the hill. Uncle Samp was
nowhere in sight, and neither Harl nor Tibb could be seen. Then she went
inside alone. She stayed a long time. We could hear her moving across the
floor. When she came out and closed the door there was a haze of smoke
behind her, blue and smelling of burnt wood.

In a moment we saw the flames through the back window. The rooms
were lighted up, and fire ran up the walls, eating into the old timbers. It
climbed to the ceiling, burst through the roof, and ate the rotten shingles
like leaves. Fletch and I watched the sapsuckers fly in noisy haste from the

black birch, and he began to cry hoarsely as the young leaves wilted and hung limp from scorched twigs. The birch trunk steamed in the heat.

When the flames were highest, leaping through the charred rafters, a gun fired repeatedly in the valley. Someone there had noticed the smoke and was arousing the folk along Little Carr Creek. When they arrived, the walls had fallen in, and Mother stood among the scattered furnishings, her face calm and triumphant.

*   *   *

William Faulkner of Mississippi is believed by many to be the South's greatest novelist. His books illustrate his belief that the South is in a state of decay. *Absalom, Absalom,* Random House, New York, 1936, tells the story of Thomas Sutpen, a planter who settled near Jefferson, Mississippi, in 1833. The narrator is Quenton Compson, a student at Harvard, who told the story to his roommate from Alberta, Canada. Sutpen was one of a family of poor whites of Scotch-Irish stock who moved into Tidewater Virginia when Thomas was ten years old. The following excerpt deals only with his boyhood, during which he came to the realization that white people were not all of the same social status. It is quoted from pp. 221-238, *passim.*

"—he was born where what few other people he knew lived in log cabins boiling with children like the one he was born in—men and grown boys who hunted or lay before the fire on the floor while the women and older girls stepped back and forth across them to reach the fire to cook, where the only colored people were Indians and you only looked down at them over your rifle sights, where he had never even heard of, never imagined a place, a land divided neatly up and actually owned by men who did nothing but ride over it on fine horses or sit in fine clothes on the galleries of big houses while other people worked for them; he did not even imagine then that there was any such way to live, or that there existed all the objects to be wanted which there were, or that the ones who owned the objects not only could look down on the ones that didn't, but could be supported in the down-looking not only by the others who owned objects too but by the very ones that were looked down on that didn't own objects and knew they never would. Because where he lived the land belonged to anybody and everybody and so the man who would go to the trouble and work to fence off a piece of it and say 'This is mine' was crazy; and as for objects, nobody had any more of them than you did because everybody had just what he was strong enough or energetic enough to take and keep, and only that crazy man would go to the trouble to take or even want more than he could eat or swap for powder and whiskey. So he didn't even know there was a country all divided and fixed and neat with a people living on it all divided and neat because of what color their skins happened to be and what they happened to own, and where a certain few men not only had the power of life and death and barter and sale over others, but they had living human men to perform the endless repetitive personal offices, such as pouring the very whiskey from the jug and putting the glass into a man's hand or pulling off his boots for him to go to bed, that all men have had to do for themselves since time began and would have to do until they died and which no man ever has or ever will like to do, but which no man that he knew had ever thought of evading any more than he thought of evading the effort of chewing and swallowing and breathing. When he was a child he didn't listen to the vague and cloudy tales of Tidewater splendor that penetrated even his mountains because then he could not understand what the people who told about it meant, and when he became a boy he didn't listen to them because there was nothing in sight to compare and gauge the tales by and give the words life and meaning, and no chance that he ever would understand what they meant because he was too busy doing the things that boys do; and when he got to be a youth and curiosity itself exhumed the tales which he did not know he had heard and speculated on, he was interested and would have liked to see the places once, but without envy and regret, because he just thought that some people were spawned in one place and some in another, some spawned rich (lucky, he may have called it) and some not, and that . . . the men themselves had little to do with the choosing and less of the regret because it never occurred to him that any man should take any such blind accident as that as authority or warrant to look down at others, any others. So he had hardly heard of such a world until he fell into it.

"That's how it was. They fell into it, the whole family, returned to the coast from which the first Sutpen had come . . . , tumbled head over heels back to Tidewater by sheer altitude, elevation and gravity, as if whatever slight hold the family had had on the mountain had broken. . . . And . . . the whole passel of them . . . slid back out of the mountains . . . across the Virginia plateau and into the slack lowlands about the mouth of the James River. He didn't know why they moved. . . . one morning the father rose and told the older girls to pack what food they had, and somebody wrapped up the baby and somebody else threw water on the fire and they walked down the mountain to where roads existed. They had a lopsided two wheeled cart now. . . . He didn't remember if it was weeks or months or a year they travelled. . . . doggeries and taverns now become hamlets, hamlets now become villages, villages now towns, and the country flattened out now with good roads and fields and niggers working in the fields while white men sat fine horses and watched them, and more fine horses and men in fine clothes, and with a different look in the face from mountain men. . . .

He had learned the difference not only between white men and black ones, but he was learning that there was a difference between white men and white men, not to be measured by lifting anvils or gouging eyes or how much whiskey you could drink and then get up and walk out of the room. He had begun to discern that without being aware of it yet. . . . [Finally they were] living in a cabin that was almost a replica of the mountain one except that it didn't sit up in the bright wind but sat instead beside a big flat river that sometimes showed no current at all and even sometimes ran backward, where his sisters and brothers seemed to take sick after supper and die before the next meal, where regiments of niggers with white men watching them planted and raised things that he had never heard of. . . . And the man was there who owned all the land and the niggers and apparently the white men who superintended the work, and who lived in the biggest house he had ever seen and who spent most of the afternoon (he told how he would creep up among the tangled shrubbery of the lawn and lie hidden and watch the man) in a barrel stave hammock between two trees, with his shoes off, and a nigger who wore every day better clothes than he of his father and sisters had ever owned and ever expected to, who did nothing else but fan him and bring him drinks. . . . [One day his father] sent him to the big house with the message. . . . He was a boy either thirteen or fourteen, he didn't know which, in garments . . . which one of his sisters had patched and cut down to fit him, and he was no more conscious of his appearance in them or of the possibility that anyone else would be than he was of his skin, following the road and turning into the gate and following the drive up past where still more niggers with nothing to do all day but plant flowers and trim grass were working, and so to the house, the portico, the front door, thinking how at last he was going to see the inside of it, see what else a man was bound to own who could have a special nigger to hand him his liquor and pull off his shoes . . . , never for one moment thinking but what the man would be as pleased to show him the balance of his things as the mountain man would have been to show the powder horn and bullet mold that went with the rifle. Because he was still innocent . . . before the monkey nigger who came to the door had finished saying what he said, he seemed to kind of dissolve and a part of him turn and rush back through the two years they had lived there, like when you pass through a room fast and look at all the objects in it and you turn and go back through the room again and look at all the objects from the other side and you find out you had never seen them before, rushing back through those two years and seeing a dozen things that had happened and he hadn't even seen them before; the certain flat level silent way his older sisters and the other white women of their kind had of looking at niggers, not with fear or dread but with a kind of speculative antagonism not because of any known fact or reason but inherited, by both white and black, the sense, effluvium of it passing between the white women in the doors of the sagging cabins and the niggers in the road and which was not quite explainable by the fact that the niggers had better clothes, and which the niggers did not return as antagonism or in any sense of dare or taunt but through the very fact that they were apparently oblivious to it, too oblivious of it. You knew that you could hit them . . . and they would not hit back or even resist. But you did not want to because they (the niggers) were not it, not what you wanted to hit. . . .

He didn't even remember leaving. All of a sudden he found himself running and already some distance from the house, and not toward home. He was not crying . . . He wasn't even mad. He just had to think, so he was going to where he could be quiet and think, and he knew where that place was. He went into the woods. He says he did not tell himself where to go: that his body, his feet, just went there—a place where a game trail entered a canebrake and an oak tree had fallen across it and made a kind of cave where he kept an iron griddle that he would cook small game on sometimes. He said he crawled back into the cave and sat with his back against the up-torn roots, and thought . . . He had been told to go around to the back door even before he could state his errand, who had sprung from a people whose houses didn't have back doors but only windows and anyone entering or leaving by a window would be either hiding or escaping, neither of which he was doing. In fact, he had actually come on business, in the good faith of business which he had believed that all men accepted. Of course he had not expected to be invited in to eat a meal . . . ; perhaps he had not ex-pected to be asked into the house at all. But he did expect to be listened to because he had come, been sent, on some business which . . . was certainly connected with the plantation that supported and endured that smooth white house and that smooth white brass-decorated door and the very broad-cloth and linen and silk stockings the monkey nigger stood in to tell him to go around to the back before he could even state the business . . .

. . . he was not mad . . . He was just thinking, because he knew that something would have to be done about it; he would have to do something about it in order to live with himself for the rest of his life . . . He thought, 'If you were fixing to combat them that had fine rifles, the first thing you would do would be to get yourself the nearest thing to a fine rifle you could borrow or steal or make, wouldn't it?' and he said Yes. 'But this ain't a ques-tion of rifles. So to combat them you have got to have what they have that made them do what the man did. You got to have land and niggers and a fine house to combat them with. You see?' and he said Yes again. He left that night. He waked before day and departed just like he went to bed: by rising from the pallet and tiptoeing out of the house. He never saw any of his family again.

He went to the West Indies.

[Here was Sutpen's design, and the rest of his life was spent in an effort to achieve it. He achieved wealth and his plantation; but the design, or per-haps the social system, brought tragedy which destroyed all that he had built.]

21

Social and Cultural Life in the New South

The love of life which had always been characteristic of Southern people persisted after the Civil War. Lack of money was no deterrent to a folk who had always found most of its pleasures in home life. Frances Butler Leigh, in her *Ten Years on a Georgia Plantation Since the War,* R. Bentley and Son, London, 1883, p. 140, gave a picture of a summer resort in South Carolina in 1869.

In July I went to South Carolina, and found my friends moved from the rice plantation to a settlement about fifteen miles distant in the pine woods, which formerly had been occupied entirely by the overseers, when the gentlemen and their families could afford to spend their summers at the North, a thing they no longer could afford, nor wished to do. The place and the way of living was altogether queerer than anything I have ever imagined. The village consisted of about a dozen houses, set down here and there among the tall pine trees, which grew up to the very doors, almost hiding one house from another. The place was very healthy and the sanitary laws very strict. No two houses were allowed to be built in a line, no one was allowed to turn up the soil, even for a garden, and no one, on pain of death, to cut down a pine tree; in this way they succeeded in keeping it perfectly free from malaria, and the air one breathed was full of the delicious fragrance of the pines, which in itself is considered a cure for most ills. In front of each house was a high mound of sand, on which at night a blazing pine fire was lit to drive away malaria that might come from the dampness of the night. These fires had the most picturesque effect, throwing their glare upon the red trunks of the pines and lighting the woods for some distance around.

The houses were built in the roughest possible manner, many of them being mere log-houses. The one we were in was neither plastered nor lined inside, one thickness of boards doing for both inside and outside walls . . . ; it was really pretty, with numbers of easy-chairs and comfortable sofas about, and the pretty bright chintz curtains and covers, which looked very well against the fresh whitewashed boards; and there was an amusing incongruity between a grand piano and fine embroidered sheets and pillow cases, relics of past days of wealth and luxury, and our bare floors and walls.

Most of the people were very poor, which created a sort of commonwealth, as there was a friendly feeling among them all, and desire to share anything good which one got with his neighbors; so that, constantly through the day, negro servants would be seen going from one house to another, carrying a neatly covered tray, which contained presents of cakes or fruit, or even fresh bread that some one had been baking. There was a meat club, which everyone belonged to, and to which everyone contributed in turn, either an ox or a sheep a week, which was then divided equally, each house receiving in turn a different part, so that all fared alike, and one week we feasted sumptuously off the sirloin, and the next, not so well, from the brisket. . . .

Many of them had their fine plantation houses, with everything in them, burnt to the ground during the war, and had no money and very little idea of how to help themselves. . . . Poor people! they were little used to such hardships, and seemed as helpless as children, but nevertheless were patient and never complained.

The woods around were full of deer, and the gentlemen hunted very often —not so much for sport as for food. They generally started about five o'clock in the morning and were aroused by a horn which was sounded in the centre of the village by the huntsman. As soon as it was heard, the hounds began to bay from the different houses, at each of which two or three were kept, no one being rich enough to keep the whole pack; but being always used to hunt together, they did very well, and made altogether a very respectable pack. One day they brought home three deer, having started ten; so for the next few days we had a grand feast of venison.

✓   ✓   ✓

Louisiana endorsed gambling by creating the Lottery in 1868. The Louisiana Lottery was much more than a social diversion. It was a big business and a political power for over twenty years. C. C. Buel, "The Degradation of a State; or the Charitable Career of the Louisiana Lottery," *The Century Illustrated Magazine,* Vol. XLIII, February, 1892, pp. 618-632, is the source of the following account. .

A drawing occurred the third day after my arrival. On that morning New Orleans was in a ferment over the local primary election for delegates to the State convention, in which election the Lottery candidate for governor got all the men chosen. But in the business section of the town the excitement over the drawing was paramount. Women venders of tickets were making their last calls at offices, and street brokers were thronging hotel lobbies and bar-rooms. As eleven o'clock approached, dealers rushed with their unsold tickets to the main office, preferring their fifteen per cent commission on the tickets they had sold to the chance of winning a great sum by becoming responsible for unsold tickets. Opposite, in a theater, the drawing promptly began. One of the boxes was occupied by ladies who took a homelike interest in the proceedings. The sparse company of men, in the body of the theater, were redolent of rum and tobacco and poor bathing facilities, and had no taste for money or clean raiment. In their character as investors they made one think of Cable's 'Sieur George, of the old French quarter near by, who was respected for a supposed trunk full of money, that proved to be a trunk full of unlucky lottery tickets.

Though the onlookers were a thin and a sad show, it was no ordinary spectacle to see General G. T. Beauregard and Lieutenant-General Jubal A. Early presiding over the wheels of fortune and producing by virtue of their ancient reputations a large part of the allurement of the Lottery. The former carried off the honors of the first pitched battle of the Confederacy, and to the last day of the struggle stood among its foremost soldiers. He had a genius for controversy, and was the object of much misrepresentation which credited him with the threat that he would "water his horse in the Tennessee River or in hell." Most Confederate soldiers think that the Tennessee should have sufficed; but they say little about the matter for the sake of a cause which remains only in sentiment. His is a job requiring only a few hours' time each month,—I will not call it easy,—the pay of which is variously estimated at $12,000 to $30,000. No matter how large the sum, it is a good bargain for the Lottery. In marshaling the forces of the smaller wheel that contains the prize slips in gutta-percha tubes, he did not wear full Confederate uniform, or medals of honor. He was simply a quiet, dignified gentlemen in civilian's dress, who in any company would be singled out for a man of distinction. He sat in a chair, received the prize tubes from a blindfolded boy, and every twentieth prize closed the wheel for the periodical stirring up. Occasionally he yielded his place to an assistant.

General Early, the other "commissioner" on a similar salary, seldom divided the honor of his office with anybody. His wheel, on the day mentioned, contained a hundred thousand numbers. It is six feet or more in diameter, and in contrast with the other wheel justifies the remark of a New Orleans accountant, who bought the lottery tickets until he visited a drawing and saw "an omnibus full of numbers, and a silk hat full of prizes," which well represents the benevolent basis of the scheme. General Early is over six feet tall; he still effects gray cloth, and, with his patriarchal beard and stoop, certainly has a saintly look, as he sits on the platform and calls off "fortune's favorites." He makes no claim to [this] saintliness, however, and it is well known that [when] he was the trusted Lieutenant of Lee and was fighting up and down the Valley with limited resources, "Old Jube" could hold down his own with any mule driver in the Confederacy. Besides being a good soldier, General Early was a careful writer; his reports are among the best-written documents in the Official Records. It is said that a prominent "daughter of the Confederacy" once took him feelingly to task for accepting a degrading position to which General Lee would not have assigned him, since Lee would have died before he would have taken it at any price.

The facts in regard to this Lottery and its personnel, no matter how indirectly put, will seem to be harshly said. To a stranger the "daily drawing" with the "policy" playing, in one hundred and eight special offices, has a look compared with which the rest of the business is divine. It is hard to speak disrespectfully of any charity, but every local shop I entered breathed the atmospheric ooze of a pawnshop, and almost every customer I saw was a fit object for charity. Some showed a tremor of excitement in asking for their favorite number or combination. The best-dressed customer I saw was a widow in her weeds, her hat having the shape of a sun-bonnet. Children are sent for tickets, sometimes in the suburbs for a long distance.

In the daily drawing, held at 4 P.M., the chances are absurdly slight for the players, and all the delusions of ignorance and fatuity are at work. On the streets may be seen trained parrakeets that for five cents will pick out a winning number. A famous play is the "washerwoman's gig," 4-11-44. On the two days preceding the primary election, it so happened that approximations to that "gig," such as a 3-11-44 and 4-11-54, were drawn, a coincidence which excited comment. Inveterate players stop children in the street and ask their age; they consult voodoo doctors; if they see a stray dog, they play a 6; a drunken man counts 14, and a dead woman 59; an exposed leg plays the mystic number 11; and to dream of a fish is a reminder to play 13. Such nonsense at this takes the place of thrift and industry with a steadily growing part of the population, as the diminished returns of the saving-banks sufficiently prove.

[In 1868] "the negro legislature of the State of Louisiana . . . passed an act to increase the revenues of the State and to authorize the incorporation and establishment of the Louisiana State Lottery Company, and to repeal certain acts now in force." . . . "the act proclaims that whereas many millions of dollars have been withdrawn from and lost to this State by the sale of Havana, Kentucky, Madrid, and other lottery tickets, policies, combinations, and devices, . . . it shall hereafter be unlawful to sell any of them . . . except in such manner and by such persons . . . as shall be hereinafter authorized." Only adepts in the philanthropic efforts could have made so neat an exposé of the harm that may arise to a State from lottery enterprises, and have so sovereign a remedy as a lottery monopoly. The act says the objects of the corporation are "to save money to the State," "to establish a reliable home institution for the sale of tickets," and "to provide means to raise a fund for educational and charitable purposes." Another clause provides that "the corporation shall pay to the Sate $40,000 per annum, to be credited to the educational fund of the State," and that "the corporation shall be exempt from all taxes and licenses from State, parish, or municipal authorities." As the capital stock was fixed at $1,000,000, in ten thousand shares of $100 each, the mind is stupefied with admiration for the sagacity that imposed a gift of $40,000 a year in return for immunity from all taxes on so large a working capital. Although the act embodies all the virtues of the opera bouffe, H. C. Warmoth, who, as governor, was at the head of the Louisiana government of those serio-comic days, neither vetoed the bill nor placed his signature to it, but, by overlooking it for the statutory lapse of time, gave the Lieutenant-Governor (a negro), and the speaker of the House the honor of certifying it to the people of Louisiana.

. . . Everybody knows that Louisiana was ruled for years by colored statesmen and white carpet-baggers, and that a shotgun cataclysm in 1874 was the sad origin of the new era. Although the Lottery people had begun to take an intimate interest in State politics, they had the merit of belonging to both political parties. But arrange matters as they might in each legislative session there would be somebody who would introduce a bill granting a new lottery charter, or withdrawing the old one. Only one of these measures, for surmisable reasons, prospered beyond a certain stage. In 1876 General Francis T. Nicholls who had left both an arm and a leg between the Rapidan and Petersburg, was nominated for Governor and was elected. Some whole veterans in Louisiana earn wages from the Lottery. Being only half a veteran, the Governor was not at heart sound on the Lottery question: so, when the legislature in the spring of 1879 actually rescinded the charter of the Lottery Company, Governor Nicholls signed the bill with his remaining arm. . . . But the repeal of the Lottery charter was annulled by an injunction issued by Judge Billings of the United States Circuit Court, who took ground at variance with decisions of the Supreme Court of the United States. And as a constitutional convention was called for the autumn of that year (1879), the Lottery very soon perceived a way to fortify itself further. Powerful interests were at work for selfish ends, and the Lottery at once allied itself with them. A strong lobby had been formed, particularly in the interests of the refunding bondholders of the Kellogg régime. New bonds had been issued to conceal the identity of millions of bonds which were regarded as fraudulent, and for that reason, there was a move to repudiate them. These allied interests carried the day in the convention, from which the Lottery emerged with a limited berth in the fundamental law of the State.

✓   ✓   ✓

Florida began to attract wealthy vacationers. Investors advertised the beauty of the semitropical plant life and the pleasant winter climate. M. B. Hillyard, *The New South,* The Manufacturers' Record Company, Baltimore, 1887, p. 224, described the beginning of the scheme for promotion of the vacation land.

The exceptional attractions of this region have induced a number of gentlemen, representing all sections of the country, to unite their efforts to open these rich resources to their appropriate uses. They have purchased some ten or twelve thousand acres of choice and selected lands along the whole course of the Homosassa River, including all the Yulee estate, and they are now expending large sums in improving these natural advantages, so as to make them available for visitors or settlers. A careful topographical survey has been made, the lands plotted and mapped, avenues and parks laid out, and works are now going on to bring to the best effect every natural point of interest or advantage. The proprietors will invite gentlemen to erect villas along the picturesque banks of the river; they will provide steam launches and pleasure boats, and open shady walks and drives paved with white shells from the gulf beaches, loading to the points of most interest and beauty; they will reserve for the present Iathloe Island, for the purpose of making it a tropical garden, where the flowers and fruit-bearing trees and rarest vines and shrubs of the gulf coast will be gathered as a type of that Mediterranean loveliness. The fertile lands most suited for general agriculture will be opened to settlers at prices that will be within the means of all. The abundance of valuable woods, such as the live oak, magnolia, red cedar and palmetto, will invite profitable industries in wood-working, such as fine finish for houses, boat building, cabinet and furniture making, &c. . . .

The means of communication and transportation which have so long been desired are now about to be made ample. The old familiar route from Cedar Keys by the gulf and river will be reopened. The Silver Springs, Ocala and Gulf Railroad is vigorously advancing . . . ; the Florida Southern Railroad is already at Brooksville . . . ; meantime a comfortable stage line will be run from Brooksville to Homosassa, connecting with the trains of the Florida Southern, and it is quite probable that another line will be run between Homosassa and Blue Spring on the north.

In anticipation of these openings, a hotel, with the best of accommodations, is to be erected by the Homosassa Company in season for the visitors who will seek this favorable opportunity for recreation, investment or permanent settlement. Indeed, the numerous applications on all these scores already received abundantly ensure the success of this enterprise.

ɟ   ɟ   ɟ

Hotels built in Florida were fabulous in size, in ornamentation, and in surroundings. Henry James visited such a hotel in 1907. Florida had become the winter vacation land of the extremely wealthy of eastern United States. The following description is from Henry James, *The American Scene,* Harper and Brothers, New York, 1907, pp. 406ff.

On a strip of sand between the sea and the jungle in one quarter, between the sea and the Lake in another, the clustered hotels, the superior Pair in especial, stand and exhale their genius. One of them, the larger, the more portentously brave, of the Pair, is a marvel indeed, proclaiming itself of course, with all the eloquence of an interminable sky-line, the biggest thing of its sort in the world . . . ; to stand off and see it rear its incoherent crest above its gardens was to remember—and quite with relief—nothing but the

processional outline of Windsor Castle that could appear to march with it.
. . . No world *but* an hotel-world could flourish in such a shadow. Every
step, for a mile or two round, conduced but to show how it did flourish;
every aspect of everything for which our reclaimed patch, our liberal square
between sea and jungle, yielded space, was a demonstration of that. The
gardens, and groves, the vistas and avenues between the alignments of palms,
the fostered insolence of flame-colored flower and golden fruit, were perhaps
the rarest attestation of all; so recent a conquest did this seem to me of
ground formerly abandoned, in the States, to the general indifference. . . .
The palace rears itself, behind its own high gates and gilded, transparent
barriers, at a few minutes walk from the great caravansaries; it sits there in
its admirable garden, amid its statues and fountains, the hugeness of its more
or less antique vases and sarcophagi—costliest reproductions of all—as if to
put to shame those remembered villas of the Lake of Come, of the Borro-
mean Islands, the type, the climate, the horticultural elegance, the contained
curiosities, luxuries, treasures, of which it invokes only to surpass them at
every point. . . .

I had been admirably provided for at the less egregious of the two hotels;
which was vast and cool and fair, friendly, breezy, shiny, swabbed and
burnished like a royal yacht, really immaculate and delightful; . . . One
could plunge, by a short walk, through a luxuriance of garden, into the
deeper depths; one could lose one's self, if so minded, in the labyrinth of
the other show. . . . you had to be financially more or less at your ease to
enjoy the privileges of the Royal Poinciana at all; enjoy them through their
range of saloons and galleries, fields of high publicity all; pursue them from
dining-halls to music-rooms, to ball-rooms, to card-rooms, to writing-rooms,
to a succession of places of convenience and refreshment, not the least characteristic of which, no doubt, was the terrace appointed to mid-morning and
mid-afternoon drinks—drinks at the latter hour, that appeared, oddly, never
to comprise tea, the only one appreciated in "Europe" at that time of
day. . . .

"Society," as we loosely use the word, is made up of the fortunate few, and
if that number be everywhere small at the best, it was yet the fortunate few
who, after their fashion, filled the frame. Every obligation lay upon me to
"study" them. . . . There were two sexes, I think, and the range of age, but,
once the one comprehensive type was embraced, no other signs of differen-
tiation. How should there have been when the men were consistently, in all
cases, thoroughly obvious products of the "business-block," the business-
block unmitigated by any other influence definite enough to name, and the
women were, under the same strictness, the indulged ladies of such lords?
. . . As for the younger persons, of whom there were many, as for the young
girls in especial, they were as perfectly in their element as goldfish in a
crystal jar: a form of exhibition suggesting but one question or mystery. Was
it they who had invented it, or had it inscrutably invented *them*?

✓   ✓   ✓

Horse racing ceased to be the universal sport of the South that it had been in ante-bellum days. Athletic events began to attract crowds of spectators. The issue of the Dallas *Morning News* published on October 1, 1935, was an anniversary edition, which contained brief stories of the news carried during fifty years of publication. What had interested Texans was probably typical of Southern interests in general. Three popular sports were surveyed in this anniversary edition.

[BASEBALL]

Texas League is Baseball's Greatest Proving Ground. Started in '88. No chronicle that covers a half century of progress in Texas could possibly be complete if it did not include the story of baseball. . . . It might easily and truthfully be said that the Texas League had proved the greatest developing ground baseball has known. Name your outstanding stars of the present days and you almost have a catalogue of graduates of this section. . . .

Sandlot baseball flourished in the State as early as 1872 and strong college teams began making their appearances in 1884, starting with the rivalry between the University of Texas and Texas A. and M. College. These teams still are recognized annually as among the best in the country in college and university circles, and they have produced many star players for the professional game.

Texas also has had its full share of strong little leagues that have served as feeding grounds for circuits of higher classification.

[FOOTBALL]

The game in the Lone Star State had its beginning with the organization of independent town teams. Regularly scheduled games were played as early as 1891 and the first major game was played on Thanksgiving Day of that year when the Fort Worth team came to Dallas and took a 24-11 licking. The contest attracted a crowd of several hundred rooters, nearly 100 of whom were women, according to newspaper accounts. From the files of *The News* the following extract was obtained:

"The excitement at times was so great that the large audience rose to its feet and with cheers and show of handkerchiefs attested its appreciation. . . ."

Intersectional games in this section date back to 1895 when the University of Texas played Tulane University in the only game of the year in the State between colleges. . . .

Football gained such importance that in 1900 the University of Texas employed two men to coach the Longhorns in the game and benefited to the extent that in November they defeated Vanderbilt at Dallas, 22 to 0.

[GOLF]

A small group of Dallas businessmen were knocking little white balls about Oak Lawn cow pastures as early as 1896. . . . H. L. Edwards and

R. E. Potter, two local businessmen, who had been introduced to the game on visits to their native England, decided to give the sport a trial here. . . .[1] The men obtained permission to use a piece of open prairie in what has since become Oak Lawn. They laid out a crude six-hole course and sent to Boston, Mass., for clubs and balls.

✔   ✔   ✔

For the women new interests developed outside their homes. The *Commercial Appeal*: Memphis, issue of February 14, 1895, was produced by women. It contained several articles which may reveal the interests of women in a large Southern city. Among them are the following:

The Menken Free Kindergarten.

Last October this free kindergarten opened its tenth year. . . . A cheerful, warm kindergarten room, with piano and other equipments, awaited these little waifs, who would otherwise frequent the streets and alleys, absorbing like a sponge evil and vice. . . . The poor toiling mothers wish to have their babies warmly housed during the cold weather, and can work with thankful hearts. The children have personal care. . . . Absent sick ones are . . . visited, and a physician gives them attention. Thirty-five or forty children are crowding the cottage. . . . Our school is named for a noble representative of the grand Hebrew race, J. S. Menken. . . . The Association is a band of strong and earnest women, and they rise in a body and thank every one—all merchants, grocers, butchers, bakers, subscribers and friends—who have assisted in the good work.

[Other Women's Organizations]

Music

The Amateur Musical Club
The Beethoven Club
The Rubenstein Club

Book Clubs

Craddock Book Club	The Nineteenth Century Club
Ingleside Club	Memphis Woman's Club
Irving Book Club	Attic Club
Leisure Hour Book Club	Cosmopolitan Club
Salon Circle	Thackeray Book Club
Vanity Fair Book Club	

✔   ✔   ✔

Altogether 48 women's clubs were mentioned and their activities reviewed. The Woman's Christian Association operated a Mission Home for Children, an employment bureau, a woman's exchange (to sell the handiwork of needy women) a boarding home for unprotected working girls, the Navy Yard Mission or reformatory for Magdalens. The United Charities of Memphis commenced work November 15, 1893.

When women began leaving their rural homes to work in cities, socially conscious women of the well-to-do class organized many clubs to aid needy workers. The Fourth Annual Report of the Commissioner of Labor, 1888, Washington, reviewed working conditions for women in large cities. The following excerpts are from pages 16, 26, 43.

CHARLESTON

In no other southern city has the exclusion of women from business been so rigid and the tradition that respectability is forfeited by manual labor so influential and powerful. Proud and well-born women have practiced great self-denial at ill-paid conventional pursuits in preference to independence in untrodden paths. . . . The special feature then, of the Charleston shops is the well-born, well-educated girl side by side in the least attractive pursuits with the "cracker." They are religious and respectable, and receive from their employers the consideration due to good conduct and efficiency. Pay is small for men, and naturally lower for women. . . . The dressmaking industry, elsewhere the sphere of working girls, is conducted almost wholly by colored women. . . .

SAVANNAH

Industrial pursuits are almost closed to girls in Savannah, partly because of a lingering prejudice against the entrance of woman into the struggle for livelihood, and partly because the chief industry of the city—the buying, handling, and shipping of cotton—affords no scope for the employment of women.

In the dry goods stores, however, girls are largely employed, and they are also found in a few bookbinderies and bakeries, in dressmaking establishments, and in the cotton mill. The laundries here, as elsewhere throughout the South, are almost monopolized by colored help. . . .

NEW ORLEANS

The Woman's Club was founded in 1884 to supply the need for an organized centre where working women could meet for mutual improvement. . . . A fund has been created for the relief of sick and distressed members, and by voluntary contributions the funeral expenses of deceased members are defrayed. The club rents a three-story dwelling containing nineteen rooms. The first floor is used for club purposes, and the upper floors rented to members. At the club rooms instruction at nominal rates is given in German, French, Latin, elocution, stenography, typewriting, calisthenics, painting, needle work, and in cutting and fitting dresses by chart. There is a library and reading room. . . . The employment bureau secures positions for copyists, teachers, bookkeepers, governesses, musicians, canvassers, agents, collectors, nurses, housekeepers, companions, dressmakers, seamstresses, cashiers, saleswomen—in fact for persons in almost all avocation save housework. . . .

✓   ✓   ✓

The emergence of women from their homes to participate in community projects accompanied the organization of women's clubs, as was noted in the following excerpt from the anniversary issue of the Dallas *Morning News,* October 1, 1935.

. . . Forty-nine years and ten months ago the first woman's club appeared in this ctiy—the Dallas Shakespeare Club, three years before the organization of the General Federation of Women's Clubs in New York State. . . .

Like wildfire the organization idea struck the women, whose suppressed ideas and ambitions had been seething for years with few outlets except church work, early temperance movements and preparations for woman's suffrage. The granting of the ballot to women enlarged the opportunities presented in early club activities, and during the last half century much of the civic, social, service and cultural progress of the country may be credited to the fresh interest and long pent-up energy of women. . . .

✓   ✓   ✓

The woman's rights movement mentioned above has been a subject of debate throughout the nation since 1848. Two Southern views of woman's suffrage are stated in the following selections.

"A Negative View of Woman Suffrage" was an address delivered before the Lee and Jackson Literary Society of the Wesleyan Female College at Staunton, Virginia, June 14, 1871, and published in the *Southern Review,* October, 1871, by Albert Taylor Bledsoe. It was reprinted in The *Commercial Appeal:* Memphis, March 4, 1895.

We have been accustomed to view the woman's rights movement as too insignificant and too absurd to deserve serious attention. But in some portions of the Border States, as well as in the universal North, this move is assuming proportions and manifesting a spirit which inspire some of our most thoughtful minds with no little alarm. They are beginning to fear that, after all, this most absurd movement may gain the ascendency in this country. . . .

The root of all this mischief is the idea that woman is the equal of man, is cast in the same mold with man, and is appointed to do the same work as man. No greater mistake could be made. . . . Let not the sphere of woman . . . be confounded with that of man, and let not her soul be unsexed to do the work of man; unless, indeed, it be our object to subvert the order of nature, to "uproar the universal peace, and pour the sweet milk of concord into hell." . . .

It may be deemed a want of gallantry in us, but still we must insist on the saligne law of intellect. For, in fact, the sun shines not more clearly in the heavens than this law does in the word of God, as well as in his works. "The man," says St. Paul, "is the head of the woman." The family, as organized by Christ, is constituted on the principle of autocracy, and not on the principle of equality in power and dominion between man and wife.

✓   ✓   ✓

The Dallas *Morning News,* October 1, 1935, reprinted an article by Pauline Periwinkle (Mrs. W. A. Callaway, Women's Editor) which appeared in the same newspaper on February 11, 1907.

There is no question but women ought to have a voice in the spending of city funds to which they contribute so much and which affect them so vitally. Whenever anything is on foot in a big way publicly—a park, a library, bonds for street improvements, etc.—the man promoters begin a hurrah about the noble women coming to the front and molding favorable public sentiment. When the bonds are voted and the money secured the noble creatures may go home and sit down. Their help and wisdom are no longer at a premium.

✓   ✓   ✓

Southern cities had their "opera houses" where the public viewed practically every New York play and listened to the concerts that were heard elsewhere in the nation. Actual participation in the theatre arts and music became prevalent in the twentieth century with the "little theatre" movement and the civic symphony orchestra. The Dallas *Morning News,* October 1, 1935, reviewed both of these trends in Dallas.

A self-contained family is the Dallas Symphony Orchestra and its 3,500 supporters. . . . Few persons beyond Dallas know of the . . . Orchestra. . . . [It] dates back circ. 1901, . . . its period of practically continuous existence began in 1911 and . . . its adult status as an all professional salaried organization has endured with few crises since 1925 . . . The Dallas Symphony enjoys few large subscriptions, none more than $1,000. The subscriptions are not donations, but actually ticket purchases en bloc. It is entirely [self-supporting] . . . on this basis. . . .

The orchestra assembles from seventy to eighty pieces with full instrumental complement. . . . [It] does a workmanlike job on a wide repertoire ranging from Bach to Honegger and has brought to its hearers almost all the music a sophisticated community requires for both academic and contemporary backgrounds.

[The year 1920] marked the demise of the old opera house and its conversion into a vaudeville theater. In the same year a group of nonprofessionals in the First Unitarian Church, inspired by Talbot Pearson, an English cotton broker, who once had acted in the estimable Liverpool Repertory Theater, produced Sardou's "A Scrap of Paper." Now amateur theatricals were nothing new in any locality. But the play produced as an institutional activity of a church strangely attracted a number of noncommunicants who merely wanted to renew acquaintance with the almost extinct spoken drama. The group felt encouraged and December, 1920, found it appearing at the Scottish Rite Cathedral as the Dallas Little Theater with the Woman's Forum standing sponsor. By 1925 a modest 200 seat playhouse had been built . . . with 2000 supporters. . . .

In the Little Theater of Dallas the spoken drama not only survived but flourished splendidly on its own scheme of economics. By 1928 it had invested in a $125,000 playhouse and had created excitement both national and local by winning three little theater tournaments on Broadway.

22

The South Has Changed

Just before World War II President F. D. Roosevelt asked the National Emergency Council to prepare a statement of the problems and needs of the South. He said that he believed the South at that time presented "the nation's No. 1 economic problem." In response to that request a report was transmitted on July 25, 1938. This report, *Report on Economic Conditions of the South,* prepared for the President by the National Emergency Council, Washington, 1938, consisting of 15 sections, was the work of Southerners, acquainted with the problems of the South and concerned with their solution, pp. 8-53, *passim.*

The paradox of the South is that while it is blessed by Nature with immense wealth, its people as a whole are the poorest in the country. Lacking industries of its own, the South has been forced to trade the richness of its soil, its minerals and forests, and the labor of its people for goods manufactured elsewhere. If the South received such goods in sufficient quantity to meet its needs, it might consider itself adequately paid. . . .

The South is losing more than $300,000,000 worth of fertile topsoil through erosion every year. This is not merely a loss of income—it is a loss of irreplaceable capital. . . .

The South is only now becoming aware of the fortune it has in its vast water resources—the value in transportation, power, fish, and game, and in health and recreation. It has just begun to consider the problems involved in conserving this many-sided resource, in curbing the destructive power of water and making it useful. . . .

The population problems of the South—the disproportion of adult workers to dependents, the displacement of agricultural workers by machines, the substitution of white workers in traditionally Negro occupations, the emigration of skilled and educated productive workers—are the most pressing of any America must face. They are not local problems alone. With the South furnishing the basis for the population increase of the Nation, with southern workers coming into other sections of the country in quest of opportunity, with the South's large potential market for the Nation's goods, these problems are national. . . .

The efforts of southern communities to increase their revenues and to

spread the tax burden more fairly have been impeded by the vigorous opposition of interests outside the region which control much of the South's
wealth. Moreover, tax revision efforts have been hampered in some sections
by the fear that their industries would move to neighboring communities
which would tax them more lightly—or even grant them tax exemption for
long periods.

The hope that industries would bring with them better living conditions
and consequent higher tax revenues often has been defeated by the competi-
tive tactics of the communities themselves. Many southern towns have found
that industries which are not willing to pay their fair share of the cost of
public services likewise are not willing to pay fair wages, and so add little
to the community's wealth. . . .

In 1936 the Southern States spent an average of $25.11 per child in schools,
or about half the average for the country as a whole, or a quarter of what
was spent per child in New York State. In 1935-36 the average school child
enrolled in Mississippi had $27.47 spent on his education. At the same time
the average school child enrolled in New York State had $141.43 spent on
his education, or more than five times as much as was spent on a child in
Mississippi. There were actually 1,500 school centers in Mississippi without
school buildings, requiring children to attend school in lodge halls, abandoned tenant houses, country churches, and, in some instances, even in cotton pens. . . .

Prior to 1936 only one State in the South gave consideration to industrial-
hygiene. Today, with the aid of Social Security funds, seven additional
States have industrial-hygiene units, and approximately 7,000,000 of the
10,000,000 gainful workers are receiving some type of industrial-hygiene
service. However, these industrial-hygiene units have started their program
only recently, and it will be some time before adequate health services will
be available. The funds now being spent for this activity in the eight States
which have industrial-hygiene services do not meet the problem of protecting and improving the health of these workers. Approximately $100,000 is
now being budgeted for this work, although it is known that the economic
loss due to industrial injuries and illnesses among these workers is hundreds
of millions of dollars.

Reports of one of the largest life-insurance companies show that more
people in the southern area than elsewhere die without medical aid. The
same company reported in a recent year a rise of 7.3 percent in the death
rate in the nine South Atlantic States, though in no other region had the
death rate risen above 4.8 percent, and in some sections it had declined.

The scourge of pellagra, that affects the South almost exclusively, is a
disease chiefly due to inadequate diet; it responds to rather simple preven-
tive measures, including suitable nourishing food. Even in southern cities
from 60 to 88 percent of the families of low incomes are spending for food
less than enough to purchase an adequate diet. . . .

The State Fair Arena, Raleigh, North Carolina, created by M. Nowiki. The American Institute of Architects in 1956 chose this glass pavilion as one of the outstanding buildings which reveal important characteristics and trends of American architecture of the past ten years.

By the most conservative estimates, 4,000,000 southern families should be rehoused. This is one-half of all families in the South. . . .

The rapidly growing population of the South is faced with the problem of finding work that will provide a decent living. Neither on the farm nor in the factory is there the certainty of a continuing livelihood, and thousands of southerners shift each year from farm to mill or mine and back again to farm. . . .

Unemployment in the South has not resulted simply from the depression. Both in agriculture and industry, large numbers have for years been living only half-employed or a quarter employed or scarcely employed at all. In the problem of unemployment in the South, the relation between agriculture and industry becomes notably clear. Over 30 percent of the persons employed on emergency works programs are farmers and farm laborers, as compared to 15.3 percent for the country as a whole. The insecurity of southern farmers is reflected in these figures. Seasonal wages in agriculture do not provide incomes sufficient to tide workers over the slack seasons. Part-time industrial work does not provide security the year round. As long as the agricultural worker cannot gain assurance of a continuing existence on the farm, he remains a threat to the job, the wages, and the working conditions of the industrial worker. . . .

Child labor is more common in the South than in any other section of the Nation, and several Southern States are among those which have the largest proportion of their women in gainful work. Moreover, women and children work under fewer legal safeguards than women and children elsewhere in the Nation.

Low industrial wages for men in the South frequently force upon their children as well as their wives a large part of the burden of family support. In agriculture, because of poor land and equipment, entire families must work in order to make their living. . . .

The farming South depends on cotton and tobacco for two-thirds of its cash income. More than half of its farmers depend on cotton alone. They are one-crop farmers, subjected year after year to risks which would appall the average businessman. All their eggs are in one basket—a basket which can be upset, and often is, by the weather, the boll weevil, or the cotton market. . . .

There has never been enough capital and credit in the South to meet the needs of its farmers and its industry. Its people have been living so close to poverty that the South has found it almost impossible to scrape together enough capital to develop its natural resources for the benefit of its own citizens.

Lacking capital of its own the South has been forced to borrow from outside financiers, who have reaped a rich harvest in the form of interest and dividends. At the same time it has had to hand over the control of much of its business and industry to investors from wealthier sections. . . .

Some of the South's credit difficulties have been slightly relieved in recent years by the extension of credit from Federal agencies—to the businessman by the Reconstruction Finance Corporation, to the farmer by the Farm Security and Farm Credit Administrations, to municipalities by the Public Works Administration. Many other agencies, ranging from the Works Progress Administration to the Soil Conservation Service, have brought desperately needed funds into the South.

The fact remains, however, that the South has not yet been able to build up an adequate supply of credit—the basis of the present-day economic system. . . .

The great natural resources of the South have been exploited with the traditional American regard for cream and disregard for skimmed milk. Perhaps no worse than in the rest of the country, but with serious effect on the South, forests have ben girdled, chopped, and burned without regard for their permanent value as timber or as conservers of the soil and rainfall. . . .

✓   ✓   ✓

Since World War II many of the conditions noted in the report of 1938 have been changed. The South is no longer a poverty-stricken region; new houses are replacing many of the substandard ones, new consolidated schools have improved educational opportunities, many new industries have sprung up, and cities are once again undergoing a boom period. These changes are the subject of the October 15, 1951, issue of *Focus,* a publication of the American Geographical Society. *Focus* is "published monthly to provide background facts and geographical interpretations of specific problems and significant events in today's news." The following article, written by Wilbur Zelinsky, was published in *Focus,* October 15, 1951.

The myth of the Old South dies hard. Ask the man in the street what the terms American South means to him, and you are likely to be regaled with magnolias, mint juleps, banjos, bales of cotton, lynchings, and the K.K.K. Turn to a well-read citizen and the response may be "The nation's economic problem number one." Actually, the popular legend and the easy epithet, whatever their past validity, have kept most of us unaware of a profound metamorphosis in Southern life, a transition that is presenting our frontier-loving country with the most recent of its great challenges. This renascence has been developing with such rapidity that its full implications have been missed even by many of its participants, but it is a change which in its vast and permanent significance to the nation ought soon to become a familiar theme to all of us.

If the changing South is not the land of the myth, what then is it, and where is it headed?

The single unifying physical element of the American South is a rather uniform climate with abundant rains . . . and long, warm growing seasons.

Landforms, minerals, and plant life vary greatly, and so do soils, which, unfortunately, average out as scarcely mediocre in fertility.

The cement that binds together these diversities is the inheritance of a unique cultural pattern and a shattering material bankruptcy from a brief heyday of plantation glory. The process of trial and error by which other American regions found their vocations a century or more ago is being re-enacted before our eyes, but more quickly and deftly. The South is profiting from its own and its neighbor's blunders and has begun to "substitute the research laboratory for the wailing wall." It is learning to capitalize on its great human resources, its considerable mineral, plant, and hydrologic treasure, and, particularly, to adapt itself profitably to a near-tropical climate favoring farming, forestry, recreation, and even industry.

Perhaps the simplest keys to these bewildering events are the recent trends in the two basic geographical elements of the region: its people and its land. In April, 1950, the South reported a population of some $41\frac{1}{2}$ million, or 28% of the nation's total. During the past half century the South has merely kept pace with the rest of the country in population growth, but in the make-up and activities of its people there have been notable changes. From 1940 to 1950 its urban population increased by 35%, the fastest rate of growth in the United States. The flight from the land has so intensified in recent years that in the 1940's about half of all Southern counties—almost all rural ones—lost population, and the South was the only section of the country to show an absolute decline in rural-farm dwellers.

Another significant change is the steadily decreasing proportion of Negroes in the South. In 1860, 38% of the people were Negroes, in 1950 only 22%, and there is every indication of a continuing drop, notwithstanding the fact that the national percentage of Negroes has remained stable.

In the past a low standard of living and inadequate medical facilities kept health levels markedly below those in the rest of the country; they have now improved sufficiently to bring life expectancy approximately up to the national figure. The population, however, is still a relatively young one, and the South continues to function in a very real sense as the seedbed of the nation—its most fertile area and largest source of out-migrants. The great exodus to the North and West (amounting to several million people), which began seriously in the 1920's, reached full flood in the past decade, with Negroes participating in very large numbers.

By virtue of much self-sacrifice the South has made advances in the quality and quantity of its educational resources that have begun to pay dividends of economic and social achievement. A sizable North-South educational differential persists, even though the South increased its school expenditures 155 times in the period 1870 to 1948, and now spends more of its income [a larger percentage] than the country as a whole; but the gap may yet be closed if Southern incomes continue to increase and the regional birth rate continues to drop.

. . . There has been a sharp rise in the income levels of Southerners in the past two decades. A certain fraction of this rise can be attributed to wartime industry and federal aid in various forms, but in large part it reflects the general strengthening of the economy. Historically, the South has functioned as the exporter of a few staple crops and raw materials and as a market for all the industrial and farm products it has been unable or unwilling to furnish itself. This unbalanced, speculative, quasi-colonial economy is now being replaced with diversified agriculture and industry. . . . The South is now supplying to itself, and even exporting, a wide variety of products in its new role as a full partner in the national economy.

Some interesting clues to the economic changes can be found in the ways in which Southern workers are employed. Although farm income has greatly increased in the past two decades, the lower proportion of workers engaged in agriculture (32% in 1940, and only 21% in 1950) indicates a distinct decline in the historic dominance of farming. Mining, the other major extractive industry, has remained stationary in terms of employment, occupying during the same period only about 3% of the regional working force.

On the other hand, the proportion of employment and income derived from the various manufacturing, service, and secondary industries has risen steadily in recent years. It is not unlikely that industrial activity (occupying more than 18% of the region's workers by 1950) may surpass agriculture during the current decade as the prime producer of wealth.

The remarkable advance of manufacturing in the Southeastern States is not merely a matter of expanding volume in the few old established industries—textiles, wood products, and tobacco—but, more significantly, a vigorous branching out into chemicals, hydroelectric energy and refined mineral fuels, transport equipment, electrical goods, metal products, and other technically advanced enterprises. Simultaneously, the older industries have upgraded their products, introduced more complex forms of manufacture, and as in the case of the Southern entry into synthetic textiles, have explored new fields of endeavor. Because of a slow start and the limitations imposed by the mineral and transport situation, there is little likelihood that the South will ever produce a Ruhr or a Pittsburgh, but the general diversification of economic activity which it seems destined to achieve may prove healthier than either its own overly agrarian past or the top-heavy industrialization of a Black Country.

The bulk of this industrial expansion has come not only through the development of war industries such as the $600,000,000 H-bomb project near Aiken, S. C., but through the establishment of branch plants of Northern businesses, and by the investment of outside capital in new enterprises within the South. To name but a few of the most recent: the Ford and General Motors plants in Atlanta, Ga.; the Camden, S. C., plant of the du Pont company, producing the new fiber, orlon; the Celanese

Corporation's acetate filament yarn plant near Rock Hill, S. C.; and the International Paper Company's rayon pulp plant near Natchez, Miss. The largest weaver of rayon, Burlington Mills, now has more than thirty plants in operation, and has recently announced plans for a new mill near Sanford, N. C. Other spectacular developments include the chemical and ore processing plants along the Gulf Coast.

The well-advertised hydroelectric power development in and around the Southern Appalachians has been the critical locational factor for surprisingly few new businesses. The majority of the new factories were drawn to the South by the opportunity of profitably supplying markets furnished by a steadily increasing population with expanding purchasing power. Some other new industries are oriented toward supplies of raw materials that are abundantly or uniquely present in the South such as petroleum, natural gas, coal, iron, phosphates, bauxite, and sulphur; others were attracted primarily by the industrial labor supply, especially by its abundance, reliability, and quality. It would seem, then, that the recent industrial boom in the South is based on conditions permanently attractive to the investor, not on a relatively evanescent wage difference, and that it is likely to continue for a good many decades. The fact that some 35% of the industrial structures contracted for in the United States between 1945 and 1948 were to be erected in the South gives some indication of the sustained strength of this movement.

The tragedy and the promise of the South are clearly marked also on the face of its land. The campaign to arrest the destruction of soil resources and to conserve and rebuild what is left continues vigorously. Now that the countryside is being renovated through contour plowing, strip cropping, and the use of cover crops designed to protect and enrich the soil, and with 56% of the nation's fertilizer bill being paid by the South, the destruction of the soil has been retarded sufficiently to minimize one of the main causes of agricultural crisis.

As the number of farms in the South has decreased, their average size has grown, permitting more intelligent and efficient management of the land. This crucial reversal of the fragmentation of holdings that had been going on since the Civil War became evident in the early 1930's with the decline in farm tenancy. From a total of 1-¾ million units operated by tenants in 1929, the number of such farms had dropped to a little over 1 million in 1944, and is probably much lower at the present time. In the face of a great loss of labor and a dearth of farm mechanization, the South can boast of the greatest relative gains in the United States (1933-1950) in the productivity of the farm worker and the per acre value of farm land.

The remarkable increase in Southern farm income from 1929 to 1948. . . . was in part a matter of governmental subsidies and rising commodity prices. In the main, however, it was due to the substantial gains in per acre yields of crops and livestock through better plant and animal selection, improved farm practices, and notably, a shift in the selection of crops. The gospel of diversification has been preached with mounting success. The acreages devoted to cotton, corn, and tobacco—the old standbys—have been curtailed; more attention is being given to peanuts, soybeans, the small grains, truck crops, citrus fruits and other tree crops, and a great variety of hay and forage crops.

But the most noteworthy trend in Southern land use today is the rapid transition to a pasture and livestock—principally beef cattle—economy. A grass-and-cattle rush has resulted from the recognition of the cheapness of potentially good pasture, the unsatisfied local demand for meat products, the possibilities inherent in new breeds of forage plants and livestock, the soil building aspects of animal husbandry, and the profit to be derived from year-round grazing with a concomitant decrease in overhead costs. The broiler industry also has made spectacular progress in parts of the South, and although egg and dairy production is only getting started, the livestock industries of the South all seem destined for prosperity.

No activity is more important to the region than growing the trees that occupy some 55% of its territory. . . . With less than one-third of the nation's forests, the South produces half of our annual timber growth (and also maintains a virtual world monopoly of turpentine and rosin). The progressive exhaustion of most of our non-Southern forests has combined with our mounting demand for wood products to give this Southern resource a particular value. Although there has been a steady drop in the amount of standing timber and a deterioration in the quality of the remnant because of reckless, haphazard cutting, of late the formulators of Southern forest policy have tried to equalize forest growth and drain, and to institute scientific tree farming. There can be no doubt that the South can double its present production by fully stocking with useful trees its great acreages of brush and abandoned land, by improved management, and by more effective fire and disease control. It could thus support its ever-expanding wood products industries and continue to export lumber to other areas. Whether this increase in output can be attained is still unclear, largely because of the presence of innumerable small farm forests holdings; but many observers are hopeful, and the progress made on large private land-holdings may be symptomatic of future possibilities.

All in all, whether we mourn the passing of the frontier and plantation folkways or rejoice in the improved welfare of the South, it appears that the Southern people are approaching the national norms. The various North-South differentials are being chipped away, unevenly to be sure, but unmistakably. The South has too long been a paradoxical land of poverty in the midst of potential plenty. Even though its inhabitants have not yet fully utilized themselves and the resources of their physical environment, the forces of a profound change are at last in visible motion everywhere, and it will not be many years before we shall have to stop calling the South poor. Mines, farms, forests, and dams can feed numerous mills scattered over the countryside and in the expanding cities; and both farming and industry are becoming varied, balanced, and profitable as they never have been before. Within this century the South is ceasing to be a national problem and is attaining its long deferred status of economic and social equality in the richest nation in the world. The process is not easy, but the wheels have begun to turn.

✓   ✓   ✓

The remarkable urbanization of the South after World War II is but a phase of the movement of people from farms to the city on a national scale. The trend appears more noticeable in the South because until World War II a majority of its people were rural dwellers and agricultural workers. The following discussion "Rapid Urbanization in the South," is from *Statistical Bulletin,* Metropolitan Life Insurance Company, New York, August, 1952, pp. 6-8.

During the 1940's there were many far-reaching changes in the population of our Southern States. The number of residents of the 16 States and the District of Columbia which comprises the South increased at a slightly lower rate than the United States as a whole—their growth being 13.3 percent, compared with 14.5 percent for the country; but underlying this moderate gain is a record of wide population shifts.

Virtually all of the South's recent increase in population occurred in urban areas. Between 1940 and 1950 its urban population increased 35.9 percent, while the rural gained only 0.2 percent. In contrast, the difference between urban and rural population growth in the rest of the country was relatively small. In fact, outside the South the increase in the urban areas was 15.2 percent and that in rural areas was 14.5 percent. Thus the difference between urban and rural population growth for the United States as a whole is accounted for almost entirely by the population trend in the South.

Among the Southern States, Texas had the highest rate of increase for urban areas, the growth for the decade from 1940 to 1950 being 58.4 percent. Other States in which this increase exceeded 40 percent were Florida, Alabama, Arkansas, and Virginia.

At the same time, several Southern States lost population in their rural areas. The loss, however, was confined to the South Central divisions. . . . The South Atlantic States, on the other hand, recorded an increase of 11.8 percent in their rural population. Unusually high rates of increase occurred in the rural areas of three states—Florida, Delaware, and Maryland. Much of this reflected the rapid growth of rural areas not too far from large cities.

As a result of the wide differences between urban and rural areas in rate of growth, the proportion of the South's population living in cities rose from 36.7 percent in 1940 to 44.0 percent in 1950. If this trend continues, it will not be long before the South has a predominantly urban population.

The most rapidly growing urban places in the South were the smaller towns and cities. In fact, the greatest relative gains were made by cities with populations between 10,000 and 25,000 in 1940. Even the smallest urban places—those with 2,500 to 5,000 inhabitants in 1940—grew faster than the cities of 100,000 or more. The rates of increase for such small towns were particularly high in Maryland, Virginia, Florida, and Alabama. Only in Texas do we find cities of 100,000 or more with unusually high rates of increase. . . .

The rapid growth of the population in smaller urban places is due partially to the great expansion of suburban areas of the large cities. Thus, while the Southern cities of 100,000 or more inhabitants in 1940 experienced an increase of 25.0 percent during the decade, the parts of the metropolitan areas that lie outside the limits of the central cities grew 68.6 percent. In fact, about one third of the South's total increase in population occurred in such satellite areas. It is thus evident that in the South, as well as in the rest of the United States, people prefer residence in the less crowded suburbs and rural areas surrounding large cities to the cities themselves. The population of satellite areas more than doubled between 1940 and 1950 for Jacksonville, Miami, Washington, Oklahoma City, and Norfolk. Other metropolitan areas in which the suburban population increased more than 70 percent were those of New Orleans, Tampa, Dallas, Baltimore, and Fort Worth.

The causes of the widespread shift to urban areas in the South are to be found in the changing emphasis from agriculture to industry in the South's economy. Stimulated by defense production and postwar prosperity, existing industries have sprung up. Chemical products, light metals, synthetic fibers, and petroleum by-products have been the chief additions to the South's industrial output. Industries which had long been established in the South—cotton mills, other textile factories, and oil wells and refineries —also have prospered. Thus, the industrial expansion of the South has not been limited to the increased production of a few items but has progressed along many fronts. Furthermore, this expansion has been general throughout the South and not concentrated in a small area. Small towns as well as large cities have benefited. Meanwhile, small-scale agriculture, as typified by the small independent farmer and the sharecropper, has decreased in relative importance in the South's economy.

This rapid industrialization has drawn people from the countryside to the cities where economic opportunities are greater. Thus, the trend toward urban areas is a manifestation of the economic progress which is raising the standard of living of the people in the South to higher levels.

1   1   1

The economic situation in the South in 1956 was the subject of the following feature article, "Story of What's Happening in the South," January 27, 1956, pp. 48-52.

The Deep South is living through an upheaval more profound, in many ways, than the Secession.

This revolution, unlike the first one, is not emotional. It is basic, and it shows every sign of enduring.

It is changing the base on which the South makes its living. In the process, traditions, habits, and ways of thinking are being plowed under.

Even the racial make-up of the Plantation States is being altered. Slowly, but surely, the white-Negro ratio is getting closer to the national picture.

All this has been a long time in coming: maybe 50 years, Southern leaders say; maybe longer. As late as 1938, Franklin D. Roosevelt considered the South to be "the nation's No. 1 economic problem." Today the measurable transition from that judgment is striking.

The Deep South is a long way from becoming the industrial powerhouse of the U. S. There are still an awful lot of poor people, with a history of hardship that goes all the way back to the Civil War.

But, economically, Southerners are gaining on the rest of the country with lengthening strides. . . .

In Alabama, Georgia, Louisiana, Mississippi and South Carolina—five "Plantation States" of the Deep South—personal income, manufacturing output and retail sales are four, five and six times what they were in 1939.

Some of these states have been advancing in various economic fields at percentage rates higher than the traditionally industrial North.

Louisiana, for example, since 1947 has outgained the nation as a whole in value of factory output. The South Carolina textile business has forged ahead of that of Massachusetts. The whole South, including the five Plantation States, tops the country in papermaking. . . .

A massive movement of population is on all over the South. Between 1940 and 1950, it has been estimated officially, a million Negroes left all the Southern States . . . where, 50 years ago, some farm counties had nine Negroes to every white resident. In many cases the preponderance has now been reduced by more than half.

One big plantation in the Mississippi Delta lost 56 per cent of its working force, almost entirely Negro, in a dozen years. A county in Alabama saw one fourth of its Negroes vanish in a decade. You hear stories of 85 tickets to Chicago being sold in a small railway depot in a single day.

The movement has economic roots. High wages in the Chicago industrial complex have drawn the young and able Negro worker away from the plantation. The older folks have lingered, creating economic stresses as the machine moves in to take over from the broad back. Social uncertainties arise, sometimes racial tensions flare under remote provocation. . . .

A way of life is disappearing—that of the close, kindly relationship between plantation master and colored servant that clung in many families for decades after the Reconstruction. Everywhere you hear nostalgic stories about how Southern families have cared for their own; still do, when they can.

But many leading Southerners believe the changing color composition of the South is, on balance, a good thing. In time, they believe, it will work out for economic betterment of all the people of the South, reduce racial tensions.

As the Negro moves out, a way of working goes with him. The sharecropper is becoming scarcer. Farm experts foresee an early end to the system by which a man traded his work for a house, a guaranteed living and a share of his crop.

Louisiana has lost more than half its farm tenants in 20 years; other Southern States, about as many. In Mississippi, six out of 10 tenant cabins are said to be vacant. Sharecroppers who have stayed are likely to work for day wages.

Now the machine rumbles onto the scene. Where a sea of aching backs once moved through the rows of bursting cotton plants, high-rigged mechanical pickers are beginning to dominate.

You can drive for miles through the Mississippi Delta and see few cotton fields picked clean by human hands. In more and more places, the picking machine has left its telltale white flags atop the rows.

The mule is dying out. The tractor is taking over everywhere. Mules are still used on smaller, hillier farms, but their numbers are declining steadily.

In three of the five Plantation States, cotton still is king. But its realm is shrunken. There is a pronounced shift to cattle and grains and other crops. Rice has moved eastward from across the Mississippi.

In 1929, there were nearly a million cotton farms in the Deep South. Today, there are just half as many.

Look at the landscape. Anyone who has not been through the Deep South recently is impressed by the change he sees today.

Rolling fallow fields are checkered by new factories—making carpets, "miracle" fabrics, chemicals—built by Northerners where no Southern hamlet ever took root.

These factories live without towns. They draw their workmen from farms dozens of miles away. They need no satellite housing, only parking space. Industry has taken the machine to the Southern farm worker, and the automobile brings the worker to the machine. . . .

Southern bankers say that new industries are opening plants in the five-State region at the rate of one a day. It is not a question of industry's moving from the North, they contend; it is a question of Northern industry's expanding in better conditions, building and supplying a hungry market.

Southerners hear the complaints of Northern industry about "unfair" inducements to industry from the South; they are aware of the concern of the union-labor organizer, who finds the Southern farm boy hard to persuade.

The South is not disturbed by these Northern complaints. But it is disturbed by what it regards as Northern pressure to hasten the process of racial equality in the South.

That is the one emotional issue below the Mason-Dixon line today. For the time being, it is red-hot. . . .

On the other hand, a lot of Southerners are too busy to brood on racial grievances. Yankees, money and business are moving into their kingdom. Living standards are surging up. In some cases, wages are strikingly higher— on a par with the North in certain big cities.

Average industrial wages in Louisiana, for example, have increased 41 cents an hour since 1950, to an average of $1.66 in June of 1955. In Baton Rouge, alive with oil and chemical plants, the rate is $2.31. Average industrial wages in Alabama are up 31 cents, to $1.49; in Birmingham, up 55 cents, to $1.90.

Compare this with average industrial pay, in 1955, of $1.89 in New York City, $1.94 in Philadelphia.

Of course, the cost of living has skyrocketed along with the pay. Family costs in Atlanta stood 101 per cent higher this year than in 1939, which was a faster rise than in Washington, D. C., or New York City. But you might figure that Southern costs of living had a lot further to go. . . .

Fifteen main railway lines, 60 truck lines, 10 major air routes pour passengers and goods in and out of Atlanta. They put the city at the crossroads of the awakening South.

The five States reached most readily from Atlanta—Georgia, Florida, Alabama, Tennessee and South Carolina—are doing 56 billion dollars' worth of business a year. A fat slice of this passes through Atlanta. Georgia itself, did 14.2 billion in business in 1954, and, of that, 6.3 billion was made by Atlanta itself. . . .

In Georgia and the other States that fit into the Atlanta trade orbit, business volume is now six times what it was in 1939. Since then, deposits of Georgia's biggest banking system, the Citizens & Southern National, have increased almost fourfold.

As in a good many prospering sections of the U. S., war plants gave the South its first real shot in the arm. The shift from cotton and tobacco has helped the process.

In Georgia alone, income from cattle, hogs, poultry and dairy products now is much bigger than from sales of cotton and tobacco. And the armed services continue to lavish contracts on the South; Georgia, for instance, got 120.6 million dollars in defense construction in the last four years. . . .

A new way of life is enveloping the cotton lands of the Deep South. None of the big changes now in progress cuts deeper than the break away from the tyranny—or benevolence—of King Cotton.

Time was when the price of a bale of cotton was the biggest worry in all five Plantation States. Cotton ruled the red clay of Georgia, the flatlands of the Delta, in between and beyond the bayous. Mules, broad backs and hoes furnished the motive power that ran the economy.

Almost everything is different now. All over the Deep South, cotton is losing out. Cattle, rice, oats, timber are stealing away the King's realm. The new ways of farming, with machinery, increased use of fertilizers, irrigation —in places where people used to complain there was too much water—have further cut down cotton's acreage.

New problems are developing with the changing agriculture. Fewer hands and backs are needed, new skills are required. New industries springing up also affect the manpower situation.

The day of the sharecropper is almost over. You can go for a long way without seeing a mule. Where cotton clings to some of its old power, tractors and cotton-picking machines rattle along the roads and into the fields. So it goes in the Mississippi Delta. But in South Carolina, even in picking season, the cotton fields look lonesome. The gaping doors of vacant tenant cabins, rotting in the weeds, tell the story. . . .

Between 1945 and 1953, the value of cattle in the 12 Delta counties in Mississippi almost quadrupled, rising from 13.3 million dollars to 50 million.

In many parts of the South, permanent grassy pastures permit cattle to be grazed outdoors most of the year.

However, many of the South's cattle are shipped north for fattening, because it is not yet economical to grow corn on a large scale in this area. Corn is the feed that is used for the final "finishing" of cattle before they are shipped to the slaughterhouse. . . .

Rice was virtually unknown east of the Mississippi River six years ago. Now it covers more than 100,000 acres in the Delta, and crop controls have been applied.

What happened? When the land went out of cotton, planters looked at their empty acres and at the broad Mississippi, across the levees beyond. They could have the water by simply stringing pipes over the levees, siphoning off as much as they wanted to irrigate their fields. So they turned to rice, which needs an abundance of water.

In Georgia and South Carolina, tobacco is doing well. Timber, too, has become a cash crop, with development of the big paper industry of the South and the arrival of synthetic-fiber plants from the North. Conservation and reforestation are coming into the picture, where neglect of woodlands once was general.

Bibliography

Abdy, E. S., *Journal of a Residence and Tour of the United States of America from April, 1833, to October 1834,* J. Murray, London, 1835, 3 vols.

Allen, James Lane, *Blue Grass Region of Kentucky,* Harper and Brothers, New York, 1892.

Alsop, George, *A Character of the Province of Maryland,* 1666, reprinted as Fund Publication No. 15, Maryland Historical Society, Baltimore, 1880.

American Historical Magazine, Peabody Normal College, Nashville, Tennessee, April 1902; July 1902.

Annals of Congress, 14 Congress, 1 Session, Gales and Seaton, 1854.

Archer, William, *Through Afro-America,* Chapman and Hall, London, 1910.

Ashe, Samuel A'Court, *History of North Carolina,* Charles Van Noppen, Publisher, Greensboro, North Carolina, 1908, 2 vols.

Asheville Citizen, September 22, 1953.

Atkinson, Edward, "Significant Aspects of the Atlanta Cotton Exposition," *Century Magazine,* Vol. XXIII, February, 1882, p. 563.

Atlantic Monthly, Vol. 36, 1875; Vol. 37, 1876; Vol. 49, 1882; Vol. 50, 1882; Vol. 51, 1883; Vol. 90, 1902; Vol. 92, 1903; Vol. 102, 1908; Vol. 103, 1909.

Audubon, John James, *Delineations of American Scenery and Character,* edited by Frances Hobart Herrick, G. A. Baker and Company, New York, 1926.

Bailey, Thomas Pearce, *Race Orthodoxy in the South,* Neale Publishing Company, New York, 1914.

Baldwin, Joseph C., *The Flush Times of Alabama and Mississippi,* American Book Co., New York, 1853.

Bandelier, Fanny, Translator, *The Journey of Alvar Nunez da Vaca and his companions from Florida to the Pacific, 1528-1536,* A. S. Barnes and Company, New York, 1905.

Bartram, William, *The Travels of William Bartram,* James and Johnson, Philadelphia, 1791; reprinted for Johnson, London, 1792.

Bassett, John Spencer, "Industrial Decay of Southern Planters," *South Atlantic Quarterly,* Durham, North Carolina, Vol. II, April, 1903, p. 107.

Beard, Mary R., *America Through Women's Eyes,* The Macmillan Company, New York, 1933.

Bernstein, Victor, "Deep South Fights, But Not for 4 Freedoms," *The Afro-American,* Baltimore, September 19, 1942. [Copyright 1942, by Field Publications.]

Beverley, Robert, *The History and Present State of Virginia,* edited by Louis B. Wright, University of North Carolina Press, Chapel Hill, 1947.

Blackwood's Edinburgh Magazine, Vol. 54, 1843; Vol. 56, 1844; Vol. 87, 1860; Vol. 89, 1861; Vol. 90, 1861; Vol. 91, 1862; Vol. 93, 1863; Vol. 97, 1865.

Blaine, James G., *Twenty Years of Congress,* The Henry Bill Publishing Company, Norwich, Connecticut, 1844, 2 vols.

Bland, Edward, *The Discovery of New Brittaine,* 1650, reprinted, Joseph Sabin, New York, 1873.

Bowie, Russell, *Sunrise in the South,* The Wm. Byrd Press, Inc., Richmond, 1942.

Brown, Alexander, Editor, *The Genesis of the United States,* Houghton Mifflin Co., Boston, 1890, 2 vols.

Brown, Frank C., *Collections of North Carolina Folklore,* Duke University Press, Durham, North Carolina, 1952.

Bruce, William Cabell, *John Randolph of Roanoke,* G. P. Putnam's Sons, New York, 1922, 2 vols.

Bryce, James, "Thoughts on the Negro Problem," *North American Review,* Vol. 153, December, 1891.

Buckingham, James S., *The Slave States of America,* Fisher, Son, & Company, London, 1842, 2 vols.

Buel, C. C., "The Degradation of a State; or the Charitable Career of the Louisiana Lottery," *The Century Illustrated Magazine,* Vol. XLIII, February, 1892.

Burgwyn, Henry K., *Considerations Relative to a Southern Confederacy with Letters to the North by a Citizen of North Carolina,* "Standard Office" print., Raleigh, 1860.

Burnaby, Andrew, *Travels Through the Middle Settlements in North America in the Years 1759 and 1760,* T. Payne, London, Third Edition, 1798.

Burt, Mary E., and Cable, Lucy L., Editors, *The Cable Story Book,* C. Scribner's Sons, New York, 1899.

Byers, Tracy, *Martha Berry, the Sunday Lady of Possum Trot,* G. P. Putnam's Sons, New York, 1932.

Cable, George Washington, *The Silent South,* C. Scribner's Sons, New York, 1907.

Calhoun, John C., "Fourth of March Speech on Compromise of 1850," *Congressional Globe,* 31st Congress, Volume XXI, Part I, p. 453.

Campbell, Sir George, "Black and White in the Southern States," *The Fortnightly Review,* Vol. XXV, New Series, March, 1879, pp. 449-468; April, 1879, pp. 588-607.

Carroll, B. R., Editor, *Historical Collections of South Carolina,* Harper and Brothers, New York, 1836, 2 vols.

Caruthers, Eli W., *A Sketch of the Life and Character of the Reverend David Caldwell,* Swaim and Sherwood, Greensboro, 1844.

Chesnutt, Charles W., "The Disfranchisement of the Negro," *The Negro Problem,* James Pott and Company, New York, 1903.

Claiborne, J. F. H., "A Trip Through the Piney Woods, 1841-42," *Publications of the Mississippi Historical Society,* quoted from the *Natchez Free Trader and Gazette,* 1842.

Clark, Walter, Editor, *State Records of North Carolina,* 1777-1790, Nash Brothers, Goldsboro, 1898, 16 vols.

Coffin, Levi, *Reminiscences of Levi Coffin, the Reputed President of the Underground Railroad,* R. Clarke and Company, Cincinnati, 1880.

Collections of the Georgia Historical Society, Savannah, Vol. II, 1842; Vol. III, 1873; Vol. XXXV, September, 1951.

Collections of the Massachusetts Historical Society, Massachusetts Historical Society, Boston, 1792-.

Colton, Calvin, Editor, *The Works of Henry Clay,* G. P. Putnam's Sons, New York, 1904, 6 vols.

Colton, Elizabeth Avery, "The Changing Emphasis in the Education of Women in the South," *Proceedings of the Thirteenth Annual Meeting of the Southern Association of College Women,* Southern Association of College Women, Raleigh, 1916.

Commercial Appeal, Memphis, February 14, 1895; March 4, 1895.

Commissioner of Labor, *Fourth Annual Report,* Washington, 1888.

Coon, Charles L., *The Beginnings of Public Education in North Carolina,* Edwards and Broughton Printing Company, Raleigh, 1908.

Cooper, Dr. Thomas, *The Case of Thomas Cooper, M.D., President of the South Carolina College,* Printed at the Times and Gazette Office, Columbia, 1831.

Craddock, Charles Egbert (Mary Noailles Murfree), *In the Tennessee Mountains,* Houghton Mifflin Company, Boston, 1884.

Current, Richard Nelson, *Old Thad Stevens,* University of Wisconsin Press, Madison, 1942.

Curry, J. L. M., *Difficulties, Complications, and Limitations Connected with the Education of the Negro,* Trustees of the John F. Slater Fund, Baltimore, 1895.

Davis, Jeff, *Jeff Davis, Governor and United States Senator. His Life and Speeches,* L. S. Dunaway, Little Rock, 1913.

Day, W. A., *A True History of Company I, 49th Regiment, North Carolina Troops, in the Great Civil War, Between the North and the South,* Printed at Enterprise Job Office, Newton, North Carolina, 1893.

DeBow's Review, New Orleans, Vol. I, 1841; Vol. IX, 1849; Vol. IX, 1850.

DeFoe, Daniel, *The Fortunes and Misfortunes of the Famous Moll Flanders,* 1722; 1840 Edition, Oxford.

DeLeon, Edwin, "The New South," *Harper's New Monthly Magazine,* Vol. 48, January, 1874.

Demaree, Albert Lowther, *The American Agricultural Press,* Columbia University Press, New York, 1941.

De Toqueville, Alexis, *Democracy in America,* 1840; Revised Edition, The Colonial Press, New York, 1900.

Dole, Nathan Haskell, Morgan, Forest, and Ticknor, Carolina, Editors, *The Roxburghe Library of Classics,* The Roxburghe Press, New York, 1904.

Drayton, John, *Memoirs of the American Revolution,* A. E. Miller, Charleston, 1821.

DuBois, William E. Burghardt, "The Talented Tenth," *The Negro Problem,* James Pott and Company, New York, 1903.

DuBois, William E. Burghardt, "Of the Training of Black Men," *Atlantic Monthly,* Vol. 90, September, 1902.

Edmonds, Richard H., *The South's Redemption,* Manufacturers' Record, Baltimore, 1890.

Edwards, Morgan, *Materials Toward a History of the Baptists in the Province of North Carolina,* unpublished manuscript in possession of the Library of the American Baptist Convention in Chester, Pennsylvania, 1772.

Elliott, E. N., Editor, *Cotton Is King, and Pro Slavery Arguments,* Pritchard, Abbott and Loomis, Atlanta, Georgia, 1860.

Evans, Maurice, *Black and White in the Southern States,* Longmans, Green and Company, London, 1915.

Examiner, The Daily Richmond, June 24, 1863.

Farish, Hunter Dickinson, *The Circuit Rider Dismounts,* The Dietz Press, Richmond, Virginia, 1938.

Faulkner, William, *Absalom, Absalom,* copyright 1936 by William Faulkner, reprinted by permission of Random House, Inc., New York.

Featherstonehaugh, George W., *Excursion Through the Slave States,* John Murray, London, 1844, 2 vols.

Fithian, Philip V., *Journal and Letters of Philip Vickers Fithian, 1773-1774: A Plantation Tutor of the Old Dominion,* edited by Hunter Dickinson Farish, Colonial Williamsburg, Inc., Williamsburg, 1943.

Fitzhugh, George, *Sociology for the South,* Morris, Richmond, 1854.

Fleming, Walter Lynnwood, *Documentary History of Reconstruction,* Columbia University Press, New York, 1906-7, 2 vols.

Flint, Timothy, *Recollections of the Last Ten Years,* Boston, 1826; Alfred A. Knopf reprint, New York, 1932.

Focus, October 15, 1951.

Foote, William K., *Sketches of Virginia, Historical and Biographical*, J. B. Lippincott Company, Philadelphia, 1856.

Force, Peter, Editor, *Tracts and Other Papers Relating Principally to the Origin, Settlement, and Progress of the Colonies in North America*, Printed by P. Force, Washington, 1844, 4 vols.

Forrest, Mary, *Women of the South Distinguished in Literature* [publisher not given], New York, 1860.

The Fortnightly Review, London, New Series, Vol. 25, 1879; Vol. 137, January-June, 1935.

Fortune, T. Thomas, *Black and White*, Fords, Howard, and Hulbert, New York, 1884.

Gilman, Caroline, *Recollections of a Southern Matron*, Harper and Brothers, 1838.

Glasgow, Ellen, *Barren Ground*, Harcourt, Brace and Company, Inc., New York, 1925, 1933, 1938.

Godkin, Edwin L., "The Republican Party and the Negro," *Forum*, Vol. VII, pp. 246-257, May, 1888.

Grady, Henry Woodfin, *The New South and Other Addresses*, edited by Edna Henry Lee Turpin, Maynard Merrill and Company, New York, 1904.

Grayson, William John, *James Louis Pettigru. A biographical sketch*, Harper and Brothers, New York, 1866.

Green, Edwin L., Editor, *Two Speeches of George McDuffie*, The State Printing Company, Columbia, South Carolina, 1905.

Hakluyt, Richard, *Explorations, Descriptions, and Attempted Settlements of Carolina, 1584-1590*, edited by David Leroy Corbitt, State Department of Archives and History, Raleigh, 1948.

Hall, Captain Basil, *Travels in North America in the Years 1827 and 1828*, Carey, Sea and Carey, 1829, 2 vols.

Hamilton, J. G. De Roulhac, Editor, *The Papers of Randolph Abbott Shotwell*, North Carolina Department of Archives and History, Raleigh, 1931, 3 vols.

Hammond, John, *Leah and Rachel, or Two Fruitful Sisters, Virginia and Maryland, 1656*, from *Peter Force's Tracts*, Vol. III, No. 14.

Harris, Joel Chandler, *Uncle Remus*, D. Appleton Company, New York, 1886.

Helper, Hinton Rowan, *The Impending Crisis*, A. B. Burdick, New York, 1857.

Hening, William Waller, Editor, *Statutes at Large*, Samuel Pleasants, Jr., Richmond, 1823, 13 vols.

Heyward, DuBose, *Porgy*, Doubleday and Company, Inc., New York, 1925.

Hickerson, Thomas Felix, *Happy Valley History and Geneology*, published by the author, Chapel Hill, 1940.

Hillyard, M. B., *The New South*, The Manufacturer's Record Company, Baltimore, 1887.

Hobbs, S. H., Jr., *Church and Community in the South*, John Knox Press, Richmond, Virginia, 1949.

Hodgson, Adam, *Letters from North America During a Tour in the United States and Canada*, Hurst, London, 1824, 2 vols.

Hooker, Richard J., Editor, *The Carolina Backcountry on the Eve of the Revolution, The Journal and Other Writings of Charles Woodmason, Anglican Itinerant*, University of North Carolina Press, Chapel Hill, 1953.

Hoyt, William Henry, Editor, *The Papers of Archibald D. Murphey*, E. M. Uzell and Company, Raleigh, 1914, 2 vols.

Humphrey, George P., *Colonial Tracts*, Rochester, New York, September 1897.

Hundley, Daniel R., *Social Relations in Our Southern States*, H. B. Price, New York, 1860.

James, Henry, *The American Scene*, Harper and Brothers, New York, 1907.

Johnston, Richard Malcolm, *Education Report, 1894-1895,* U. S. Government, Washington, D. C., 1895.

Jones, Hugh, *The Present State of Virginia,* London, 1724; reprinted for Joseph Sabin, New York, 1865.

Joyner, J. Y., "The Public School and the Future," North Carolina Society of New York, *Speeches,* New York, 1908.

Kemble, Frances Anne, *Journal of a Residence on a Georgia Plantation,* Harper and Brothers, New York, 1863.

Kendrick, Benjamin B., *The Journal of the Joint Committee of Fifteen on Reconstruction,* Columbia University, New York, 1915.

Kennedy, John Pendleton, *Swallow Barn,* Carey, Philadelphia, 1832.

Kennedy, John Pendleton, Editor, *Journals of the House of Burgesses of Virginia, 1761-1765,* The Colonial Press, E. Waddey Company, Richmond, 1907.

Kitson, James, "Iron and Steel Industries of America," *The Contemporary Review,* Vol. LIX, May 1891.

Lanier, Sidney, "The New South," *Scribner's Magazine,* quoted from Centennial Edition, *Sidney Lanier,* Johns Hopkins Press, Baltimore, 1945, 10 vols.

Lawson, John, *History of North Carolina, Containing the Exact Description and Natural History of that Country Together with the Present State Thereof . . . ,* 1714, reprinted, O. H. Perry and Co., Raleigh, 1860.

Leigh, Frances Butler, *Ten Years on a Georgia Plantation After the War,* R. Bentley and Son, London, 1883.

Lewis, Hylan, *Blackways of Kent,* University of North Carolina Press, Chapel Hill, 1955.

Locke, John, "An Essay Concerning the True, Original, Extent and End of Civil Government," reprinted in *The World's Great Thinkers, Man and State: The Political Philosophers,* edited by Saxe Commins and Robert N. Linscott, Random House, New York, 1947.

Longstreet, Augustus Baldwin, *Georgia Scenes,* Harper & Brothers, New York, 1875 Edition.

Ludlow, Helen W., "The Hampton Normal and Agricultural Institute," *Harper's New Monthly Magazine,* Vol. XLVII, October, 1873.

Lyell, Sir Charles, *A Second Visit to the United States,* Harper and Brothers, New York, 1850, 2 vols.

McMahon, John V. L., *An Historical View of the Government of Maryland,* F. Lucas, Jr., Cushing and Sons, and W. and J. Neal, Baltimore, 1831.

McRee, Griffith J., *Life and Correspondence of James Iredell,* D. Appleton and Company, New York, 1857, 2 vols.

Marshall, C. K., "Home Education in the South," *DeBow's Review,* New Series, Vol. I, New Orleans, 1841.

Mathews, John L., "The Farmers' Union and the Tobacco Pool," *Atlantic Monthly,* Vol. 102, 1908, pp. 482-491.

Meek, A. B., *Songs and Poems of the South,* Goetzel, Mobile, 1857.

Meek, A. B., *Romantic Passages in Southwestern History,* Goetzel, Mobile, 1857.

Michaux, Francois Andre, *Travels to the West of the Allegheny Mountains,* B. Crosby and Company, London, Second Edition, 1805.

Mississippi Historical Society Publications, 1898-1914, Jackson.

More, Sir Thomas, *Utopia,* quoted in the *Roxburghe Library of Classics,* edited by Nathan Haskell Cole, Forrest Morgan and Caroline Ticknor, The Roxburghe Press, New York, 1904.

Morning News, Dallas, October 1, 1935.

Moses, Montrose J., *The Literature of the South,* T. Y. Crowell and Company, New York, 1910.

Muir, John, *A Thousand-Mile Walk to the Gulf,* Houghton, Mifflin Company, New York, 1916.

Munford, Mary-Cooke Branch, "The Southern Woman's Work for Education; a Record and an Interpretation," *Proceedings,* Conference for Education in the South, Raleigh, 1909.

Nelson, Henry L., "Industrial Daybreak in the South," *International Review,* Vol. 12, January, 1882.

New Orleans Christian Advocate, August 11, 1866.

New York Christian Advocate, May 23, 1867.

New York Times, March 15, 1954; May 23, 1954; November 26, 1954; November 26, 1955.

Odum, Howard, *Rainbow Round My Shoulder: the Blue Trail of the Black Ulysses,* Bobbs Merrill and Company, New York, 1928.

Official Records, Government Printing Office, Washington, Series I, Vol. I; Series I, Vol. XLIV; Series I, Vol. XLVII.

The War of the Rebellion, Official Records of the Union and Confederate Armies, Government Printing Office, Washington, 1880-1901, 70 vols. in 128.

Olmstead, Frederick Law, *A Journey in the Seaboard Slave States,* Dix and Edwards, New York, 1856.

Otken, Charles H., *The Ills of the South,* G. P. Putnam's Sons, New York, 1894.

Page, Thomas Nelson, "Marse Chan, A Tale of Old Virginia," *In Ole Virginia,* Charles Scribner's Sons, New York, 1887.

Page, Thomas Nelson, "The Southern People During Reconstruction," *Atlantic Monthly,* Vol. 88, September, 1901.

Page, Thomas Nelson, *The Negro: The Southerner's Problem,* Charles Scribner's Sons, New York, 1904.

Page, Walter Hines, "The Rebuilding of Old Commonwealths," *Atlantic Monthly,* Vol. 89, May, 1902.

Palmer, William P., *et al.,* Editors, *Calendar of Virginia State Papers,* printed under the authority and direction of H. W. Flournoy, Sec. of the Commonwealth, Richmond, 1875, 11 vols.

Paulding, James Kirke, *Letters from the South, Written During an Excursion in the Summer of 1816,* J. Eastburn and Company, New York, 1817, 2 vols.

Pickering, Danby, *The Statutes at Large,* from the Thirty-ninth of Q. Elizabeth, to the Twelfth of K. Charles II, inclusive, J. Bentham, Cambridge, 1763.

Pierson, Hamilton W., *In the Brush; or Old-Time Social, Political, and Religious Life in the Southwest,* D. Appleton and Company, New York, 1881.

Pipes, William H., *Say Amen, Brother. Old-Time Negro Preaching: A Study in American Frustration,* The William Frederick Press, New York, 1951.

Poteat, Edwin McNeill, Jr., "Religion in the South," *Culture in the South,* edited by W. T. Couch, University of North Carolina Press, 1934.

Proceedings of the Twelfth Annual Meeting of the Southern Association of College Women, Raleigh, 1915.

Progressive Farmer, January 19, 1888; February 2, 1888; May 15, 1888; July 31, 1888; August 2, 1889; September 10, 1889.

Public Laws of the State of North Carolina, Raleigh, 1854-55.

Raleigh News and Observer, March 1, 1954.

Ravenel, Henry Edmund, *Ravenel Records,* The Franklin Printing and Publishing Company, Atlanta, 1898.

Report on Economic Conditions of the South, prepared for the President by the National Emergency Council, Washington, 1938.

Reports of Committee of the Senate of the United States, Third Session, 1894-95, No. 986.

Resolutions of Virginia and Kentucky, Penned by Madison and Jefferson, Robert I. Smith, Richmond, 1835, p. 64.

Richardson, James D., *A Compilation of the Messages and Papers of the Presidents, 1789-1902,* published by Authority of Congress, Washington, 1902.

Riley, B. F., *A History of the Baptists in the Southern States East of the Mississippi,* American Baptist Publishing Society, Philadelphia, 1898.

Rowland, Dunbar, Collector and Editor, *Jefferson Davis, Constitutionalist, His Letters, Papers and Speeches,* Mississippi Dept. of Archives, Jackson, Mississippi, 1923, 10 vols.

Russell, William H., *My Diary North and South,* Bradbury and Evans, London, 1863, 2 vols.

Saunders, William L., Editor, *Colonial Records of North Carolina, 1662-1776,* P. M. Hale [etc.,] Raleigh, 1886-90, 10 vols.

Second Annual Report of the Commissioner of Labor, 1886, Washington, 49th Congress, 2nd Session, House of Representatives, Ex. Doc. 1, Part 5.

Sensing, Thurman, "The South Has No Race Problem," *Charlotte Observer,* September 11, 1944.

Sheldon, William DuBose, *Populism in the Old Dominion, Virginia Farm Politics, 1885-1900,* Princeton University Press, Princeton, 1935.

Shotwell, Randolph Abbott, *The Papers of Randolph Abbott Shotwell,* See Hamilton, J. G. de Roulhac.

Simms, William Gilmore, "How Sharp Snaffles Got His Capital and Wife," *Harper's New Monthly Magazine,* October, 1870, pp. 667-687.

Sledd, Andrew, "The Negro: Another View," *Atlantic Monthly,* Vol. 90, July, 1902.

Smedes, Susan Dabney, *Memorial of a Southern Planter,* James Pott and Company, New York, 1888.

Smith, Buckingham, Translator, *Narratives of the Career of Hernando de Soto,* edited by Edward G. Bourne, Williams Barker Company, New York, 1904; reprinted, 1922, Allerton Book Company.

Smith, Captain John, *Works,* edited by Edward Arber, *The English Scholar's Library,* The Editor, Birmingham, England, 1884.

Somers, Robert, *The Southern States Since the War,* Macmillan and Company, London and New York, 1871.

Southern Christian Advocate, May 24, 1867.

Southern Literary Journal, Charleston, South Carolina, Vol. III, February 1838; Vol. III, April, 1838; Vol. II, July, 1836.

Southern Historical Collection, *Diary* of David Schenck, May, 1858, Library of the University of North Carolina, Chapel Hill, North Carolina.

Statistical Bulletin, Metropolitan Life Insurance Company, New York, August, 1952.

Stickney, William, Editor, *Autobiography of Amos Kendall,* 1872, Lee and Shepard, Publishers, Boston.

Still, James, *River of Earth,* The Viking Press, Inc., New York, 1941.

Stowe, Robert Lee, Sr., *Early History of Belmont and Gaston County, North Carolina,* privately published, Belmont, 1951.

Talbot, Sir William, Translator and Editor, *The Discoveries of John Lederer, in Three Several Marches from Virginia to the West of Carolina, 1669-1670* (London, 1672) reprinted, Rochester, 1902.

Taylor, John, *Arator, Being a Series of Agricultural Essays,* J. M. Carter, Baltimore, 1817.

Taylor, Richard, *Destruction and Reconstruction,* D. Appleton and Company, New York, 1879.

Thacher, James, *Military Journal of the American Revolutionary War from 1775 to 1783,* Hurlburt, Kellogg & Company, Hartford, 1861.

Thompson, Holland, *From Cotton Field to Cotton Mill,* The Macmillan Company, New York, 1885, 1899 edition.

Thorpe, T. B., "Cotton and Its Cultivation," *Harper's New Monthly Magazine,* New York, 1850-, Vol. 8, March, 1854.

Toulmin, Harry, *The Western Country in 1793,* edited by Marion Tinling and Godfrey Davies, The Huntington Library and Art Gallery, San Marino, California, 1948. Used with permission of the Huntington Library and Art Gallery.

Turnbull, Robert James, *The Crisis,* A. E. Miller, Charleston, October, 1827.

Twain, Mark, *The Adventures of Huckleberry Finn,* C. L. Webster and Company, New York, 1885, 1899 edition.

Twain, Mark, *Life on the Mississippi,* 1874; De Luxe Edition, The American Publishing Company, Hartford, 1899.

United States Bureau of Education, *Circular of Information,* No. 2, 1888.

United States News and World Report, United States News Publishing Corporation, Washington, January 21, 1956.

Urban, John W., *Battle Field and Prison Pen,* Hubbard Brothers, Philadelphia, 1882.

Waddell, Alfred Moore, *A History of New Hanover County and the Lower Cape Fear Region,* 1723-1800.

War of the Rebellion. A Compilation of the Official Records of the Union and Confederate Armies, Government Printing Office, Washington, 1880.

Washington, Booker T., *My Larger Education,* Doubleday Page and Company, Garden City, 1911.

Washington, Booker T., "The Fruits of Industrial Training," *Atlantic Monthly,* Vol. 92, September, 1903.

Watson, Tom, *Tom Watson's Magazine,* Vol. I, 1905.

Webb, William A., "Report," *Proceedings* of the Twelfth Annual Meeting of the Southern Association of College Women, Southern Association of College Women, Raleigh, 1915.

"Webster-Hayne Debate," *Gales and Seaton's Register of Debates in Congress,* 1825-1837, 2 Vols., Gales and Seaton, Washington, D. C., Vol. VI.

Weston, George M., *The Poor Whites of the South,* D. C. Buell and Blanchard, Washington, 1856.

Wheeler, John H., *Historical Sketches of North Carolina,* Lippincott, Grambo and Company, Philadelphia, 1851, 2 vols.

Williams, Ben Ames, Editor, *A Diary from Dixie,* Houghton Mifflin Company, Boston, 1950.

Wilson, Edwin Mood, *The Congressional Career of Nathaniel Macon,* James Sprunt Historical Monographs, No. 2, University Press, Chapel Hill, 1900.

Wolfe, Thomas, *Look Homeward, Angel,* Charles Scribner's Sons, New York, 1929.

Yeardley, Francis, "Narrative of Excursions into Carolina, 1654," reprinted in *State Papers of John Thurloe,* Vol. II, Thomas Birch, London, 1742.

Zeigler, Wilbur G., and Grosscup, Ben S., *The Heart of the Alleghenies or Western North Carolina,* Alfred Williams and Company, Raleigh, 1883.

Index